Why You Need This New Edition

Six Good Reasons to Buy Eshleman/Bulcroft, *The Family*, 12th Edition

1. Expanded discussion of **inter-institutional relationships involving families** (e.g., educational institutions, occupational settings, community contexts, political systems, welfare states, etc.).

2. **Reframing of social class differences** as differences based on socioeconomic status and environmental conditions and using a broader distinction between wealthy families versus working families versus families in poverty.

3. Merging of chapter on African American families with chapter on ethnic group differences and a more theoretical treatment of **race and ethnicity as they relate to family life.**

4. Expanded scope of cross-cultural boxed features to include a wider range of societies beyond China and Sweden and **more integration of cross-cultural research throughout.**

5. New boxed features on **transnational families** that covers migrant families, families in diaspora communities, families formed across national boundaries, etc.

6. **Updated research and statistics throughout** with revisions in statistical presentations to improve clarity, meaningfulness and interpretation.

PEARSON

The Family

TWELFTH EDITION

The Family

TWELFTH EDITION

J. Ross Eshleman

Professor Emeritus
Wayne State University

Richard A. Bulcroft

Western Washington University and
Franklin College Switzerland

Allyn & Bacon

Boston   Columbus   Indianapolis   New York   San Francisco   Upper Saddle River
Amsterdam   Cape Town   Dubai   London   Madrid   Milan   Munich   Paris   Montreal
Delhi   Mexico City   Sao Paolo   Sydney   Hong Kong   Seoul   Singapore   Taipei   Tokyo

Publisher: Karen Hanson
Assistant Editor: Mayda Bosco
Editorial Assistant: Courtney Shea
Executive Marketing Manager: Kelly May
Marketing Assistant: Elaine Almquist
Production Editor: Claudine Bellanton
Manufacturing Buyer: Debbie Rossi
Cover Administrator/Designer: Joel Gendron
Editorial Production and Composition Service: Elm Street Publishing Services
Interior Design: Carol Somberg

Credits appear on page 623, which constitutes an extension of the copyright page.

Many of the designations by manufacturers and sellers to distinguish their products are claimed as trademarks. Where those designations appear in this book, and the publisher was aware of trademark claim, the designations have been printed in initial caps or all caps.

Library of Congress Cataloging-in-Publication Data

Eshleman, J. Ross.
     The family / J. Ross Eshleman, Richard A. Bulcroft.—12th ed.
        p.   cm.
     Includes bibliographical references and index.
     ISBN-10: 0-205-57874-8 (alk. paper)
     ISBN-13: 978-0-205-57874-0 (alk. paper)
     1. Families.   2. Marriage.   I. Bulcroft, Richard.   II. Title.

HQ515.E83 2010
306.85'—dc22

                                                    2009038696

10 9 8 7 6 5 4 3   RRDW   15 14 13

Allyn & Bacon
is an imprint of

www.pearsonhighered.com

ISBN-13: 978-0-205-57874-0
ISBN-10:   0-205-57874-8

Contents

PART IV   *Life Course Conditions and Changes in Families*   338

Preface

This edition marks my second revision of *The Family*. I continue to try to remain faithful to the strong institutional focus and empirical research orientation of the text while expanding the focus to include more social psychological content and more information from qualitative studies. In the previous edition, I worked to remove much of the functionalist orientation that often comes with institutional approaches to the family, and I introduced considerable new social psychological content in the chapters on premarital and nonmarital relationships and marriage. In this edition, I continue to move the text away from a traditional functionalist approach by placing more emphasis in the early chapters on the concept of institutions as socially constructed phenomena shaped by a dynamic process of individuals and families attempting to adapt to changing environmental conditions but constrained in their adaptation by strong cultural narratives and societal power structures. I also have continued the last edition's expansion of the social psychological material by revising the chapters on parenting and parent–child relationships to incorporate theories and research on fertility decision making, parental role identity, attachment processes, and parenting styles.

In another long-term shift in orientation I have continued my attempt to contextualize our knowledge of American families by presenting information about similar trends and developments in other parts of the Western world. Although the text retains and improves on information about American families in particular, this new context highlights how American families often are shaped by the same sociological processes as other Western countries and how American families are distinctive.

In addition to making progress on these long-term transformations of the material, I have worked to make major revisions to the statistical data presentations throughout the text. I have found that students have a difficult time reading, understanding, retaining, and studying countless numbers and statistics if they are presented without sufficient context or explanation. Therefore, I have tried to reduce the content to the essentials that illustrate clearly articulated points about the state of families today and changes that have occurred in family life over time. To do this I have eliminated the absolute numbers and instead highlighted percentages and rates to better convey the incidence and prevalence of conditions or the differences between groups. I have also tried to simplify many of the tables and figures by eliminating or condensing categories that do not provide additional understanding. In the process of making these revisions, I have also updated all of the statistical information throughout the text using the latest numbers from *The 2009 Statistical Abstract of the United States* and other current data sources. The statistics presented throughout the text were the most recent available in early 2009.

Not only have the statistics been updated, but many recently published empirical research findings have been incorporated. As has always been the case with *The Family*, students are given the most up-to-date information about family life based on some of the best studies available. This information is not just presented in general form, however. A major strength of this text always has been and continues to be the way in which research is presented. Students aren't asked to just take the author's word for the knowledge conveyed, but are instead given details about how the study was done as well as some of the strengths or limitations of the information. In the process, they are given more information about how to interpret the meaningfulness of statistical presentations and the validity of social research findings, making them better consumers of social science research and better critical thinkers.

Last, but not least, I have devoted considerable effort to revising the boxed features throughout. My goal was to make these inserts more meaningful and pertinent to the material in the main body of the text. In keeping with the goal of providing a more global contextualization of the American family, I have expanded the *Cross-Cultural Perspective* features to include countries other than just China and Sweden. Students will now find information in these features on different aspects of family life in countries such as Israel, India, the Republic of Georgia, Ireland, Mexico, England, Vietnam, New Zealand, Australia, and broader regions such as Western, Central and Eastern Europe; Arabia; and Latin America. This more global focus also applies to many of the *News Item* inserts; although these have been revised primarily to stimulate discussion of current topics and controversies such as same-sex marriage and adoption, sexuality, online dating services, the effects of the economic crisis on wedding rituals, declining birthrates, sex control in fertility decisions, breast-feeding, the use of foreign workers as nannies, the existence of mid-life crises, elder abuse, the meaningfulness and misuse of divorce statistics, blended families, welfare reform, and the effects of the economic crisis on families of color.

Third, the *Family Diversity* features have been revised to more consistently highlight the ways that some groups differ from what we know based on representative studies of the population as a whole. Although considerable information about diversity is included in the main body of the text itself, these features highlight marriage and family life among African Americans, Hispanic Americans, Native Americans, gays and lesbians, later life couples, and those living in rural areas.

Finally, I have added a new set of features to this edition: *TransNational Families*. These features demonstrate how the world has become a more cosmopolitan place and show how the family has become less of a national institution and more of a global institution defined by the forces of globalization and adaptations made by people who purposefully cross borders in their day-to-day lives. Topics covered in the *TransNational Families* features include: international adoption, undocumented immigrants crossing borders, mail-order brides and international dating and matchmaking services, filial responsibility among Chinese immigrant families, family life and rituals among Indian and Pakistani diaspora communities in the United States and Great Britain, family life among migrant groups such as the Roma of Central and Eastern Europe and Mexican migrant laborers in the United States, and divorce in the transnational context of Hong Kong, to name but a few.

*H*ighlighted Changes to the Twelfth Edition

In addition to the broader changes discussed above, several chapters received substantial changes and two chapters (Chapters 5 and 6) were merged, reducing the total number of chapters to 15. Although statistics and research were updated in all chapters, the following describes the more significant changes in selected chapters:

Chapter 1—Discussions of institutions as socially constructed; the meanings, practices and consequences of polygyny; and modified-nuclear versus modified-extended families have been revised and expanded. Material on incest has been moved to the discussion of the fifth function of kinship systems—the regulation of sexual relationships.

Chapter 2—The discussion of how industrialization, capitalism, and modernity have altered the conditions of life and the ways that individuals and families adapt to them has been revised and expanded. I've also expanded discussion of the interdependence between families and other institutions:

- Politics—the importance and development of legal definitions of marriage and family; different types of welfare regimes and their consequences for families; the significance of immigration policies for families; and the impact of international conflicts and military involvement on families.
- Community—the significance of rural versus urban contexts
- Economy—the importance of perceptions of need versus actual need; work-family and family-work spillover; and women's labor force participation
- Education—the co-evolution of mandatory public schooling and the emergence of private versus public spheres; the impact of educational patterns on the timing of marriage and parenthood; the potential for culture conflict between schools and families; the role of education on the development of economic, human, social and cultural capital; and the impact of family capital accumulation on the effectiveness of parental involvement in schools
- Religion—the different ways of conceptualizing and measuring religion and religiosity, and a summary of how religion and religiosity affects family life
- Media—expanded discussion of the role of the Internet in family life.

Chapter 4 has been reorganized around the concept of socioeconomic status rather than traditional Marxist concept of social class. In it I discuss three broad areas of difference across socioeconomic statuses: cultural beliefs and values shaped by status location, environmental and ecological contexts, and the availability of economic, human, social, and cultural capital for goal attainment and survival. I've extensively revised material under new headings: Wealthy Families, Working Families, and Families Living in Poverty. The latter section includes information on family structure and marriage promotion policies to help families in poverty, but more tangential material on single parenting is now found in the chapters on fertility and parenting.

Chapter 5—Chapters 5 and 6 have been combined to better convey the theoretical significance of race and ethnicity as sources of variation in families as opposed to simply describing each major race and ethnic group. The content has been reorganized around two dimensions distinguishing families of color from others: cultural heritage and historical experiences, and current ecological contexts (especially socioeconomic status).

Chapter 10 now focuses more on fertility values and behaviors with a section on the value of children and pronatalism. The meanings of and trends in birth rates and fertility rates; childlessness/childfreeness; and unwed parenthood in the United States and elsewhere are now discussed in more detail.

Chapter 11—The coverage of parenting role identities has been moved from Chapter 10 to Chapter 11. Values and behaviors, including discussions of evolutionary perspectives, attachment theory, and parenting styles are also discussed in further detail.

Supplements

Instructor's Manual and Test Bank (ISBN: 0-205-57888-8)
Revised by Denise Donnelly of Georgia State University, this essential instructor tool includes detailed Chapter Overviews; Focus for each chapter; Student Objectives; Chapter Outlines; Lecture Launchers, Classroom Activities, and Additional Resources. The Text Bank contains over 1200 questions in True/False, Multiple Choice, Short Answer, and Essay formats. This supplement is available to adopters at *www.pearsonhighered.com*.

My Test (ISBN: 0-205-57889-6)
This computerized software allows instructors to create their own personalized exams, to edit any or all of the existing test questions and to add new questions. Other special features of this program include random generation of test questions, creation of alternate versions of the same test, scrambling question sequence, and test preview before printing. For easy access, this supplement is available to adopters at *www.pearsonmytest.com*.

Power Point Presentations (ISBN: 0-205-79752-0)
Each chapter of the textbook is accompanied by approximately 20 to 30 slides that communicate the key concepts in that chapter. They are available to adopters at *www.pearsonhighered.com*.

Note to Students

This text was not designed to give you definitive answers. There are none. The study of families is an ongoing enterprise with advances in knowledge often followed by steps backward. My goal, instead, is to try to expand your understanding of families beyond the very strong native knowledge you already have based on your own personal experiences and belief systems. This is not to say that your experiential knowledge is wrong, but I ask you to consider the possibility that your personal knowledge may be limited in scope and potentially biased by your hopes and desires.

Another goal is to impress on you the care that social scientists take to assure they are not imposing their own values and beliefs on you, while at the same time making it clear that great room for creativity exists when constructing explanations for otherwise unbiased empirical findings. We reject the idea that a single explanatory system or perspective can fully explain the reality of relationships, marriage, and family life—at least at this stage in our knowledge—although we also reject the idea that any explanation or observation of reality is equally valid. It is true that every person has a right to hold his or her own opinion, but it is also true that some opinions are more informed and more reflective of empirical reality than others. We believe that through the proper application of scientific methods and the ongoing critical questioning of data and theories, our understanding of relationships, marriage, and family life will increasingly approximate reality—and our opinions will become more informed. As a result, we place a strong emphasis in this text on theoretical understandings and empirical research issues, and encourage you to use these tools to be more critical of your own understandings of the world.

Finally, this text was written for an academic analysis of families and not as a self-help guide. We do not intend to prescribe any particular way of life or give you direct guidance as to how to solve any problems you may encounter with relationships, marriage, parenting, or any other aspect of family life. In fact, we reject the idea that a single set of prescriptions can be developed that would be valid for all individual circumstances. Rather than try to prescribe how you should live out your relationships, we have opted to give you what we know to be the best information available about how relationships and family life are structured within Western societies, how they are influenced by changes in other institutions, how the culture supports the arrangements and rearrangements of relationships among institutions, how larger social structures and cultural expressions shape and constrain our behaviors in relationships and families, and how our relationships and family lives are continuously unfolding and changing as we act purposefully within them. By arming you with this knowledge and understanding, we believe you will become better able to make choices and shape more rewarding relationships and family lives.

Acknowledgments

I would not have been in a position to take on this text if it were not for my wife, Kris Bulcroft. Kris has not only given me the emotional (and many times financial) support I needed to develop my career in family sociology, but has also been my closest collaborator over the past twenty years. I have relied on her insights many times in developing my own work and have benefited from her generosity in including me as a collaborator in projects on which she was working.

I would also like to acknowledge the families I have lived in throughout my life. Having grown up in a traditional, large (eight children), two-parent family, I have gained an understanding of the complexities and the sometimes tumultuous nature of family life. Although my life growing up was rewarding in many respects, I know first-hand that many of the public images of the traditional family are oversimplified in their portrayal of an idyllic life. In contrast, the family I formed through my own marriage has been far from traditional and has given me a greater appreciation of the diversity of family life. The birth of my daughter, Anastasia Polda, gave me an opportunity to understand and experiment with the nature of parenthood and the possibilities of being involved more fully as a caregiving parent than I had been taught through culture or had experienced myself while growing up. The incorporation of a close friend, the late Mary Paez, as part of our family showed me that family was much more than just kinship and demonstrated the strength that comes from a less exclusive notion of family. Finally, by opening up the boundaries of our family even further and incorporating foreign exchange students Sasha Simkova, Olga Kurochkina, Laurie Vandervilt, Marie Vervaille, and Delphine Hoegy as surrogate daughters, I gained a greater appreciation of the rewards that come from a vital family life open to change and variation. Each of these young women greatly enriched our family life and made us all better for it. As a result, I am not one who argues that the family is in decline because I see the family with a much wider lens. I hope this more inclusive perspective is reflected in the text.

At the professional level, I would like to thank my many colleagues who have participated in the Theory Construction and Research Methodology workshops that have preceded the annual meetings of the National Council on Family Relations. Through their participation, they have greatly expanded my own perspectives on marriage and family life and given me the opportunity to develop my theoretical and methodological abilities. Karen Bradley, chair of the Department of Sociology at

Western Washington University, also deserves great thanks for supporting my request for leave so that I could complete the revisions for this edition, as does Franklin College of Switzerland for providing me with the office space and supplies needed to complete this work. I would also like to thank the following reviewers for their comments on the twelfth edition:

Kyong Hee Chee, Texas State University–San Marcos
Theresa Gonzalez, Queens College of CUNY
Kwaku Obosu-Mensah, Lorain County Community College
Nancy Reeves, Widener University
Ovetta Robinson-Heyward, Midlands Technical College
Daniel Romesberg, University of Pittsburgh
Meifang Zhang, Midlands Technical College

Finally, I would like to thank my Publisher, Karen Hanson, and her editorial and production staff—especially Mayda Bosco who showed me much patience while also prodding me to meet deadlines. I am also indebted to Claudine Bellanton, my production editor, Julie Low who worked hard and creatively to find the best possible photos, and Karin Kipp and Lauren Traut from Elm Street Publishing Services for their copyediting assistance.

Richard A. Bulcroft

The Family

TWELFTH EDITION

part I

Understanding Marriages and Families across Time and Place

chapter 1

Defining the Family
Institutional and Disciplinary Concerns

What Is a Family? Is There a Universal Standard?
What Do Contemporary Families Look Like?

Ross and Janet have been married more than forty-seven years. They have two children, a daughter-in-law and a son-in-law, and four grandsons. Few would dispute the notion that all these members are part of a common kinship group because all are related by birth or marriage. The three couples involved each got engaged, made a public announcement of their wedding plans, got married in a religious ceremony, and moved to separate residences, and each female accepted her husband's last name. Few would question that each of these groups of couples with their children constitutes a family, although a question remains as to whether they are a single family unit or multiple family units.

More difficult to classify are the families of Vernon and Jeanne and their children. Married for more than twenty years, Vernon and Jeanne had four children whom have had vastly different family experiences.

Their oldest son, John, moved into a new addition to his parents' house when he was married and continues to live there with his wife and three children. Are John, his wife, and his children a separate family unit, or are they part of Vernon and Jeanne's family unit?

The second child, Sonia, pursued a career in marketing and never married. She realized in her middle twenties that she was more attracted to women than she was to men and developed a long-term committed relationship with another woman, Elaine. Both religious persons, Sonia and Elaine had a "commitment ceremony" presided over by an Episcopal minister eight years ago and have been living together ever since. They have a child, James, whom Sonia conceived through artificial insemination. Are Sonia, Elaine, and James a family?

Sonia's younger brother Jim married Terry when he was 18 after fathering her child, Cody. They divorced a year later and both have now remarried. Where is the family here? Are they one big family or separate families? Which family does Cody belong to? Can Cody belong to two different families?

Finally, the youngest daughter Yvette also has a child, Nathan, who was born when she was still a teenager. Nathan's father did not initially take responsibility for Nathan and never married Yvette. Today, Yvette and Nathan live in an apartment nearby with Yvette's new boyfriend, but Nathan's father has begun to take an interest in Nathan and often visits with him. Are Yvette and Nathan a family? Is Yvette's new boyfriend who lives with her a part of her family? What about Nathan's dad? Is he a part of Yvette's family? Is he a part of Nathan's family?

Questions to Consider

What do you perceive a marriage and/or a family to be? If couples live together, is it a marriage? Does fathering or conceiving a child automatically make you part of that child's family? What if you never marry or are divorced and live alone with a child? Can individuals form a family based on a same-sex relationship?

How do you know where one family begins and another ends? Can people be part of different families at the same time? What is the difference between a family and a kinship group?

What difference does our definition of a family make in terms of society and societal functioning? What difference does it make in individuals' lives?

*T*he family. What is *the family*? Or should the question be: "What are *families*?" Does the family consist of one female legally married to one male? Is the family restricted to groups that have children born within wedlock; a husband, employed full time, serving as the primary provider and ultimate authority; and a wife who is a full-time mother and homemaker? Or does the family include a single parent, divorced or never married, raising his or her children? Does the family include a wife who is employed full time and a husband who chooses to be the primary child rearer? Is a childless couple a family? Is the family any cohesive, loving, sexually exclusive unit, bound until death? Or is the family sometimes less than cohesive, even conflict ridden and abusive? Do members of the family always live together?

Traditionally, and legally, *the family* refers to two or more persons related by birth, marriage, or adoption who reside together in a household. This definition is how the U.S. Census defines families. It is a definition that emphasizes the *structural dimension* of families because it focuses on the requirements for membership and the spatial arrangements of members. But families can also be, and often are, defined in terms of their functional significance as a societal institution (i.e., what they do for society) or in terms of their unique relational characteristics (i.e., how their members interact with each other). For example, we might define the family as an institution responsible for procreation and the socialization of children. This definition emphasizes the *functional dimension*. Or, we might define a family as any social group in which the members love each other, are highly interdependent, and have a commitment to each other and a strong sense of loyalty. This definition emphasizes the *relational dimension*.

Regardless of which dimensions we use, it is important to keep in mind that these definitions are not true in any metaphysical sense. Societies have created terms such as *family* to refer to some aspect of social reality or an ideal reality. These terms, like all terms, are **social constructions**—classifications of reality agreed on by members of a social group. Because all social constructions come about through a process of agreement among group members, they are to some degree arbitrary. Different groups may, and often do, define the family in different ways. What shapes these definitions is the way the society or societal subgroup is structured, that is, how it has chosen to accomplish necessary tasks for survival and how power is distributed in the group. Thus, to some degree the definitions reflect adaptations to environmental circumstances and previous societal conditions, but they are also the product of cultural innovations and a process by which those in positions of power and privilege promote definitions that serve their own interests and values.

As Judith Stacey notes, the family is a symbol linked to an **ideology**,[1] where ideology refers to a value system linked to a position in the power structure of society. Those in positions of power promote certain values and behaviors that give them legitimacy and create a sense of normalcy and naturalness to the social order on which their power is based. The way in which social institutions such as the family are defined reflects the dominant value system. It is part of the ideology. These definitions maintain the current social order by setting the criteria for what is considered deviant. From a sociological perspective, deviance is not a moral issue as much as it is a social construction premised on what behaviors are defined as *normative* (or normal). Behaviors (or social arrangements) considered deviant are discouraged through *negative sanctions*. In this way, the current order is maintained. In the case of the family, some traditional definitional elements—such as the ideology that families should be small and based on a marital unit (two parents), that marriage should be between a man and a woman, that men should be providers and women nurturers, that the older generation should have more decision-making authority and command more respect, and that children should be disciplined rather than reasoned with—can be linked to the relative power of different interest groups in society. These groups can be based on gender (men versus women), generation (older versus younger), sexual preference (heterosexual versus same sex), and social class (owner versus worker), as well as others.

Viewing selected patterns of behavior or institutions as not necessarily fixed entities has led a number of scholars to question whether the word *family* is even a meaningful concept, since it implies images of heterosexual couples, love, permanence, children, sexual exclusivity, homemakers, legal unions, and intergenerational continuity. Such scholars have questioned whether these images are anything more than a perceived idealism that is inconsistent with the realities of today's relationships: remarriages, dual careers, childless couples, one-parent households, same-sex unions, gender inequalities, abusive partners, and intergenerational disruptions. It is suggested that families be considered less in terms of structure and stability and more in terms of ongoing process and change, less in terms of traditional images and standards by which everything else is judged and more in terms of close

---

[1]Judith Stacey, *In the Name of the Family: Rethinking Family Values in the Post-Modern Age* (Boston: Beacon Press, 1996).

The meaning of marriage in the United States has been changing for two centuries. These changes have led to a more recent trend toward the acceptance of same-sex relationships as eligible for legal recognition through marriage.

relationships and sexually bonded primary relationships.[2] The former terms suggest a traditional view held by a select segment of the population, whereas the latter suggest a broader, more comprehensive, and more accurate portrayal of the reality of human, close, primary, and sexually bonded relationships. In recognition of the variation in societal arrangements and definitions, the leading professional organization for those studying and working with families—the National Council on Family Relations—actually changed the name of its journal in the year 2000 from *The Journal of Marriage and the Family* to *The Journal of Marriage and Family*.

One difficulty with expanding our notion of family, however, is finding terms or concepts that differentiate family from nonfamily relationships and experiences. *Family realm* has been suggested as a term that differentiates familial types of human relationships from nonfamilial types such as political, economic, medical, educational, military, and artistic relationships.[3] More recently, the concept of *family transcendence* has been introduced as a unifying theme for family realm characteristics.[4] The transcendent reaches beyond the senses and invites holistic inquiry into connections and dimensions of location and meaning that heretofore have not been seen as appropriate for scientific inquiry. Jan Trost proposes a system of dyadic units to define and conceptualize family.[5] Individuals might define what their own families consist of and may include two men who cohabit, an ex-spouse, parents-in-law, stepparents, siblings, friends, and even pets. Any dyad (two persons) or set of dyads could be considered a family. Although we recognize the philosophical foundations and critical value of the family transcendence approach, we are not ready to discard scientific inquiry. We find more value in the concept of family realm insofar as we believe it is possible to identify aspects of family groups or systems that distinguish them from other types of groups or systems without necessarily endorsing one form of family group (i.e., family institution) over another.

Thus, this book views the family as both a *social institution* and as a *scientifically meaningful category* of social groups. Various nation states in the world

[2]John Scanzoni, Karen Polonko, Jay Teachman, and Linda Thompson, *The Sexual Bond: Rethinking Families and Close Relationships* (Newbury Park, CA: Sage Publications, Inc., 1989). See also Jaber F. Gubrium and James A. Holstein, *What Is Family?* (Mountain View, CA: Mayfield, 1990); and Jan Trost, "Do We Mean the Same by the Concept of Family?" *Communications Research* 17 (August 1990): 431–443.

[3]Ivan F. Beutler, Wesley R. Burr, Kathleen S. Bahr, and Donald A. Herrin, "The Family Realm: Theoretical Contributions for Understanding Its Uniqueness," *Journal of Marriage and the Family* 51 (August 1989): 805–816.

[4]Howard M. Bahr and Kathleen Slaugh Bahr, "A Paradigm of Family Transcendence," *Journal of Marriage and the Family* 58 (August 1996): 541–555.

[5]Jan Trost, "Family from a Dyadic Perspective," *Journal of Family Issues* 14 (March 1993): 92–104; and Jan Trost, "Family Structure and Relationships: The Dyadic Approach," *Journal of Comparative Family Studies* 27 (Summer 1996): 395–408.

define "the family" differently. These diverse definitions can be seen by the different ways they assign rights and responsibilities and implement social policies based on legal and/or biological ties. These **institutional definitions** are the product of both unique aspects of adaptation and politics in each nation state as well as more global processes and conditions. We will examine these family and family-like patterns to try to understand how and why these institutional definitions have come about. But we will also approach the family as an entity with certain systemic properties that distinguish it from other types of groups, using what might be called an **analytical definition** of the family. Such a definition highlights key elements of group structure and relationships that make life in families different from life in other types of groups. For example, we could argue that families are unique because they have both emotional and instrumental functions. That is, they are groups where members have to be concerned about and care for the feelings of other group members at the same time that they have to direct the actions of members and control their behaviors in order to achieve group goals and accomplish group tasks. Therefore, family groups require unique solutions for task accomplishment and the maintenance of social order within the group. We see such a definition as less biased toward members of a particular culture and more useful in coming to an understanding of how individuals act differently in families and how family groups function differently from other types of groups in society. In shaping this definition, we will not be so specific that we fail to recognize the diversity of family arrangements, but we also will try not to be so inclusive that any social group can be classified as a family. To do the latter would give us no guidelines for our subject of interest and, we believe, would ignore the reality of social groups.

We begin this chapter and text by distinguishing between definitions of the family as an institution and as a social group or system. As sociologists, we are concerned with the ways in which institutional definitions of the family are constructed, but we are also interested in increasing our understanding of the dynamics of social groups or systems with characteristics that we might define as family-like. We then review terminology that might help us distinguish between different types of family institutions and groups. Knowing where one family ends and another begins can be important for understanding the dynamics of the interactions that take place within them. As we will discover, these boundaries are not universally defined and are not always clear. Distinguishing between kinship groups and families is also important.

Although the title of this text remains *The Family*, we recognize that the family as a social group includes marriages as well as groups that do not fit traditional notions of what marriages and families are or should be. Many relationships (same sex, cohabitors, fictive kin, unmarried parents, and the like) fulfill responsibilities basic to social system functioning or that exhibit structural and relational characteristics that distinguish them from other types of groups and unite them in terms of their internal system dynamics. Current research findings have been incorporated in an effort to understand the similarities as well as the differences among the norms, values, and behaviors that characterize marriage and family-type relationships.

*F*amily as a Social Institution

Frequent reference has been made by both scholars and others to the family as the most basic of all social institutions, linked closely to the supporting institution of marriage. What does this mean?

Lisa McIntyre defines a **social institution** as "a set of ideas about the way a specific important social need ought to be addressed."[6] Thus, the concept of an "institution" refers to specific areas of human social life that have become broadly organized into discernible patterns and supported by agreed upon expectations or standards for goals and behavior. What constitutes a "social need" can vary from time to time and from place to place. Although it can be argued that certain fundamental needs must be met in all societies (e.g., the recruitment of new members, the nurturance and socialization of children, and the maintenance of social solidarity and some level of social order), we maintain a position of neutrality on this point so as not to imply needs based on our own cultural perspective and interests (e.g., a need to suppress political resistance, the need to maintain a hierarchical system of gender relations, etc.). All that we can know with certainty is that societies organize their activities and relationships in response to environmental demands and politically influenced collective perceptions, and these organized responses become reinforced through socialization experiences, value and belief systems, and social norms enforced by sanctions. Furthermore, we are open to the possibility that the development of institutions is not constrained by the boundaries of nation states. Although both local and national politics certainly play a major role in how the family is defined as an institution, in the end such definitions must be responsive to the demands of an increasingly interdependent global environment.

More importantly, we also maintain a position of neutrality with respect to the inherent necessity of any institution in society. Although it may be possible to identify a small set of institutions that have existed in some form across all known societies and time periods, this in itself does not argue that such institutions are necessary for societal survival or even optimal for human life. In addition, the variations in structures, functions and relational patterns found across societal contexts within what is nominally called the same institution (e.g., "the family") is sufficient to argue that no single institutionalized pattern of relationships is essential.

A related term, **institutionalize**, is a verb that means to establish patterned and predictable behavior. The emergence of patterned and predictable behaviors is a complex process shaped by both individuals living their day-to-day lives under common environmental demands and constraints and structures of power in society that allow some groups to alter the behaviors of other groups to better serve their self-interests. As patterns of life begin to emerge, they are either adopted by an increasing number of people and recognized as legitimate or they find less support and are abandoned. Which occurs depends on the adaptive value of the patterns as well as their implications for those in positions of power. For example, although nonmarital childbearing appeared to be a new emerging pattern of life in American society in the late twentieth century, it never achieved institutional status and has declined steadily since the 1990s. A similar fate awaited the emergence of so-called "serial monogamy" where high divorce rates coupled with high remarriage rates suggested a new pattern where lifelong marriage was rejected in favor of a pattern of more conditional commitments. Like nonmarital childbearing, this pattern of divorce and remarriage has also experienced a decline because it failed to meet the needs of individuals and the broader society and/or it was not compelling enough to overcome the influence of powerful interest groups (e.g., men, religious groups) that benefitted from a model of lifelong martial commitments. Cohabitation, on the

---

[6]Lisa J. McIntyre, *The Practical Skeptic: Core Concepts in Sociology*, 2nd ed. (Boston: McGraw Hill, 2002), 106.

other hand, may be in the process of becoming institutionalized as more and more young people today choose to cohabit before marriage and the nature of these cohabitations becomes more patterned, predictable, and accepted. Similarly, it could be argued that child socialization through daycare has emerged as an institutionalized pattern in response to a modern industrial society where women have taken on more vital and powerful economic roles.

The institutionalization process does not occur without repercussions for existing societal institutions. The emergence of new patterns of organization in family life creates limits and demands on, as well as opportunities for, the ways other institutions are organized. Similarly, changes in the organization of other institutions have implications for the organization of families. This interdependency of institutions in society is perhaps best illustrated by the changes that resulted from the needs of a modern capitalist economy to incorporate more women into the labor force and the corresponding power that women gained as a result of their new economic roles. As women were drawn into the labor force, they were also drawn out of their families, creating an organizational crisis for an existing family organization that had been based on a gendered division of labor with women responsible for home and child care. How did families respond? They began by seeking out relatives and others to help them care for their youngest children. As the need grew, however, new institutions—daycare centers—came into existence and flourished. This new institutional option for child care in turn made possible increasing involvement of women in economic careers, which has further empowered them to bring about a reorganization of role responsibilities in their families vis-à-vis their husbands. Although this is a significant oversimplification of the institutionalization process that occurred in the late twentieth century, it hopefully conveys the complexity and interdependencies involved in institutionalization. As new institutions arise to meet new needs or as an outcome of societal conflict between interest groups, existing institutions often are redefined and could even become obsolete. Thus, the redefinition of an institution such as the family or its complete elimination does not necessarily mean the downfall of society. It may simply reflect the reorganization of the ways we address societal needs.

Few institutions have received more recognition and criticism than the family, and marriage as its central component. Both have been claimed to be the solution to problems, on the one hand, and the basic cause of problems, on the other hand. For example, in the late 1990s, a number of professional family scholars claimed that marriage is an institution in decay and basically responsible for the increases in violent crime, child neglect and abuse, the psychological pathology of children and youth, alcohol and drug abuse, poverty, and even declining SAT scores.[7] And if families and marriages are the cause of the problems, their solution resides in the same institution. Marriages are to be made stronger by reclaiming the ideal of marital permanence, declaring out-of-wedlock childbearing wrong, having children grow up with two parents, and increasing the time parents spend raising their children.[8] In brief, they argued, it is important to stress traditional family values (although we should note that the term *traditional* often is used in a selective manner and with little regard for historical facts; see Chapter 2).

---

[7]David Popenoe, Jean Bethke Elshtain, and David Blankenhorn, *Promises to Keep: Decline and Renewal of Marriage in America* (Lanham, MD: Rowman and Littlefield Publishers, Inc., 1996).

[8]Ibid., 308.

CROSS-CULTURAL *Perspective*

Global Similarity and Diversity

There is a great deal of both similarity and diversity of family life across nations around the globe based on similarities and differences in environmental conditions, how basic survival needs are met, the nature of belief systems, and location in a system of globalization and world interdependence (core versus peripheral economic position). In each chapter, we will try to convey some of these differences and similarities by showcasing a different cultural pattern in these "Cross-Cultural Perspective" features. We will consider both differences in nation states as well as differences based on regions. We have tried to find examples that represent marriage and family life across eleven regions that, although not homogeneous, we believe share some important common characteristics:

North America (United States and Canada): post-industrial, modern, affluent, strong religious influence (Protestant), high geographic mobility, racial and ethnic diversity, high inequality (United States only)

Central and South America (including Mexico and the Caribbean): mostly agricultural with large industrial urban centers, peripheral economies, high poverty, traditional, strong religious influence (Catholic)

The United Kingdom and Ireland: post-industrial, modern, affluent, weak religious influence (except Ireland–Catholic), large immigrant populations, high inequality

Scandinavia and Northern Europe: post-industrial, modern, affluent, weak religious influence, gender egalitarian, low inequality, high welfare expenditures

Western Europe (France, Germany, Austria, Switzerland): post-industrial, modern, affluent, weak religious influence, moderate inequality, moderate welfare expenditures, large immigrant populations

Southern Europe (Spain, Italy, Greece): industrial, early modern, less affluent, strong religious influence (Catholic/Greek Orthodox), low welfare expenditures

Central and Eastern Europe (Czech and Slovak Republics, Poland, Ukraine, Hungary, Romania, Serbia, Croatia, etc.): agricultural and industrial, less affluent, post-communist, ethnic populations

Arabia and the Middle East: non-industrial, traditional, strong religious influence (Islamic), male-dominated, communal

Africa: subsistence agriculture, peripheral economies, high poverty, traditional, ethnic populations, communal

Asia (India, China, Japan, Korea, Southeast Asia): agricultural and industrial, traditional, strong religious influence (Hindu, Islamic, Confucian, Buddhist), male-dominated, high population density, communal

Oceania (New Zealand, Australia, South Pacific Islands): agricultural and industrial, modern, weak religious influence, racial and ethnic diversity

Our intention in presenting these examples is not to characterize all families within a nation or region based on single studies, but to sensitize you to the vast diversity of marriage and family life and try to stimulate an interest in why differences occur. Although we are always looking for theories that can explain marriage and family life across time and place, we also recognize that it would be short-sighted to base those theories only on studies done in North America or even the group of so-called "modern" societies. Most of the material in the body of this text relies on research done in North America. Therefore, we will rely on these "Cross-Cultural Perspective" features to extend our understandings beyond these limited horizons.

As we will discuss later, such assertions are based on correlations among aggregate indicators incapable of demonstrating or testing the relationship between individual family breakdowns and specific child outcomes (e.g., criminal behavior). Furthermore, the causal timing is difficult to establish. For example, is it family breakdown that causes poverty or poverty that leads to family breakdown? Houseknecht and Sastry[9]

---

[9]Sharon K. Houseknecht and Jaya Sastry, "Family 'Decline' and Child Well-Being: A Comparative Assessment," *Journal of Marriage and the Family* 58 (August 1996): 726–739.

TRANSNATIONAL FAMILIES

What Is a Transnational Family?

One limitation with restricting our search for diversity in marriage and family life to a comparison of nation states or regions of the world is that such an approach assumes the effectiveness of national boundaries in defining the limits of social life. Primarily as a result of economic expansion and globalization processes, families today find themselves acting in multiple nations either as whole units crossing borders or as fragmented units with members living in different nations. Realization of this blurring of national boundaries and its impact on how we study societies and social institutions has lead to the emergence of a new developing paradigm in sociology called cosmopolitanism (see Ulrich Beck, *Cosmopolitan Vision*. Translated by Ciarin Cronin. Cambridge: Polity Press, 2006). In each chapter, we explore in the feature "TransNational Families" how an increasingly cosmopolitan world has affected families. We do this by looking at the ways families are constructed and defined as a result of their members' psychological and behavioral participation in multiple nations.

In these segments, we will look at research and theory focused on a variety of different types of transnational families: families formed through international marriages or adoptions, families living in one nation but participating economically or otherwise in another, families living in one nation but recreating their home culture within that nation (diaspora families), families living in one nation but having members living in another (e.g., astronaut or satellite families), and families that regularly cross national borders usually for economic reasons (e.g., migrant labor families in the United States or Roma families in Central and Eastern Europe). Each of these types of families faces unique circumstances and needs to reconstruct what it means to be a family without a single and clear cultural or institutional reference.

caution us about accepting at face value such across-the-board deleterious outcomes for child well-being as asserted by Popenoe. In a comparative study of the relationship between family decline and child well-being in four countries (Sweden, United States, the former West Germany, and Italy), the results do not indicate unequivocal support for the thesis that countries ranked higher on family decline will rank lower on child well-being. Although, in general, children are better off when they live in a society in which traditional family patterns are strong, there are exceptions. Sweden, for example, which had the highest family decline score, did not demonstrate a high level of negative outcomes for children compared with other countries with lower levels of family decline.

In thinking, then, about the needs families (or any societal institution) are called on to fulfill, it is important to keep in mind the many ways that a society might choose to fulfill the same needs. This substitutability of structures is referred to as **functional equivalence**.[10] It is, thus, impossible to argue that a society must have a family subsystem in order to survive, and it is even less defensible to argue that only one form of a family system is viable or optimally adaptive for societal survival. Families may be unique in their organization around serving both the instrumental needs of society and the long-term emotional needs of their members (i.e., their combination of emotional and instrumental functionality), but to designate any specific functions as necessary components of the family (e.g., reproduction, child nurturance and socialization, economic production, etc.) based on current or past societal arrangements would be to

---

[10]Nancy Kingsbury and John Scanzoni, "Structure-Functionalism," in Pauline G. Boss, William J. Doherty, Ralph LaRossa, Walter R. Schumm, and Susan K. Steinmetz, *Sourcebook of Family Theories and Methods: A Contextual Approach* (New York: Plenum Press, 1993), 195–217.

reify (make more real or justified than they are) those cultural systems. We believe it may be possible for a society to be functional without an organized family system, but we also believe the family as a type of system has certain generic characteristics that make it highly suitable for fulfilling certain societal needs that often arise.

Popenoe has suggested that textbooks such as this be rewritten to portray marriage with children as a desirable social goal and not simply as one of many viable lifestyle alternatives. We agree that on a personal level such goals and values may be of worth, but they may not be of equal worth to all across all social contexts. We also believe that taking such a monolithic view ignores the importance of context in understanding social institutions and contributes to the dominance of one cultural group's values over others. The intent of this book is not to advocate any particular marital or family value or lifestyle. Rather, the intent is to examine how attitudes and values about what is acceptable and ideal come about, as well as to understand the diversity of family groups and systems.

Families as Systems and Groups

The term **family system** is used in sociology much as physicists and biologists speak of solar or biological systems. In each instance, the word *system* means a configuration of interdependent parts. All systems, whether living or nonliving, have characteristic organizations and patterns of interdependence and are comprised of and embedded within a set of subsystems. The nature of their organization and interdependencies is what distinguishes one type of system from another.

In nonliving systems (e.g., vending machines, automobile engines, etc.), organizational characteristics and patterns of interdependence are determined by outside forces and are unchangeable. In the case of living systems such as the family, however, change can and does come about from external forces (e.g., societal pressures and needs) as well as internal ones (e.g., individual pressures and needs). To complicate matters even further, these external and internal forces do not operate independently in shaping the family system. External forces are reacted to and processed by the individuals in a family system in a way that reflects their own internal pressures and needs. Similarly, as family systems shape themselves to address the pressures and needs derived from their members, they interact with their environments in ways that reflect societal pressures and needs, resulting in different system configurations under various environmental conditions and, over time, a potential change in other societal subsystems. One need only look at the uneven effects of industrialization and capitalism on families at different locations in the larger social system and the rise of public educational and daycare systems to see how families change in response to external pressures as well as how they reciprocally influence the social system within which they are embedded.

To treat the family as a social system is to note its form of social organization and the nature of its interdependencies, that is, to construct an *analytical definition*. The basic units, therefore, of a marital or family system are not persons but the interrelated statuses (positions) and the established patterns of expectations (roles) that accompany those statuses. Although people are part of the system, it is the statuses, roles, norms, ways of ranking, means of social controls, and values (all abstractions) of those people that are significant in examining social systems.

The interrelated statuses in the family system potentially include, among others, parent–child, husband–wife, uncle–aunt, grandparent–grandchild, father–mother, and brother–sister relationships. Each of these status combinations implies a set of mutual role expectations, obligations, and rights that are worked out by those in the relationships in a way that addresses broader family system concerns as well as their own individual wants and needs. The regularities of these expectations, obligations, and rights across families in similar social locations and with similar membership characteristics are of primary interest to the sociologist. To illustrate this interest, the comparison of same-sex couples to heterosexual couples is instructive.

In many ways, the marital relationship of a same-sex couple will mirror the marital relationship of a heterosexual couple who occupy the same position in the larger social system (e.g., social class, ethnicity, geography, etc.). Add a child to the mix and both sets of couples will experience similar changes to their relationship. As we will discuss later, these similarities derive from such common conditions as the intergenerational nature of marriage, the unique mixture of primary and secondary group functions fulfilled in the context of marriage, the high levels of interdependence across domains found in marriage, and the expectations for duration and high levels of commitment that develop in marriages. Like heterosexual couples, same-sex couples will need to alter their interactions to adapt to common pressures in their environment as well as their common concern for fulfilling their individual psychological needs within the context of their relationship and the demands of maintaining a relationship under conditions of long-term commitment.

This is not to say that both marriage systems will be identical or that any particular spousal status combination, regardless of sexual orientation, will organize their marriage exactly the same way. The combination of sexes in a marriage sets the conditions for marital organization by virtue of the fact that society is structured along the lines of sex and members of society are expected to act in different ways accordingly. It is also the case that sexual orientation has been an organizing principle in most societies (both as a legitimate status as well as a deviant status). This then acts as a crosscurrent in designating an individual couple's location in the larger social system. As a result, a same-sex marital couple of the same ethnicity, social class, and geographical location should also be expected to look different from its heterosexual counterpart and this difference will occur regardless of the individuals involved (i.e., regardless of their morality or psychological makeup). Similarly, a same-sex male couple should be expected to look different from a same-sex female couple by virtue of different gender socialization experiences and different levels of discriminatory treatment in the larger society. There will also be individual differences across couples who are similar in all aspects of their social location whether homosexual or heterosexual in orientation. These individual differences often stem from the personality traits of those involved in the marriage and are treated more fully by psychologists. For sociologists, however, these individual differences are treated as residual and are assumed to vary randomly across all types of couples.

We believe the uniqueness of the family as a system (i.e., the characteristics that distinguish it from other types of systems) lies in three sets of factors—structural, functional, and relational. These factors will serve as our analytical definition of the family and will set the parameters for what we cover in this text and what we include as family theory and research.

First, at the structural level, families are to some degree intergenerational groups. In the case of a parent and his or her child, the intergenerational nature of the family structure is obvious. By virtue of this intergenerational connection, there

news item

'Remarkable' Gay Marriage Win for Iowa

Iowa is the first state in America's conservative heartland to allow same-sex marriage. (Reuters) In the United States supporters of same-sex marriage have recently notched up some big victories. But it is the Iowa Supreme Court's decision to allow gay marriage that is seen as groundbreaking.

Iowa has become the first state in the socially conservative American heartland to allow same-sex couples to exchange vows. "I think it is important that we're seeing a state that's not on the coast and in many ways is the heart of our country," said Camilla Taylor, a Chicago-based lawyer for the gay rights group Lambda Legal which was involved in the Iowa case.

Kenji Yoshino, a constitutional law professor at New York University, said it was a remarkable decision. "This is a remarkable decision not only because it occurred in the Midwest, but also because it was seven-zero," he said.

"The three prior courts to rule in favour of same-sex marriage were four-three decisions, in California, in Connecticut and in Massachusetts.

"So I think that while on the one hand this is a more tempered opinion, on the other hand it was a more aggressive opinion in that there was absolutely no toe-hold for naysayers to find in the opinion.

"This makes the opposition to same sex marriage much more like opposition to interracial marriage. Basically the Iowa Supreme Court was communicating…[that] there just isn't an argument here that we're willing to credit."

David Yepsen, a political columnist at the Des Moines Register newspaper in Iowa, says Iowans are comfortable with the notion of gay marriage.

"I mean this is the Middle West," he said. "There's room to spread out. There's a real ethic of leave me alone.

"Yes, they're deeply religious but not necessarily in a conservative way. There's many tolerant Christians in Iowa who even though they aren't gay or lesbian simply believe in the notion of leaving people alone.

"It's not harming them if a gay couple wants to get married. So, I think add all of that together and you get an environment in which this sort of thing can happen and will be accepted."

The National Organisation for Marriage has launched a new ad campaign called A Gathering Storm, which uses actors to portray so-called everyday people who talk about how gay marriage would affect their lives.

Bryan English, the director of public relations for the Iowa Family Policy Centre, says the country is being dragged into a constitutional crisis.

"Finally here in Iowa, at the very least, there are some folks in Government and people running for office who are standing up saying 'enough is enough'," he said.

"We're governed by a constitution, not by seven justices in black robes sitting behind the bench, and it's time to put them back in their place.

"The people of Iowa and really the people around the country just never thought that the Iowa Supreme Court would be so bold as to ignore the law and ignore the constitution and rule the way they did," Mr. English said.

The battle over gay marriage in America is far from over, and the Iowa ruling has pushed the battle into the nation's heartland.

Source: Kim Landers for Australian Broadcasting Corporation, May 10, 2009. http://www.abc.net.au/news/stories/2009/05/10/2565732.htm?section=world

---

is an inherent role organization and structure of rights and obligations stemming from the members' capabilities and dependencies. This structure sets the stage for intergenerational relationships that will impact the child's later marriage, with or without children. Although parents are not part of their child's marriage in modern industrial societies, they nevertheless alter the conditions of social organization within the marriage through the transmission of culture, the conditions of support outside the system, and the intrusiveness of outsiders in the marital system. These are structural conditions unlike those found in other social systems (e.g., educational systems, occupational systems, etc.).

Second, at the functional level, it has already been noted that families are unique in their functionality at both the emotional and instrumental levels. As discussed later, families are both primary and secondary groups. As a result, the nature of the interactions that occur within families is modified as members must accomplish tasks efficiently as well as be attentive to the emotional needs of their members. This is one of the problems with applying rational economic models to help families better accomplish their goals. What works within an economic system may not work within a family system because the latter is unique in its need to meet the primary emotional needs of its members. The levels of emotional and instrumental functionality will vary from society to society and from time to time as other social systems may augment one or the other functions or put additional pressure on the family system to meet individual emotional or instrumental needs to a different degree, but the duality of the functionality in families is unmatched by other social systems.

Finally, families have certain relational qualities that distinguish them from other types of groups. We have no basis to argue that families are inherently places of loyalty, love, and affection. In fact, Straus[11] has argued that families can be "crucibles of violence." Instead, Straus points to the relational qualities of family life that provide the basis for distinguishing families from other types of groups. Families are characterized by extremely high levels of interdependence across a variety of domains (emotional, psychological, physical, behavioral, economic, social, etc.). This interdependence may not be voluntary and may even be resisted by family members, but it nevertheless exists and influences family members' reactions to each other. In addition to this interdependence, families are characterized by expectations for duration. Although many couples today eschew the traditional marital vow of "until death do us part" and some replace it with the vow of "for as long as our love shall last," in all cases couples enter into marriage and begin families with the expectation that their union is not temporary and will outlive other relationships or involvement in other systems such as school, work, community, and church. As noted later in the discussion of social exchange theory, this relational quality is important insofar as it conditions the interactions that occur in families both in terms of the exchange of valued resources and the interdependence of identities.

Primary versus Secondary Groups

Sociologists view groups as the core of their attention. They speak of in- and out-groups, primary and secondary groups, formal and informal groups, large and small groups, minority and majority groups, open and closed groups, organized and unorganized groups, independent and dependent groups, voluntary and involuntary groups, and others. Some of these constructs are more useful to understanding family systems than others. One distinction that appears particularly important for understanding families is primary versus secondary group relationships.

A **primary group** consists of a small number of people who interact in direct, personal, and intimate ways. Primary-group relationships are facilitated by (1) face-to-face contact, (2) smallness of size, and (3) frequent and intense contact. Unlike most primary groups, the family is special because it is so essential, both to individuals and

---

[11]Murray Straus and Suzanne K. Steinmetz, *Violence in the Family* (New York: Harper and Row, 1974).

to society, and its formation usually is legitimized by the community through religious and legal rituals. Although most other primary groups can disband voluntarily, the dissolution of the family group generally is accomplished through institutionalized means.

Much of the importance of marital, family, and kinship groups lies in their function as primary groups.[12] What functions does a primary group serve?

1. For most individuals, the primary group serves as the basic socializing agent for the acquisition and internalization of beliefs and attitudes.
2. Primary groups constitute the chief focus for the realization of personal satisfaction and fulfillment. In modern society, the family, perhaps more than any other source, influences its members' general sense of well-being, companionship, ego worth, security, and affection. This primacy of the family as a primary group may lie in the lack of alternative stable primary groups in a highly mobile, industrial, and capitalistic society. Unfortunately, involvement in primary groups, although necessary, may not always lead to satisfactory outcomes for individuals. Most people, when away from home for the first time, experience homesickness or a nostalgia for the primary group from which their immediate ties have been severed. Others experience relief at being freed from the oppression that primary ties can also create.
3. Primary groups, such as families, are also potentially important agents of indirect **internal social control** (social control brought about by the learning of rules and principles for behavior and maintained by internal psychological processes rather than outside pressures or threats of punishment). Primary groups have an extraordinary power to teach prosocial values, convey lessons of social responsibility, and bring about voluntary conformity because most people depend on other primary group members for meeting their psychological needs and for realizing meaningful social experiences.

The opposite of the primary group is the **secondary group**. Many if not most involvements in school, work, and the communities are characterized not by the intimate, informal, and personal nature of primary groups but rather by impersonal, segmental, and utilitarian contacts. Secondary groups basically are goal oriented rather than person oriented. For instance, the personal life of a bus driver, or a classmate, or an insurance salesperson is not of major significance in fulfilling the goals established for interactions with these people.

Of course, families also have a secondary component. In the past, families were relied on to produce what was necessary for subsistence and survival or to function as a political or military unit. The transference of wealth and external social control are two other secondary functions that families have been known to fulfill. Today, families are, for the most part, no longer *economic production units*, but they still function within the economic system as *consumption units* (e.g., they purchase houses, furniture, automobiles, etc.) that require rational organization of economic activity. They are also given other secondary group functions such as the direct external social control of members (both children and spouses) and the transference of wealth through inheritance.

In modern societies, such as those found in the United States and elsewhere (e.g., Canada, Western Europe, Scandinavia, Australia and New Zealand), most

---

[12]Note in particular William Marsiglio and John H. Scanzoni, *Families and Friendships: Applying the Sociological Imagination* (New York: HarperCollins, 1995).

TRANSNATIONAL FAMILIES

Therapeutic Concerns in Transnational Families

The process of economic globalization was made possible by advances in information and transportation technologies, a breakdown in the political power of nation-states, and the drive of advanced capitalism to seek out cheaper sources of materials and labor for production. With this economic globalization has come a parallel globalization of social relations that has increased the exchange of peoples across borders and made possible a new kind of immigration experience.

Celia Falicov, a clinical psychiatrist in San Diego California, notes how these new immigrants from Latin America, the Caribbean, and Asia differ from those of the past who moved to the United States primarily from Europe. In particular, she notes how early immigrants had to make a clean break from their countries of origin and from family and kin left behind. Although this created many "broken hearts" and adjustment difficulties, these older immigrants faced a clearer set of parameters to confront in their lives. Modern day immigrants, on the other hand, can take advantage of technologies and more open borders to maintain relationships with others in their home countries. This presents a different set of challenges: "Links across borders bring about the ambiguities of living with two hearts instead of a broken heart." (158). She highlights three sets of challenges that must be confronted.

The first is to recognize the unique ways that transnational families construct meaning in their lives. These families lack the advantage of family rituals and redundant interactions that give us a sense of coherency as a family and a sense of continuity of who we are over time. They are in a chronic state of "ambiguous loss" wherein family members are psychologically present but physically absent. This can result in many types of relational stress as family members are unclear about how they should act relative to each other. Although these families often create positive attachment behaviors in their children through communal parenting strategies in their home country, it is also important not to romanticize the strength of community ties and to recognize that home country conditions are not always favorable to optimal child development. Relational stress also occurs because separations are difficult and can cause high levels of guilt and resentment in family members. Also, reunions will not always be amicable. Members of a transnational family can become strangers to each other as a result of their prolonged separations. Expecting "family" type interactions upon reunion can lead to disappointment and conflict. Finally, transnational families must deal with "acculturative stress" as the receiving culture is more likely to have more egalitarian norms with respect to gender as well as have less age-based hierarchies than immigrants' home cultures. As a result, spousal and family relations may become more strained as members lack a shared set of values related to their gender and age position in the family

The second set of challenges involves their community context. Many immigrants place great importance on giving back to their home communities or making up for past deficiencies. There are also both positive and negative aspects to the ethnic communities within which many transnational families "rebuild" their home culture. These communities are positive insofar as they establish support networks and fend against discrimination. They can also be negative, however, insofar as they inhibit integration and sustain cultural values inconsistent with their new social context.

Finally, therapists and others need to recognize that transnational families often are faced with high levels of discrimination, suspicion, and subordination. As a result, issues of power and identity are likely to be significant, especially when they come into contact with agencies or persons of authority in the receiving culture.

Source: Celia J. Falicov, "Working with Transnational Immigrants: Expanding Meanings of Family, Community, and Culture," *Family Process*, 46 (2007), 157–171.

relationships in the public domain have become more rational, formal, and impersonal. As a result, marriage and family groups have taken on new importance in the emotional lives of their members and have become increasingly vital to individual health and happiness.[13] Of course, they have also maintained secondary functions related to day-to-day survival needs as the individuals involved need to coordinate their secondary survival activities to maintain these increasingly critical primary relationships. Thus, when families fail in modern societies, the results often are devastating. The absence or loss of familial networks as primary sources of social support has been linked to a wide range of negative outcomes: school truancy, accidents, suicides, commitment to mental hospitals, pregnancy disorders, coronary disease, and even lack of recovery from all types of illnesses. An argument could be made that, without families, survival in a modern society would be doubtful. This idea has been fairly well substantiated with infants and adults who have no family or close friends. One possible conclusion from all of this is that, rather than being in a state of decay or losing its significant functions and becoming obsolete, the U.S. family may be fulfilling a primary-group function that has seldom been more crucial and important in maintaining personal and social stability and well-being.

Characteristics of Marriage, Family, and Kinship Systems

Marriage, family, and *kinship systems* are institutionalized social arrangements in all known societies. However, the nature of the arrangement differs greatly across societies, over time, and even within a given society at a specific time. As noted earlier, how a society defines the family as an institution is determined partly by societal needs and partly by systems of power and conflict.

To understand how a society or cultural group defines a family requires a consideration of how it defines the boundaries of institutions. Who is or is not included as part of a marriage, family, or kinship group has implications for individual well-being, interaction patterns within the group, and other social institutions. In this section, we will discuss the variety of ways societies draw the boundaries of marriage and of family and kinship groups. We will also consider the system of social relationships shaped by those boundaries by presenting several "ideal types" of marriage, family, and kinship systems found around the world and throughout history. An explanation of and caution about ideal types are in order, however, before we begin.

Ideal Types

Ideal-type constructs always represent the ends, the extremes, or the poles of a continuum. Use of the word *ideal* is not meant to imply what is good, best, valuable, perfect, or desirable. Rather, ideal types are hypothetical constructs based on pure, definitive characteristics. Used hypothetically, ideal types provide contrasting qualities with which to characterize any social phenomenon. *Patriarchal/matriarchal, arranged marriage/free choice marriage, endogamy/exogamy, primary/secondary, individual/familial*, and *rural/urban* are examples of qualities of ideal types. In

---

[13]Ulrich Beck and Elisabeth Beck-Gernsheim, *The Normal Chaos of Love* (Cambridge: Polity, 1995).

ideal-type terms, the pure characteristics of either extreme may not exist anywhere in the world. Most marriages, families, and kinship systems fall somewhere on a continuum between the polar extremes.

The concept *ideal type* was systematically developed by the German sociologist Max Weber.[14] He was careful to point out that, first, value connotations should be avoided. The prefix *ideal* denotes a constructed model, not evaluation or approval. This term makes no suggestion as to what ought to be or what norm of conduct warrants approval or disapproval. Second, an ideal type or ideal construct is not an average. An *average* denotes a central tendency; an *ideal* is an extreme. A society might be characterized as having an autonomous mate selection system because most individuals in the society are allowed to choose their own marriage partners, but this does not mean that it fits the ideal type perfectly. As you will learn later, in every autonomous system there is some degree of restriction on choice. We classify the society as autonomous because the patterns of marriage partner selection come closest to the autonomous end of the continuum of ideal types. Third, as mentioned, an ideal type does not reflect reality. It is an abstraction, a logical construct, a pure form; thus, by nature, it is not found in reality.

In short, an ideal type provides a standard to use to assess what any phenomenon would be if it always or never conformed to its own definition. Thus, ideal types enable social scientists to make valid and precise comparisons among societies, institutions, and families separated in time and place. They enable those who study the family to have a methodological tool that provides assistance in examining, for instance, the upper or lower classes, African American or white American families, or arranged or free choice mate selection. In the sections that follow, ideal types are used to examine variations in marriage, family, and kinship systems around the world and across historical time periods.

Boundaries of Marriage

Throughout the world, marriage is an institutional arrangement between persons, generally males and females, who recognize each other as husband and wife or intimate partners. Marriage is a strictly human social institution and assumes some permanence and conformity to societal norms.

About forty years ago, anthropologist William Stephens said marriage is (1) a socially legitimate sexual union, begun with (2) a public announcement, undertaken with (3) some idea of performance, and assumed with a more or less explicit (4) marriage contract, which spells out reciprocal obligations between spouses and between spouses and their children.[15] For the most part, these same normative conditions exist today, although many marriage-like relationships are not defined by everyone as socially legitimate, are not begun with any type of announcement, are not entered into with the idea of permanence, and do not always have clearly defined contracts (written or nonwritten) as to what behaviors are expected. Thus, debate exists as to whether certain types of intimate relationships (such as among same-sex partners or unmarried cohabitors) are socially and legally recognized as marriages or families.

---

[14]Max Weber, *The Methodology of the Social Sciences*, trans. and ed. Edward H. Shils and Henry A. Finch (New York: The Free Press, 1949).

[15]William N. Stephens, *The Family in Cross Cultural Perspective* (New York: Holt, Rinehart and Winston, 1963), 7.

As noted earlier, any institutional definition is, in a certain sense, arbitrary. Most current definitions of marriage exclude persons in same-sex relationships, persons such as children, and persons who do not meet the social or cultural norms that specify what marriage is and who the legitimate partners are. In fact, many phenomenological, conflict, and feminist theorists (see Chapter 3) call into question the very use of labels such as *marriage*, *family*, and *kin*. The suggestion is that the very use of a label reifies a reality that ignores the historic origins and the range of meanings given to marriage and family by persons in their day-to-day lives.

Recognizing the danger of reifying the concept, let us turn our attention to historical and cross-cultural variations in marriage patterns, particularly as related to the number of persons involved.

Typology of Marital Systems

Marital status (single, married, separated, widowed, divorced) and number of spouses (none, one, more than one) are two major components of the boundaries of marriage. With a change in marital status and the number of spouses come variations in marital interaction patterns; living and sleeping arrangements; exclusivity of sexual interactions; the likelihood of and number of children; patterns of support, decision making, and authority; and male/female roles, to mention a few.

Sociologists and anthropologists have long used a typology of marital systems that focuses on the number of spouses allowed and preferred in a marriage and the gender of multiple spouses when allowed. The broadest distinction is between monogamous and polygamous systems. The suffix *-gamy* refers to marriage or a union for propagation and reproduction. Thus, *monogamy* (single), *bigamy* (two), *polygamy* (several or many), *allogamy* (closely related), *endogamy* (within), and *exogamy* (outside or external) describe the nature of marriage. **Monogamy** refers to marriage to a single spouse. **Polygamy** refers to marriage to several or many individuals; **bigamy** (marriage to two spouses) is a specific type of polygamy. Theoretically, there could be two or more wives (**polygyny**), two or more husbands (**polyandry**), or two or more husbands and wives (**group marriage**). Each of these is a polygamous marriage, as distinguished from a monogamous (one-spouse) marriage.

Before exploring each of these types further, it is important, once again, to note that these terms were constructed by social scientists to classify marriage systems under specific cultural conditions. Simply because these terms utilize the suffix *-gamy* does not mean that our conception of marriage systems has to be restricted to systems designed for propagation and reproduction. In fact, as we will see, the boundaries of marriage systems are constructed in societies for reasons having very little to do simply with propagation and reproduction of human children. Thus, nothing prevents us from using these same terms to refer to same-sex couples or those who do not desire to have children.

Monogamy

To most Americans, the most traditional as well as the most proper form of marriage is *monogamy*: one man to one woman (at a time). Throughout the world, this form of marriage is the only one universally recognized and is the predominant form even within societies where other forms exist. However, it should be noted that historically, on a societal basis, only a small percentage of societies in the world have been designated as strictly monogamous (monogamy as the required form).[16] Monogamy is the predominant form in most societies because in societies where other forms are allowed or even preferred, most men are too poor to have more than one wife and the ratios of men to women make widespread practice of multiple spouses difficult.

Although the United States is designated as strictly monogamous, it is possible for Americans to have more than one husband or one wife. Because monogamy has never achieved perfect stability, certain married persons end their relationships and most of them remarry. Thus, the second spouse, although not existing simultaneously with the first, is sometimes referred to as fitting into a pattern of **sequential or serial monogamy** or remarriage. Thus, in U.S. society, it is both legally and socially approved to have more than one wife or more than one husband, as long as they occur sequentially and not simultaneously. Whether or not this practice is preferred or highly institutionalized, however, remains to be determined.

Polygamy

From the perspective of families in North America, polygamy is a nontraditional family form, but for most of the world this form of marriage is traditional and preferred. As mentioned previously, there are three possible types of polygamy: *polygyny*, *polyandry*, and *group marriage*. The frequency with which marriage to a plural number of spouses occurs normatively (as an expected or desired type of marriage) was investigated in the late 1950s in a classic study by George Murdock. In a world sample of 554 societies, polygyny was culturally favored in 415 (77 percent), whereas polyandry was culturally favored in only four (less than 1 percent): Toda, Marquesas, Nayar, and Tibet.[17] Research over the years has never uncovered a society in which group marriage was clearly the dominant or most frequent form.

Before exploring patterns and explanations of polygamy across societies, several words of caution are needed concerning polygamy. First, it is necessary to maintain a clear distinction between ideology and actual occurrence. Occasionally, in the United States and elsewhere, groups advocate the right to have as many or as few spouses as desired, and when multiple-spouse marriages or communes are located and studied, the results are exploited by the mass media and given considerable attention. It seems, however, that the uniqueness or rarity of the situation attracts the attention rather than any commonality or acceptance.

Second, multiple spouses (except in group marriage) are only possible on a large scale when an unbalanced **sex ratio** (number of males per one hundred females) exists. Only if the sex ratio is high will polyandry be possible, and only when it is low will polygyny be possible. Such situations can be artificially created by increasing the permitted age at marriage for one sex (or making marriage more difficult by increasing its prerequisites) and decreasing it for the other (or easing requirements), and to some extent societies attempt to do this. This manipulation of the sex balance of available spouses, however, cannot be done without significantly increasing the number of single persons of one sex.

Third, polygamy is highly regulated and normatively controlled, as are all forms of marriage. Rarely does it involve a strictly personal or psychological motive.

---

[16]George P. Murdock, "World Ethnographic Sample," *American Anthropologist* 59 (August 1957): 686.
    [17]Ibid.

Polygamy has been illegal in the United States since 1878. Although groups that practice polygamy today identify themselves with Mormonism, the Mormon church rejected polygamy more than a century ago. In 2008, the U.S. government raided a polygamous compound of the Fundamentalist Church of Jesus Christ of Latter-Day Saints (FLDS) in Eldorado, Texas, and removed more than 200 women involved in polygamous marriages and their more than 400 children.

Rather, polygamy is likely to be supported by the attitudes and values of both sexes and linked closely to the sex ratio, economic conditions, and belief systems.

Fourth, polygamy has many forms and variations of normative structure that determine who the spouse should be. Polygamous marriages often are nonconsanguineous, meaning that the multiple spouses involved in a single marriage are not related to each other by blood. Equally or even more likely, however, are consanguineous marriages where the multiple spouses are blood relatives. In most cases, the relationship is at the level of first or second cousins,[18] but occasionally it is closer. For example, in some cases, all the multiple husbands are considered brothers (*fraternal polyandry*) or all the multiple wives are sisters (*sororal polygyny*). A levirate and sororate arrangement existed in the ancient Hebrew family. The **levirate** was a situation (technically, sequential monogamy) in which the wife

---

[18]Shuji Sueyoshi and Ryutaro Ohtsuka, "Effects of Polygyny and Consanguinity on High Fertility in the Rural Arab Population in South Jordan," *Journal of Biosocial Science* 35.4 (October 2003): 513–526.

married the brother of her deceased husband, whereas the **sororate** was a situation in which the preferred mate for a husband was the sister of his deceased wife.

Polygyny

In the early 1980s, Welch and Glick selected fifteen African countries to illustrate the incidence (polygynists per hundred married men), intensity (number of wives per polygynist), and general index (number of wives per married man).[19] The incidence of polygyny per hundred men was typically between twenty and thirty-five; that is, from about one in five to one in three married men had more than one wife. The intensity ranged from 2.0 to 2.5, which indicates that most polygynists had two wives rather than three or more. And for each country as a whole, the general index (number of wives per married man) ranged from 1.1 to 1.6, which indicates that most men, even in highly polygynous countries, had only one wife. Since then other researchers have demonstrated similar levels of polygyny. In one survey of African countries, 1993–1996 rates of polygynous marriage ranged from 18.6 percent (Zimbabwe) to 49.6 percent in Guinea. Furthermore, in spite of considerable social change and urbanization, most African countries experienced only modest reductions in polygyny, with Kenya leading the way with a 10 percent reduction in polygyny between 1977–1982 (29.5%) and 1993–1996 (19.5%).[20] In Arab countries, polygyny is less widely practiced with rates ranging from 3.7 percent in Lebanon (1986) to somewhere between 11.1 and 19.1 percent in Algeria (1993).[21] When translated into the number of women involved in polygynous marriages, estimates in both Arabia and Africa are in the range of 40–50 percent.[22]

Kanazawa and Still argue that if resource inequality among men is great, women choose to marry polygynously as this strategy maximizes their outcomes from marriage. If there is a high level of inequality between men and only a limited number of men with wealth, then polygamous marriage increases the available marriage slots for women to marry into wealth. If resource inequality among men is small, women have less to gain in marrying polygynously and less to lose in marrying monogamously and so choose to marry monogamously.[23] Thus, shifts from polygyny to monogamy will only occur in response to a decline of inequality among men. A criticism of this theory is that it places all of the impetus for marriage choice on women and ignores male choices. Alternatively, Sanderson argues that polygyny results primarily from males' desire for sexual variety, which has evolved because it enhances the likelihood of male reproductive success.[24] Whether these or other theories are correct, it does appear that a negative correlation exists between polygyny and women's status across societies. Polygyny is more common in countries such as

---

[19]Charles E. Welch III and Paul C. Glick, "The Incidence of Polygamy in Contemporary Africa: A Research Note," *Journal of Marriage and the Family* 43 (February 1981): 191–193.

[20]Ian M. Timaeus and Angela Reynar, "Polygynists and Their Wives in Sub-Saharan Africa: An Analysis of Five Demographic and Health Surveys," *Population Studies* 52.2 (July 1998): 145–162.

[21]Sueyoshi and Ohtsuka, "Effects of Polygyny and Consanguinity on High Fertility in the Rural Arab Population in South Jordan," 513–526.

[22]Ibid., 513–526; and Solene Lardoux and Etienne Van de Walle, "Polygyny and Fertility in Rural Senegal," *Population: English Edition* 58.6 (Nov.–Dec. 2003): 717–744.

[23]Satoshi Kanazawa and Mary C. Still, "Why Monogamy?" *Social Forces* 78 (September 1999): 25–50.

[24]Stephen K. Sanderson, "Explaining Monogamy and Polygyny in Human Societies: Comment on Kanazawa and Still," *Social Forces* 80 (September 2001): 329–336.

Africa and the Middle East where women's status is low and less common in Western and more highly industrialized countries with a more egalitarian ethic.

Why have more than one wife? Many circumstances and motives contribute to polygyny. Polygyny appears to be a privilege of the wealthy. Often, having several wives is a mark of prestige, distinction, and high status. The chiefs, the wealthy, the best hunters, and the leaders get second and third wives. In Israel, throughout the Old Testament period, polygyny was practiced but often was restricted to men who were rich, occupied leading positions, or had some other claim to distinction. Even today in the Middle East, the common man has only one wife but wealthy men are more likely to have more than one. Such a motivation leads to a type of polygyny known as **affluent polygyny**. This type is widely practiced among middle- and upper-class males in Arab countries and contains many elements of control and exploitation of women. An alternative form of polygyny based on more practical concerns might be called **intervention polygyny**. Here, women choose to enter into polygynous marriages or to accept polygynous marriages because doing so resolves marital problems stemming primarily from the failure to produce male children.[25]

Other reasons given for polygyny include wife capture (where the men from one village literally take wives from another village), economic value of wifely services, and, in some instances, religious revelation. The frequently cited example of Mormon polygyny originated in a religious revelation to Joseph Smith, the founder of the Church of Jesus Christ of Latter-Day Saints (the Mormon religion). Interestingly, some of the factors that led to the occurrence of polygyny in this religion were the same factors that led to its being outlawed. Namely, the Mormon faith was begun and maintained by devout conviction to carrying out God's will; it was ended by a revelation from God to the president of the church forbidding the continuation of polygyny.

Christianity stamped Western society in a similar manner by outlawing polygyny. Polygyny was frequent among the pre-Christian tribes of Europe as well as in Old Testament Hebrew accounts. Gideon, the Israelite judge, had many wives who bore him seventy sons (Judges 8:30). King David had several wives (Samuel 25:39, 43; II Samuel 3:2 ff., 5:13), and King Solomon had a huge number of wives (I Kings 9:16; Song of Solomon 6:8).

The desire for children (especially male children) and the need to enhance their survival is greatly enhanced by polygyny. By sharing childbearing responsibilities, each family unit can produce more offspring at the same time that total fertility is reduced.[26] This reduction in total fertility (the number of children a woman bears in a lifetime) comes about because of a number of factors ranging from reduced frequency of intercourse; competition dynamics between wives; extended breast-feeding creating conditions of lactational amenorrhea (absence or suppression of menstruation while breastfeeding); and longer birth intervals.

In addition to reduced fertility (and the potential health benefits to mothers and children that result from less frequent childbearing and longer birth intervals), there may be other advantages to polygyny. Although most people in western societies would expect jealousy, competition, and conflict as disruptive factors among multiple

---

[25]Augustine Nwoye, "The Practice of Interventive Polygamy in Two Regions of Africa: Background, Theory and Techniques," *Dialectical Anthropology* 31.4 (December 2007): 383–421.

[26]Sueyoshi and Ohtsuka, "Effects of Polygyny and Consanguinity on High Fertility in the Rural Arab Population in South Jordan," 513–526; and Lardoux and Van de Walle, "Polygyny and Fertility in Rural Senegal," 717–744.

wives, a study from Ibadan, Nigeria, where polygyny is very common, indicated that co-wives get along fairly well. When wives were asked how they would feel if their husbands took another wife, some 60 percent said they would be pleased to share the housework, husband care, and child rearing and to have someone to gossip and "play" with.[27] Perhaps for this reason, in Nigeria, the number of plural wives was found to be related to the stability of marriage.[28] However, unions with two wives were more stable than those with three or more wives. Despite an ideology of equity among all the wives, it is likely that, when there are more than two, differentiation increases among the wives on the basis of age, education, family wealth, and so on. Marriage to a third or fourth wife, thus, seems to intensify co-wife conflict and economic constraints.

On the negative side, polygyny, especially affluent polygyny, appears to have many negative psychological consequences for both mothers and children. Bedouin Arab women in polygynous marriages where found to have more psychological problems and marital distress than those in monogamous marriages, and their children also had more psychosocial problems and performed more poorly in school.[29]

What about polygyny in the United States today?[30] The most frequently cited sources of polygyny are those of certain Mormon fundamentalists living in "underground" family units in Utah and neighboring states. These dissident Mormons have no affiliation with the mainline Church of Jesus Christ of Latter-Day Saints. The number of these marriages is unknown.

Polyandry

Polyandry, the marriage of one woman to more than one man at the same time, appears quite rare. Stephens has made several generalizations about polyandry. First, polyandry and group marriage tend to go together; where one is found, the other will likely be found.[31]

Second, co-husbanding is fraternal. In the few cases in which the husbands are not brothers, they are clan brothers; that is, they belong to the same clan and are of the same generation. Among the Todas, a non-Hindu tribe in India, it is understood that when a woman marries a man, she becomes the wife of his brothers at the same time. Among the Yanomama Indians living in northern Brazil, a wife may have other recognized sexual unions with the consent of her husband. The most frequent union is with the husband's younger brother, who, until he acquires his own wife, has a quasi-right to his older brother's wife. The husband may also consent to share his wife with other males, kin or non-kin, who may be recognized as secondary husbands throughout their lives.[32]

---

[27]Helen Ware, "Polygyny: Women's Views in a Traditional Society, Nigeria 1975," *Journal of Marriage and the Family* 41 (February 1979): 188.

[28]Anastasia J. Gege-Brandon, "The Polygyny–Divorce Relationship: A Case Study of Nigeria," *Journal of Marriage and the Family* 54 (May 1992): 285–292.

[29]Alean Al-Krenawi and John R. Graham, "A Comparison of Family Functioning, Life and Marital Satisfaction, and Mental Health of Women in Polygamous and Monogamous Marriages," *International Journal of Social Psychiatry* 52.1 (Jan 2006): 5–17; Alean Al-Krenawi and Vered Slonim-Nevo, "Psychosocial and Familial Functioning of Children from Polygynous and Monogamous Families," *The Journal of Social Psychology* 148.6 (December 2008.): 745–764.

[30]See Irwin Altman and Joseph Ginat, *Polygamous Families in Contemporary Society* (New York: Cambridge University Press, 1996).

[31]Stephens, *The Family in Cross Cultural Perspective*, 39–49.

[32]John D. Early and John F. Peters, *The Population Dynamics of the Mucajai Yanomama* (New York: Academic Press, 1990), 40.

Third, an economic inducement is often mentioned. A man tries to recruit co-husbands so they will work for him. In other instances, co-husbandry is practiced for economic security or as an answer to a land shortage. When several men marry one woman, the fragmentation of holdings, especially land, is avoided. Cassidy and Lee argued that economic factors are the key to understanding the very existence of polyandry.[33] That is, the two most important antecedents to polyandry appear to be (1) extreme societal poverty with harsh environmental conditions and (2) limited roles for women in the productive economy.

Where polyandry does exist, there is frequent mention of female infanticide. It is a curious anomaly that male infanticide is rarely, if ever, mentioned in the literature. Female infanticide eliminates the wife surplus among polyandrous families; however, male infanticide does not seem to be used to eliminate the husband surplus in polygynous societies.

Group Marriage

Group marriage exists when several males and several females are married simultaneously to each other. Except on an experimental basis, this is an extremely rare occurrence and may never have existed as a viable form of marriage for any society in the world.

The Oneida Community of upstate New York has been frequently cited as an example of a group marriage experiment (see Family Diversity box). In the mid-1800s, the Oneida practiced economic and sexual sharing based on spiritual and religious principles. The group was an experimental religious community and not representative of U.S. society at the time. In addition, similar to most group marriages on record, the timespan of this experiment was limited. Rarely do such arrangements endure beyond one or two generations.

Group marriage has various difficulties that include getting all members to accept each other as spouses; avoiding jealousy over status, privileges, affection, and sex; and problems related to housing, income, children, privacy, and division of labor in general. What's more, when group marriage does exist, the strong negative reactions of outside persons force anonymity and secrecy. Thus, it seems reasonable to assume that group marriage will never become very popular.

Boundaries of the Family

It could be said that all marriages are families but not all families are marriages. And certain functions expected in the marital relationship (coitus or sexual intercourse) are taboo among certain family members (such as between brothers and sisters). As marriages differ structurally in the number of spouses, families differ structurally in size and composition.

Typology of Family Systems

One controversy in the family literature has focused on the extent to which families, particularly in the United States, are, and traditionally have been, small, isolated, independent units as opposed to large, interdependent networks. The extremes usually are represented by a nuclear/extended dichotomy, with modified nuclear and modified extended as intermediate positions. The major characteristics of these

---

[33]Margaret L. Cassidy and Gary R. Lee, "The Study of Polyandry: A Critique and Synthesis," *Journal of Comparative Family Studies* 20 (Spring 1989): 1–11.

Family Diversity

Group Marriage in the Oneida Community

The Oneida Community began in New York in 1848 with approximately twenty-five members. The leader, John Humphrey Noyes, gave up law to enter the ministry. He preached that human beings were capable of living sinless lives based on a spiritual equality of all persons: materially, socially, and sexually. Monogamy was a sign of selfish possessiveness.

Under the charismatic leadership of this man, the group grew and prospered. The emphasis was on *we* rather than on *I*. Economically, there was self-sufficiency and equal ownership of property. The Oneida made traps, marketed crops in cans and glass jars, did silk spinning, and manufactured silverware. To eliminate feelings of discrimination and sexual inequality, jobs were rotated.

The group differed from most other communal groups in its *group marriage*, or pantogamous (marriage for all), relationship. It was felt that romantic love made spiritual love impossible to attain and gave rise to jealousy, hate, and the like; therefore, everyone should literally love everyone else. Requests for sexual relationships were made to a central committee. A go-between, usually an older woman, would get the consent of the requested female (women rarely made requests), and, if agreed upon, the couple would go to the woman's bedroom.

Any discord or problem among the Oneida was handled daily in a practice known as *mutual criticism*, in which the followers would subject themselves to criticism by the rest of the group. The criticized member would sit quietly while the others listed his or her good and bad points. The result was said to be a catharsis, a spiritual cleansing, with remarkably successful outcomes.

When Noyes left the group for Canada in 1879, for whatever reason (outside pressures, age, health, intra-commune strife), the group marriage practice came to an end. However, the economically successful venture continued.

On November 20, 1880, the group incorporated as Oneida Community, Ltd., to succeed Oneida Community. The present title, Oneida Ltd., was adopted in 1935.

Today, Oneida Ltd. is listed on the New York Stock Exchange (symbol OCQ). The company manufactures and markets a variety of tableware items, including silver-plated and stainless steel products, china dinnerware, and gift items such as glass stemware and barware. It is an international corporation with facilities throughout the world including Australia, Asia/Pacific, Canada, Mexico, Latin America, the Middle East, Africa, and Europe. In 2001, the company had sales of more than $500 million, had nearly 4,600 employees, had a stock range of between $10 and $20, and was paying a small dividend.

This company, resulting from a mid-nineteenth-century utopian community, would make Noyes proud today. His children and grandchildren have prospered well. Although group marriage is out, profits are in.

---

family types are outlined in Table 1.1 (page 28). The solution to this controversy lies in questions related to geographical isolation, economic independence, and social autonomy—in other words, in physical, economic, and social boundaries that separate one unit from another. Do families live separately from kin? Do other relatives outside the nuclear unit provide financial assistance or aid in times of need? Do kin provide significant emotional support, visiting patterns, and social activities?

A related controversy is whether the emergence of an isolated, independent, and autonomous nuclear family leads to high divorce rates; to the need for more public assistance programs for people who are aged, for single parents, or for families in poverty; and to an increase in personal instability (alcoholism, suicide, mental illness, and the like). This latter controversy cannot be answered simply. It is first necessary to understand the characteristics of each type of family system and how different family systems might have unique adaptive advantages under different

Table 1.1

Typology of Family Structures

NUCLEAR AND CONJUGAL	MODIFIED NUCLEAR AND MODIFIED EXTENDED	EXTENDED
Small size	Intermediate size	Many kin
Geographic isolation	Kin within easy visiting distance	Geographic proximity
Minimal kin contact	Regular contact	Daily contact
Family autonomy	Family autonomy with kin influences in decision making	Intergenerational authority
Economic self-sufficiency	Considerable exchange of goods and services	Economic interdependence
Nonkin models of socialization	Kin, friendship, nonkin models of socialization	Kinship network as model for socialization
Emotional support and protection from nonkin		Kinship complete source of emotional support and protection

environmental and social conditions. To treat the family as an institution voluntarily constructed by its members without external pressures and constraints would be to ignore the realities of the social world.

Nuclear and Conjugal Families

Both nuclear and conjugal families characterize the family unit in its smallest form. Generally, this form includes the husband, the wife, and their immediate children. The terms *nuclear* and *conjugal* are at times used interchangeably; however, they are not truly synonymous. A **conjugal family** must include a husband and wife. A **nuclear family** may or may not include the marriage partners but consists of any two or more persons related to one another by birth (blood), marriage, or adoption, assuming they are of the same or adjoining generations. Thus, a brother and sister or a single parent and child are both nuclear families but would not, technically speaking, be conjugal families.

Because most persons marry, it is likely that, during their lifetimes, they will be members of two different but overlapping nuclear families. The nuclear family into which someone is born and reared (consisting of self, brothers and sisters, and parents) is termed the **family of orientation**. This is the family unit in which the first and most basic socialization processes occur. When an individual marries, he or she forms a new nuclear (and conjugal) family—a **family of procreation**. This family is composed of the individual, his or her spouse, and their children.

Extended Families

The term **extended family** refers to family structures that extend beyond the nuclear family. As stated, there may be multiple nuclear family groupings within the

CROSS-CULTURAL *Perspective*

Extended Families in China

The clan system of traditional China was extremely important to the maintenance of ancestral linkages and group solidarity. A *clan*, sometimes referred to as a *tsu*, included all persons with a common surname who traced descent from a common ancestor. The tsu operated through a council of elders; it often involved several thousand persons—sometimes entire villages.

The significance that this large clan group had for the family can be seen in the functions the clan performed: lending money to members, helping individual families pay for extravagant weddings and funerals, establishing schools, exercising judicial authority, acting as a government agent in collecting taxes, and maintaining ancestral graves and tsu property. The clan performed most of the functions generally associated with government: taxes, law enforcement, schools, welfare, and so on. As one might guess, the tsu came under serious attack when the revolutionary government came into power.

In the contemporary Chinese family, extended family relationships show signs of change. Logan and others say there have been fundamental changes in family relationships in urban China. Arranged marriages have become less common, women are treated more equitably by their co-residing mothers-in-law than before, and there is greater autonomy for both the parent and child generations. Yet co-residence remains nearly as high in China as in some other East Asian countries—thus, much higher than in the West.

One state policy that may have deep impacts on the extended family and on intergenerational relations is the one-child family policy. Population control in the 1980s and 1990s sharply reduced fertility, with an immediate impact on the presence of grandchildren and eventual effects on the number and possibly on the gender of adult children. Clearly the one-child family will force many older people to live alone.

On the other hand, as they have fewer children, parents and grandparents may invest more in each child and, therefore, increase the likelihood of reciprocal support in old age. An only child may feel more obligation to parents. Logan and colleagues say some data suggest that parents with only one child are more likely to prefer co-residence than those with more than one and that only children are especially likely to live with parents.

See: Paul Chao, *Women Under Communism: Family in Russia and China* (Bayside, NY: General Hall, 1977); John R. Logan, Fuqin Bian, and Yanjie Bian, "Tradition and Change in the Urban Chinese Family: The Case of Living Arrangements," *Social Forces* 76 (March 1998): 851–852; and John R. Logan and Fuqin Bian, "Family Values and Coresidence with Married Children in Urban China," *Social Forces* 77 (June 1999): 1253–1282.

---

extended family. Sometimes the terms *consanguine families* and *joint families* are used interchangeably with *extended families*. Both consanguine and joint families are extended families; however, the emphasis in the **consanguine family** is on blood ties rather than marital ties. Thus, in a consanguineous marriage, the two partners have at least one ancestor in common, such as a marriage between third cousins or closer relatives.

Generally, it is assumed that consanguineous marriages decline in response to the forces of modernization and industrialization. But some recent evidence from Iran suggests this may not always be the case. Factors, such as an increased pool of cousins (due to lower infant mortality, for example), may actually lead to an increase in consanguinity when modernization takes place.[34]

---

[34]Benjamin P. Givens and Charles Hirschman, "Modernization and Consanguineous Marriage in Iran," *Journal of Marriage and the Family* 56 (November 1994): 820–834.

The term **joint family** is not used as frequently today as in times past. The term has most often been used to describe large families in India when at least two brothers, with their own wives and children, lived together in the same household. The joint family was *consanguine* in that the brothers were related by blood and extended in that the wives of the brothers (sisters-in-law) and their children (nephews, nieces, and cousins) lived together. The family was *joint* in that there existed a common treasury, common kitchen and dining room, and common deities. This Indian form of joint family was usually patrilineal and patrilocal and emphasized filial and fraternal solidarity.

The smallest variety of extended family is the **stem family**. Normally, a stem family consists of two families in adjacent generations, joined by economic and blood ties. This type of family is quite common in Japan where, despite rapid urbanization, approximately 25 percent of middle-aged married couples live with one spouse's parents.[35] These stem families are most common if the marriage was arranged, the husband was the oldest son, and/or the wife was the oldest daughter and had no brothers.

Dr. Vern Bengtson, in his Burgess Award Lecture to the National Council on Family Relations, argued that family relationships across several generations are becoming increasingly important in American society. His arguments for this statement include (1) the demographic change of population aging, which results in "longer years of shared hours" between generations; (2) the increasing importance of grandparents and other kin in fulfilling family functions; and (3) the strength and resilience of intergenerational solidarity over time.[36]

Modified-Nuclear and Modified-Extended Families

A number of writers have suggested that the isolated nuclear family, as well as the traditional large extended family, are largely fictitious. That is, families of procreation as well as never-married single, widowed, and divorced persons actually maintain sufficient independence to be defined as distinct units but also function within a network of other nuclear families and social networks, offering services and gifts and maintaining close contact.[37] Thus, the idea of a modified form of nuclear or extended family has developed.

Although no clear consensus exists on where to mark the distinction between a modified-nuclear and a modified-extended family, it is clear that each type takes an intermediate position between the isolated, independent, small nuclear unit and the interdependent co-resident kin network of the extended family (see Table 1.1 on page 28). In an extended typology of family extendedness, a **modified-nuclear family structure** would be one where families of procreation retain considerable autonomy (e.g., independent decision making about organization of family work, socialization practices, and budgetary matters) yet maintain a coalition with other nuclear families with which they engage in a high level of exchange in terms of contact levels, financial assistance,

[35]Yoshinori Kamo, "Husbands and Wives Living in Nuclear and Stem Family Households in Japan," *Sociological Perspectives* 33 (1990): 397–417.

[36]Vern L. Bengtson, "Beyond the Nuclear Family: The Increasing Importance of Multigenerational Bonds," *Journal of Marriage and the Family* 63 (February 2001): 1–16.

[37]Eugene Litwak and Stephen Kulis, "Technology, Proximity and Measures of Kin Support," *Journal of Marriage and the Family* 49 (August 1987): 649–661; and Naomi Gerstel, "Divorce and Kin Ties: The Importance of Gender," *Journal of Marriage and the Family* 50 (February 1988): 209–219. See also the classical article on this topic by Marvin B. Sussman, "The Isolated Nuclear Family: Fact or Fiction," *Social Problems* 6 (Spring 1959): 333–340.

Extended family networks exist in all societies. Even in North America, the transmission of property, the proximity of residence, and the formal and informal contacts made through calls, visits, and gifts demonstrate the presence and importance of extended kin networks. Some families have reunions on a regular basis to bring old and new members together.

and in-kind assistance (e.g., child care, home maintenance, etc.). In modified-nuclear families, the different units may include other kin (e.g., a grandmother, adult siblings, or grandchildren), but do so more as a means of providing or receiving assistance than as fully integrated members of the family system. For the most part, modified-nuclear family systems maintain separate households but typically live in close proximity to one another or experience periods of more intense interaction co-residence with kin. The family living arrangements of many Latino immigrant families in the United States most resemble this type of family system.[38]

In contrast, in a **modified-extended family structure,** considerably less autonomy exists among the separate units. How children are socialized or how finances are accumulated and dispersed in one parental unit are decisions that need to be coordinated with other units. In a modified-extended family, co-residence is more likely to occur, but with considerable latitude for independent living and decision making within smaller units. When separate residence occurs, these family systems demonstrate high levels of economic interdependency. Filipino and Cambodian-American immigrant families perhaps best exemplify the co-residential nature and high economic interdependency present in these types of families.[39]

---

[38]Susan Blank and Ramon S. Torrecilha, "Understanding the Living Arrangements of Latino Immigrants: A Life Course Approach," *International Migration Review* 32.1 (Spring 1998): 3–19; and Jennifer VanHook and Jennifer Glick, "Immigration and Living Arrangements: Moving Beyond Economic Need Versus Acculturation," *Demography* 44.2 (2007): 225–249.

[39]Gay Becker, Yewoubdar Beyene, Edwina Newsom, and Nury Mayen, "Creating Continuity through Mutual Assistance: Intergenerational Reciprocity in Four Ethnic Groups," *Journals of Gerontology Series B: Psychological Sciences and Social Sciences* 58B.3 (2003): 151–159.

CROSS-CULTURAL *Perspective*

Nuclear Families in Sweden

According to Popenoe, the case for Sweden's world-leading move away from the traditional nuclear family is based on five main factors:

1. A low rate of marriage
2. A high rate of cohabitation
3. A high rate of family dissolution
4. A small household size
5. The extensive move of mothers into the labor force

In spite of these changes, Popenoe suggested the Swedish family is strong and established. Most men and women want to live as couples and have not turned against the idea of permanent monogamous dyads. Most women still want to have and do have children. Children are born into a society that has an enviable record in its public child-care policies. Fathers and mothers, in greater numbers than anywhere in the Western world, take parental leave from employment.

The degree of Swedish familism is shown as well by the extent to which social life continues to revolve strongly around gatherings of relatives. It seems that the Swedish women's movement has never had much of the antifamily sentiment found in the U.S. movement. In short, while the form or structure of the family has changed and will likely continue to do so, families are alive and well in Sweden.

See: David Popenoe, "Beyond the Nuclear Family: A Statistical Portrait of the Changing Family in Sweden," *Journal of Marriage and the Family* 49 (February 1987): 173–183.

Glick and others[40] suggest that the long-term downward trend in the percentage of extended family households in the United States came to a halt during the 1980s. One key factor in this change is immigration. Changes in national origin of the immigrant population have influenced increased rates of extended family living among all immigrants since 1970. Immigrants from countries closer to the United States and that are likely to send labor migrants (Mexico and Latin America) have contributed significantly to the increase in extended households. But increases in immigration from Asian countries have also made significant contributions to increasing family households. The result is a widening gap between immigrants and natives in the proportion of the U.S. population residing in extended family households.

The following section contains a closer examination of the boundaries of the kinship network and intergenerational relationships and the major importance they hold for most people today.

Boundaries of Kinship

Kinship systems involve patterns of rights, obligations, and constraints that govern the relationships between individuals in societies based on ties of blood, marriage, or adoption. Kinship norms vary widely across societies and most govern patterns

---

[40]Jennifer E. Glick, Frank D. Bean, and Jennifer V. W. Van Hook, "Immigration and Changing Patterns of Extended Family Household Structure in the United States," *Journal of Marriage and the Family* 59 (February 1997): 177–191.

of residency (e.g., where newly married couples live relative to each spouse's parents) and property relationships (e.g., inheritance of private property). These norms are important elements in how power is structured and maintained in societies, especially with respect to age and gender. Kinship systems are more elaborate and consist of more rules and norms in societies where economic production is centered around genealogical relations. In modern industrial societies, kinship takes on less significance, although such ties still maintain significance for the well-being of individuals and families. In the sections that follow, we will examine some of the key areas of life that kinships systems govern in societies and the variation that exists in how societies structure their kinship relations.

Functions of Kinship Systems

Keeping in mind our earlier discussion of the substitutability of institutions and the concept of functional equivalence, kinship groups and systems have tended to fulfill certain functions even when the kinship network is indistinguishable from other institutions. Some of the key functions that kinship systems have served in the past include:

1. Property holding and inheritance
2. Housing and residential proximity
3. Keeping in touch and gift giving
4. Affection, emotional ties, and primary relationships
5. Regulation of sexual relationships

A brief examination of each of these five aspects of kinship group regulation follows.

Property Holding and Inheritance

The holding, ownership, and control of property and the transmission of property from one owner to another are issues of central concern to family sociologists and anthropologists in general and to conflict theorists and feminists in particular. Property ownership is directly related to wealth and power, and inheritance has implications for how wealth and power are transmitted. Within family systems, this transference is directly linked to inheritance and the rules of descent.

At birth, each person inherits two separate bloodlines; thus, a key issue in most societies (less so in the United States and other Western societies) is whose bloodline, the mother's or the father's, is the more important. If the descent pattern is **unilineal**—as is true in most societies in Asia, India, and Africa—the name, property, authority, and marriage controls are traced through one line, usually the father and his bloodline. This pattern is **patrilineal** and helps to preserve male power in a society by concentrating property resources among men. A **matrilineal** pattern—a unilineal system that traces the lineage through the female line—is found much less frequently. Where it is found, however, women are likely to have more power in the family and the society; although as we shall see later, sometimes societies construct elaborate residence rules that preserve male power and privilege even when property is owned by and transferred through the female line. Finally, the system of descent most prevalent in modern societies (such as the United States), where more equality exists between the sexes, is the **bilateral** system in which power and property are transferred through both the mother's and father's lines to both males and females.

One key exception to this pattern is name. In the United States, both genders tend to assume the names of their fathers, and most wives take their husbands' family names on marriage. This, too, may be in a process of changing, albeit slowly. Female college students were far more accepting of nontraditional name choices and more tolerant of choices made by others.[41] Even so, more than 80 percent of females said that if they marry, they plan to change their last name to that of their husband. Women planning to marry at a later age and expecting nontraditional work roles were less likely than other women to want to change their last name to that of their husband.

Patterns of descent take on special significance to many feminists and conflict theorists (see Chapter 3) for several reasons. First of all, most family systems throughout the world tend to perpetuate power and wealth through successive generations, that is, the rich stay rich and the poor stay poor. Also, most family systems differentiate this power and wealth between the sexes, with males receiving preferential treatment. The result is that class and sexual inequalities are built into most family systems, such that the inequalities come to be viewed as natural and legitimate. In other words, some families have the right to be wealthier than others, males are expected to be dominant, and females are supposed to submit to their male counterparts.

Housing and Residential Proximity

All family systems have rules of residence that establish who lives where and with whom. Because husbands and wives come from different families and most spouses choose to share the same residence, to achieve this one or both individuals must move.

The most common residential pattern is **patrilocal**, in which the bride changes residence and lives with the parents of the groom. In the **matrilocal** pattern, which is much less frequently found, the newlywed couple lives with the parents of the bride. In most Western countries, including the United States, far more common than either of the preceding are the **bilocal** system, in which the couple lives near the parents of either spouse, and the **neolocal** system, in which the couple lives in a home of their own that may be located apart from both sets of parents. Perhaps the most unusual type of residence rule, found in societies with matrilineal descent systems, is avunculocal. In the **avunculocal** system, a son goes to live with his maternal uncle (his mother's brother) when he attains adulthood and his new wife goes to live with him there when they are married. In this way, the property is handed down through the female line, but the property is controlled by a male of her line. The male who inherits the property then accepts his sister's adult male child (his nephew) into his household and this child will inherit the property in the next generation. His own male child will go to live with his wife's brother to continue her line. In this way, the property remains in the control of the males of each generation, but male heirs to the property continue to be provided by the same female line from generation to generation. Such a system preserves male power in a society where the property is invested in women.

---

[41]Laurie K. Scheuble and David R. Johnson, "Marital Name Change: Plans and Attitudes of College Students," *Journal of Marriage and the Family* 55 (August 1993): 747–754. Note also David R. Johnson and Laurie K. Scheuble, "Women's Marital Naming in Two Generations: A National Study," *Journal of Marriage and the Family* 57 (August 1995): 724–732.

CROSS-CULTURAL *Perspective*

Mexico

Family life in Mexico is of particular interest to family sociologists in the United States. As a border country to the United States, Mexican social institutions and cultural belief systems are a major source of social and cultural diversity in American family life due to historical patterns of annexation and contemporary patterns of immigration. One dimension of Mexican family life that has received considerable attention in both academic and popular press writings is the nature of Mexican kinship relations. As we will note later in Chapter 5, the Mexican-American family system is less extended in form than is popularly believed and comes closest to being a modified nuclear family. Nevertheless, the importance of kin relationship among Mexican Americans is well documented. In particular, much has been made of the system of godparenting—*comadrazgo*—and the role of unrelated godparents—*comadre* and *compadre*—in the successful adaptation of Mexican-American families. Although kinship relations have been studied extensively among Mexican-Americans, less is known about how these relationships function among contemporary Mexican families. Are the patterns of kinship relations and supports found in the United States simply a product of unique adaptations to American society, or do they have their roots in the Mexican system of social institutions and cultural beliefs?

A recent study by Shawn Malia Kana'Iaupuni, Katherine Donato, Theresa Thompson-Colon and Melissa Stainback explored how immediate and extended kinship relations function among economically marginalized families in ten villages in Mexico. Using data from the first wave of the Health and Migration Survey, they were interested in the characteristics of social networks and how those networks impacted child health. They found that although high contact and co-residence with *immediate kin* (mothers, siblings, children) results in high levels of emotional supports, the effects of *immediate kin* on financial support in impoverished Mexican families are negative. In contrast, high levels of contact and co-residence with *extended kin* has a significant positive impact on both emotional and financial support. They also found that high levels of extended family co-residence played an important role in promoting more positive health outcomes among children.

They conclude that the strong cultural expectations for reciprocity among extended kin and the diversity of life circumstances (especially in terms of resource availability) introduced into Mexican extended kin relationships by the custom of the comadrazgo make these relationships important resources to families trying to adapt to impoverished economic conditions. Unlike immediate kin, these extended kin members are less likely to be dependent on the household and are more likely to have resources they can contribute to the common well-being of household members.

Source: Shawn Malia Kana'Iaupuni, Katherine M. Donato, Theresa Thompson-Colon and Melissa Stainback, "Counting on Kin: Social Networks, Social Support, and Child Health Status," *Social Forces*, 83 (2005), 1137–1164.

The pattern of residence takes on a special significance for the third and fourth aspects of kinship, namely, obligation and emotional ties among kin. Helping patterns and showing affection to grandparents, parents, and siblings take on different character depending on whether the people involved share the same building, live in the same neighborhood or community, or reside hundreds of miles apart. Research on transnational families, however, suggests that such obligations can withstand vast geographical distances in a world made smaller by technology.[42]

---

[42]Celia J. Falicov, "Working With Transnational Immigrants: Expanding Meanings of Family, Community, and Culture," *Family Process* 46 (2007):157–171.

Data from the 1980s suggest that residence patterns in the United States show a surprising degree of local concentration. In the study of Middletown, for example, taking any resident of the city at random, the odds were one in five that a brother or sister also lived in the city; one in three that one or both parents lived there; and two in five that a more distant relative (a grandparent, aunt, uncle, or cousin) lived there.[43] The respondents' immediate families were especially concentrated, with 54 percent of the grown children, 43 percent of the parents, and 31 percent of the brothers and sisters living right in Middletown.[44] These percentages increased considerably when a 50-mile radius was used to establish residence. Thus, although a newlywed couple may establish a residence separate from their parents, it tends to be in geographical proximity to parents and siblings.

Keeping in Touch and Gift Giving

Around the world, it is expected that kin communicate or keep in touch, particularly with parents, to a lesser extent with siblings, and even less so with other relatives such as aunts, uncles, and cousins. Many extended families have a person who could be considered a **kinkeeper**, usually a female, who works at keeping the family members in touch with one another.[45]

In the 1980s, the main determinants of the amount of interaction between relatives in Middletown were the distance between their homes and the closeness of their relationships. With increasing distance, visiting was replaced by telephone calls, which was replaced by letter writing. Almost no one corresponded regularly with cousins, except perhaps through exchanging Christmas cards. Consistently, women did more joint activities with parents and other kin than did men.

In the new millennium, with advances in Internet availability and usage, the importance of distance as a determinant of contact with both friends and relatives is only slightly reduced. In a study of "Netville"—a new and highly "wired" suburb of Toronto, Canada—contact with kin among new residents was only increased by Internet usage when distances were within 50 to 500 kilometers. The greater availability and use of the Internet in this community had less impact at shorter or greater distances.[46] Furthermore, other studies have shown little impact of Internet usage on kinship exchanges[47] and a maintenance of the traditional allocation of kinkeeping tasks (even those involving Internet connections) to women.[48]

In addition to the maintenance of social contacts, it often is expected that services or gifts be shared among relatives as gestures of goodwill and kindness. Gift giving, whether with friends or family, tends to cement social relationships. The gifts may be material or nonmaterial: presents of food (having guests for dinner), lodging (offering guests a place to stay in one's home), and care or help. Data from the Netherlands that examined gift giving in Western societies revealed that gifts are

---

[43]Theodore Caplow et al., *Middletown Families* (New York: Bantam Books, 1982), 206.

[44]Ibid., 203.

[45]K.L. Fingerman, "The Role of Offspring and In-Laws in Grandparents' Ties to Their Grandchildren," *Journal of Family Issues* 25 (2004) 1026–1049.

[46]Keith Hampton and Barry Wellman, "Long Distance Community in the Network Society: Contact and Support Beyond Netville," *American Behavioral Scientist* 45.3 (November 2001): 476–495.

[47]Valentina Hlebec, Katja Lozar Manfreda, and Vasja Vehovar, "The Social Support Networks of Internet Users," *New Media & Society* 8.1 (February 2006): 9–32.

[48]Bonka Boneve, Robert Kraut, and David Frohlich, "Using E-mail for Personal Relationships: The Difference Gender Makes," *American Behavioral Scientist* 45.3 (November 2001): 530–549.

given approximately to the same extent to extended kin and to friends, but gifts to friends seem to be given more out of affection than out of obligation.[49] Gift giving to extended kin is more obligatory, but at the same time it is more enduring than giving to friends.

These patterns may be undergoing change, however, as conditions of modernity break down obligations based on family and kinship and replace them with obligations of the state to individuals. In Sweden, arguably the most modern of nation states, kinship obligations are more motivated by and dependent on emotional bonds than on need or obligation. This shift in motivations for gift giving may be attributable not only to the emergence of a modern welfare state that relieves families of much of their obligations to support kin but also to a transformation of the meaning of family relations from bonds of obligation to bonds of psycho-emotional content and love.[50]

Affection and Primary Relationships

Affection and primary relationships are the emotional dimensions of visits, calls, and letters. *Affection* means being emotionally close to kin. Women seem to be the "specialists" in affectionate kin relationships. In Middletown, as elsewhere, women expressed more affection than men for every category of relative. The distribution of affection was highest for mothers, next highest for fathers and near siblings, and lowest for best-known cousins.

With age, the affection dimension seems to increase between children and parents but weaken with kin such as cousins. In Middletown, the increased closeness to parents was attributed to children's own maturity, their parental experience, the belated recognition of the emotional debt they owe, the relaxation of parental authority, the increased needs of parents, and the expectation of bereavement. It can be said that, in Middletown, as well as elsewhere, most people feel good about their parents, love them, and make sacrifices for them when necessary.[51] And, there has been little evidence of any weakening of kinship ties during the past fifty years.

Regulation of Sexual Relationships

The most widely used example of a universal norm is a taboo on **incest**. All societies forbid sexual relations between persons in certain kinship positions, particularly those within and closest to the nuclear family: father and daughter, mother and son, brother and sister, stepfather and stepdaughter, and the like. Violations of these norms arouse strong feelings among the kinship group as well as in the larger society. In societies organized primarily around family ties, it is unsettling to imagine the confusion of statuses and role expectations that would result if fathers and daughters or mothers and sons had offspring. Consider, for example, a female child born to a mother–son relationship. The child would be a daughter to her brother, a sister to her father, a granddaughter to her own mother, a stepdaughter to her grandfather, and so forth. Should her father, who is also her brother, discipline her as a parent or treat her as a sibling? Could she marry her stepfather, who is her

---

[49]Aafke Komter and Wilma Vollebergh, "Gift Giving and the Emotional Significance of Family and Friends," *Journal of Marriage and the Family* 59 (August 1997): 747–757.

[50]Ulla Bjomberg and Hans Ekbrand, "Financial and Practical Kin Support in Sweden: Normative Guidelines and Practice," *Journal of Comparative Family Studies* 39.1 (Winter 2008): 73–95.

[51]Caplow et al., *Middletown Families*, 220.

grandfather, if he divorced her mother? In modern societies, however, such distinctions of position in families may have less importance. Why then a continuation of this taboo against incest? Perhaps the reason lies in the heightened focus and value on the psycho-emotional development and well-being of individuals as well as the required intimacy in family relations and the extreme power differences between parents and children. Without strong normative guidelines against incest, the potential for negative psycho-emotional consequences from the abuse of trust in close relationships is increased.

In addition to kinship sexual restrictions, all societies also forbid intermarriage between certain kinship group members. The circle of prohibited relatives for marriage does, however, vary widely in different societies. One extreme, ancient Egypt, permitted brother–sister and father–daughter marriages. The other extreme may be represented by the traditional clan system of China and by certain extended families in India, where the prohibition extended to a very wide group of relatives, including cousins to the sixth degree. In between is the (not uncommon) practice of cousin marriage, which many societies practice as a means of strengthening cultural continuity across generations by assuring that both husbands and wives have been socialized in the same context of beliefs, values, and norms. In fact, Martin Ottenheimer argues that the American prohibition against cousin marriage is based less on concerns about genetics and health outcomes and more on the desire to disrupt this practice among immigrants and thereby increase levels of assimilation into the dominant value system of the time.[52]

---

[52]Martin Ottenheimer, *Forbidden Relatives: The American Myth of Cousin Marriage*, (Urbana, IL: University of Illinois Press, 1996).

Summary

1. Traditionally and legally, *the family* refers to two or more persons related by birth, marriage, or adoption and who reside together in a household. This definition emphasizes membership criteria or the *structural* component of families. It was noted as well that families can also be defined *functionally* in terms of what they do and *relationally* in terms of the nature of their members' interactions with each other. Regardless of which dimension of family life is emphasized, however, it is important to keep in mind that definitions of the family are social constructions and, therefore, arbitrary to some degree.

2. From a sociological perspective, we are interested in families as both *institutions* and social *systems* or *groups*. The family, as a social institution, is an organized, formal, and regular system of carrying out certain tasks in society. The family is defined by a wide system of norms that organizes family units into stable and on-going social systems. These norms reflect societal needs but are also shaped by systems of power and conflict because how a society defines its institutions has impli-cations for structures of power, inequality, and conflict in the society. As sociologists, we are interested in how these norms develop, are maintained, and change.

3. In addition to the institutional definitions of family that develop in a society, we are also interested in families as analytical units or as special types of social groups with predictable characteristics that help us understand their behavior and the behaviors of their members. As social systems or groups, families can be characterized by their intergenerational composition, their mix of both primary and secondary functions, and their relations of interdependence and duration. As a primary group, the family is small in size and has frequent and intense contact among members. As a secondary group, its relations are more formal and involve the impersonal contacts that characterize much of an individual's life.

4. In studying and comparing family systems across societies and cultures, sociologists utilize ideal types. Ideal-type constructs provide a means of illustrating the range of perspectives between two extremes along

a continuum. This tool can be used to examine major issues in the U.S. family, evaluating traditional and nontraditional norms. Each issue involves conflict as a result of social change; that is, traditional patterns coexist with nontraditional patterns. If there were no change or if there were total change, no conflicts or issues would exist.

5. The boundaries of marriage are not always precise and clearly defined, and a great deal of variation exists within and across societies in both the definition and the practice of marriage. The major variations in marriage are based on the number of spouses, specifically the practice of either monogamy or polygamy. Polygyny and polyandry, two forms of polygamy, occur in a wide range of contexts and take numerous forms. The plural spouses may be brothers or sisters, may marry simultaneously or sequentially, and may perform various functions. Although polygyny is very common, polyandry is quite rare. Group marriage also occurs extremely infrequently and may never have existed as a viable and lasting form of marriage for any society in the world.

6. As with marriage, the boundaries of the family also vary considerably. How the boundaries of the family change will depend on the needs of the society, the needs and preferences of the individuals in the family, and the structures of conflict and power.

7. One typology of family structures differentiates the nuclear/conjugal unit from a variety of extended units. Some of these include families of orientation and procreation; modified-nuclear and modified-extended families; and consanguine, joint, and stem families.

8. The boundaries of kinship serve as an extension of those of the marital and family units. A universal taboo on incest consists of norms that specify eligible sexual and marital partners.

9. Kinship systems have key functions and characteristics that include property holding and inheritance, housing and maintenance of residential proximity, obligation or helping in time of need, and affection and emotional ties.

Having considered the concept of the family as a social construction, the next chapter looks at how the family has been structured and defined in the United States historically and today. The purpose of Chapter 2 is to examine the variety of family experiences and definitions in contemporary U.S. society and to provide an understanding of how family structures are not independent of the structures of other institutions. We will also consider briefly some of the key issues in contemporary U.S. family life that will be addressed more fully throughout the book.

Key Terms and Topics

Social constructions p. 5
Ideology p. 5
Institutional definitions p. 7
Analytical definition p. 7
Social institution p. 8
Institutionalize p. 8
Functional equivalence p. 11
Family systems p. 12
Primary group p. 15
Internal social control p. 16
Secondary group p. 16
Ideal-type constructs p. 18
Monogamy p. 20
Polygamy p. 20
Bigamy p. 20
Polygyny p. 20
Polyandry p. 20
Group marriage p. 20
Sequential or serial monogamy p. 21

Sex ratio p. 21
Levirate p. 22
Sororate p. 23
Affluent polygyny p. 24
Intervention polygyny p. 24
Conjugal family p. 28
Nuclear family p. 28
Family of orientation p. 28
Family of procreation p. 28
Extended family p. 28
Consanguine family p. 29
Joint family p. 30
Stem family p. 30
Modified-nuclear family structure p. 30
Modified-extended family structure p. 31
Kinship systems p. 32
Unilineal p. 33
Patrilineal p. 33
Matrilineal p. 33

Discussion Questions

1. If the meaning of *family* is socially constructed, does this mean the definition is totally arbitrary and we can define a family any way we want? Or can we talk about "the family" as a necessary part of existence in human societies?

2. What is meant by the phrase *family as a social institution*? Do long-term committed relationships formed by same-sex couples, single mothers with children born outside of marriage, cohabiting couples, and married working mothers who put their children in daycare for 40 hours each week constitute legitimate families?

3. What do changes in American society such as increases in the prevalence of cohabitation and the use of daycares to care for and socialize children tell us about the institution of "the family"? What do these changes and comparisons with other modern societies tell us about the institutionalization process and the changeable nature of institutions and their relationships with other institutions in a society?

4. Differentiate *family groups* from *family systems*. Since systems are abstractions, of what relevance are family systems to understanding the family?

5. Describe what would likely happen to a person who was removed from all primary-group relationships. Why are such relationships so crucial?

6. Define the terms *marriage* and *family* in a way that would be comprehensive enough to include marriages and families in most societies in the world. How are the two terms similar and different? How do marriage and family differ from other groups and relationships? Should gays and lesbians be able to marry, divorce, adopt children, and form families? Why?

7. Why is monogamy so strongly stressed in the United States as the appropriate form of marriage? What is your theory for monogamy as opposed to polygyny? What advantages or disadvantages do monogamy, polygyny, polyandry, and group marriage have for adults in the United States?

8. In societies where polygamy is culturally accepted, polygyny appears to be far more common than polyandry. Why? What factors explain exceptions that occur?

9. Think of your own kin group. How many persons in it do you know (uncles, cousins, and so on)? With how many kin do you have contact via email and the Internet? With how many do you exchange birthday or holiday greetings? How many do you visit regularly? Based on your personal experience, is the extended family merely a thing of the past or is it alive today as well?

10. How would you explain the universal norm of a taboo on incest? Within your own kinship system, what relatives (second cousins, stepsiblings, and so forth) are considered to be legitimate sexual or marital partners?

11. What arguments will feminists and conflict theorists likely make about traditional unilineal descent and inheritance systems?

Further Readings

Adams, Bert, and Trost, Jan. *Handbook of World Families*. Thousand Oaks, CA: Sage Publications, 2005.

A cross-cultural look at recent empirical research on families in 25 different countries around the world divided by region.

Carlson, Allan. *American Way: Family & Community in Shaping of American Identity* Intercollegiate Studies Institute, 2003.

Examines the different ways that debates about the definition of family and family life have been used in political discourse to support and promote national identity and national policies in America.

Carsten, Janet, ed. *Cultures of Relatedness: New Approaches to the Study of Kinship*. Cambridge, MA: Cambridge University Press, 2000.

Nine anthropologists describe what "being related" does for people in localities such as Africa, China, India, Alaska, and Europe.

Cherlin, Andrew J. *The Marriage-Go-Round: The State of Marriage and the Family in America Today*. NY: Knopf, 2009.

One of the foremost scholars in the area of family sociology examines the process of de-institutionalization in the area of marriage and family life.

Dorow, Sara K. *Transnational Adoption: A Cultural Economy of Race, Gender and Kinship*. NY: New York University Press, 2006.

One of the few sociological examinations of a widespread practice in American families—transnational adoptions—this book considers how this transnational family practice intersects with traditional notions of kinship and shows how these families are redefining kinship outside of a national context.

Leeder, Elaine J. *The Family in Global Perspective: A Gendered Journey*. Thousand Oaks, CA: Sage Publications, 2004.

An examination of family life around the globe in comparison to Western families done from a gendered perspective with an emphasis on globalization.

Lehr, Valerie. *Queer Family Values: Debunking the Myth of the Nuclear Family*. Philadelphia: Temple University Press, 1999.

A look at the values centering around gay and lesbian politics: family agendas, rights, children, and other issues.

Murdock, George P. *Social Structure*. New York: Free Press, 1965.

Although recommended reading for a general and excellent cross-cultural perspective on family structure, the book also extensively analyzes sexual patterns and incest.

Smith, William L. *Families and Communes: An Examination of Nontraditional Lifestyles*. Thousand Oaks, CA: Sage Publications, 1999.

An exploration of a variety of practices including monogamy, polygamy, and group marriage as implemented by intentional communities in dealing with family life.

Zaretsky, Natasha. *No Direction Home: The American Family and the Fear of National Decline, 1968–1980*. Chapel Hill: University of North Carolina Press, 2007.

Another look at how debates about the family intersect with constructions of national identity.

chapter 2

U.S. Families

Historical Origins, Changes, and Contemporary Issues

Contemporary Views on the Changing Family

Tom and Ethel were married in 1942 and had their marriage blessed one year later by the Roman Catholic Church. She was 21 years old and he was 22. She graduated from high school in Warwick, Rhode Island, and never attended college, whereas he never completed high school and followed a path set by his father and grandfather, who were both well-respected horsemen on the Canadian racetrack circuit. Tom's parents had eleven children, six boys and five girls. Most of the boys found careers on the racetrack like their father and grandfather before them. Tom's family life was strict but full of freedom to play with his brothers and sisters outside the purview of his mother and father—with eleven children and the need to keep food on the table, it was sometimes difficult to keep up with what they were all doing. While Tom's father was training horses, his mother was operating a kitchen on the track to earn extra income. It was a hard life, but one that created strong bonds between the siblings. All but one of Tom's brothers and sisters moved away from home when they became adults and got married. Many moved to the United States. His sister Florence never married. Tom's father died the same year Tom and Ethel were married, and his mother lived another eighteen years in her own home with Florence.

Ethel was the only child of Robert Reynolds and Eva Ward. Her father was eleven years older than her mother and both had been in previous marriages. He had four or five children from his first marriage and she brought three children to the marriage. Ethel's father died when she was 3 years old. Since there was no Social Security in those days, Ethel's mother had to work and left her two youngest children in the care of their older sister who was 11 years old at the time. When the neighbors complained, they were placed in a Catholic orphanage. They did not remain there long, however, and were moved to a state-sponsored foster home where Ethel lived with John and Johanna Moroney Cullinan until she was married.

Life was hard for Ethel growing up, and her family was deeply impacted by the Great Depression. She still speaks of the lessons in life she learned from growing up in that time and has a deeply embedded sense of how the government can help others in times of need. She also speaks of the importance of family life, although her definition of the family goes well beyond the simple notion of a husband and wife with their biological children. Although she never knew her stepsiblings from her father's first marriage very well, she often talks about wanting to find out more about them. She also recalls the importance of boarders in her family life because her foster parents had to rent out rooms to make ends meet.

Tom and Ethel were married almost twenty-six years and had eight children. For the first fifteen years of their marriage, they moved frequently from town to town as the racetrack seasons changed. Shortly after their last child was born, Tom died of leukemia. With many mouths to feed at home, Ethel remarried soon thereafter. This was followed by one other remarriage. Her second and third husbands (to whom she was married for two and twenty-seven years, respectively) also passed away before her. All eight of Ethel's children are still living and all have been married, with only one divorce among them. Ethel now has nineteen grandchildren (an average of two per child) and fifteen great-grandchildren. Five of her children live nearby and many of her adult grandchildren do as well, but she lives independently in the home that she and Tom bought in 1949.

Questions to Consider

Do the family histories of Tom and Ethel meet your image of the "traditional" family?

Do you think our contemporary image of the "traditional" family is an accurate representation of families of the past? If not, where does this image come from and why has it been promoted?

What do you think are the major issues facing families today? How are they different from those that families had to face in the past?

*F*amilies in the United States are perhaps as diverse as anywhere in the world. Yet, most of us have an image of what a family is and should be. This image, perhaps best illustrated by popular television shows of the 1950s (e.g., *Father Knows Best, Leave It to Beaver*, and *Ozzie and Harriet*), is one of a loving, two-parent family with children. The father is the breadwinner and "head," the stay-at-home mother cares for the house and children and is the loving and supportive wife, and the children, while exhibiting occasions of sibling rivalry and mischief, are basically conforming and obedient. Does this image comply with what we know about the family of the 1950s? Or is it the product of nostalgia for a better time? Family historians have shown that this image is one that may have fit a minority of mostly middle-class families but is far from an accurate portrayal of family life during that time for most Americans.[1]

Looking further back, the image of family life is characterized by a high degree of stability over time and strong intergenerational relationships. Family life since colonial times is looked back on as full of loving relationships and strong commitments. Surely these images must be accurate?

Although it is true that colonial America was characterized by strong community ties and a strong sense of intergenerational responsibility, demographic (population) and social forces worked against the reality of a stable, intergenerational family pattern. Many parents didn't live long enough to experience a three-generational family life, especially given a high age at marriage and a low life expectancy.[2] Families were mostly nuclear in Western Europe and the American colonies and often expanded in size by the incorporation of nonkin (including servants, apprentices, and slaves). When property was owned by families and productive (agricultural areas), simple extended forms such as stem and joint families emerged, but in most areas this was not an adaptive family form.[3]

As for stability in family structure over time, many families went through numerous re-formations, usually due to the premature death of a parent (often during childbearing) or as the result of desertions and involuntary separations.[4] Although most breakdowns in family structure were due to death, the fact remains that the likelihood of children experiencing family disruptions through loss and addition of adult family members was probably greater in the past than it is today. It was also rare in most of Western Europe and the American colonies for families to live in the same location for more than two generations. In fact, the house was the defining unit in a community and not the family that lived within.[5]

Finally, the image of a cohesive family life where members looked out for each other and provided each other with all of their psychological and emotional needs may be more of a projection stemming from our own anxieties, desires, and expectations about family life today. Although love was certainly present in these early families, interactions in them were much more instrumental in nature and highly organized through a hierarchy of patriarchal control. Families during the colonial period in American history were not private places. The practice of "gadding" whereby individuals felt free to enter each other's homes for unannounced visits speaks to the public nature of family life.[6] The need for a private family was less because community relations were more personal themselves. It is only in late modern society, where such personal ties are more tenuous, that we look to the family to compensate and thereby build walls around our families to maintain the privacy of those relationships.

---

[1]There have been several books written in recent decades on the families of the 1950s and feelings of nostalgia for family life during that time period. See Arlene Skolnick, *Embattled Paradise: The American Family in an Age of Uncertainty* (New York: Basic Books, 1991); Stephanie Coontz, *The Way We Never Were: American Families and the Nostalgia Trap* (New York: Basic Books, 1992); and John R. Gillis, *A World of Their Own Making* (New York: Basic Books, 1996).

[2]John Demos, *A Little Commonwealth: Family Life in Plymouth Colony* (New York: Oxford University Press, 1970).

[3]Rosemary O'Day, *The Family and Family Relationships, 1500–1900* (Hampshire, England: MacMillan Press Ltd., 1994).

[4]Roderick Phillips, *Untying the Knot: A Short History of Divorce* (Cambridge: Cambridge University Press, 1991).

[5]O'Day, *The Family and Family Relationships, 1500–1900*; Gillis, *A World of Their Own Making*.

[6]Gillis, *A World of Their Own Making*.

The anxieties we feel today that lead to these inaccurate constructions of history are not new. As Gillis notes, "...the fragmentation, instability, and discontinuity that we feel so keenly today has been part of the European experience of family life since at least the late Middle Ages. Europeans who came to the Americas carried a dream of caring and cooperation with them but were unable to realize it in the new land. Throughout the seventeenth and eighteenth centuries, family unity and continuity remained elusive on both sides of the Atlantic, and, in the great industrial and political upheavals of the nineteenth century, it became even more so."[7]

As you will learn in the next section, the modern Western (including American) family is unique in human history and the expectations that we place on our own family life have led us to imagine a past that fits those expectations better than what we experience ourselves. The images we have constructed are of the **families we live by** as opposed to the **families we live with**.[8] Different historical periods (e.g., the Victorian era and the era of the Great Depression) have witnessed different constructions of the families they live by and such constructions have reflected anxieties and desires for the future more than they have been an accurate reflection of the past. These images are of the **prescriptive family** in the time period when we live (a family life we *expect* to have) and often bear little resemblance to the **descriptive family** that we *actually experience*.[9]

Although maintaining such images may help us confront the challenges of our time, it is equally important to maintain an awareness of history so that we do not fall prey to the trappings of nostalgia and thereby fail to realize the potentialities for family life in our current and future societal context. Rather than cry out about the decline of the family and bemoan the loss of a family life that never existed (or existed for only a few), it might be best to understand how our family lives have been and are now being affected by our social and cultural context so that we can better realize our goals and needs within our families, whatever forms those families may take. It is important that we do not fail to adapt and meet our human needs in the name of preserving an ideal image of family life that never existed and that might not function within our current life circumstances. To help us arrive at the necessary understandings of our past, a brief history of the Western family is provided next.

*H*istorical Origins of the Modern Family in Europe and America

Although a rich literature covers the history of the family in America, we believe greater insight is gained by considering the contemporary American family as an example of a broader class of societies that have been described as *late modern*. This perspective allows us to not only take a longer time perspective, but it also allows us to see changes in the American family as the product of generalizable social and cultural forces rather than idiosyncratic historical events. As O'Day[10] has noted, many commonalities exist in the development of the family across northern Western societies (especially English, French, and American) that would justify a grouping of their histories. Such an approach also expands our perspective in terms of seeing the "American" family as less exclusively a product of national identity and more increasingly a product of global conditions and processes.

---

[7]Ibid., 7.
[8]Ibid.
[9]O'Day, *The Family and Family Relationships, 1500–1900*.
[10]Ibid.

For most people, family life was hard and hierarchical in the nineteenth and early twentieth centuries. The images we have of early historical periods are often distorted by our own desires and concerns.

O'Day also notes, however, that sufficient idiosyncrasies exist both within and across these societies to caution against blanket generalizations of family forms or histories. With this caution in mind, we will now look at how the Western family of late modern society has evolved. We will then conclude with a discussion of the current state of the late modern family. To help understand these changes, we identify three important and highly interdependent causal forces:

1. The movement from an agricultural to an industrial mode of production, which brought with it a high degree of differentiation and specialization of work and a relocation of production activities from inside the family (family businesses and family self-sufficiency) to separate production facilities outside the control of the family (factories and public businesses). This movement also brought about a shift in how status in society was obtained from an **ascribed status** system where one's position, rights and responsibilities were based on family connections and determined at birth to an **achieved status** system where one's position, rights and responsibilities were based on individual accomplishments independent of family relationships. As a result of these changes, other institutions (economic, educational, health care, governmental, etc.) were formed and took over many of the essential functions that families served for individuals and society. Families were no longer *units of production* and became smaller and less powerful over their members' behaviors.

2. The decline of **feudalism** (a primarily agricultural system whereby ownership was concentrated in the hands of a few elite groups and commoners worked the land to support the elites and provide for their own subsistence) and the emergence of **capitalism** (a primarily industrial system whereby ownership of the means of production was concentrated in the hands of those who could most successfully produce profit and where the production of profit became the primary motivation for economic activity). This transition "freed" laborers from their indentured servitude to land owners, but also placed them in a position of competition with one another for paid positions and made them more vulnerable and susceptible to exploitation. These changes are significant because they brought about: (a) a greater centralization of market activity outside the control of families, local communities, and even national governments; (b) the emergence and development of a labor market based on a system of wages that it was in the interest of employers to suppress in order to survive and achieve the goal of producing profit; (c) a gradual decline in importance of factors such as race, ethnicity, gender and age in determining economic outcomes as concerns about maximizing profit overrode concerns about social or cultural backgrounds when making hiring and promotion decisions; and (d) the potential for

the commoditization (the giving of economic value to things) of individuals and personal relationships. As a result of these changes, families became less organized around kinship ties. Families became *units of consumption* and had to become more self-sufficient in a free marketplace. In addition, the decline in the significance of age and sex as determinants of economic outcomes meant a transformation of relationships within families as older generations and men lost much of their bases for power over other family members.

3. The decline of a **traditional mode of action** (action based on previously established standards) and the rise of a **rational mode of action** (action based on logical means–ends relationships). This cultural change supported the movement to an industrial mode of production, the emergence of modern democracies, and the development of modern capitalism. Most significantly, the emergence of rational modes of action called into question existing methods and hierarchies in society (including those within the family) and replaced established practices with ones that clearly advanced individuals' self-interests. People no longer did things because that was the way they were always done. They needed to see that their actions had some logical relationship to some desirable outcome. They also came to judge themselves in terms of the measurable outcomes of their actions. As a result, society became more egalitarian but also more individualistic and *reflexive* (self-evaluative) and, as will be noted later, may have created a crisis of both self-definition and emotional authenticity. Without tradition to guide actions, family formation and maintenance processes could no longer be taken for granted, were no longer as strongly governed by social norms, and became less certain and more in need of rational management. In addition, individual growth and development became essential goals of both marital and parenting relationships, reshaping the dynamics between spouses and between parents and their children.

In historical studies of the family throughout Western Europe, the logical beginning point would be the **prefeudal family** (prior to the fifth century), followed by the **medieval family** of feudal society (fifth through the fifteenth centuries), and then the modern family of the fifteenth through twenty-first centuries. The dates affixed to these periods are not absolute as one system often melded into another over several generations, and vestiges of previous systems are still present even today in the late modern family. We use them here to roughly approximate when new patterns of family life began to emerge.

Prefeudal Family Life

Information on family life in Europe prior to the period of feudalism is less clear than for periods later than this. Although elements of the modern family could be found in the homes of the Roman elite prior to the fall of the Roman Empire,[11] it is reasonable to assume that family life among commoners (especially in the further reaches of the empire) and among most of society in earlier times was organized around kinship groups that were stable over time. The dominant mode of production was broadly agricultural within a subsistence economy organized around kinship units and maintained through traditional action rather than rational action. Under these conditions, family life was stable within and across generations and families functioned as primary production units on land owned and passed down through kinship lines.

---

[11]David Herlihy, *Medieval Households* (Cambridge, MA: Harvard University Press, 1985).

Marriage and parenthood occurred early in life and families tended to be large and extended. These families, or kinship groups, had highly developed ascribed status hierarchies based on generational status and gender. The focus of life, including family life, was on survival under current environmental conditions rather than on the emotional and psychological growth of individuals. These were communal societies.

Medieval Family Life

The emergence of feudalism saw a breakdown in the control of kinship units, at least among commoners, and a greater centralization of economic activity, although the mode of production was primarily agricultural and social action was still based primarily on tradition. During the feudal period, the kinship system lost much of its authority in society (outside the ranks of the elites) and the foundations for extended family life were undermined by the accumulation of property by just a few. This period saw the emergence of the **European marriage pattern**—a pattern of low marriage rates and high age at marriage—in Northern and Western Europe.[12] The economic foundations for early marriage were no longer present. As a result, many children never married and large extended families became demographically difficult to achieve due to the low life expectancy and the late age of marriage for children. This is not to say that families did not maintain their extended kinship ties; these ties often were essential for survival but were maintained for primarily instrumental reasons ("cupboard love") and were no longer a basis for organizing family life.[13] As a result, large nuclear families prevailed that served many different functions for society and family members but had reduced significance in terms of economic and political functions.

The role of the church in family life during this period was perhaps greater than prior to feudalism but was nonetheless minimal outside of the lives of the elite. The emerging church saw marriage as a necessary evil but elevated the state of celibacy (a nonsexual lifestyle) above that of the family.[14] From its earliest days, the Catholic Church was "more interested in the individual soul" than it was in the sanctity of an ideal family unit.[15] Families were promoted only as a means of exercising control over their individual members and providing for proper socialization into religious beliefs. As Gillis notes:

> Until the late Middle Ages, high holiness and family life had seemed incompatible. Only then did married persons begin to be canonized. It was also then that mother saints and father saints became imaginable...and the Holy Family... became a central feature of Christian worship....At first [however,] the Holy Family was imagined as an extended kin group, consisting of infant and mother, the maternal grandmother, Saint Anne, and various cousins. The matrifocality of this imagined family seems to have reflected the realities of early medieval family life...[and t]he high evaluation placed on extended kin ties was consistent with the feudalistic effort to forge a political and economic order that would transcend the interests of the nuclear family.[16]

---

[12] John Hajnal, "European Marriage Patterns in Perspective," in D.V. Glass and D.E.C. Eversley, *Population in History: Essays in Historical Demography* (London: Edward Arnold, 1965); and Hajnal, "Two Kinds of Pre-Industrial Household Systems," *Population and Development Review* 8 (1982): 449–494.

[13] O'Day, *The Family and Family Relationships, 1500–1900*.

[14] Phillips, *Untying the Knot*.

[15] O'Day, *The Family and Family Relationships, 1500–1900*, 30.

[16] Gillis, *A World of Their Own Making*, 28.

Modernity and the Family

The feudal period began to give way to modernity as a more central marketplace emerged and the mode of production began shifting from agricultural to industrial. The emergence of the stock market signified a shift to a capitalistic economy based on the accumulation of profit rather than the provision of basic subsistence needs. These changes occurred in affinity with a shift in modes of social action from *traditional* to *rational*. No longer were individuals content to follow the ways of tradition. A growing belief in the well-being of the individual began to unfold in the early modern period (beginning around the fifteenth century) and continued to become more widespread and elaborate as the period of modernity progressed with events such as the Protestant Reformation in the sixteenth century and the great revolutions of the eighteenth and nineteenth centuries largely attributed to this cultural transformation.

With this shift came a change in how we viewed and lived in our families. With the dissolution of feudal estates and the emergence of a new marketplace, individual nuclear families were required to become self-sufficient. Throughout the early modern period (until the mid-nineteenth century), husbands and wives worked together in economic production activities often centered in the home. Thus, husbands were highly involved in the day-to-day affairs and management of the household and in parenting as well. This was especially true for those less well off. Although community organization and regulation of marriage and family life was still strong, it began to dissipate and emerging ideals of free choice in partner selection and marriages based on love began to appear. For a large segment of the population (those not among the elite), parental influence over choice of marriage partners was eroded and individuals were given increased choice. Marriages did not occur, however, without some outside regulation and without consideration of economic feasibility. During the latter part of this early modern period (late 1700s and early 1800s), there was tremendous innovation in marriage. Many times, informal marital arrangements took place only to be formalized once economic position had been achieved and/or a child was born.[17]

The role of the church in defining marriage and family life grew considerably during the early modern period. "By the fourteenth and fifteenth centuries,...St. Joseph was coming to have a place in the Holy Family, eventually displacing Saint Anne. Images of the Nativity were becoming more common, foregrounding the nuclear family of procreation....Mary's maternity became more fully developed, and Joseph acquired...a more youthful image, making his paternity plausible for the first time."[18] Most likely a response to the Protestant Reformation as well as Catholic secular philosophers such as Erasmus, this image elevated the importance of love and togetherness among nuclear family members. The idea of the "spiritualized household" was later prominent in the sermons and writings of Puritan leaders in the American colonies.[19] Thus, the importance of the conjugal relationship and the mother–child relationship grew, as did the significance of the nuclear family household, but it wasn't until later in the nineteenth century that we see a much more articulated linkage between conjugal and mother–child love and religious beliefs.

---

[17]John R. Gillis, *For Better, For Worse: British Marriages, 1600 to the Present* (New York: Oxford University Press, 1985).

[18]Gillis, *A World of Their Own Making*, 29.

[19]O'Day, *The Family and Family Relationships, 1500–1900*, 41.

During the Victorian period of the late nineteenth century, major changes occurred in family life. Industrialization, urbanization, and immigration were creating massive disruptions of the social order and increasing emphasis was placed on the family as a "haven in a heartless world."[20] The conjugal relationship became even more important and came under increasing scrutiny. Conjugal love became equated with love of God and a **cult of domesticity** arose, wherein women were seen as the protectors of morality both in terms of their husbands and their children. It was during this period that motherhood first took on the significance that we give it today and became linked with the concept of womanhood. It was also during this time that men's and women's roles became more clearly differentiated between private and public domains.[21]

Many of the functions that families had performed in earlier times were beginning to be lost to the **public sphere** of institutions during the Victorian era and the family began to be more specialized in dealing with **private sphere** issues such as psychological and emotional need gratification and fulfillment. This trend continued throughout the twentieth century as society became increasingly differentiated and specialized. Adding to the growing reliance on the family for personal need gratification and fulfillment was the fact that community ties were eroded by social and geographical mobility, increasing diversity, the growth of suburban communities, and an increased cultural emphasis on individual development and fulfillment. As society had become more formal and more rational, a crisis of identity began to be felt[22] and the emphasis was shifted from an **instrumental self**, premised on what one "did" or one's status in the community and broader society, to an **expressive self**, premised on one's individuality, emotional and psychological need fulfillment, and system of informal intimate relationships.[23] As Beck and Beck-Gernsheim[24] suggest, because of the growing rationality of the public world and the breakdown of life-long community relationships, the only place to find the meanings of this expressive self in the late modern society of today might be in the context of marriage and family life.

At the same time as the nuclear family took on this new function, the institutional controls and regulations that previously existed over relationship formation and maintenance patterns were dismantled.[25] As a result, relationships became more expressive and egalitarian (equal) between men and women and parents and children. However, individuals were also left to themselves to create families now essential for defining the authentic self. Individuals today work to construct personal biographies of their lives through marriages and family events; in doing so, they relieve anxieties about the meanings of the self. As a result, rituals such as marriages, honeymoons, birthdays, and anniversaries take on added significance. Unfortunately, this new function performed by marriages and families places added pressure on family members to meet each other's needs, and the ability of marriages to survive under these pressures may have been compromised.

---

[20]Peter Laslett, *The World We Have Lost* (London: Methuen and Co., Ltd., 1965).

[21]Barbara Ehrenreich and Dierdre England, *For Her Own Good* (Garden City, NY: Anchor, 1978). See also Ann Oakley, *Becoming a Mother* (New York: Schocken, 1979).

[22]Anthony Giddens, *Modernity and Self-Identity* (Cambridge: Polity, 1991).

[23]Marlis Buchmann and Manuel Eisner, "The Transition from the Utilitarian to the Expressive Self: 1900–1992," *Poetics* 25 (1997): 157–175.

[24]Ulrich Beck and Elisabeth Beck-Gernsheim, *The Normal Chaos of Love* (Cambridge: Polity, 1995).

[25]Ibid.

As we continue to live in this late modern period, we continue to struggle with both meeting each other's needs in marriage and family life and finding our own selves in these same relationships. There are many positive outcomes of modern relationships (especially in the areas of gender equality, personal autonomy, and emotional and psychological significance), but there are also considerable pressures. How we deal with those pressures will determine the future of the family. Do we continue to place responsibility for marital and family happiness on the individuals involved, or do we redefine other social institutions to help relieve some of the pressures individuals feel in their relationships? Some would argue that we need to go back to an earlier time when families were not under such pressures. But is this possible, and what would be the societal implications for making such a move? Can we just redefine our family lives as if we lived in a vacuum, or do we need to realistically take into consideration the interdependence that exists between families and other institutions and ways of life?

In the following sections, we will look more closely at the state of contemporary American families, their relationships with other institutions, and some of the major issues today's families face.

Characteristics of Contemporary U.S. Families

The United States Bureau of the Census is a primary source of demographic (population) data about the size and makeup of families in this country. At 12:30 A.M. on March 5, 2009, The U.S. Census Bureau's "American Factfinder" website estimated the total resident population of the United States to be almost 306 million (305,943,069). Although large, this represents less than 22 percent of the world population of over 6.7 billion. In terms of sex, the population is nearly evenly divided with 49.8 percent male and 50.2 percent female.[26]

According to the U.S. Census Bureau's 2007 Population Estimates, only 66 percent of the population consisted of non-Hispanic whites alone (not mixed with any other race group), 12.3 percent was non-Hispanic black only, 4.3 percent was non-Hispanic Asian only, .8 percent was exclusively non-Hispanic Native American, .1 percent was non-Hispanic Native Hawaiian or Pacific Islanders, and 1.4 percent was of mixed race and non-Hispanic origin. Thus, the remainder of the population (15.1 percent) consisted of individuals of Hispanic origin of various races (although 92 percent of this Hispanic population is exclusively white). In the year 2000, only 11.8 percent of the U.S. population identified themselves as Hispanic. Thus, as a result of this nearly 28 percent increase in relative population growth, Hispanics are now the largest minority group in the United States. More details about race and ethnic population characteristics will be presented in Chapter 5 along with a discussion of the meaning of these categories in terms of how they relate to family diversity.

Numbers of Families and Households

The term **family**, as used in census reporting, refers to a group of two or more persons related by birth, marriage, or adoption and who reside together in a household. A family is different from a **household**. A household consists of all persons who occupy

---

[26]U.S. Bureau of the Census, "American FactFinder," http://factfinder.census.gov/home/saff/main.html?_lang=en, March 5, 2009.

a housing unit. A house, an apartment or other group of rooms, or a single room is regarded as a housing unit when it is occupied or intended for occupancy as separate living quarters. A household includes related family members and all other unrelated persons, if any, such as lodgers, foster children, wards, and live-in employees. A person living alone in a housing unit or a group of unrelated persons sharing a housing unit is also counted as a household. Thus, not all households contain families. In addition, some households can contain more than one family. When a married couple or a parent and child unit live in a household headed by someone else (a parent, other relative, or other nonrelative) they are referred to as a **subfamily**. Such arrangements are not uncommon in countries without adequate housing stock to accommodate newly married couples (e.g., Italy and Spain) and have increased at a greater rate than householder families in the United States over the past fifty years, albeit for different reasons (i.e., single parents living with parents or grandparents).[27]

In 2007, there were 116 million U.S. households; 67.8 percent (78.4 million) were *family households*, a decrease in family households from 85 percent in 1960. This decrease in the proportion of households containing families can be attributed to the fact that people are marrying less, are less likely to have children, and are more likely to live alone or with an unrelated person. These related trends can be seen in a decline from 87.4 percent to 75.2 percent in the proportion of households containing married couples; a decline from 48.7 percent to 31.7 percent in the proportion containing children under 18 years old; a small increase from 1.9 percent to 5.6 percent in nonfamily households containing more than one person (e.g., roommates or cohabiting couples without children); and a doubling from 13.1 percent to 26.8 percent of households containing single individuals living alone. The only categories of *family* household types to increase during this period since 1960 were male headed householders with a child or other dependent family member (an increase from 2.4 percent of households in 1960 to 4.4 percent in 2007) and female headed householders with a child or other dependent family member (an increase from 8.4 percent to 12.4 percent).[28]

The stacked bar chart in Figure 2.1 (page 54) shows how the proportions of different household types have changed since 1960. A look at the bottom two bars shows how sharply marriage has declined during this time period, especially marriages that include children under 18 still living at home (the second bar segment from the bottom). Although the decline has occurred in every decade, the decade from 1970 to 1980 appears to be a significant transition point, with much more moderate declines in married households occurring since 1980. A similar pattern of changes (although increases rather than decreases) can be seen in the categories of nonfamily households. These and other longer term trends in marriage will be discussed in greater depth in Chapter 6. At this point, however, it would be safe to say that the U.S. population has undergone a profound transition resulting in a condition where households including married couples still predominate, but where increasing numbers of people (young and old) are living alone or in alternative family and nonfamily households. As Figure 2.2 (page 55) shows, this transition is not unique to the United States. In comparison to other industrialized countries, the United States falls somewhere in the middle with respect to the percent of its population that is

---

[27]U.S. Bureau of the Census, *The 2008 Statistical Abstract*, "Table 58: Households, Families, Subfamilies, and Married Couples," http://www.2010census.biz/compendia/statab/cats/population/households_families_group_quarters.html.
    [28]Ibid.

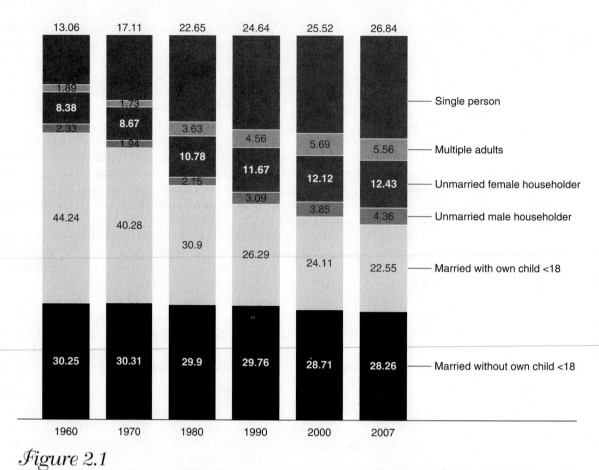

Figure 2.1

Households by Type: Selected Years, 1970–2007 (percentage distribution)

Source: U.S. Bureau of the Census, The 2008 Statistical Abstract, "Table 58: Households, Families, Subfamilies, and Married Couples," http://www.2010census.biz/compendia/statab/cats/population/households_families_group_quarters.html.

married (with or without children) and isn't even highest when it comes to single parents living with children.

Sizes of Families and Households

Given the changes noted above in household composition, it should be of little surprise to learn that the average size of households in the United States has changed as well. The average number of persons per household in 2007 was 2.56. This represents a considerable decrease since the earliest census reports were taken. In 1890, the average size of a household was 5.4. In 1940, it had shrunk to 3.3, where it remained through 1960. Thus, the average household size today is less than half of what it was at the end of the nineteenth century. Similarly, the average size of families also decreased during the twentieth century. Although comparable census data on **family size** is more difficult to obtain for 1890 due to a greater blurring of the definitional distinction between family and nonfamily households, the average family size in 1960 was 3.67 compared to 3.13 in 2007.[29]

---

[29]Ibid.

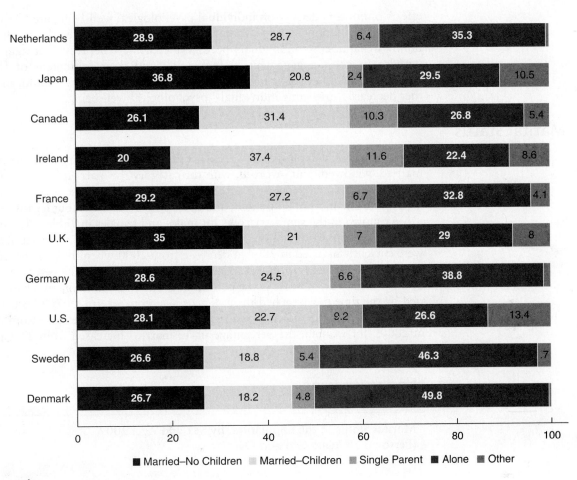

Figure 2.2

Household Type by Selected Countries

Table 1294–Percent Distribution of Households by Type and Country
http://www.2010census.biz/compendia/statab/cats/international_statistics/population_households.html

This decrease in average household size may have some positive influence on the interaction of its members and the social connectedness with others outside the household. In a longitudinal study of more than 1,200 respondents living in the Toronto metropolitan area, increasing household density tended to have negative effects on both men's and women's psychological well-being. These effects varied, however, depending on the type of psychological outcomes measured and the degree of household density. As density increased from below-average levels to average levels (0–2 persons per room), women's depression also increased as did men's aggressiveness combined with withdrawal symptoms. With further increases in household density (beyond two persons per room) both of these gender-specific symptoms increased at an even greater rate.[30] Obviously, the consequences of the

---

[30]Wendy C. Regoeczi, "Crowding in Context: An Examination of the Differential Responses of Men and Women to High Density Living Environments," *Journal of Health and Social Behavior* 49 (Sep.): 254–268.

effects of housing density on individual psychological well-being are likely to be felt at the level of family system dynamics as well and may even be the result of altered family dynamics. As individuals become increasingly depressed or aggressive and withdrawn, their engagement in family life and their fulfillment of family role responsibilities are likely to suffer. Such changes in family life should, in turn, further decrease those same individuals' psychological well-being.

Marital Status

Census classification of marital status identifies four major categories: never married, married, widowed, and divorced, with the category for married including those who live with their spouse (over 90 percent of this category), those who live apart from their spouse in another household, and those who are married but legally separated.

As shown in the summary rows for males and females in Table 2.1, among those 18 and older in the population, 59.9 percent of all men and 56.7 percent of all women were currently married in 2007, a decrease from 2000 when the percentages married were 61.5 and 57.6, respectively. Almost all of this decline in the percent married can be attributed to an increase in the percent of the adult population who had never married by the time they reached their current age. For men in 2007, 28.6 percent were never married by the time they reached their current age (an increase from 27 percent in 2000); for women, the percentage never married increased from 21.1 percent to 22 percent over this same seven-year period. With respect to widowed and divorced

Table 2.1

Marital Status of the Population, by Sex and Age: 2007
(Personal 18 Years Old and Over)

	TOTAL	NEVER MARRIED	MARRIED	WIDOWED	DIVORCED
MALE	100.0	28.6	59.9	2.5	8.9
20 to 24 years old	100.0	86.9	12.2	0.1	0.8
30 to 34 years old	100.0	32.4	61.1	0.1	6.4
40 to 44 years old	100.0	16.9	70.3	0.5	12.3
55 to 64 years old	100.0	6.8	77.2	2.2	13.8
65 to 74 years old	100.0	4.3	78.4	7.7	9.6
75 years old and over	100.0	3.7	71.4	20.0	4.9
FEMALE	100.0	22.0	56.7	9.8	11.5
20 to 24 years old	100.0	76.4	21.8	0.2	1.7
30 to 34 years old	100.0	24.0	67.2	0.6	8.1
40 to 44 years old	100.0	12.9	70.4	1.5	15.2
55 to 64 years old	100.0	6.6	66.0	9.0	18.4
65 to 74 years old	100.0	4.0	56.9	26.2	13.0
75 years old and over	100.0	3.4	32.2	58.2	6.3

Source: U.S. Bureau of the Census, The 2009 Statistical Abstract, "Table 56: Marital Status of the Population by Sex and Age" http://www.2010census.biz/compendia/statab/cats/population/marital_status_and_living_arrangements.html.

statuses, the overall percentages for both men and women were small (2.5 and 8.9 percent for men, and 9.8 and 11.5 percent for women). There was virtually no change for men between 2000 and 2007; but a slight decrease in the likelihood of currently being widowed and increase in the likelihood of being divorced for women. Although divorce rates increased significantly in the 1970s (see Chapter 14), a leveling off and slight decline in these rates in the intervening decades combined with high remarriage rates has resulted in a relatively small proportion of the adult population currently living in a divorced state.[31]

Of course, these percentages are affected by the age distribution of the population. Since the median age at first marriage in 2007 was 27.7 for men and 26 for women,[32] it is likely that many of those who are currently never married will eventually marry sometime in their lifetime. Marital history data on birth cohorts (all those born in the same year) from 1935–1939 through 1980–1984 has shown that the vast majority of first marriages occur before the age of 40 regardless of historical period.[33] As a result, the percent never married among those currently 40–44 years old should be a better indicator of the number of people choosing never to marry. As can be seen in Table 2.1, among those in the 40–44 age group, 16.9 percent of males and 12.9 percent of females remain never married. This number drops drastically for those in the 55–64 age group, but this decrease is likely due to what social scientists call *cohort effects*. That is, their low rates of never married status are most likely due to the fact that they were making decisions about whether or not to marry during an earlier decade (the 1960s), prior to a time when American society and the institution of marriage underwent significant changes making marriage less likely or desirable. It is highly unlikely that those in the 40–44 age group in 2007 will exhibit such a low rate of never marrying when they reach the ages of 55–64.

In addition to the likelihoods of marriage for those in the younger age groups, the data in Table 2.1 also show differences in the postmarital status of men in women in later life. Women 55 and older are much more likely than their male counterparts to be either widowed or divorced. These differences can be attributed to the longer life expectancy of women and the greater likelihood that a man who is widowed or divorced will remarry and do so sooner than a woman who is widowed or divorced.

Family Income

In each census, every household member age 15 and over is asked the amount of income received in the preceding calendar year from sources such as wages or salaries, self-employment, unemployment compensation, Social Security, dividends, interest, rental income, child support, public assistance or welfare payments, and other periodic income. This income is before taxes but does not include amounts from sources such as the sale of property (stocks, bonds, houses, or cars),

---

[31]U.S. Bureau of the Census, *The 2009 Statistical Abstract*, "Table 56: Marital Status of the Population by Sex and Age," http://www.2010census.biz/compendia/statab/cats/population/marital_status_and_living_arrangements.html.

[32]U.S. Bureau of the Census, "Median Age at First Marriage, 1890–2007," http://www.infoplease.com/ipa/A0005061.html, 2009.

[33]U.S. Bureau of the Census, *Survey of Income and Program Participation (SIPP)*, 2004 Panel, Wave 2 Topical Module, "Table 1: Marital History by Sex for Selected Birth Cohorts, 1935–39 to 1980–84," http://www.census.gov/population/www/socdemo/marr-div/2004detailed_tables.html, 2004.

Family Diversity

Alternative Definitions of "The" Family

Governments play a major role in how family life is defined in the cultural meaning system of a society. Not only do they put into law criteria for defining marriage and family rights and responsibilities, but they also influence cultural definitions and even academic scholarship on the family by the ways they collect data on their population. An example of how something as simple as a census definition can alter our understandings of family life and the diversity of family life in modern societies is offered by Kathryn Harker Tillman and Charles B. Nam. Using data from the Netherland Kinship Panel, they show how a more expanded census definition of the family can lead to different conclusions about the effects of modernity on the integrity and meaningfulness of family life. In particular, they show that by including unmarried cohabiting adults (heterosexual or same-sex

couples) in the criteria for what constitutes a family and by including families that cross household boundaries, the image that emerges is one that includes (1) more families in the population than would otherwise be reported, (2) larger family sizes, and (3) a better understanding of the living conditions of the elderly that finds many living in separate households but still incorporated into the families of their adult children. There are also policy implications of changing the census definition to be more inclusive of the diversity of family forms. For example, we gain a better understanding of the sources of financial and other support available to children (especially those in poverty), and we gain a better understanding of intergenerational relations in later life that can be useful in enhancing the lives of the elderly.

Source: Tillman, Kathryn Harker and Charles B.Nam. (2008). "Family Structure outcomes of alternative family definitions," Population Research and Policy vReview, 27, 367-384.

borrowed money, tax refunds, gifts, or lump-sum inheritance or insurance payments. The total income of a household is the sum of the amounts received by all income recipients in the family. In 2006, the median household income was $48,201, with family households reporting over $11,000 more ($59,894) and nonfamily households reporting almost $20,000 less ($29,083). Much of this difference can be attributed to the fact that family households are more likely to include two or more income earners, as one-earner households reported a median income of $39,309 compared to a median income of $74,513 among two earner households. Of course, family households are more likely to include one or more dependents, so the amount of income required to maintain a comparable standard of living is also greater. Within the category of *family* households, those including a married couple had the highest median income ($69,716), followed by those with an unmarried male householder ($47,078) and those with an unmarried female householder ($31,818).[34] These median values do not convey a complete picture of household income, however, as there is considerable variation, or inequality, in income in the United States. Approximately 25 percent of all households earn less than $25,000 a year, while 19 percent earn $100,000 or more. As might be expected, family households, and in particular those with a married couple, are more likely to be at the high end of the income distribution, with almost half of married couple households reporting incomes in excess of $75,000. In contrast, 22 percent of unmarried female family householders report incomes of under

---

[34]U.S. Bureau of the Census, *The 2009 Statistical Abstract*, "Table 670: Money Income of Households—Distribution by Current Income Level and Selected Characteristics," http://www. 2010census.biz/compendia/statab/cats/income_expenditures_poverty_wealth/household_income.html.

$15,000 and 39 percent fall below an income of $25,000. Unmarried male family householders are less likely than unmarried female family householders to report incomes under $25,000, but more likely than married couple householders to do so.[35] The consequences of these considerable income discrepancies for family life will be discussed in greater detail in Chapter 4.

Contemporary U.S. Families and Other Social Institutions

It appears obvious that relationships exist between family systems and other systems, yet these linkages frequently are ignored in family studies. As we saw in our brief review of historical changes in families in Western societies, families change in their structure, functions, and internal relationships in response to and in conjunction with changes in political, community, economic, educational, religious, and other institutions. As families change to meet their needs, they also bring about changes in these other institutions and sometimes stimulate the creation of new institutions. For example, as the economy changes, so do employment rates and family spending patterns. As wars affect international relations, so do they affect divorce rates. As political decisions determine policies related to health and welfare, so do they affect attitudes toward one-parent families and child-support responsibilities. And as education, employment, and the advancement of fertility-control methods modify the opportunities and options available to women and men, these changes affect male–female, husband–wife, and parent–child interactions and expectations.

Politics and the Family

Political systems impact families in a variety of ways. The most obvious is through the explicit actions of the state and its various regulatory bodies. The *state* is defined by civil laws and policies created by legislators that have either been appointed or elected by the citizenry. These laws and policies are enforced by agents of local, state, and federal governments. The state (political system) influences families through laws that both directly regulate and support families and laws that indirectly regulate and support families by restricting or designating rights to individuals in areas such as property and inheritance, health care decision making, and even the rights to have a say in the disposition of individuals' bodies after death. In addition, states affect families through their relations to other states and, in particular, their engagement in international conflicts.

Families are directly regulated through laws that govern marriage, including the choice of spouse, the number of spouses, the age at which marriage is permissible, the necessity of a blood test, the acceptance or nonacceptance of common-law marriages, the prohibition or acceptance of same-sex marriages, which relationships are seen as incestuous, and the soundness of the proposed partners' mental conditions. Families are also regulated through laws that specify the rights and duties of parenthood, such as those that relate to contraception, pregnancy, abortion, custody of children, and abuse. Other regulations of families relate to factors such as divorce and separation as well as economic factors, such as the distribution of property. Some of these laws are very general and establish guidelines or boundaries of permissible behavior; others are very precise and specific and carry legal and civil sanctions.

---

[35]Ibid.

Why are these legal definitions of marriage and family status so important? Leading up to the 2008 vote on the California initiative to prohibit same-sex marriage (Proposition 8), the campaigns for and against the initiative raised over $60 million, an amount that exceeded spending on every other political contest in the country other than the presidential race.[36] Why have groups invested so much in arguing and advocating their positions with respect to legal definitions of marriage and family status?

There is much to be gained or lost at both group and individual levels as a result of the outcomes of these contests. Existing power and privilege hierarchies based on social class, gender, religious group membership, and other characteristics are sustained by the rules governing institutions and individual behaviors within institutions. How marriage and family membership is legally defined has implications for the preservation and advancement of social class hierarchies insofar as those hierarchies are premised on family status and inheritance (see Chapter 4). Men have much to lose vis-à-vis women insofar as existing definitions of family and expectations about family relationships favor men's independence and greater access to family income earning roles that put them at an advantage in negotiations with their partners over desired outcomes and give them greater control over their partners' behaviors (see Chapters 9 and 13). Religious groups have much to gain or lose insofar as a specific definition of family and family relationships between spouses and between parents and children is integrated into a broader set of values and beliefs. Finally, at the individual level, much is at stake in these debates insofar as many other rights, privileges, opportunities, and personal dignity are linked to the right to marry or form a family through giving birth or adopting children. During recent debates about the legalization of same-sex marriage, the significance of the state in directly and indirectly shaping and supporting the family was made clear by the presentation of evidence that more than a thousand public rights and benefits are codified into law contingent on marital status.[37]

The state also influences family life through the formulation of social policies such as social welfare, immigration, and policies designed specifically to address family-related concerns. It has long been recognized that a balancing act exists between the state, the economy, and the family as institutions responsible for the welfare of individuals. How nation states resolve this balance has led to a typology of welfare states into three types: social democratic, conservative, and liberal.[38] **Social democratic welfare regimes** provide benefits based on citizenship alone. Be it income security, health care, child care, elder care, or any other type of support, all members of society are eligible for the same level of benefit regardless of their ability to pay for it themselves. Such systems have high levels of taxation with high levels of benefit provision resulting in many positive consequences for children and others. Since the state assumes responsibility for providing support, these systems are less linked to marital or family status. As a result, countries with social democratic welfare regimes (e.g., Sweden and other Scandinavian countries) tend to have

---

[36]Justin Ewers, "California Same-Sex Marriage Initiative Campaigns Shatter Spending Records," http://www.usnews.com/articles/news/national/2008/10/29/california-same-sex-marriage-initiative-campaigns-shatter-spending-records.html, October 29, 2008.

[37]National Gay and Lesbian Task Force, www.thetaskforce.org/theissues/issue.cfm?issue.ID=14, 2005.

[38]G. Esping-Andersen, *1999 Social Foundations of Postindustrial Economies* (Oxford: Oxford University Press).

CROSS-CULTURAL *Perspective*

Welfare Regimes and Family Patterns in Europe

Although the countries of the European Union generally provide more welfare support to their populations than the United States, these countries nevertheless vary in the nature of their welfare regimes and the levels of support they provide. Like the United States, the United Kingdom is a liberal welfare regime providing low levels of support and relying on the market place to provide needed supports to individuals and families. On the opposite end of the spectrum, the countries in the far north (e.g., Sweden, Norway, Finland, and Denmark) are social democratic regimes, relying on the state to provide support at relatively high levels. Most of the remaining countries fall somewhere in between these two groups in levels of support, but most rely heavily on the family (and especially women in families) as a source of informal support.

What are the consequences for families of these different levels and types of support? A recent analysis by Joachim Vogel of differences in family life across sixteen countries in the European Union shows some significant impacts in a variety of areas of family life. In general, countries in the north have an earlier age at which adult children leave the home (especially men); a lower age at first union formation but higher age at

first marriage; higher levels of living alone throughout adulthood; lower marriage rates; higher rates of long-term cohabitations; higher levels of total fertility (due mostly to recent steep declines in fertility in the southern countries); smaller difference in the employment status of mothers versus fathers of young children; higher levels of the elderly living independently of their children and grandchildren; and somewhat higher divorce rates, although there has been a steep increase in divorce in the southern countries.

Do these changes suggest a demise of the family in social democratic welfare state regimes? If by "family" one means a system of economic and instrumental relationships and obligations, then the answer would have to be *yes*. Much of the social obligations placed on family members to support each other are taken over by the state in social democratic welfare regimes. This does not mean, however, that all levels of mutual support have disappeared. As another study by Ulla Bjornberg and Mia Latta shows, financial support among family members still exists in Sweden, but has changed in terms of the motivations given for providing support. Instead of support based on obligation in the presence of need, it is now based on affective ties and is largely independent of need.

Sources: Vogel, Joachim, "The Family," *Social Indicators Research*, 64 (Dec. 2003), 393–435; Bjornberg, Ulla and Mia Latta, "The Roles of the Family and the Welfare State: The Relationship between Public and Private Financial Support in Sweden," *Current Sociology*, 55, (May 2007), 415–445.

---

low rates of legal marriage (although long–term, stable cohabitations are quite frequent). In contrast, a **liberal welfare regime** places responsibility for social support on a free market system. In liberal regimes, taxation and state provided support are low. Individuals are expected to contract for support and insurance against problems through private sources. Only those in extreme need can receive assistance from the state. Such a means-tested approach to providing benefits results in high levels of stigmatization and lower levels of support, both for individuals and families. The United States, Canada, and the United Kingdom come closest to fitting this model. Finally, the **conservative welfare regimes** focus their attention on the family as a provider of support, but attempt to equalize support across families through income redistributive tax policies and supplements for needed supports such as child care. Social support and benefits are linked to family status and participation of family members in the labor force. The state provides considerable economic transfers to equalize family economic conditions but does not provide benefits otherwise. Conservative welfare regimes (such as in France and Germany), tend to promote family formation and provide levels of benefits somewhere between those of social democratic and liberal regimes.[39]

In addition to welfare policies, immigration policies have become important determinants of family life for large segments of modern global societies such as the United States. Undocumented workers and the failures of U.S. policies to deal with the desire and motivation of many from Mexico and Central America to immigrate to the United States has been the source of much political debate in recent years. In spite of strong economic incentives for undocumented workers to cross the border into the United States—fueled by business interests in reducing wages by hiring workers from Mexico and Central America—the United States has done little to develop a realistic and humane immigration policy to accommodate foreign workers and their families. The consequences of this failure can be found in the challenges faced by many undocumented women in truly transnational families as they attempt to manage relationships with their children "back home." Based on a previous study by Hondagneu-Sotelo[40] and another by Hongangeu-Sotelo and Avila,[41] Melanie Nicholson intensively interviewed thirteen women who immigrated without documentation to New York State.[42] These women moved to the United States to join their husbands who, themselves undocumented, had moved to the United States previously in pursuit of a livelihood for their family. Due to the risks involved both in crossing the border and in the neighborhood contexts within which these immigrants find housing, these mothers chose to leave their children behind in the care of relatives. This situation created considerable anxiety for these mothers and forced them to reconceptualize their ideas of motherhood. Although they were unable to fulfill the white, middle-class, western standard of "exclusive and intensive motherhood," these mothers still managed to maintain a positive view of their mothering activities insofar as they maintained ongoing contact with and decision making in their children's lives, had an expanded and more communal notion of providing nurturance and care, and incorporated their wage-earning activities as critical components of their ability to enhance the life outcomes of their children. Nevertheless, the situation is a difficult one for them to endure in order to improve their life conditions back in their home countries when they return.

Another way in which immigration policies can affect families is through the impact they have on gender relationships and control and violence in those relationships. As Margaret Abraham[43] shows, based on her work for a South Asian community-based women's organization in New York City, immigration policies in the 1960s encouraged many Indian professionals (mostly men) to immigrate to the United State where they were able to develop a strong identity as a "model minority" due to their success in the labor force, especially in relation to other minorities

---

[39]John Myles, "How to Design a 'Liberal' Welfare State: A Comparison of Canada and the United States," *Social Policy and Administration* 32. 4 (1998): 341–364.

[40]Hondagneu-Sotelo, *Gendered Transition: Mexican Experiences of Immigration* (Berkeley: University of California Press, 1994).

[41]Hondagneu-Sotelo and Ernestine Avila, "I'm Here, but I'm There: The Meanings of Latina Transnational Motherhood," *Gender and Society* 11 (1997): 549.

[42]Melanie Nicholson. "Without Their Children: Rethinking Motherhood among Transnational Immigrant Women," *Social Text* 24 (Fall 2006): 13–33.

[43]Margaret Abraham, "Domestic Violence and the Indian Diaspora in the United States," *Indian Journal of Gender Studies* 12 (May–Dec. 2005): 427–451.

such as African Americans and Hispanics. That initial migration later led to an increase in the numbers and diversity of Indian migrants throughout the remainder of the century, primarily through family reunification provisions. Although this provision for reuniting families was positive, the population of Indian immigrants became more socioeconomically diverse and many unmarried male Indian immigrants found it difficult to find marital partners who fit their cultural ideals of submissiveness, docility, and sexual constraint. As a result, many sought wives in India and contracted for arranged marriages with women living in India. Given the lack of prior knowledge of their new spouse, the high level of isolation of the wife who no longer has a community of relatives around her, and the potential for these new wives to adopt elements of their new culture that challenge traditional norms, many South Asian women were confronted with control attempts by their husbands, violence, and a desire to leave their marriage due to a lack of compatibility, personal safety and well-being, and satisfaction.

Two policy initiatives made the situation faced by these women worse. The first was the 1986 Immigrant Marriage Fraud Amendment that granted only conditional residence status to new spouses for a two-year period in order to prevent people from getting married only because they wanted to immigrate. The result of this law is that it made South Asian women more dependent on their husbands and less able to leave a controlling or abusive relationship for fear of being deported for marriage fraud. Subsequent changes to immigration law in 1990 and the creation of the Violence Against Women Act in 1994 and 2000 helped relieve some of the issues these women faced. However, in 2001, a new policy initiative designed to fight against terrorism, The Patriot Act, once again created a similar situation for many South Asian immigrant women. Since the Patriot Act made it easier for authorities to deport immigrants with little cause (especially those from eastern countries and the Middle East), South Asian women once again found themselves hesitant to leave or even report abusive situations. To do so would create an opportunity for officials to examine backgrounds more closely and potentially deport for even minor irregularities. Reporting abuse in marriage might also invite greater scrutiny by officials of other family members and put them at risk of deportation, an untenable situation in a culture that emphasizes loyalty and obligation to family members.

Finally, political systems impact families through their maintenance of a military and their engagement in international relationships and conflicts. Jay Teachman and his colleagues have explored the various ways that life course and family factors affect military enlistment as well as the ways the military experience affects marital and family transitions.[44] In addition, the recent war in Iraq has increased our concern with how wars fought on foreign lands affect family life at home, especially in a technological environment with rapid communication of information and pictures. One particular study of these effects was done by Alesia Montgomery. In her analysis of war-time advice given to families by psychologists and others, she noted how the

---

[44]Jay D. Teachman, Vaughn R.A. Call, and Mady Segal Wechsler, "Family, Work, and School Influences on the Decision to Enter the Military," *Journal of Family Issues* 14.2 (1993): 291–313; Vaughn R.A. Call and Jay D. Teachman, "Life-Course Timing and Sequencing of Marriage and Military Service and their Effects on Marital Stability," *Journal of Marriage and the Family* 58.1 (1996): 219–26; Jay D. Teachman and Lucky Tedro, "Divorce, Race, and Military Service: More than Equal Pay and Equal Opportunity," *Journal of Marriage and Family* 70.4 (2008): 1030–44; and Jay D. Teachman, "Race, Military Service, and Marital Timing: Evidence from the NLSY–79," *Demography* 44.2 (2007): 389–404.

observations of war can have negative impacts on family members with no direct connection to the war, especially children. She cautions, however, that the kind of advice we give to families to help them cope also has implications for the political discourse around the justification for war and efforts to resist war. In particular, she agrees with the advice that children's exposure to graphic news about the war should be monitored and restricted. However, she also argues that an avoidance of discussions about the war, its justifications, and its consequences for individuals may not be as healthy as much of the advice given would imply. Instead, she argues that engagement with issues about the justifications for war and participation in antiwar protests and other resistance activities can also have beneficial effects on helping children and families cope successfully with the situation.[45]

Community and the Family

Another important context for understanding families and other institutions is the type of community within which those institutions are embedded. In modern industrial societies, an important distinction has emerged between life in rural communities versus life in urban communities. In more recent decades, the emergence of suburbs has added yet another dimension and source of variation in social life.

The U.S. Census defines rural communities as those consisting of fewer than 2,500 people living outside a metropolitan area of 50,000 or more. Such communities predominated in the United States through much of the nineteenth century, but large-scale immigration and internal migration fueled by industrialization during the late nineteenth and early twentieth centuries transformed the landscape to one where most people live in urban environments. This transformation subsided in the second half of the twentieth century to the point where the rural population has consisted of about 20 percent of the population since 1990.[46] For the most part, these areas are characterized by a farm or agricultural economy, although in the United States today very few small farms are still in operation and most people in rural communities either work in nonfarm employment or supplement their farm income through nonfarm employment. Today, the states with the largest percentage of rural population include traditional farm states such as Mississippi, Alabama, Arkansas, Kentucky, Montana, South Dakota, and North Dakota as well as states not typically thought of as farming centers, such as Maine, Vermont, New Hampshire, and West Virginia.[47] Nevertheless, rural communities continue to maintain much of their unique character, as first described by the German sociologist Ferdinand Toennies.

In his analysis of the massive societal changes occurring in the nineteenth century, Toennies made a distinction between **Gemeinschaft** societies and **Gesellschaft** societies. The former type referred to societies based on agricultural production and the latter to societies created by industrialization and urbanization. In Gemainschaft societies, relationships were primary and communal in nature. Individuals knew each other personally from birth and maintained intimate bonds

---

[45]Alesia F. Montgomery, "Therapeutic vs. Political Frames: The Influence of 'Witnessing' The U.S.–Iraq War on Family 'Agitation,'" *Sociological Perspectives* 51 (Fall 2008): 605–627.

[46]U.S. Bureau of the Census, *The 2009 Statistical Abstract*, "Table 28: Urban and Rural Population by State," http://www.2010census.biz/compendia/statab/cats/population/estimates_and_projectionsstates_metropolitan_areas_cities.html.

[47]Ibid.

with a diverse number of others throughout their lives. Such societies were characterized by high levels of mutuality in terms of self-definition, destinies, and conditions of life. As a result, there was a high level of consensus about values and beliefs and a strong emphasis on obligation to the community and conformity to group norms. In Gesellschaft societies, on the other hand, high levels of differentiation in the industrial production system along with high levels of geographical mobility created differences among individuals, destroying much of the mutuality that existed in the rural environment and reducing the opportunities for life-long personal bonds and self-definition through neighborhood relationships. Individuals became more focused on individual interest and less on communal interests. Relationships were maintained only insofar as doing so advanced individuals' personal goals and interests.[48]

What are the consequences of **rural versus urban community** contexts for family life? First, in rural communities, the family is a central institution around which all life revolves. As such, there are strong norms concerning family formation, organization, and commitment, and these norms tend to be integrated with norms concerning appropriate behavior based on age and gender and a strong regulation of sexuality outside of marriage. Second, rural communities exhibit high levels of involvement in all institutions (e.g., family, church, school, and voluntary organizations) resulting in high levels of personal bonds and mutual knowing outside the immediate nuclear family. The nuclear family is less of an "island" of personal bonding in an otherwise impersonal world. Third, rural communities tend to be more conservative when it comes to accepting change. Change threatens the established order and is potentially disruptive of personal relationships. As a result, the acceptance of new or alternative family life styles is much slower to occur. Same-sex relationships, nonmarital sexuality, cohabitation, single parenting, and divorce are more heavily frowned upon and are likely to be negatively sanctioned.

Evidence of the stronger family norms existing in rural communities and the resistance to alternative family arrangements can be found in a recent analysis of the National Survey of Family Growth. In a study of over 10,000 women living in metro, nonmetro (suburban), and rural communities, the authors found lower incidences of cohabitation and divorce in the rural and nonmetro communities. They also found that nonmetro and, especially, rural women were more likely to get married, marry earlier (about one year earlier on average), have their first child within the context of marriage, and have an earlier first birth.[49]

In another study comparing farm and nonfarm families in rural Iowa with urban families in Los Angeles, the high level of interdependence and mutuality of rural environments was demonstrated with respect to levels of contact and aid giving between adolescents and their grandparents. With respect to paternal grandparents, the percent of adolescents who reported some contact or help from grandparents during the previous year was 81 percent among rural farm adolescents, and 63 percent among rural nonfarm adolescents. In contrast, only 20 percent of the urban adolescents reported either some contact or help from their paternal grandparents. A similar pattern was found for maternal grandparents,

---

[48]Ferdinand Toennies, *Gemeinschaft and Gesellschaft*. Translated and edited by Charles P. Loomis (New York: Harper & Row, 1898/1963).

[49]Anastasia R. Snyder, Susan L. Brown, and Erin P. Condo, "Residential Differences in Family Formation: The Significance of Cohabitation," *Rural Sociology* 69.2 (2004): 235–260.

TRANSNATIONAL FAMILIES

The Roma

On September 27, 2003, a 12-year-old Romani girl, Ana Maria Cioaba, was wed to a 15-year-old Romani boy in an arranged marriage in Sibiu, Romania. The Roma are a nomadic people from the Punjabi region of Northwest India who settled throughout Europe between the twelfth and fifteenth centuries, principally in Central and Eastern Europe and Spain. In earlier historical periods, the Roma frequently crossed borders seeking a livelihood through trade, foraging for food and other materials, agricultural work, and entertainment. As a "foreign" people of color, the Roma experienced a history of discrimination, prejudice, and persecution. They often were the scapegoats of nations experiencing problems and were cast into slavery or physically marked as outcasts. In more recent times, they were persecuted with the Jews in Nazi Germany (large numbers were put to death in gas chambers) as well as by the communist governments of the old Soviet states. Today, the Roma are mostly a settled people, although they continue to exhibit high levels of migratory activities either to escape persecution or seek temporary or seasonal employment in door-to-door sales, agriculture, arts and crafts, or entertainment fields. Family life among the Roma is traditionally matricentric, but strongly patriarchal. Although arranged marriage can occur, it is not frequently practiced. Large numbers of Roma live in segregated settlements in rural areas characterized by extremely poor living conditions. Due to low life expectancies, early marriage patterns, high fertility, and the migratory nature of men's economic activities, these settlements consist of a disproportionate number of young women and children. Large numbers of Roma can also be found living in extreme poverty in large urban centers, while still others have escaped their conditions of poverty and often are indistinguishable from the majority population among whom they live and work.

The marriage of Ana Maria Cioaba was a significant event—it was highly publicized and condemned in the Romanian media as well as through media outlets across Europe and even in the *New York Times*. Unfortunately, this news coverage highlighted the "exotic" nature of the event and of Roma culture in general and cast the Roma as both foreign and primitive. As Alexandra Oprea points out, this reaction of the media had many negative consequences for the Roma people and for Roma women in particular. Although the outrage expressed in news reports about the marriage of a 12-year-old girl was focused on defending girls and women against mistreatment and subjugation (some cast the event as one of statutory rape), she notes that the latent function of the reports in Romania was to highlight the difference between the "primitive" Roma and the more sophisticated and modern Romanian population at a time when Romania was seeking to improve its image for membership in the European Union. In news outlets outside of Romania, the latent function of these reports was to address fears throughout Europe about the loss of national identity due to increasingly free movement of peoples across borders. Even among those who defended the Roma in the face of this event did so in a manner that was not necessarily helpful for changing conditions among the Roma. Roma "traditional culture" was presented as homogeneous and sacred even though there is great variety in cultural practices across Roma communities, and the subordinate position of women in traditional Roma culture is neither sacred nor universally accepted.

Sources: The Roma Dosta! Campaign, http://www.dosta.org; Roma in the Czech Republic, http://romove.radio.cz/en/clanek/18241; Alexandra Oprea, "The Arranged Marriage of Ana Maria Cioaba, Intra-Community Oppression and Romani Feminist Ideals: Transcending the Primitive Culture Argument," *European Journal of Women's Studies*, 12 (2005), 133–148.

but the differences were smaller, especially for comparisons involving the farm adolescents. Further analysis of their data revealed that much of the difference in contacts and aid giving could be explained by greater geographical distance from grandparents and higher divorce rates in the urban and nonfarm contexts; although a residual difference remained suggesting that intergenerational relations, and family relationships in general, are integral parts of the rural culture and way of life.[50]

Finally, the consequence of a rural community context for satisfaction with family life was demonstrated in a recent analysis of the U.S. General Social Survey. In this study, the family life satisfaction scores for rural residents were significantly higher than they were for urban residents. Furthermore, these satisfaction scores could be largely explained by levels of community satisfaction, as rural respondents reported more satisfaction with their community as well. Perhaps these higher satisfaction levels can be explained by a higher level of contact and exchange with family members and neighbors in rural communities. This is suggested by the fact that measures of contact with family and friends helped offset the lower satisfaction levels of urban residents but had no effect on the rural residents where such contacts are already likely to be strong.[51]

All of this is not to say that rural communities are without their problems. In a modern society where family farm production is no longer viable and power and resources are concentrated in cities, those living in rural communities often can be marginalized. Considerable poverty exists in rural America, and many families and individuals are isolated in their communities as a result of relatives and others having moved to the urban centers in search of employment and a different way of life. As city life becomes increasingly expensive, there has also been movement of the urban poor and welfare recipients to rural communities in search of less expensive housing. This increasing "impoverishment" of the rural landscape is exacerbated by the fact that social services for those in need are more expensive and difficult to provide, resulting in fewer resources when problems (such as violence, sexual abuse, depression, child problem behavior, and substance abuse) occur in families.

Economy and the Family

Perhaps as much as any other institution, the economic system influences family organization and interaction. The economy is the component of society concerned with the creation, distribution, and consumption of goods and services. The family contributes labor and skills and in turn receives wages or other forms of compensation (prestige, insurance, services, etc.). At a macro level of analysis, the economic system in a modern capitalistic society such as the United States has a broad impact on family life through the dynamics of social class relations. As discussed in Chapter 4, one's social class position not only determines one's financial resources but also has impacts on values and belief systems, lifestyle choices, behavioral expectations, socialization experiences, social networks, neighborhood environments, and other aspects of social life that impact family experiences. Beyond the effects of social class, problems in macroeconomic systems (e.g., high unemployment rates, inflation, recessions, and economic depressions) can have profound and diverse effects on families.

---

[50]Valerie King, Merril Silverstein, Glen H. Elder Jr., Vern L. Bengtson, and Rand D. Conger, "Relations with Grandparents: Rural Midwest versus Urban Southern California," *Journal of Family Issues* 24.8 (November 2003): 1044–1069.

[51]John F. Toth Jr., Ralph B. Brown, and Xiaohe Xu, "Separate Family and Community Realities? An Urban-Rural Comparison of the Association between Family Life Satisfaction and Community Satisfaction," *Community, Work & Family* 5.2 (2002): 181–202.

At a more micro level, stress is a well-documented result of receiving inadequate wages or other compensation. And financial stress, in turn, has pernicious consequences for both adults and children.[52] Poor mental health, erosion of self-image, increased risk of suicide, alcohol-related disease, divorce, and child abuse are some of the negative consequences for adults. Children have also been found to exhibit a range of emotional and behavioral problems. Recent studies, however, suggest that negative outcomes of economic conditions on families are largely mediated through parental perceptions. In one study of low-income, mostly single mothers in Wisconsin, *total income* and *income from government supports* alone had no direct effects on children's social outcomes (defined as "positive behaviors" and "problematic behaviors"), although levels of *instrumental support availability* (reliability of sources of support from other people) and *financial management strategies* (availability of active bank accounts, bank credit, etc.) did have modest effects. More importantly, the lack of all four types of resources affected the likelihood that parents would perceive more difficulties meeting both *basic needs* and *modest extras* ("financial wants"), and both of these perceptions had significant negative effects on child outcomes. These negative effects were themselves mediated through the parent's general stress levels, depressive symptoms, and feeling of efficacy—all of which reduced their levels of control over children and their responsiveness in parenting.[53] In another long-term study of two-parent families, these negative consequences of parents' perceived economic hardship on children were shown to persist into early adulthood.[54]

In addition to general levels of stress due to a lack of economic resources, the economy interacts with family life through the workplace itself. In Chapter 4, we will discuss how the nature of work in different social classes impacts parenting styles. At a more general level, however, there have been numerous studies of how work stress "spills over" into family life (**work-family spillover**) and how family life stress "spills over" into work life (**family-work spillover**). These effects can be either negative or positive. *Negative* spillover occurs when stress, fatigue, or negative mood states from one realm affects a person's behaviors in his/her roles in the other realm. *Positive* spillover occurs when some skill (e.g., time management) or cognition (e.g., positive outlook) developed in one realm enhances one's role performance in the other realm. In a recent study of how nonstandard work schedules impact family life, it was shown that working a night shift has a negative impact on spousal relationships and that this affect can largely be credited to an increase in negative work-family spillover (increased fatigue). Weekend work, on the other hand, had no negative effect on marital relationships for white-collar workers, but did increase work-family spillover for blue-collar workers.[55]

---

[52]Patricia Voydanoff, "Economic Distress and Family Relations: A Review of the Eighties," *Journal of Marriage and the Family* 52 (November 1990): 1099–1115; and David T. Takeuchi, David R. Williams, and Russell K. Adair, "Economic Stress in the Family and Children's Emotional and Behavioral Problems," *Journal of Marriage and the Family* 53 (November 1991): 1031–1041.

[53]Rashmita S. Mistry, Edward D. Lowe, Aprile D. Benner, and Nina Chien, "Expanding the Family Economic Stress Model: Insights from a Mixed-Methods Approach," *Journal of Marriage and Family* 70 (2008): 196–209.

[54]Juliana M. Sobolewski and Paul R. Amato, "Economic Hardship in the Family of Origin and Children's Pscyhological Well-Being in Adulthood," *Journal of Marriage and Family* 67 (2005): 141–156.

[55]Kelly D. Davis, W. Benjamin Goodman, Amy E. Pirretti, and David M. Almeida, "Nonstandard Work Schedules, Perceived Family Well-Being, and Daily Stressors," *Journal of Marriage and Family* 70 (2008): 991–1003.

Yet another way the economic system impacts families can also be found in levels of work involvement. Specifically, comparative levels of work involvement by husbands and wives can have significant effects on the division of household labor, power relations, parenting effectiveness, marital satisfaction, and marital stability. Many of these effects will be discussed in greater detail in Chapter 9 (The Marital System). As a preface to that discussion, however, it is instructive to know how comparative levels of work involvement by husbands and wives have changed in recent decades.

After World War II, the expanding economy and demand for labor led to a major increase in women's labor force participation. Although African American women had long maintained a place in the labor force, white women were now joining them in employment. This trend was further spurred by rising expectations for living standards requiring two incomes. As a result, the percentage of women active in the labor force has increased from 37.7 percent in 1960 to 59.3 percent in 2007.[56] For married women, the increase in labor force participation has been even greater; increasing from 30.5 percent in 1960 to 61.6 percent in 2007 (see Figure 2.3). This increase would have been even greater if not for a large number of older women who no longer had children living at home and who dropped out of the labor force in earlier decades, never developed the skills needed for employment, and/or subscribe to an older model of appropriate roles for men and women. As can be seen in Figure 2.3, the increases in labor force participation among younger women with children at home have been extremely steep, although they have leveled off since the early 1990s. For women with a child under the age of 6 at home, women's labor force participation has increased from 18.6 to 61.5 percent. For women with a school-age child between 6 and 17 at home, the rate has also increased steeply from

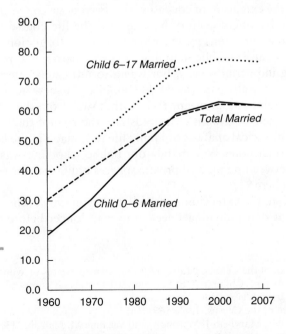

Figure 2.3

Labor Force
Participation Rates of
Married Women:
1960–2007

[56]U.S. Bureau of the Census, "Table 569: Civilian Population—Employment Status by Sex, Race, and Ethnicity," http://www.2010census.biz/compendia/statab/cats/labor_force_employment_earnings/labor_force_status.html.

39 percent in 1960 to 76.2 percent in 2007.[57] Interestingly, this rate is higher than the employment rate for all men in the civilian labor force (73.2 percent).[58]

As a result of these increases in women's labor force participation, there has also been a dramatic increase in dual-earner couples and "unconventional earning patterns" among dual-income couples. In an analysis of over 18,000 marital households of couples between the ages of 25 and 54, Sara Raley and her colleagues found a dramatic decrease in "husband as sole provider" households from 56 percent in 1970 to 24 percent in 2001 and a more than doubling of "equally shared income provisioning" from 9 percent in 1970 to 24 percent in 2001. Most of the change in the former category occurred between 1970 and 1990, but most of the increase in equal sharing has occurred since 1990. The percentage of households where the wife is either the majority or the sole income earner increased even more during this period from 4 percent to 12 percent, although this arrangement remains rare. Thus, although women are making greater contributions to family income (both in absolute and relative terms), in the majority of households in 2001 the husband was either the sole breadwinner or the primary breadwinner. Further continuation of these trends can be expected, however, given that younger women and those with more education are more likely to be either equal partners or primary or sole providers.[59]

Education and the Family

Like other family-institution relationships, the relationship between the family and the educational system is also reciprocal. At a very basic level, schools affect families by shaping the rhythms of everyday life in families. At a macro level, the emergence of public education at the primary and secondary school levels in the late nineteenth century and the extension of educational expectations and requirements beyond high school in the twentieth century have altered the life course of individuals in ways that have had implications for marriage and family formation and for parenting. The advent of mandatory public schooling occurred partially in response to the needs of the emerging industrial society, but was also intricately interwoven with the emergence of new family patterns of life among the new middle classes. Requiring children to attend school meant their withdrawal from the labor force and focused attention on their developmental needs and the role of the family in meeting those needs. In an historical analysis of family life in Canada in the late nineteenth century, Gordon Darroch notes how mandatory public schooling was part of the emerging distinction between public and private spheres of life and the relegation of women to the private sphere.[60]

In addition, the extension of schooling beyond high school in the late twentieth century meant that individuals needed to wait longer before they could begin their

---

[57]U.S. Bureau of the Census, "Table 578: Employment Status of Women, by Marital Status and Presence and Age of Children," http://www.2010census.biz/compendia/statab/cats/labor_force_employment_earnings/labor_force_status.html.

[58]U.S Bureau of the Census, Table 569.

[59]Sara B. Raley, Marybeth J. Mattingly, and Suzanne M. Bianchi, "How Dual Are Dual-Income Couples? Documenting Change from 1970 to 2001," *Journal of Marriage and Family* 68 (2006): 11–28.

[60]Gordon Darroch, "Domestic Revolution and Cultural Formation in Nineteenth-Century Ontario, Canada," *History of the Family* 4.4 (1999): 427–445.

occupational careers, which means that they needed to wait longer before they could establish the economic foundations for marriage. As a result, there has been a substantial increase in the average age at first marriage since the early 1950s that has likely contributed to changes in premarital intimate relationships and the increase in cohabitation.

At a more micro level, the ways in which the school day and the school year are structured pose logistics problems for parents as they need to find ways to balance work outside the home with the need to care for children when they are not attending school. A change in the length of the school day or in the length of the school year is likely to have repercussions for family life and bring about strong reactions from parents who would be required to alter their schedules and role responsibilities. Schools also group students according to their ages and sometimes their abilities. Family life changes when young children enter school, become active in school endeavors, and move through the K–12 system. At each school level, children and their parents are exposed to different expectations for behavior and involvement in activities outside of school. These new expectations can come into conflict with family expectations and often times force changes in family responsibilities and power relationships that can result in conflict when family change does not occur. Finally, schools don't only take children through an established curriculum of academic subjects, but also focus heavily on the so-called hidden curriculum, teaching civic and moral responsibility. The extent to which this hidden curriculum focuses on obedience to rules versus individual moral decision making, respect for authority versus questioning authority, success through competition versus through cooperation, and other areas of potential value controversy is likely to either reinforce or disrupt family value systems. Such impacts can affect levels of cohesiveness in families and either facilitate or impede the attainment of parents' socialization goals.

Finally, education has implications for family life by shaping individuals' human, social and cultural capital. **Capital** refers to accumulated goods or resources that can be used to satisfy human needs, respond to stressor events or crises, and acquire additional resources in the future. Although active debate still exists in the discipline about the meaning of *capital* as a concept,[61] sociologists often make a distinction between four types of capital: *economic, human, social*, and *cultural*. **Economic capital** refers to the economic resources one has accumulated such as savings accounts, houses, credit lines, stocks and bonds, and other forms of wealth. **Human capital** refers to skills and abilities one has accumulated such as abilities to read, write, and perform quantitative operations. It also includes general and specialized knowledge one has accumulated that can be used to facilitate social outcomes (e.g., more effective parenting, greater communication, and conflict management, etc.) as well as economic ones (e.g., performance in specialized occupational careers). **Social capital** refers to the network of social relationships (e.g., kinship networks, friendship networks, community networks, political networks, etc.) that can be used to help monitor external environment, find assistance in times of need, and create opportunities for enhancing or expanding goals and outcomes. Lastly, **cultural capital** refers to cultural experiences (e.g., travel to foreign countries, visits to museums, attendance at concerts, etc.), language usage and linguistic styles, knowledge of

---

[61]Annette Lareau and Elliot B. Weininger, "Cultural Capital in Educational Research: A Critical Assessment," *Theory and Society* 32 (2003): 567–606.

topics deemed important by powerful groups in society, and lifestyle preferences that are "institutionalized…signals…used for social and cultural exclusion."[62] Cultural capital is useful insofar as it conveys worth to others and thereby shapes their expectations, their evaluations, and their willingness to comply with one's wishes.

Formal schooling directly affects levels of human, social, and cultural capital through its skill and knowledge building activities, its organization of social relationships among students, and its exposure of students to particular types of cultural experiences and value systems. These impacts can be seen in the effects of education on economic outcomes and economic capital building as well as in the positive effects of education on marital and parenting effectiveness and success.

With respect to the reciprocal effects of family on education and schooling, there is extensive literature demonstrating how the quality of family life and the resources of parents can enhance the educational outcomes of their children. Having economic and other resources increases the likelihood of a more enriched home environment: access to books, computers, and other educational resources; physical space and privacy needed for study; less stress at home to distract from learning; and more effective involvement of parents in learning and educational pursuits. Considerable attention has been given to the effects of parental school involvement on child outcomes. The idea that parental involvement in their children's education both in and out of the school setting will bring about more positive educational (e.g., grades, test performance, and reduced dropout rates) and social (e.g., lower delinquency rates) outcomes is widely accepted in the population and by many professional educators. As Thurston Domina has noted, the assumption that parental involvement will be a positive force in children's educational outcomes has been at the core of major educational policy reforms of both Republican and Democratic administrations from the Reagan administrations Educate America Act (1986) to the Clinton administration's Elementary and Secondary Education Act (1996), to the No Child Left Behind Act of George W. Bush (2002).[63] Recent sociological research, however, tempers enthusiasm for this panacea to poor educational performance by students.

Although there is evidence that shared book reading and parental teaching of reading and writing skills in the early preschool years has positive consequences for children's reading levels in first and third grade,[64] evidence of positive educational outcomes from parental involvement in later schooling (both in terms of helping students at home and participating in school activities, conference, etc.) is lacking. For the most part, this research has focused on parental involvement as a source of both social and cultural capital that students can use to transform their relationships with teachers, obtain the needed help in making school adjustments and learning material, and receive higher grades. From a social capital perspective, involvement in schools should enhance parents' knowledge of how their children are performing and what their needs are. This should make them more effective in either helping their children directly or finding the needed help for their children to succeed. From a cultural capital viewpoint, parental involvement

[62]Michele Lamont and Annette Lareau, "Cultural Capital: Allusions, Gaps and Glissandos in Recent Theoretical Developments," *Sociological Theory* 6 (1988): 156.

[63]Thurston Domina, "Leveling the Home Advantage: Assessing the Effectiveness of Parental Involvement in Elementary School," *Sociology of Education* 78 (2005): 233–249.

[64]Monique Senechal and Jo-Anne LeFevre, "Parental Involvement in the Development of Children's Reading Skill: A Five-Year Longitudinal Study," *Child Development* 73 (2002): 445–460.

Questions with the Sereno Family

Recipients of NIU's Alumni Award

A longtime Naperville family recently was honored with Northern Illinois University's 2009 Outstanding College of Liberal Arts and Sciences Alumni Award—an award that traditionally goes to an individual. The Sereno family, which includes six siblings, is not only unique in that they received this award, but also because all six children graduated from NIU, each has gone on to earn his or her doctorate, and all have successful careers.

The matriarch of this family, Rena Sereno, was born in Naperville in 1932. In 1972, Sereno paved her family's way at NIU by beginning work on her master's degree in art education. One by one, her children followed until the last graduated from NIU in 1986. The Sereno children didn't stop their education there, though. All went on to graduate school, and all have received their doctorates, which is even more impressive considering that NIU could find no record of any other family with six siblings who all have their doctorates.

As for Rena, she did not stop educating herself after receiving that master's degree thirty-three years ago. She currently has 197 graduate credits at NIU and continues her education by frequently attending lectures and presiding on the board of directors of ALPHA, Friends of Antiquity at NIU, which has brought in guest lecturers to the campus for more than thirty years.

1. *How did you encourage education in your family?* There's no secret formula. You have to be excited yourself about learning and new things. I have seen people who have no resources whatsoever raise wonderful children. It was from the attitude in the house.

2. *What is your greatest accomplishment?* My children. Who else can stand in front of six children, all with their Ph.D. s, who are all beautiful, handsome, gorgeous and feisty?

3. *You have traveled all over the world. What do you learn from your travels?* I have been in 31 countries in Europe. I don't go to lounge around. I go to see the art. I see everything. The first trip I took to Europe, I saw 60 museums and 55 cathedrals. When my baby was 10 years old, I took my first overseas course for six weeks.

4. *When they were young, did your children understand your desire to continue your education?* They wanted me to go to school. They wanted me to be a teacher. Children want to participate in what you're doing if it's exciting.

5. *What is your parenting advice for those raising kids today?* Be with them. I see kids today. They're not out in the yard. They're not playing. They go to all kinds of classes. My classes were in the backyard.

Source: *The Naperville Sun*, Naperville, IL, http://www.suburbanchicagonews.com/napervillesun/news/1567140,five-questions_na051009.article

---

should also help shape how teachers perceive their children and thereby improve their children's relationships with teachers, teachers' positive bias in evaluating their children's knowledge and abilities, and their children's sense of belonging in school. A strong sense of belonging and positive performance and evaluation in school should in turn reduce delinquency rates among children whose parents are more involved.

Recent studies of large populations and of minority groups call into question the extensiveness of the impact that parent involvement makes in child educational and social outcomes. For example, Domina found in an analysis of the National Longitudinal Survey of Youth that parental involvement had positive consequences on the achievement test scores and lack of problem behaviors of elementary school children, but the effects on achievement test scores were completely explained by the socioeconomic status of the parents.[65] Thus, it was more a matter of family economic capital having an impact than it was a matter of social and cultural capital enhanced through parental involvement levels. In another study of low-income children, parental involvement in schooling positively influenced their children's relationships with teachers, which in turn positively influenced their feelings about school and their perceived competency in reading and math.[66] However, in spite of evidence that perceived academic competence leads to academic achievement,[67] this study was unable to demonstrate significant improvements in grades or standardized test scores for students with high levels of parental involvement. Perhaps more importantly, a number of studies focusing on minority groups suggest that any positive effects of parental involvement may be limited to those who are from majority, high status groups.[68] According to Lareau and her colleagues, what is important is the level of cultural capital that parents can transfer to their children as a result of their involvement, and this depends on the degree to which parental attitudes, values, perceptions, and interactional styles reflect the standards of the school and its teachers and administrators.[69]

Finally, there is some evidence that schools can moderate the negative impacts of high-risk family environments on children. In a recent analysis of data from the National Educational Longitudinal Study and the National Longitudinal Study of Adolescent Health, John Hoffman and Mikaela Dufur found that high-quality school environments (e.g., schools perceived as "fair" and caring and trusting of students, and function well) can compensate for a lack of parental involvement in the school and effectively reduce delinquency rates that would otherwise result from poor academic performance and values.[70] Thus, families do play an important role in students' educational and social outcomes, but their roles are limited and they are not the sole determinants of those outcomes.

Religion and the Family

According to data collected in 2007 by the Pew Forum on Religion and Public Life, over 83 percent of adult Americans report an affiliation with some religious group, with 51 percent reporting that their "present religion" is Protestant (17 percent Baptist), 24 percent reporting Catholic, almost 2 percent Mormon, almost 2 percent Jewish, and the remainder reporting other religions (including eastern religions and

---

[65]Domina, *Leveling the Home Advantage*, 233–249.

[66]Eric Dearing, Holly Kreider, and Heather B. Weiss, "Increasing Family Involvement in School Predicts Improved Child-Teacher Relationships and Feelings About School for Low-Income Children," *Marriage and Family Review* 43 (2008): 226–254.

[67]J.C. Valentine, D.L. DuBois, and H. Cooper, "The Relation between Self-Beliefs and Academic Achievement: A Meta-Analytic Review," *Educational Psychologist* 39 (2004): 111–133.

[68]William H. Jeynes, "The Effects of Parental Involvement on the Academic Achievement of African American Youth," *The Journal of Negro Education* 74 (2005): 260–274; Gabriel P. Kuperminc, Adam J. Darnell, and Anabel Alvarez-Jimenez, "Parent Involvement in the Academic Adjustment of Latino Middle and High School Youth: Teacher Expectations and School Belonging as Mediators," *Journal of Adolescence* 31 (2007–2008): 469–483; and Michele Lamont and Annette Lareau, "Cultural Capital: Allusions, Gaps and Glissandos in Recent Theoretical Developments," *Sociological Theory* 6 (1988): 156.

[69]Lamont et al., *Cultural Capital*, 156.

[70]John P. Hoffman and Mikaela Dufur, "Family and School Capital Effects on Delinquency: Substitutes or Complements?" *Sociological Perspectives* 51 (2008): 29–62.

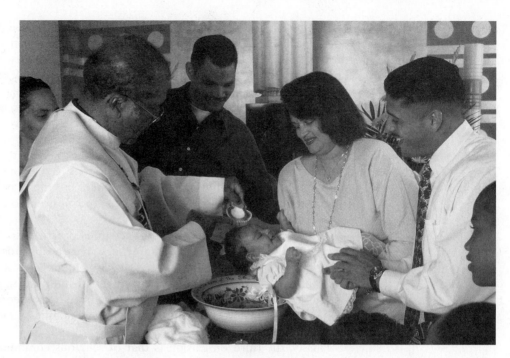

Religious teachings and behaviors, including prayer, play an important part in the lives of most persons around the world. Many family rituals including births, weddings, rites of passage into adulthood, and death are sacred events and are religious in nature.

new age groups).[71] Although these data do not show levels of religious participation, it would be safe to say that the United States is one of the most religious nations in the world, and this high level of religiosity is likely to have profound effects on family life.

Cross-culturally as well as historically, the relationship between the religious system and the family system has been reciprocal. In most societies, many family celebrations are religious in nature. Religious norms also influence speech patterns, nonmarital as well as marital sexuality, male and female roles, husband–wife and parent–child relations, and so forth. Marriage contracts, baptisms, and death rituals frequently involve the clergy and religious organizations. Not only do religions and religious organizations affect the ways people live their lives in families, but family organization and patterns of life affect the integrity and viability of religious organizations. Through family involvement in religious organizations and ceremonies, religious communities are created. Through marriage and subsequent child rearing, new and stable sources of religious group membership are secured. Through parenting practices and socialization of children, the values and beliefs of the religious organization are sustained, strengthened, and protected. Obviously, religious institutions have a substantial stake in the formation and preservation of family systems, but what are the mechanisms through which religion affects families and how strong is this effect?

---

[71]U.S. Bureau of the Census, *The 2009 Statistical Abstract*, "Table 74: Religious Composition of U.S. Population: 2007," http://www.2010census.biz/compendia/statab/cats/population/religion. html.

In a recent review of the literature on families and religion, David Dollahite, Loren Marks, and Michael Goodman argue that religion is a multidimensional construct that needs to be considered in its full complexity.[72] The first dimension consists of beliefs. Different religious groups have different beliefs about the nature of men and women, the proper forms of relationships, the appropriateness and moral correctness of different types of behaviors, and even the nature of the universe and the origin of species. Individuals perceive each other, their relationships and the world around them through the filtered lenses of their religious beliefs and these perceptions are likely to affect the way they form intimate relationships and families and respond to each other in the context of their marriages and families. Although there are differences in these beliefs across religious groups, the differences between religious and nonreligious groups are perhaps most profound.

The second dimension consists of religious practices such as prayer and other outward expressions of faith. Such practices are perhaps most significant insofar as they create ritual practices in families that can function as a source of certainty in uncertain times, group solidarity, regular social interaction, and opportunities for communication. As family systems and family stress theorists and practitioners would argue, such practices may be critical to families making successful adjustments to potentially stress-producing situations.[73]

Finally, the third dimension is that of religious community. Through involvement in religion, individuals and families develop extensive networks outside their family that can serve as important sources of support in times of need. Many of the positive effects of religion, and especially religious involvement, on family outcomes are most likely the result of this third dimension.

Another way of thinking about the second and third dimensions of religious influences is through the concept of *religiosity*. In their review of previous attempts to measure religiosity, Marie Cornwall and her colleagues identified three major components of religiosity: cognitive (strength of belief and orthodoxy), affective (an emotional attachment to one's religious identity), and behavioral (enactment of beliefs, enactment of rituals, and participation in religious institutions).[74] Other social psychologists have focused more exclusively on the cognitive and emotional components.[75]

The consequences of these three dimensions of religiosity for family life are likely to be varied. High levels of orthodoxy, for example, are likely to create a strong sense of coherence in families but may also reduce flexibility in family systems—a condition that may create high functionality under stable environmental conditions but put families at risk in more fluid situations where change might be

---

[72]David C. Dollahite, Loren D. Marks, and Michael A. Goodman, "Families and Religious Beliefs, Practices, and Communities: Linkages in a Diverse and Dynamic Cultural Context," M. Coleman and L. Ganong (Eds.), *Handbook of Contemporary Families: Considering the Past, Contemplating the Future* (Thousand Oaks, CA: Sage Publications).

[73]Pauline Boss, *Family Stress Management: A Contextual Approach* (Thousand Oaks, CA: Sage Publications, Inc., 2nd ed., 2002); and Froma Walsh, *Normal Family Processes* (New York: The Guilford Press, 3rd ed., 2003).

[74]Marie Cornwall et al., "The Dimensions of Religiosity: A Conceptual Model with an Empirical Test," *Review of Religious Research* 27.3 (1986): 226–44.

[75]Stephen Joseph and Deborah Diduca, "The Dimensions of Religiosity Scale: 20-Item Self-Report Measure of Religious Preoccupation, Guidance, Conviction, and Emotional Involvement," *Mental Health, Religion & Culture* 10.6 (2007): 603–8.

beneficial.[76] High levels of emotional involvement and commitment can have positive consequences in terms of sustaining individuals and families under stressful circumstances through a strong *transcendent value system,*[77] but at the same time may result in less of the flexibility required for adapting to those circumstances. Finally, the potential positive aspects of the behavioral component of ritual practice and institutional involvement have already been discussed, but here too there may be negative consequences insofar as religious institutions can place heavy demands on individuals' time, energy, and financial resources that can detract from the needs of the family system.[78]

As religious organizations have become increasingly vocal on family values, it can be asked what impact religious affiliation has on specific behaviors and family outcomes. That religious institutions exercise influence over behaviors such as intercourse risk and contraceptive use is clear from the many studies of adolescent fertility and fertility-related behaviors. Young women with ties to established denominations are less likely than their nonreligious counterparts to become sexually involved during adolescence. Brewster and others[79] pooled data from two national surveys and found that religious affiliation serves as a "gatekeeping" function. That is, its impact is primarily on the timing of *first* intercourse. The risk of later intercourse and decisions to use contraception, however, are unaffected by religious affiliation. In addition to its impact on adolescent sexual behavior, Dollahite and his colleagues site evidence that religion has generally positive effects in a number of areas of marriage and family life. Overall, religion and religiosity have positive impacts on marital and family satisfaction, sexual satisfaction, communication, conflict management, commitment, and stability. Religious parents also tend to demonstrate higher levels of parenting functioning and effectiveness and father involvement, and their children have fewer problem behaviors. On the other hand, more religious persons have less gender equality in their marriages, although religious wives are not dissatisfied with this arrangement. There is also some evidence that religious families are more accepting of spousal abuse but there is no clear evidence that these marriages are more or less susceptible to violence. In terms of parenting, religious parents tend to be more authoritarian, less open-minded, and less flexible. Although these parenting styles may be more functional under stable environmental conditions, research on parenting has shown that authoritarian parenting styles have more negative consequences for children and are less effective in modern societal contexts.[80]

Mass Media and the Family

Today, the mass media can be considered an emerging social system and social institution. The mass media includes newspapers, magazines, television, radio, films, and most recently computers and the Internet.[81] The media presented to a

---

[76]David H. Olsen and Dean M. Gorall, "Circumplex Model of Marital and Family Systems" in Froma Walsh, *Normal Family Processes* (New York: The Guilford Press, 3rd ed., 2003: 459-486).

[77]W. Robert Beavers and Robert B. Hansom, "Measuring Family Competnece: The Beavers Systems Model," in Froma Walsh, *Normal Family Processes* (New York: The Guilford Press, 3rd ed., 2003: 487-514).

[78]Dollahite et al., *Families and Religious Beliefs, Practices, and Communities.*

[79]Karin L. Brewster, Elizabeth C. Cooksey, David K. Guilkey, and Ronald R. Rindfuss, "The Changing Impact of Religion on the Sexual and Contraceptive Behavior of Adolescent Women in the United States," *Journal of Marriage and the Family* 60 (May 1998): 493–504.

[80]Dollahite et al., *Families and Religious Beliefs, Practices, and Communities.*

[81]Robert Hughes, Jr. and Jason D. Hans, "Computers, the Internet, and Families," *Journal of Family Issues* 22 (September 2001): 776–790.

widely dispersed public (the *mass*) is a source of information, but it is far more than "just" information. The media influences our attitudes toward the legitimacy of different marital and family structures, such as single parenthood or same-sex marriages; marital and family behaviors, such as parenting and human sexuality; and even our definitions of self. In a modern society, the media reflects back to us our concerns, anxieties, and continually evolving values with respect to relationships, marriage, and family life. It is a reflection of our social condition and not simply a source of information. But it is not an unfiltered lens. Those in positions of power in society have tremendous influence over what images are presented. In a capitalistic society (one based on the principle of profit maximization in the economic sphere), control over the media is exercised by those who pay for the advertising and fund the arts and sit on boards of directors. Although the images they allow to be presented must ultimately "sell" and, therefore, need to reflect the concerns and realities of the public, there is much room for excluding or altering images that do not serve their self-interests or that present values inconsistent with their own.

Television seems to draw the most attention, since it is found in 98.2 percent of the homes in the United States and is the primary media source immediately accessible to children and adults on a day-to-day basis. Census data show that as of 2007, 94.2 percent of adults watch television, 82.9 percent listen to the radio, 73.9 percent read newspapers, and 67.4 percent access the Internet.[82] These numbers are fairly comparable to levels of media access in the year 2000—with the exception of newspaper reading (down by 6 percent) and access to the Internet, which has increased by 22 percent in just seven years. Perhaps more importantly, television viewing and reading newspapers appear to be developing into activities of the elderly as opposed to young adults; listening to the radio and accessing the Internet are methods of media access most common among young adults versus the elderly. In 2007, 65 percent and 91.3 percent of adults between the ages of 18 and 24 read newspapers and watched television, respectively; the comparable numbers for those 65 and older were 78.8 percent and 97.1 percent. For radio listening and Internet usage, the age trends were in the opposite direction with 88.7 percent and 80.5 percent of young adults using these respective mediums; and 62.2 percent and only 30.2 percent of the elderly using them. These statistics only reflect media usage by adults. It is reasonable to assume that both television watching and, to a lesser extent, Internet usage are activities engaged in by a large majority of children and adolescents. In fact, many families use television as an electronic baby-sitter. Volti says that children in the United States spend more time in front of a television set than they do in school.[83] Since children are exposed to so much television, of particular concern is its impact on them. Looking at something such as violence, Volti indicates that by age 18, the average adolescent has watched about 18,000 people being strangled, smothered, stabbed, shot, poisoned, blown up, drowned, run over, or beaten to death. It is possible that they view ten times as many armed robberies and assaults. Given these numbers, it should not be totally surprising that at the turn of the twenty-first century, several media reports included teenagers shooting their classmates, rapes and

---

[82]U.S. Bureau of the Census, *Statistical Abstract of the United States: 2001*, 121st ed. (Washington, DC: U.S. Government Printing Office, 2001), no. 1127, 705.

[83]Rudi Volti, *Society and Technological Change* (New York: St. Martin's Press, 1995), 196.

beatings on college campuses, and the use of violence as an acceptable solution to personal or social problems in dating, the home, or elsewhere.

Regardless of the medium used, the media is an important source of influence regarding values, norms, and expectations related to family life. Feminist theorists and scholars in particular have expressed concern over how the mass media serves as a powerful force in reinforcing cultural expectations of males and females and of gender stereotyping. **Stereotypes** are widely held beliefs about the character and behavior of all members of a group that seldom correspond to the facts. They usually are oversimplified summary descriptions.

Gender stereotypes are not always consistent but in general let us know that males and females are not only different but also are unequal. Advertising frequently portrays men as dominant figures and women as sex objects. Magazines directed at adolescent girls feature articles and ads focused on being beautiful, thin, and popular, while those directed at males feature being muscular and successful in sports. Music frequently portrays males as aggressive and domineering, females as dependent and nurturing. Some even argue that music not only stereotypes popular gender images but also focuses exclusively on men, with females as irrelevant or as background displays for men. Television, too, features far more males than females and frequently portrays the wife as dependent on and submissive to her authoritative, decision-making husband.

These recurring images make the mass media a powerful force in shaping our ideas of gender and interpersonal relationships. Ideas are conveyed that men are more important than and superior to women; that the elderly who are underrepresented on television and in advertisements are of little consequence and can be ignored; and that women should do the housework, raise the children, and not disturb the husband while he is watching sports events on television. In one study of print media portrayals of women's competing roles at work versus in families, Arielle Kuperberg and Pamela Stone found evidence to suggest the development of a "new feminist mystique" premised on the idea that as "liberated" actors, women can now "choose" to stay home and take care of children (i.e., to "opt out" of career roles), and this choice is both a valued and natural one.[84] These articles contained little mention of the inflexibility of workplaces to accommodate women's dual roles nor of the role and importance of fathers as co-parents with equal levels of involvement. They also are exclusively focused on white, middle- and upper-class women. Given that these images do not reflect the actual choices of most new mothers (including white middle- and upper-class women), it is difficult to argue that they are reflecting lived realities. Instead, they are constructing a new ideology about women and their roles in families (postfeminism). Although women themselves are involved in this ideology building enterprise, they are most likely responding to contingencies in their lives shaped by gender relations and workplace conditions.

These ideology-building processes are not restricted to the print media. In another study of a popular Internet website for women (iVillage.com), a similar process of ideology building around postfeminism was observed.[85] At this site, visited by one in seven women who use the Internet, four recurring themes arise

---

[84]Arielle Kuperberg and Pamela Stone, "The Media Depiction of Women Who Opt Out," *Gender & Society* 22.4 (2008): 497–517.

[85]Worthington, Nancy, "Women's Work on the World Wide Web: How a New Medium Represents an Old Problem," 3.1 (2005): 43–60; and Royal, Cindy, "Framing the Internet: A Comparison of Gendered Spaces," *Social Science Computer Review* 26.2 (2008): 152–69.

from the tips provided to women struggling with the conflicting expectations about the priority of their work and family roles. Women are advised to "accommodate rather than challenge the assumption that housework is primarily their responsibility." They are also exposed to stories of the "exceptional father" who helps out rather than the stay-at-home father who conveys a different norm about home and child care responsibilities; nontraditional wage labor arrangements that make it possible for women to do both rather than renegotiate their marital roles; or exposure to products that women can use to deal with the negative consequences of trying to manage both work and family roles responsibilities ("commodity feminism").

You may argue that these stereotypes are simple media portrayals and in "real life" people don't believe them. But research suggests that recipients of the media are influenced by what is presented. This may be best illustrated by the effects of advertising on sales of products or the influence of spending millions of dollars in campaigns to generate votes. Research on the effects of violence has arrived at similar conclusions. It should be noted that people rarely imitate exactly what they see in films or on television. Yet, what they see does socialize them to become sensitized to violence and makes it more acceptable for husbands to dominate wives and parents to hit their children. In addition to the ideological aspects of media, increased communication technologies have more direct behavioral impacts on families. With respect to marital partners, the increased use of Internet and e-mail and the increased availability of cell phones and pagers increase the potential for work life to spill over into family life and for family life to spill over into work life. Although there is the potential for technology to increase flexibility in work and family roles and thereby positively influence both family and work relationships, research shows the effects are primarily, if not exclusively, negative. Persistent communication use increases negative work-to-family spillover, which in turn increases negative affect and decreases family satisfaction.[86] With respect to parenting, the increased availability of the Internet also poses new problems for parents in supervising and monitoring their children's exposure to inappropriate information and values counter to those of their family system. Monitoring children's Internet use is particularly challenging for parents who lack technical knowledge equivalent to their children.[87]

*I*ssues and Changes in Contemporary U.S. Families

There can be little dispute that the family in U.S. society has changed and will continue to change. This notion is widely acknowledged in the mass media and has been documented by empirical research. The trajectory of this change, however, is not necessarily linear. Social change in attitude and behaviors is a more complex process of action, reaction, and counterreaction. Arland Thornton and his colleagues have documented the more complex nature of changes in attitudes about marriage and family life in two studies: one an examination of three

---

[86]Noelle Chesley, "Blurring Boundaries? Linking Technology Use, Spillover, Individual Distress, and Family Satisfaction," *Journal of Marriage and Family* 67 (2005): 1237–1248.

[87]Rong Wang, Suzanne M. Bianchi, and Sara B. Raley, "Teenagers' Internet Use and Family Rules: A Research Note," *Journal of Marriage and Family* 67 (2005): 1249–1258.

decades of changing norms and values concerning American family life from the late 1950s through the late 1980s,[88] and the other a similar examination focusing on the period from the mid-1970s through the late 1990s. Using a broad range of data sets in both studies, Thornton documented a weakening between the late 1950s and the early 1980s of the imperatives to marry, to remain married, to have children, to restrict intimate relations to marriage, and to maintain separate roles for males and females. However, between the mid-1970s and the late 1990s, he found a strengthening of support for marriage and family life in the form of increased commitments to a good marriage and family life, a greater preference for marriage among young people, an increased expectation among young people that they would get married someday, and stronger belief among both males and females that parenthood (motherhood and fatherhood) is a fulfilling experience. He also found no further reduction in attitudes against extramarital sex.

At the same time as this strengthening of support for marriage and family life was occurring, however, Americans continued their movement toward a view that these relationships are more voluntary than obligatory, should be more equal than hierarchical, and should involve more individual freedoms. As a result, Americans have continued to become more tolerant of alternative marriage and family arrangements such as cohabitation, dual earner families and shared family roles, unmarried childbearing, single parenting, and divorce. At the same time, however, they believe that cohabitations should be undertaken more as a step toward marriage rather than a relationship of convenience, that men have primary responsibility for earning income while women have primary responsibility in the home, that having a child outside of marriage is better than having an abortion or giving up a child for adoption, that having two parents is better than having just one, and that divorce should only be undertaken with good reasons and is harmful to children when it does occur. With respect to the future of marriage and family life, Thornton and Young-DeMarco conclude:

> "…perhaps the biggest question facing Americans in the future—at both the private and public levels—is the integration of the principles of equality, freedom and commitment with family, marriage and children. How do people choose among the principles…when these highly valued goods become mutually exclusive rather than mutually reinforcing options? How do people take advantage of the freedom to pursue their own individual goals and aspirations while at the same time maintaining family commitments and responsibilities?"

In this section, we will examine some of the significant issues debated about marriage and family life in the United States today.

Meaning of Marriage and the Family

The most basic issue in studying the family is the meaning of marriage and the family. This issue involves debates about the fundamental purposes or functions of marriage and families as well as disagreements about the sources of legitimate authority in answering questions of marital and family life. It also questions whether marriage itself is necessary.

---

[88]Arland Thornton, "Changing Attitudes toward Family Issues in the United States," *Journal of Marriage and the Family* 51 (November 1989): 873–893.

Traditional social norms view marriage and family life as either a given truth based on past practices and religious beliefs or as a reality premised on the idea of social obligation. The most traditional social norm, which represents one extreme of the ideal-type construct, views marriage as a *sacred* phenomenon. That is to say, the family and marriage are divine and holy institutions created and maintained by God, Yahweh, or some supreme being greater than men and women. The phrase "Marriages are made in heaven" is, in many ways, consistent with this perspective.

This traditional social norm was most widely prevalent prior to the dawn of modernity in Western societies and still is prevalent in some form in non-Western societies today. It is maintained in today's society through the institution of religious organizations. Non-Western religions have long emphasized and prescribed kinship relations, marriage, and family life. Western religions (especially Catholicism), however, have only more recently come to promote the role of marriage and family life in the hierarchy of behaviors associated with salvation. Although marriage is a sacrament in the Catholic Church today, the importance of marriage as a status in life was long subordinated to the status of singlehood and celibacy. Even the concept of the "holy family" is a relatively recent (fifteenth-century) development in the Catholic Church as communal relationships were emphasized as taking priority over marriage and family ties. Indeed, it may have been the advent of Protestantism and the growth of secular philosophies that led the Catholic Church to adopt a more pro-family position.[89]

Regardless of these historical developments, religious organizations today uphold principles by which many define and live their marital and family lives. Basic to this view is the idea that authority on all family and religious matters stems from God and is administered by religious officials. Guidelines for appropriate marriage and family form, function, and behavior can be found in the teachings of prophets and the written records of God's word. As such, information gained through scientific investigation is irrelevant to determining the appropriate form and functions of marriage and the family. The family functions as an instrument of God's will and a source of socialization and cohesion for the community of believers.

A second traditional norm, one present in the earliest societies but articulated most clearly and widely at the turn of the twentieth century and into the early 1900s, views the meaning of marriage and the family as being rooted in *social* obligations. The social meaning of marriage, like the sacred meaning, represents traditional norms. Instead of God, authority stems from human beings, as represented by the kin group, community, the church as a social institution, and society in general. In this context, primary values of marriage and the family are to maintain social respectability, conform to kin and community wishes, and maintain a proper image within society. Thus, what other people think is very important but only within a specific cultural context. Divorce, nonmarital sex, single parenthood, black/white intermarriage, and so forth are not forbidden or approved per se but may vary from one racial, ethnic, community, or network to another. Conformity to the norms of one's social category or group brings approval and acceptance; nonconformity brings disapproval.

---

[89]O'Day, *The Family and Family Relationships, 1500–1900*; Gillis, *A World of Their Own Making.*

A third meaning of marriage stems from the development of modernity and suggests that families and marriages exist for the *individual*. From the modernity position, the source of authority regarding marriage and family life is the rational (means–end) relationship between marriage and family institutions and the well-being of the individuals in them. Tradition and the sacred are not to be trusted as sources of knowledge and only scientifically accumulated knowledge is acceptable. Social obligation factors into reasoning about marriage and family forms and behaviors but only insofar as those obligations relate to the sustainability of individual well-being. There is an inherent liberalism and pluralism in the modern perspective in that a single model of marriage and family life cannot logically address each individual's unique circumstances. If someone chooses to marry outside his or her race, religion, ethnic group, social class, or educational level, that is his or her business. Similarly, choosing a marriage-like relationship by cohabiting, either heterosexually or homosexually, is also a private, personal decision. According to this view, being happy in a marriage or intimate relationship is what determines success. Marriages and families function for the well-being of their members and when that well-being is threatened, the system becomes dysfunctional. Neither God nor society can dictate personal behavior nor can they force someone to endure an unsuccessful marriage or relationship. Within this meaning, the source of authority is the person alone; each individual is responsible for his or her own success or failure.

Thus, there are at least three basic ideal-type meanings of marriage and the family, all of which exist today. To some persons and groups, marriage is sacred; to others, marriage is a social contract and success is viewed in terms of conformity to societal demands; and to still others, marriage is a highly personal, highly individualistic concern. There seems to be an increasing movement since the 1970s toward this third meaning of individual interests and personal concerns, although American society continues to be a pluralistic one. As a result, debates about marriage and family life will continue to be confounded by the fact that people will be "framing" the debate in different terms, focusing on different sets of outcomes and using different criteria for assessing those outcomes.[90]

Family Functions

Critics of U.S. society who assume the family has broken down base some of their argument for this breakdown on the loss of family functions. Throughout history, the family has been the major social institution, serving functions such as economic production, protection, education, and recreation. Given the loss of functions the family traditionally performed, it is argued that the increasing specialization and complexity of modern society have led to a dehumanizing and fragmentizing process. As a result, much of the economic, legal, and other interdependencies that formed the basis for marriage and family life have been lost, leaving families vulnerable to breakup and leaving children at risk.[91]

Many people in U.S. society today are committed to the idea that traditional functions of the family should be maintained. That is, familism should have priority

---

[90]Vincent Price, Lilach Nir, and Joseph N. Cappell, "Framing Public Discussion of Gay Civil Unions," *Public Opinion Quarterly* 69 (2005): 179–212.

[91]David Popenoe, "Marriage and Family in the Scandinavian Experience," *Society* 43 (2006): 68–72.

over individualism, education should be centered in the home, children should care for their aging parents, prayer and religious rituals should be basic parts of daily family life, recreation should involve the family as a unit, and affection should be shared relatively exclusively among family members.

Emergent patterns of family behavior, however, suggest that many traditional family functions are now performed by other agencies. The economic function has shifted to the factory and office. Prestige and status are associated more with performance or achievements of the individual family member than with the reputation of the family name. Teachers, daycare employees, and even television have become substitute parents and are responsible for educating children of all ages. Police, reform schools, Social Security, Medicare and Medicaid, unemployment compensation, and other types of social programs provided by the state have replaced the traditional protective function. Professional priests, rabbis, and clergy have assumed responsibility for the religious function. Little League baseball, company bowling teams, TV watching, and women's tennis groups, for example, have replaced the family as a source of recreation. One could even argue that the restaurant industry (especially fast-food outlets) has begun to substitute for the family as a source of basic nutrition, a trend that has developed in response to growing pressures on the time of family members and accompanied by a decline in family rituals around dining.[92] Although many would argue that the family is still the basic source of affection among members and the primary setting for producing children, one does not have to look far to discover that both functions are easily served outside its boundaries.

Are these changes bad for society, families, or individuals? Again the answer often lies within a particular source of accepted authority. As we will show throughout this book, many of the measurable outcomes of such changes show that these changes have probably enhanced individual, family, and social life given other changes in material conditions of social life. But are these the outcomes that are important to base our evaluations on and is reliance on the scientific method for determining such value positions even accepted as legitimate? We believe so, but our position as social scientists is clearly in the modernist tradition and may not be accepted by all.

To be sure, not only losses have taken place in family functions; gains have occurred as well. With the breakdown in stable communities over time and place in late modern society, the family and peer groups, for example, have increased in importance as sources of emotional support. Within these primary group boundaries, members may increasingly find a therapeutic milieu for personal and physical health problems. Families increasingly may be responsible for developing members' competence in the use of community and nonfamily resources. Existence in complex, highly specialized societies requires knowledge of the range of options available, an ability to make sound choices, and flexibility toward new technologies and ideologies. Thus, major family functions continue to be the *stabilization of adults* and the *socialization of the members*, but socialization entails teaching members' competence in a changing, complex society and world unlike any that have ever existed.

---

[92]Kerry J. Daly, *Families and Time: Keeping Pace in a Hurried Culture* (Thousand Oaks, CA: Sage Publications, 1996).

Same-Sex Marriage and Parenthood

One of the central debates in political elections over the past decade has been the issue of same-sex marriage. Recent legislation in the United States at the federal level (The Defense of Marriage Act, 1997) has sought to limit marriage to the union of one man and one woman. At the state level, 33 U.S. states have passed constitutional amendments or laws enforcing similar limits on access to marriage, and 28 states either restrict the rights to adopt a child to heterosexual couples (Florida), restrict "second-parent" adoptions (adopting the child of one's unmarried partner), or are judged to be generally hostile toward same-sex parents' appeals to adopt a child.[93] On the other hand, the past decade has seen the legalization of same-sex marriage in several Western and Northern European countries (Belgium, the Netherlands, Spain, Norway, and, most recently, Sweden), Canada, South Africa, and several U.S. States (Massachusetts, Connecticut, Vermont, New Hampshire, Maine, and Iowa). The supreme court of California also struck down restrictions on same-sex marriage in 2008, but those restrictions were reimposed through a voter referendum later that year, which, at the time of this writing, is still under review by the California court as to its constitutionality. New Zealand and the United Kingdom still restrict marriage to heterosexuals, but extend equivalent marriage benefits to gays and lesbians through the legalization of "civil unions."

Public opinion research conducted by numerous polling organizations in the United States has demonstrated a slow, but methodical, transformation of public opinion about same-sex marriage and same-sex adoption. In a review of polls conducted by the Gallup Organization, the Pew Forum, and Angus-Reid, a Canadian public interest group—Ontario Consultants on Religious Tolerance— found that opinions about same-sex marriage have become more favorable in the United States over the past decade. In 1996–1997, only 27 percent of the U.S. population favored same-sex marriage and 65–68 percent opposed it. By the middle of 2008, the number in favor had risen to 38–44 percent and the number opposed had decreased to 49–53 percent. As they note, this change in public opinion (about 1 percent per year) mirrors the change that occurred in attitudes toward interracial marriage between 1948 (when California became the first U.S. state to legalize interracial marriage) and 1991 (when opposition to interracial marriage became a minority opinion for the first time). Attitudes toward same-sex adoption have also shifted over the past decade, from 46 percent in favor and 47 percent opposed in 2000 to 53 percent in favor and 39 percent opposed at the end of 2008.[94]

Opinions about same-sex marriage and changes in these opinions are not uniform across all groups, however. In an in-depth poll of public opinion in 2003 by the Pew Research Center For The People & The Press, opinions in favor of same-sex marriage were found to be stronger among young people 18–30 years old (about a 50/50 split in opinions) versus those 40 and over (over 60 percent opposition); those with college degrees (about a 50/50 split versus a 67–27 opposition);

---

[93]Lambda Legal, "Overview of State Adoption Laws," http://www.lambdalegal.org/our-work/issues/marriage-relationships-family/parenting/overview-of-state-adoption.html.

[94]Ontario Consultants on Religious Tolerance, "Trends in Attitudes Towards Same-Sex Marriage (SSM) and Civil Unions," http://www.religioustolerance.org/hom_poll5.html.

those with low levels of religious commitment (46 percent in favor versus 17 percent among those with high religious commitment); and those who have had personal contacts with gays and lesbians (39 percent in favor versus 21 among those without such contacts). More favorable attitudes were also found among those living in the east versus the south and among whites and Hispanics versus Blacks.[95]

Given differences in attitudes among subgroups, it is not surprising to find that religious and conservative political attitudes underlie much of the opposition to same-sex marriage. In addition to these general effects, however, a perception that heterosexual marriage is under threat by societal changes has an independent effect on opposition to same-sex marriage.[96] The importance of this concern about the viability of heterosexual marriage can also be found in the Canadian debate that led to the legalization of same-sex marriage. As Claire Young and Susan Boyd found in their analysis of the legal debate and proceedings in Canada, a key element to the success of the same-sex marriage proponents was the recognition of the importance of marriage as an institution. It was this recognition of the importance of marriage that highlighted the significance of the rights being denied to same-sex partners. As they note, however, in making this argument, the proponents of same-sex marriage may have set back the movement to redefine marriage in a way that was less patriarchal and restrictive.[97]

The debate over same-sex marriage is likely to continue for a number of years. As same-sex couples gain the right to marry, the issue becomes more salient and polarizing and there is often a public opinion backlash.[98] Given the support found among young people, however, it is likely that same-sex marriage will continue to find increasing support and legal recognition.

Marital- and Gender-Role Differentiation

Whether dealing with same-sex families or heterosexual families, a key component to family life is gender. Since families are where we first develop and play out daily our identities and gender is a key component of all identities, ideas about the appropriateness and "naturalness" of different behaviors based on gender are a constant element in all family relationships. Ideas about what is natural or appropriate for men and women, however, are in a state of flux in modern societies. Modern technologies reduce biological imperatives for men and women to act differently and assume different role responsibilities. In addition, there is a greater concern for individual freedom and maximization of individual development and potential. As a result, there is much ambiguity and confusion about gender and, correspondingly, about marital and parenting roles, goals, and behaviors. There is also more conflict today about marital roles, both within individual families and at the societal level.

[95]The Pew Research Center for the People & The Press, "Religious Beliefs Underpin Opposition to Homosexuality," http://www.pewforum.org/publications/surveys/religion-homosexuality.pdf.

[96]Stacey M. Brumbaugh, Laura A. Sanchez, Steven L. Nock, and James D. Wright, "Attitudes Toward Gay Marriage in States Undergoing Marriage Law Transformation," *Journal of Marriage and Family* 70 (2008): 345–359.

[97]Claire Young and Susan Boyd, "Losing the Feminist Voice? Debates on the Legal Recognition of Same Sex Partnerships in Canada," *Feminist Legal Studies* 14 (2006): 213–240.

[98]Ontario Consultants on Religious Tolerance, Trends in Attitudes Towards Same-Sex Marriage (SSM) and Civil Unions.

Couples in the United States confront many conflicting issues that involve traditional versus emerging norms and behaviors. Issues of love, sexual behavior, intermarriage, living together before (or instead of) marriage, family planning, children, and financial independence are just a few that they face.

This conflict stems from the fact that traditional male and female roles inside and outside the family have been differentially rewarded and convey different amounts of power and privilege. As the traditional basis for power and privilege based on gender has broken down, it has opened up the opportunity for women to contest their subordinate roles and compete for roles that command more resources, power, and privilege. The confusion and uncertainty about role definitions of male and female genders become very evident when students are asked to define and list characteristics of masculinity. It often is difficult, first, to list characteristics and, second, to reach agreement about them. Traditionally, no such difficulty was likely to exist. The male/husband/father was the head of the family, its main economic support, and its representative in the community. The female/wife/mother provided support by caring for the children and maintaining the home, but she remained silent and even passive. In short, the male was the boss, the breadwinner, and the aggressive partner, whereas the female was the subservient helpmate.

These traditional norms, which endorse a patriarchal family, are supported today by religious fundamentalist groups,[99] which interpret literally words such as

[99]Harold G. Grasmick, Linda Patterson Wilcox, and Sharon R. Bird, "The Effects of Religious Fundamentalism and Religiosity on Preference for Traditional Family Norms," *Sociological Inquiry* 60 (November 1990): 352–369.

those of the Apostle Paul in his letters to the Ephesians and the Colossians. To the Ephesians, Paul said:

> Wives submit yourselves unto your husbands for the husband is the head of the wife. Therefore as the church is subject unto Christ so let the wives be to their own husbands in everything.[100]

To the Colossians, Paul was very clear on the proper hierarchy of power and authority within the family. He wrote:

> Wives submit yourselves unto your own husbands, as it is fit in the Lord. Husbands, love your wives and be not bitter against them. Children, obey your parents in all things: for this is well pleasing unto the Lord.[101]

This traditional role pattern is consistent with the sacred meaning of marriage. The source of authority is God, not human beings.

For fundamentalist Christians, the traditional expectations of appropriate marital and gender roles are clear and unmistakable. Women are expected to make marriage, home, and children (the private sphere) their primary concerns. Wives take their husband's name, share his income, and rely on him for status and identity. Women should be sympathetic, caring, loving, compassionate, gentle, and submissive, which in turn makes them excellent wives, mothers, nurses, and teachers of young children.

In contrast, men financially support their wives and children through their participation in the public sphere of life. To be masculine is to be self-reliant, strong, verbally and physically aggressive, dominant, and muscular. Men are risk takers, decision makers, and protectors. The ideal male is hardworking, responsible, achieving, and reliable. In addition, heterosexuality is greatly stressed in interests and activities, and departures from this lifestyle are strongly condemned.

The traditional norm of differentiated male/female roles across public and private spheres of life has come into serious question over the past few decades, both in terms of historical evidence and contemporary practice. The historical evidence is clear that such differentiation was more a product of the Victorian era of the late nineteenth century than it was an accurate representation of how men and women divided tasks in earlier periods of time. Nevertheless, the sacred norm persists in spite of significant changes in contemporary society. Although **androgyny** (a condition of no gender-role differentiation) has not been achieved, pressures exist to move in that direction. Factors such as nonfamilial roles made available to women, an increasingly egalitarian emphasis in intimate family and nonfamily relationships, changing beliefs in both work and play, and changing patterns of socialization and education have led to nontraditional attitudes and behaviors as appropriate for males and females.

Although the labels may vary—*androgyny, unisex, gender justice, sexual equality*—the message is similar: men and women increasingly are pursuing their similarities, experiencing the thrill of escaping from traditional gender-role

---

[100]Ephesians 5:22–24.
[101]Colossians 3:18–20.

stereotypes, and choosing to behave as *equal partners*. Both sexes are behaving in ways that are instrumental as well as expressive, assertive as well as yielding, and masculine as well as feminine.

The transition from gender-role differentiation to androgyny or from complementary to egalitarian-type marriage is far from complete. But as women's participation in the world of paid employment has grown, household and child-rearing responsibilities are shared by husbands and wives, and each sex is thinking and behaving more and more in ways traditionally linked to its opposite.[102] Some of these changes will be described more fully throughout the book, as gender is a component of most chapters.

Other Contemporary Issues

An extensive number of issues not likely to be classified as marriage or family issues per se have a direct bearing on family life. At the most general level, every social policy and social problem is family related: pollution, health care, taxation, immigration, affirmative action, student loans, school prayer, burning the flag, homelessness, crime, terrorism, and so forth. Families are instrumental in the socialization process by which individuals learn what issues are important as well as how to view or approach them. Likewise, social events, social circumstances, and social policies tend to influence people's behaviors and lifestyles. This is especially true in understanding the diverse and unique patterns of family life in different social class, community, race, and ethnic contexts (see Chapters 4 and 5). Before exploring these dynamics, however, we need to consider how social scientists obtain and organize knowledge about marriage and family life. This will be the topic of discussion in Chapter 3.

---

[102]See, for example, Constance L. Shehan and John H. Scanzoni, "Gender Patterns in the United States: Demographic Trends and Policy Prospects," *Family Relations* 37 (October 1988): 441–450.

Summary

1. Historical research on families has shown that our images of the family of the past are largely inaccurate and may be more of a reflection of our own contemporary issues and concerns about the family. Every historical period appears to have socially constructed a prescriptive family image to address dominant individual and cultural concerns about social life. These images provide guidelines for individual behaviors. They are the families we live by rather than more descriptive images of the families we live with.

2. American families share many common characteristics with those found in other Western societies and are to a large degree the product of similar social conditions of late modernity. The historical development of the American family can, therefore, be seen as part of a larger social process linked to three major developments: the change from an agricultural to an industrial mode of production (and corresponding shift from an ascribed to an achieved status system), the change from a feudal economic system to one based on capitalism, and the decline in traditional modes of action and rise in action based on the rational principle of means–end relationships.

3. The emergence of feudalism during the medieval period of Western history was accompanied by a major

shift in family life from large and complex units based on extended kinship relations and communal obligation to large, but simpler, nuclear units. This shift in family structure was facilitated by the emergence of the European marriage pattern of low marriage rates and high ages of first marriage.

4. With the emergence of industrialization, capitalism, and modernity, family life became even more nuclear, private, and isolated from the community. Modernity brought about a shift in emphasis from an instrumental self defined by formal public roles and statuses to an emotional self premised on individuality, emotional and psychological fulfillment, and the maintenance of informal intimate relationships. The family became a haven in a heartless world and a place that individuals needed to fulfill their needs for emotional expression, psychological development, and personal biography.

5. The religious significance of marriage and family life also shifted during these historical periods. Prior to modernity, the church viewed marriage as necessary only in the context of the need for procreation and religious socialization and control. Celibacy was more highly esteemed, and systems of kinship and lineage were more heavily emphasized. The concept of the nuclear "holy family" first came into religious doctrine during the early modern period and was highly consistent with other social developments of that time.

6. Contemporary families in the United States are highly diverse. Census information provides extensive data on this diversity as it relates to the number of families and households, marital status, size of families, family income, and so forth. Major trends in the American population include fewer family households, more subfamilies, fewer married couple households, decreased household and family size (2.56 and 3.13, respectively), and decreased marriage likelihoods (although a leveling off in divorce). In addition, income disparities remain large, with 19 percent earning $100,000 or more and 25 percent earning $25,000 or less. Married couple households had the highest incomes, while single-female-headed households had the lowest.

7. To understand contemporary families, it is important to consider the links between families and other institutions. Cross-culturally as well as historically, major connections have existed at a macro level between basic systems within all societies. Some of the key institutional links include those between the family and the political system, the community, the workplace and economy, the educational system, and religious institutions. It is also important to recognize the role of the media in family life.

8. The more dominant issues confronting the institutional definition of the family in modern American society include debates about what is the appropriate source of authority for defining what constitutes a family (the sacred, the social, or the individual; conflicts over the appropriate functions that families should serve in modern society versus those served by other institutions (e.g., educational systems, daycares, etc.); issues about who is included in families (especially the place of same-sex individuals and their participation in family life through marriage and adoption rights); and ongoing conflicts at both the cultural and individual family level over the appropriate roles of men and women in families.

Having considered the relative nature of family definitions and the diversity of families around the world and within the United States, we will now shift our focus to the discipline of sociology itself. Chapter 3 considers the role of theory and research methodology in our understanding of families and our ability to process the tremendous amount of information that we receive in our daily lives about the state of families today.

Key Terms and Topics

Discussion Questions

1. Historical evidence points to the inaccuracy of our image of the "traditional" family of the past (both recent and distant). What are some of the key components of the contemporary image of the traditional family that we live by, and why do you think we have constructed an image with these elements when they do not reflect the realities of the families that we live with?

2. How did the forces of industrialization, capitalism, and modernity shape the contemporary American family?

3. This chapter included a discussion of many changes that have occurred in American families in recent decades. Select several of the changes given and ask the question, *why*? For example: Why does the United States have some of the highest marriage and divorce rates among the world's industrialized countries? Why has there been an increase in median age at marriage over the last twenty years? Why has there been an increase in persons living alone over the same time period?

4. How are family issues intertwined with political ones? Why do nation states have a profound interest in how the family is defined?

5. How do rural communities differ from urban ones? What are some of the advantages of living one's family life in a rural community? What are the advantages of living family life in an urban center? What about suburban life?

6. What are the various ways economic conditions impact families? How have changes in the composition of the workforce over the past fifty years affected family life? How have family changes over that same period affected economic growth and expansion?

7. What is the concept of "capital" as used by sociologists? How are the different forms of capital important in terms of how education affects family life and in terms of the effectiveness of families in optimizing the outcomes of their children in the educational sphere?

8. How important is religion in family life? What are some of the different ways in which religion and religiosity impact families?

9. How does the media impact families? Does the media shape families or do family preferences and patterns determine what is portrayed in the media? With continued advances in information technologies, what will the future family look like?

10. Consult five married adults and ask about their perceptions of the most important issues in marriage and the family today. Do the same with five single adults. Compare results.

11. Why do marriages exist today? What is their purpose? What or who should be the ultimate authority?

Further Readings

Browning, Don S. and Clairmont, David A., eds. *American Religions and the Family: How Faith Traditions Cope with Modernization and Democracy.* New York: Columbia University Press, 2007.

An examination of how family change has consequences for religious instiutions and belief systems and the strategies used by those with religious faith to counteract those consequences.

Casper, Lynne, and Bianchi, Suzanne M. *Continuity and Change in the American Family.* Thousand Oaks, CA: Sage Publications, Inc., 2001.

Focusing on data since the 1970s, a description is provided of areas of rapid change and of greater continuity.

Coleman, Marilyn, and Ganong, Lawrence H., eds. *Handbook of Contemporary Families: Considering the Past, Contemplating the Future.* Thousand Oaks, CA: Sage Publications, 2004.

A collection of theoretical and empirical literature reviews by leading researchers and theorists in the field of family studies on issues confronting contemporary families.

Comfort, Megan. *Doing Time Together: Love and Family in the Shadow of the Prison.* Chicago, IL: University of Chicago Press, 2008.

Based on interviews with women whose partners were in prison, this study looks at the ways that the criminal justice system intersects with families along gender and racial lines.

Coontz, Stephanie. *Marriage, a History: How Love Conquered Marriage.* London: Penguin Books, 2005.

A historical perspective on marriage from ancient times to today. Coontz again confronts the myths of marriage and family life in the past by documenting how marriage for love is a recent invention of modern societies and how the emotional things we value in a quality marriage today were missing in the past but also make modern marriage more fragile.

Drago, Robert W. *Striking a Balance: Work, Family, Life.* Boston, MA: Dollars & Sense Publishers. 2007.

A look at strategies used by families to avoid work-family spillover.

Ganong, Lawrence H., and Coleman, Marilyn. "Considering the Past, Contemplating the Future: Family Diversity in the New Millennium," *Journal of Family Issues* 22 (September and October 2000): Part I, pp. 683–809 and Part II, pp. 815–939.

Two special issues cover family diversity and nontraditional lifestyles and change.

Gillis, John R. *A World of Their Own Making: Myth, Ritual, and the Quest for Family Values.* New York: Basic Books, 1996.

A reconstruction of the history of the myths, rituals, and other cultural practices of the Western family from the late Middle Ages to the present.

Hareven, Tamara K. *Families, History, and Social Change.* Boulder, CO: Westview Press, 2000.

A historian examines continuity and change in life course and cross-cultural perspectives.

Jagger, Jill, and Wright, Caroline. *Changing Family Values.* New York: Routledge, 1999.

A look at family values and the backlash against single mothers, lesbian and gay families, masculinities, and the changing family.

Rosenfeld, Michael J. *The Age of Independence: Interracial Unions, Same-Sex Unions, and the Changing American Family.* Cambridge, MA: Harvard University Press, 2007.

An examination of census data on changes in the transition period between adolescences and adulthood since 1960 combined with qualitative interviews to show how this extended period of transition has contributed to the emergence of new family forms and how the emergence of less traditional lifestyles has led to increased independence of young people.

Scanzoni, John H. *Designing Families: The Search for Self and Community in the Information Age.* Thousand Oaks, CA: Pine Forge Press, 2000.

A book that sets the issue of change in families in a historical and cross-cultural perspective and places the issue of household diversity in community perspective.

Stone, Pamela. *Opting Out: Why Women Really Quit Careers and Head Home.* Berkeley, CA: University of California Press, 2007.

What leads women in high–paying, successful careers to leave it all behind and decide to spend more time caring for their children and partners' needs? Using interviews with career women who have opted out, Pamela Stone explores their reasoning.

Teachman, Jay D., Tedrow, Lucky M., and Crowder, Kyle. "The Changing Demography of American's Families," *Journal of Marriage and the Family* 62 (November 2000): 1234–1246.

A decade review article that describes recent changes in the composition, economics, stability, and diversity of families in America.

Thornton, Arland, and Young-DeMarco, Linda. "Four Decades of Trends in Attitudes toward Family Issues in the United States: The 1960s through the 1990s," *Journal of Marriage and Family* 63 (November 2001): 1009–1037.

An excellent examination of five national data sets revealing trends in attitudes and values in the United States over four decades.

Watters, Charles. *Refugee Children: Towards the Next Horizon*. New York: Routledge, 2008.

A thorough analysis of existing and original research on the growing refugee population living in Europe today. This book considers the experiences of children as a result of their displacement and the reactions they receive from their new communities.

chapter 3

Marriage and the Family
Disciplinary and Theoretical Approaches

Discovering and Understanding Families:
Methods and Theories

Ross and Richard understood early in their careers the importance of scientific research and theory in understanding social structure and processes in families.

One of the early influences on Ross was his Ph.D. advisor, the late A.R. Mangus, who wrote an article titled, "Role Theory and Marriage Counseling." Ross was impressed with how Mangus applied the symbolic interaction frame of reference (more specifically role theory) to marriage and family counseling. He made it clear how human conduct is organized and goal-directed and how problems between persons (such as in marriage) are a function of role perceptions, role expectations, and role performances. He noted the importance of significant others in the development of our social self and alerted us to be sensitive to interpersonal and social processes rather than simple psychological ones.

As Ross's training continued, he became aware of how different theories at a *macro* level (theories that look at how whole societies function, such as conflict theory and structural-functionalism) direct us toward asking different questions than those raised at a *micro* or interpersonal level (theories that look at how individuals interact in families, such as symbolic interaction and social exchange theory). Later, Ross tuned in to the issues that feminists and sociobiologists were raising and became keenly aware of how what we see (and find) is highly dependent on the theoretical frame of reference we use. In short, he came to believe that nothing is as practical as a good theory, whether it pertains to research, teaching, assisting couples or persons with problems, or aiding us as we live our personal lives.

Initially attracted to the philosophical and theoretical aspects of sociology at the macro level of analysis, Richard discovered the value of research at the micro level of analysis through an undergraduate course on family violence. Under the guidance of his undergraduate advisor, Murray Straus, Richard learned how answers to important questions could be found in the matrices of coefficients obtained from the statistical analysis of carefully and numerically measured traits or characteristics of individuals who participated in research studies. He also learned how those coefficients had little meaning if there was no theoretical context for interpreting them. The variety of family violence theories stimulated the imagination and expanded understandings of this important phenomenon. No single theory alone seemed to explain it all. It took a combination of different macro- and micro-level theories to give a complete picture, and each theory demanded the measurement and analysis of a different set of concepts or variables.

Later as a graduate student, Richard's interest in theory expanded primarily through the tutelage of the late Ruben Hill and his interactions with scholars and fellow graduate students at the Minnesota Family Studies Center. Here he learned the importance of and techniques for formalizing theory. He also gained an appreciation for approaches to studying families that were not "scientific" but were nonetheless valuable for understanding families and avoiding biases introduced in scientific knowledge by his own value system and position in society as a white male. For most of his career, he worked within the scientific paradigm using quantitative methods to answer specific micro-level research problems derived from formal theories. More recently, however, he has become more intrigued by the insights gained from a post-structural or postmodern approach that emphasizes a more interpretative process applied to macro-level cultural data.

This chapter focuses heavily on research methods and theory. Who cares? Of what use are they? What is gained from a knowledge of research methods and statistical analysis techniques? Methods and statistics are the "tools" of the social scientist. They are the basis for gaining and evaluating knowledge. Thus, an understanding of their logic, strengths, weaknesses, and interpretations is essential. What about theory? In the simplest terms, theory is our explanation for whatever takes place. At a personal level, we have theories about why males and females behave differently, how to discipline children, what makes a good marriage, or why some marriages end before death. Unfortunately, these innate theories are limited by our bounded experiences. At an academic level, theory provides logically interrelated propositions that explain some process or outcome, directs us toward establishing hypotheses for testing across a wide variety of contexts and individual experiences, and in general, guides our research questions and methods.

Questions to Consider

What do you think the "scientific method" is? Should we use science as our standard for what constitutes knowledge about families? Are other sources of knowledge valid? What about religion as an alternative source of knowledge about families? What would it mean if we rejected science as the standard for accumulating knowledge about families?

The scientific approach assumes all phenomena can be measured using quantitative methods (by applying numbers to traits). Can you think of any marriage or family phenomena that maybe can't be measured or that would be too difficult to measure?

It was mentioned that nothing is as practical as a good theory. Explain. What would be your theory as to why some sort of marriage/family system exists in every society, the factors people consider important in choosing a partner, or why domestic violence takes place? Does the same theory apply to all three areas?

*A*lthough the authors of this text were both trained as sociologists, the area of marriage and the family reaches far beyond the limited concerns of sociology. Because families have played such a significant role in our personal, social, and cultural lives and because families have provided the context within which biological reproduction has occurred in most human societies, scholars, writers, artists, and practitioners from a wide array of disciplines have been interested in marriage and family life. Table 3.1 illustrates some of the disciplines that are concerned with

Table 3.1

Selected Disciplines Involved in Study of the Family and Family-Related Issues

DISCIPLINE	ILLUSTRATIVE TOPICS
Anthropology	Families in developing societies; cross-cultural studies; evolution; kinship
Biology	Human growth; genetics; conception and reproduction
Child development	Infant growth; learning; personality formation
Counseling	Family therapy; interpersonal relationships; vocational guidance
Demography	Marriage, birth, and divorce rates; mobility patterns
Economics	Family finance; consumer behavior; standards of living
Education	Family life; marriage preparation; child development; sex education
English	Family through literature and mass media
Gerontology	Family life of the elderly; intergenerational links; kin-support systems
History	Family origins, trends, and patterns over time
Home economics	Housing; nutrition; ecology; child development
Law	Marriage; divorce; abuse; adoption; welfare; child custody
Psychology	Interpersonal relationships; learning; human development
Public health	Venereal disease; maternal and infant care; preventive medicine
Religion	Morality; marriage vows; love; sex; religious training
Social work	Family, child, maternal, and aging assistance
Sociology	Family systems; interpersonal relationships; social change

families, family-related issues, and the topics associated with each. Clearly, no single discipline or profession dominates the topic of marriage and the family. In fact, the subject itself is highly interdisciplinary. In recent decades, a separate discipline has emerged—family science—that tries to capture that inderdisciplinarity, at least with respect to the social sciences and applied fields.

The use of new interdisciplinary approaches may lead to closing some of the gaps that separate disciplines and may bring forth new concepts and new meanings; yet, each discipline will continue to focus attention in a specific direction. The anthropologist will focus on family patterns in a cross-cultural and national context. The counselor, usually in an applied context, will attempt to assist individuals, couples, and groups in resolving conflicts and modifying attitude or behavioral problems. The educator will attempt to convey ideas and elicit thoughts on child development, preparation for marriage, sexual concerns, and parental functioning. The historian will examine family patterns, events, and changes over time. The politician will formulate policies and enact laws to deal with child care, marriage, and parenting. The social worker will direct knowledge and skills toward assisting families with problems of income, health, and behavior.

A complete understanding of marriages and families and effective interventions in marriages and families requires knowledge gained from all of these disciplines. For example, scholars from the humanities have long been interested in the family realm. Poets, theologians, philosophers, linguists, artists, musicians, and others have portrayed various aspects of intimate relationships and family life and these portrayals convey collective sentiments about how family life is and should be experienced in different times and places. All cultural expressions of a given time and place contribute to the construction of *cultural narratives* (or stories with moral meaning) through which, or in relation to which, individuals interpret their own lives and experiences in families. These narratives are not simply reflections of peoples lived experiences, however. Rather, they are interpretations of lived experiences shaped by their appeal to collective sentiments and feelings and existing power hierarchies in the societies within which they are produced. Today, all forms of media—from magazines and newspapers to soap operas and situation comedies on television to dramas in movies—similarly convey values about families and family life and have been of significant interest to family sociologists, especially those who come from more critical and feminist perspectives (see discussion later in this chapter).[1]

Even knowledge about biological processes can be critical to a full understanding of marriage and family life. The rapidly developing reproductive technologies such as *in vitro* fertilization, artificial insemination, frozen embryos, sperm banks, genetic engineering, ovum transfer, cloning, and surrogacy have profound implications for the family.[2] Other scientific advances have similar potential to alter

---

[1]See, for example, Su Holmes, "'Riveting and Real—a Family in the Raw': (Re)Visiting the Family (1974) After Reality TV," *International Journal of Cultural Studies* (2008): 193–210; Michelle Janning, "Public Spectacles of Private Spheres," *Journal of Family Issues* 29 (2008): 427–436; and Debra C. Smith, "Critiquing Reality-Based Televisual Black Fatherhood: A Critical Analysis of Run's House and Snoop Dogg's Father Hood," *Critical Studies in Media Communication* 25 (2008).

[2]See Alan Booth, Douglas A. Granger, Allan Mazur, and Katie T. Kivlighan, "Testosterone and Social Behavior," *Social Forces* 85 (2006): 167–191; and Martin Voracek, Stefan G. Dressler, and John T. Manning, "Evidence for Assortative Mating on Digit Ratio (2d:4d), A Biomarker for Prenatal Androgen Exposure," *Journal of Biosocial Science* 39 (2007): 599–612.

personal well-being and interpersonal interactions in dramatic ways, including the ability to select the sex of an offspring or even manipulate the child's appearance and capacities, the donation and transfer of organs from one person to another, and the availability of mind-altering drugs to treat most pains and illnesses.

Sociology of the Family

Sociology per se is devoted to the study of how society is organized, including its social structures and social processes. The primary units of investigation include human groups, social systems, and institutions. A sociology of families seeks to explain the social order and disorder of families by examining their system and group properties. A sociology of families is interested in many related topics: how families are organized, how families as social systems are sustained and modified, how family relationships are formed and changed, how the components within families are interrelated, and how families are interdependent with other groups or systems.

A sociological approach to the family differs from the psychological approach. Whereas the latter is primarily concerned with the behavior of individuals as a product of physiological and mental processes, sociology is interested in the social forms and structures within which individual behavior takes place. The separation of **psychology** and **sociology** is not always clear, however. In fact, both claim a subfield of social psychology that attempts to articulate the interplay between psychological and sociological structures and processes. Each of these three branches of social science, then, has a different emphasis.

For the most part, a sociology of families does not focus on the motivations and perceptions of individuals nor does it emphasize how each individual is unique or has experiences different from those of anyone else. Rather, the sociological focus is on the context in which those individual experiences operate and how individual thinking and behavior are shaped by social and cultural forces. All people, as social beings, exist in a larger structural and organizational network that creates limits or contingencies on their individual choices and behaviors and exerts powerful influences on their lives. The languages people speak, the things that make them feel good or guilty, and the way they respond to the opposite gender are highly patterned. In their efforts to understand social life, sociologists question the obvious, seek patterns and regularities, and look beyond individuals to social interactions and group processes. They do not deny that differences exist between individuals and groups such as families and they do not believe human behavior is strictly "determined" by social context. They do, however, see individual and group behavior as reflective of and reactive to social contexts, making an understanding of these contexts essential to a full understanding of individual and group behaviors.

Uses of Family Sociology

Of what use is a sociological approach to the family, particularly since most people have no intention of becoming either sociologists or family specialists? First of all, family sociology does with families what sociologists do with social life: It questions the obvious, seeks patterns and regularities, and assesses individual behavior in the context of a larger society. Thus, family sociology becomes useful in understanding existing behaviors, in presenting new ways of viewing life, and in acquiring knowledge about relationships and families in the United States and around the world. This has traditionally been used to describe a *basic* or *concrete* approach to family study. The emphasis of this approach is less on applying or using the knowledge and more on obtaining it. From this perspective, persons involved in the acquisition of knowledge do not devote their time and attention to its direct, day-to-day application. Knowledge, from this extreme, is sought for its own sake.

What about the opposite extreme, application or performance—working with couples, solving family problems, and so forth—without the knowledge? Uninformed intervention, no matter how well intended, can be both dangerous and damaging; taking family social science or family sociology courses can help prevent this. Certainly, no one would want to drive a car across a bridge built by someone with no training in the basic principles of physics or be treated by a physician with no training in the biological sciences. So too, "do-gooders" in the family realm, who have no training in the social sciences, should be regarded with skepticism. Thus, a second important use of family sociology is in applying the knowledge gained within a framework of sound theory and research.

The third and perhaps most important use of family sociology is at a personal level. All people are brought up in a social context (for example, poor, only child, single parent, Hispanic American) that plays a major part in who and what they are and will become. In their intimate relationships, many people have specific ideas as to what they want and need from parents, partners, and children. Although sociology cannot provide answers and solutions to all personal problems, it can provide some assistance and direction in dealing with the complex social world in which people live. How can this be done?

A knowledge of family theories and awareness of research findings can add to one's critical-thinking and problem-solving skills by providing the information needed to analyze a situation, make informed decisions and judgments, and resolve conflicts or difficulties. As C. Wright Mills[3] noted in his influential book *The Sociological Imagination*, sociology teaches us to look outside the norm and to question our taken-for-granted world. This process of questioning our assumptions is at the heart of what we value in our modern society and call *critical thinking*. Family sociology can also enhance one's interpersonal skills, which help in managing everyday life and dealing with others. Understanding the values, roles, norms, and behaviors common to people of a particular ethnic group or who practice a nontraditional lifestyle can increase sensitivities and improve one's interaction with them. Finally, family sociology can help people *understand* themselves. People are social animals and can understand themselves only by studying the social context in which they live. It is true that knowledge of the social constraints that hinder people can make them feel trapped, frustrated at their inability to control their lives, and angry at the social injustices and inequalities that surround them. But only through understanding the society and the social context in which they exist can people truly understand themselves.

Thus, family sociology and more specifically sociological research on marriages and families, aims to produce three types of knowledge or knowledge for three distinct purposes:

1. *Descriptive*, presenting information about how frequently some family phenomenon or event occurs in the population or detailing the process by which those phenomena or events come about so that we can gain an understanding of them.

---

[3]C. Wright Mills, *The Sociological Imagination* (New York: Oxford University Press, 1959).

2. *Explanatory*, demonstrating why some family phenomenon or event occurs so we or others can bring about change in those that are negative or stability in those that are desirable.

3. *Evaluative*, recommending what programs or policies are effective once we develop and implement a course of action to address marital and family problems.

Social Science Approach to the Family

Generally, the social sciences include sociology, anthropology, psychology, economics, and political science. Sometimes history, geography, and linguistics are added to this list. Designating these disciplines as "sciences" is more an expression of their dominate paradigm than an expression of how knowledge is obtained by all of those working in each area. For example, most sociologists adopt a scientific approach to studying families, but others (such as phenomenologists, postmodernists, and many feminists) explicitly reject science as biased and subjective and prefer to utilize a more interpretive and qualitative methodology. In the recent *Sourcebook of Family Theory & Research*, the editors distinguish between three types of *epistemologies* (ways of knowing) in family sociology: scientific, interpretive, and critical. Each makes a contribution to our ability to explain and predict, understand, and change social conditions that impact individuals' lives and therefore has value as an approach to "knowing."[4] The dominant epistemology found in sociology is the scientific one and is therefore the one we will focus on here; although, in doing so, we do not wish to imply that the scientific epistemology is more valuable than the other two.

There is a common assumption throughout the work of most of those working in the social sciences that knowledge must be based on a set of principles shared with the natural sciences of biology, chemistry, and physics. The phenomena studied—social systems, psychological processes, economic systems, or political institutions—may be different, but each shares a common challenge of conceptualizing and measuring phenomena without physical form and each adopts a common strategy for the discovery and testing of knowledge. Science is not defined by its subject matter but is determined by its assumptions about and methods for obtaining knowledge.

At the heart of the **scientific approach** is the philosophy of **positivism**, which states that all phenomena, including social phenomena, have certain regularities and uniformities that operate independently of the researcher or observer and that these patterns can be discovered and knowledge tested through objective observation. Science is predicated on the assumption that there is a real world and that things exist and happen naturally and consistently. These things can be demonstrated and verified; thus, they are empirically knowable and testable. The scientific approach also assumes, however, that there are limits to our knowledge. We can never "prove" our theories are right. This is true in both the natural sciences and the social sciences. Any system of knowledge (or theory of reality) is only true to the extent that it has been tested and applied. The possibility always remains that improvements in our ability to observe, changes in the context of our observations

---

[4]Vern L. Bengtson, Alan C. Acock, Katherine R. Allen, Peggye Dilworth-Anderson, and David M. Klein, eds., *Sourcebook of Family Theory & Research* (Thousand Oaks, CA: Sage Publications, 2005).

(in time or space), or the expansion of our applications of existing knowledge could result in *anomalies* (facts that don't fit existing theories) that require the modification or complete reformulation of our theories.

Another source of uncertainty in our knowledge stems from the realization in modern sciences (including modern physics) that causal processes are *probabilistic* rather than *deterministic* in nature. That is, we cannot say with certainty that something exists or that changing the state of some phenomenon will necessarily bring about a change in some outcome. We can only say that there is a *probability* that some phenomenon exists in a specific location or that changing some trait will increase or decrease the *likelihood* that some outcome will result.

Thus, the aims and goals of a social science approach to the family are to establish more or less general and probabilistic relationships. These relationships must be based on empirical observation, and findings must be considered tentative and open to multiple interpretations. In addition, as minority and feminist social scientists caution, we must not assume the knowledge we gain based on a scientific processes is entirely value free. Although we may be more or less certain of the unbiased nature of collecting data and evaluating research hypotheses using scientific methods (see discussion to follow), the nature of the questions we ask, the explanations we propose, and the conclusions we draw based on empirical data are all subject to our own personal and cultural biases.[5] As such, the scientific approach needs to be balanced by knowledge gained through the use of interpretive and critical epistemologies such as those discussed at the end of this chapter.

Relationship between Research and Theory: The Scientific Process

Given the open nature of all scientific knowledge, the relationship between research methods and theoretical knowledge is best conceptualized as a cyclical one (see Figure 3.1). According to this model, social scientists continually are engaged in a process of *discovering new knowledge* (formulating and reformulating theories) based on observed regularities in social life and *testing existing knowledge* through the *a priori* (before observation) derivation of testable *hypotheses* (predictions of reality) from theories, which is followed by making observations according to fixed rules and procedures. The former activity of discovery is called **exploratory research** and involves a logical process known as **induction** (the derivation of general and abstract knowledge from particular and concrete observations). The latter process of testing is called **explanatory research** and involves the logical process known as **deduction** (the derivation of particular and concrete predictions from general and abstract principles or theories of reality).

---

[5]See Ramona Faith Oswald, Libby Balter Blume, and Stephen R. Marks, "Decentering Heteronormativity: A Model for Family Studies," in Vern L. Bengtson, Alan C. Acock, Katherine R. Allen, Peggye Dilworth-Anderson, and David M. Klein, eds., *Sourcebook of Family Theory & Research* (Thousand Oaks, CA: Sage Publications, 2005), Chapter 6, 143–165; and Lee Ann DeReus, April L. Few, and Libby Balter Blume, "Multicultural and Critical Race Feminism: Theorizing Families in the Third Wave," in Vern L. Bengtson, Alan C. Acock, Katherine R. Allen, Peggye Dilworth-Anderson, and David M. Klein, eds., *Sourcebook of Family Theory & Research* (Thousand Oaks, CA: Sage Publications, 2005), Chapter 18, 447–468.

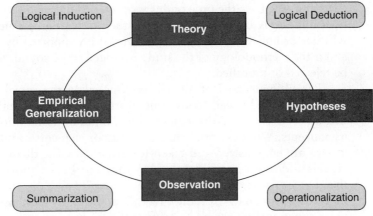

Figure 3.1

The Scientific Process: The Relationship between Theory and Research

Source: Adapted from Wallace, Walter, L. *The Logic of Science in Sociology.* New York: Aldine de Gruyter, 1971.

An example of this process can be found in recent research on the North American honeymoon.[6] Using historical methods to try to understand the elaborateness of and regularities found in contemporary North American honeymoons, the researchers studied popular press articles published over a period of a hundred years. In reading through these articles, they discovered patterns at different historical periods that appeared to coincide with significant changes in the sociocultural environment. Specifically, they detected an increased anxiety about honeymoons at the same time that anxieties about marriage were also increasing. In an apparent response to those anxieties, they also found changes in the normative honeymoon experience, such as an increased elaborateness of the ritual and an increased rationality or planfulness of the experience. Based on these observations, and the application of broader theoretical work on social processes in modern societies,[7] they developed a theory of honeymoons premised on the assumption that relationships in modern society have become more risky and the personal nature of that risk has also increased. As a result, we have become more susceptible to messages of risk reduction through rational planning and more inclined to ritualize the transition to marriage in order to feel more secure.

Now that the theory has been developed, it is being tested by applying it to a study of the content of personals ads in different sociocultural contexts. If it is true that relationships in modern societies are more risky and if we respond to risk with rational planning and ritual, then personals ads in more modern contexts (e.g., states like Connecticut and New Jersey versus states like Arkansas and Mississippi) should more fully articulate desirable characteristics of potential partners and the writer's own personal traits as well as more fully express elements of a ritualized

---

[6]See Kris Bulcroft, Linda Smeins, and Richard Bulcroft, *Romancing the Honeymoon: Consummating Marriage in Modern Society* (Thousand Oaks, CA: Sage Publications, 1999); and Richard Bulcroft, Kris Bulcroft, Karen Bradley, and Carl Simpson, "The Management and Production of Risk in Romantic Relationships: A Postmodern Paradox," *Journal of Family History* 25 (2000): 63–92.

[7]See Ulrich Beck, *Risk Society: Towards a New Modernity* (Beverley Hills, CA: Sage Publications, 1992); and Ulrich Beck and Elisabeth Beck-Gernsheim, *The Normal Chaos of Love* (Cambridge, MA: Blackwell Press, 1995).

romantic script. At the time of this writing, one of the authors of the earlier study of honeymoons is currently examining the content of online personals ads to test whether or not this hypothesis (prediction) is supported by observation. If it is not and if the methodology of the study is judged to be sound, then the theory needs to be rejected or modified.

The ultimate goal of all sciences, including the social sciences, is to develop clear, articulate, logically consistent, abstract, and generalizable **theories**. The *clarity* of a theory is obtained through specification of its assumptions and the definition of its concepts. What essential characteristics or elements of human behavior or social groups are emphasized and taken for granted by the theory? What motivates individuals and/or groups to act the way they do? In the above example, it is assumed that modern societies are inherently "risky" and that individuals will always be motivated to manage or reduce risk. In addition to these assumptions, what do we mean when we use words to label realities? For example, what is the meaning of "risk"? What is meant by the word "ritual"? What are some examples of each? The *articulation and logical consistency* of a theory refers to the extent to which causal processes are specified in the form of propositions and how the different relationships specified in the theory's propositions fit together without contradicting each other. Again, in the foregoing example, does the theory specify how and why increased relationship risk in the society produces or causes the increased elaborateness of honeymoons and does this explanation make logical sense? Finally, the degree of *abstraction and generalizability* of a theory refer to the extent to which a theory's assumptions and concepts are specified in ways that allow them to refer to a wide variety of concrete observable phenomena that share important essential characteristics. For example, can the theory of honeymoons be applied to help understand the emergence of large weddings or more elaborate family rituals such as birthdays and honeymoons in modern societies? Does this theory also relate to explanations of other rituals in nonmodern societies? Does the theory also help explain phenomena in modern societies other than rituals (e.g., the emergence of rational dating and matchmaking services) that might also stem from the assumption of increased risk? If so, then the theory has a high level of generalizability.

The abstractness and the generalizability of a theory go hand-in-hand. A more abstract theory tends to increase its degree of generalizability. For example, a theory of honeymoons that specifies historical time periods as an explanation for the rise of honeymoon resorts is less useful than a theory that sees the rise of honeymoon resorts as just one concrete indicator of a more abstract idea—the elaboration of ritual—and sees this elaboration of ritual as not simply the result of concrete historical time periods but also as the result of a more abstract idea represented by changing historical periods—modernity. As a result, a translation of the theory of honeymoons into one of the effects of modernity on the elaboration of ritual in personal relationships expands the generalizability of the theory. Now the same explanation can be applied to other aspects of the honeymoon (such as the popularity of cruises, the degree of romantic symbolism, the amount of money spent on honeymoons, etc.) as well as to other phenomena (such as the elaboration of weddings, the celebration of birthdays and anniversaries, and the content of personals ads, to name just a few).

It is the abstraction and generalizability of theories that make them so valuable to us. Rather than carry around with us a litany of experiential memories or research findings of how specific situations affect our behaviors so that we can make informed decisions in our lives, it is much more efficient to condense that knowledge in the form of theories and then derive predictions for the results of different alternative actions based on those theories. Given their value, then, it is important to have a fuller understanding of their component parts.

Assumptions

Assumptions are the heart of a theory in that they specify the fundamental truths about the world from which all other aspects of the theory derive their meaning. For example, one of the theories we will discuss later is called *social exchange theory*. The most essential assumption of this theory is that all humans (regardless of race, ethnicity, nationality, religion, or other cultural distinction) are *rational hedonists* and will act accordingly. That is, in making decisions about how to act, all humans rationally calculate how their behaviors will advance their own self-interests, or allow them to maximize rewards and minimize costs. They will then act in ways that give them the greatest benefit. Of course, the theory itself is not this simple as there are many subtleties to the rational calculation of costs and benefits (such as the consideration of long-term versus short-term benefits, the value that humans place on relationships as sources of stabilization in their reward-cost outcomes, the norms that arise as a result of an aggregate of individuals all seeking their own self-interest, etc.). Nevertheless, this fundamental assumption distinguishes social exchange theory from other theories and tells us to focus on certain aspects of situations (the structure of potential rewards and costs) in predicting others' behaviors. Other theories begin from a different set of truths about reality and will tell us to focus on different aspects of the same situation. For example, *symbolic interaction* assumes that individuals act the way they do because they need to maintain a consistent and positive concept of themselves. Thus, it is not the potential rewards and costs of a situation that determine behavior but the perception of the individual about whom he or she is in the situation and how others expect him or her to act.

A good way to think about assumptions (and theory in general) is to use the metaphor of a house or building. The final structure of a house or building (the structure of our theoretical explanation) is determined by how the foundation (set of assumptions) is constructed. The layout of the foundation (square, rectangular, L-shaped, circular, etc.) and the strength and depth of the materials used will determine both the shape and the height possibilities for the final structure. How the foundation is laid will also limit or expand the possibilities for materials used in building the structure (size of brick that can be used, the possibility of masonry stone, the size of lumber that can be used, etc.). In theoretical terms, these building blocks represent the concepts of the theory. Thus, assumptions also play a role in what concepts are used and how they are defined (discussed later).

Concepts and Variables

A **concept** is an abstract symbol, such as a word or phrase, that enables a concrete and observable phenomenon to be perceived in a certain way. Concepts are tools by which one can share meanings and highlight important aspects of reality. As symbols, concepts derive their meaning by way of agreement among a community of interacting individuals who desire to use the concepts to convey their experiences and observations. They are, in a sense, social constructions, and their meanings are specific to the communities that construct and use them. Thus, the same word can convey different meanings for different communities.

One major distinction between communities that use words to convey meanings about marriage and family life is the distinction between the scientific and nonscientific communities. Many of the terms we will use in this text and that are used in the social sciences to refer to marriage and family phenomena are also part of our everyday language (e.g., love, power, commitment, etc.). Within the social science community, however, the meanings of these words may be different or, at least, more specific. Therefore, it is important to pay close attention to how social scientists define and use these terms so that you have a clearer understanding of the meaning of their findings and theories. A second distinction of communities that is important to keep in mind is between disciplines and between theoretical perspectives within the social sciences. For example, even though both psychologists and sociologists use the concept of identity, they often do so in very different ways. For the psychologist, identity is a more central and fixed characteristic of the mind; for the sociologist, identity often is viewed as more transitory, situated (specific to various role relationships), and emergent in the interactions between individuals. Even within sociology, the same term can be used to refer to different phenomena. (See the sections on structure-functionalism and symbolic interactionism for a discussion of how the term role is used differently in these two perspectives.)

Although there are many concepts that transcend theoretical perspectives (e.g., family of orientation, social differentiation, group cohesion, etc.), there are also many concepts unique to particular theoretical perspectives or that have unique meanings in different theoretical contexts. For example, within the social exchange perspective, the concepts of reward and cost are essential given the assumption that humans are motivated to maximize the former and minimize the latter. These concepts are less applicable within the symbolic interactionist perspective, however, as concepts highlighting dimensions of the self become more critical given the assumption that humans are motivated to maintain a consistent and positive self-concept. Without specifically stated conceptual definitions and explicit instructions for **operationalization** (translating abstract meanings of concepts into procedures for measurement), the applicability of the theory to our lives as we live them and the testability of the theory will be lost.

Concepts are also unitary (parts of a whole) and, thus, do not explain, predict, or state relationships. Often, they are grouped together in what have been called **conceptual frameworks** (groupings of concepts that reflect similar assumptions about reality and highlight different aspects of reality relative to those assumptions), but the groupings only suggest the potential for causal relationships rather than any specification of such causality. Concepts can also be linked together in **typologies** to convey a more complex aspect of reality—social process—but these clusters do not specify any causal linkages. Typologies are used heavily by *family system theorists* to denote regularities in family systems across a variety of different conceptual dimensions simultaneously. For example, we might talk about competent families versus borderline families based on how family members relate to each other in terms of power, role expectations, control, boundaries, communication patterns, and so on. Certain combinations of these traits can result in a holistic family unit that adapts well versus poorly, that achieves or fails to achieve its goals, that produces normal versus deviant behaviors, and so on. Each dimension might make a separate contribution to specific outcomes, but the mix of traits along all dimensions taken together might be what is more important.

Concepts that represent degrees or values are referred to as **variables**. *Husband* is a concept; *years married* is a variable. A variable may be classified as independent (the presumed cause) or dependent (the presumed effect). The independent variable is antecedent to or simultaneous with the dependent variable. For instance, *family income* (a variable) may be dependent on (the presumed effect of) the *number of years of education* (the presumed cause).

Because use of a particular concept affects what is seen, concepts must be constructed in ways that do not distort reality. An extremely difficult task for the family scholar is to label phenomena in ways that avoid undesired connotations. Consider the implications made in a book about the family that uses terms such as *honky*, *WASP*, and *paleface*. Also, notice the obviously different connotations of labels or concepts such as *nigger*, *colored*, *Negro*, *black*, and *African American*.

Propositions and Hypotheses

A **proposition** is a statement about the nature of the relationship between two or more abstract concepts representing some aspect of reality. If assumptions are the foundations of theories and concepts the basic building blocks, propositions specify how those blocks should be connected. For example, in social exchange theory a well-established proposition might be: "The greater the resources, the greater the power." This is a proposition in that it specifies a relationship between two phenomena in abstract terms. Neither resources nor power can be directly measured—both are abstractions from more concrete realities. *Resources* might be defined as anything that can increase the rewards and minimize the costs of the other. This could include such measurable phenomena as income, wealth, occupational prestige, and education. *Power* can be defined as any outcome of interaction that reflects the ability of one person to fulfill his or her desires despite the other's resistance. Measurable phenomena that reflect power might be the observation of how much one person talks in a conversation versus the other, how often one person interrupts the other during a conversation, how decisions ultimately get made in the relationship relative to initial value positions, or how much housework each partner in the relationship does on a regular basis. This proposition is logically derived from the assumption that individuals are rational hedonists and are motivated to maximize rewards and minimize costs. Power comes about because the other person in the relationship gives his or her compliance in exchange for the desired rewards that the other's resources can provide (thus maximizing profits) and the other only expends his or her resources if he or she receives something of value (realization of desired outcomes) in return.

Ultimately, in order for a theory to be tested its propositions must be translated into a form that allows for empirical observation. A proposition that has been so translated is called a **hypothesis**. Thus, a testable hypothesis would be "The greater the *relative income* of one spouse versus the other, the greater the *amount of times the spouse with more resources will interrupt* the other in a problem-solving interaction."

Hypotheses and propositions are identical, with the exception that hypotheses carry clear implications for testing or measuring the stated relations. Hypotheses serve as an important branch between theory and empirical inquiry. One of the ways we judge the merits of a proposition (and by implication the theoretical assumptions from which it was derived) is whether or not the hypothesized empirical relationships derived from its assumptions are observed. Therefore, it is essential that the logic we use to justify our propositions is valid and that the phenomena that we measure (as specified in the hypothesis) are valid representations of the abstract concepts found in the proposition. If either has questionable validity, then we cannot draw any firm conclusions from our research results (see the discussion of measurement validity and reliability in the section that follows).

Research Methods and Statistical Concepts

Where one begins in the scientific process—with observation or with theory—depends on what is already known about the phenomenon studied and the purpose of the research. When little is already known, the social scientist is likely to start with *qualitative* observations to describe and explore reality and generate theories or explanations for the phenomenon of interest. When more is known about or when theories are used to try to explain some phenomenon, the social scientist relies on *quantitative* observations.

Qualitative observation is a process in which the researchers don't know ahead of time (a priori) what factors will be important to observe and cannot, therefore, use any specific measures to quantify (put into numbers) those factors. In fact, the factors that might be important to quantify might not have any measures yet developed. For example, in the honeymoon research cited earlier, the researchers didn't even have a concept of elaborateness of ritual in their mindset and no such concept previously existed in the social sciences. As they conducted their observations, they needed to develop this concept to capture several distinct and concrete phenomena they were observing (symbols of romance, exotic locations, constructed fantasies, high levels of monetary expenditures, architectural development of sites, etc.) that seemed to occur together and in response to a common stimulus. Of course, this interpretive process is subject to the researchers' own biases and preconceptions. They could see commonalities in objects and events that are marginal at best—and doing so in a conscious or unconscious attempt to prove their own theory or to confirm their own values or beliefs.

In **quantitative** research, the approach is quite different. Here, the researchers already know what they want or need to observe. As a result, specific measures can be used or developed for use in doing these observations in an unbiased way. The researchers must first specify what observable phenomena measure concepts of interest beforehand in order to assign numerical values. They cannot change the measure afterward if their observations do not support their hypothesis. In addition, since the measures have numerical value, statistical procedures can be used to assess the quality and consistency of their observations.

Although qualitative studies are very important in the social sciences because they generate new knowledge and ways of constructing reality, the definitive answers about the validity of theories lie in the application of quantitative methods to test hypotheses derived from theories once they are formulated. Quantitative research is also important in that it can provide information about the larger population of individuals and families outside the immediate observational field of the researcher. As a result, those interested in describing the degree of occurrence of different marriage and family phenomena in the larger population must also rely on quantitative methods. Therefore, we present next a brief description of the two major quantitative research designs used in the social sciences and then discuss four major methodological concerns about the application of quantitative methods. Finally, we will briefly explain some of the statistical concepts used by quantitative researchers to summarize their findings. It is essential to the critical evaluation of

news item

Girl Driven Research Project Is a Mosaic of Learning and Growth

A large mosaic of tile and glass dominates the facade of the North Sheridan Road building that's home to the Girl Driven Research Project. Inside, the youths who come here on weekends, after school and during the summer also have created mosaics that line the halls. It's a fitting adornment in a place where young women take ideas that may be rough around the edges and figure out if they can be pieced together to form something more substantial and cohesive.

The Girl Driven Research Project is based out of Alternatives, a 38-year-old youth and family-oriented agency on the city's North Side. The project, part of the agency's Girl World programming, helps girls build self-esteem in part by teaching them to think critically about the issues affecting their neighborhoods. The goal is for them to plan a community research project, centered on social justice, so they can study it thoroughly and recommend solutions to problems. Over the last several years, the girls' projects have examined beauty and body image; the epidemic of girls fighting; and, among other projects, the social, religious and peer pressures that lead to conformity.

This year, the project's 10 teens—who are 13 to 18 years old and come from neighborhoods around the city— researched racial profiling. They looked at the ways it plays out in student-teacher interactions as well as interactions among their peers. As part of their research, the girls created one survey for students and another for adults. Both were checked thoroughly for sound research methodology by expert researchers. The girls collected data from about 300 respondents. The students then pored over the data....The students will present their findings on racial profiling later this month at a social justice expo sponsored by the organization Chicago Youth Initiating Change. The young women also will make a presentation during a career conference that Girl World is hosting May 30....

After last year's girls completed their project on conformity, they spent the summer putting together recommendations. They then used part of their funding to offer a grant to another organization that implemented the recommendations.

This summer, the project's girls hope to do the same, as well as assemble a team to come up with an action plan.

Visit "Exploring Race," at chicagotribune.com/race, to learn more about the survey and Alternatives.

Source: The Chicago Tribune, http://www.chicagotribune.com/news/columnists/chi-trice-11-may11,0,7836843.column Reprinted with permission of the Chicago Tribune; copyright the Chicago Tribune, all rights reserved.

knowledge gained from the social sciences about family life that one has an understanding of these methodological designs, concerns, and statistical concepts. Not all social science research is good research and much of the information about families that we are exposed to in the popular press is particularly susceptible to flaws in methodological design or in the interpretation of statistical results.

Quantitative Research Designs

The two major research designs used to test theoretically derived hypotheses are *experiments* and *surveys*. In **experiments**, units of study (for example, individuals) are brought into a standardized and highly controlled setting where they usually are randomly assigned to two or more groups (a process called **randomization**). One group (the experimental or treatment group) receives a treatment or stimulus designed to bring about some predicted outcome. The other group (the control group) does not receive the stimulus (or receives some other stimulus not expected to bring about the same outcome). After the stimulus (or stimuli) are given, the two groups are observed on the outcome measure to see if any differences exist. If they do, then it can be assumed that the reason for the difference is that one group received the stimulus and the other didn't. This assumption can be made because the random assignment of units to groups means that any preexisting differences between units should be equally distributed across the groups (the groups are very likely to be the same before the stimulus is applied) and the standardization of the settings assures the experiences of both groups are the same in all other respects other than the stimulus received.

Experiments are not used much in family sociology because many of the phenomena of interest cannot be easily or ethically manipulated. For example, if you are interested in studying the effects of cohabitation on later marital success, you couldn't very well randomly assign couples to groups and demand that one group live together before marriage and the other not. Even if you could, it would not be possible to control all the conditions of their lives by making them live their marriages in the same setting (as was done in the Jim Carrey movie *The Truman Show*). In addition, sometimes we are interested in just describing the entire population on some family characteristic rather than testing some causal process. Therefore, family sociologists rely mostly on survey research designs.

In **surveys**, the researcher selects an entire population or a subset of the population to study and then has participants answer questions on a survey either by selecting answers on a questionnaire (on paper or online) or by verbally responding to an interviewer on the telephone or face-to-face. The questions used are designed to measure the experiences the respondents have had and their background characteristics and social conditions. The researcher then looks for patterns in the responses to assess whether or not having had certain experiences corresponds with having had other experiences. For example, do those who experienced cohabitation before marriage also have a greater likelihood of experiencing low levels of marital quality and higher levels of divorce? If so, then, assuming other conditions are met (see section on *causal validity* later), it is assumed that the one experience (cohabitation) caused the other (poor quality and high divorce) to occur. This method of analyzing the results of survey research is called *correlation* and is described more in the section on statistical concepts that follows.

Sample Selection

Sampling is the process by which we select our units of observation—things, people, relationships, groups, or whole societies. Because it would be impossible to study everyone in a population (unless we were only interested in a very limited group such as college students at a single institution), researchers rely on the observation of a subset of units in their studies. This subset is called the *sample*. The major concern in this process is that we do not allow ourselves as researchers to make the decision of whom or what is to be observed. The reason for this is that we may choose to include or exclude individual units because we consciously or unconsciously think they are more likely to confirm or reject our preconceived ideas about reality.

There are two related criteria for judging the adequacy of sampling—representativeness and generalizability. **Sample representativeness** refers to whether or not the researcher has included a true cross-section of the larger population he or she is trying to describe. For example, did the researcher include the same number of African Americans and Hispanics in his or her sample as exist in the larger population? If 13 percent of the population is Hispanic, is the sample also 13 percent Hispanic? If not, then the sample is not representative. **Sample generalizability** refers to the extent to which the sample was selected in a way that allows the researcher to say that the results found for the sample would have a high likelihood of also being found if he or she studied the whole population. It is impossible to have a generalizable sample if you cannot establish that the sample is also representative, but more is needed. Even if it is representative, were the units selected in an unbiased manner? If the researcher selected units based on his or her own assessment of appropriateness, then the results may not be generalizable even if all relevant groups in the population are proportionally represented. In addition, were there enough units selected to avoid the problem of selecting only those that lie at one or the other extreme of reality? Samples must be large enough to avoid this problem. With increased sample size, the likelihood of getting only one extreme or the other decreases and the likelihood of getting "typical" units in the sample increases.

To assure that a sample is representative and generalizable, researchers select a large enough set of units for their samples and do so using **random selection** procedures. Basically, a random selection procedure is like flipping a coin or throwing dice to decide who is in the sample and who is not. Thus, the researcher can't choose to study only people who might confirm his or her hypothesis or otherwise bias the results because they share a common trait (they were friendly looking) that led the researcher to choose them instead of others. Units are selected independently in a way that gives every unit in the population an equal likelihood of being included in the sample.

Thus, in assessing the results of any research study of the family, you need to be aware of how large the sample was and how it was selected. The larger the study and the more truly random the selection process, the greater the faith you can have that the results are representative of and generalizable to the larger population and not just specific to the units that were studied.

Measurement Concerns

Measurement is the process by which we assign numbers to characteristics or traits of the units studied in order to classify them and detect relationships between their traits using statistical techniques. As was the case in selecting a sample, the scientific method requires that the researcher not be allowed to make personal judgments when classifying the units studied because he or she may attach meanings to observations biased in favor of his or her own preconceptions or values. There are two related concerns when assessing the adequacy of measurement in a study—*measurement reliability* and *measurement validity*.

Measurement reliability refers to whether or not the results obtained from one observer or at one point in time can be replicated by a second observer or second observation at a later point in time (assuming that no change has occurred between measurement time points). If they can be replicated, then we say that the measure is reliable and can be trusted. If not, then we cannot trust our results because they could vary from one observer or observation to the next even though the phenomenon observed has remained the same. This criterion for measurement is one we use in our everyday life. For example, if you were in a car accident, you would want to get as many witnesses as possible to testify to having seen the same unfolding of events leading to the accident. The more people corroborate your story of what happened, the more believable your story is to others. This is true for observations made by quantitative measures as well. As a result, social scientists have methods for assessing the reliability of their measure based on the idea of repeated observations at the same time or over short intervals of time.

Measurement validity refers to whether or not what you measured is indeed what you intended to measure. This is a more difficult idea to grasp because most social science concepts are not physical in nature. How does one measure what a person is thinking or a pattern of behaviors that reoccurs over time between individuals? The problem of measurement in the social sciences is more serious than in the natural sciences because the phenomena studied are so abstract and must be translated into something concrete that can be observed. A person's values, attitudes, or state of mind can only be assessed by getting him or her to react to a question or set of questions on a questionnaire. The answer (what participants say to an interviewer or what they circle on a questionnaire) is a behavior that can be observed and recorded, but we must then make a leap of faith that what they said or circled reflects some value, attitude, or mental state that they hold in their mind. For example, I might measure your level of depression by asking you whether or not you have trouble sleeping at night. If you say "yes," does this mean that you are more depressed, or could you have responded this way because you have been having back problems recently that make sleeping more difficult, or could it mean both things?

This is the problem of validity and it applies to the measurement of social phenomena as well as individual mental ones. In a famous study of suicide by the nineteenth-century French sociologist Emile Durkheim,[8] the rate of suicide found in a community was used to measure the degree of social solidarity and cohesion present. Was this a valid measure? The validity of a measure can be assessed by looking for the consistency between the measurement procedure and how the concept is defined and by comparing how it classifies units relative to already established facts about reality. Thus, in both cases, the trust that we can put in the results of research studies is enhanced by the use of multiple indicators of the concepts we are attempting to measure and the explicit testing for consistency in measurement and predictability of measurement outcomes with already established facts.

Causal Validity

An often overlooked issue in social research (especially sociological surveys) is that of *causal validity*. **Causal validity** refers to the trust one has that an observed relationship between two variables occurs because one is causal to the other. What does it mean to say that something is causal? The best way to think of the idea of causality is to think of a force. When one thing causes another, it means that it exerts a force on it that brings about a certain systematic and predictable change. If, therefore, a variable X *exerts a force on* another variable Y, then we should see some systematic change occurring in Y whenever X changes in a particular direction and by a certain amount.

Unfortunately, X and Y can change systematically and predictably together for other reasons. One is that instead of X exerting a force on Y, Y could be exerting a force on X. For example, if a researcher finds that children of divorced parents have higher levels of problem behavior, does this mean that divorce *causes* problem behavior in children, or could the child's problem behavior have somehow contributed to the parents getting a divorce? This problem can be referred to as a problem of **causal ordering**. The question is not easily answered. Not only do you

---

[8]Emile Durkheim, *Suicide: A Study in Sociology*, translated by George Simpson and John A. Spaulding (New York: Free Press, 1951)

need to show a systematic pattern of *covariation* between these two variables, but you must also be able to demonstrate that change in one preceded change in the other.

Experimental designs establish causal order very efficiently because the researcher can set up the circumstances such that no difference in the outcome exists prior to introducing some stimulus and then can observe whether or not some change occurs afterward as a result. Experimental studies of the effects of viewing television violence on children's violence toward a punching bag can clearly establish that the viewing of the violence preceded the violent behavior and that it wasn't the child's previous violent tendencies that produced the likelihood of viewing the violent television program. This is because the researcher can control who watches the violent programs. As noted earlier, this is not so possible for most sociological research problems looking at marriage and family phenomena. Instead, sociological researchers more often rely on survey methods in which they ask people about their marital experiences and their child's problem behaviors after they have already occurred. These kinds of **cross-sectional designs** often have questionable causal validity because they can't easily and clearly establish which changed first. One way to overcome this problem is to study the same units multiple times so that the timing of changes in marital status and child problem behavior can also be observed. This type of research design is called a **longitudinal design**.

Even if you could establish the causal ordering of these two phenomena (divorce and child behavior problems), there is another threat to the causal validity of this finding. It could be that both are the outcome of the same underlying cause. It could be, for example, that poverty puts pressure on marriages and this pressure causes divorce. It could also be that poverty puts pressure on children and exposes them to more examples of deviance and as a result causes higher levels of problem behavior regardless of whether or not the child's parents get divorced. Thus, a researcher is likely to find that when divorce occurs, the levels of child problem behavior go up, but this could simply be because both divorce and problem behavior are responding to change in the third variable—poverty. If this is the case, then we would say the relationship between divorce and problem behavior is **spurious** (noncausal).

Again, experimental designs are capable of avoiding this problem of spuriousness or causal validity. In an experiment, the researcher can randomly assign individuals to groups and thereby ensure the same proportion of poor people in each group—the one that will be forced to get a divorce and the one forced to stay together. As a result, if the divorced group shows higher levels of problem behavior afterward, it cannot be due to preexisting differences in their poverty levels.

In surveys, it is only possible to test for possible sources of spuriousness rather than rule them out completely. This is done by introducing **control variables** and then holding those variables *constant* (nonchanging) when looking for causal relationships between other variables. For example, if we measured poverty in our survey, we could later separate our sample into two groups, those who are poor and those who are not. If we were to find that children from divorced homes had higher problem behavior scores within each group, then we would know the effect was not spurious due to the effects of poverty. Unfortunately, an unknown number of other variables could have a similar effect on the results (race, ethnicity, geographical location, religiosity, education of parents, neighborhood conditions, etc.) and may not have been controlled for or even measured in the survey. Therefore, you can never be certain about the causal validity of results obtained from surveys, whether cross-sectional or longitudinal, and you always need to assess survey research find-ings by asking what variables were controlled for and considering whether or not any important sources of spuriousness were omitted from the study. We will return to this issue later in greater detail when we discuss the research findings on the effects of cohabitation on later marital quality and success (Chapter 7).

Ecological Validity

The final methodological issue to be sensitive to when assessing the results of social research on families is **ecological validity**. The term is used to refer to the generaliz-ability of research results to the natural setting of human behavior. This is different than sampling generalizability. In this case, the reference is not to the sampling of units but to the real nature versus artificiality of the setting where the study was conducted. For example, experiments usually are low in ecological validity because they create an artificial setting, such as when they study violent behavior by seeing if a child will hit a punching bag after watching a violent film. The question arises in these situations whether or not the same outcome would have been observed in the natural setting. In this example, the children who viewed the violent film may have hit the punching bag more, but did the film-watching experience truly resemble the everyday experience of watching violence in television programs, and is hitting a punching bag the same thing as hitting the child next door or in school? These are questions of ecological validity. This is one area where surveys tend to be better than experiments because they attempt to capture natural behaviors occurring in natural situations.

Statistical Concepts

Increasingly, sociology and the social sciences in general have become much more reliant on the application of statistical procedures for summarizing their research observations and testing their theories. The sophistication of these statistical proce-dures, however, goes well beyond the previous training of most of you who are tak-ing this course. Nevertheless, it is useful to know some basics about statistical analyses so that you can better interpret the results of research you may read later on or may encounter summaries of in the popular press. We will cover next five key statistical analysis ideas or principles.

First, it is important to understand the difference between frequencies and percentages. A **frequency** is simply a count of something based on a researcher's ob-servations. As such, it has little meaning because it doesn't take into consideration the possibility that something could have been observed. For example, if we were to say that there were 4.7 million unmarried couple households (cohabitating couples) in the United States in the year 2000, you might say "Wow! That's a lot!" But if you consider there were over 47 million couple households of both the unmarried and married type in the population during the same time period, you might conclude that it is a problem but not one that indicates any major breakdown in marriage as an institution. After all, the vast majority of couple households (over 90 percent) are marital couple households. This is why we calculate and use **percentages** (the number of occurrences divided by the number of units in the population) when reporting on the occurrence of some family phenomenon or when looking for dif-ferences in the occurrence of some phenomenon across different groups.

Second, we often want to compare distinct groups in society on some outcome. One of the most frequent comparisons we make is between men and women. We

TRANSNATIONAL FAMILIES

Research on Transnational Families

The study of transnational families is complicated by the fact that family members are spread across national boundaries, may not have fluency in the researcher's language, often are highly mobile, and live in a culture that often is hostile to their presence. Not only do these conditions present access problems for researchers, but they also bring into focus the validity of measures based on previous studies of Western populations. Therefore, research on transnationals often involves a mix of both qualitative and quantitative methods and the employment of special procedures for accessing and measuring families. Yan Ruth Xia, Zhi George Zhou, and Ziolin Xie describe some of these challenges and the strategies they used to overcome them in their study of Chinese immigrant families.

The first challenge they note is accessing subjects. Chinese immigrants, like other immigrants, often are living in vulnerable socioeconomic conditions requiring a high level of attention to necessities for survival that do not include responding to research study requests. They also are not accustomed to revealing personal or family related information to outsiders. To overcome these problems, the researchers took a gradual approach in their study. First, they worked on building relationships in the immigrant community by becoming involved in church, school, and community events. They also attempted to increase levels of trust and reciprocity obligations by offering workshops on marital relations and parenting. After a period of involvement in the community, they then used "snowball sampling" techniques to gather a sample large enough for their study. This technique involved asking a small number of families to participate first and then asking those families to recommend others who might be willing to participate. Although this approach is less than ideal, since the results are likely to lack ideal levels of representativeness and generalizability, the researchers note that this is a limitation that most studies of these communities will have to deal with given the challenges of access. They also attempted to overcome the problems of measurement equivalence by first conducting semi-structured interviews that gave respondents an opportunity to express their own perceptions of family life without having to fit themselves into categories that may only apply to Westerners.

Source: Yan Ruth Xia, Zhi George Zhou, and Ziolin Xie. "Strengths and Resilience in Chinese Immigrant Families: An Initial Effort of Inquiry," in Vern L. Bengtson, Alan C. Acock, Katherine R. Allen, Peggye Dilworth-Anderson, and David M. Klein, eds., *Sourcebook of Family Theory & Research* (Thousand Oaks, CA: Sage Publications, 2005), 108–111.

make these comparisons because we attach some causal significance to the group to which one belongs. For example, being a woman means you are exposed to a different set of socialization experiences and current opportunities than you would be exposed to as a man. We make these comparisons by calculating means (averages) or percentages for some measured outcome variable in each group separately. For example, we might find that the average time women spend doing housework is 17.5 hours per week, whereas men spend on average only 10 hours doing the same type of work. Alternatively, we might summarize our observations differently by noting that women do 75 percent of all the housework, whereas men only do 25 percent. In either case, if we find a difference, we will conclude that there is something about a person's gender that causes this difference to occur.

Many differences have been found between men and women in both psychological and sociological studies. It is important to note, however, that the size of the difference usually is very small, and frequently the comparison of a particular woman with a particular man will show the opposite of what the comparison of averages or percentages will show. This is because not all women are the same and not all men are the same. Thus, finding a group difference only suggests a tendency or a probability for a particular man to be different from a particular woman. There will be many exceptions to the rule, however.

Third, sometimes the things we measure involve more than just a few groups. For example, if we are interested in the effects of education on the level of decision making a wife has in her marriage, we have a wide range of education and decision-making patterns to consider. In this situation, researchers use **correlational techniques**. These techniques are premised on the idea that if education causes an increase in decision-making power, then when you compare one woman to another, if you find a difference in their educations, then you will also find a systematic or predictable difference in their decision making. If the dominant pattern is one in which a difference on one variable (education) usually is accompanied by a difference on the other variable (decision making) in the *same direction* (higher education–higher decision making or lower education–lower decision making), then we call it a **positive relationship** (or a positive effect or a positive correlation). If the dominant pattern is one in which the difference on one is in the *opposite direction* from the difference on the other (higher education–lower decision making or lower education–higher decision making), then we call it a **negative relationship** (or a negative effect or a negative correlation). The extent to which this pattern is fixed and holds across all possible comparisons of units in our study is called the **strength of the relationship**. If there are many exceptions to the pattern (e.g., most of the time the pattern is positive, but many times scores on the two variables change in opposite directions), then it is a weak relationship. If there are very few exceptions, then it is a strong relationship. Correlations and many other similar statistics in sociology are standardized and range from 0 (no relationship) to 1 (extremely strong relationship—no exceptions). Correlations are also preceded by a sign to tell whether the relationship is positive or negative. Thus, the possible range of values is between –1 and +1, with both a –1 and a +1 indicating extremely strong relationships but in opposite directions, and a coefficient near 0 (either positive or negative), indicating a very weak or nonexistent relationship. Since social behavior is determined by so many forces, it is very rare that correlations exceed +/–.30, although few researchers would accept as important coefficients below +/–.10.

Finally, the strength and direction of effects found in observational studies such as surveys are not the researcher's only concern. Recall that in surveys the researcher is relying on a sample of units from a larger population. Therefore, even if he or she finds a strong relationship in his or her study, the question remains as to *whether or not that finding can be generalized to the larger population*. We can never know this for sure, but statisticians have developed a method for telling us the probability that our sample results cannot be generalized or are based on a sample that might be unique in some way from the rest of the population. We call these statistical techniques **inferential statistics**, and they can take many different forms. In all cases, however, the statistic calculated is compared to a table of coefficients that tell us the *probability* that our results are *not generalizable* beyond their application to the sample of units observed. Thus, whenever evaluating the results from quantitative research on the family, you need to ask about this probability of nongeneralizability (also known as **significance**). Social scientists do not accept results with a probability of nongeneralizability that is more than 5 percent. In other words, the significance of a result must be less than .05 ($p < .05$ or $s < .05$) before we can make generalizations to the larger population. The significance of a result is proportional to the strength of the effect and the size of the sample it was based on. When observed effects are strong or when the sample is large, there is a greater chance that the results will be significant and generalizable. Thus, if the sample is extremely large (10,000 or more), very weak effects will be significant even though their weakness will mean they aren't very explanatory.

Theories and Frames of Reference

Theories of marital and family life presented in this text and elsewhere often are limited in scope as they attempt to provide explanation for a specific outcome or state. For example, there are theories of marital power, family violence, divorce, divorce effects on children, and other phenomena. These theories often are just models that specify systems of causal relationships that bring about the phenomenon studied. In other words, they represent systems of logically interrelated propositions or hypotheses that provide an explanation for why something occurs. These causal models are then tested more or less fully through the observation of the variables involved and an analysis of their interconnectedness or patterns of regularity. Often researchers do not specify their initial assumptions nor link their theories with others used to explain different phenomena. This does not mean, however, that researchers operate independently of each other or that we cannot accumulate knowledge and theoretical principles across areas of study. In most cases, researchers utilize assumptions from one or more of a limited number of broad theoretical perspectives or frameworks and identifying which of these perspectives is used can help the reader interpret the meaning and significance of their results.

The theoretical perspectives used in the sociological study of marital and family phenomena can be divided into three groupings. First, there are two perspectives (*structure-functionalism* and *conflict theory*) that we can label as **macro theories** in that they are most widely applicable to problems of family change and stability across societal contexts and see individual behavior in families as determined by the structures within which those individuals are embedded. The second grouping of perspectives (*symbolic interactionism* and *social exchange theory*) can be classified as **micro theories** in that they factor in individual motivations and see marital and family phenomena as the direct outcome of individuals negotiating with each other to realize desired goals. These interactions may be influenced by larger social structures, but the emphasis is on how those structures are interpreted and reacted to by the individuals in them. Third, there are two perspectives (family systems theory and *family development theory*) that are more explicitly **multilevel theories** in that they attempt to incorporate both macro-level and micro-level processes.

No single perspective is necessarily more valid than another. Although it sometimes may be possible to develop a unified theory of marital and family life, sociology has not yet achieved that point. Some theories may have broader applicability or more support, but all also have sufficient deficiencies to explain fully all of the phenomena of interest to family social scientists. A better way to think of these perspectives is as a set of lenses for viewing reality. Each lens highlights different aspects of that reality and is therefore necessary to gain a full understanding and explanation.

It is also important to keep in mind that these theories are just social constructions or stories that fit reality to a greater or lesser extent. There may be perspectives yet to be developed that more accurately and fully capture reality. Since these are social constructions, we should also not be fooled into thinking that any theory represents the "truth" and we should be cautious about how these stories might have been formulated in a way that advances our own self-interests or that is limited by our own biases in perspective. It is always possible that a completely different set of assumptions, concepts, and propositions could fit reality as well as one that fits that same reality perfectly. To reinforce this idea, we conclude this section with a discussion of nonscientific and poststructural perspectives used in family studies.

Structural-Functional Frame of Reference

The **structural-functional frame of reference**, sometimes called *structure–functionalism* or just *functionalism*, was a dominant theoretical orientation in sociology up until the 1970s and is still used today, although to a much lesser extent. Within the family area, the scope of this approach is very broad as it provides a framework for dealing with relationships within the family (husband, wife, sibling, etc.) as well as influences on the family from other systems within society (educational, religious, occupational, etc.) and long-term change and stability in family systems.

The structural-functional frame of reference has been most articulated by the early American sociologist Talcott Parsons,[9] although key philosophical elements and assumptions can be clearly traced to eighteenth-century *organicism*, the early nineteenth-century sociologists Auguste Comte, Herbert Spenser, and Emile Durkheim, and the early twentieth-century tradition of British anthropology represented by Radcliffe-Brown and Bronislaw Malinowski.[10]

The philosophical position of **organicism** proposed the idea that "society, like the body, is a cohesive whole served by its parts."[11] This idea of the whole being more than the simple sum of its parts is at the very heart of structure-functionalism and it relegates the motivations and perceptions of individuals to a residual position in explaining social behavior. Comte, Spenser, and Durkheim all developed the organic analogy in their analyses of society and extended it by developing concepts to capture many of the qualities of the whole such as cohesion, consensus, solidarity, differentiation, and the conscious collective. In particular, Durkheim contributed the idea that social institutions and behaviors were *social facts* and could be studied independently of the persons who participated in them. He also linked the health of social institutions to the degree of social solidarity and social order in a society and thereby the health of the society as a whole. Spenser took the organic analogy even further as he proposed a theory of social evolution borrowed from biological evolutionary theory and premised on the principle of *survival of the fittest*. Accordingly, the structure of social institutions evolved over time in response to environmental conditions and could, therefore, be considered functional.

In addition to the assumption that the whole is greater than the sum of its parts, structure-functionalism assumes that social structures arise in response to functional needs defined by the conditions of survival. Society is viewed as a "system" with four "defining properties": (1) a differentiated set of roles, (2) a shared value system, (3) clearly defined boundaries linking individuals in a common system together in meeting their basic survival needs, and (4) a tendency to reach and maintain a

---

[9]Talcott Parsons, *The Social System* (Glencoe, IL: The Free Press, 1951).

[10]Nancy Kingsbury and John Scanzoni, "Structural-Functionalism," in Pauline G. Boss, William J. Doherty, Ralph LaRossa, Walter R. Schumm, and Suzanne K. Steinmetz, *Sourcebook of Family Theories and Methods: A Contextual Approach* (New York: Plenum Press, 1993), Chapter 9, 195–217.

[11]Ibid., 199.

condition of equilibrium or stability in structure.[12] In order for members of a differentiated society to work together to achieve survival, a shared system of values is considered critical. Once a system of relationships is established for meeting survival needs, it is then essential for that system to be maintained and for deviance from values and norms to be suppressed (this is the **equilibrium assumption**). In order to deal with the problem of deviant behavior by self-interested individuals, social control mechanisms are also seen as essential.

The term *structure* is central to this perspective and refers to the system of more or less stable role relationships among members of a society—relationships dictated by the survival needs of the society and learned and maintained by the construction of societal norms (expectations held by all members of the society for each other's behaviors). These roles may be further organized in the form of social institutions like the family that address certain specific functional needs (e.g., the recruitment and training of new members, the stabilization of adult personalities).[13] Thus, both the essential nature of institutions and the normative arrangement of roles within them can be derived directly from an analysis of the survival needs of the society and the observation of how current arrangements are meeting those needs. Since structures are linked to specific functions, their existence and current form are often seen as *necessary* and any shift toward their dissolution or change in form is often considered a threat to the survival of the society and the well-being of societal members.

The term *function* is also central to this perspective but is more difficult to define. In our common vernacular, the function that something serves is simply an expression of what it does or what effect it has. For example, one function of a college degree might be to get a job. This would be a **manifest function** in that it is explicitly stated and recognized by members of our society and both educational and work institutions are structured in a way that can be directly related to this outcome. Other functions of educational institutions are more indirect and less recognized. For example, attending college keeps unemployed young people off the streets and thereby functions for the society as a source of social control. Attending college also provides a context for meeting potential marriage partners and so functions as a mate selection institution. These latter functions are called **latent functions**.

The structure-functionalist perspective recognizes both manifest and latent functions of institutions but does so in a more specific manner. Although we know the function of an institution or set of role relationships by observing what they do after the fact, the structure-functionalist attempts much more than simple description. The functions specified must also be related to the survival needs of the society or the particular institution within a society. It is the functional need that brings about the structures observed.

It has been suggested that, for individual members, some manifest functions of the family are to provide basic personality formation, basic status ascription, nurturant socialization, and tension management. For the larger society, some manifest functions are to replace members, to socialize the members to the norms and values of the society, and to act as an agent of social control. In terms of latent functions, the idea of the traditional family might be sustained today because it serves to give

---

[12]Ibid.

[13]Talcott Parsons and Robert F. Bales, *Family Socialization and Interaction Process* (New York: The Free Press, 1955), 16–17.

individuals a greater sense of stability and certainty in an otherwise changing and uncertain modern society where societal consensus has broken down. From this perspective, it could be argued that the current cultural discourse about the demise of "the family" actually is a reflection of our collective sense of societal disorganization in other areas than an argument based on a clearly drawn connection between a particular family form and societal survival needs.

In addition to the concepts of structure and function, the concept of *social solidarity* is also considered important from this perspective. **Social solidarity** refers to individuals' motivations to participate in the system and fulfill their role responsibilities. Durkheim proposed two types of social solidarity—*mechanical* and *organic*. **Mechanical solidarity** is found in preindustrial societies and is premised on the commonality of life experiences and values of members of a social system. **Organic solidarity** is more critical in industrial societies where individuals have become so differentiated in their role responsibilities that they lack the commonality of both experiences and values that held them together in prior times. In these highly differentiated societies, the "glue" that holds members together is a sense of their interdependence with one another. That is, we are all individuals with unique circumstances and needs, so we need to develop a *collective conscience* (a common worldview) that recognizes our need for each other. It doesn't matter so much what type of solidarity develops as long as it does develop. According to this perspective, without solidarity it will be impossible for a society to maintain high levels of interdependence and its survival (along with the survival of its members) will, therefore, be threatened.

Finally, the structure-functionalist perspective has developed concepts to refer to the structural arrangements of its members. Three of these worth discussing here are the concepts of social roles, norms, and social differentiation.

A **social role** is a set of *prescribed* (determined and ordered by societal needs) behaviors associated with one's position in the social structure. For example, one of the roles associated with being a husband (a position in the institution of marriage) might be the "breadwinner" (the person responsible for going to work every day, performing tasks at work, and bringing home and distributing his wages). It doesn't matter who the person is that occupies this position, his roles will always be the same. If they were different because he wanted to do something else, then there would be no basis for order in society and society would, therefore, cease to survive. These roles are, therefore, reinforced by **social norms**, sets of expectations for behavior held by the majority of societal members and enforced through sanctions. When individuals deviate from the norms, then societal members punish them in some way. When they comply, they are rewarded.

Social differentiation relates to the concept of roles in that it conveys the extent to which individuals in society have separate and distinct roles. This distinctiveness comes about when societies specialize, or divide up the tasks necessary for survival into their component elements and then assign individuals responsibility for completing only one aspect of the task repeatedly. Another term for social differentiation is the **division of labor**. The application of this concept to the functionalist explanation for family roles has been at the heart of criticisms of the perspective as too conservative. Using data from anthropological studies and small group research, Parsons and his colleagues[14] proposed that there was a natural and universal

---

[14]Robert Bales and Paul Slater, "Role Differentiation in Small Decision-Making Groups," in Talcott Parsons and Robert Bales, *Family Socialization and Interaction Process* (Glencoe, IL: The Free Press, 1955), 259–306.

division of labor in marriage whereby men performed **instrumental roles** (roles that required nonemotional rational behavior such as working outside the home, managing money, fixing machinery, and generally working with things) and women performed **expressive roles** (roles that required emotional involvement and expressiveness such as caring for children, preparing meals to sustain health, and generally meeting the emotional needs of family members). This division was natural because the role responsibilities were contradictory (you couldn't do one effectively while also doing the other), and men and women had different biological capacities to do each type of activity. Unfortunately, this research was significantly flawed as were the conceptualizations of instrumental and expressive roles.

The argument that structure-functionalism is too conservative goes beyond this one example of the specialized division of labor in marriage. Sociologists using this perspective began to see flaws in their assumptions about the commonality of values in society (today we see many examples of pluralistic societies) and began to see the importance of power in shaping institutions in ways that didn't necessarily promote societal survival but instead promoted the interests of those with the power.

The theoretical reasoning of this perspective also came under criticism as being *teleological* (circular) in that the function served by a structure is considered to be the cause of the structure, but the only way to determine a structure's function is after the fact. As a result, all stable structures are given justification through a search for what functions might be assigned to them. Without an independent means for determining a society's functional needs prior to the rise of social structures, the theory becomes untestable, and existing structures are given much more legitimacy and truth value than they deserve.

A third criticism of this perspective is its adherence to the notion that only one structural arrangement can meet the functional needs of the society. This criticism is a bit muted, however, by Robert Merton's introduction of the concept of **functional equivalence**, which holds that alternative institutional arrangements can substitute for those previously established to meet a given societal need.

Finally, structure-functionalism has been seen as too preoccupied with the problem of stability and has ignored or problematized the fact that societies experience quite a bit of change. Change is seen as a negative indicator of societal health, when in fact it may result in better adaptation to the environment and better living conditions for the majority of society's members. John Scanzoni[15] illustrates how this conservative bias has informed recent applications of functionalist thinking in contemporary criticisms of emerging alternative (or diverse) family forms. He argues that we need to be more aware of the process by which new families are actively constructed and undergoing continuous change as individuals adapt to their environments and satisfy their needs. Such a constructivist perspective rejects the functionalist idea of a single "functional" family fitted to a stable ecological environment and instead recognizes a "diversity" of families whose success or failure depends on their members' abilities "to think critically and creatively and to engage in problem solving and negotiation."[16]

Today, structure-functionalism is no longer used explicitly in social research on the family. In fact, it is disappearing as a topic in textbooks used to teach family

---

[15]John Scanzoni, "From the Normal Family to Alternate Families to the Quest for Diversity with Interdependence," *Journal of Family Issues* 22 (2001): 688–710.

[16]Ibid., 699.

theory.[17] Nevertheless, it is a perspective that underlies many demographic, cross-cultural, and biosocial explanations of family life and institutional variations. It is also a perspective that shares many assumptions with still viable theories such as ecological theory and systems theory (see discussion of systems theory later in this chapter).[18]

Social Conflict Frame of Reference

Perhaps the most basic assumption of a **social conflict frame of reference** is that conflict is natural and inevitable in all human interaction. Thus, rather than stressing order, equilibrium, consensus, and system maintenance, as does functionalism, the focus of a social conflict frame of reference is conflict management. Conflict is not viewed as bad or disruptive of social systems and human interaction; instead, conflict is viewed as an assumed and expected part of all systems and interactions.

The classic case for social conflict theory originated with Karl Marx.[19] Marx believed in **economic determinism**. He believed that the fundamental logic of the economic system of a society set in motion social processes that determined all other aspects of social systems from political to religious to familial to cultural. Although he undertook broad historical analyses of different economic systems, he focused mostly on modern capitalistic economies, which he saw as premised on the dialectical logic of two classes in constant conflict—a small **bourgeoisie** that owned the means of production and a much larger **proletariat** (workers) that was exploited and oppressed as a necessary consequence of the need to generate profit in a free and competitive marketplace. All noneconomic institutions in society were seen as either the outcome of this struggle or in support of the more powerful bourgeoisie. This included the family, which, according to Marx's colleague Frederick Engels,[20] helped sustain the ability of the bourgeoisie to exploit and oppress the proletariat by structuring unequal gender relationships whereby women provided free labor in the home to care for workers and this allowed the owners to increase their level of exploitation of their husbands. Thus, conflict was structured and inevitable in the relationships between men (and women) and would both generate social order as well as bring about significant change (for Marx this change would be revolutionary).

Max Weber, another German sociologist, also contributed to the development of this perspective by noting alternative sources of conflict in society. Rejecting the economic determinism of Marx, Weber believed that society was comprised of many groups with different values and interests in competition with each other

---

[17]See for example James M. White and David M. Klein, *Family Theories*, 2nd ed. (Thousand Oaks, CA: Sage Publications, 2002).

[18]See the discussion of demographic theories by Suzanne M. Bianchi and Lynne M. Casper, "Explanations of Family Change: A Family Demographic Perspective," in Vern L. Bengtson, Alan C. Acock, Katherine R. Allen, Peggye Dilworth-Anderson, and David M. Klein, eds., *Sourcebook of Family Theory & Research* (Thousand Oaks, CA: Sage Publications, 2005), 93–117; Elaine Leeder, *The Family in Global Perspective* (Thousand Oaks, CA: Sage Publications, 2004); and James M. White and David M. Klein, *Family Theories*, 2nd ed. (Thousand Oaks, CA: Sage Publications, 2002), Chapters 4, 5, and 8.

[19]Karl Marx, *The Communist Manifesto*, trans. Samuel Moore (Baltimore: Penguin, 1967), originally published in 1849 with Friedrich Engels; C. Wright Mills, *The Marxists* (New York: Harcourt, Brace, 1948); and Rolf Dahrendorf, *Class and Class Conflict in Industrial Society* (Stanford: Stanford University Press, 1959).

[20]Freidrich Engels, *The Origins of the Family, Private Property and the State* (New York: International Publishers, 1964).

(including economic interest groups). He also saw the possibility that one group could gain power over another and this process was not predetermined by the group's location in the economic system. Thus, for Weber, the key issue was power relations and how one group is able to legitimize its values and interests over others and thereby gain power.[21]

Conflict theory is primarily a macro-level theory in that it sees the behaviors of individuals as shaped by their location in the social system and sees the source of social change in processes operating at the level of the social system rather than as an outcome of individual initiative. Conflict theorists have also given a great deal of attention to processes of conflict management at the micro level as well, but that work is largely compensatory, as any source of change in the nature of the conflict in a group must come from changes in its structural context. We can learn better how to manage our conflicts and in doing so enhance the quality of our lives, but we cannot eliminate the sources of underlying conflict without changing our position in the larger social structure.

There are four fundamental assumptions of social conflict theory: (1) Conflict is *endemic* (always present) in all social groups; (2) conflict shapes institutions and relationships; (3) conflict is a source of both order and change; and (4) the expression of conflict can be a positive force in relationships.

To assume that conflict is endemic to all social groups is not to say that fighting or the expression of conflict will always occur or be present. Conflict theorists talk about two types of conflict—*structured* and *expressed*. This assumption refers to **structured conflict**, the existence of differences in interests and values among members of a group. This type of conflict is structured in the sense that regardless of what values and interests we express in our relationships, our fates are determined by the interest groups to which we belong.

Two important types of interest groups that shape interactions within families are age and gender-based groups. Our age group membership is important in considering intergenerational relationships in families. For example, how we relate to our aging parents will be shaped by what sources of support are available from the government to meet their needs. To the extent that there are many services, the nature of our relationships with our parents is likely to be more congenial. If services are not available, however, then pressure will be applied on the children to provide support. This obligation, although readily accepted by the children, will certainly involve the neglect of their own interests and may interfere with their ability to live their family lives according to their own interests. Thus, an underlying structural conflict will exist between generations. With respect to gender, structural conflicts also exist by virtue of the fact that our society is gender stratified. Because men receive greater rewards from their work, have more opportunities, and are granted more rights in a patriarchal society, all heterosexual marital couples have to manage their relationships under a system of inequality. Even the most egalitarian couple must work to achieve a state of equality in their relationship in the face of the husband's greater sources of power and privilege.[22] We cannot change these

---

[21]Keith Farrington and Ely Chertok, "Social Conflict Theories of the Family," in Pauline G. Boss, William J. Doherty, Ralph LaRossa, Walter R. Schumm, and Suzanne K. Steinmetz, *Sourcebook of Family Theories and Methods: A Contextual Approach* (New York: Plenum Press, 1993), Chapter 15, 357–380.

[22]Pepper Schwartz, *Peer Marriage: How Love between Equals Really Works* (New York: The Free Press, 1994).

circumstances by our own volition, but we can learn techniques for better dealing with their consequences. If we wish to make more basic changes, we will need to address this unequal distribution of resources across different interest groups in society. The issue of gender conflict in families will be addressed in greater detail in Chapter 9.

The second and third assumptions that conflict shapes institutions and relationships and that conflict is a source of both order and change are complementary. On the one hand, certain forms of relationships and institutions are shaped and stabilized by the competition between interest groups. If one group has greater power, it can assert its values and interests over another. This doesn't mean all families in society will look the same as those of the dominant group, however. Rather, it is assumed that the form that family life takes in the less powerful group in some ways is in the interest of the more powerful group. On the other hand, conflict can destabilize relationships and institutions as well. This is most likely to occur when power differences between groups are reduced.[23] For example, the high rates of divorce in the United States in the 1960s through 1980s could be attributed, from this perspective, to the equalization of power between men and women in society. Note that the explanation for rising divorce rates lies at the macro level and has little to do with changes in the individual motivations or moralities of those getting divorced.

Is peace and order better than conflict and change? The fourth assumption says order is not necessarily good and change is not necessarily bad. The expression of conflict can have many positive consequences for relationships insofar as it exposes dissatisfactions and inequalities that can then be addressed through bargaining and negotiation and it often leads to ideas for how to change a relationship to enhance the satisfactions of those involved.

This assumption that conflict and change can be good is a fundamental distinction between functionalism and conflict theory. In brief, from a social conflict perspective, the family is not the haven posited by an order perspective such as functionalism (see Table 3.2). Functionalists, who see the family as the primary socialization agent of youth, are viewed by conflict theorists as promoting a false consciousness by teaching youth to accept the inequalities between the sexes and classes as natural. Functionalists also see the family as perpetuating the same "life chances" from one generation to another (the rich stay rich and the poor stay poor), whereas conflict theorists feel this perpetuation maintains and promotes inequality based on ascription rather than achievement. Functionalists believe the isolated nuclear family is consistent with the mobility needs of a capitalist society; conflict theorists believe mobility is disruptive to individual members and their emotional needs. Finally, functionalists, who see the modern family as tranquil, passive, and in a state of equilibrium with other units of society, are seen by conflict theorists as promoting a system fraught with potential and actual conflict. Conflict—inevitable in society, in the family, and in interpersonal relationships—leads to change.

Symbolic Interaction Frame of Reference

Symbolic interaction frame of reference describes a particular and distinctive approach to the study of the group life and personal behavior of human beings. As a social-psychological frame of reference, symbolic interactionism addresses two

---

[23]Roger V. Gould, *Collision of Wills: How Ambiguity about Social Rank Breeds Conflict* (Chicago: University of Chicago Press, 2003).

Table 3.2

Duality of Social Life: Assumptions of the Order and Conflict Models of Society

	ORDER MODEL	CONFLICT MODEL
Question	What is the fundamental relationship among the parts of society?	
Answer	Harmony and cooperation	Competition, conflict, domination, and subordination
Why	The parts have complementary interests.	The things people want are always in short supply.
	Basic consensus on societal norms and values	Basic dissensus on societal norms and values
Degree of integration	Highly integrated	Loosely integrated
		Whatever integration is achieved is the result of force and fraud.
Type of societal integration	Gradual, adjustive, and reforming	Abrupt and revolutionary
Degree of stability	Stable	Unstable

Source: U.S. Bureau of the Census, The 2009 Statistical Abstract, "Table 56: Marital Status of the Population by Sex and Age" http://www.2010census.biz/compendia/statab/cats/population/marital_status_and_living_arrangements.html.

issues—socialization and social interaction—both of which are of central concern to the family. The first issue, **socialization**, focuses on how individuals become social and on how human beings obtain and internalize the behavior patterns and ways of thinking and feeling of the society and culture in which they live. The second issue, social interaction, is basic to socialization itself and to all aspects of life; it focuses on the importance of symbols in interaction, the self in relation to others, and the social interchanges between individuals and groups.

Two of the earliest proponents of this perspective—Charles Horton Cooley and George Herbert Mead—argued that we represent our world using symbols that have no inherent meaning. Instead, we must develop a system of meanings to represent the world, and those symbols only have meaning to the extent that others react to them the same way that we do or that we intend them to. Therefore, social interaction is both necessary and possible only through the development of a common system of meanings. One meaning that is essential and that takes priority over all others is the meaning of who we are—that is, the self. Cooley used the term *looking glass self* to capture the idea that we need a reflection from others to know who we are. This reflection is not a physical one but a behavioral one. We learn about our self and we maintain a self-concept by observing and manipulating the reactions of others toward us.

The distinctiveness of symbolic interactionism lies in its assumption that meaning can only be found in the consequences of action. It is neither a product of the mind nor a preexisting reality. Rather, the meaning of things—including social behavior, social relationships, and social institutions—must be found in the interactions between individuals. Social structure is, therefore, *emergent*. This means, for example, that a husband and wife relationship can only be described as unequal or unfair to the extent that they themselves define it as such. The wife might be doing most of the housework and the husband might have considerably more leisure time and decision-making power, but if in their symbolic negotiations over the meaning of this situation they interpret her additional work as a "gift" and justify his leisure time and decision-making power as justified by his work status, then they will act in their relationship based on a "reality" of equality. Thus, the study of individuals and their perceptions and behaviors is essential to any study of society or social groups like families.

LaRossa and Reitzes[24] identify seven assumptions of this perspective:

1. Human beings act toward things on the basis of the meanings that the things have for them.
2. Meaning arises in the process of interaction between people.
3. Meanings are handled in and modified through an interpretive process used by the person in dealing with things he or she encounters.
4. Individuals are not born with a sense of self, but develop self-concepts through social interaction.
5. Self-concepts, once developed, provide an important motive for behavior.
6. Individuals and small groups are influenced by larger cultural and societal processes.
7. It is through social interaction in everyday situations that individuals work out the details of social structure.

Thus, all human interaction in groups such as families can be seen as motivated by the search for common meanings or interpretations of reality and, in particular, the search for consistency of meaning of the self through the reactions of others.

Concepts from the social interaction framework are used extensively throughout this book. There are three that warrant discussion here—*self-concept*, *identity*, and *role*. Others will be discussed in later chapters as we use this perspective to explain marital and family behaviors.

The **self-concept** is a definition individuals carry with them and continuously recreate through interactions with others. It includes information about how they expect themselves to act and how others expect them to act in different situations. The distinctiveness of the symbolic interaction framework lies in the fact that it sees the self as a set of internalized expectations based on past and current interactional processes. Unlike psychological personality theories that see the self as more immutable (unchangeable) and the outcome of early life experiences, symbolic interactionists see the self as more fluid and *situated* (variable across situations). To capture the idea that the self is both the product of previous experiences and an ongoing project of social interaction, Mead used the terms *I* and *Me*. The *I* comprises the subject self that is acting in the present situation and actively reconstructing the

---

[24]Ralph LaRossa and Donald C. Reitzes, "Symbolic Interactionism and Family Studies," in Pauline G. Boss, William J. Doherty, Ralph LaRossa, Walter R. Schumm, and Suzanne K. Steinmetz, *Sourcebook of Family Theories and Methods: A Contextual Approach* (New York: Plenum Press, 1993), Chapter 6, 135–160.

self through those actions; it is the active and spontaneous aspect of the self. The *Me*, on the other hand, is the object self that the individual reflects on and cognitively constructs. It is a more or less coherent amalgamation of previous interactional experiences (actions and corresponding reactions from others) melded with interpretations of one's own actions and reactions of others in the present situation as they unfold. Thus, the self is an ongoing project of interpretation and reinterpretation based on interactional experiences. As such, it is emergent within those experiences. It is in this sense that West and Zimmerman[25] have argued that gender (as an aspect of the self) is not something we are born with or that is the inexorable outcome of early life experiences but is instead an ongoing project of interaction. As a result, they argue that we should not talk about "being" a gender but should instead talk about how we are "doing gender" or creating gender differences every time we choose to act in particular ways.

A closely related concept to self-concept is that of **identity**. Again, the symbolic interactionist uses identity in a distinctive way from most psychological theories. For the symbolic interactionist, there is not one identity but as many identities as there are systems of relationships that one is involved in. For example, the governor of Washington State, Christine Gregoire, not only constructs her self-concept in terms of her identity as governor but also as a daughter, a sister, a friend, a wife, a worker, and a mother. These are all separate identities comprised of sets of expectation for how she should behave in relationships with different groups of others. They do not exist independently of each other, however, as they must be integrated in her self-concept in a way that is consistent and noncontradictory. Sometimes contradictions in expectations do arise, however, and she will have to choose which set of expectations she complies with or will have to negotiate a change in those expectations with the others with whom she has relationships. To help her make decisions in these cases, she will have organized her separate identities into an **identity hierarchy** and will give priority to those expectations associated with the identities that are highest in her hierarchy. This occurred in 2000 when she chose not to run for the U.S. Senate because her elderly mother needed her attention and her identity as a daughter superseded her identity as a politician.

The expectations associated with identities are captured in the concept of role. This concept is used within both a structural-functional framework and an interactionist framework. However, its use varies significantly. For the structure-functionalist, the concept of role is an institutional or structural concept and refers to societal expectations necessarily attached to positions or statuses that people occupy in a social system. These expectations are derived from a functional analysis of societal survival needs and the institutionalized structures for meeting those needs. As such, roles are culturally defined expectations and exist independently of any given person. Individuals may deviate from their roles, but they cannot change or negotiate them.

The symbolic interactionist does not reject the idea that roles are culturally defined. As the sixth assumption listed earlier states, "Individuals and small groups are influenced by larger cultural and societal processes."[26] The difference in this perspective lies in the source of those cultural definitions and the deterministic nature of their influence on individuals in social relationships such as marriages and families. Culturally defined role expectations are seen as the outcome of individuals interacting

---

[25]Candyce West and Don H. Zimmerman, "Doing Gender," *Gender and Society* 1 (1987): 125–151.

[26]LaRossa and Reitzes, "Symbolic Interactionism and Family Studies," 144.

together and constructing an image of what is appropriate behavior for those in their position. They reflect those individuals' attempts to live and manage their lives in the face of similar environmental circumstances, but they are neither necessary nor deterministic. Individuals do not necessarily comply with culturally constructed role expectations nor do they necessarily see those expectations in the same way. The expectations (roles) are developed in interaction. The emphasis here is on process.

Using heterosexual dating relationships as an example might clarify the use of the concept of role in symbolic interactionist terms. To begin with, individuals enter into dating relationships with a set of preconceived expectations for how they should behave. For example, the man might perceive that he is expected to hold the door for his date and pay the bill for dinner. These expectations were internalized through observations of others involved in dating, exposure to cultural images of others in dating relationships, and previous dating experiences. Not all individuals are exposed to the exact same set of expectations or cultural images, however, since these expectations are seen as interactively generated and are not viewed as universally necessary for societal survival. Thus, when he attempts to hold the door or pay the bill, his date might react negatively or prevent him from fulfilling this self-expectation. Her behavior would be consistent with her own self-expectation that a woman should be self-reliant and assertive in her interactions with men. Her behavior, then, creates ambiguity in the dating relationship. The man must reassess his role expectations as a romantic partner (and as a man) and negotiate with his date to arrive at an agreement about how they expect each other to behave. In the process, they develop a new set of role expectations. This process is not a simple one, however, because, as noted earlier, one's role expectations in one identity must be consistent with role expectations in other identities (in this case, he must consider how changes in his behavior might reflect on his definition of self as a man). Thus, the question of self-definition is always central to social interaction and shapes our negotiations concerning roles.

Given this perspective's focus on individual perceptions and interactional processes in creating meanings, how are we to view or define marriage or family? At one level, we can study the family as a social construction to determine what common pressures individuals in families experience in their role relationships. We can also examine commonly held role expectations associated with individuals' positions in other socially constructed institutions such as school, work, and neighborhood. Such an analysis can be used to identify issues that might arise in marriages and families due to conflicts in these expectations. This would be consistent with what might be called the *structural school* of symbolic interactionism. Alternatively, we could study marriages and families simply as ongoing contexts of negotiated meanings. Such an approach emphasizes the process by which selves are constructed within the context of marriages and families (as defined by the individuals in them) and is less concerned with finding common structures of expectations that individuals must react to or negotiate. This latter approach might be called the *process school* of symbolic interactionism.

Social Exchange Frame of Reference

Seldom does a day pass in which certain social exchanges do not take place. Work, gifts, cards, affection, and ideas are given in hopes of getting something in return. Certain exchanges, such as many economic ones, are institutionalized and predetermined, clarified in precise terms prior to the exchange. For instance, one can exchange fifty cents for a newspaper or eighty dollars for a membership in the National Council on Family Relations. Other exchanges, including the type found in the **social exchange frame of reference**, leave unspecified the exact nature of the return, although an expectation for return—an expectation of reciprocity—does exist, even when denied or disavowed. For example, neighbors who lend tools, friends who buy dinner, and politicians who promise lower taxes all expect something in return.

The social exchange theory, also known as social choice theory or rational choice theory, rests on the belief that human beings are *rational hedonists*, which means that they are motivated in their actions by the need to maximize their rewards and minimize their costs and they do so in a way that involves a process of calculation and comparison of alternatives. Although it may be true that persons exist who selflessly work for others with no thought of reward, such "saints" are rare, and even they seek social or perhaps spiritual approval. Social exchanges are voluntary social actions contingent on receiving rewarding reactions from others and will cease when the actual or expected reactions are not forthcoming.

Social exchange theory has followed two differing schools of thought regarding this process, best represented by George Homans[27] and Peter Blau.[28] Homans, the recognized initiator of exchange theory, represented a perspective consistent with that of behavioral psychologists who believe in *psychological reductionism* (a belief that all social phenomena can be accounted for by simply aggregating the self-motivated actions of individuals) and *reinforcement theory*, in which the focus is on actual behavior that is rewarded or punished by the behavior of other persons. Humans, like animals, react to stimuli based on need, reward, and reinforcement. Unlike structure-functionalism or conflict theory, they do not automatically act in accordance with societal or interest group needs.

Blau differed considerably from Homans and represented a perspective more consistent with that of the symbolic interactionists. That is, social exchange is seen as more subjective and interpretative. Exchange, like interaction, is a creative process that occurs between actors. Although humans want rewards, the choices and decisions they make are affected by social influences, such as friends or kin. The human mind responds subjectively to stimuli through conceptualizing, defining, valuing, reflecting, and symbolizing. This school of thought, then, leads logically to a second assumption of social exchange theory, that "humans use their expectations for rewards and costs to guide their behavior."[29] These expectations are based on their interpretation of the value of different rewards and costs, their assessment of the probabilities of obtaining rewards and avoiding costs, and, as we will discuss later, the interdependencies that develop in exchange relationships that occur over time.

A third assumption of this perspective is that the "standards that humans use to evaluate rewards and costs differ from person to person and can vary over the course of time."[30] These rewards and costs can be economic in nature (money) or

---

[27]George C. Homans, *Social Behavior: Its Elementary Forms* (New York: Harcourt, Brace and World, 1961); George C. Homans, "Social Behavior as Exchange," *American Journal of Sociology* 63 (May 1958): 597–606.

[28]Peter M. Blau, *Exchange and Power in Social Life* (New York: Wiley, 1964); Peter Blau, "Justice in Social Exchange," *Sociological Inquiry* 34 (Spring 1964): 193–206.

[29]Ronald Sabatelli and Constance Shehan, "Exchange and Resource Theories," in Pauline G. Boss, William J. Doherty, Ralph LaRossa, Walter R. Schumm, and Suzanne K. Steinmetz, *Sourcebook of Family Theories and Methods: A Contextual Approach* (New York: Plenum Press, 1993), Chapter 16, 396.

[30]Ibid.

can be in the form of love (emotional response, personal attraction), status (respect, prestige, social acceptance and approval), services, goods, or information.

An important concept of this perspective related to the ability to give another rewards and costs is that of **resources**. Sabatelli and Shehan define resources as any commodity, material or symbolic, that can be transmitted through interpersonal behavior and gives one person the capacity to reward another. Specific resources (money, position, physical assets, personality, education, social skills) may be more applicable in one exchange than in another and may have different values in different exchanges. The worth of a resource can be accurately assessed only through participation in actual social markets. Therefore, socialization in exchange and bargaining skills is vital to maximizing the use of available resources. As we will see in Chapter 9, the balance of resources in a relationship can have important consequences for power and decision making in that relationship.

Both Homans and Blau agreed that what is important is that each party in the exchange receive something perceived as equal to or greater than that which is given. This is referred to as *reciprocity*. Thus, a fourth assumption is that all social exchange involves a mutually held expectation that reciprocation will occur (the **norm of reciprocity**).[31] When it does not, the exchange relationship is likely to be perceived as unjust or unfair (what Homans called the principle of *distributive justice* and Blau termed *fair exchange*).

Finally, two other prominent exchange theorists—Thibault and Kelley[32]—emphasized the interdependencies that get created in exchange relationships. Based on their contributions, three additional assumptions can be specified. First, "[s]ocial exchanges are characterized by interdependence, that is, the ability to obtain profits in a relationship is contingent on the ability to provide others with rewards[.] Second, [t]he emergent experiences of relationships guide subsequent exchanges[.] And third, [t]he dynamics of interaction within relationships and the stability of relationships over time results from the contrasting levels of attraction and dependence experienced by the participants in the relationship."[33]

Thus, in studies of marriage and family life from this perspective, the relationships between family members are governed by and contingent on the maximization of rewards and minimization of costs in the context of a certain balance of resources between members, expectations for how much each person can get and deserves given his or her own resources and previous levels of rewards and costs obtained in the relationship, the perceived probability of rewards and costs in the future, and an assessment of the rewards and costs involved in dissolving the current relationship and getting involved in an alternative. It doesn't matter how we think about this process, however. It is possible, and likely, that we will interpret our own exchange behavior in terms of having little to do with rewards and costs, but those behaviors will nevertheless be predictable based on just such an analysis.

The family literature is filled with many examples of social exchange. In Chapter 6 we will discuss the importance of marriage markets in determining when, whom, and whether or not individuals choose to get married. In Chapter 7 we will discuss how social exchange processes explain and predict the development of nonmarital romantic relationships and how the higher incidence of premarital

---

[31]Ibid.

[32]John W. Thibaut and Harold H. Kelly, *Interpersonal Relations: A Theory of Interdependence* (New York: Wiley, 1978).

[33]Ronald Sabatelli and Constance Shehan, "Exchange and Resource Theories," 396.

CROSS-CULTURAL *Perspective*

World Systems Theory and the Family

The understanding of family life in other cultures requires that we move beyond an anthropological analysis and take into consideration the ways countries influence each other in a global society. One of the first theories to recognize this dynamic was Wallerstein's "world systems theory." Essentially, this theory states that we live in an era where the world is divided into two or three segments defined by a relationship to the production of wealth. At the "core" of the world system are the western industrialized countries characterized by free laborers who negotiate a value for their work with the owners of the means of production. At the periphery are the less developed nations of the world who have very little bargaining power for their labor and are exploited by the core for cheap labor and material resources. The

significance of this theory for understanding families in other cultures lies in the role of the nuclear family in this process of exploitation. Large extended families of early self-sustaining agricultural societies were obstacles to the acceptance of new modes of production. It was only through the advancement of the nuclear family model that men became free to engage in work in industry and raw material extraction as women provided the needed supports at home to sustain them and their children. In a sense, a system of cascading exploitation developed, where global capitalists exploited men in the periphery who, in turn, exploited women and children in families. As this system has developed further, the exploitation by core countries has expanded even further through the location of large scale manufacturing in the urban centers of peripheral countries and the expansion of the tourism industry, both of which now also exploit women and children in families directly.

Source: Elaine Leeder, *The Family in Global Perspective: A Gendered Journey*, Thousand Oaks, CA: Sage Publications, 2004.

sexual behavior by engaged females can be explained as an exchange of sex on the part of the female in return for commitment on the part of the male. Throughout the text, we will also note the value of different types of resources and the exchange processes at work in understanding authority and power, husband–wife interaction, mate selection, kin relationships, sexual patterns, parent–child conflict, and the like.[34]

Family Systems Frame of Reference

Although both the macro and micro approaches previously discussed can and have been used to study both types of phenomena, their primary focus and fundamental assumptions reflect one or the other level of analysis. Some family theories (family systems theory and family development theory), however, attempt to explicitly incorporate both micro and macro processes.

The **family systems frame of reference** views families as living systems that respond to environmental pressures, but do so in interaction with the effect of the perceptions and motivations of individual family members. Each family system

---

[34]For information on social exchange theory from the perspective of the family, see John N. Edwards, "Familial Behavior as Social Exchange," *Journal of Marriage and the Family* 31 (August 1969): 518–526; F. Ivan Nye, ed., *Family Relationships: Rewards and Costs* (Beverly Hills: Sage Publications, 1982); and Chester A. Winton, *Frameworks for Studying Families* (Guilford, CT: Dushkin Publishing Group, Inc., 1995), Chapter 4, 111–130.

must adapt to its environmental conditions in order to survive but must also change its structure and modify its processes of adaptation to account for the needs and desires of its members. In contrast to structure-functionalism, the systems perspective sees families as in a more or less continuous state of **morphogenesis** (or ongoing change and adjustment) and not as a static institution trying to maintain equilibrium (or a state of no change). Furthermore, the members of the family system are not simply cogs in the machinery. That is, their perceptions of family circumstances and needs will vary, and they will willfully bring about system morphogenesis. Thus, any explanation for family behavior and family organization must take into account the psychological state of family members and the interactional dynamics discussed in the symbolic interactionist and social exchange frameworks previously. Family change can come about from within as well as from without.

The true value of this framework is in how it treats the system from a *holistic perspective*. Like macro theories, the systems framework assumes the whole is greater than the sum of its parts. For example, a two-person family consisting of two individuals with aggressive psychological tendencies may actually exhibit low levels of aggressive interactions because to do otherwise might endanger the system's ability to meet its goals, whereas a two-person family with less aggressive personalities might be able to manage and, therefore, allow higher levels of conflict. Unlike macro theories, however, the source of system goals and system change can be found in the self-reflexive character of its members and cannot be simply inferred from an analysis of environmental conditions.

The systems perspective attempts to specify the mechanisms by which families adapt to their internal and external conditions by specifying such concepts as communication systems (cybernetics) and feedback processes. **Feedback** is a central concept in this framework and refers to the process by which families monitor their outputs relative to goals and then incorporate those outputs as inputs and react to them by making system adjustments, either in terms of members' behaviors, structured processes, or the goals themselves. For example, parents monitor their children's behavior inside and outside the home relative to a standard for what they want to produce through their parenting behaviors and procedures. When children deviate from that standard by misbehaving, the parents may make an adjustment by escalating their level of directives and controls (e.g., directly supervising their homework activities or limiting their outside behaviors with curfews). To the extent that these procedures extinguish the deviance, this would be an example of **negative feedback** or a "deviation-attenuating loop." Sometimes, however, the family system might try to extinguish the deviance through existing procedures, but the attempt produces even more deviance on the part of the child. This often happens during the transition from childhood into adolescence as the child has psychological needs and social pressures to be more independent. When parents recognize this fact and, instead of escalating the level of existing rule enforcement, actually change the very nature of the rules to accommodate the child's developmental needs, then the system is exhibiting a "deviation-amplifying loop" or **positive feedback** whereby morphogenesis occurs.[35]

---

[35]Gail G. Whitchurch and Larry L. Constantine, "Systems Theory," in Pauline G. Boss, William J. Doherty, Ralph LaRossa, Walter R. Schumm, and Suzanne K. Steinmetz, *Sourcebook of Family Theories and Methods: A Contextual Approach* (New York: Plenum Press, 1993), Chapter 14, 325–353.

In addition to family processes of self-regulation, this framework attempts to specify family structures that best facilitate goal achievement and system adaptation processes. One of the more popular systems models for specifying adaptive structures is that of David Olson and colleagues.[36] This model focuses on three dimensions of system structure and process—cohesion, flexibility, and communication. According to this model, families that are extreme in cohesion (too much togetherness or too much separateness) and flexibility (too flexible or too rigid in structure) will be the most susceptible to crises and problems of adaptation. Too much cohesiveness can cause family members to be too resistant to change or innovation for fear of disrupting the well-being of other family members, whereas too much separateness in the family can result in family members having little motivation to act for the betterment of the whole or having little tolerance for other family members' negative behaviors. With respect to flexibility, too much flexibility can lead to chaos and an inability to organize members' behaviors to meet stressors in the environment, whereas too much rigidity can make it impossible for a family to change its rules and role relationships to meet environmental or internal demands. Communication is important because clear lines of communication are essential for the family to monitor itself and negotiate any changes in cohesion and flexibility needed for adaptation.

Developmental Frame of Reference

The **developmental frame of reference** covers a very broad area and tends to be both macro- and microanalytic in nature. The peculiar character of this approach lies in its attempt to account for both changes in the family system as well as changes in patterns of interaction over time. Traditionally, it was characterized as a linear model with expectable and sequential stages. The major conceptual tool among family scholars for this time analysis has been termed the *family life cycle*.[37] Today, frequent reference is made to the term life course in dealing with changes and differences over time.

The most systematic, widespread, and long-term use of the family lifecycle idea has been provided by Evelyn Duvall, who attempted to provide a link between *lifecycle stages*[38] and the *developmental-task concept*.[39] A **developmental task** is one that arises at or about a certain period in the life of an individual. Successful

---

[36]David H. Olson, Candyce S. Russell, and Douglas H. Sprenkle, *Circumplex Model: Systematic Assessment and Treatment of Families* (Binghamton, New York: Haworth Press, 1989).

[37]For a discussion and empirical evaluation of this concept, see Paul C. Glick, "The Family Life Cycle and Social Change," *Family Relations* 38 (April 1989): 123–129; Graham B. Spanier and Paul C. Glick, "The Life Cycle of American Families: An Expanded Analysis," *Journal of Family History* 5 (Spring 1980): 97–111; and Joan Aldous, "Family Development and the Life Course: Two Perspectives on Family Change," *Journal of Marriage and the Family* 52 (August 1990): 571–583.

[38]See, for example, Gunhild O. Hagestad, "Demographic Change and the Life Course: Some Emerging Trends in the Family Realm," *Family Relations* 37 (October 1988): 405–410; and Tamara K. Hareven and Kanji Masaoka, "Turning Points and Transitions: Perceptions of the Life Course," *Journal of Family History* 13 (1988): 271–289.

[39]Evelyn M. Duvall and Brent C. Miller, *Marriage and Family Development*, 6th ed. (New York: Harper and Row, 1985), Chapter 3.

achievement of the task leads to individual happiness, social approval, and success with later tasks, whereas failure leads to unhappiness, disapproval, and later difficulties. Developmental tasks have two primary origins: physical maturation and cultural pressures and privileges.[40] The developmental tasks an individual faces over a lifetime are innumerable. Many of them are delineated in human development textbooks.

The developmental theory contends that, like individuals, families also face tasks at given stages in the family lifecycle. A family's developmental task is "a growth responsibility that arises at a certain stage in the life of a family, the successful achievement of which leads to present satisfaction, approval and success with later tasks whereas failure leads to unhappiness in the family, disapproval by society, and difficulty with later family developmental tasks."[41] For a family to continue to grow as a unit, it needs to satisfy, at a given stage: (1) biological requirements, (2) cultural imperatives, and (3) personal aspirations and values.

Duvall[42] recognized and depicted the **family lifecycle** as consisting of eight stages:

Stage 1 Married couples (without children)
Stage 2 Childbearing families (oldest child, birth–30 months)
Stage 3 Families with preschool children (oldest child, $2\frac{1}{2}$–6 years)
Stage 4 Families with schoolchildren (oldest child, 6–13 years)
Stage 5 Families with teenagers (oldest child, 13–20 years)
Stage 6 Families as launching centers (first child gone to last child leaving home)
Stage 7 Middle-aged parents ("empty nest" to retirement)
Stage 8 Aging family members (retirement to death of both spouses)

These stages are determined by the age and school placement of the oldest child up to the launching stage (6), after which the situation facing those remaining in the original family is the determinant. This type of scheme explicitly fails to recognize multiple-child families, overlapping stages, the death of a spouse, and many other variations in families including those of ethnically and racially diverse populations.[43] Nevertheless, it is an informative theory insofar as it highlights sources of change in families that come about due to the internal developmental changes experienced by family members, time dependent social processes (such as impacts on expectations over time based on previous levels of rewards received or satisfactions experienced in a relationship), and predictable changes in life conditions based on the way that the life course is structured in different societies. [44]

---

[40]Ibid., 47.

[41]Ibid., 61.

[42]Ibid., 26.

[43]Peggye Dilworth-Anderson and Linda M. Burton, "Rethinking Family Development: Critical Conceptual Issues in the Study of Diverse Groups," *Journal of Social and Personal Relationships* 13 (August 1996): 325–334.

[44]For information on the developmental approach from the perspective of the family, see James M. White, *Dynamics of Family Development, A Theoretical Perspective* (New York: The Guilford Press, 1991); Roy H. Rodgers, *Family Interaction and Transaction: The Developmental Approach* (Englewood Cliffs, NJ: Prentice-Hall, 1973); and Chester A. Winton, *Frameworks for Studying Families* (Guilford, CT: Dushkin Publishing Group, Inc., 1995), Chapter 1, 9–43.

Alternative Perspectives

Over the course of the past several decades, a reaction has taken place in sociology and other disciplines (across the social sciences, humanities, and arts) against the structures of knowledge that have been generated by the application of the modern principles of rationality and science. These perspectives are not so much alternative theoretical frames of reference for constructing causal models of reality as they are paradigms for challenging biases and inequalities structured into the very theories that science produces. As such, they challenge the very foundations of knowledge and offer an alternative methodology for "knowing" to that offered by the scientific method. Two of these paradigms—*postmodernism* and *feminism*—are discussed next.

Postmodernism

Postmodernism is a difficult perspective to articulate because it assumes many different forms in social thought and artistic expression. The important characteristics of this perspective from our standpoint as sociologists, however, are found in its rejection of rationality and science as the foundation for knowledge. Postmodernists see scientific knowledge (and theories) as simply grand narratives that have been socially constructed to give meaning to a diversity of individual human experiences.[45] In contrast to positivism, they do not accept the idea that there is a reality that can be known through observation and the testing of logically derived hypotheses. The **grand narratives** of science have as much validity as any other "story" that we might construct to explain the events in our lives. Furthermore, they point out that grand narratives are shaped by power in society and are a source of dominance for one group over another[46] insofar as they provide an interpretive framework for our experiences that serves the interests of the groups that shape them.

The construction of grand narratives, then, assumes a place of priority over individual narratives or the narratives of minority groups in society. Thus, all we can do as sociologists of the family is to uncover how dominant socially constructed narratives (be they scientific ones or nonscientific ones) shape our understandings of the relationships between individuals and social groups and then bring to light the narratives of other individuals and groups (e.g., women, racial minorities, etc.) and elevate their status to scientific theories and other dominant narratives. This methodology could be called "critical" in that it does not seek to uncover truth or reality but instead seeks to challenge existing interpretations of reality, with a special concern for looking at how power relations are structured in those narratives. There is also a heavy emphasis in this approach on the interpretive analysis of cultural representations (e.g., popular press literature, art forms, architecture, etc.) and individual lived experiences and interpretations of those experiences.

---

[45]Jean Francoise Lyotard, *The Postmodern Condition: A Report on Knowledge*, translated by Geoffrey Bennington and Brian Massumi (Minneapolis, MN: University of Minnesota Press, 1984).

[46]Michel Foucault, *Power/Knowledge: Selected Interviews and Other Writings*, 1972–1977, edited by Colin Gordon (London: Harvester, 1980).

A central concept of postmodernism is *reflexivity*. Unlike previous historical periods in which knowledge was either a natural given or the product of scientific investigation, postmodernists see knowledge as a project of lived experiences, in which we examine our own behaviors and attempt to fit them into an interpretive framework. This **reflexivity** is reflected in the very nature of the postindustrial/late modern/postmodern society that spawned this perspective. In contemporary U.S. and Western European societies, we reflect on our experiences and construct reality accordingly. As a reflexive society, then, we become responsible for constructing the very meaning of our existence. These meanings cannot be found in any objective sense in our positions in a social structure (as would be the case in structure-functionalism, conflict theory, and social exchange theory) or even in the emergent nature of our interactions with others (as is the case in symbolic interactionism).

Feminism

Like postmodernism, **feminism** is more of a paradigm for knowledge than a theoretical frame of reference organized around a uniform set of assumptions and interrelated concepts. A variety of feminist theories and perspectives exists,[47] but they all assert that gender is basic to all social structures and organizations. The impetus for those working in this paradigm is a simple question: And what about women?[48] Answers to this question are based on ideas that the experiences of women are different from those of men, are unequal (less privileged) to those of men, and that women are actively oppressed (restrained, subordinated, used, and abused) by men.

Related to these ideas are basic assumptions of feminist thought, as discussed in an article in a special issue of *Family Relations* on feminism and family studies:

1. Women—or any group defined on the basis of age, class, race, ethnicity, disability, or sexual preference—are oppressed.
2. The personal is political. In other words, nothing is exclusive to women's personal lives; everything has social ramifications. The social system imposes a reality on everyday life and is not separate from it. Social structure must be taken into account.
3. Feminists have a double vision of reality: they need to be successful in the current system while working to change oppressive practices and institutions.[49]

---

[47]Marie Withers Osmond and Barrie Thorne, "Feminist Theories: The Social Construction of Gender in Families and Society," in Pauline G. Boss, William J. Doherty, Ralph LaRossa, Walter R. Schumm, and Suzanne K. Steinmetz, *Sourcebook of Family Theories and Methods: A Contextual Approach* (New York: Plenum Press, 1993), Chapter 23, 591–621.

[48]Patricia Madoo Lengermann and Jill Niebrugge-Brantley, "Contemporary Feminist Theory," in George Ritzer, *Contemporary Sociological Theory* (New York: Alfred A. Knopf, 1988), 282–325.

[49]Alexis J. Walker, Sally S. Kees Martin, and Linda Thompson, "Feminist Programs for Families," *Family Relations* 37 (January 1988): 17–22. See also Katherine R. Allen and Kristine M. Baber, "Starting a Revolution in Family Life Education: A Feminist Vision," *Family Relations* 41 (October 1992): 378–384; and Linda Thompson and Alexis J. Walker, "The Place of Feminism in Family Studies," *Journal of Marriage and the Family* 57 (November 1995): 847–865.

Family Diversity

A Phenomenological Analysis of Female Sexuality

Phenomenological approaches seem highly appropriate for understanding how people construct their own reality. They often are used to examine meanings and experiences about which little is known or that are fraught with erroneous assumptions and misinformation. Thus, Judith Daniluk, writing in the *Psychology of Women Quarterly* (1993: 53–69) revealed how she interviewed women in a group setting for two to three hours once a week for eleven weeks to determine how they experience their sexuality and what meanings they associate with these experiences.

All the women struggled with the reality that to be female, as defined in our culture, is to be unworthy, flawed, and somehow deficient. Four primary contextual sources were identified as highly disenabling in defining and constructing their experiences of their sexuality. These included the influence of medicine, religion, sexual violence, and the media.

The experience of these women with *medicine* and medical professionals was one of having their power and dignity undermined, resulting in feelings of anger, loss, and helplessness. Normal female functions were pathological and the women felt blamed for their illnesses. Their experience with *religion* was

one of making them feel guilty. Religious conceptions of the female body and bodily processes left the women feeling dirty and shameful: punishment was viewed as God's response to female sexual desire and expression.

The women's experience with *sexual violence* in the form of rape, incest, verbal abuse, and sexual harassment resulted in all participants feeling victimized. Male ownership and prerogative were perceived as the guiding principle in a society that seems to discount women's needs for and right to safety. Fear—combined with feelings of betrayal, anger, violation, and self-blame—characterized many of their memories. The *media* was a more subtle but pervasive source of influence in the women's experience of their sexuality. Television, music, movies, magazines, and videos all represented unrealistic standards of beauty and behavior.

In spite of these themes of cultural oppression, the women were able to access positive life- and self-affirming experiences. Areas of central importance to women for experiencing their sexuality included sexual expression, reproduction, body image, and intimate relationships. Rather than de-emphasizing differences between men and women, the perceived road to sexual self-esteem was viewed as a celebration of differences and the experiences unique to women.

Myra Marx Ferree[50] challenged family studies to rethink two notions: (1) that families can be understood separately from the economic, political, and other systems of male power and (2) that families are unitary wholes in which conflicts of interest between men and women are disregarded. The first notion questions the separateness between public and private, where fundamentally different social relations exist in families more than in the rest of society. This idea supports the false notion that the family is a private world, in which women take center stage, appear to have unlimited power, and are held responsible for everything—from the quality of the marital relationship to the mental health of the children and even to the prevention of male violence.

---

[50]Myra Marx Ferree, "Beyond Separate Spheres: Feminism and Family Research," *Journal of Marriage and the Family* 52 (November 1990): 866–884. See also Greer Litton Fox and Velma McBride Murry, "Gender and Families: Feminist Perspectives and Family Research," *Journal of Marriage and the Family* 62 (November 2000): 1160–1172.

Feminist theory notes that women are not merely different from men but are less privileged and subordinated to them. The source of change in women's status in families may lie in the larger women's movement to change structures of inequality outside the family.

The second notion questions the solidarity myth, according to which the family is a unitary whole in which everyone shares a standard of living, class position, and set of interests. The reality is that conflicts of interest exist by gender, and feminist thought recognizes this. In the words of Ferree, the feminist perspective "redefines families as arenas of gender and generational struggles, crucibles of caring and conflict, where claims for an identity are rooted, and separateness and solidarity are continually created and contested."[51]

Feminist theorists, while not denying the economic inequalities argued by Marxian theorists, do not blame all male–female inequalities on economic systems. Some feminists have substituted the word *patriarchy* for *bourgeoisie* and even for *sex roles*. Sex roles, with their theme of different but equal tasks and power, downplay the structured inequality (male dominance) that is pervasive. Male dominance exists in its own right and cuts across all economic and class lines. In addition, male dominance implies oppression of females and sexism. The source of this oppression and sexism is in the home, where women, employed or not, find that housework and home are part of the same system. Until women increase their independence from men and gain resources (power, money, education, job opportunities, etc.) that improve their status, the family will never be an egalitarian institution.

Appraisal and Expansion of Contemporary Family Theory

The reader should not think the scientific and nonscientific perspectives presented here are the only frames of reference in family sociology. Udry, Booth, and others, for example, suggest that parenthood, gendered behavior, sexual development, courtship and mate selection, marital status and marital conflict, health, occupation choice, and other behaviors will be increasingly influenced by biological choice: a biosocial theory.[52]

The turn of the century may be a time of theoretical synthesis: an integration of macro and micro ideas, a joining of structural and exchange theories into a network theory, or a blurring of distinct theoretical boundary lines, as theories borrow heavily from one another and new or revived ideas come to the fore.

What ideas? Notions of rationality are once again challenged. Humanists are pressing for the involvement of social scientists in efforts toward achieving social

---

[51]Ibid., 880.

[52]J. Richard Udry, "Biosocial Models of Low-Fertility Societies," *Population and Development Review* 22 (1996): 325–336; and Alan Booth, Karen Carver, and Douglas A. Granger, "Biosocial Perspectives in the Family," *Journal of Marriage and the Family* 62 (November 2000): 1018–1034.

justice and improving social conditions. Many critical and feminist scholars have no desire to subject their theories and ideas to the positivistic (recognizing only matters of proof and fact) principles of science.

Katherine Allen and others argue that family scholars must take bolder steps to engage the tensions between our heritage of positivist science and its postmodern challenges. They argue that our theories, methods, and substantive issues need to be relevant to the diversity of families we study. Our subjective experiences need to be acknowledged. And we need to recognize the critical intersections of race, class, gender, sexual orientation, and age in defining and dealing with family diversity. [53]

---

[53]For a discussion of alternative postmodern perspectives on families, see Vern L. Bengtson, Alan C. Acock, Katherine R. Allen, Peggye Dilworth-Anderson, and David M. Klein, eds., *Sourcebook of Family Theory & Research* (Thousand Oaks, CA: Sage Publications, 2005), Chapters 1, 6 and 18.

Summary

1. A wide range of disciplines, approaches, and selected frames of reference is used in the study of the family. The marriage and family area is highly interdisciplinary; no single discipline either asks all the questions or provides all the answers. This book uses a social science orientation with a major concentration focused on a sociology of the family.

2. Of what use is a sociology of the family? It alerts one to question the obvious and assess individual behavior in the context of the larger society. It enables one to obtain a body of knowledge about persons, relationships, and family structures. It assists one in applying this body of knowledge to work with persons and families. It can be very useful on a personal level in improving critical thinking and problem-solving skills, interpersonal skills, and communication skills. And, finally, family sociology should help people understand themselves and the social context in which they live.

3. The scientific approach is one means for evaluating knowledge about reality that is widely accepted in modern societies. This approach assumes there is a reality that can be known and is based on the principle of positivism, which holds that all knowledge must be tested by evaluating predictions based on empirical observations. The scientific approach asserts that all knowledge is tentative and subject to further testing.

4. The scientific process involves a continuous circle of exploration and testing of new explanations for phenomena. The goal is to construct theories that are clear, well articulated, logically consistent, abstract, generalizable, and in agreement with observed realities.

5. Scientific theories consist of a set of assumptions that are statements about the basic nature of reality and that tell us what aspects of reality to focus our attention and explanations on. Based on these assumptions, each theory develops a set of concepts that can be used to classify aspects of that reality consistent with the assumptions. Finally, the explanation for why things happen can be found in the propositions that link the concepts of the theory in a set of interrelated causal processes.

6. An understanding of how social scientists conduct their studies to test theories is critical to the confidence we have in those studies. Two major designs are used in the social sciences—experiments and surveys—and four major methodological concerns that any consumer of social science information needs to consider are sample selection (representativeness and generalizability), measurement (reliability and validity), causal validity (causal ordering and spuriousness), and ecological validity. Although experiments yield the most unequivocal results about causal relationships, they are weak in terms of representativeness, generalizability, and ecological validity.

7. In addition to how studies are done, a consumer needs to also be aware of some basic statistical concepts—especially correlation—and other strength of relationship statistics and inferential statistics (issues of statistical significance).

8. One of the most dominant theories or frames of reference in sociology is the structural-functional theory. This frame of reference uses the social system as the basic autonomous unit of which the family is a

subsystem. All systems have interdependent parts (structures) that do certain things for the individual or society and have various social consequences (functions). The basic task of functional analysis is to explain the parts, the relationship among the parts and the whole, and the functions performed by or that result from the relationship formed by the parts. Some important concepts in this perspective are manifest and latent function and the idea of functional equivalence.

9. A second frame of reference is social conflict. Two significant issues in this perspective are the view of conflict (a) as natural and inevitable and (b) as a major factor that can lead to social change. Conflict theory is particularly applicable to a further understanding of marital relationships, power, the division of labor, and conflict but sees these relationship dynamics as the product of societal forces rather than individual characteristics or motivations. Conflict theory can be used to study more than just conflict. It also helps us understand the absence of expressed conflict in relationships.

10. The symbolic interaction frame of reference addresses two basic issues, both of central concern to the family: socialization and social interaction. The basic premises of this approach are (a) that human beings act toward things on the basis of the meanings things have for them, (b) that these meanings are derived from interaction with others, and (c) that these meanings are modified through an interpretive process. Each human being is unique unto himself or herself, understood only in his or her social context, is neither inherently good nor bad, and responds to self-stimulating or symbolically interpreted stimuli. The concept of the self is essential to understanding the behaviors of individuals.

11. The social exchange framework helps explain why certain behavioral outcomes occur, given a set of structural conditions and interactional potentialities. Two different approaches to social exchange were examined in this chapter: one consistent with a behavioral frame of reference and the other with an interactionist frame of reference. Although the central assumption of this perspective is that humans are rational hedonists, it doesn't mean that we always try to maximize our immediate rewards in interaction with others. Often, we sacrifice for others as a strategy to maximize long-term rewards or to reciprocate rewards given to us in the past.

12. The family systems frame of reference is similar to the macro perspectives in that it sees the family as a holistic unit that requires a consideration of its context and organizational needs. Unlike the macro perspectives, however, this perspective also sees family organization as shaped by the individual characteristics, actions, and preferences of its members.

13. The developmental frame of reference has the peculiar characteristic of attempting to account for change in the family system and change in patterns of interaction over time with the use of concepts such as the family lifecycle and family life course.

14. Both the postmodern and the feminist frames of reference challenge existing scientific knowledge about the family. They argue that even science contains a potential for value bias in the interpretation of observations and in the types of stories created to make sense of those observations. In particular, a feminist frame of reference recognizes that the experiences of women are different, unequal, and oppressed as compared to those of men. Families cannot be understood apart from other systems of male power, nor are families unitary wholes in which conflicts of interest between men and women can be disregarded.

Now that important methodological issues and cautions have been addressed and the major theoretical perspectives reviewed, the remainder of the text will examine the empirical literature on various aspects of contemporary families. As we do so, we will refer many times to the theories and concepts discussed in this chapter. The next three chapters look at the nature and circumstances of family life across different social class, racial, and ethnic groups.

Key Terms and Topics

Disciplines involved in family study p. 97	Exploratory research p. 102
Psychology p. 99	Induction p. 102
Sociology p. 99	Explanatory research p. 102
Scientific approach p. 101	Deduction p. 102
Positivism p. 101	Theories p. 104

Discussion Questions

1. Because no one discipline has all the answers to any family-related question, why isn't all research of an interdisciplinary nature? What problems exist in interdisciplinary research?

2. Of what value is a social science approach to the family? Within the social sciences, compare and contrast how psychology, social psychology, social

anthropology, and sociology approach the family as an area of study.

3. Differentiate between terms in the following pairs: concepts and variables, hypotheses and propositions, and conceptual frameworks and theories.

4. Discuss the major functions of the family in the United States. How are these different from the functions of families thirty years ago? What functions will the family likely perform thirty years from now?

5. Is conflict natural and inevitable in all marriages and families? Is conflict essential for change? Explain.

6. What types of assumptions and issues are basic to a symbolic interaction frame of reference? What difference does it make to assume that humans must be studied on their own levels, that the human infant is asocial, and the like? Relate these ideas to marriage and the family.

7. Write a paragraph on "Who I am." Begin by listing the statuses you occupy. Take this list of statuses, and write one or two social expectations appropriate to each status. After reflection, write about the following: Which role expectations do you personally find displeasing? Are there conflicts between different expectations or between your personal preferences and social expectations? How do you handle them?

8. What exchanges can you identify in explaining male–female sexual behaviors, husband–wife spending patterns, and parent–child disciplinary behaviors? What is given and received in each exchange? Can you think of examples in which no reciprocity is expected or given in return for a favor or gift? If so, what are they?

9. Identify which stage of the family lifecycle your family is currently in (either you and your parents and siblings or you and your spouse and/or children). Identify the central problems, concerns, and tasks of a family at this particular stage.

10. Describe some basic assumptions of the feminist perspective. What contributions does this approach make to family studies and how people think about families?

Further Readings

Bengston, Vern L., Acock, Alan C., Allen, Katherine, Dilworth-Anderson, Peggye, and Klein, David. *Sourcebook of Family Theory and Research*. Thousand Oaks, CA: Sage, 2005.

A discussion of the state of theoretical and methodological development in different areas of marriage and family studies with case studies illustrating the use of theory and methods in each area.

Boss, Pauline G., Doherty, William J., LaRossa, Ralph, Schumm, Walter R., and Steinmetz, Suzanne K. *Sourcebook of Family Theories and Methods: A Contextual Approach*. New York: Plenum Press, 1993.

A sociohistorical contextual approach to family theories, tracing their origins, assumptions, major concepts, research examples, and applications to families.

Carter, Betty, and McGoldrick, Monica, eds. *The Expanded Family Life Cycle: Individual, Family, and Social Perspectives*. 3rd ed. Boston: Allyn and Bacon, 1999.

An extensive overview of a wide range of individual, family, and social issues as related to the family life course. Examples of nine major theories applied to formulate and test empirical research questions. Includes perspectives from human development.

Chibucos, Thomas R., Leite, Randall W. and Weis, David L., eds. *Readings in Family Theory*. Thgousand Oaks, CA: Sage Publications, 2004

An anthology of classic and contemporary articles demonstrating the application of contemporary theories in the study of the family today.

Coltrane, Scott, and Collins, Randall. *Sociology of Marriage and the Family; Gender, Love, and Property*. 5th ed. Belmont, CA: Wadsworth/Thomson Learning, 2001.

A sociology text that incorporates conflict and feminist perspectives into family issues and studies.

Evans, Judith. *Feminist Theory Today*. Thousand Oaks, CA: Sage Publications, 1995.

An examination of "schools" of feminist theory since the mid-1960s and some of the problems within them.

Fine, Robert. *Cosmopolitanism*. New York, NY: Routledge, 2007.

A summary and discussion of the emerging theoretical paradigm of cosmopolitanism, a paradigm that attempts to reframe the study of social institutions as resulting from forces that transcend national boundaries.

Greenstein, Theodore N. *Methods of Family Research*. Thousand Oaks, CA: Sage Publications, 2001.

A readable and concise treatment of the research process with a focus on a wide range of methodological issues in studying families.

Sussman, Marvin B., Steinmetz, Suzanne K., and Peterson, Gary W., eds. *Handbook of Marriage and the Family*. 2nd ed. New York: Plenum Press, 1999.

A second edition of the handbook covering theories and methods, family diversity, and family linkages with other institutions.

White, James M. and Klein, David M. *Family Theories*, 2nd edition. Thousand Oaks, California, Sage Publications, 2002.

Seven theoretical frameworks from the perspectives of sociology and family studies are presented: exchange, symbolic interaction, family development, systems, conflict, ecological, and feminism.

part II

Sociocultural Contexts and the Diversity of Families in the United States

4

Social Class Variations

Survival on Public Assistance

Dal is a 30-year-old single mother of four children between the ages of 6 and 12. She has been off and on welfare several times since age 18 but has been on steadily for the past five years. She was married for several of those years, but her husband got involved in drugs and was not financially or emotionally responsible to her or the children.

According to Dal, public assistance is providing the help she needs to raise her children and serves as a stepping-stone for her to eventually become financially able to manage on her own. As she said: "Finances have always been a problem, but thanks to welfare we have been always able to have a home, food, and clothes. I know that I am poor but seldom feel totally helpless. I am able to get the things the children really need, and I don't believe they feel they are worse off than others. While the amount we get has increased, it typically has been about $600 a month. Of that, $325 goes for rent, $60 for electric and gas, and I have about $200 after those expenses are taken out. This I use for transportation to a part-time job, phone, some child care, and household items like cleaning stuff. We also get medical coverage for the children and about $340 in food stamps, which gets reduced if I earn too much. I can understand why, but it does upset me because it takes away any incentive for me to work more. But I feel good knowing I earn money and gain work experience I can use.

"Thanks to the help I get from my aunt, grandmother, mother, and an elderly church friend, I've been able to do a lot better than most. They would help sometimes with money, transportation, or with the children. My friend from church was, and is, especially important in providing emotional support and encouraging me when I am ready to give up. We pray together a lot. It is because of her that I hope to complete my degree in social work and go into gerontology.

"I really appreciate the assistance I've been given. I believe mothers should be encouraged to work but they must be given the tools to accomplish it. If cuts are made and more programs are eliminated, a lot of people, myself included, will never be able to go to school or get out of poverty."

Questions to Consider

Politicians in the late 1990s took great pride in announcing how much the welfare rolls had been reduced. How do you think Dal's life, and opportunities for school and for her children, would be different had she not been able to receive public assistance?

Dal indicated that her food stamp allotment is reduced if she earns "too much." What are the arguments for and against this policy?

*P*erhaps the most pervasive influence on peoples' lives in a modern industrial society is their location or position in the social class system. Simply put, social class refers to a system of unequal distribution of wealth, prestige, and power based on one's position in a system of economic production. What people believe and value, what lifestyles they live, what environmental challenges they need to face, and what resources they possess to meet those challenges all are shaped by whether or not they own and control the system of production versus supply their labor in exchange for wages; and, if the latter, by the nature of the work they do and the compensation they are able to demand in exchange for their labor. In this chapter, we will examine the meanings and consequences of social class: what it is, how it is determined, and how families who comprise general class categories experience and express differing lifestyles. The chapter will end with a discussion of family mobility—changing lifestyles by moving from one class category to another.

Meaning of Social Class

Sociologists have long been concerned with the question of how and why inequalities arise in societies and how those inequalities affect the lives of individuals and the organization of social institutions. Inequalities in opportunity, wealth, prestige, and power can be found in all societies to some degree. To the extent that these inequalities are determined based on some systematic process and integrated into the organization or structure of institutions, sociologists refer to them as a system of *social stratification*. Thus, **social stratification** is defined as a ranking of persons and groups in a hierarchy of unequal social positions. Similar to the use of the term stratification in geology, it refers to an arrangement of different strata or layers where those occupying the same strata or layer possess many of the same fundamental characteristics and those in different layers possess different characteristics. In geology, the different strata are determined by forces in the physical environment such as climate change, volcanic activity, erosion, glacial movements, etc. In sociology, the strata are determined by social forces such as political might, religious influence and economic activity.

Two of the theories described in the previous chapter, the *structural-functional* and the *conflict* theories, are particularly relevant to understanding the stratification system. A **structural-functional perspective** views stratification as both an inevitable and a necessary feature of society. The assumption is that all societies have a wide range of tasks that need to be performed. These tasks are essential for the stability and maintenance of that society but carry different levels of prestige and rewards. Some individuals must collect garbage, repair plumbing, and assemble automobiles while others must teach students, plan defense strategies, and perform heart surgery. Those tasks that require greater levels of skill and training, that require more dedication and motivation to perform, and that are more important to the functioning of the society are likely to be more highly rewarded. This unequal distribution of social rewards is defined as *functional* for society because it enables all roles and tasks to be completed, with those that demand the most scarce talents performed by the most able and skilled persons.

For many years, this structural-functional perspective was predominant among sociologists. However, other people have questioned why some families are highly rewarded with inherited fortunes when they perform little of value to society; why film stars and athletes earn millions each year for doing work that is viewed as less important than that done by social workers, scientists, and even the president of the United States; and why poor families live in poverty from one generation to the next. Sociologists have also raised value-oriented questions about the justice of unequal rewards and the fairness of assignment by birth of certain groups to positions of low prestige, wealth, and power. An awareness of these and other inequities among persons and families led conflict theorists to reject the structural-functional view of a stratified society.

Conflict theorists believe a stratified society leads to dissatisfaction, alienation, and exploitation, not stability and order. From this perspective, the origins of social inequality and stratification can be found in previous and ongoing struggles between broad classifications of people in society who share similar interests, values, beliefs, and lifestyles—**interest groups**. These groups could be defined based on age, gender, race, ethnicity, religious orientation, family or kinship affiliation, or other shared characteristics. As economic, political, and other environmental conditions of life change, different interest groups gain or lose advantage in the struggle to advance their own interests usually at the expense or gain of opposing interest groups. Once an advantage is gained, social institutions and cultural belief systems (ideologies) are restructured to enhance and maintain the group advantage. Most importantly, wealth, prestige, and power are redistributed unequally based on group membership and levels of support for the group's interests. Thus, systems of inequality are not necessary for societal functioning and can be changed through political, economic, and other forces.

Prior to the emergence of modern industrial capitalistic societies, systems of stratification were based on political and religious forces. In a **social caste** system, the remnants of which still exists to some degree in India today, one's position in the system is determined at birth based on family connections. Such systems can be found in agricultural societies where property ownership, economic production, and political power is concentrated in families and where religious beliefs have arisen to support and legitimate an unequal distribution of wealth, prestige, and power based on family inheritance. Since the single determinant of one's position in the system of stratification is one's family of orientation, there is no possibility of movement from one caste position to another either across generations or within a single generation. In sociological terms, social caste systems provide no opportunities for *social mobility*. A closely related system of stratification found in feudal systems is called an **estate system**. Like the caste system, the estate system is also based on family connections but with some opportunities for social mobility, primarily through an intermediate estate between land owners and nonowners—the clergy.

The political, religious, and economic foundations of caste and estate systems are undermined with the emergence of a system of industrial production and a modern capitalistic economic system where ownership and economic rewards are based on the ability to produce profit rather than on family connections. As Karl Marx has shown in his historical analysis of economic systems, the modern capitalistic system contains two inherent and diametrically opposing interest groups or **social classes**: those who own the means of production (*the bourgeoisie class*) and those whose labor constitutes the means of production (*the proletariat class*). Since owners can only maintain their position by producing greater profit in a system of open market competition with other owners and profit depends on reducing the costs of production, which is found primarily in the costs of labor, one group's gain requires the other group's loss. This inherent conflict in economic relations then reverberates throughout the social system and can be seen in differences in cultural beliefs and values, lifestyle preferences, environmental conditions of life, and the organization of social institutions such as government, families, legal and criminal justice systems, education, health care, and so on.

Since Karl Marx first developed his theory of class conflict, other conflict theorists have modified and expanded our understandings of social stratification processes in modern industrial capitalistic societies. For example, Max Weber has argued that economic competition is only one dimension of conflict and that other interest groupings of individuals need to be considered. Thus, conflicts between groups defined by shared characteristics, such as race, ethnicity, religion, and gender, need to be considered in understanding social inequalities. Whether or not class differences will eventually overpower these other group differences, as Marx suggests, remains an open question. Therefore, we will focus on social class effects on family life in this chapter and deal with other group inequalities in other chapters.

Determination of Social Class

From a Marxist perspective, social class is determined by examining who manages, oppresses, and controls in contrast to those who are managed, oppressed, and controlled. Some have suggested, however, that such a view is too simplistic and may not reflect how capitalism has evolved since Marx first proposed his thesis. In particular, the emergence of a modern stock market has seemed to blur the lines of ownership of companies and given rise to a new "managerial" class.[1] In addition, the highly differentiated nature of the modern industrial system has given rise to a multitude of intermediary positions (e.g., professionals, craftsmen, clerical workers, manual laborers, service workers, farmers, etc.) that are unequally rewarded and

---

[1]For a discussion of changing views of social class boundaries see Michael Gilding, "Families and Fortunes: Accumulation, Management Succession and Inheritance in Wealthy Families," *Journal of Sociology* 41 (2005): 29–45.

that constitute unique interest groups in their own right.[2] Thus, in advanced capitalistic societies there are manual workers with substantial investments in the ownership of corporations through stock shares and there are professionals who may have no ownership interests in corporations yet are distinct from manual workers in their economic and cultural interests. These developments are not to say that social classes no longer exist. Rather, they caution us to be aware of over-generalizing the effects of social class based on ownership position, relying on ownership as a marker of social class, and assuming that the conditions of life within social class groupings are uniform.

The studies of Middletown (Muncie, Indiana), which are among the most famous community studies in sociology, used two classes: the business class and the working class.[3] Most people think in terms of three classes: upper, middle, and lower. The classic work by August Hollingshead, entitled *Elmtown's Youth*, subdivided the community into five classes: upper, upper middle, lower middle, upper lower, and lower lower.[4] Given the greater complexity of social class systems in modern capitalistic societies, however, sociologists have moved away from simplistic categorization of class position such as upper class, middle class, working class, and so on. Instead, the focus in recent decades has been on measuring and assessing the effects of *socioeconomic status* (SES) on individuals' lives and families. **Socioeconomic status** is a classification of one's position in a modern system of inequality based on levels of education, occupational prestige, and income. These three characteristics are significant in modern industrial societies insofar as they shape one's values and beliefs, environmental context, and opportunities in life. Sometimes their effects are considered together as a single construct and other times they are considered as individual and unique influences on social outcomes. Finally, in the context of family studies, the increased involvement of women in the workforce has added yet another degree of complexity to the understanding of social class effects as the independent statuses of a husband/father and wife/mother may be unique, cumulative, or counteracting.

In the sections that follow, we will examine the impacts of social class on family life by organizing the discussion based on three broad groupings: **wealthy families**, **working families**, and families in poverty. Although we recognize that many "wealthy" families consist of actively employed members, life in these families is primarily organized by their position in the system of ownership in society. The modern stock market, as noted above, has allowed more individuals from other class groups to participate in ownership, but there still remains a network of individuals and families who control the majority of shares in modern corporations and much of their economic activity and interest is centered in family life.[5] The working classes have become more diversified in their interests, but this has been less the case among the ownership class. In contrast, "working" families have greater diversity often based on the levels of education they possess, their occupational involvements, and their income. As a result, we will focus

[2]See David B. Grusky, "Social Stratification," in Edgar F. Borgatta and Rhonda J. V. Montgomery (eds.), *Encyclopedia of Sociology*, 2nd edition (NY: Macmillan Reference USA, 2000): 2807–2821.

[3]Robert S. Lynd and Helen Merrell Lynd, *Middletown* (New York: Harcourt, Brace and World, 1939); Robert S. Lynd and Helen Merrell Lynd, *Middletown in Transition* (New York: Harcourt, Brace and World, 1937); and Theodore Caplow et al., *Middletown Families* (New York: Bantam Books, 1982).

[4]August B. Hollingshead, *Elmtown's Youth* (New York: Wiley, 1949).

[5]Michael Gilding, "Families and Fortunes: Accumulation, Management Succession and Inheritance in Wealthy Families," *Journal of Sociology* 41 (2005): 29–45.

more on these independent socioeconomic status effects when discussing these families. Finally, families in poverty face unique circumstances in life shaped primarily by their struggle to survive in the face of inadequate resources and opportunities. Knowing how these conditions shape their survival strategies is important to understanding their family lives and finding ways to help them more effectively.

Consequences of Socioeconomic Status to Families

The significance of socioeconomic status stems from some of its consequences. In addition to influencing one's chances to live (including the likelihood of being born in the first place), to live through the first year, to not die prematurely, and to reach retirement age, socioeconomic status influences one's early socialization, role expectations and role projections, values, standards of appropriate behavior, and likelihood of mental illness. In addition, it affects educational opportunities (type of education available, the motivation to get it, the likelihood of doing so) and outcomes (the ends for which education is meant). Dropout rates, scores on intelligence tests, grades, occupational/vocational aspirations, and almost all other factors related to education are also related to socioeconomic status. Most significantly, socioeconomic status both determines and results in important differences in influence, power, and opportunities.

Similar consequences of status hold true for marriages and families. Position in the socioeconomic status hierarchy affects the age at which one is likely to marry, the success of that marriage, the meanings attached to sexual behavior, the size of family, the recreation engaged in, the type of food eaten, the discipline and care given to children, sleeping arrangements, and contraceptive use. Regardless of race, ethnicity, or gender, differences in behaviors are evident at varying status levels. In fact, Hughes and Perry-Jenkins document important status differences in family processes and interactions that have been overlooked in family life education programs and, thus, decrease their effectiveness.[6]

The reasons why socioeconomic status has these effects can be found in three broad categories of factors: cultural beliefs and values; environmental or ecological contexts; and the availability of economic, human, social and cultural capital to realize goals and adapt to social contexts. Because of the group interests involved, one's status position will lead individuals and families to endorse certain beliefs and values that support and protect those interests. Although it is important to recognize that a single status group will have a diversity of beliefs and values, it is still possible to recognize overarching frameworks within which those differences play out.[7] For example, those from a long line of wealthy families may not share exactly the same set of values as those who have more recently joined their elevated social group when it comes to policies for helping people in need, yet both groups will likely endorse the values of individual responsibility, competition, and protecting the integrity of private ownership of property in the solutions they endorse.

What Marx called the *material conditions* of life play an important role in shaping our beliefs and values. These include even our notions of what constitutes a family. Bettina Becker and Nickie Charles show how individuals from different

---

[6]Robert Hughes, Jr. and Maureen Perry-Jenkins, "Social Class Issues in Family Life Education," *Family Relations* 45 (April 1996): 175–182.

[7]David B. Grusky, "Social Stratification," 2807–2821.

TRANSNATIONAL FAMILIES

Social Class and Family among the Indian Diaspora in New York

New York City contains a large population of immigrants from India as a result of two waves of immigration—one in 1965 and the other in 1990. As a result of these two waves of immigrants and the conditions they faced upon arrival, strong Indian communities were established within the city. These communities allowed their residents to maintain their cultural practices, cohesiveness, and identity in the face of what often was a hostile environment to newcomers. Maintaining their ethnic identity also was made possible by advances in information technology and transportation that allowed them to maintain ongoing contact and economic interdependence with their family relations in India. The socioeconomic makeup of these communities, however, is far from homogeneous. Because of immigration policies and economic conditions at the time, earlier immigrants were mostly professionals who often were successful in finding professional jobs. Later immigrants, however, came to America more for reasons of family reunification and often either lacked sufficient training to succeed in the American economy or were unable to convert their training into highly rewarded positions as a result of discrimination and changes in the economy. As a result, the conditions of life are different for families of the Indian diaspora. While those with more resources participate fully in the protective and supportive environment of ethnic communities, those who are more disadvantaged economically often are marginalized. This marginalization comes about because lower status immigrants feel as though the class structure of their community makes them susceptible to exploitation by higher status members and participation in the diaspora community only increases their sense of failure and self-blame.

Source: Gauri Bhattacharya, "The Indian Diaspora in Transnational Context: Social Relations and Cultural Identities of immigrants to New York City," *Journal of Intercultural Studies,* 29 (February 2008), 65–80.

social status backgrounds construct ideas about families. For example, higher status families need to rely less on extended kin for their day-to-day survival and realization of goals. As a result, their concept of family tends to be more nuclear and exclusive of kinship ties. Families in lower status groups, however, are more likely to include extended family and nonfamily ties in their ideas of what constitutes a family and emphasize the importance of support giving as a criterion for family membership. These groups are even willing to exclude fathers of children from family membership if they are not providing support. Thus, definitions of family come about through everyday experiences—what they call "doing families."[8]

Elements of the environmental or ecological context within which families live their lives are also shaped by social status position. Some socioeconomic groups must confront less certain environments involving high levels of risk. For others, neighborhoods and communities may be safe and enriching places for enhancing family life and outcomes. In a recent study of neighborhood characteristics, those who were among the highest 2 percent of income earners in the United States were found to live in low density neighborhoods outside of central cities where they owned larger detached homes and in areas with higher proportions of married persons with children, majority white or Asian residents, and residents with higher levels of education and greater occupational prestige. They were also more likely to have men who were actively employed and women who could stay home and care

---

[8]Bettina Becker and Nickie Charles, "Layered Meanings: The Construction of "the Family" in the Interview." *Community, Work and Family* 9 (May 2006): 101–122.

for the home and children.[9] Obviously, these environments will present fewer stressors, greater social cohesion and supports, provide a safer environment for raising children, and make possible options in family life and parenting not as easily pursued in less stable and crime-filled neighborhoods.

Finally, the availability of economic, human, social and cultural capital is unequally distributed based on social status position. As noted in Chapter 2, capital is a term that refers to things one possesses or accumulates that can be used to produce desired outcomes. In the economic sphere, capital consists of things such as monetary savings, ownership of natural resources, and factories with a certain production capacity. These possessions can then be used to produce products that can then be sold in the marketplace to gain profit that can then be turned back into the accumulation of additional capital for enhanced production capabilities. In the social sphere, a similar process occurs although the nature of capital and the outcomes produced are different.

Economic capital is similar in both spheres and consists of things such as income, wealth, home and vehicle ownership, and so on. In the social sphere, however, outcomes such as a higher quality of life, health, and developmental outcomes for children and adult family members are "produced." Monetary resources can be used to purchase such things as better schools for children and better neighborhoods and housing for family life. Home ownership also facilitates physical and psychological health and provides a better context for enhanced learning and child development. Even ownership of a vehicle can translate into increased goal production insofar as having a car opens up possibilities for employment in locations more distant from home and child care options that make it possible for two parents to work and thereby accumulate even greater economic resources.

Human, social, and cultural forms of capital are also unequally distributed based on socioeconomic status. For example, differences in economic rewards associated with property ownership or occupational position can be used to enhance the knowledge and skills of family members (human capital) and extend social ties that can be used for support in times of need (social capital). Economic resources can also lead to enhanced opportunities in the economic and political spheres of life and increase exposure to and involvement in cultural environments that foster values, beliefs, and lifestyle preferences more valued by elites (cultural capital) and that constitute eligibility requirements for entry into higher status positions and enhanced living environments.

Social Categories of Families

Wealthy Families

Wealthy families have been identified as the *very rich*, the *upper class*, and the *ruling class*. Compared to other categories of families, relatively few recent data are available on the wealthy. This group of families, although small in number relative to other groups, is large in power and influence. They possess enormous economic and social resources. They have a network of affiliations on important boards in banking, insurance, and manufacturing. The wealthy are the elite who own and control the means of production and make the rules for workers to follow.

---

[9]Barrett A. Lee and Matthew Marlay, "The Ride Side of the Tracks: Affluent Neighborhoods in the Metropolitan United States," *Social Science Quarterly* 88 (September 2007): 766–789.

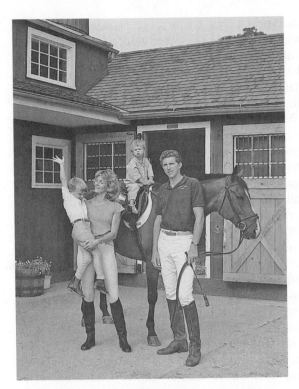

Upper-class parents have a disproportionately large share of the total wealth and income of a nation. Many of these families have been wealthy for several generations, hold a significant amount of power and influence, and engage in country club and recreational activities unavailable to the lower classes.

The family structure of the very rich is interesting and can be linked to the requirements of maintaining their social class position. As Michael Gilding has pointed out, "fortunes are rarely vested in individuals alone. For a variety of reasons—notably, tax minimization, business partnerships,...inheritance, and protection against bankruptcy and criminal proceedings—they are usually spread out among groups of individuals. Most commonly,...related though kinship."[10] As a result of the importance of family ties to the concentration of wealth in modern capitalist societies, Gilding identified several cultural and social features of the family life of the wealthy. Through interviews with individuals who were in the "Rich 200" list of the wealthiest individuals and families in Australia, he found that concerns about wealth accumulation, management succession, and inheritance lead to a heightened emphasis on the trust and loyalty that comes with family ties, the value of placing family interests over individual gratifications, the willingness of family members to work hard in the interest of family wealth accumulation, the cohesiveness of family ties that facilitates goal-directed activities, and the greater willingness of family members to take risks. At the same time, these individuals noted the potential risks in relying on family ties such as the potential for interpersonal conflict and the overreliance of children on inheritance of property from their parents. As a result, they also placed a high value on setting limits for their children while also fostering their independence and self-sufficiency.[11]

Gilding's findings are consistent with the findings of other researchers who describe wealthy families as extremely lineal and concerned with who they are rather than what they do. They are quite ancestor oriented and conscious of the boundaries that separate the "best" families from the others. *The Social Register* (names of upper-class families) is used even today to consolidate upper class repute, support class cohesion, and maintain "good breeding" in their interest in continuity of lineage.[12] Families are obviously the units within which wealth is accumulated and transmitted.

The importance of family ties and social networks in maintaining wealth and consolidating power can also be seen in the extensive role of wealthy women as "gatekeepers" of many of the institutions of the very rich. They launch children, serve as board members at private schools, run social and service clubs, and facilitate marriage pools through events such as debuts and charity functions. Susan Ostrander conducted interviews with thirty-six upper-class women and found that they held a clear preference for being with people like themselves (such as through

[10]Michael Gilding, "Families and Fortunes: Accumulation, Management Succession and Inheritance in Wealthy Families," 30.

[11]Ibid., 29–45.

[12]David B. Broad, "The Social Register: Directory of America's Upper Class," *Sociological Spectrum* 16 (1996): 173–181.

private and exclusive clubs, by invitation only), felt a sense of being better than other people (materially, morally, and in terms of volunteer work and contributions to the community), and conveyed an awareness that people define and judge them by who they are rather than by what they do.[13]

At this class level, women accommodate and support their husbands enabling them to better manage the economic and political affairs of society and to perpetuate the dominance of the upper class. Perhaps because of their high level of involvement in family and social roles and their corresponding lack of involvement in the all-important economic activity that directly maintains their class standing, these wives—like traditional wives in the lower classes—held a subordinate position to their husbands, had an unequal voice in family decisions, and maintained sole responsibility for home and family. An important difference, however, is that at this class level, women did not perform the nitty-gritty tasks of housework and child care. Women of other races and classes did such work for them. Without doubt, the upper class is very gender segregated. Interestingly, this gender separation is an accepted fact, virtually unchallenged by upper-class women. Why? Ostrander suggested that perhaps the gains of *gender* equality are not enough to balance the losses of *class* equality.

By any measure, this category of wealthy persons is the smallest numerically of all social classes in the United States but has the highest prestige and influence. Since the wealthy are at the very top of the class hierarchy, the members maintain their positions by preserving symbols of status, such as genealogies, biographies of ancestors, heirlooms, and records of ancestral achievement. The wealthy also maintain their position by carefully controlling the marriage choices of their children.

Working Families

When most Americans are asked to what class they belong, they will likely respond "middle." Relatively few people can honestly respond "wealthy," and few people want to admit to being "poor," even if it's true. Furthermore, a response of "middle class" generally carries positive connotations, implying that, while some people occupy higher occupational statuses and more prestigious positions, other people obviously occupy lower positions. Traditionally, middle-class families formed the linkage between powerful, wealthy families and the working-class, less powerful, poorer families. From a Marxian perspective (see Chapter 3), the middle class is composed of the *bourgeoisie*, those who own small amounts of productive resources and have control over their working conditions in ways not found among the *proletariat*, those working-class people who work for wages. Today, the term *middle class* is more likely to refer to people employed as professionals or corporate and government bureaucrats usually without possession of productive resources; whereas the working classes are employed in manual and service work. As noted previously, however, the distinctiveness of these class divisions has become blurred in modern capitalism. Nevertheless, differences remain between those who fall closer to the top of the socioeconomic hierarchy and those who fall closer to the bottom. In this section, we will consider the various mechanisms through which socioeconomic status affects families who depend on salaries or wages for their livelihoods as opposed to those who depend primarily on accumulated wealth or those who depend on systems of social support.

Simply based on general position in the socioeconomic hierarchy a number of differences can be identified among working families. For those residing closer to

---

[13]Susan A. Ostrander, *Women of the Upper Class* (Philadelphia: Temple University Press, 1984).

Blue-collar, or working-class, families tend to conform closely to traditional images of husband and wife roles, such that the husband is the principle provider and final authority. Because work is highly influenced by swings in the business climate, families often suffer great hardship during economic downturns.

the top of the hierarchy, levels of investment in the existing social system are high as these individuals and families are more likely to own homes, have financial investment portfolios, and rely on incomes contingent on a stable social and economic environment. They are also more likely to receive salaries rather than hourly wages. With this stable resource base is likely to come a range of amenities that lessen the shock of unanticipated crisis events: medical coverage, pension and retirement plans, bank credit, investment income, and the like. Higher levels of income and greater job security also allow for some discretionary spending and leisure activities. In addition, those closer to the top of the hierarchy are likely to be motivated in their individual and family behaviors by the real possibilities of moving upward as well as the real dangers of moving downward in the hierarchy.

In contrast, those who reside at the lower levels of socioeconomic status are almost completely dependent on the swings of the business cycle in the wage/price/profits system; thus, the economic stability enjoyed by higher status families is less prevalent among lower status families. Most income is received from wages earned by the hour, the piece, the day, or the week. To supplement the incomes of husbands, many wives are employed outside the home. Unlike a sizable proportion of working wives from higher status positions, however, wives at lower status levels are more likely to work out of economic necessity than desire for a career. Perhaps consequentially to these differences in socioeconomic conditions, higher status families tend to be very conscious of social values, involved in the major issues brought on by social change, and tend to uphold moral standards. They are also likely to believe strongly in values that lead to success in modern capitalism such as individualism, independence, autonomy, and rational planning to achieve goals. Such value systems reinforce existing systems of social and economic relations and can provide the cultural capital needed to realize further advancement. In contrast, those working families who reside closer to the bottom of the status hierarchy have less invested in existing systems of social and economic relations and have less potential for moving upward and more potential for falling into poverty. As a result, they are likely to be less involved in issues of social change and more focused on maintaining a sustainable quality of life. They will be less focused on the future and more on the present. Here the focus is likely to be on allegiances, loyalty, and adaptability rather than individualism, autonomy, and rational planning.

These differences in values and orientations are reflected in socioeconomic differences in marital and parenting roles and child rearing. Those residing at the high end of the hierarchy are more likely to value women's independent career pursuits and downplay the importance of exclusive mother-child dependencies. Beliefs in self-determination and autonomy may explain why employed professional women tend to express reactions against full-time mothering and give work a higher priority in their lives.[14] Families at the lower end of the hierarchy are more likely to conform to the traditional roles of husband and wife. The husband's role is to be a good provider and, as the primary wage earner, he is the final authority and disciplinarian. The wife's role is to do the housework and rear the children. Although she often is employed, her employment is considered "necessary" rather than inherently meaningful and secondary to her husband's work activities. Women at the lower levels of the hierarchy are more likely to enjoy full-time motherhood and to give family roles higher priority than work roles.

Families near the top of the hierarchy are also more likely to espouse the ideal of equality between husband and wife, and this seems to be an important indicator of marital conflict if it is not shared. In contrast, for lower status wives, a more consistent indicator of frequency of marital conflicts is not equity but the division of feminine tasks. In other words, for a lower status wife, conflict is avoided when she does "the women's work" whereas for a higher status wife conflict arises when her husband is not taking on, in her view, his "fair share" of family work.[15]

With respect to child rearing, those who reside closer to the top of the hierarchy are more likely to stress that children stay in school and parents make major sacrifices to keep them there. In fact, the importance of academic success among more affluent parents can involve a great deal of emotional work as they struggle to motivate their children to get into private schools and work the system to give their children every advantage that comes from their superior social and cultural position in spite of a belief that school admissions should be based solely on merit. In addition to dealing with the emotional ambivalence created by this situation, these parents also find themselves having to deal with the emotional consequences of a child that fails to meet the high expectations set for him or her because of family socioeconomic position.[16] At the lower end of the status hierarchy, the role of children is definitely subordinate to that of parents or the welfare of the family as a whole. These parents are more likely to expect that children will contribute to their own economic welfare (and sometimes the welfare of the entire family) as soon as they are able. Thus, children will need to get jobs while still in high school and are more likely to leave school after fulfilling the minimum legal requirements or, at most, after completing high school. Boys and girls are taught to be self-sufficient, to be tough-minded, and to be able to compete for personal rights and privileges. Perhaps because their educational and occupation career prospects are more limited, boys at lower status levels have heterosexual experiences earlier and have intercourse more frequently than boys from higher status families. For girls, they are more likely to marry early, often because of premarital pregnancy. Although these girls may desire love, they get babies.

Neighborhood Context

In addition to the advantages that come from having sufficient income to achieve family goals, those with higher socioeconomic status are also advantaged by their

---

[14]Beverly H. Burris, "Employed Mothers: The Impact of Class and Marital Status on the Prioritizing of Family and Work," *Social Science Quarterly* 72 (March 1991): 50–66.

[15]Maureen Perry-Jenkins and Karen Folk, "Class, Couples, and Conflict: Effects of the Division of Labor on Assessments of Marriage in Dual-Earner Families," *Journal of Marriage and the Family* 56 (February 1994): 165–180.

[16]Tiffani Chin, "'Sixth Grade Madness': Parental Emotion Work in the Private High School Application Process," *Journal of Contemporary Ethnography* 29 (April 2000): 124–163.

access to communities that are more resource rich and secure and free of environmental risks and stressors. The significance of this aspect of socioeconomic status was highlighted by William J. Wilson in his seminal analysis of inner-city poverty.[17] Also, as Urie Bronfenbrenner recognized in his ecological theory of human development, variations in community and neighborhood environments can have profound and long lasting effects on children and their psychological development.[18] These effects can be either direct or mediated by the impacts of neighborhood environments on family dynamics. As Tama Lebenthal and Jeanne Brooks-Gunn point out, neighborhoods can affect individual and family outcomes in two fundamental ways. Neighborhoods vary in the extent to which they provide quality **institutional resources** that are easily accessible (e.g., good schools, quality day care, health care facilities, and social and recreational opportunities). The availability of resources can both reduce the potential for experiencing stressor events as well as help families adapt successfully to stressors when they occur. Neighborhoods also vary in what they call their **normative/collective efficacy**, or the degree to which they are characterized by conditions of social organization versus disorganization (e.g., levels of unemployment, poverty, crime, and geographical mobility among neighborhood residents, crime rates and levels of victimization, presence of deviant subcultures in the community, etc.).[19] These factors can have significant consequences for both disrupting individual psychological well-being and family functioning as well as for placing demands on families to organize their activities in ways that will facilitate adaptation to their unique contexts. In other words, a low level of normative/collective efficacy in the community context may or may not cause families to become dysfunctional, but at the least, it is likely to alter the way that they adapt and function, making certain aspects of family organization (e.g., family cohesion, family flexibility, family size, parental structure, etc.) more important in some contexts versus others.

The impacts of neighborhood contexts shaped by socioeconomic status have been studied most extensively with respect to parenting and child outcomes. In one comparison of a more affluent community in the Southeastern United States with a less affluent community in the Midwest, parents in the former context expressed more positive perceptions of and satisfaction with their community context as measured by their perceptions of the availability of community formal resources (such as schools and after school programs), quality informal relationships among community members, neighborhood safety and freedom from drugs, and high levels of "welcoming values" among community residents. These more positive perceptions increased life satisfaction, perceived family functioning, higher role balance, and lower levels of work-family conflict.[20]

Given these effects of neighborhood perceptions on parents and their perceptions of family functioning, it would not be surprising to find that neighborhood

---

[17]William J. Wilson, *The Truly Disadvantaged: The Innercity, the Underclass, and Public Policy* (Chicago, IL: University of Chicago Press, 1987).

[18]Urie Bronfenbrenner, *The Ecology of Human Development* (Cambridge, MA: Harvard University Press, 1979).

[19]Tama Leventhal and Jeanne Brooks-Gunn, "Changing Neighborhoods and Child Well-Being: Understanding How Children May Be Affected in the Coming Century," *Children at the Millenium: Where Have We Come From, Where Are We Going?* 6 (2001): 263–301.

[20]Marcie Pitt-Catsouphes, Shelley M. MacDermid, Rona Schwartz, and Christina Matz, "Community Contexts: The Perspectives and Adaptations of Working Parents," *American Behavioral Scientist* 49 (June, 2006): 1400–1421.

context affects the effectiveness of parenting as well. In another study by Laura Plybon and Wendy Kliewer, the links between neighborhood context, family stress and child outcomes was shown in a study of urban school age children. In this study, objective measures of low poverty and low crime in communities were correlated with lower levels of family stress and lower family stress was correlated with lower levels of child externalizing problem behaviors. Furthermore, statistical tests showed that the lower levels of stress found in families in the low poverty/low crime communities effectively explained or accounted for the effects of poor community contexts on child behavior problems. Finally, this study showed that, to the extent that families are able to maintain high levels of family cohesion or togetherness in poorer and crime ridden neighborhoods, they can effectively reduce the negative effects these environments have on child behaviors.[21]

Another way that community context affects parenting outcomes is through the direct effect on parental psychological distress. Several studies have shown that measures of perceived neighborhood stress, neighborhood risk or danger, and levels of neighborhood problems have significant negative effects on parents' psychological well-being and these negative effects on parental well-being account for lower levels of effective parenting such as low levels of monitoring and less consistency in disciplining children.[22] In turn, these lower levels of effective parenting explain much of the negatives effects of poor neighborhoods on child outcomes.[23]

Finally, community context not only alters the likelihood of parents engaging in positive parenting behaviors, but it also shapes what types of parenting behaviors will be more or less effective. Ronald Simons and his colleagues tested three hypotheses regarding the differential effectiveness of parental control and corporal punishment parenting techniques in different community contexts. The first set of hypotheses concerned the effectiveness of parental control under high- and low-risk neighborhood conditions. On the one hand, high levels of control might be more effective when there is more to gain (that is, when there is a high level of crime and delinquency in the community context). They called this the *buffering hypothesis*. On the other hand, it might be that high levels of community crime and delinquency override the effectiveness of parenting. They called this the *evaporation hypothesis*. What they found was that their data supported the evaporation hypothesis, suggesting that parents are ineffective at counteracting the negative effects of high-risk neighborhoods on their children regardless of how much they attempt to control their children's behaviors.

---

[21]Laura E. Plybon and Wendy Kliewer, "Neighborhood Types and Externalizing Behavior in Urban School-Age Children:Tests of Direct, Mediated, and Moderated Effects," *Journal of Child and Family Studies* 10 (December, 2001): 419–437.

[22]B. A. Kotchick, S. Dorsey, & L. Heller, "Predictors of Parenting Among African American Single Mothers: Personal and Contextual Factors," *Journal of Marriage and Family* 67 (2005): 448–460; N. E. Hill and Herman-Stahl, "Neighborhood Safety and Social Involvement: Associations With Parenting Behaviors and Depressive Symptoms Among African American and Euro-American Mothers," *Journal of Family Psychology* 16 (2002): 209–219; Alexandra Loukas, Hazel M. Prelow, Marie-Anne Suizzo, and Shane Allua, "Mothering and Peer Associations Mediate Cumulative Risk Effects for Latino Youth." *Journal of Marriage and Family* 70 (2008): 76–85; and Rebecca M. B. White, Mark W. Roosa, Scott R. Weaver, and Rajni L. Nair, "Cultural and Contextual Influences on Parenting in Mexican American Families," *Journal of Marriage and Family* 71 (February 2009): 61–79.

[23]K. J. Conger, M. A. Rueter, and Rand D. Conger, "The Role of Economic Pressure in the Lives of Parents and Their Adolescents: The Family Stress Model." In R. K. Silbereisen and L. J. Crockett (Eds.), *Negotiating Adolescence in Times of Social Change* (New York: Cambridge University Press, 2000): 201–223.

Family Diversity

The Long Arm of the Farm

Out of 133 stressful occupations in America, farming ranks as the 12th most stressful. In addition, the potential for *work-family spillover* and *family-work spillover* can be expected among the highest as well, given the integration of farm work with family life. Because of the tenuous nature of farm work and the high level of integration with family life, farming families place a great value on self-sufficiency, work ethic, community integration, traditional gender roles, stability, low levels of conflict, and religiosity. Farm families also are likely to react differently to economic stressors, both in their personal lives and in the lives of their communities.

Using data from the Iowa Youth and Families Project, Raymond Swisher and his colleagues looked at the aftermath of the farm crisis of the 1980s to see if farmers were more exposed and more vulnerable to economic stressors relative to those in nonfarm occupations. They hypothesized that farm families would be exposed to more economic and job-related stressors as a result of the nature of their jobs and the economic conditions of the times. They also predicted that farmers would suppress conflicts in their families in order to maintain order and calm in the face of stressors and be more exposed to stress experiences by those in their communities: kin and friends. Finally, they predicted farmers would also be more vulnerable

to the stressors faced by their kin, but would be less vulnerable to stressors experienced by friends. This latter prediction is based on the idea that farmers would find downward comparisons a valuable coping technique in the face of their own stressor events.

The results of this study showed that farmers do indeed experience more economic stressor events in their lives and are more likely to have friends and kin who have experienced stressors. Farmers are also more likely to be negatively impacted by stressor events and those of their *kin*, but, as predicted, they are less negatively impacted than nonfarmers by negative economic events experienced by their *friends*. This supports the downward comparison hypothesis. Finally, farmers are less likely to experience conflict in their families, although when conflict occurs, their well-being is more negatively affected than it is for nonfarmers.

Thus, the value placed by farmers on stability in family life plays a central role in their ability to deal with the high levels of chronic stressors they must confront. This stability, however, makes them vulnerable to family crisis should the stability be disrupted by conflict.

Source: Raymond R. Swisher, Glen H. Elder, Jr., Frederick O. Lorenz, and Rand D. Conger. "The Long Arm of the Farm: How an Occupation Structures Exposure and Vulnerability to Stressors across Role Domains," *Journal of Health and Social Behavior*, 39 (March 1998), 72–89.

Their third hypothesis concerned the effectiveness of corporal punishment (e.g., physical punishment) on children under conditions where such parenting techniques are used rarely versus extensively by other community residents. They predicted that when corporal punishment is not used extensively by other parents in the community that it will be considered illegitimate and create negative reactions and rebellion in children. In contrast, in neighborhoods where corporal punishment is widely used, it will be considered legitimate and will therefore be more effective as a parenting technique. Their findings were consistent with this *legitimacy hypothesis* as corporal punishment had negative effects on children's behaviors only in the context where it was used less frequently by other parents.[24]

---

[24]Ronald L. Simons, Kuei-Hsiu Lin, Leslie C. Gordon, Gene H. Brody, Velma Murry and Rand Conger, "Community Differences in the Association Between Parenting Practices and Child Conduct Problems," *Journal of Marriage and Family* 64 (May 2002): 331–345.

Educational Attainment

In addition to income and neighborhood context effects, differences in educational attainment represent a third major determinant of differences in family life based on socioeconomic status. Status attainment in a modern industrial economy is, to a large extent, based on one's achievements in the workplace and the extent to which one's occupational role is valued and rewarded; and access to work and occupational roles is restricted based on human and other forms of capital accumulated through educational attainment. As a result, one's location in the socioeconomic status hierarchy also reflects differences in educational resources that also have important implications for family life.

The importance of educational attainment for family life lies in three areas. First, education provides access to other resources and opportunities. Not only is education an important entry requirement to more highly rewarded occupational positions, but it also enhances access to sources of informal and formal social support in times of need. Through education individuals learn more about public and private sources of social support and develop the skills and value systems that enhance their ability to negotiate with institutions to obtain the supports they need to enhance their marital and parenting outcomes. This effect is best exemplified in the greater effectiveness of parental involvement in schools found among parents with higher levels of socioeconomic status.

Second, highly educated individuals are also more likely to develop more modern and less conventional values, attitudes, and lifestyles. As a result, they are more likely to choose lifestyles considered deviant by the majority opinion (e.g., choosing not to have children), place greater value on individual development within the context of marriage, place greater value on gender equality in marriage, and be more willing to end a relationship when it fails to live up to expectations. These attitudes, values, and lifestyle preferences should not only change how they approach and act in relationships, but also affect their attraction to different social and cultural environments such as those found in urban areas. As such, they will have more potential partners to choose from when looking to form relationships as well as greater access to alternative relationships and lifestyles (e.g., remaining single) once they are in long-term relationships. Such access to alternatives is an important factor in shaping power dynamics in relationships and likelihoods of relationship dissolution.

Third, education directly affects marital and parenting relationships by providing the cognitive capabilities and background knowledge needed to successfully understand the developmental capabilities of children and the environmental contingencies affecting one's partner as well as the skills needed to manage children and negotiate with one's partner. As a result, more educated partners should experience more successful marriages and more educated parents should experience more successful parenting outcomes. Such effects have been observed in two recent studies.

Using a large representative sample in Norway, Torkild Lyngstad found that in a modern society such as Norway (and the United States) where divorce is an acceptable alternative to a bad marriage, higher levels of educational attainment reduces the likelihood of divorce. He attributes this effect to the cognitive and relationship skills that spouses develop through education. The effect of spouses' own education is different than the effect he observed for *parental* education. Although one's own educational attainment reduced the likelihood of divorce, coming from a family where one's *parents* had higher levels of education actually increased the likelihood of divorce among those in this sample. He attributes this effect to the more modern and less conventional attitudes developed by their parents because they were educated during a time when divorce was less acceptable and they passed on these more liberal attitudes to their children. As a result, children of more highly educated parents are more likely to develop higher personal gratification expectations for marriage and less negative attitudes about divorce than children of less educated parents. These higher expectations and less negative attitudes toward divorce then increase their likelihood of divorcing when their expectations are not met. Thus, they argue that education increases the likelihood of divorce in low-divorce cultures, such as in early periods of time or in less modern and more traditional contexts (e.g., in Catholic countries such as Italy), but reduces the likelihood of divorce in more modern and divorce-accepting contexts. These contrasting effects are then attributable to the dual influences of education on values and attitudes, on the one hand, and on skills and capabilities on the other.[25]

With respect to parenting, the effects of education are noted in an analysis of a large U.S. national data set—the National Longitudinal Survey of Youth (NLSY). In their analysis of later waves of these data focusing on parents with children between the ages of 6 and 7, Mikaela Dufur, Toby Parcel, and Benjamin McKune found that mothers who have higher levels of educational attainment are less likely to have children who exhibit high levels of problem behaviors. This effect of education is completely explained by the higher levels of cognitive skills and higher levels of self-esteem found among the more educated parents.[26]

Work and Occupations

As noted in Chapter 2, the importance of work and occupations for family life can best be understood in the context of work-family spillover. Work conditions and role demands can either interfere with (negative spillover) or facilitate (positive spillover) family role performance. When work roles make demands on marital partners and parents that make it more difficult to fulfill family role expectations, a condition of **role conflict** results. This role conflict can cause psychological distress, inadequate fulfillment of roles, family stress, and declines in marriage and family life satisfaction. On the other hand, work roles can provide marital partners and parents with important opportunities for developing their cognitive capacities and developing values that make them better marital partners and/or more effective parents.

Work and occupational conditions vary significantly based on socioeconomic status. At a very general level, those who work in higher status occupations can expect to experience greater work role flexibility (e.g., time and place demands of work), an organizational structure that is more supportive of individual and family needs, greater support from supervisors and coworkers, and more free hours at work for potentially dealing with personal and family needs. In a recent study of over 1,000 employed parents, E. Jeffrey Hill found that these conditions of work have important consequences for family life insofar as they increase perceptions of work as facilitating family roles; reduce levels of perceived work-family role conflict; reduce individual stress; and increase levels of marital, family, and general life satisfaction.[27]

---

[25]Torkild Hovde Lyngstad, "Why Do Couples with Highly Educated Parents Have Higher Divorce Rates" *European Sociological Review* 22 (February 2006): 49–60.

[26]Mikaela J. Dufur, Toby Parcel, and Benjamin A. McKune, "Capital and Context: Using Social Capital at Home and at School to Predict Child Social Adjustment," *Journal of Health and Social Behavior* 49 (June 2008): 146–161.

[27]E. Jeffrey Hill, "Work-Family Facilitation and Conflict, Working Fathers and Mothers, Work-Family Stressors and Support," *Journal of Family Issues* 26 (September 2005): 793–819.

In addition to general work conditions, the types of occupations found in higher status positions can also impact family life. One important distinction between higher and lower status occupations is that of white-collar versus blue-collar jobs. **White-collar jobs** usually are salaried positions requiring higher levels of educational training. They typically are professional or managerial positions in business, education, or government. **Blue-collar jobs,** on the other hand, are made up of individuals classified in the U.S. Census as employed in precision production, craft, and repair; machine operating, assembling, and inspecting; transportation and material moving; and handling, equipment cleaning, helping, and laboring. Service jobs are generally also classified as blue-collar occupations. Formal education beyond a high school or trade school is not generally required to learn the manual skills necessary for these positions. Physical health is quite crucial to blue-collar workers, since many jobs depend on the ability to perform physical labor.

A widely studied area showing differences between those in white-collar versus blue-collar positions is in parent–child relations and child-rearing practices. Typically, white-collar positions require individuals to (1) deal more with the manipulation of ideas, symbols, and interpersonal relations; (2) be involved in work that is more complex and requires great flexibility, thought, and judgment; and (3) be less closely supervised and rewarded for experimenting and innovation. In contrast, blue-collar positions typically require individuals to: (1) deal with the manipulation of things or inanimate objects rather than people or ideas; (2) be involved in work that involves low levels of cognitive functioning and flexibility and little independent thought or decision making; and (3) be more closely supervised and rewarded for conformity to rules and regulations of work activity. Nearly fifty years ago, Melvin Kohn suggested that these differences in the occupational work activities and settings of fathers would spill over into family life, and, in particular, parenting techniques with respect to disciplining children. In his research, he showed that parents in families where the father was employed in a white-collar profession were more likely to use reason, verbal threats, or withdrawal of rewards to punish a child or solicit the child's compliance.[28] In contrast, blue-collar parents were more likely to rely on physical punishment. Since his earlier studies, these findings have been replicated by other researchers in the United States[29] as well as in Germany and the Netherlands.[30]

At the heart of Kohn's reasoning was the idea that by experiencing different working conditions, members of different occupational groupings come to see the world differently and to develop different conceptions of social reality and desirable personality characteristics as well as different aspirations. White-collar values are likely to include self-direction, freedom, individualism, initiative, creativity, and self-actualization. Thus, parents encourage in their children *internal* standards such as

---

[28]Melvin Kohn, "Social Class and Parent–Child Relationships: An Interpretation," *American Journal of Sociology* 68 (January 1963): 471–480; and Melvin Kohn, *Class and Conformity* (Homewood, IL: Dorsey, 1969).

[29]See Tom Luster, Kelly Rhoades, and Bruce Haas, "The Relation between Parental Values and Parenting Behavior: A Test of the Kohn Hypothesis," *Journal of Marriage and the Family* 51 (1989): 139–147.

[30]Robert C. Williamson, "A Partial Replication of the Kohn-Gecas Nye Thesis in a German Sample," *Journal of Marriage and the Family* 46 (November 1984): 971–979; and Maja Dekovic and Jan R. M. Gerris, "Parental Reasoning Complexity, Social Class, and Child-Rearing Behaviors," *Journal of Marriage and the Family* 54 (August 1992): 675–685.

consideration, curiosity, and self-control. Discipline is based on the parents' interpretation of a child's motive for a particular act.[31]

Later, this reasoning was extended to include differences in how occupational activities also shape cognitive styles and abilities that in turn make different styles of parenting more or less feasible. Specifically, the nature of white-collar work with ideas and people involves greater *substantive complexity,* and this complexity fosters greater *intellectual flexibility* in the parent, which in turn makes the use of reasoning in parenting more likely.[32] In several recent studies that extended Kohn's thesis to older workers[33] and to the effects of mothers' occupational characteristics,[34] the effects of occupational substantive complexity on cognitive functioning have been well documented. In addition, these effects on cognitive functioning have been linked to positive child outcomes.[35] In fact, the complexity of work is an important conditional factor in understanding the effects of single parenting and mother employment on children. As Menaghan and her colleagues have shown, when mothers (including single mothers) are employed in more substantively complex occupations, their children experience fewer adverse effects in terms of cognitive stimulation and behavior problems.[36]

Families Living in Poverty

To understand how families organize themselves and adapt under conditions of poverty, it is first necessary to understand what those conditions involve and how social scientists determine which families fall into this category when they conduct their research. The measurement and reporting of poverty is both a sociological and social policy concern as well as a political one. From a sociological/social policy viewpoint, we are interested in knowing how individuals and families end up living in and adapting to conditions where they are unable to sustain a minimal standard of living and lifestyle as set by the values and norms of their culture. In so doing, programs can be developed to better help those in need. Determining what

---

[31]In contrast, lower-class or blue-collar workers deal more with the manipulation of physical objects, require less interpersonal skill, have more standardization of work, and are more closely supervised. This leads to values of conformity to external standards such as orderliness, neatness, and obedience. Discipline is based on the consequences of the child's behavior rather than on the interpretation of motive for the behavior.

[32]See Carmi Schooler, "Psychological Effects of Complex Environments during the Life Span: A Review and Theory." In Carmi Schooler and K. Warner Schaie, eds., Cognitive Functioning and Social Structure over the Life Course (Norwood, NJ: Ablex Publishing Corp., 1987): 24-49.

[33]C. Schooler, M. S. Mulatu, and G. Oates, "Occupational Self-Direction, Intellectual Functioning, and Self-Directed Orientation in Older Workers: Findings and Implications for Individuals and Societies," *American Journal of Sociology* 110 (2004): 161–97.

[34]Toby L. Parcel and Elizabeth G. Menaghan, "Early Parental Work, Family Social Capital, and Early Childhood Outcomes," *American Journal of Sociology* 99 (January 1994): 972–1009; and Elizabeth G. Menaghan and Toby L. Parcel, "Social Sources of Change in Children's Home Environments: The Effects of Parental Occupational Experiences and Family Conditions," *Journal of Marriage and the Family* 57 (February 1995): 69–84.

[35]Dufur, Parcel, and McKune, "Capital and Context: Using Social Capital at Home and at School to Predict Child Social Adjustment," 146–161.

[36]Elizabeth G. Menaghan, Lori Kowaleski-Jones, and Frank L. Mott, "The Intergenerational Costs of Parental Social Stressors: Academic and Social Difficulties in Early Adolescence for Children of Young Mothers," *Journal of Health and Social Behavior* 38 (March 1997): 72–86.

this level is can be a difficult task as each cultural group sets its own standards and there is a considerable gap between what is minimal and what is optimal. The task is complicated even further, however, by the interest that nation states have in representing their societal conditions in the most beneficial light.[37] For modern nations (and more wealthy segments of those nations), the interest usually is in trying to minimize representations of poverty in order to *legitimize* governments and those in power and prevent rebellions. However, in so-called "developing" societies (and less well-off areas of modern nations), this interest in maintaining a positive image is counteracted by the need to document a case for external assistance. As a result of these conflicting interests, a number of different poverty measures have been developed.

Meaning and Measurement of Poverty

For global comparisons of nation states, poverty is measured by the United Nations in order to assist with the administration of its development programs and generally monitor social conditions throughout the world. They do this in two different ways, one for developing countries and one for more modern societies (countries in the Organization for Economic Cooperation and Development—OECD). The **human poverty index for developing countries** is based on three factors: the probability of a birth not surviving to age 40, the adult literacy rate, and a combined measure comprised of access to improved water sources and the proportion of children under weight for their age. The **human poverty index for developed countries**, on the other hand, is based on four factors: the probability of a birth surviving to the age of 60, the adult functional literacy rate, the proportion of the population with disposable household incomes in the lowest 25 percent for the country as a whole, and the rate of long-term unemployment lasting twelve months or more.[38] Using this latter measure, the 2007–2008 Human Development Report lists the United States as ranking seventeenth out of nineteen of the developed countries in the world for which this measure was obtained. Thus, this ranking reflects one of the highest levels of human poverty among this group of modern nations. By comparison, Iceland had the lowest rate of human poverty among developed nations, followed by Norway, Australia, Canada, Ireland, Sweden, Switzerland, Japan, the Netherlands, and France (in that order).[39]

Individual countries such as the United States also calculate their own poverty rates for monitoring and social welfare administration purposes. In the United States, poverty is measured based on a formula developed in 1963–1964 and has only been slightly modified since. Using the most extreme minimal standards for nutrition set by the Department of Agriculture at the time, the costs of purchasing food to meet those standards (the Economy Food Plan), and data from 1955 on what proportion of their income families spent on food, Mollie Orshansky developed a measure that assumed

---

[37]For an interesting summary of debates over the measurement of poverty in the United States, see Gordon M. Fisher, "The Development and History of the U.S. Poverty Thresholds: A Brief Overview," *GSS/SSS Newsletter* [Newsletter of the Government Statistics Section and the Social Statistics Section of the American Statistical Association] (Winter 1997): 6–7. http://aspe.hhs.gov/poverty/papers/hptgssiv.htm.

[38]United Nations, "Human Development Report 2007/2008," http://hdr.undp.org/en/reports/global/hdr2007-2008/

[39]United Nations, "Human and Income Poverty: OECD Countries, Central and Eastern Europe and the CIS," http://hdrstats.undp.org/en/indicators/27.html.

families would always and in all times spend about a third of their income on food and, as a result, would require a minimum income that was three times the cost of purchasing the minimal amount of food required for survival. In spite of the unrealistic nature of this assumption (consider the increased costs in housing, clothing and transportation in today's society relative to the smaller increases in food costs) and the exceptionally low standard set for minimum nutrition, this measure has withstood many efforts at revision. Today, this measure is used to establish *poverty thresholds* and *poverty guidelines* that vary based on the number of people in the family, the age of the head of household, and the number of children in the family.

Poverty thresholds are used for statistical monitoring purposes and establish a minimum level of income needed for survival based on the *pre-tax* income of all related members of a family living together in a household derived from all public and private sources, but excluding noncash assistance (such as food stamps, Medicaid, and public housing) and capital gains and losses. These thresholds vary based primarily on the size of the family and the number of children present but are *identical regardless of what state one resides in and what the cost of living is in each state*. They are also the measure used when talking about the official poverty line. **Poverty guidelines** are simplified versions of poverty thresholds used for program administration purposes. Other than some minor statistical corrections and publication dating (e.g., the 2009 poverty guidelines are equivalent to the 2008 poverty thresholds and both are based on data collected in 2006), the poverty guidelines have the advantage of being adjusted based on whether or not one lives in the forty-eight contiguous states versus living in Hawaii or Alaska (thus, there are three sets of guidelines that correspond to a single set of thresholds).

As illustrated in Table 4.1 (page 166), the average poverty threshold in 2008 for a family of four consisting of two adults and two children under age 18 was $21,834 or less than $2,000 a month. Remember that this threshold is for *pre-tax* income and must be distributed to pay for all family expenses such as food, clothing, housing, transportation, heating, electricity, and so on. Obviously, the poverty threshold is only identifying families in the most extreme need and as a result, many researchers and program administrators frequently use a cutoff point for determining poverty that is higher (e.g., from 125 percent to 200 percent of the poverty threshold). For one person under age 65, the poverty threshold in 2008 was $11,201; for a two-person household without children under 18 it was $14,417; and for a three-person household consisting of a single parent family with two children, it was $17,346. For a family of nine, consisting of two adults and seven children, it was $47,278.

According to the 2009 Statistical Abstract published by the U.S. Census Bureau, 12.3 percent of all *persons* living in the United States in 2006 lived below the poverty level, and 16.8 percent lived below 125 percent of the poverty level. These levels represent increases from the year 2000 when the percent of all persons living below these levels were 11.3 and 15.6 percent, respectively. They also represent a giving back of over half of the gains made in reducing poverty since 1980 when the percent of persons living below the poverty threshold was 13 percent.[40] For *families,* the percentage falling below the poverty threshold in 2006 was 9.8 percent, with 13.4 percent falling below 125 percent of the threshold. These rates are

---

[40]U.S. Census Bureau, "Table 689: People Below Poverty Level and Below 125 Percent of Poverty Level by Race and Hispanic Origin: 1980 to 2006," *2009 Statistical Abstract* http://www. 2010census.biz/compendia/statab/tables/09s0689.pdf.

Table 4.1

Poverty thresholds by size of family: 2008

SIZE OF FAMILY UNIT	POVERTY THRESHOLD
One person (unrelated individual)	
Under 65 years	$11,201
65 years and over	$10,326
Two persons (no children under age 18)	
Householder under 65 years	$14,417
Householder 65 years and over	$13,014
Two adults and one child under 18 (3 persons)	$17,330
One adult and two children under 18 (3 persons)	$17,346
Two adults and two children under 18 (4 persons)	$21,834
Two adults and three children under 18 (5 persons)	$26,338
Two adults and four children under 18 (6 persons)	$30,288
Two adults and five children under 18 (7 persons)	$34,901
Two adults and six children under 18 (8 persons)	$39,270
Two adults and seven children under 18 (9 persons)	$47,278

Source: U.S. Census Bureau, "Poverty Thresholds for 2008 by Size of Family and Number of Related Children Under 18 Years," http://www.census.gov/hhes/www/poverty/threshld/thresh08.html.

increases from 2000 levels of 8.7 and 12.2 percent, respectively.41 The higher rates of poverty found among persons rather than families can be explained by the fact that many of the persons living in poverty are children who live in families. In 2006, 16.9 percent of all *children* under age 18 lived below the poverty threshold. Like the rates of persons and families, this too represents an increase from 2000 when the percent of children living below the poverty threshold was 15.6 percent.42 In short, one in every ten families in the United States was classified as having an income below the most extreme minimum required for sustaining itself in 2006, and the poverty rate among these families impacted almost 17 percent of all the children in the country during that year.

It is also useful to understand how poverty is disproportionately distributed across race and ethnic groups in the United States and for those in different family structures. In 2006, the poverty rate for non-Hispanic white families was 8.0 percent and 7.8 percent for Asian and Pacific Islander families. In contrast, poverty rates were considerably higher for Hispanic-origin families (18.9 percent), and black families (21.6 percent).43 Among families with a female householder with no husband

---

[41]U.S. Census Bureau, "Table 693: Families Below Poverty Level and Below 125 Percent of Poverty by Race and Hispanic Origin: 1980 to 2006" *2009 Statistical Abstract* http://www.2010census.biz/compendia/statab/tables/09s0693.pdf.

[42]U.S. Census Bureau, "Table 690: Children Below Poverty Level by Race and Hispanic Origin: 1980 to 2006," *2009 Statistical Abstract* http://www.2010census.biz/compendia/statab/tables/09s0690.pdf.

[43]U.S. Census Bureau, "Table 693: Families Below Poverty Level and Below 125 Percent of Poverty by Race and Hispanic Origin: 1980 to 2006"

present, these poverty rates were considerably higher, although the race and ethnicity differences remained. The percentages increased to 25.1 for non-Hispanic white families, 15.4 for Asian and Pacific Islander families, 36.0 for Hispanic-origin families, and 36.6 for black families. Finally, poverty has a curvilinear relationship with age, with middle-aged individuals (45–54) experiencing the lowest rates of poverty (7.8 percent) compared to younger individuals (16.9 percent for those under 18) and those who are older (10.3 percent for those 75 and older).[44]

Feminization of Poverty

Given the high rates of poverty found among single parents and the elderly (both disproportionately composed of women), it is of little surprise to find that a gender gap exists in poverty. In 2006, 13.6 percent of women in the United States lived below the poverty threshold, compared to only 11.0 percent of men. This difference reflects a long-term trend in poverty in the United States as well as in other modern Western countries—a trend referred to as the **feminization of poverty**. David Brady and Denise Krall document this trend (both in terms of the proportions who are in poverty and in the intensity of the poverty differences) in the United States and in eighteen other Western societies going as far back as 1969.[45] In the United States, as well as in the vast majority of countries they studied, the gap exists for working-aged

More women than men live in poverty in the United States today due largely to the low sex ratio of elderly men to elderly women and the high prevalence of single parenting among younger women.

---

[44]U.S. Census Bureau, "Table 694: Families Below Poverty Level by Selected Characteristics: 2006," *2009 Statistical Abstract* http://www.2010census.biz/compendia/statab/tables/09s0694.pdf.

[45]David Brady and Denise Kall, "Nearly Universal, but Somewhat Distinct: The Feminization of Poverty in Affluent Western Democracies, 1969–2000," *Social Science Research* 37 (2008): 976–1007.

women, but is even larger when the elderly are included. Countries with the highest levels of feminized poverty include Ireland, Austria, Norway, the United Kingdom, and the United States. Countries with the lowest gender gap in poverty include Belgium, Finland, the Netherlands, Sweden, and Switzerland. Switzerland was the only country in their study that showed no feminization of poverty among all adults as well as among working adults only.

Brady and Krall identify three possible explanations for this gender gap in poverty. The *liberal economic theory* argues that gender differences in poverty are a function of poor economic conditions and poverty levels in general. That is, when economic growth occurs it will reduce poverty in all segments of the population and differences between men and women in terms of employment levels and income will disappear. The *structural theory* argues that even with economic growth, the gender gap in poverty levels will remain because the elderly and those with children (especially single parents) are restricted in their ability to assume productive economic roles equivalent to those of middle aged individuals without family dependents. Since women make up a disproportionate number of the elderly and single parents, the gender gap remains but could be reduced or eliminated through the enactment of social policies and welfare income transfers to those with children and the elderly. Finally, the *power resource theory* argues that even with increased welfare assistance the gender gap will remain because patriarchy is structured in the state as well as in the economic sphere. Thus, when welfare policies are instituted, they often are aimed at addressing concerns of men by providing additional unemployment benefits or redistributing earned income rather than improving public services for and increasing income transfers to women and children.

Brady and Krall's research showed no significant change in the gender poverty gap with changes in poverty in general, thus rejecting the liberal economic theory. They did find support for the structural theory, however, as female unemployment, female single parenting, and a low sex ratio in the elderly population (more women than men among the elderly), all predicted larger gender gaps in poverty. The power resource theory received only limited support as social security transfers directly reduced the gender poverty gap but other measures of women's empowerment across societies had no effect and social welfare provisions (as found in Scandinavian countries) had a strong impact on both men's and women's poverty that did reduce the gender gap to some degree.

Given the strong association between rates of single parenting and rates of poverty, much of the research on the causes and consequences of poverty and policies enacted to reduce poverty have focused on this subgroup. Thus, the problem of poverty has become a problem of resolving high rates of single parenting in the population and, more generally, reinforcing traditional family norms and behaviors.[46] This conflagration of problems will be discussed in greater depth later in this chapter, although it is safe to say at this point that the problem of poverty is too complex to resolve with a simple solution of reducing the number of single mothers and elderly women in the population.

Significance of Poverty for Families

The challenges of poverty are similar to those faced by lower status working families in terms of inadequate resources to maximize family goals, risky neighborhood

---

[46]Melanie Heath, "State of our Unions: Marriage Promotion and the Contested Power of Heterosexuality," *Gender and Society* 23 (February 2009): 27–48.

environments, and, for the *working poor*, unsupportive work environments, insecure wages, and high potential for work-family spillover. Due to the extreme nature of their conditions, however, the problems of living in poverty are qualitatively different from those faced by lower status working families earning a *living wage*.

For individuals and families, living in poverty means adjusting to conditions where there are very few opportunities for escaping one's socioeconomic context or achieving even minimal personal or family goals. Also, in a modern capitalistic society, poverty often is considered the outcome of individuals' own failures to take advantage of opportunities. The responsibility for one's poverty lies with the individual and often is attributed to personal and moral failings. As a result, a great deal of stigma is attached to being poor. Third, those attempting to maintain and find meaning through marriage and family relationships are confronted with extreme levels of risk. Finding a marital partner with whom one can maintain a quality relationship, enduring the economic stressors that increase the risk of divorce, successfully managing children's risky environments outside the home, and constructing a meaningful and enriching home life are all made more difficult, and therefore more personally significant, by conditions of poverty. Finally, high levels of male unemployment, male incarceration, divorce, and births outside of marriage make men more marginal in poor families. This marginality contributes to the strong cultural emphasis on the mother–child dyad as the core of family life and the greater openness among poor mothers to include as "family" various relatives and friends (usually other women) with whom they have daily contact and close emotional contact.[47]

At an individual level, conditions of poverty often create high levels of chronic stress and reduced psychological well-being. Continual worrying about finding the means to avoid hunger and homelessness combined with restrictions on viable options for relieving stress can result in high levels of depression and substance abuse among the poor. Lack of capital and access to opportunities for advancement to higher status levels compounds these effects by creating high levels of hopelessness. In addition, the inadequacy of income earning activities among men and the high work demands placed on women (especially single mothers) can lead to feelings of failure to be a good spouse or a good provider.

Children also suffer as a result of poverty. Greg Duncan and his colleagues examined how childhood poverty affects the life chances of children.[48] They summarize the literature in addition to analyzing two sets of national data of U.S. households. The literature and their own findings showed that (1) family income has wide-ranging negative effects on children, and these effects are particularly strong with respect to achievement and ability-related outcomes rather than with measures of health and behavior; (2) early childhood appears to be the stage in which family economic conditions matter the most; and (3) the impact of family income on completed schooling appears to be larger for children in low-income families than those in high-income families. These effects are not only the result of disrupted family life among the poor but also contribute further to the challenges of maintaining a family among this group.

---

[47]Becker and Charles, "Layered Meanings: The Construction of 'the Family' in the Interview," 101–122.

[48]Greg J. Duncan, W. Jean Yeung, Jeanne Brooks-Gunn, and Judith R. Smith, "How Much Does Childhood Poverty Affect the Life Chances of Children?" *American Sociological Review* 63 (June 1998): 406–423.

The impacts of poverty on individual stress and well-being are likely to spill over into the realm of relationships and family dynamics. Indeed, the negative psychological effects on parents may account for the negative outcomes experienced by children in poverty. As noted in Chapter 2, the Family Economic Stress Model explains poor outcomes for children living in low socioeconomic conditions as being a result of the economic stress and resulting psychological distress experienced by parents. In a study by Rashmita Mistry and colleagues, this Family Economic Stress Model was examined using a sample from an antipoverty demonstration project in Milwaukee, Wisconsin, where participants had extremely low income levels and high dependence on public assistance programs. Using measures of perceived income inadequacy, they found that both were affected by different economic resources and both affected perceived lack of control over children and perceived responsiveness to children as a result of general psychological stress, depression, and feelings of self-efficacy. In addition, the negative impacts of income inadequacy on parenting control and responsiveness then accounted for higher levels of problem behavior and lower levels of positive behavior in the children from families with the lowest level of financial and other supports.[49]

One other important finding from this study was the discovery that perceived income inadequacy in the area of borderline discretionary spending on family "wants" (e.g., going somewhere "just for fun") independently predicted parental psychological distress in addition to the perceived inadequacy of income to meet family needs (e.g., groceries, transportation, housing, clothing, etc.). This finding confirms previous studies that have shown that, for a number of reasons, providing for modest wants as well as needs is essential to maintaining a positive self-perception as a good parent, helping children adjust emotionally to their impoverished environments, and providing opportunities for structuring "family time" where parent–child interaction and communication (and presumably parenting) can be enhanced.

More specific impacts of poverty on family dynamics have also been noted with respect to role performance problems and, in particular, the gendered division of labor in poor families. In a Hungarian study of how men and women experience poverty differently, Eva Fodor highlights how poverty disproportionately impacts the family lives of women, even among those who are married. Not only do women take on more of the budgeting responsibilities in poor families, but they also have to devote more time to role activities in their traditional domains of shopping (bargain hunting), home, food and clothing production, child care, and kinship and friendship network maintenance. Unlike working families and the wealthy, they have little or no discretionary income to waste and none to spend on items or services that might reduce home and care-giving tasks. To add to their burden even further, she notes that women living in poverty not only struggle to maintain a positive self-image as a good wife and mother under difficult circumstances, but they also often take on an additional emotional burden of caring for their husbands' greater emotional needs brought on by their perceived "failures" to achieve the traditional male expectations for being a good provider.[50]

---

[49]Rashmita S. Mistry, Edward D. Lowe, Aprile D. Benner, and Nina Chien, "Expanding the Family Economic Stress Model: Insights from a Mixed-Methods Approach," *Journal of Marriage and Family* 70 (February 2008): 196–209.

[50]Eva Fodor, "A Different Type of Gender Gap: How Women and Men Experience Poverty," *East European Politics and Societies* 20 (2006): 14–39.

CROSS-CULTURAL *Perspective*

Extended Families as a Strategy of Adaptation in Eastern Europe

The historical pattern of family composition in Eastern Europe has diverged from the pattern generally found throughout western and northern Europe where a "European marriage pattern" has been observed consisting of low rates of marriage and increased age at marriage. As a result, in the period prior to industrialization, family life was mostly nuclear in the west and north. In Eastern Europe, however, evidence suggests that extended families persisted and continued through much of the period of soviet domination due to housing shortages. What is the situation in Eastern Europe today, and is it related to lifestyle preferences or to socioeconomic conditions? Patricia Ahmed and Rebecca Jean Emigh attempted to determine the answers to these two questions in a study of household composition in five postsocialist East European countries: Bulgaria, Hungary, Poland, Romania, and Russia. In doing so, they put forward two hypotheses: (1) a preferences hypothesis that states household formation is the result of a strong preference based on biology, cultural beliefs, or some other set of factors

and (2) an adaptation hypothesis that states households form because they facilitate economic survival and enhance economic goals.

With respect to patterns of household formation in these countries, Ahmed and Emigh found that although most households are not extended, substantial minorities are, and these extended households are more common among the poor and among the Roma and poor subgroups. These results suggest that the adaptation hypothesis is more valid. In a further analysis of their data, Ahmed and Emigh provide additional evidence to support adaptation as a reason for continued extended households. For example, families that can realize their preferences—the wealthy and families of the well educated—show a significant tendency to be more nuclear, suggesting a preference for that type. In addition, the Roma, who have a cultural heritage that would favor extended households, tend not to differ from non-Roma households when socioeconomic conditions are held constant. In contrast, families whose adaptation would be most served through the additional support found in extended households—poor families, households with single parents, and households with retirees—are significantly more likely to be extended even when they also consist of groups that would otherwise prefer a nuclear family form.

Source: Patricia Ahmed, Rebecca Jean Emigh, "Household Composition in Post-Socialist Eastern Europe," *International Journal of Sociology and Social Policy,* 25 (2005), 9–41.

Survival of Families in Poverty

One of the principle means by which poor families (and especially poor single mothers) have been observed to manage family life without the assistance of a husband/father who can rely on a steady and livable wage is through a reliance on a support network of family and friends. As Carol Stack observed over thirty-five years ago in her study of black single mothers in New York City, one survival strategy used is captured by the cliché "What goes round comes round."[51] That is, clothing, furniture, food, appliances, money, and kids are shared among individuals and households. People give what they can and take what they need.

---

[51]Carol B. Stack, *All Our Kin: Strategies for Survival in a Black Community* (New York: Harper & Row, 1974), Chapter 3, 32–44.

These exchange patterns result in a *fictive kinship*, by which friends are turned into family. **Fictive kinship** refers to a network of persons which whom one is not related by birth, adoption, or marriage but who have rights and responsibilities equivalent to those who are so related. The swapping of goods and services results not merely in the norms of reciprocity that seem prevalent in most social exchanges, but also in stable friendships that pattern those of kin. As Stack found:

> Non-kin who live up to one another's expectations express elaborate vows of friendship and conduct their social relations within the idiom of kinship. Exchange behavior between those friends "going for kin" is identical to exchange behavior between close kin.[52]

These findings were replicated in a later national study of African Americans, which found support networks from both family and friends to be important sources of tangible assistance.[53] These networks are not just coincidentally helpful, but are necessary for survival.

One needs to be cautious as to the ability of kin (or even fictive kin) to assist those in poverty, however. One study showed that intergenerational support to contemporary young African American mothers may not be as abundant as past theorizing intimated. When kin support was available, welfare reforms provided an opportunity for black women to establish economic independence and mobility. But in many cases, kin support was absent or sorely lacking and, in these instances, welfare reform left many mothers with no support of any kind.[54] In another study of poor and lower class women living in rural trailer parks, Margie Kiter Edwards found that "hard-living women" who were less successful at maintaining family identity than more successful "settled women" reported much poorer relationships with friends and kinship members.[55] Thus, there is variability among the poor in the extent that they can utilize network support as an adaptation strategy, but having such supports can be an important resource for successful adaptation.[56]

Given the greater reliance on friends, family, and public agencies as sources of financial and other supports, it is not surprising to find that women in poor families who are making successful adaptations spend a good deal of effort at managing these relationships. The problem is not a simple one, however, as the involvement of outsiders in the family can threaten family boundaries and any sense of coherence as a family. Such threats also come about as a result of

---

[52]Deborah L. Padgett, "The Contribution of Support Networks to Household Labor in African American Families," *Journal of Social Issues* 18 (May 1997): 40.

[53]Ibid., 227–250.

[54]Katrina Bell McDonald and Elizabeth M. Armstrong, "De-Romanticizing Black Intergenerational Support: The Questionable Expectations of Welfare Reform," *Journal of Marriage and Family* 63 (February 2001): 213–223.

[55]Margie L. Kiter Edwards, "We're Decent People: Constructing and Managing Family Identity in Rural Working-Class Communities," *Journal of Marriage and Family* 66 (May 2004): 515–529.

[56]For a recent study of the causes and consequences of social support networks among the disadvantaged, see also: Kristen Harknet, The Relationship between Private Safety Nets and Economic Outcomes among Single Mothers," *Journal of Marriage and Family* 68 (February 2006): 172–191.

difficulties maintaining family privacy in high density neighborhoods and the challenge of fending off the negative consequences of social stigmas against the family as a whole and one's children in particular. In Kiter Edwards's research on trailer park families, she notes four important strategies that poor wives and mothers engage in to manage family identity: familial boundary maintenance (managing support systems with family members and friends); territorial boundary maintenance (managing and protecting private family space for engaging in family interaction and socialization activities); mobility restriction (managing their children's outside activities, friends, and relationships with authorities); and social restrictions (managing how others perceive one's family to create a positive image and thereby enhance opportunities and reduce the potential for negative consequences).

A third adaptation strategy employed by poor families involves the construction of family time. Carolyn Tubbs, Kevin Roy, and Linda Burton looked at how low-income families constructed "family time" in spite of the obligatory pressures of family economic maintenance activities and the lack of discretionary income to purchase opportunities for "free" time. Using ethnographic data from seventy-four poor families (less than 200 percent of the poverty line) in the Chicago component of the Welfare, Children and Families study, these researchers show that mothers in poor families not only value, but go to extraordinary lengths to make time for family interactions involving their children. Some of the techniques they used involved developing daily routines or rituals (e.g., family dinners, religious practices, bedtime routines, television watching) that provided opportunities for their children to have "talk time" with a parent; rearranging meal times as well as creating meal-time subgroups (e.g., staggered eating schedules to fit parents' irregular or nonoptimal work hours) to assure that all members of the family had opportunities to express their needs; structuring "play time" with their children to assist with their development and deal with their emotional needs; and providing treats to help define their children's "specialness." These strategies not only assisted with the adjustment and development of their children, but also helped parents feel a greater sense of control and effectiveness as parents—and as human beings.[57]

Programs and Policies to Help Families in Poverty

As noted in Chapter 2, the United States is a liberal welfare regime. As such, it is characterized by low levels of welfare benefits, complex requirements and regulations that restrict access to aid to only the very needy and that are designed to prevent welfare fraud, and high levels of social stigma attached to the receipt of aid. Although there are many types of aid available for different groups of needy individuals, the greatest welfare expenditures in the United States consist of Supplemental Security Income (SSI) for the elderly and disabled, Medicare and Medicaid, Food Stamps, the Earned Income Tax Credit (EITC) for low-income wage earners, and the **Temporary Assistance for Needy Families (TANF)** program targeted to help families with dependent children (formerly known as Aid to

---

[57]Carolyn Y. Tubbs, Kevin M. Roy, and Linda M. Burton, "Family Ties: Constructing Family Time in Low-Income Families," *Family Process* 44 (2005): 77–91.

Families with Dependent Children—AFDC). Of course, these forms of social welfare overlook other types of assistance that governments provide that don't support the poor such as lower tax rates for capital gains than income, interest deductions on multiple home loans, and ceilings on the amount of social security tax paid (effectively reducing their tax rate), to name just a few. Meyer, while noting race, class, and marital status biases linked to noncontributory benefits, shows that these benefits are most advantageous to middle- and upper-class white women.[58] Is this government support "welfare for the rich"?

In the context of the present discussion of families living under poverty, it is the programs that target low-income families that are of most interest here. The National Center for Children in Poverty reports that in 2006, there were one million adults, 1.8 million families, and 3.2 million children receiving this form of assistance. The total expenditure in 2006 just for "basic assistance" through this program was $9.9 billion.[59] These levels of aid and expenditures are considerably lower than in the predecessor to this program—AFDC—which was significantly changed as a result of congressional action in the mid-1990s as part of the Republican "Contract with America" and the Clinton administration's initiative to transform "welfare as we know it" through the **Personal Responsibility and Work Opportunity Reconciliation Act (PRWORA)** passed in 1996. Much of the rhetoric espoused during these welfare reform movements was focused on five themes or issues: (1) that these programs contributed to a **culture of poverty** that undermined values and beliefs in hard work as an avenue to self-sufficiency and success and contributed to the intergenerational transmission of poverty and welfare dependency; (2) that the incentive structure of these programs (based on number of children in the household relative to the number of adults) encouraged further childbearing and a flight from marriage to avoid losing benefits; (3) that encouraging aid recipients to work will reduce their dependency, counteract the culture of poverty, and help them escape conditions of poverty; (4) that the causes of poverty can be found in the lack of motivation among women, and particularly single mothers, to marry their partner or child's father and remain in marital relationships; and (5) that marriage enhances both family income and positive outcomes for children. In evaluating the success of these reforms, then, it is first necessary to evaluate each of these assumptions.

First, do public assistance programs such as AFDC and TANF contribute to a "culture of poverty" that undermines the work ethic and contribute to the intergenerational transfer of poverty and welfare dependency? There appears to be evidence to support a very limited contribution of parent welfare to the likelihood that their children will also be on welfare sometime in adulthood. Data from a large, national representative sample revealed that although three-quarters of welfare recipients did not grow up in households that received welfare, those raised in households that received welfare were more likely to receive welfare when they became adults. The authors suggest that this intergenerational connection has little to do with welfare per se but has much to do with economic class. Lower-class

[58]Madonna Harrington Meyer, "Making Claims as Workers or Wives: The Distribution of Social Security Benefits," *American Sociological Review* 61 (June 1996): 449–465.

[59]National Center for Children in Poverty (NCCP), "Temporary Assistance for Needy Families (TANF) Cash Assistance," http://www.nccp.org/profiles/index_36.html.

parents are limited financially in terms of the opportunities and resources they can offer their children.[60]

This suggestion has been supported by a recent study of welfare recipients in the state of Louisiana.[61] In this sample, having a mom on welfare significantly predicted a reduced likelihood that the recipient would move off welfare during the study period. The effect, however, was not due to a failure to adopt work ethic values. There was no effect of either mother's previous work history or mother's earlier welfare status on the welfare recipients' work ethic values and beliefs. Instead, the intergenerational effect of mother's welfare dependency on adult child dependency was mediated through the effect of impoverished conditions on the child's ability to accumulate human capital needed for later educational attainment and gainful employment. The authors of this study conclude that these findings support a **structure of poverty** explanation for intergenerational transmission rather than a *culture* of poverty explanation. Thus, programs that support single mothers will not have negative side effects on their children's later values and beliefs and programs that help create a healthy environment and provide educational opportunities for single parents and their children are likely to be more effective.

The second assumption made by those who have advocated for limitations on welfare benefits for single mothers and their children is that providing generous benefits is counterproductive insofar as those benefits are incentives for women to remain unmarried and to have more children. There is some recent evidence from the **Fragile Families and Child Well-being Study** [62] that suggests a slight reduction in the likelihood of marriage among those receiving TANF benefits versus those who do not. These effects are found even after controlling for sociodemographic characteristics, but the difference in likelihood is small and the effect disappears after these women are no longer receiving benefits.[63] It seems obvious that welfare benefits would reduce the economic motivation to marry and thereby suppress marriage rates. What is less obvious is whether or not this is a negative consequence. This study was unable to control for the types of partners each of the groups of women were confronted with and it did not assess differences between the TANF group and the controls with respect to the later marital and child outcomes each group experienced. These outcomes are addressed by other studies discussed later.

With respect to the assumed incentive that welfare benefits provide for single mothers to have more children, the results of a study by Mark Rank soundly reject this assumption. He found that women on welfare have a rate of fertility

---

[60]Mark R. Rank and Li-Chen Cheng, "Welfare Use across Generations: How Important Are the Ties That Bind?" *Journal of Marriage and the Family* 57 (August 1995): 673–684; and Lisa Greenwell, Arleen Leibowitz, and Jacob Alex Klerman, "Welfare Background, Attitudes, and Employment among New Mothers," *Journal of Marriage and the Family* 60 (February 1998): 175–193.

[61]M. A. Lee, Joachim Singelmann, and Anat Yom-Tov, "Welfare Myths: The Transmission of Values and Work among TANF Families," *Social Science Research* 37 (2008): 516–529.

[62]For more details about this important study of families at risk in urban centers of the United States conducted by the Bendheim-Thoman Center for Research on Child Wellbeing at Princeton University, go to http://www.fragilefamilies.princeton.edu

[63]Julien O. Teitler, Nancy E. Reichman, Lenna Nepomnyaschy, and Irwin Garfinkel, "Effects of Welfare Participation on Marriage", Center for Research on Child Wellbeing Working Paper #2205–24, See a brief of this research at: http://www.fragilefamilies.princeton.edu/ffpubs.asp.

considerably below that of women in the general population. Furthermore, the longer a woman remains on welfare, the less likely she is to give birth.[64] The women themselves suggested that their financial and social situations are not conducive to having more children. The economic, social, and psychological costs of becoming pregnant and having a child are perceived as clearly outweighing the benefits. Given these findings, one could ponder the economic, social, and psychological implications of formulating policy, as many states have done, that eliminates public funding for pregnant women (particularly those in poverty) to obtain abortions.

Like the two assumptions preceding it, the assumption that encouraging work through the rules associated with receiving benefits will help recipients get off welfare and escape poverty also is of questionable validity. Most people believe that mothers in poverty and on welfare should work and some studies indicate that greater amounts of public assistance income reduce the probability of being employed.[65] Yet, about one-third of welfare mothers are working, and half of all single mothers have some contact with the labor market. In addition, one study of African American women with children under age 6 found that those with relatively low levels of education and low earnings, and those never married all had a reduced probability of being employed regardless of how much public assistance income they received.

National data reveal that only very large and unrealistic increases in maternal employment would significantly reduce child poverty rates.[66] The solution to the poverty problems resides not only in encouraging parent work but also in creating jobs that pay a family wage. The "welfare trap" is not one of dependency but one in which welfare pays better than low-wage work. Thus, it is essential that those who do work can earn a living wage, can be secure in their jobs, and can avoid future pregnancies and births. This means removing barriers to employment by assuring affordable child care, health insurance coverage, fair and favorable tax policies, child-support payments, and the like.

Are Marriage Promotion Policies the Answer?

The final two assumptions made by those who advocated for substantial changes in welfare policies targeting low-income mothers and their children both involve a tying together of marital status, poverty, and negative outcomes for children. These assumptions were embedded in the 1996 PRWORA welfare legislation but became more prominent in the George W. Bush administration's Healthy Marriage Initiative of 2005. This initiative, funded as part of the Deficit Reduction Act, provides $150 million each year to promote marriage primarily among single parents and provide counseling and other services to help those in troubled marriages to overcome their difficulties and stay together. Although programs that enhance social and psychological counseling services to families in trouble are surely needed

---

[64]Mark P. Rank, "Fertility among Women on Welfare: Incidence and Determinants," *American Sociological Review* 54 (April 1989): 296–304.

[65]Marta Elliott and John F. Packham, "When Do Single Mothers Work? An Analysis of the 1990 Census Data," *Journal of Sociology and Social Welfare* 25 (March 1998): 39–60.

[66]Daniel T. Lichter and David J. Eggebeen, "The Effect of Parental Employment on Child Poverty," *Journal of Marriage and the Family* 56 (August 1994): 633–645.

and can be effective, the main focus of this legislation was to reinforce traditional marriage and encourage single mothers on welfare to marry and thereby no longer require the assistance of welfare.

As noted above, one assumption behind this initiative (and the fourth assumption of "welfare reformers") is that single mothers need to be motivated to marry. That somehow their welfare dependency has left them without the desire to form a long-term, committed heterosexual relationship with their child's father. Research studies using the Fragile Families data set again refute this assumption. A majority of poor single mothers and, to a lesser extent, fathers in the Fragile Families study believed it is (1) better to get married than live together and (2) better for children if parents are married. They also had a strong desire to get married and felt strongly that they would get married.[67] Furthermore, the desire to get married and the expectations for marrying the child's other parent are not just the result of a desire to cast themselves in a more positive light on a survey instrument given that they had just engaged in a non-normative behavior (giving birth outside of marriage)—**social desirability bias**.[68] As Gibson-Davis, Edin, and McLanahan report, the level of desire and expectation for marriage go down slightly several months later when these couples are interviewed in a less formal manner, but the levels are still high enough to expect a good number of these unmarried mothers to get married in the near future.

In spite of these positive attitudes toward marriage, an analysis of data obtained from these same unmarried mothers three years later shows that very few managed to fulfill their desires and expectations. Fewer than 15 percent eventually married in the intervening time period in spite of the fact that 51 percent were living with the child's father at the time of the child's birth, and another 32 percent were in romantic relationships with the child's father who "visited" frequently.[69]

Given their strong support for and desire to marry, what are the reasons for remaining unmarried and susceptible to continued welfare dependency and poverty? There are two major barriers to marriage that these unmarried mothers are confronted with. First is their strong attitudes and concerns about what is needed to have a viable marriage. As Gibson-Davis, Edin, and McLanahan show, these women had three sets of concerns about getting married: financial, relational, and the potential for divorce. Financially, they felt that marriage required financial stability, asset accumulation, and high levels of financial responsibility on the part of the marital partners. They also felt that having enough to afford a real wedding was an important prerequisite for marriage. Relationally, these women saw marriage as a long-term commitment—the "ultimate" relationship—that required clear readiness on the part of the partners and a trial period of cohabitation to assure that they were ready. Finally, there was a clear fear of getting into a marriage that would ultimately lead to divorce. Many believed in the sanctity of marriage, and most

[67]Wendy Sigle-Rushton and Sara McLanahan, "Is Marriage a Viable Objective for Fragile Families?" Center for Research on Child Wellbeing Working Paper #2005–9, See a brief of this research at: http://www.fragilefamilies.princeton.edu/ffpubs.asp.

[68]Christina M. Gibson-Davis, Kathryn Edin, and Sara McLanahan, "High Hopes but Even Higher Expectations: The Retreat from Marriage among Low income Couples," *Journal of Marriage and Family* 67 (December 2005): 1301–1312.

[69]Maureen R. Waller and H. Elizabeth Peters, "The Risk of Divorce as a Barrier to Marriage among Parents of Young Children," *Social Science Research* 37 (2008): 1188–1199.

believed marriage should be a lifelong relationship and wished to avoid the stigma and hurt that can result from divorce.[70]

Compounding the effects of these strong attitudes and concerns are the personal and structural barriers these women faced. On a personal level, 35 percent of mothers and 31 percent of fathers reported some health limitation.[71] In addition, almost 25 percent of these parental dyads included a member who suffered from clinical levels of depression, another 5 percent had generalized anxiety problems, 21 percent reported at least one member with a drug or alcohol problem, 9 percent reported experiencing domestic violence in the previous year, and 10 percent involved a father who was a violent offender.[72] At a structural level, barriers to marriage include social and economic conditions that put potential marriages at risk and that limit the potential profitability of marriage such as low educational attainment of mothers and fathers, high unemployment and incarceration rates among fathers, and low wages among working fathers.

Ultimately, these data suggest that programs to simply promote marriage at the attitudinal level are likely to be ineffective. Poor unmarried mothers appear to have strong positive attitudes about marriage but are making reasoned and rational decisions not to get married based on the potential for their marriage to be successful given their personal traits, their partners' traits, and their socioeconomic circumstances.

The wisdom of this decision-making process is suggested by one additional innovative analysis of the Fragile Families data set by Maureen Waller and H. Elizabeth Peters.[73] These researchers first used almost 1,200 *married* respondents in the study to estimate a prediction model for the likelihood of divorce three years after the birth of their child. This model included predictors such as low age at marriage, low education, father's incarceration history, high relationship conflict with father, low shared social network involvement, and residence in a city with high divorce rates. Using this model, they then created a measure for the 3,700 *unmarried* mothers in the study called the **propensity for divorce**. When this measure was entered into a model to predict the likelihood of marriage among these unmarried mothers, they found that the most significant predictors of the likelihood of an unmarried mother marrying within three years of the birth of a child were: not being black, high rates of religious attendance, employed status of the father at birth of child, high father wage at the time when the child was born, and having a high propensity for divorce at the time the child was born. Thus, poor unmarried mothers recognize that marriage for them is a very risky proposition due to their personal, structural, and cultural situation and appear to be making decisions based on a rational assessment of that risk.

The final assumption behind recent attempts to reform welfare for poor families and promote marriage is that doing so will create a better environment for children by reducing poverty and its resulting stress, increasing father involvement,

---

[70]Gibson-Davis, Edin, and McLanahan, "High Hopes but Even Higher Expectations: The Retreat from Marriage among Low Income Couples," 1301–1312.

[71]Sigle-Rushton and McLanahan, "Is Marriage a Viable Objective for Fragile Families?"

[72]Bendheim-Toman Center for Research on Child Wellbeing, "Barriers to Marriage among Fragile Families," *Fragile Families Research Brief* 16 (May 2003), http://www.fragilefamilies.princeton.edu/ffpubs.asp.

[73]Waller and Peters, "The Risk of Divorce as a Barrier to Marriage among Parents of Young Children," 1188–1199.

and increasing the effectiveness of parenting. Unfortunately, this assumption has only partial support, as the situation faced by poor single mothers in trying to be good parents is more complex and cannot be resolved with a simple measure such as getting married. For example, Christina Gibson-Davis shows that among Fragile Families mothers,[74] it was their socioeconomic circumstances that affected their parenting behaviors and not whether or not they were married, cohabiting, or parenting alone. For fathers, family structure effects were more pronounced, but it was new cohabiting partners (not biological fathers) who showed the highest levels of engagement and cooperation in parenting. Gibson-Davis explains these conflicting results with previous studies showing significant family structure effects by noting that they control for selection effects into marriage. As she concludes: "... marriage does not appear to be the key determinant of parenting behavior for either fathers or mothers...and care should be taken not to confound the institution of marriage with the characteristics of those who choose to wed."[75]

Gregory Acs also confronts this issue and marriage promotion policies directly[76] in a study using the National Longitudinal Survey of Youth, a large national representative data set. In this study, he compares the impacts on young children (ages 2–11) from living in six types of families: stable marriage families, unstable marriage families (those that ultimately experience divorce at the later point in time), blended families, families of cohabiting biological parents, families of cohabiting social parents (one partner is not the child's parent), and single-parent families. Acs also looks at how transitioning into a married parent family from either single-parenting or cohabiting parents impacts children. By comparing children in stable versus unstable families, his results tell us something about the value of parents "staying together" for the children and the potential results of programs that make divorce more difficult or simply encourage couples to stay together. By comparing outcomes from situations where parents stay unmarried to those where they get married, his results tell us something about programs that promote unmarried women's marriage to their child's father.

For the entire sample, his results show some support for promoting marriage as young children in both stable and unstable marriage families do better on a variety of cognitive and behavioral measures than children from cohabiting and single-parent families. This effect is greater for stable marriages but does exist to a smaller extent for even the unstable marriages. Acs also finds that although the transition to marriage is initially detrimental to young children, these negative effects are offset by the advantage of living in a family with married parents.

On the other hand, his results also question the validity of the marriage benefit to children among those living in poverty. When Acs restricts his sample to only those living below 200 percent of the poverty line, he finds most of the advantage of living in a married parent family disappears, especially when that relationship is unstable. He also finds negative effects of making a transition to

[74]Christina M. Gibson-Davis, "Family Structure Effects on Maternal and Paternal Parenting in Low-Income Families," *Journal of Marriage and Family* 70 (May 2008): 452–465.

[75]Gibson-Davis, "Family Structure Effects on Maternal and Paternal Parenting in Low-Income Families," 463.

[76]Gregory Acs, "Can We Promote Child Well-Being by Promoting Marriage?" *Journal of Marriage and Family* 69 (December 2007): 1326–1344.

a married parent family that are greater than any positive advantage gained by living with two married parents. Finally, Acs's results show that the effects of mothers' education are substantially greater than the effects of marital status of parents. As a result, he concludes that marriage promotion programs are unlikely to be highly effective in enhancing child outcomes among the poor and that programs promoting the educational attainment of mothers will have much greater impacts.

Given the questionable assumptions behind recent welfare reforms, what happens to families and children who have been on Temporary Assistance to Needy Families, or its predecessor, AFDC, who have either forcefully or voluntarily left the program? Meyer and Cancian found substantial diversity in economic well-being five years after leaving.[77] Women who were working when they exited from AFDC did better, as did those who were married or had a partner, those with higher earning potential and higher education, and those with fewer or older children. Although some families achieved modest levels of economic success, 41 percent remained poor even five years after an exit from AFDC. These results highlight the distinction between leaving welfare and leaving poverty. The authors conclude that reforms targeted at reducing caseloads may do relatively little to enhance economic success.

In conclusion, cuts in governmental food, housing, and health benefits clearly hit those living below the poverty level the hardest and will likely increase the need for assistance across generations. The obvious solution to poverty in general and the feminization of poverty in particular is to increase standards of living. But how?[78] This may be achieved by either expanding benefits or increasing income. Given the public and political outcry against welfare and public assistance, the answer clearly will not come from expanding benefits. Realistic solutions include education and employment—but employment that pays well enough to lift the family and the children within it out of poverty. Higher wages for those working, as well as investments in education, are two very important factors in getting people off of welfare and on to economic independence.[79] Ironically, in the light of recent attempts to solve the problem of poverty through marriage promotion efforts, research strongly suggests that solving the problem of poverty by removing the social and economic barriers to self-sufficiency through employment in living wage jobs is likely to have a profound positive effect on the creation and maintenance of two-parent families.

Social Mobility: Changing Family Lifestyles

One fundamental characteristic of families and social stratification is the extent to which there is opportunity to move from one class to another. Although **social mobility** often is thought to mean *social improvement*, mobility can be upward,

---

[77]Daniel R. Meyer and Maria Cancian, "Economic Well-Being Following an Exit from Aid to Families with Dependent Children," *Journal of Marriage and the Family* 60 (May 1998): 479–492.

[78]See Alvin L. Schorr, "Ending Poverty," *American Behavioral Scientist* 35 (January/February 1992): 332–339; and Catherine S. Chilman, "Working Poor Families: Trends, Causes, Effects, and Suggested Policies," *Family Relations* 40 (April 1991): 191–198.

[79]Kathleen Mullan Harris, "Work and Welfare among Single Mothers in Poverty," *American Journal of Sociology* 99 (September 1993): 317–352.

news item

Nanny Trap Is Suspiciously Selective

The allegations of nanny mistreatment against Ruby Dhalla raise questions not only about the Liberal MP's cred but also about sexism and child care....

Consider: South of the border, a string of both men and women have been nailed over the years. Most recently, Timothy Geithner, U.S. President Barack Obama's treasury secretary, was criticized for having a housekeeper whose immigration papers expired while in his employ.

At the same time, business consultant Nancy Killefer declined a senior cabinet position, ostensibly because she hadn't paid her nanny's unemployment premiums in a timely fashion back in 2005.

(He's in. She's out. Hmm.)

That wealthy and powerful people sometimes take advantage of vulnerable workers, who struggle to support families back home until they can bring them to Canada, is completely reprehensible.

But it happens. From all appearances, it happens all the time. So has nary a single male Canadian MP ever mistreated his gardener, dogwalker, snow shoveller? Does every male pol pay his housecleaner decent wages, above the table? Does every nanny in every male legislator's household perform just the work she was hired to do?...

One of the reasons there are so few women in Parliament—truly, we have just about the worst record in the developed world—is because of the lack of child care. What's more, women are also usually burdened with looking after aging, ailing parents. Just last month, White House communications director Ellen Moran was the first senior Obama adviser to step down, citing her marriage and two toddlers as the reason.

Now you'd think the Obamas, all things considered, would have onsite daycare. But no. Indeed, Michelle Obama's mother Marian Robinson was roped in, initially reluctant to leave her lifelong Chicago home, to look after her granddaughters Malia and Sasha. Not many parents are so fortunate to have such reliable back-up.

Admittedly, in Dhalla's Mississauga home, there are no children. There is just her, her brother Neil, and their mother Tavinder, who doesn't seem to be either particularly disabled or infirm.

At least not so much as to qualify for the Live-In Caregiver program.

Fears now among women who have emailed me are that, whatever happens to the nanny program, it will not make it easier for them.

First, because Canadians who want child care will have to jump through more bureaucratic hoops, with more possibilities for legal errors.

Second, because immigrant women hoping for better lives won't get the chance to earn them if Canadian parents play it safe by avoiding the live-in program.

Either way, it will be women—and children—who will pay the price.

Source: The Toronto Star, http://www.thestar.com/News/Canada/article/628987.

downward, or lateral. The first two types (upward and downward) are referred to as *vertical social mobility*, and the latter (lateral) is referred to as *horizontal social mobility*.

Generally, horizontal social mobility is used to refer to movement to a different occupation within a similar social strata or class. A residential or geographical move may be social mobility of a horizontal nature as well, and one that has significant consequences. For example, children who live with only one parent or with stepparents were found to experience both (1) more residential mobility and (2) a higher school dropout rate than children living in two-parent families.[80] As much

[80]Nan Marie Astone and Sara S. McLanahan, "Family Structure, Residential Mobility, and School Dropout: A Research Note," *Demography* 31 (November 1994): 575–584.

as 30 percent of the difference in the risk of dropping out of school between children from stepfamilies and children from intact families was explained by residential mobility.

Likelihood of Vertical Social Mobility

The likelihood of vertical social mobility is a function of three separate phenomena. First is the *opportunity structure* to which the individual has access. This is the organizational structure of a society that defines the ultimate achievement possibilities for the individual as well as the channels available to realize achievement. Different opportunity structures apply to different individuals, groups, and subcultures within the same society. However, the structure of the society—including the presence or absence of jobs, the availability of educational and training programs, and other social characteristics—will, in large part, determine the extent to which mobility occurs.

The second component of the likelihood of vertical social mobility is the *individual*. Personality characteristics—such as intelligence, motivation, motor skills, and value systems—determine the individual's capacity for exploiting the opportunity structure and influence the likelihood of mobility.

The third component may be termed the *frictional factor*, that is, two identically equipped individuals who confront the same opportunity structure may nevertheless attain disparate levels of mobility. These factors, inherent in neither the individual nor the opportunity structure, may be referred to as chance, luck, or fortune.[81]

The first factor in the likelihood of vertical social mobility, the opportunity structure, seems more crucial to understanding the low achievements of poor children and families than either psychological factors (such as personality type and motivation) or simple good fortune. What are the chances for mobility?

Extent of Vertical Social Mobility

The American dream suggests that, in this land of opportunity, anyone can go from "rags to riches." The widespread belief is that hard work, endurance, and motivation will enable anyone to move up on the social-class ladder. The fact is that social mobility and equal opportunity have probably never been as attainable as U.S. citizens have believed. But recent data have suggested that social mobility in U.S. society is increasing.

It has been estimated that one of every four or five persons moves up at least one social-class level during his or her lifetime. The greatest amount of upward mobility occurs among blue-collar workers. What is less frequently recognized and studied is downward mobility.

Patricia Smith, in two articles (one with the subtitle "Sinking Boats in a Rising Tide"), notes that over two separate three-year periods, in spite of a growing economy, a substantial minority of Americans (5 to 20 percent) experienced downward income mobility.[82] A large share of the downward mobility came from the middle

---

[81]Bradley R. Schiller, "Stratified Opportunities: The Essence of the 'Vicious Circle,'" *American Journal of Sociology* 76 (November 1970): 427.

[82]Patricia K. Smith, "Recent Patterns in Downward Income Mobility: Sinking Boats in a Rising Tide," *Social Indicators Research* 31 (1994): 277–303; and Patricia K. Smith, "Downward Mobility: Is It a Growing Problem?" *American Journal of Economics and Sociology* 53 (January 1994): 57–72.

and lower classes. Women who separated or divorced faced the highest risk of downward mobility. The factors that increased the odds of downward mobility included female headship, minority headship, family dissolution, nest leaving, and having a household head who works in mining, construction, manufacturing, transportation, trade, or farming. The factors that lowered the odds included having a college-educated head of household, retaining the same household heads, and having them working in professional, technical, or operative occupations or in the finance, insurance, or real estate industries.

Downward mobility involves more than a loss of job and drop in income. It includes a loss of occupational prestige and demotion from one's place in society, as well. Marriage, child rearing, divorce, widowhood, and employment of wives all affect families and the status they hold. The experience of family disruption during a male's childhood substantially increases his odds of ending up in a lower occupational stratum.[83] For women, divorce is a particularly traumatic event that leads to downward mobility. Most victims of downward mobility, male or female, express feelings of anger, dismay, and injustice.

Empirical studies of social mobility have suggested several general conclusions:

1. Most children will ultimately live at the same class level as their parents.
2. A substantial proportion of sons and daughters will experience some mobility. One study of three generations found that each successive generation of offspring had higher occupational attainment than the one before.[84]
3. Upward mobility is more prevalent than downward mobility.
4. When mobility does occur, it will likely be a shift to a class level adjacent to that of the individual's parents; that is, short-distance mobility is more common than long-distance mobility.

Consequences of Social Mobility

Few people are immune to the possibility of downward social mobility, and many would likely embrace the opportunity for upward social mobility. With this opportunity comes a better job, a higher income, a more luxurious home, a more prestigious neighborhood, opportunities to travel, better clothes, a new car, freedom from debt—in short, a more luxurious and refined lifestyle. Many, if not most, people believe that education is one means to obtain these rewards. Within U.S. society, with its fairly open-class system and its increasing requirements for specialized and highly trained technicians and experts, "brain power" frequently means higher status. But a closer investigation of the open-class system shows that not all consequences of mobility, even upward social mobility, are positive. In various ways, the costs of upward social mobility may be great and the penalties quite severe.

Many students discover that their increased education (a potential contribution to upward social mobility) has some disruptive effects. The most obvious is likely to be an increasingly estranged relationship with parents. Many students find that, as they become more educated, their beliefs and values change in ways that may

[83]Timothy J. Biblarz and Adrian E. Raftery, "The Effects of Family Disruption on Social Mobility," *American Sociological Review* 58 (February 1993): 97–109.

[84]Timothy J. Biblarz, Vern L. Bengston, and Alexander Bucur, "Social Mobility across Three Generations," *Journal of Marriage and the Family* 58 (February 1996): 188–200.

conflict with those of their parents, particularly if their parents are working-class people of limited formal education. The paradox of this situation is that these are frequently the types of parents who make major sacrifices to provide college education for their children. The painful consequence is that their children become socially distant from them.

In some instances, marriage itself may be threatened by upward social mobility. The wife who works to assist her husband in completing his education may find that his value system and lifestyle change while hers remains more static. Success in business may encourage certain husbands to seek the friendship of more sophisticated or like-minded females. Career-oriented wives may discover that, with increased economic and social opportunities, they can be self-sufficient and independent, perhaps eliminating the need or desire for a husband. Career women may discover men whose values and behavior patterns are more to their liking than those of their husbands. These and many other examples of upward social mobility illustrate how this supposedly desirable phenomenon may disrupt husband–wife relationships.

Summary

1. *Social stratification* is a defined as a ranking of persons and groups in a hierarchy of unequal social positions. Two theories particularly relevant to understanding social class are the structural-functional and conflict theories. Functionalist theory asserts that a stratified system is inevitable and necessary for the fulfillment of tasks needed to maintain a society. Conflict theory holds that a stratified system is not inevitable and leads to injustices, dissatisfaction and conflict between groups competing to realize their group interests. Stratification comes about because certain interest groups gain an advantage over other groups and then structure society and create cultures to support their advantaged position. Interest groups can be based on one's age, gender, race, ethnicity, religion, relationship to production activities (the type of work one does), or any of a number of different factors.

2. *Social class* is only one type of social stratification system and is based on one's relationship to the means of production. Other types are **caste** and **estate** systems. Social class is based on whether one is an owner of the means of production or one is a worker in the system of production. In modern societies, this distinction is not always clear because ownership often is dispersed to share holders throughout the population. Nevertheless, it is still useful to distinguish between wealthy families, those who work for salary or wages for a living (working families), and those who either do not work or who work for wages that are insufficient for sustaining a livelihood (families in poverty). A more useful concept for understanding modern capitalistic societies is *socioeconomic status*—a continuous measure of one's location in the stratification system based on education, occupational prestige, and income.

3. The significance of socioeconomic status for families lies in the ways that it structures opportunities and power in society and thereby shapes cultural beliefs and values, environmental or ecological contexts, and the availability of economic, human, social, and cultural capital to realize goals and adapt to social contexts.

4. Wealthy families have been identified as the very rich, the upper class, and the ruling class. This elite group owns and controls majority shares in corporations either individually or through a network of family and kin. Wealthy families are concerned with who they are and serve to protect their names and resources. They care a great deal about family ties because those ties are critical to their ability to concentrate their wealth and maintain their privileged position in society.

5. It is no longer useful to make distinctions between middle and working class families as the boundaries between these groups have become more blurred in modern capitalism. Working families consist of those who must rely on salaries or wages in order to maintain a minimal or greater standard of living. Great diversity exists among working families based on their general level of prestige and economic resources (economic capital); the types of neighborhood they live in and that shape their opportunities,

resources, and challenges; the level of education they have attained; the types of work they do and the occupational environments they are employed in; and the levels of human, social, and cultural capital they have accumulated for achieving their individual and family goals.

6. Because they have more potential to move up in the hierarchy and more to lose by moving down, higher socioeconomic status is associated with a greater consciousness about social values and social change and a greater emphasis on individualism, independence, autonomy, and rational planning to achieve goals. These values differences are reflected in the greater value placed on equality in marital relationships; greater psychological, emotional, and financial investments made in their children; and childrearing values and behaviors that foster independence of thought and action in their children.

7. Higher socioeconomic status is also associated with higher levels of institutional resources in the local community and greater normative/collective efficacy in the neighborhood context. These more favorable conditions are reflected in lower levels of individual and family stressor events, improved ability to react to stressor events and avoid stress, greater parenting efficacy, and more positive parenting outcomes.

8. The higher educational attainment levels found among higher status families influences family life in three ways: (1) increased access to resources and opportunities that enhance marriage, parenting, and family life in general; (2) the development of more modern and less conventional values that alter perceptions about the significance of marital and family relationships and make higher status families less responsive to traditional social norms; and (3) greater cognitive capacity, background knowledge, and social skills that can enhance marital and parenting outcomes.

9. In general, higher social status work and occupational positions will involve lower levels of negative work-family due to greater role flexibility, a more individual and family supportive workplace, and more free hours at work do deal with necessary family tasks. In addition, higher status occupations are ones that tend to involve working with ideas and people rather than working with things. These workers are also more likely to be encouraged and rewarded for innovation and independence of thought. These conditions of work have been shown to increase the cognitive flexibility of parents and influence their parenting values and practices in ways that facilitate their children's development and success in modern societies.

10. The United States has one of the highest poverty rates in the modern world. Even using a measure of poverty that is extremely conservative, almost 10 percent of families and 17 percent of children under the age of 18 live below the official poverty line, and poverty is particularly high for young and older Americans, blacks and Hispanics, single parents, and women. The higher rates of poverty for women today are found throughout the modern world; this new trend is referred to as the feminization of poverty.

11. Poverty presents many of the same challenges to family life as in lower status working families, but these challenges are considerably greater. Families living in poverty need to adapt to high levels of social stigma and high levels of individual distress resulting from their extreme economic conditions. As a result, they are more open to an expanded definition of family that may incorporate unrelated others and may exclude fathers if they don't provide support. They also need to go to unusual steps to create a sense of family and provide opportunities for "family time."

12. Given the high number of single mothers and their children living in poverty and on welfare, much concern has been expressed recently in how to more effectively design welfare programs. Unfortunately, much of this discussion has focused more on reducing the welfare roles than on solving the problem of poverty. Research on the effectiveness of recent welfare reform initiatives—especially those focused on promoting marriage as a solution—shows that most of the assumptions made by these reforms are not valid. The problem of poverty (and its negative consequences for children) cannot be solved by encouraging single mothers to marry. In fact, programs that help the poor get the education they need to be productive in the work force and that increase the wages for low-income workers are likely to be more effective in reducing poverty as well as in encouraging more two-parent families.

13. What are the chances for and consequences of family social mobility, upward or downward? Upward social mobility in the United States has probably never been as widespread as widely believed, but it seems to be increasing. While seen as desirable by most persons, upward mobility can result in new recognition and social prestige or may bring rejection and social isolation.

This chapter has shown how family life is shaped by the conditions of one's social-class position and how different meanings of family may emerge from very different conditions of life across social classes. Chapter 5 continues this theme but looks at race and ethnicity as another defining characteristic that shapes the conditions of our lives and thereby affects the nature of families.

Key Terms and Topics

Social stratification p. 146

Structural-functional perspective p. 147

Conflict theorists p. 147

Interest group p. 147

Social caste p. 147

Estate system p. 148

Social classes p. 148

Socioeconomic status p. 149

Wealthy families p. 152–154

Working families p. 154–163

Institutional resources p. 157

Normative/collective efficacy p. 157

Role conflict p. 161

White-collar jobs p. 162

Blue-collar jobs p. 162

Human poverty index for developing countries p. 164

Human poverty index for developed countries p. 164

Poverty threshold p. 165

Poverty guidelines p. 165

Feminization of poverty p. 167

Fictive kinship p. 172

Temporary Assistance for Needy Families (TANF) p. 173

Personal Responsibility and Work Opportunity Reconciliation Act (PRWORA) p. 174

Culture of poverty p. 174

Structure of poverty p. 175

Fragile Families and Child Well-being Study p. 175

Social desirability bias p. 177

Propensity for divorce p. 178

Social mobility p. 180

Discussion Questions

1. What is social stratification, how does it come about in societies, and how is it related to the concept of social class?

2. What is socioeconomic status, what are its three major components, and in what ways is one's position in the socioeconomic hierarchy significant for family life?

3. What are the key issues and concerns of the wealthy and how do those issues and concerns affect the ways that the wealthy construct their families?

4. What are some of the key dimensions along which people with different levels of socioeconomic status differ from each other and how do those differences impact their family lives?

5. How do differences in income and prestige affect the values and concerns of working families and how do those values and concerns affect their family lives?

6. How are differences in educational attainment important for family functioning?

7. How do difference in socioeconomic status in terms of the nature of work and occupational activities (especially differences between white collar vs. blue collar workers) impact marital and parenting relationships among working families?

8. How is poverty measured internationally and nationally? What do you think about the adequacy of these measures for identifying those whose lives are impacted by severe negative economic conditions?

9. What is the feminization of poverty and how has it come about in modern societies?

10. How does poverty impact families and what strategies do poor families use to adapt to their situation?

11. What assumptions underlie recent changes in welfare programs in the United States? What does research tell us about the validity of these assumptions?

12. What factors foster upward social mobility? Downward social mobility? Why are many consequences of upward social mobility disruptive to kin and community ties?

Further Readings

Duncan, Greg J., Huston, Aletha C. and Weisner, Thomas S. *Higher Ground: New Hope for the Working Poor and Their Children*. New York, NY: Russell Sage Foundation, 2007.

A description and analysis of a program in Milwaukee, Wisconsin initiated by activists and business leaders to address the problems of poverty among single mothers.

Edin, Kathryn and Kefalas, Maria. *Promises I Can Keep: Why Poor Women Put Motherhood Before Marriage*. Berkeley, CA: University of California Press, 2007.

A study involving in-depth interviews with over 160 single mothers discussing the dilemma they face in weighing marriage versus parenting concerns.

Elder, Glen H., and Conger, Rand D. *Children of the Land: Adversity and Success in Rural America*. Chicago: University of Chicago Press, 2000.

An investigation of the role that farming plays in adaptations to change and in the developmental experiences of the young.

Haour-Knipe, Mary. *Moving Families: Expatriation, Stress and Coping*. New York: Routledge Press, 2001.

A detailed exploration of how families cope with the stresses of moving to a new culture.

Henrici, Jane, ed. *Doing Without: Women and Work After Welfare Reform*. Tucson, AZ: University of Arizona Press, 2006.

Nine case studies of women living in poverty and confronting new welfare policies requiring work involvement.

Kowaleski-Jones, Lori and Wolfinger, Nicholas H., eds. *Fragile Families and the Marriage Agenda*. New York, NY: Springer, 2006.

An examination of the proposition that government interventions can and should be used to raise marriage rates and address the problems of poverty.

Lareau, Annette. *Unequal Childhoods: Class, Race, and Family Life*. Berkeley: University of California Press, 2003.

An ethnographic study of how parents in different social classes differentially guide and direct their children's lives inside and outside the home.

Orrange, Robert M. *Work, Family and Leisure: Uncertainty in a Risk Society*. Lanham, MD: Rowman and Littlefield Publishers, 2007.

Based on in-depth interviews with advanced law and MBA students, this study explores the impacts of modern society on life course expectations around work, family and leisure.

Rosier, Katherine Brown. *Mothering Inner-City Children: The Early School Years*. New Brunswick, NJ: Rutgers University Press, 2000.

A book about low-income, inner-city black mothers, their children, and the various neighborhoods in which their lives are embedded.

Seccombe, Karen. *"So You Think I Drive a Cadillac?": Welfare Recipients' Perspectives on the System and Its Reform*. Boston: Allyn & Bacon, 1999.

Based on the stories of forty-seven women, the book provides an insightful look at what it is like to be poor and live on welfare.

Shirk, Martha, Bennett, Neal G., and Aber, J. Lawrence. *Lives on the Line: American Families and the Struggle to Make Ends Meet*. Boulder, CO: Westview Press, 1999.

Stories of ten low-income American families engaged in a struggle to overcome the barriers created by poverty.

Simon, Rita J., ed. *A Look Backward and Forward at American Professional Women and Their Families*. Lanham, MD: University Press of America, 2000.

Part I focuses on women and the American family, including home schooling, countercultural womanhood, joint custody, and obstacles that keep men from their families.

White, Lynn, and Rogers, Stacy J. "Economic Circumstances and Family Outcomes: A Review of the 1990s," *Journal of Marriage and the Family* 62 (November 2000): 1035–1051.

A decade-review article that looks at the consequences of economic circumstances on family formation, divorce, marital quality, and child well-being.

Wilson, William Julius. *The Ghetto Underclass: Social Science Perspectives*. Newbury Park, CA: Sage, 1993.

Wilson and other leading social scientists cover family patterns, sexual behavior, immigration, and homelessness of the urban underclass.

5

Race and Ethnic Variations

Father of Three, Husband to None

"I'm Larry, a 23-year-old African American male, high school graduate, and full-time employee as a security and electrical technician. I have never been married but have three children, ages 7, 4, and 3, by three mothers. I was responsible for two other pregnancies, both of which ended before birth. Prior to the first pregnancy, I guess I had sex with about twenty different women.

"My oldest boy was conceived when I was 15. The mother was 18. I only slept with her one time in my life and she got pregnant. I wanted her to have an abortion but she refused. I accepted paternity, pay child support each month, and see my son regularly.

"Several years later, I had a daughter by my first love and the only woman I was ever committed to. We were in high school together and I was very happy about her pregnancy. Since she was only 16, we both agreed not to get married but continued to see each other for another year or so. During this time, I continued to have sex with other women and my third child, a son, was conceived before my daughter was born.

"I gave money to the mother of my third child to have an abortion but she wouldn't do it. I'm not close to her at all and, although I provide support to my two oldest children, I don't help financially with this child. Anyway, she makes more money than I do.

"No, none of the five pregnancies by me were planned. And although I have had sex with probably 130 to 150 women, the last two years I have always carried a condom and have used one every time I had sex. I don't want any more children and the disease thing is real scary. About one-third of the women I've had sex with have come on to me. I respect women, and if they want sex, so do I. I'll do whatever they want. But I will never sleep with a woman who doesn't want to. I've never picked up a prostitute but have agreed to give some money to several women to move the relationship along a bit faster. I'd have to spend it on them anyway.

"My goal is to get a college education and degree. I'll probably get married within the next three years to the mother of my second child. None of the mothers of my children have ever been married but this one is real nice. I do a lot with my daughter, with the other child she has, and with my oldest son and want them all to do well in school."

Questions to Consider

What are/should be the roles and responsibilities of Larry toward his children and their mothers? Do unique factors exist in the African American culture that make the position and roles of men different than in the larger society? How do you think African Americans differ from other ethnic groups in this respect?

How do you explain the lower marriage rates and higher single-parent rates that exist among African American, Hispanic, and Native American women when compared to whites and Asian Americans? Does the larger society hold a responsibility to provide support for single parents and children in poverty, regardless of race or ethnicity?

*I*n this chapter, we will examine the meaning and significance for family life of social classifications of people into groups based on their outward physical appearance (race) and/or their cultural origins (ethnicity). At the outset, however, it is important to clarify the meanings of these two classification systems and why they are significant factors in understanding family life.

*M*eanings of Race and Ethnicity

Race is accepted by most people (including many scientists and scholars) as a way to classify people based on shared physical characteristics that reflect a common evolutionary history and hidden genetic traits resulting from generations of adaptations to environmental conditions. As a result, individuals from the same race are assumed to be more similar to each other than to others of different races and are assumed to possess similar capabilities and behavioral predispositions different from those of other races.[1]

Basing their classifications primarily on three physical traits—skin color, hair texture, and facial traits—physical anthropologists of the past distinguished between three basic racial groups: Caucasoid (white), Negroid (black), and Mongoloid (Asian). Over the course of the past century, scientists have looked to find what they presumed to be the differences in intellectual and physical capabilities that reflected

---

[1]The discussion in this section is based on an excellent and highly readable discussion of the meaning of race by Susan Pitchford Susan Pitchford in the *Encyclopedia of Sociology*: Susan R. Pitchford, "Race," in Edgar F. Borgatta and Rhonda J.V. Montgomery, eds. *Encyclopedia of Sociology*, 2nd edition (NY: Macmillan Reference USA, 2000).

the underlying genetic differences correlated with these outward physical trait differences. Over the years, a number of differences were detected. However, in more recent decades, all of this earlier work was called into question as methodological deficiencies were noted and inherent bias detected in the formulation of research questions, the measurement of capabilities, and conclusions drawn from the results. Today, most scientists conclude there is no evidence to support intellectual and other capability differences between race groups. In fact, the very meaningfulness of race as a genetic/biological classification system has come into question with evidence that different racial groups do not share distinct and homogeneous evolutionary histories and the differences in genetic traits are greater within racial groups than between racial groups.

Race nevertheless remains an important predictor of outcomes for individuals in their lives, and significant differences can be found between racial groups today in terms of their family lives. It is important to understand these differences, however, as the outcome of the ways that individuals with certain physical traits are "defined" by the societies they come into contact with. In other words, **race** is a *social construction* based on outward physical traits <u>assumed</u> to reflect differences in physical and intellectual capabilities as well as values, beliefs, attitudes, and predispositions to act in different ways under similar circumstances. These social constructions develop as a result of historical circumstances of intersection between *cultural* groups and power dynamics in place as members from one culture come in contact with another. Once group membership is defined, individuals from those groups are expected to act in particular ways and are constrained from access to opportunities and valued social roles. As a result, arbitrary and majority serving definitions become real in their consequences for the groups so defined.

Why then continue to use race in the study of human behavior? Some argue that continuing to use race as an explanatory variable in studies of psychological conditions or social institutions only perpetuates a myth that race differences are indeed inherited and uniform. Although we sympathize with this argument, social constructions and their consequences are of central concern to sociologists. The differences based on race are no less real than the differences found between other groups (e.g., men versus women, catholic versus protestant, north versus south, etc). They are also no more invariable and possess no less within group variability than comparisons made between other types of groups. Therefore, we will examine race differences in family life, but we do so without assuming these differences are in any way an outcome of genetics, biology, or evolutionary history. The fact that many blacks in America shared a common immigration and assimilation history can explain why differences in family life with other racial groups have emerged. In fact, this is why we group together the discussion of race differences with the discussion of ethnic differences. We will argue that both types of differences are the result of shared historical and cultural experiences and current environmental adaptations.

Historical Context

The cultural heritage and history of interaction with the dominant culture play an important role in understanding and explaining current differences in family life between race and ethnic groups. In the pages that follow, we will explore some of the key defining cultural elements and experiences that set the context for how the members of four major race and ethnic groups—African Americans, Hispanic

Americans, Asian Americans, and Native Americans—have adapted to their current environmental contexts. In exploring these cultural elements and experiences, however, we need to keep in mind that a rich diversity of histories exists within each group as well as across the groups. For example, African Americans consist of those who came to America from the African continent mostly involuntarily as a result of slavery but also voluntarily as well. In addition, a sizable proportion of the African American population also has its origins in the Caribbean, especially the island country of Haiti. Among Hispanic Americans, the diversity of historical origins may be even greater, ranging from former residents of Mexico who were annexed into the United States, to Mexican immigrants who came to America in search of employment often at the encouragement of American businesses and governments, to refugees and others from Central and South America (many who came to escape persecution or civil strife), to Puerto Ricans who became nationalized after the Spanish-American War, to Cubans among whom many were business owners fleeing the nationalization of their businesses under Fidel Castro.[2] Among the Asian population, the diversity includes early immigrants from mainland China; well established and often professional immigrants from Japan and India; and more recent immigrants from Korea, the Philippines, and Southeast Asia—many of whom immigrated following the Korean and Vietnam wars.[3] There is great diversity even among the Native American population, for example, the distinction between coastal and plains Indians, to name just one.

Why are historical origins important? As a result of unique adaptations to regional environmental conditions, unique histories of contact with different cultures and unique institutional innovations, groups from different areas develop their own set of values, beliefs, and perspectives on the world and their relationships in the world. These values, beliefs, and perspectives then guide their future behaviors and adaptations to new environments. For each race/ethnic group, we will discuss the values, beliefs, and perspectives they brought with them prior to contact with the current majority Anglo or European American culture. Three key dimensions of variation in values we will discuss include *collectivism/communalism*, *familism*, and *patriarchy*.

Collectivism/communalism refers to the belief that each member of the society has an obligation to the whole of society and places the common good over their own individual needs. In collectivistic societies, there is a high degree of shared responsibility for meeting individual and societal needs. **Familism** is closely related to collectivism, but refers to the kinship group. In familistic cultures, there is a strong obligation to place the fulfillment of family roles over the fulfillment of both individual needs as well as community needs. In addition, this familism could apply to a wide range of extended family relations (as in the Asian family system) or to a more circumscribed group of immediate nuclear family members and a limited number of close relatives (as in the Hispanic culture). **Patriarchy** is a third important element of race/ethnic group cultural difference. In patriarchal societies, a strong belief is held that the male members of the society should have more authority and decision-making power and that boys are more valuable than girls.

---

[2]Linda Citlali Halgunseth, "Continuing Research on Latino Families," in Marilyn Coleman and Lawrence H. Ganong, eds. *Handbook of Contemporary Families* (Thousand Oaks, CA: Sage Publications, 2004), 333–351.

[3]Masako Ishii-Kuntz, "Asian American Families: Diverse History, Contemporary Trends, and the Future," in Marilyn Coleman and Lawrence H. Ganong, eds. *Handbook of Contemporary Families* (Thousand Oaks, CA: Sage Publications, 2004), 369–384.

The second component of the historical context of race/ethnic group differences is each group's unique history of interaction with the dominant culture. Each of the race/ethnic groups we will discuss has had a unique set of circumstances to deal with, as a result of their own history of interactions with the European settlers in America. Some, like African Americans, have had to deal with slavery and migrations to large urban centers in the North at times when conditions were not favorable to finding success in those centers. Others, such as Mexican Americans, have had to deal with the displacement from their lands and isolation in urban ghettos (**barrios**) or with high levels of ongoing migration in search of seasonal employment in agriculture. Native Americans have also had to deal with displacement from their lands, but to rural and less productive areas. They also had to deal with active interventions by governments to force full *assimilation* and *acculturation* through the systematic removal of their children from their parental homes and into boarding schools where they would learn "correct" moral values and skills to prepare them for life in the "new world" of the majority white population. Still later, Native Americans also had to face the challenges of large-scale migration to urban centers in search of earning a livelihood. Finally, Asian Americans have had to endure immigration policies that prevented early immigrant men from bringing their wives and children with them when they came to America. In addition, Japanese Americans have had to make adjustments to deal with displacement to internment camps during World War II. Each of these experiences and many others altered the landscape of possibilities and placed constraints on each group's struggles to establish patterns of family life.

One important outcome of historical interactions between race/ethnic groups and the dominant cultural group of European Americans is the degree to which these experiences have led to acculturation and assimilation. **Acculturation** refers to "the adaptation by an ethnic group of the cultural patterns of the dominant, or majority, group. Such acculturation encompasses not only external cultural traits, such as dress and language, but also internal ones, such as beliefs and values."[4] **Assimilation**, on the other hand, involves "the entry of an ethnic group's members into close, or primary, relationships with members of the dominant group."[5] High levels of acculturation often are seen as a prerequisite for assimilation, although highly multicultural societies such as Canada allow groups to retain their cultures while experiencing full or nearly full participation in social relationships. Historically in the United States, the idea of acculturation as essential for assimilation is captured by the idea of a "melting pot" where cultural differences are dissolved into a single American culture. Unfortunately, that culture looks much more like the culture of white European Americans than it does to other race/ethnic groups.

Current Ecological Context

The idea that race/ethnic group differences are directly derived from their originating cultural differences and/or their historical experiences alone fails to recognize the importance of immediate environments in explaining contemporary differences in family life between groups. As William Julius Wilson first noted in his influential

---

[4]Richard D. Alba, "Ethnicity," in Edgar F. Borgatta and Rhonda J.V. Montgomery, eds., *Encyclopedia of Sociology*, 2nd edition (NY: Macmillan Reference USA, 2000), 842.
[5]ibid, p. 842.

news item

Homeownership Losses Are Greatest Among Minorities, Report Finds

After a decade of growth, the gains made in homeownership by African-Americans and native-born Latinos have been eroding faster in the economic downturn than those of whites, according to a report issued Tuesday by the Pew Hispanic Center. The report also suggests that the gains for minority groups, achieved from 1995 to 2004, were disproportionately tied to relaxed lending standards and subprime loans....

The decline in homeownership among [minority] groups,...reflects both high foreclosure rates and lower rates of home buying.

Even with the decline, the rate for all groups together remains higher than before the boom, with nearly 68 percent of American households owning homes last year, up from 64 percent in 1994.

The gaps between white and minority households remain significant, however, with homeownership rates for Asians (59.1 percent), blacks (47.5 percent) and Latinos (48.9 percent) well below the 74.9 percent among whites.

Like previous studies, the report found that blacks and Hispanics were more than twice as likely to have subprime mortgages as white homeowners, even among borrowers with comparable incomes. In 2006, the last year of heavy subprime lending, 17.5 percent of white home buyers took subprime loans, compared with 44.9 percent for Hispanics and 52.8 percent for blacks.

These loans, which typically require little or no down payment and are meant for borrowers with low credit scores, made homeownership possible for many black and Hispanic families during the boom years, but also led to high rates of foreclosure. "Basically, that gap was closed on poor loans that never should have been made and wound up harming folks and their neighborhoods," said Kevin Stein, associate director of the California Reinvestment Coalition, an organization of nonprofit housing groups.

African-Americans and Latinos remain more likely than whites to be turned down for mortgages, with 26.1 percent of applications from Hispanics rejected in 2007, 30.4 percent of applications from blacks and 12.1 percent of applications from whites.

Though there were no figures available on the race or ethnicity of homeowners in foreclosure, the researchers found that counties with high concentrations of immigrants had particularly high foreclosure rates.

But the research did not suggest that high rates of immigration on their own caused high levels of foreclosure, Mr. Kochhar said. High unemployment, falling home prices, subprime loans and high ratios of debt to income all contributed...

Source: John Leland, *New York Times*, May 13, 2009.

---

book, *The Declining Significance of Race,*[6] the current socioeconomic conditions faced by African American families is a much more powerful predictor of individual and family outcomes than their racial characteristics. In other words, a white family and a black family placed in the same socioeconomic conditions of poverty would look more similar to each other than two white families or two black families living in different socioeconomic conditions. As discussed in Chapter 4, socioeconomic status has significant implications for family life insofar as it shapes the resources or capital families have to survive and achieve their goals and shapes the risks and challenges they must face in their immediate environments. To the extent that race/ethnicity overlaps with socioeconomic status, it becomes necessary to disentangle the effects of the latter before attributing race/ethnicity differences in family life to culture or other factors.

---

[6]William Julius Wilson, *The Declining Significance of Race: Blacks and Changing American Institutions* (Chicago: The University of Chicago Press, 1980).

Of course, the reason why race/ethnicity overlaps with socioeconomic status has much to do with the historical experiences of these groups and the socially constructed definition of their race/ethnicity. What the majority believes about the characteristics of those from groups different from themselves leads to expectations and behaviors toward minorities that, in turn, lead to their disadvantaged socioeconomic position. Negative impressions and bias toward members of minority groups (**prejudice**) leads to negative and exclusionary behaviors (**discrimination**) that limit opportunities and contribute to negative or deviant identities. In fact, the effects of prejudice and discrimination appear to impact minorities independently of socioeconomic status. In a test of Wilson's "declining significance of race" thesis, Michael Hughes and Melvin Thomas note that even after controlling for the effects of socioeconomic status, race differences remain with respect to overall quality of life, happiness, marital happiness, feelings of isolation, mistrust, and poor health.[7] These effects also extend to living environments. For example, Douglass Massey and Nancy Denton have documented the high level of residential segregation that still exists in the United States today based on minority status.[8] This **residential segregation** comes about primarily as a result of "white flight" from urban areas with high proportions of minorities as well as bank lending policies and other social forces. As a result, blacks and other minorities are left living in more impoverished environments where schools are underfunded and where greater levels of social disorganization exist. As noted in Chapter 2 and Chapter 4, high risk environments pose significant challenges to family life. Race/ethnic minority groups often attempt to respond to these challenges through the creation of ethnic communities or the creation of an alternative system for maintaining social order.

African American Families

Before 2001, the African American population was the largest racial/ethnic minority group in the United States and was surpassed in that year for the first time by Hispanic Americans. Because of unique historical and social experiences, many African Americans have lifestyles and value patterns that differ considerably from those of the European American majority. The relations between whites and blacks in the United States have been the source of a number of major social issues in the past several decades: busing, segregation, job discrimination, quotas, affirmative action, and interracial marriage, to mention a few.

Historical Context

The historical context that has shaped the environmental conditions faced by African Americans today as well as their strategies of adaptation can be summarized by three transitions:

1. Africa to the United States
2. Slavery to emancipation
3. Rural and southern areas to urban and northern areas

---

[7]Michael Hughes and Melvin E. Thomas, "The Continuing Significance of Race Revisited: A Study of Race, Class and Quality of life in America, 1972–1996," *American Sociological Review*, 63 (December 1998), 785–795

[8]Douglass Massey and Nancy Denton, *American Apartheid: Segregation and the Making of the Underclass* (Cambridge: Harvard University Press, 1993).

From Africa to the United States

Three factors in the transition from Africa to the United States have profound relevance for blacks. First is *color*, the factor that is the most influential characteristic of African American people in U.S. society. Color identifies blacks as such. Black Americans who can "pass" as white due to fair coloring are confronted with a different set of interactions than those with dark coloring who cannot "pass." In fact, it appears that color is not merely a question of black or white. Skin tone (complexion) itself has been found to have significant effects on educational attainment, occupation, and income among African Americans.[9] Findings by Hill suggest that color bias (colorism) rather than family background may be responsible for the bulk of color differences in the socioeconomic status of African American men.[10] Darker-skinned blacks are at a continuing disadvantage and experience more discrimination than fair-skinned blacks in the contemporary United States.

The second factor in the transition from Africa to the United States is **cultural discontinuity**. The system of behavior that was socially learned and shared by members of African society was not applicable to the social conditions they faced in the United States. It is perhaps difficult, if not impossible, to find any other group who came or were brought to the United States and faced such a disruption of cultural patterns. Yet many African cultural patterns were maintained. Thus arose the concept *African American*.

The third factor is *slavery*. Again, unlike almost all other groups in the United States, the Africans did not choose to come. With few exceptions, Africans came only as slaves. The impact slavery had on family patterns and norms at the time it occurred as well as the significance slavery has for understanding African American families today has become an issue of controversy. For example, some writers have emphasized the instability of marriage and family ties, the disruption of husband–wife and kin networks, the extent of matricentricity, and the lack of authority of fathers. Others suggest the slave family was considerably stronger than has been believed. It was not patterned by instability, chaos, and disorder but rather by two-parent households. While females headed a somewhat higher proportion of African American families than was true for other racial and ethnic groups, slavery was not the sole explanation. Economic conditions, in general, had a significant impact on the black family structure. Black males had high mortality rates, and females with children faced extreme difficulties in marrying or remarrying.

Although there has been disagreement about the nature of the slave family, most scholars would agree that the history of slavery in the United States continues to have a major impact on the African American family today. In the United States, slavery conferred inferiority. The slave had no legal rights, marriages were not licensed, many female slaves were sexually used or abused, and **miscegenation**—a term referring to the marriage and interbreeding between members of different races that violated the social norms of the times—was frequent.

From Slavery to Emancipation

In 1863, the Emancipation Proclamation, issued by Abraham Lincoln, freed the slaves in all territories still at war with the Union. No longer could individuals be

---

[9]Verna M. Keith and Cedric Herring, "Skin Tone and Stratification in the Black Community," *American Journal of Sociology* 97 (November 1991): 760–778.

[10]Mark E. Hill, "Color Differences in the Socioeconomic Status of African American Men: Results of a Longitudinal Study," *Social Forces* 78 (June 2000): 1437–1460.

sold away from their families. Marriages among blacks were to be legalized and recorded. At least in theory, the slave was free from servitude, bondage, and restraint. For thousands of African Americans, however, emancipation brought with it the freedom to die of starvation and illness. In numerous ways, this transition presented a crisis for many black families.

At least three patterns of family life emerged from this crisis.

1. The majority of African Americans remained on plantations as tenants of their former owners, receiving little or no wages for their labor.
2. Families that had been allowed to establish common residence worked common plots of ground for extra food for the family. Families where the man was an artisan, preacher, or house servant made the transition with the least difficulty.
3. In situations where only loose and informal ties held a man and woman together, those ties were severed during the crisis of emancipation, even despite the presence of children. In search of work, many men banded together and wandered the countryside. Females were established as the major productive and dependable family element. This pattern was perhaps the most disruptive of family life.

Steven Ruggles, in tracing the origins of the contemporary pattern of single parenthood in the African American family, suggests several historical explanations. First, it could have been a response to the socioeconomic conditions of extreme poverty and inadequate employment opportunities faced by newly freed blacks after the Civil War and by free blacks in 1950. Second, the pattern could reflect a difference in social norms between blacks and whites, either developed through the experience of slavery or as a result of dissimilarities between European and African culture.[11]

From Rural and Southern Areas to Urban and Northern Areas

The movement of African Americans from rural areas and from the South has, in general, followed the rest of the population; however, very few African Americans have migrated to western states, with the exception of California. In 1930, about four-fifths of all African Americans lived in the South, compared to slightly more than half (55.3 percent) in 2003. Likewise, a change has occurred in the transition to metropolitan areas. In 1960, 64.8 percent of all black families lived in metropolitan areas. By 1970, this figure had increased dramatically to 79.1 percent, and by 2003, it had increased to 87.5 percent. Fifty-two percent of all African American families currently live in central cities, 36 percent live in the rings around central cities, and 12 percent live in rural (nonmetropolitan) areas.[12]

Who cares? What is the significance of moving to the North and residing in metropolitan areas with a majority residing in central cities? One consequence is a heavy concentration of poverty. The loss of low-skill manufacturing jobs during the 1970s and the shift toward jobs that require more education and higher skills produced a sharp rise in the concentration of poverty in many inner-city neighborhoods. The growth of poverty and increasing levels of social disorder in ghettos also helped fuel the outmigration of middle-class and working-class families, thus deepening the impoverishment of these neighborhoods.

---

[11]Steven Ruggles, "The Origins of African-American Family Structure," *American Sociological Review* 59 (February 1994): 136–151.

[12]U.S. Bureau of the Census, *Current Population Reports*, P20-541, "The Black Population in the United States: March 2002" (Washington, DC: U.S. Government Printing Office, 2002), Figures 1 and 2.

A study of African American families living in the inner city revealed a strong link between neighborhood poverty and social isolation.[13] Residents of poorer neighborhoods had fewer friends who were stably employed or college educated and more who were on public assistance. They confirmed the contention that residents of high poverty neighborhoods are deprived of conventional role models and important social network resources, particularly access to informal job networks.

Another factor making these migration patterns significant revolves around blacks' selectivity: Not all ages of African Americans were caught up in the movement to urban areas or to the North, nor were complete families. The industrial pool preferred young men, which had a tremendous impact both on the community left behind and on the community into which African Americans migrated. Family life was affected by disrupting the nuclear family and by geographically separating extended family ties. African American males, in particular, brought with them to the city or the North aspirations for economic improvement; for many, these dreams were not fulfilled. Unlike a person from the middle class, who will relocate due to a job offer, the lower-class male is more likely to migrate because of current unemployment or an irregular work schedule.

On the other hand, the consequences of the shift from rural/southern to urban/northern areas have not all been negative. Many stabilizing factors and positive aspects have resulted. Although the city often is portrayed as a center of evil in U.S. society, in a very real sense it has been the center of hope for some African Americans—providing better schools, better social welfare services, better medical and public health facilities, and more tolerance for racial minorities.

Stewart Tolnay has shown that northern urbanites with "southern origins" have exhibited more traditional family patterns than nonmigrants.[14] When compared with northern-born blacks, southern migrants had more children living with two parents, more ever-married women living with their spouses, less family disruption, higher rates of participation in the labor force, and, thus, less unemployment, poverty, and welfare dependency. Why? It is true that economic opportunities and higher wages may have played a part, but these conditions already existed for native-born northerners. Other explanations include a selective migration factor in which the more able, ambitious, and determined were the ones who migrated. Perhaps southern migrants may have been more religious than their northern-born counterparts, which decreased the likelihood of marital disruption and nonmarital motherhood. Whatever the reasons for the more traditional family patterns, the evidence yields no support for the assumption that southern migrants to the North carried with them or contributed to a "dysfunctional family culture."

Socioeconomic Context

Some would argue that the single most important variable to understanding the African American family today is social class. Many family forms are more likely to be the consequence of class rather than either race or ethnicity. Major differences

---

[13]Bruce H. Rankin and James M. Quane, "Neighborhood Poverty and the Social Isolation of Inner-City African American Families," *Social Forces* 79 (September 2000): 139–164.

[14]Stewart E. Tolnay, "The Great Migration and Changes in the Northern Black Family, 1940 to 1990," *Social Forces* 75 (June 1997): 1213–1238. See also Thomas C. Wilson, "Explaining Black Southern Migrants' Advantage in Family Stability: The Role of Selective Migration," *Social Forces* 80 (December 2001): 555–571.

Whiteness, Social Class, and Parenting in Urban London

To focus on race and ethnic minorities is to highlight "difference." But difference from what? Social scientists have attempted to uncover unique cultural values associated with different race and ethnic groups, but what are the values that distinguish those who are White? The use of terms Anglo American or European American are designed to convey some common cultural histories and shared values among the white population, but in fact those histories are varied and Anglo and European cultures of the past have become more diffuse. Some have even argued that "whiteness" is an empty category requiring actions by the white population to define itself in relationship to the minority "other."

One interesting study of how this process plays out in families was conducted by Diane Reay and her colleagues in London and two other nearby communities. In this study, they examined the school choices of white middle-class parents and, in particular, those who chose to send their children to multi-ethnic comprehensive urban schools. What they found among these parents was a high value placed on "multiculturalism" and a strong desire to expose their children to different cultures as a way to parent responsibly and ethically according to their multicultural values.

At the same time, however, they found a strong theme of instrumentality in these parents' behaviors and motivations. Their choice of school, and the encouragement they gave their children to develop friendships with children from other cultures, played into another set of values. They saw their choices as better preparing their children to compete in the new global and diverse economy and as a way of enhancing their children's social confidence and self-esteem (relative to the greater number of poor performing minority children). They also saw their choices as a means for distinguishing themselves from other white working class children who were inferior to their children's minority friends in terms of their display of appropriate behavior and their valuing education, ambition and achievement.

In examining the ways that these white parents guided their children's involvement in minority cultures, the authors noted the ambivalence involved in espousing multicultural views at the same time that they were concerned about their children's own safety. They effectively limited their children's acceptance of the minority culture, choosing instead to select and nurture ties with minority children who held the "correct" values. In doing so, these parents not only reaffirmed their children's "white" cultural values, but also reaffirmed their superiority over working class children (both white and minority) who did not share their values.

Finally, they acknowledge that some positive consequences come about for those minority children who become involved with white middle-class children, but these positives are outweighed by the extent to which other minority values not shared with the dominant white middle class culture are suppressed. They conclude their analysis by citing Marx's thesis that ethical behavior is constrained by a system of unequal distribution of resources. As they note: "When the white middle classes make choices that are directed towards the common good, greater benefits and value still accrue to them rather than to their class and ethnic others. This is a case of trapped in privilege and constitutes powerful evidence that we need effective policies that work towards the dismantling of economic and social privilege." (1055)

Source: Diane Reay, Sumi Hollinghorth, Katya Williams, Gill Crozier, Fiona Jamieson, David James, and Phoebe Beedell, "'A Darker Shade of Pale?' Whiteness, the Middle Classes and Multi-Ethnic Inner City Schooling," *Sociology*, 41 (2007): 1041–1060.

seem to exist within the African American family if a distinction is made between those living below the poverty level and those living in the middle class of the sub-culture. It is the African American middle class that is seldom publicized. This is a stratum of two-parent units in which most marriages are stable and where husbands have a high school education or better and occupy positions in business, government, or education. These families are basically more similar than dissimilar to the dominant white family form that exists in U.S. society.

The shift from a negative to a positive social status has prompted a shift in the approach to and the interpretation of African American families. The traditional model of the African American family projected a negative stereotype, one of the family as a monolithic lower-class entity, as a social problem in itself, as a pathology of out-of-wedlock births and broken homes, as centering around the female as a dominating matriarch, and as including males with low self-esteem. The emerging model challenges these negative views, stressing that the African American family comprises a variety of types at different social-class levels; rejecting the social problem and pathology orientation as an expression of middle-class ethnocentrism; viewing the family as having strengths such as egalitarianism, self-reliant males, strong family ties, and high achievement orientations; and finally, being worthy of study as a form of social organization in its own right.

The old model of the African American family was vividly portrayed more than thirty-five years ago by Daniel Patrick Moynihan in his now classic **Moynihan Report**.[15] He contended that there had been a serious weakening in the African American social structure and that there was a trend away from family stability in lower socioeconomic levels. Moynihan concluded in his report that the structure of family life in the African American community constitutes a **tangle of pathology** and that at the heart of the deterioration of the fabric of African American society is the deterioration of the family. Thus, the major block to equality, according to this report, was the matricentric family. The implication is that young African American children grew up and were reared in mother-centered families without the helpful influence of both parents. This, in turn, Moynihan argued, was a major reason that African Americans were making only limited gains during the prosperous 1960s.

Billingsley and others disagreed directly and strongly with Moynihan's central tenet.[16] They contended that the African American family was not a cause of the "tangle of pathology" but rather that it was an absorbing, adaptive, and amazingly resilient mechanism for the socialization of its children and the civilization of its society.

Have specific shifts occurred for African Americans, from a negative to a positive social status, as portrayed primarily by census data in regard to employment, income, and education? Note particularly (1) the tremendous gains made in recent years in the United States for both black males and females and (2) the major disparities that still exist between blacks and whites.

Employment

An increasing number of African Americans have entered positions of leadership in the professions, in business, and in government. The number and rate of unemployed

---

[15]Daniel P. Moynihan, *The Negro Family: The Case for National Action* (Washington, DC: U.S. Government Printing Office, U.S. Department of Labor, 1965).

[16]Andrew Billingsley, *Black Families in White America* (Englewood Cliffs, NJ: Prentice Hall, 1968), 33.

African Americans have overshadowed these gains, however. For many years, the unemployment rate among blacks was double the rate of the population as a whole. That is, if the national unemployment rate were 5 percent, one could assume a 10 percent rate for blacks. In 2007, the annual average unemployment rate was 3.3 for white adults, 6.2 for black adults, 4.6 for Hispanic adults, and only 2.8 for Asian adults. Although these rates are considerably lower than in previous years, the unemployment rate for blacks remained nearly twice that of whites.[17] Black females had an unemployment rate slightly lower than black males but more than twice as high as white females. But it should be noted that black females who are employed are overrepresented in service, clerical, and blue-collar jobs that generally are low status and pay low wages. For the population as a whole, evidence has not supported the widespread belief that a double-negative status (being both black and female) provides an occupational advantage.

It may be of interest that not only is the unemployment rate higher for black females than white females, but Browne showed that for the first time in the late twentieth century, black women also participated in the labor force at lower rates than white women.[18] Historically, black women have maintained a strong presence in the labor force because their incomes were essential to supporting their families. The lower rate of labor force participation among black women today is explained by black–white differences in human capital, dropping out of school, the presence of young children, and factors such as long-term welfare. Welfare recipients and never-married mothers are less likely to participate in the labor force than are women without these attributes.

Historically, African American women have had high rates of employment compared to white women, but their jobs have been disproportionately in working class or service type jobs

Income

There is no doubt that the African American population has made substantial social status gains over the past fifty years in terms of occupation, education, and income. Yet regardless of absolute gains, blacks remain significantly deprived when compared to whites at the same income level. The economic gap that separates whites and blacks in the United States is growing, despite all efforts of recent years.

According to census data (see Table 5.1 on page 202), the dollar gap between blacks and whites has remained relatively constant in the last quarter century, with the biggest increase in the gap coming in the decade of the 1990s. In 1970, the median white family income was $10,236 and

---

[17]U.S. Census Bureau, *The 2009 Statistical Abstract* "Table 607—Unemployed and Unemployment Rates by Educational Attainment, Sex, Race, and Hispanic Origin," http://www.2010census.biz/compendia/statab/cats/labor_force_employment_earnings/unemployed_persons.html.

[18]Irene Browne, "Explaining the Black-White Gap in Labor Force Participation Among Women Heading Households," *American Sociological Review* 62 (April 1997): 236–252.

Table 5.1

Median Incomes of White, Black, Hispanic, and Asian families, 1970–2007 (in current dollars)

YEAR	WHITE	BLACK	RATIO: BLACK TO WHITE*	HISPANIC	ASIAN
2007	$54,920	$33,916	62	$38,679	$66,103
2000	53,256	34,204	64	35,050	56,026
1995	42,646	25,970	61	24,570	46,356
1990	36,915	21,423	58	23,431	42,246
1985	29,152	16,786	58	19,027	NA
1980	21,904	12,674	58	14,716	NA
1975	14,268	8,779	62	9,551	NA
1970	10,236	6,279	61	NA	NA

*Ratio means black income as a percentage of white income.

NA = Not Available

Source: U.S. Bureau of the Census, *Current Population Reports*, Series P60-213, "Money Income in the United States: 2000" (Washington, DC: U.S. Government Printing Office, September 2001), Table 4; and U.S. Bureau of the Census, *Statistical Abstract of the United States*, 2001, 121st ed. (Washington, DC: U.S. Government Printing Office, 2001), no. 669, 437; DeNavas-Walt, Carmen, Bernadette D. Proctor, and Jessica C. Smith, U.S. Census Bureau, *Current Population Reports*, P60-235, "Income, Poverty, and Health Insurance Coverage in the United States: 2007" (Washington, DC: U.S. Government Printing Office, 2008).

the median black family income was $6,279, 61.3 percent that of whites and a dollar gap of $3,957. By 1980, after widely heralded social reforms, blacks made significant gains in income but relative to whites they fell still further behind. Although black income increased by 300 percent to $12,674 and white income increased by only 200 percent to $21,904, these differential percentage gains were not enough to maintain, no less overcome, the initial gap in earnings as relative black income fell to 57.9 percent that of whites and the dollar gap more than doubled to $9,230. By the year 2007, however, blacks had regained some ground in earnings as the median income for white families more than doubled to $54,920 while for black families in nearly tripled to $33,916. Still, black income was at a level only slightly more equal relative to whites (61.8 percent) and the actual dollar gap increased to $21,004.

More important than the gap in median income is the difference between blacks and whites in terms of incomes sufficient to maintain families. In 2007, nearly one in four persons (24.5 percent) in the black population were classified as below the poverty level in the United States compared to less than one in ten (8.2 percent) of the white population.[19] Figures such as these lead many social scientists to argue that what is often perceived as a racial issue is very much an economic one.

---

[19]DeNavas-Walt, Carmen, Bernadette D. Proctor, and Jessica C. Smith, U.S. Census Bureau, *Current Population Reports*, P60-235, "Income, Poverty, and Health Insurance Coverage in the United States: 2007" (Washington, DC: U.S. Government Printing Office, 2008).

What implications do figures such as these have for family life among African Americans? Broman has shown that blacks are significantly less likely than whites to feel that their marriages are harmonious and black women are less likely to be satisfied with their marriages than white women.[20] One key explanation for these patterns centered on financial factors: increased marital well-being was associated with satisfaction with the family's financial well-being. In general, an established sociological finding positively relates socioeconomic status to marital stability. Thus, based strictly on economic factors, we could expect a high rate of marital disruption among black families (shown in Chapter 14).

Education

Transition from a negative to a more positive social status can also be seen by examining the percentages of African Americans age 25 and over who have obtained a high school and/or college education. In 2007, 81.9 percent of black males and 82.6 percent of black females had completed four years or more of high school. The same year, 18 percent of black males and 19 percent of black females had completed four years or more of college. The high school figures are about two and one-half times the comparable 1970 percentages of 30.1 and 32.5 for black males and females, respectively, and show greater percentage increases than those for whites (see Table 5.2). The college figures are more than three times the comparable 1970 percentages but all are considerably lower than

Table 5.2

Persons Age 25 and over Completing Four Years or More of High School and College by Sex and Race: 1970–2007 (in percent)

YEAR	WHITE		BLACK		HISPANIC		ASIAN	
	MALE	FEMALE	MALE	FEMALE	MALE	FEMALE	MALE	FEMALE
Completed High School								
2007	85.3	87.1	81.9	82.6	58.2	62.5	89.8	85.9
1990	79.1	79.0	65.8	66.5	50.3	51.3	84.0	77.2
1980	69.6	68.6	50.8	51.5	47.3	45.8	NA	NA
1970	54.0	55.0	30.1	32.5	37.9	34.2	NA	NA
Completed College								
2007	29.9	28.3	18.0	19.0	11.8	13.7	55.2	49.3
1990	25.3	19.0	11.9	10.8	9.8	8.7	44.9	35.4
1980	21.3	13.3	8.4	8.3	9.4	6.0	NA	NA
1970	14.4	8.4	4.2	4.6	7.8	4.3	NA	NA

NA = Not Available

Source: U.S. Bureau of the Census, *The 2009 Statistical Abstract*, "Table 222- Educational Attainment by Race, Hispanic Origin, and Sex. http://www.2010census.biz/compendia/statab/cats/education/educational_attainment.html.

---

[20]Clifford L. Broman, "Marital Quality in Black and White Marriages," *Journal of Family Issues*, 26 (May 2005): 431–441.

those for whites. These changes are quite dramatic for the timespan involved. Generally, as economic conditions and educational attainments improve, the incidence of family disorganization decreases, family life becomes increasingly stable, aspirations for children become higher, and conformity to the sexual mores of society increases.

Patterns of Family Life

Today, the most predominant family pattern among African Americans is the single-parent family, with the vast majority of these being female- or mother-headed families. In 2007, 53 percent of African American families in the United States were female householders with no husband present and another 5 percent were male householders with no wife present. Only 42 percent were two-parent families. In contrast, 75 percent of white families and 69 percent of Hispanic families with children present were two-parent families (see Figure 5.1). These distributions have not changed substantially since 1980.[21]

Given the high number of single-parent families among African Americans, it is useful to divide the discussion of family patterns into two types: (1) the matricentric female-headed pattern and (2) the two-parent pattern. Although these patterns refer primarily to the nuclear family unit, they do not exclude other relatives. Not uncommon among African American nuclear families is the presence of nephews, aunts, grandparents, cousins, and other adult relatives. These extended kin, plus unrelated kin living in as roommates, boarders, or guests, exert a major influence on the lifestyles of African American families.

Three points must be made at this juncture in the discussion: (1) there is a wide range of family structures beyond these two patterns, (2) perhaps more important than structure per se is the degree of parental involvement, and (3) the African American family institution is extremely resilient. Neither the mother-centered nor any other type of family is necessarily "falling apart"—the black

Figure 5.1

Family Groups with Children under 18 Years Old by Race and Hispanic Origin

Source: U.S. Census Bureau, The 2009 Statistical Abstract. "Table 66. Family Groups With Children Under 18 Years Old by Race and Hispanic Origin" http://www.2010census.biz/compendia/statab/cats/population/households_families_group_quarters.html

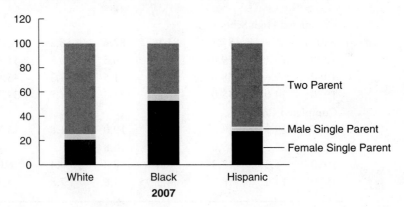

[21]For chapters on African American families, see Harriet Pipes McAdoo, "African-American Families," in Charles H. Mindel, Robert W. Habenstein, and Roosevelt Wright, Jr., eds., *Ethnic Families in America*. 4th ed. (Upper Saddle River, NJ: Prentice-Hall, Inc., 1998), Chapter 15; and Ronald L. Taylor, "Black American Families," in Ronald L. Taylor, ed., *Minority Families in the United States: A Multicultural Perspective*, 2nd ed. (Upper Saddle River, NJ: Prentice-Hall, Inc., 1998), Chapter 1.

family is capable of major adaptations to the historical and contemporary social conditions confronting it.[22]

Matricentric Female-Headed Family Pattern

The **matricentric female-headed family pattern** is one in which the female is the dominant member. The female may be a mother or grandmother who resides with children, usually without the continuous presence of a husband or father. Early motherhood, lack of education, and insufficient income lead to the characterization of this family pattern as "multi-problemed" and families living below the level of poverty are most likely to fit this pattern.

Families headed by females without husbands comprise a sizable proportion of low-income families. About two-thirds of all black female-headed households with no husband present were below the poverty level. Clearly, regardless of race, female-headed households and poverty are highly interrelated. It is debatable whether the family structure of the female householder with no husband present explains the family's poverty or whether the poverty explains the family's structure. Most likely, each contributes to the other, and governmental policies contribute to both.

The proliferative growth of female-headed households leading up to 1980 was one of the most significant changes in the black family over the past five decades,[23] although, as noted above, there has been little growth in the proportion of this form of family among blacks since 1980. One of the most visible reasons for the dramatic increase in households headed by women has been a corresponding increase in out-of-wedlock births. While the rates of nonmarital sexual activity of black and white women are converging, black females initiate intercourse at an early age, are more likely to have unprotected intercourse, and are less likely to marry or have an abortion if they become pregnant.

A less visible reason than out-of-wedlock births for the increase in female-headed households is related to the shortage of men relative to the number of women during the marriageable years (a low sex-ratio). A greater prevalence of men (higher sex-ratio) was associated with higher marriage prevalence for black women, higher prevalence of husband–wife families, higher percentages of children living in husband–wife families, and higher percentages of marital births.[24]

In addition to the negative effect of a shortage of men on marriage and two-parent families was the positive effect of men's economic status on marriage prevalence and marital births for black women. For women, however, higher economic opportunities and public assistance levels were associated with lower marriage prevalence and fewer marital births. In brief, fewer marriages and more out-of-wedlock births seem to be related to (1) a shortage of black men, (2) a lower socioeconomic status of black men who are available, and (3) a higher educational and economic status for black women.

---

[22]U.S. Census Bureau, *The 2009 Statistical Abstract* "Table 66. Family Groups with Children Under 18 Years Old by Race and Hispanic Origin," http://www.2010census.biz/compendia/statab/cats/population/households_families_group_quarters.html.

[23]Ann M. Nichols-Casebolt, "Black Families Headed by Single Mothers: Growing Numbers and Increasing Poverty," *Social Problems* 33 (July/August 1988): 306–313.

[24]Cynthia M. Cready, Mark A. Fossett, and K. Jill Kiecolt, "Mate Availability and African American Family Structure in the U.S. Nonmetropolitan South, 1960–1990," *Journal of Marriage and the Family* 59 (February 1997): 192–203.

One of the most significant changes over the past several decades among African American families is the growth of single-parent, primarily female-headed households. Yet the family, regardless of structure, remains the key agent of childhood socialization and source of meaningful relationships.

Black women desire marriage but appear to resist marrying men with fewer educational and economic resources than they have.

How much of a shortage of men exists and how is it accounted for? According to the U.S. Bureau of the Census, in 2007 the sex ratio for blacks was 91.2, or about 91 males for every 100 females. For whites, the ratio was 98.3, or 98 males for every 100 females. Since there is an excess of black males at birth, the shortage of males must be attributed both to higher infant mortality rates (which in 2005 was 13.7 per 1,000 live births compared to 5.7 for whites[25]) and a considerably greater mortality rate of young black males through homicide, accident, suicide, drug overdose, and war casualty. In addition, black males who are divorced or separated due to military service, unemployment, or institutional confinement (such as prison or mental hospitals) and those with serious alcohol or drug problems are also removed from the "marriage market." Factors such as these magnify the serious disadvantages of black women in choosing from the eligible and desirable males in the marriage pool or in staying married.

In U.S. society, it is widely believed that children cannot be adequately socialized unless they are reared in two-parent families. Although there is little question that having two parents makes parenting easier and potentially more successful, there is no guarantee that having two parents will lead to successful child outcomes, and evidence suggests that single parents can be successful in rearing children who display prosocial behaviors and are successful adults. Willie alerts us to overcome ethnocentrism and to be conscious of an approach (such as phenomenology) that recognizes that the behavior and family structures of individuals and groups tend to be functions of the situations and circumstances in which they find themselves. And if black populations are subdominant in the power structure, this situation may require or result in adaptive forms that differ from those found among whites or the dominant group in power.[26]

One method used successfully by black single mothers is the use of social support networks. In a recent study of African American single mothers living in inner-city New Orleans, Louisiana, Beth Kotchick, Shannon Dorsey, and Laurie Heller found that high levels of environmental stressors such as gangs, physical fighting, drugs and alcohol use, shootings, substandard housing conditions, and other indicators predicted

[25]U.S. Census Bureau, *The 2009 Statistical Abstract* "Table 111—Infant Mortality Rates by Race—States," http://www.2010census.biz/compendia/statab/cats/births_deaths_marriages_divorces/deaths.html.

[26]Charles V. Willie, "Social Theory and Social Policy Derived from the Black Family Experience," *Journal of Black Studies* 23 (June 1993): 451–459.

higher levels of maternal stress, less positive parenting and more problem behaviors among their children. These effects were moderated, however, by the presence of a strong support group of family and friends. In other words, when there was a strong support group, neighborhood stressors had no significant effect on either parenting or child outcomes. The negative impacts of neighborhood were only found among those who did not have support networks.[27]

Two-Parent Family Pattern

Family stability, life satisfaction, and personal happiness do not depend on a **two-parent family pattern,** but not unlike the effect for whites, marriage itself appears to contribute to the life satisfaction of black adults.[28]

The number of affluent African American families is on the rise. These families are likely to include two parents, one or both of whom are likely to be college-educated professionals.

In contrast to single-parent families, married couple families are more likely to be middle-class or higher-income working-class families. Males are likely to have more stable employment and assume an active role in decision-making and child-rearing responsibilities. The two-parent intact African American family has been relatively neglected by most social scientists. Perhaps this family pattern has been ignored because these families are relatively stable, conforming, and achieving, and cause few problems to anyone. The presence of two parents increases the likelihood of having two adult wage earners, which improves levels of income and other economic resources. As indicated previously, a direct link appears to exist between economic resources and family structure, including among African American families.

It appears that families in which both husband and wife are present are those from which African American leaders emerge. A three-generation analysis of the social origins of contemporary black leaders in the United States revealed that most of these individuals were reared in stable families; 67.8 percent lived with both parents (15.3 percent lived with their mothers, 4.1 percent with their fathers, 5.6 percent with relatives, and 4.9 percent with other people).[29] Interestingly, these eminent blacks were also predominantly the descendants of families characterized by antebellum (before the Civil War) freedom, lighter skin, urban residence, and higher educational and occupational attainment. It is in the two-parent family pattern that the father plays

[27]Beth A. Kotchick, Shannon Dorsey, and Laurie Heller, "Predictors of Parenting among African American Single Mothers: Personal and Contextual Factors," *Journal of Marriage and Family*, 67 (May 2005), 448–460.

[28]Mookherjee, Harsha N. "Marital Status, Gender, and Perception of Well-being," *Journal of Social Psychology* 137.1 (1997): 95–105.

[29]Elizabeth I. Mullins and Paul Sites, "The Origins of Contemporary Eminent Black Americans: A Three-Generation Analysis of Social Origin," *American Sociological Review* 49 (October 1984): 672–685.

a more dominant role and that the children develop a greater identification with him. The role of the father as playmate, teacher, and disciplinarian to his children is less likely to be fulfilled in the matricentric form of family organization, even when the father is present.

Hispanic American Families

As noted earlier, Hispanics are the fastest-growing segment of the U.S. population, and this growth has sparked considerable interest in this segment of the population at a political level as well as an academic one. Also as noted earlier, the category **Hispanic American** includes a diversity of peoples: those who classify themselves as Mexican American (64.1 percent), Puerto Rican (9.0 percent), Cuban (3.4 percent), Dominican (2.7 percent), Central and South American (13.2 percent), and "Other Hispanic" (7.6 percent) from Spain or other Spanish-speaking countries (see Figure 5.2). Also included in this "other" category are those who simply identify themselves as *Spanish American*, *Hispanic*, or *Latino* and do not identify a specific country of origin.

Historical Context

The term "Hispanic" refers to a variety of cultural groups who share a common native language of Spanish as a result of Spanish colonization in the Americas. Primarily, this group consists of natives of Mexico, Puerto Rico, Cuba, the Dominican Republic and

Hispanics are now the largest minority group in the United States, although they represent a diverse group with a variety of cultural traditions and unique historical experiences.

Figure 5.2

Hispanics by Origin: 2006

Source: U.S. Bureau of the Census, Current Population Reports, Series P20-535, "The Hispanic Population in the United States: March 2001" (Washington, DC: U.S. Government Printing Office, 2001), Figure 1, p. 1.

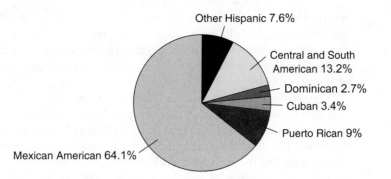

Other Hispanic 7.6%

Central and South American 13.2%

Dominican 2.7%

Cuban 3.4%

Puerto Rican 9%

Mexican American 64.1%

other parts of Latin America. These cultural groups are also referred to under the label "Latino/a," which also includes non-Spanish speaking groups in other parts of Central and South America.[30] Given the diversity of cultural groups represented by these terms, it is difficult to characterize them as a single cultural group other than to identify commonalities based on environmental conditions and, more importantly, the influence of Spanish colonization on their native cultures. Also, given the imbalanced distribution of Hispanic Americans in the United States noted above, most of what we know about this ethnic group comes from research done on Mexican Americans. With these cautions in mind, we will first consider the historical context for Hispanic American family life today and then examine how current environmental conditions play a role in the ongoing construction of Hispanic families.

In terms of the cultural belief systems in place before Hispanic Americans were either incorporated into U.S. society or immigrated to the United States, the four defining features mentioned at the outset of this chapter stand out: collectivism/communalism, familism, patriarchal ideology, and matricentrism.

Strong *collectivistic/communalistic* values come from the mostly rural way of life led by these groups prior to colonization. These cultural values, however, were disrupted by colonization and enslavement in Spanish households. In addition, the impacts of Spanish Catholicism shifted the emphasis to a valuation of family ties over communal ones. As a result, Hispanic Americans also place a high value on *familism* with particular focus on the nuclear family unit but with strong obligations to grandparents and to a lesser extent other extended kinship relations.

The one exception to this focus on the modified-nuclear or modified-extended family is the strong role that godparents (**compadres** and **comadres**) play in Hispanic American family life. The general patterns of **compadrazgo** are associated primarily with infant baptism but may also apply to first communion, marriage, and other rituals. At these times, ties are established between parents and godparents and child and godparents. Traditionally, expectant parents selected a married couple from among close friends or an extended-family member to be the child's sponsors. An invitation to be a sponsor was a special honor that was not to be refused. Through the baptism ceremony, a major social bond was established between the parents and godparents (co-parents), which brought them into a relationship that was expected

---

[30]This section relies heavily on a summary of Hispanic American family history and contemporary research found in Linda Citlali Halgunseth, "Continuing Research on Latino Families," in Marilyn Coleman and Lawrence H. Ganong, eds. *Handbook of Contemporary Families* (Thousand Oaks, CA: Sage Publications, 2004), 333–351.

to last a lifetime. The godparent was expected to take care of the physical and spiritual needs of the child in the event the parents could not perform these essential duties. Williams determined, however, that today the *compadrazgo* ceremony no longer serves to sustain the "fictive kinship system," as traditionally defined.[31] Many of its elements have disappeared or been modified.

Two other themes found in Hispanic American culture are those of *patriarchy* and *marianism*. Hispanic American men have traditionally adhered to an ideal of manliness (**machismo**) equated with authority, strength, and sexual virility and prowess. The man was the patriarch who made the important decisions. He was strong and brave. He could seek other sexual partners, but his wife could not. One possible source of this ideology may be found in the relationship between Spanish colonizers and their native slave women. Children of such unions were referred to as mestizos[32] and these unions were characterized by a severe imbalance of power such as is incorporated in the concept of machismo. The concept of machismo, however, goes beyond how men treat women in stereotypical dominating ways such as being "macho." It also includes viewing men as providers, protectors, and representatives of their families. Manly characteristics include being courageous and being respectful of women. The cultural practice of machismo has been found, for example, to have an effect on condom use and the prevention of AIDS.[33] Since the use of condoms appears to be more a male prerogative than a female one, condom use was found to depend on how well males took charge of obtaining and using condoms in fulfilling certain aspects of the machismo role.

Mexican American women have traditionally played (and somewhat still continue to play) a complementary role in the home. A "good woman" was one who married, had children, and stayed home to care for her children and her husband. Wives and daughters were subordinate to their husbands and fathers, a role pattern highly reinforced by the religious belief system, that of the Roman Catholic Church. The religious origins of this ideology and family pattern are reflected in the term used to capture it—**marianism**. In addition to the subordination of women in the family, however, marianism includes a respect for mothers as sacred and the recognition that mothers are the focal point of family life—matricentrism.[34]

To what extent do these gendered patterns of family life exist today? When compared to non-Hispanic American families, it seems that Mexican American husbands still exert power over wives and that women still fulfill the majority of child care and household tasks. Husbands and fathers, however, have been shown to have a definite interest in children's behavior, placing great importance on their being independent, exercising self-control, obeying, getting along with others, and succeeding in athletics. Nevertheless, findings by Oropesa challenge stereotypical descriptions of the position of wives in Mexican families as necessarily subordinate

---

[31]Norma Williams, *The Mexican American Family: Tradition and Change* (Dix Hills, NY: General Hall, 1990), 44.

[32]Linda Citlali Halgunseth, "Continuing Research on Latino Families," in Marilyn Coleman and Lawrence H. Ganong, eds. *Handbook of Contemporary Families* (Thousand Oaks, CA: Sage Publications, 2004), 333–351.

[33]James K. Mikawa, Pete A. Morones, Antonio Gomez, Hillary L. Case, Dan Olsen, and Mary Jane Gonzales-Huss, "Cultural Practices of Hispanics: Implications for the Prevention of AIDS," *Hispanic Journal of Behavioral Sciences* 14 (November 1992): 421–433.

[34]Linda Citlali Halgunseth, "Continuing Research on Latino Families," in Marilyn Coleman and Lawrence H. Ganong, eds. *Handbook of Contemporary Families* (Thousand Oaks, CA: Sage Publications, 2004), 333–351.

to husbands.[35] Husband dominance is said to be neither universal nor insurmountable. The typical wife does not feel excluded from most decisions and is likely to feel that she shares decision making with her husband. Equally misleading is the claim that husbands typically use force to maintain an atmosphere of intimidation within the home (although 19 percent of the respondents said their partners have hit them). Wives' education was found to foster lower risks of violence, equalitarian decision making, and satisfaction with decision making.

Traditional cultural beliefs and practices still survive today among Hispanic Americans, but they have been adapted and modified as a result of interactions with the dominant European American culture and the requirements of adaptation to the dominant systems of social and economic relations in the United States. Differences across subgroups of Hispanic Americans in these historical processes are a source of considerable diversity in social and family life among those sharing this ethnic identification.

The Mexican American experience can be divided into four groups: Chicanos, legal immigrants, braceros, and undocumented immigrants. The term **Chicanos** is a contraction of *Mexicanos* (pronounced "meschicanos" in the ancient Nahuatl language of Mexico). More than one million Mexican Americans are descendants of the native Mexicans who lived in the Southwest before it became part of the United States following the Mexican American War. These natives became Americans in 1848, when Texas, California, New Mexico, and most of Arizona became U.S. territory. These four states plus Colorado contain the largest concentrations of Mexican Americans today. Although they were already settled in these states, language barriers and noncompatible skills resulted in many being displaced into urban ghettos called *barrios*, where ethnic communities often were established limiting the extent of acculturation to the dominant culture. Most urban Mexican Americans today live in California, especially Los Angeles.

A second group of Mexican Americans arrived in the United States as a result of large-scale migration in the early 1900s caused in part by the Mexican Revolution and unsettled economic conditions in Mexico, as well as by the demand for labor on cotton farms and railroads in California. The lives of these early legal immigrants were more disrupted and they often found themselves isolated in rural areas. The third group were the **braceros**, participants in an early type of "guest worker" program in the United States. Before the minimum wage law was passed, agricultural employers preferred braceros to local workers because the Mexicans could be paid less and were not a burden to the federal government as they returned to Mexico when their services were no longer needed. Finally, a large number of undocumented immigrants arrive from Mexico every year in search of employment or family reunification. These immigrants face high levels of vulnerability and risk in their personal and family lives because they lack the protection of the state.

As a result of these earlier historical experiences, Mexican Americans can be divided into two groups: those who have stable residence patterns and live in strong ethnic communities in towns and cities throughout the Southwest United States and those who participate in migrant labor activities in mostly rural agricultural areas, especially along the western coast of the United States. In addition, more recent

---

[35]R. S. Oropesa, "Development and Marital Power in Mexico," *Social Forces* 75 (June 1997): 1291–1317.

migratory experiences of Mexican Americans have led to a third group—those who migrated to areas in the South and Midwest where they sought out jobs primarily in the meat industry. These new immigrants have found some economic success as they are likely to experience much lower rates of poverty than their counterparts elsewhere.[36]

The historical experiences of the other three major Hispanic groups are not as varied as the Mexican American experience, but they are distinct from the other subgroups. Puerto Ricans have had a long history if active migration between Puerto Rico and the Eastern United States. These patterns often involved the separation of men from families as they sought out employment on the mainland and sent back money to their families. These patterns were reinforced with the annexation of Puerto Rico as a territory of the United States after the Spanish American War in 1917. As a result, many Puerto Ricans moved more permanently to urban centers such as Boston, New York and Miami where they often encountered discrimination in employment and housing and had to adapt to impoverished living conditions. In contrast, a large number of Cuban Americans immigrated to the United State to escape the Castro regime's nationalization of businesses. Thus, many of these immigrants were more well-off economically and had previously developed business interests with the United States. They mostly settled in the Miami area and established strong Cuban communities in hopes of returning someday. Since that initial wave of immigrants, however, increasing numbers of Cubans have sought political refuge in the United States resulting in a greater economic diversification of this subgroup of Hispanic Americans. Finally, Hispanic Americans from Central and South America are among the most recent immigrants to the United States and have much less developed ethnic communities to help them adapt. Many of these immigrants are political refugees attempting to escape persecution and armed conflicts in their home countries.

Socioeconomic Context

As with African American families, Hispanic American families must be understood in the context of their current socioeconomic conditions: levels of unemployment, income, and educational attainment.[37] As stated earlier, the unemployment rate for African American males and females generally is more than twice that of white Americans. For Hispanic Americans, the unemployment rate tends to fall between the rates for whites and blacks (4.6 vs. 3.3 and 6.4, respectively). As was shown in Table 5.1, the median income of Hispanic families ($38,679) in 2007 was about 70 percent of the median income of all white families ($54,920). In 2006, 18.9 percent of Hispanic families lived below the poverty line. As shown in Figure 5.3, this rate was three times that of the all–white, non-Hispanic population (6.2 percent), with considerable variation by region of origin. Poverty rates were

---

[36]Martha Crowley, Daniel T. Lichter, and Zhenchao Qian, Beyond Gateway Cities: Economic Restructuring and Poverty among Mexican Immigrant Families and Children," *Family Relations*, 55 (July 2006): 345–360.

[37]Readers with a particular interest in Hispanic ethnic minorities should see Charles H. Mindel, Robert W. Habenstein, and Roosevelt Wright Jr., eds., *Ethnic Families in America*. 4th ed. (Upper Saddle River, NJ: Prentice-Hall, Inc., 1998), Chapters 7–9; and Ronald L. Taylor, ed., *Minority Families in the United States: A Multicultural Perspective*. 3rd ed. (Upper Saddle River, NJ: Prentice-Hall, Inc., 2002), Chapters 4–6.

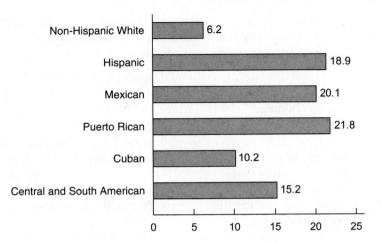

Figure 5.3

People Living Below the Poverty Level, by Detailed Hispanic Origin: 2007 (in Percent)

Source: U.S. Bureau of the Census, The Hispanic Population in the United States: March, 2002 Detailed Tables (PPL-165), Tables 14.1 and 14.2. www.census. gov/population/www/ socdemo/hispanic/ ppl-165.html.

highest for Puerto Rican-origin and Mexican-origin families (21.8 percent and 20.1 percent, respectively) and lowest for Cuban-origin families (10.2 percent).[38]

A report by the Urban Institute indicated that in spite of persistent and growing Latino poverty, most national policy discussions fail to address poverty issues relevant to the Latino/Hispanic experience.[39] Why? Five reasons are given below.

1. *Misperceived identity.* Even though 64 percent of U.S. Latinos are native-born, most are perceived as immigrants, thus being seen as temporary or "unfairly" competing for scarce resources.
2. *No attention to the working poor.* Most reform efforts have been directed to the "underclass" of nonworking poor, overlooking the problems of the Latino poor, most of whom are working.
3. *Geographic concentration.* Three-fourths of all Latinos live in five states (California, Florida, Illinois, New York, and Texas); thus, directives are toward local rather than national efforts.
4. *Political participation.* Only one-third of Latinos are registered to vote (compared to 64 percent of African Americans and 70 percent of white non-Hispanics).
5. *Differences among subgroups.* Highlighting differences among ethnic groups in factors such as employment, welfare use, and female-headed households has obscured larger, underlying themes common to the poverty experience of Latinos.

Yet, as indicated, the poverty rate, particularly among subgroups such as Puerto Rican-origin families, is very high. This appears to be related, at least in part, to two factors:

1. There is a heavy concentration of Puerto Ricans living in cities and working in low-paying full-time jobs, working in part-time jobs, or without a job at all. In New York City, for example, initially the city provided access to jobs that required few skills and little education; however, many of these types of manufacturing industries have left New York.

---

[38]U.S. Census Bureau, *The 2009 Statistical Abstract* "38—Social and Economic Characteristics of the Hispanic Population: 2007," http://www.census.gov/compendia/statab/cats/population/elderly_racial_and_hispanic_origin_population_profiles.html.

[39]Maria Enchautegui, "Policy Implications of Latino Poverty," *The Urban Institute/Policy and Research Report 25* (Winter/Spring 1995): 10–12.

2. In greater numbers than other Hispanics, Puerto Ricans form families without benefit of marriage; the result is a high proportion of families maintained by females with no spouses present.

These two factors, parental work/employment patterns and family structure/female-headed households as related to poverty were examined with a focus on Latino children.[40] Daniel Lichter and Nancy Landale suggest that Puerto Rican and black children pay a high price for the "breakdown of the family" if it is measured strictly in terms of economic well-being. Family structure alone accounted for 55 percent of the differences between Puerto Ricans and whites in child poverty, and when family structure was combined with parental work patterns, 78 percent of the difference in child poverty was explained. The lack of parental work and the low rate of labor force participation among Puerto Rican women have exacerbated the child poverty problem.

Unfortunately, employment is not only a problem for Puerto Rican women but for men as well. Puerto Rican men have a low rate of labor force participation and a high rate of unemployment relative to both non-Latino whites and to other Latino groups. This precarious economic situation contributes to the high rate of union dissolution and the high rate of nonmarital childbearing among Puerto Rican men. Moreover, results underscore the critical role of employment in fathers' abilities to support their children.[41] It is not that fathers desire to abdicate responsibility for their offspring but that they are unable to contribute financially and be involved in the care of their children. This was especially the case for nonresidential fathers.

What about the educational attainment of Hispanic Americans? As was shown in Table 5.2, over 85 percent of white persons and more than 80 percent of black persons age 25 and over have completed four years or more of high school. For Hispanic Americans, the rate drops to about 60 percent. As to college completion, more than one-fourth of white persons had four years or more of college compared to more than 18 percent of black persons and more than 12 percent of Hispanics.

Patterns of Family Life

As we saw in Figure 5.1, about 69 percent of all Hispanic-origin family households consisted of married couples and slightly more than one-fourth (28 percent) were maintained by females with no husbands present. The married-couple figures are below those for whites and considerably higher than those found for blacks. Correspondingly, the figures for female-householder families are higher than they are for whites but considerably lower than they are for blacks.

Again, considerable differences can be seen by country of origin. Nearly 80 percent of Cuban-origin and 70 percent of Mexican-origin families consisted of married couples, while only slightly over half of Puerto Rican–origin families were such. This may be due to the prevalence of nonmarital cohabitation among Puerto Rican women. National data revealed that Puerto Ricans are more accepting of informal cohabitation both with and without intentions to marry, and have greater tolerance

---

[40]Daniel T. Lichter and Nancy S. Landale, "Parental Work, Family Structure, and Poverty among Latino Children," *Journal of Marriage and the Family* 57 (May 1995): 346–354.

[41]Nancy S. Landale and R. S. Oropesa, "Father Involvement in the Lives of Mainland Puerto Rican Children: Contributions of Nonresident, Cohabiting and Married Fathers," *Social Forces* 79 (March 2001): 945–968.

TRANSNATIONAL FAMILIES

Hardship and Resiliency among Latino Migrant Labor Families

Regularly crossing national boundaries for employment is a reality for many families around the world, especially those who live in less economically advantaged locations. One such group is the Latino (mostly Mexican) migrant family in the United States that crosses the border from Mexico each year to work on harvests in large agricultural areas of California, the Southwest, the Northwest and elsewhere. It is a group of particular interest because it consists largely of family units that migrate rather than just individuals. Although 81 percent of U.S. farm workers are Latinos, this group is largely overlooked in research studies. One such study was done by Jose Ruben Parra-Cardona and his colleagues using qualitative interview data from the Michigan subsample of the "Rural Families Speak Multistate Study." Of particular interest in this study was the ways that migrant labor families adapt to their challenging social contexts. In the field of family therapy, the term "resilience" is used to capture capabilities that families possess that allow them to make such adaptations.

In a series of interviews with 13 women from migrant labor families, six themes were noted in this study. The first involved high levels of satisfaction with life in spite of their conditions. This satisfaction was derived from a perception that things were either better or had the potential to be better than what they had experienced in Mexico. The second involved the ethos of working hard ("Trabajando duro"), not for personal wages or gain but as a source of pride and responsibility to others. Third, these respondents noted the challenges to family life and child education arising from the need to move at a moment's notice based on agricultural needs. Fourth was the ongoing challenges of discrimination and exploitation that they faced. These

forces resulted in inconsistencies in pay and health benefits and frequently having to deal with employers who promised one thing but changed conditions once the laborers had arrived from another distant location. They also resulted in farm worker families being exposed to dangerous chemicals in the workplace and other dangerous conditions without recourse to labor union or legal support. Fifth was another value expressed by these families—"moving up in life." These families had no opportunities for status mobility, but they did see the potential for making improvements in their daily lives through learning English, seeking employment with higher wages and better working conditions, and so forth. Finally, the last theme—"Estando todos juntos" (being all together)—reflects the strong emphasis in the Latino culture on the values of *colectivismo* and *familismo*. These values lead to less of a focus on the inability of individuals to attain income and more emphasis on how their work contributed to the well-being of their family and community.

Thus, although wages and living conditions were poor, working conditions dangerous, and social supports generally lacking, these families were able to maintain a resiliency because their cultural value system led them to find meaning in their work in terms of its contribution to the community and the family rather than just through the wages they received. They also were able to reframe their situation "to make meaning of adversity" (372). They saw their situation as one that offered opportunities for improvement—especially with respect to escaping from poorer conditions in Mexico—and they held out hope and optimism for a better future.

Source: Jose Ruben Parra-Cardona, Laurie A. Bulock, David R. Imig, Francisco A. Villarruel, and Steven J. Gold, "'Trabajando Duro Todos Los Dias': Learning from the Life Experiences of Mexican-Origin Migrant Families," *Family Relations,* 55 (July 2006): 361–375.

of nonmarital childbearing and sexual relations.[42] In contrast, Mexican Americans are generally tolerant of informal unions only as a precursor to marriage. Mexican Americans adhered most strongly to the marriage ideal, and girls were traditionally socialized to believe that marriage "is part of God's plan" and should be their major

---

[42]R.S. Oropesa, "Normative Beliefs about Marriage and Cohabitation: A Comparison of Non-Latino Whites, Mexican Americans, and Puerto Ricans," *Journal of Marriage and the Family* 58 (February 1996): 49–62.

life objective. To the Mexican American girl, marriage often is portrayed as an affirmation of womanhood.

A study in New York City suggested that among the Puerto Rican-origin population, these informal unions resemble marriages.[43] Although they are not legal marriages, the study showed that women in these unions were more similar to married women than single women in respect to childbearing behavior and employment and educational pursuits. These nonmarital unions (cohabitants) among women of Puerto Rican background served as an important component of premarital childbearing as well. Cohabitation not only increased the risk of a completed premarital pregnancy but also living in a nonmarital union reduced the odds of marriage between the time of getting pregnant and birth of the child.[44]

The high rate of poverty and the low median family income for Puerto Ricans are directly linked to their heavy concentration in New York City in low-paying jobs and to the lower number of married-couple households. A majority of Puerto Rican-origin families with no husband present live below the poverty level.

The lowest rate of poverty among Hispanic American groups exists among families of Cuban origin. This is partially explained by the large number of full-time employed wives (more workers per family) and by the approximately 400,000 Cubans who immigrated to the United States within a decade of the Marxist revolution led by Fidel Castro. Most of these immigrants settled in Miami and many were highly educated and professional people.[45]

Another contributing factor to high poverty rates among Hispanic Americans is their unusually high fertility and large numbers of persons per household. It is not unusual for Hispanic American families to have three or more children; most other American families have one or two. In 2007, for example, 16 percent of Hispanic-origin family households had three or more children, compared to 8 percent in non-Hispanic white families and 12 percent in black families. This pattern was particularly strong among Mexican American families, followed by Puerto Rican and then Cuban families.[46]

Two-Parent Family Patterns

One of the most debated aspects of Hispanic American family life today involves conflicting evidence regarding the *extendedness* of Hispanic American families. The opposing positions in this debate are best summarized by the concepts of *superintegration* and *disintegration*. The **superintegration hypothesis** is that Hispanic American families (and especially Mexican American families) place strong cultural values on familism and patriarchy and display high levels of involvement in the Catholic religion. These values should increase levels of coresidence and interaction with extended kin as well as place strong obligations on families to provide mutual support to each other in the

---

[43]Nancy S. Landale and Katherine Fennelly, "Informal Unions among Mainland Puerto Ricans: Cohabitation or an Alternative to Legal Marriage?" *Journal of Marriage and the Family* 54 (May 1992): 269–280.

[44]Wendy D. Manning and Nancy S. Landale, "Racial and Ethnic Differences in the Role of Cohabitation in Premarital Childbearing," *Journal of Marriage and the Family* 58 (February 1996): 63–77.

[45]Ronald L. Taylor, ed., *Minority Families in the United States: A Multicultural Perspective.* 3rd ed. (Upper Saddle River, NJ: Prentice-Hall, 2002), Chapter 6.

[46]U.S. Census Bureau, *The 2009 Statistical Abstract* "Table 63 - Families by Number of Own Children Under 18 Years Old," http://www.census.gov/compendia/statab/cats/population/households_families_group_quarters.html.

form of money, emotional support and in-kind instrumental support (e.g., child care, home and auto care, etc.). Communal values of Catholicism and the integration provided through involvement in church activities should also enhance these extended family relations. In contrast, the **disintegration hypothesis** holds that with increasing levels of acculturation into dominant cultural values and lifestyles and high levels of economic stress and poverty, the idealized notion of the Hispanic American extended family no longer applies. According to this argument, Hispanic American families are beginning to look more like white families in terms of preferring a nuclear family form and placing limits on exchanges with extended family members. In addition, limited resources for providing for their immediate family members and for sustaining contacts with relatives should dampen the levels support giving as well as levels of interaction with relatives.

Numerous studies comparing Hispanic Americans to Anglo Americans in terms of coresidence, visiting and interaction levels, and support provision were summarized by Natalia Sarkisian, Mariana Gerena, and Naomi Gerstel.[47] There summary shows highly conflicted results often dependent on the samples and measures used and the degree to which alternative explanatory factors were controlled for. In their own study using the national Survey of Families and Households, they also found that the answer to this debate is more complex than a simple cultural explanation can provide. For example, they did find that Hispanic families (Mexican American

Mexican American families place a high value on familism in which the welfare of the family supersedes personal interests. Themes of family honor and unity characterize the extended family network.

---

[47]Natalia Sarkisian, Mariana Gerena, and Naomi Gerstel, "Extended Family Ties among Mexicans, Puerto Ricans, and Whites: Superintegration or Disintegration?" *Family Relations*, 55 (July 2006): 331–344.

and Puerto Rican) were more integrated than white families in terms of coresidence and living near kin, but there were no significant differences when predicting levels of financial or instrumental help after controlling for socioeconomic status. In addition, they found that measures of cultural values such as gender ideology, extended familism, and church attendance could not account for the differences they found in coresidence and living nearby.[48]

In a later analysis using the same data set but breaking down their analysis by gender, they found that Mexican American women exhibited higher levels of instrumental support giving than white women, although there were no differences between men. They also found that neither Hispanic men nor Hispanic women were more likely than their white counterparts to have contact with extended family relations and that levels of financial support giving (using a measure more sensitive to small amounts of aid) were higher for whites.[49]

Thus, Hispanic American family patterns with respect to extended kin relations are not as distinct as many believe, at least when taking into consideration the effects of different socioeconomic status. Since the socioeconomic status of Hispanic Americans is lower than that of whites, levels of financial assistance are limited and they display less of this type of support giving. On the other hand, lower socioeconomic status increases the likelihood of coresidence and living close to other family members due to the greater efficiencies realized and the lower levels of geographical mobility involved. This closer residence, in turn, enhances levels of instrumental support giving.

These changes from traditional patterns of kinship relations have been shown to have a major impact on the quality of grandparent–grandchild relationships as well. The transition from traditionalism to acculturation in Hispanic American families often alienates grandchildren from their grandparents. When adult grandchildren are more acculturated than their grandparents, they report less frequent interaction with them and a decline in affection toward them over time.[50]

Asian American Families

As of 2007, about 5.4 percent of the resident U.S. population (16.2 million) was characterized by the U.S. Census as Asian, Native Hawaiian, or Pacific Islander—alone or in combination with another racial group.[51] Like Hispanic Americans, **Asian Americans** are not a homogeneous group but a diverse collection of ethnic minorities with distinct cultures, languages, and historical developments. The Asian and Pacific Islander population in the United States includes persons from at least twenty-nine Asian countries and twenty identified Pacific Island cultures from the Far East, Southeast Asia, the Indian subcontinent, and the Pacific Islands.

---

[48]Ibid.

[49]Natalia Sarkisian, Mariana Gerena, and Naomi Gerstel, "Extended Family Integration among Euro and Mexican Americans: Ethnicity, Gender, and Class," *Journal of Marriage and Family*, 69 (February 2007): 40–54.

[50]Teresa W. Julian, Patrick C. McHenry, and Mary W. McKelvey, "Perceptions of Caucasian, African-American, Hispanic, and Asian-American Parents," *Family Relations* 43 (January 1994): 30–37.

[51]U.S. Census Bureau, *The 2009 Statistical Abstract* "Table 6—Resident Population by Sex, Race, and Hispanic Origin Status, http://www.census.gov/compendia/statab/cats/population/estimates_and_projections_by_age_sex_raceethnicity.html.

In spite of tremendous diversity among Asian American families, child-rearing patterns tend to emphasize obligation to family, obedience, and a desire for educational achievement.

The groups most often classified under the category of Asian include persons who identify their origin or background as Chinese (23.7 percent), Filipino (18.1 percent), Asian Indian (16.4 percent), Vietnamese (10.9 percent), Korean (10.5 percent), Japanese (7.8 percent), and other Asian (12.6 percent) including Laotian, Cambodian, Thai, or Hmong.

The term **Pacific Islanders** appears as a subcategory in the U.S. Census and on affirmative-action forms and the like, but Pacific Islanders are not an ethnic group.[52] Almost no one wakes up thinking of themselves as a Pacific Islander. Some may think of themselves as Polynesian, Melanesian, or Micronesian, but most identify as Tongas, Samoans, Maoris, or Fijians, and even they are **multiethnic** within each person. But according to the census, Pacific Islander Americans (.4 percent of the population) include persons who identify as Native Hawaiians (35.3 percent), Samoan (22.8 percent), Guamanian (14.5 percent), and Pacific Islanders (27.3 percent). Relatively few of the Pacific Islanders are foreign born; of course, Hawaiians are native to the United States.

Historical Context

Without exception, each Asian group differs in ancestry, language, culture, and recency of immigration. Some groups, such as the Chinese and Japanese, have had sizable numbers of members in the United States for several generations, whereas others, such as the Vietnamese, Laotians, and Cambodians, are comparatively recent immigrants. Asian Americans are heavily concentrated in California and Hawaii,

---

[52]Paul R. Spickard and Rowena Fong, "Pacific Islander Americans and Multiethnicity: A Vision of American's Future," *Social Forces* 73 (June 1995): 1365–1383.

with sizable proportions of the total in New York, Texas, Illinois, and New Jersey as well. More than 90 percent live in metropolitan areas.

The earliest Asian group to immigrate to the United States was the Chinese. The year 1852 marked a surge of immigrant men from China mostly to the Western United States to work as laborers in mines and on building railroads. These early immigrants were prohibited from bringing their wives and families, and those restrictions as well as others were further reinforced by the Chinese Exclusion Act of 1882 and the National Origin Act of 1924. Given the low wage nature of these jobs and the lack of families, large Chinese ethnic communities arose in large metropolitan areas. Some of these early and later immigrants from China and elsewhere did manage to bring families, however, through the use of private entrepreneurs.

During World War II, Asian Americans were regarded with suspicion and often subject to prejudice and discrimination. Large numbers of Japanese Americans were displaced from their homes and communities and put in internment camps. After the war, however, immigrants from Asia found some success as the 1965 Immigration Reform Act led to an influx of well-educated and professional Asians who brought their families with them. These immigrants found the value systems they brought with them to be highly consistent with the dominant European American value system in that they included such traits as diligence, punctuality, self-discipline, high achievement, politeness, and respect for authority. They also entered American society at a time when their skills fit well with the needs of the economy.

A third group of Asian immigrants followed the Vietnam War. These more recent immigrants came primarily from Southeast Asia to escape persecution and poor living conditions. Lacking the educational training, professional skills, and language proficiency of the earlier immigrant groups, they found considerably less success. In addition, later immigrants from India joined them as part of family reunification programs. Since many of these immigrants also lacked the education and skill sets of the immigrants in the 1960s, it created much more socioeconomically diverse Asian communities.

With respect to family related value systems, Asian Americans brought with them a strong sense of collectivism/communalism, a strong sense of filial responsibility and extended familism, and high levels of patriarchy. These value systems made assimilation into the middle class more difficult, but Asian Americans have found greater levels of assimilation with whites than any other ethnic group and exhibit high levels of intermarriage with whites (see Chapter 6).

Socioeconomic Context

As with African Americans and Hispanic Americans, Asian American families can be better understood by examining a number of general social status characteristics. Asian Americans are younger than the white non-Hispanic population but are older than those of Hispanic origin. As of 2006, their median age was about 33.7, compared to 39.6 for the white non-Hispanic, 30.6 for the black, 26.7 for those of Hispanic origin, and 28.9 for the Native American population in the United States.[53]

---

[53]U.S. Census Bureau, *The 2009 Statistical Abstract* "Table 8—Resident Population by Race, Hispanic Origin, and Age," http://www.census.gov/compendia/statab/cats/population.html.

Asian Americans are better educated than the population as a whole. As of 2007, 89.8 percent of the males and 85.9 percent of the females have four years or more of high school, compared to about 85.3 and 87.1 percent for whites, 81.9 and 82.6 percent for blacks, and 58.2 and 62.5 percent for Hispanics (review Table 5.2). The image of Asians as good students seems to be supported by higher-than-average Scholastic Achievement Test scores in mathematics, for example. These higher test scores are reflected in Asian Americans' extremely high levels of college attendance and graduation. Over 55 percent of Asian males and 49 percent of Asian females over the age of 25 have attained a college degree compared to only 30 percent of white males and 28 percent of white females. And with a higher level of education tends to come a higher median income. In 2006, the median household income for Asian Americans was $64,238, more than $13,000 greater than that for whites ($50,673).[54]

Unfortunately, the grouping together of the Asian and Pacific Island populations masks discrepancies among the subgroups. For example, only 5.3 percent of the persons of Japanese origin were below the poverty level. In comparison, the poverty levels for those of Chinese, Asian Indian, and Vietnamese descent ranged from 11.1 to 27.9 percent. A greater proportion of Filipino (26.2 percent) and Vietnamese (32.9 percent) persons had a family size of six or more members, whereas a lesser proportion of Korean persons had a family of six or more (5.5 percent). And 17.2 percent of Vietnamese persons and 12.8 percent of Korean persons rated their health as only fair or poor (rather than very good or good) in contrast to the 6.1 to 17.4 percent of Chinese, Filipino, and Japanese who gave the same rating.[55]

Patterns of Family Life

In 2006, Asian and Pacific Islanders in the United States had a married couple rate (80.4 percent) just slightly above the white population (80.1 percent) but considerably higher than the Hispanic (67.8 percent) and black (46.6 percent) populations. Likewise, the rate of female households with no husband present was quite low at 11.8 percent when compared with Hispanics at 22.6 percent and blacks at 44.8 percent.[56]

Particularly among Chinese American, Japanese American, and Filipino American marriages, there is a high level of family stability and a greater degree of permanence than among Hispanic American and African American marriages. Divorce rates are low, and strong kinship associations are high. Most Asian American populations have entrenched norms and role expectations pertaining to caring for older relatives, particularly parents, many of whom live in the same household as their adult children.

---

[54]U.S. Census Bureau, *The 2009 Statistical Abstract* "Table 669—Money Income of Households—Median Income by Race and Hispanic Origin, in Current and Constant (2006) Dollars: 1980 to 2006," http://www.2010census.biz/compendia/statab/cats/income_expenditures_poverty_wealth.html.

[55]JoAnn Kuo and Kathryn Porter, "Health Status of Asian Americans: United States, 1992–94," *National Center for Health Statistics* (Hyattsville, MD: Centers for Disease Control and Prevention, no. 298, August 7, 1998): 5–6.

[56]U.S. Census Bureau, *The 2009 Statistical Abstract* "Table 55—Marital Status of the Population by Sex, Race and Hispanic Origin," http://www.2010census.biz/compendia/statab/cats/population/marital_status_and_living_arrangements.html.

CROSS-CULTURAL *Perspective*

Chinese Filial Piety, Identity Conflict and Elder Care in Oceania

Australia and New Zealand have experienced numerous waves of immigrants from mainland China and Taiwan over the past 150 years. Migrations began with the gold rush in the mid-1800s and continued with post–World War II migrations, university and labor force expansion efforts in the 1980s, and accommodations extended to those fleeing communist restrictions on free speech and potential nationalization of businesses and wealth in Hong Kong and Taiwan. As a result, Oceania has in recent years had to deal with ethnic diversity in both its population of youth and its elderly. The problems confronted by both of these groups are intertwined through the concept of *filial piety* and the part it plays in the levels of cultural *identity conflict* experienced by youth and the extent to which the younger generation is providing adequate care for the elderly. Two recent studies provide some insight into these problems.

The first study looked at how family related variables and intergroup relationship variables impact the levels of identity conflict experienced by Chinese youth living in New Zealand and Singapore. Defining **identity conflict** as a "type of intrapersonal struggle...[characterized by a] subjective feeling of being 'torn apart' between two or more different commitments" and resulting from living in a cultural environment alien to the cultural environment of one's early socialization, this study predicted that high levels of filial piety would cause identity conflict for Chinese youth living in these foreign settings

because the obligations to parents and grandparents it entails run contrary to the Western cultural emphasis on egalitarianism, democracy, and personal freedom. As expected, they found that among youth between the ages of 16 and 26, high commitment to filial piety significantly increased feelings of identity conflict, even after controlling for several "intergroup" variables such as perceived discrimination, perceived acceptance into the dominant culture, and a sense of cultural continuity in their transition.

A second study looking at Chinese elderly in Brisbane, Australia demonstrates how the assumption of strong values of filial piety in the Chinese Australian community is not necessarily a valid assumption and has led to a neglect of this vulnerable population. This study found high levels of social isolation among this ethnic sub-group due in large part from a lack of attention and care in their adult children's homes and a failure of transportation and social welfare systems to attend to their needs on the assumption that they were being provided for in their children's homes. Elderly parents in this study appeared to be aware of the ways in which filial piety had been transformed in the modern Chinese ethnic context from an obligation and right to a voluntary responsibility taken on by their adult children. Divested from their powerful position derived from property ownership, the Chinese elderly in Brisbane were dependent on the adult children's goodwill, a condition that their children made aware to them and that they respected by not complaining and by quietly accepting their isolated conditions.

Sources: En-Yi Lin, "Family and Social Influences on Identity Conflict in Overseas Chinese," *International Journal of Intercultural Relations*, 32 (2008): 130–141.; and David Ip, Chi Wai Lui, and Wing Hong Chui, "Veiled Entrapment: A Study of Social isolation of Older Chinese Migrants in Brisbane, Queensland," *Aging and Society*, 27 (2007): 719–738.

Some of the traditional cultural norms, such as speaking the native language, patriarchal authority, rigid role expectations for wives and children, and the heavy emphasis on childhood obedience and loyalty to parents, bring with them intergenerational strains. Second- and third-generation children tend to assimilate culturally. They are likely to accept English as their dominant language, adopt the dress codes and musical preferences of their peers (many of whom are not of

Asian descent), and pick up various dating and sexual patterns that are at odds with traditional and parental values.

The significance of language in parent–child relationships was seen in a study of more than 600 adolescents whose parents were immigrants from Asian and Latin American backgrounds.[57] Adolescents who shared a common language with their parents had the closest relationships with them and were the most likely to discuss their present and future concerns with them. Second-generation (U.S.-born) adolescents were more likely to use English in their conversations with parents, many of whom lacked the degree of comfort with and fluency in English their children possessed. The results were higher levels of parent–adolescent conflict, less emphasis on parental authority, greater difficulty on the part of parents to appreciate their children's viewpoints, and often an embarrassment to the children of their "accented" parents and their inability to aid them with U.S. social issues.

One indication of cultural assimilation is seen in the significant increase in the degree of intermarriage between Asian Americans of different Asian nationalities and with non-Asians. A study of intermarriage by six Asian American groups (Japanese, Chinese, Filipino, Korean, Asian Indian, and Vietnamese) revealed some interesting findings.[58] Among five of the six groups, Asian men showed a greater propensity than Asian women to marry endogamously, that is, within their own group (Asian Indians were the exception). Among these six groups, Japanese were by far the most likely to be intermarried, with half of the men and more than half of the women having spouses who were not Japanese. Filipino and Korean women had high intermarriage rates as well. Although the wars in Korea and Vietnam brought with them numerous marriages of Korean and Vietnamese women to white and black U.S. servicemen, these "war brides" were a small proportion of the total Asian intermarriages.

Native American Family System

Suzan Shown Harjo notes that for over 500 years, Native Americans were referred to as "Indians."[59] They were, and remain, several hundred tribes or nations with 300 separate languages and dialects. The population at the time Columbus landed in 1492 was estimated at about 10 million. As of 2007, about 1.5 percent (4.5 million) of the U.S. population claimed Native American and Alaska Native origins.[60]

Exact patterns of growth are difficult to determine, but census data suggest the Native American population may be increasing at a rate four times the national

---

[57]Vivian Tseng and Andrew J. Fuligni, "Parent-Adolescent Language Use and Relationships among Immigrant Families with East Asian, Filipino, and Latin American Backgrounds," *Journal of Marriage and the Family* 62 (May 2000): 465–476.

[58]Sean-Shong Hwang, Rogelio Saenz, and Benigno E. Aguirre, "Structural and Assimilationist Explanations of Asian American Intermarriage," *Journal of Marriage and the Family* 59 (August 1997): 758–772.

[59]Suzan Shown Harjo, "The American Indian Experience" in Harriette Pipes McAdoo, *Family Ethnicity: Strengths in Diversity* (Newbury Park, CA: Sage, 1993), 199.

[60]U.S. Census Bureau, *The 2009 Statistical Abstract* "Table 6—Resident Population by Sex, Race, and Hispanic Origin Status, http://www.census.gov/compendia/statab/cats/population/estimates_and_projections_by_age_sex_raceethnicity.html.

Native American families maintain strong patterns of inter- and intrafamiily cooperation and sharing. Conceptions of time and living in harmony with nature illustrate departures from Western norms.

average. This is due to factors such as a rise in the birthrate, a reduction in infant mortality, and a greater number of persons identifying themselves as having Native American ancestry. Eschbach claims that over the past few decades, an increasing portion of the census-identified Native American population consists of individuals not identified as such previously and not native to the regions where most reservations are located. He cites a more than sixfold increase in population between the 1960 and 1990 census figures for these "non-reservation" Native Americans, and suggests that this be understood most appropriately as a new emergence of ethnic identification, or at least as reflecting changes in the expression of an ethnic identification. (Migration from other areas played only a small role in this population growth.)[61]

Historical Context

As with African Americans, Hispanic Americans, and Asian Americans, it is inaccurate to view Native Americans as a homogeneous people. While sharing many values in common, they have distinct languages, tribal customs, family forms, life-course rituals, patterns of lineage, and kinship relationships. For example, many tribes have a kinship descent pattern that is patrilineal, but among the Hopi the

---

[61]Karl Eschbach, "Changing Identification Among American Indians and Alaska Natives," *Demography* 30 (November 1993): 635–652; and Jeffrey S. Passel, "The Growing American Indian Population, 1960–1990: Beyond Demography," *Population Research and Policy Review* 16 (1997): 11–31.

pattern is matrilineal. Many tribes have a postmarital residence pattern that is patrilocal, but again, the Hopi are matrilocal. Nevertheless, as with the other major racial/ethnic/minority groups, some general characteristics of Native Americans will be presented.

Within the **Native American** population are hundreds of distinct tribes or nations. The largest group, the Cherokees, comprise about 16 percent of the Native American population. The second largest group, the Navajo, comprise about 12 percent. Other large groups, ranging from 2.3 to 5.5 percent of the Native American population, include the Sioux, Chippewa, Choctaw, Pueblo, Apache, Iroquois, Lumbee, and Creek tribes.[62] Most Native Americans live in the western regions of the United States: California, Arizona, Oklahoma, New Mexico, Washington, and Alaska.

Walter Kawamoto and Tamara Cheshire attempt to capture Native American cultural beliefs using a relatively common American Indian term "**seven generations.**"[63] This term is used to refer to how decisions an individual makes in his/her life will affect the tribe over the following seven generations. As such, it conveys strong cultural values of collectivism/communalism and generational piety. Although there may be great variation in Native American family life from tribal group to tribal group in terms of levels of patriarchy versus matriarchy and levels of family extendedness, these two themes seem to be consistently represented in Native American culture.

In addition, there appears to be a centrality of women in the village and family life of American Indians in both the American plains and the coastal regions of the Northwest. The traditional role of men was in the external affairs of the community, particularly in finding sources of food through hunting and fishing activities and in protecting the community and negotiating with others outside the community. The role of women was in the center of the community and was generally focused around local food and clothing production, cultural transmission through storytelling, and cooperative child care.

Unfortunately, of all ethnic groups in the United States, the culture of Native Americans may have been the most disrupted as a result of contact with the dominant European American society and culture. While the experience of most minorities in the United States involved a struggle to gain position in the melting pot—social acceptance, economic power, and equal rights—the experience of the American Indian was the opposite, involving a struggle to avoid subjugation and to reserve their land, water, traditions, and unique legal rights.[64] Unlike any other minority group in the United States, Native Americans have negotiated over 600 treaties with the United States government and have ceded billions of acres of land and untold natural resources.

Harjo states that assimilation for Native Americans involved overt cultural genocide through official efforts to destroy native languages, traditions, customary laws,

---

[62]*Statistical Abstract of the United States*, 2000, nos. 43 and 44, p. 45.

[63]Walter T. Kawamoto and Tamara C. Cheshire, "A Seven-Generation Approach to American Indian Families," in Marilyn Coleman and Lawrence H. Ganong, eds. *Handbook of Contemporary Families* (Thousand Oaks, CA: Sage Publications, 2004), 385–393.

[64]Harjo, "The American Indian Experience," pp. 199–207. The information in this section comes primarily from this source.

dress, religion, and occupations. This was done in three major ways: (1) through federal franchising of tribal lands to Christian denominations for proselytizing and sectarian "social work"; (2) through an imposed educational system designed to separate children from their families and instill in them nonnative values; and (3) through federal efforts to break up tribal landholdings, turn Native Americans into individual landowners, and impose taxes on their lands.

Dealings with the educational system extend back to the early 1800s, when a congressional appropriation for natives' education was set aside in a **"civilization fund."** In 1871, President Grant delegated specific reservations to churches that had the aim of stripping Native American people of their religious ceremonies (including the Sun Dance and the Ghost Dance), forbidding them to speak their native languages, and separating children from their parents (for up to twelve years) by sending them to off-reservation boarding schools or placing them in foster homes. Harjo notes that until recently, educational efforts were based on the premise that Native American people are inferior to white people. Children were taught that their traditions were savage and immoral. Unfortunately, not only did these experiences destroy Native American cultures but they also lead to the development of risky health behaviors among youth who lacked the traditional controls and directives of their native culture and often were exposed to abuse in boarding schools and foster homes.[65]

Today, Native American education is increasingly under tribal control as a result of education reform acts passed in the 1970s and cultural history is now taught on the reservations. But U.S. history books used nationwide by most students in public grade schools, high schools, and colleges relegate Native American matters to a few pages or, at best, a chapter. Near Thanksgiving, non-Native American schools may set aside a day or week for "Native American awareness."

Many issues other than education are pertinent to understanding Native Americans and their family life today. Take land, for example. Not only were nomadic tribes confined to restricted areas, but major efforts were made to allocate land to individual families, to make them farmers, and therefore to have them become more "civilized." Promises were made to irrigate these lands (much of them desert or semiarid and not suitable for cultivation), most of which were never fulfilled.

Perhaps the issues surrounding the Native American experience can best be summed up by Harjo, who wrote:

> ...the taking of land, forced relocation, an institutionally racist educational system, removal of Indian children from their homes, U.S. government paternalism, obstacles to self-governance, stripping of tribal recognition, and denial of religious freedom—continue to place great stress on Indian families. Symptoms of these policies are, not surprisingly, high unemployment and alcohol and drug abuse.[66]

Socioeconomic Context

According to U.S. Census data, less than half (40 percent) of the Native Americans live on reservations, trust lands, or tribal designated areas. Federal American

---

[65]Walter T. Kawamoto and Tamara C. Cheshire, "A Seven-Generation Approach to American Indian Families," in Marilyn Coleman and Lawrence H. Ganong, eds. *Handbook of Contemporary Families* (Thousand Oaks, CA: Sage Publications, 2004), 385–393.

[66]Harjo, "The American Indian Experience," pp. 199–207.

Indian **reservations** are areas established by treaty, statute, or court order and are recognized as territories in which the tribes have jurisdiction. **Trust lands** are associated with a particular tribe but located outside reservation boundaries and are held in trust by the federal government. **Tribal-designated statistical areas** have no specific land base or trust lands but provide statistical areas on which census data are tabulated. The remaining 60 percent of Native Americans live in cities or communities apart from the designated areas listed. Increasingly, Native Americans are leaving the reservations and rural areas for urban employment and schooling.

One startling characteristic of Native Americans is the median age and life expectancy of Native Americans. In 2006, the median age was 30.3 (compared to the median age of 36.6 for the rest of the population).[67] The life expectancy is estimated to be just over 50 (compared to the white life expectancy of about 75). A high rate of infant mortality; alcoholism; tuberculosis, diabetes, and other diseases; psychological distress; suicide; crime; and accidental death all contribute to this low life expectancy.

Although most of the student-age Native American population is enrolled in school, the dropout rate is high. Less than 6 percent of the entire Native American population in 2000 was enrolled in college, with females making up 58 percent of that number. Exactly half of the college students (50 percent) were attending two-year colleges and half were attending four-year colleges. Increases in educational attainment by Native Americans are most pronounced in metropolitan areas.[68]

In general, low educational achievement, combined with a large proportion of men and women relegated to service and unskilled jobs, results in Native Americans having one of the lowest median family incomes of any ethnic minority in the United States. A report by the Urban Institute revealed that they have the poorest-quality housing in the United States as well.[69] The number of Native Americans living in inadequate housing in tribal areas is about 40 percent, nearly seven times the percentage for all U.S. residents.

Patterns of Family Life

In 2007, 58.6 percent of all Native American family households were comprised of married-couple families.[70] This was below that of Hispanic Americans, Asian Americans, and white Americans but above that of blacks (refer to Figure 5.1). The

---

[67]U.S. Census Bureau, *Facts for Features*, "American Indian and Alaska Native Heritage Month: November 2008," http://www.census.gov/Press-Release/www/releases/archives/facts_for_features_special_editions/012782.html.

[68]Karl Eschbach, Khalil Supple, and C. Matthew Snipp, "Changes in Racial Identification and the Educational Attainment of American Indians, 1970–1990," *Demography* 35 (February 1998): 35–43.

[69]"American Indian Housing," *The Urban Institute/Policy and Research Report* (Spring 1996): 7–9.

[70]U.S. Census Bureau, *Facts for Features*, "American Indian and Alaska Native Heritage Month: November 2008," http://www.census.gov/Press-Release/www/releases/archives/facts_for_features_special_editions/012782.html.

CROSS-CULTURAL *Perspective*

New Zealand's Native Peoples: The Maori

The native people of New Zealand—the Maori—have not been subjected to the same level of systematic isolation and weakening of their cultural beliefs as have the native peoples elsewhere—such as the United States and Canada. In a historical study of how the Maori have been treated by the welfare state in New Zealand, Bronwyn Labrum notes that the Maori have long been treated as equals under various welfare regimes between 1944 and 1970. The New Zealand governments of the past as well as those today continue to try to maintain a high level of respect for Maori peoples and culture. Much of this respect has been based on a high degree of integration of Maori into urban life and public recognition of the heroism and prowess displayed by the Maori during World War II. Nevertheless, the Maori remain significantly disadvantaged in New Zealand society today and not unlike early well-intended policies to help native populations in the United States and Canada, New Zealand welfare provisions have had unintended consequences that have contributed to their disadvantage.

In spite of the desires of the New Zealand government to provide for the needs of the Maori, welfare policies were structured in a way that led to this group being "problematized." The programs designed to help the Maori assimilate into New Zealand culture and the large proportion of this population living in urban areas made the Maori, and their "foreign" culture, more visible to the larger population. Labrum identifies housing policies as one particular area where good intentions backfired. These policies attempted to put Maori families into homes designed for nuclear families in neighborhoods of the *Pakeha* majority population. Such an arrangement was inconsistent with the Maori culture of large families, extended family relations and their openness to including others in their households. As a result, many problems arose in these neighborhoods when neighbors complained that their new neighbors lacked the "respect" for their property expected by middle class standards and that houses were overcrowded with visitors and late night socializing. Other aspects of Maori culture that were made more visible and defined as "problematic" as a result of this conscious incorporation into welfare were Maori traditions such as early ages at marriage, informal marriage traditions, and informal fostering and adoption practices.

Source: Bronwyn Labrum, "Developing 'the Essentials of Good Citizenship and Responsibilities' in Maori Women: Family Life, Social Change, and the State in New Zealand, 1944–70," *Journal of Family History*, 29 (2004): 446–465.

high rates of single parenting occur in spite of the fact that Native Americans had a high age at first intercourse.[71]

Despite tribal differences, kinship ties are of supreme importance, and extended family networks remain as a constant. The members of these extended family households may or may not reside in single housing quarters and function as an economic unit by sharing economic resources such as rent or groceries.[72] This is possible because those who don't live together live near one another. These members engage in obligatory mutual assistance and actively participate in important ceremonial events.

---

[71]Walter T. Kawamoto and Tamara C. Cheshire, "A Seven-Generation Approach to American Indian Families," in Marilyn Coleman and Lawrence H. Ganong, eds. *Handbook of Contemporary Families* (Thousand Oaks, CA: Sage Publications, 2004), 385–393.

[72]Michael Yellowbird and C. Matthew Snipp, "American Indian Families," in Ronald L. Taylor, ed., *Minority Families in the United States*, 227.

Families derive their identity from family relations, tribes, land-base positions, and highly valued clan relationships between individuals.

The division of household labor, especially among groups such as the Navajo, appears to be more egalitarian than in most ethnic/cultural groups. Hossain reports that although mothers spend more time in household labor than fathers, fathers' involvement is noticeably high.[73] Navajo fathers report high levels of participation in cleaning, feeding, and playing with their babies. They have a sense of competence and self-confidence in their family network that fosters sensitivity to their children and involvement in household labor. Home is a priority and husbands are expected to participate in household labor and help their wives maintain family possessions (the traditional family ideology of matriarchy gives Navajo mothers ownership of land and other properties in the family).

Elders, too, play a special role in Native American communities and families. Children are taught to respect and assist them. Grandparents participate actively in the training of grandchildren, nephews/nieces, and other extended relatives and assume much of the responsibility for passing on the cultural heritage, including language, tribal rituals, and family traditions. Of particular relevance is the teaching of living in harmony with nature and having respect for the land. Other values—many that depart from the European American culture—include a conception of time as a blend of the past and future.

As with Asian Americans, interracial marriage is common. Eschbach identified six regions as having high rates of intermarriage: the Northeast, Northwest, South, California, Prairie, and Midwest.[74] (Places with low rates included Alaska, Arizona, New Mexico, North Carolina, and the northern plains states.) In regions where the intermarriage rate was high, in 1990 more than three-fourths of married Native Americans were married to non-Native Americans. Among people under age 25, that figure was nearly 80 percent.

Wilkinson[75] suggests these intermarriage alliances, other than changes in identification, are a result of a number of social conditions: residence in metropolitan areas, new occupational opportunities, frequency of contact with other ethnic groups, higher educational status, and the desire for and perceptions of the possibility of assimilation.

We might anticipate that as more Native Americans leave the reservations for urban areas, values of time, sharing, cooperation, and responsibility for one another are likely to lessen. As more women are employed outside the home, traditional gender roles are likely to break down. As some members are successful in obtaining higher levels of education and income, the gap between the "haves" will contrast even more sharply with the "have nots" who live in substandard housing and rely on government assistance just to survive. These and other changes will lead to continuing diversity, not only between tribal groups and families but within them as well.

---

[73]Ziarat Hossain, "Division of Household Labor and Family Functioning in Off-Reservation Navajo Indian Families," *Family Relations* 50 (July 2001): 255–261.

[74]Karl Eschbach, "The Enduring and Vanishing American Indian: American Indian Population Growth and Intermarriage in 1990," *Ethnic and Racial Studies* 18 (January 1995): 89–108.

[75]Doris Wilkinson, "Family Ethnicity in America," in Harriette Pipes McAdoo, ed., *Family Ethnicity: Strengths in Diversity* (Newbury Park, CA: Sage, 1993), 44.

Summary

1. Race is a socially constructed classification system that assumes differences in outward physical appearance represent internal genetic, biological, and psychological capabilities and predispositions. Research and theoretical logic argue against the validity of these assumptions. Instead, race is best treated like ethnicity as a way to classify people from different cultural backgrounds, with differences between groups attributed to these different backgrounds and the ways in which the groups have intersected with majority culture and societal conditions.

2. In order to understand race/ethnic group differences, it is important to understand their cultures prior to contact with the dominant European American culture as well as the unique historical experiences they have had as a result of those contacts. Three important cultural themes that distinguish minority race and ethnic groups from the dominant European American culture are collectivism/communalism, familism, and patriarchy. These three themes play an important role in understanding how families from these groups have adapted to American society. Two other important concepts are acculturation and assimilation. These represent the degree to which race/ethnic groups have adopted dominant cultural values and integrated into the system of social relationships among those from the dominant culture, respectively.

3. In addition to preexisting cultures and historical experiences, it is also important to consider the possibility that race/ethnic differences are really the outcome of current ecological conditions, often brought about as a result of prior historical experiences. In particular, the effects of social class, prejudice, discrimination, and segregation are all significant and explain many of the race/ethnic differences observed in family life.

4. African American families have been and still are affected by cultural traditions brought to America by their ancestors, the ways in which they used those traditions to adapt to slavery, the ways that slavery introduced new cultural traditions as a result of adaptation to the conditions of slavery, and the impacts of the great migration. In addition to these cultural traditions and historical experiences, African American families are in the process of actively adapting to their current ecological contexts. These contexts are not uniform, however. Although low socioeconomic status, high levels of poverty, and high risk neighborhoods confront many African American families, there has also been growth in recent years in the black middle class. As a result, two family patterns have emerged: the matricentric female-headed family pattern and the two-parent family pattern.

5. The Hispanic American population is made up of groups with ties to Mexico, Puerto Rico, Cuba, Central and South America, and other Spanish-speaking countries. Major differences exist among these groups in terms of their cultural heritage and historical experiences, but all are influenced by values of collectivism/communalism, familism, and patriarchy. The collectivistic aspects of Hispanic culture are captured by the concept of the *compadrazgo*, which involves the incorporation of friends and extended family members into the lives of children and their parents. Familism in Hispanic American culture involves a high level of obligation and responsibility to family members (especially immediate family and grandparents). The patriarchal tradition is captured with the concepts of *machismo* and *marianism*.

6. There are significant differences between Hispanic groups in terms of their socioeconomic conditions. Although Cuban Americans are the best off financially, they still have lower status than whites. Puerto Ricans and Mexican Americans are considerably less well off and have high rates of poverty.

7. Data on household types among Hispanic Americans have shown that numbers of married couples and female householders fall between those of the white and black populations. As with other groups, the proportion of female-headed families that live below the level of poverty is very high. Male and female roles in the Mexican American family, although still highly traditional, are exhibiting change. Particularly among professional women, marital decision making appears to be becoming more egalitarian, and the traditional *machismo* pattern among men seems to be lessening. Levels of extended family integration are higher for Hispanic Americans versus whites, but there is no evidence to support a superintegration hypothesis. Support networks of both whites and Hispanic Americans are shaped and constrained by socioeconomic conditions.

8. As with Hispanic Americans, Asian Americans are a very diverse collection of ethnic minorities. Chinese and Filipinos are the largest groups, with sizable numbers of Japanese, Asian Indian, Korean, Vietnamese, Hawaiian, Laotian, Cambodian, Thai, Hmong,

Samoan, and Guamanian. Asian Americans, when compared with the other groups considered, have higher levels of education and median family incomes. Select groups, such as the Chinese, Japanese, and Filipinos, have high levels of family stability and low divorce rates.

9. Native Americans are made up of several hundred tribes. The majority reside in western regions of the United States, but Native Americans can be found in any state and most cities. Compared to the other groups considered, Native Americans have a lower median age and shorter life expectancy. Despite tribal

differences, kinship ties, the role of the elders, and the sacredness of the land are values shared among most Native Americans. Adherence to many traditional values becomes more difficult as increasing numbers of Native Americans intermarry and move to urban areas.

In the next chapter, we begin our exploration of the family life course by looking at patterns of marriage and partner selection before discussion processes of interaction in premarital and nonmarital relationships in Chapters 7 and 8.

Key Terms and Topics

Ethnicity p. 190

Race p. 191

Collectivism/communalism p. 192

Familism p. 192

Patriarchy p. 192

Barrios p. 193

Acculturation p. 193

Assimilation p. 193

Prejudice p. 195

Discrimination p. 195

Residential segregation p. 195

Cultural discontinuity p. 196

Miscegenation p. 196

Moynihan Report p. 200

Tangle of pathology p. 200

Matricentric female-headed family pattern p. 205

Two-parent family pattern p. 207

Hispanic Americans p. 208

Compadres and comadres p. 209

Compadrazgo p. 209

Machismo p. 210

Marianism p. 210

Chicanos p. 211

Braceros p. 211

Superintegration hypothesis p. 216

Disintegration hypothesis p. 217

Asian Americans p. 218

Pacific Islanders p. 219

Multiethnic p. 219

Identity conflict p. 222

Native American p. 225

Seven generations p. 225

Civilization fund p. 226

Reservations p. 227

Trust lands p. 227

Tribal-designated statistical areas p. 227

Discussion Questions

1. What is the meaning and significance of race in understanding human social behavior?
2. What are the various factors that need to be considered when trying to understand or explain race and ethnic differences in family life?
3. What contemporary family characteristics can be traced directly to African heritage? How does under-

standing slavery in the United States contribute to understanding current patterns of African American family life?

4. What is meant by "the declining significance of race?" What does the evidence tell us about this hypothesis?

5. What cultural aspects are generally shared by different Hispanic American groups? What cultural and socioeconomic factors distinguish these different subgroups?

6. How have historical experiences shaped the family lives of Mexican Americans and Puerto Ricans in different ways?

7. What is the debate around superintegration versus disintegration with respect to Hispanic American extended family networks? What does the data say about this debate?

8. How would you explain the higher levels of education and median family income among Asian Americans than among other groups considered?

9. How have the cultural heritage and historical experiences of Asian Americans shaped their success in America and in their family lives? Why would it be incorrect to assume that all Asian Americans have achieved success?

Further Readings

Benokraitis, Nijole V. *Contemporary Ethnic Families in the United States*. Upper Saddle River, NJ: Pearson Education, Inc., 2002.

   A collection of forty-six articles published in the past decade that deals with values, gender roles, parenting, class, violence, and other topics involving ethnic families in the United States.

Browne, Irene, ed. *Latinas and African American Women at Work: Race, Gender, and Economic Inequality*. New York: Russell Sage Foundation, 1999.

   A series of articles documents how race and gender intersect to disadvantage black and Latino women.

Chow, Claire S. *Leaving Deep Water: The Lives of Asian American Women at the Crossroads of Two Cultures*. New York: Dutton, 1998.

   An insightful investigation of the families, relationships, and lives of Asian American women as they bridge two contrasting cultures.

Coleman, Marilyn and Lawrence H. Ganong, eds. *Handbook of Contemporary Families* (Thousand Oaks, CA: Sage Publications, 2004)

   Contains many chapters on contemporary family life and five chapters on race and ethnic minorities.

Coles, Roberta L. *Race and Family: A Structural Approach*. Thousand Oaks, CA: Sage Publications, 2005.

   A different approach to looking at race and ethnic families that focuses on structural factors that unify and distinguish these groups. The emphasis is lesson specific group histories and more on sociological processes that have created commonalities in family organization as well as differences.

Hamer, Jennifer. *What It Means to Be Daddy: Fatherhood for Black Men Living Away from Their Children*. New York: Columbia University Press, 2001.

   An investigation of what black live-away fathers do as fathers and an explanation for their behavior.

Katz, Elizabeth G., and Correia, Maria Cecilia, eds. *The Economics of Gender in Mexico: Work, Family, State, and Market*. Washington, DC: World Bank, 2001.

   Gender issues in the Mexican economy are examined over the life course.

Kitano, Harry H.L., and Daniels, Roger. *Asian Americans: Emerging Minorities*. 3rd ed. Upper Saddle River, NJ: Prentice Hall, 2001.

   An excellent source detailing Asian immigration to the United States, including the Chinese before and after 1943, the Japanese before and after 1946, Filipinos, Asian Indians, Koreans, Pacific Islanders, and Southeast Asians.

Ladner, Joyce A. *The Ties That Bind: Timeless Values for African American Families*. New York: J. Wiley, 1998.

   An investigation of the values, standards, and traditions of black families.

Landry, Bart. *Black Working Wives: Pioneers of the American Family Revolution*. Berkeley, CA: University of California Press, 2000.

   The author takes a look at middle-class black families with a focus on working women and wives.

Logan, Sadye L., ed. *The Black Family: Strengths, Self-Help, and Positive Change*. 2nd ed. Boulder, CO: Westview Press, 2001.

   A look at the strengths of black families and at the ways to create and promote positive change.

McAdoo, Harriette Pipes, ed. *Black Children: Social, Educational, and Parental Environments*. 2nd ed. Thousand Oaks, CA: Sage Publications, 2002.

A series of articles focusing on the social contexts and circumstances surrounding the lives of African American children.

McCubbin, Hamilton I., Thompson, Elizabeth A., Thompson, Anne I., and Futrall, Jo A., eds. *Resiliency in African American Families*. Thousand Oaks, CA: Sage Publications, 1998.

A focus on why African American families succeed in spite of adversities and crisis.

McLoyd, Vonnie C., Cauce, Ana Mari, Takeuchi, David, and Wilson, Leon. "Marital Processes and Parental Socialization in Families of Color: A Decade Review of Research," *Journal of Marriage and the Family* 62 (November 2000): 1070–1093.

A decade-review article looking at demographic trends, marital and parental processes, and future directions of African, Latino, and Asian American families.

Taylor, Ronald L., ed. *Minority Families in the United States: A Multicultural Perspective*. 3rd ed. Upper Saddle River, NJ: Prentice-Hall, 2002.

Chapters are devoted to a range of minority families in the United States, including black, West Indian, Mexican, Puerto Rican, Cuban, Chinese, Japanese, Korean, Native American, and others.

part III Relationship Formation Processes and Nonmarital Relationships

chapter 6

Partnering and Marriage Formation

An Interracial, Interfaith Relationship

Preston and Julie have had a relationship with one another for approximately seven years and recently became engaged. They purchased a townhouse in Maryland and are living there together. Preston, age 32, received both a B.A. and an M.B.A. from Duke University. Julie, age 30, graduated from the University of Massachusetts at Amherst and is working on a master's degree in conflict resolution. He is in a management position with Ford Motor Company and she, certified in human resource management, does consulting and training in that area. Preston is African American and Protestant. Julie is white and Jewish.

Preston and Julie met in Washington, DC, where they were both employed by the Sheraton Corporation. They dated for more than two years before she took a position in Atlanta, Georgia, and he returned to school in Durham, North Carolina. For the next three years, they carried on a long-distance relationship until he got a position in Michigan and she moved there to be with him.

Although of different racial and religious backgrounds, both share a basic core value of desiring an inclusive society and a belief that all individuals deserve to be treated with respect. For Preston, race was not an issue. He assumed he would marry within his race but had previously dated white, Hispanic, Asian, and Native American women. On the other hand, Julie had never dated outside of her race. She said that was surprising because she had lived in heterogeneous communities and was open to the possibility. But when she met Preston, new possibilities opened up. He was unlike any man she had ever met: patient, calm, understanding, down to earth, intelligent, and easy to talk with about anything. To Preston, Julie was attractive, warm, open, funny, and very smart.

How did their parents and friends react to the relationship? For Preston, parents and friends presented no problem. Many of his friends were of different races and had dated others from diverse racial and ethnic backgrounds. His parents, active in the military and who themselves adopted a boy of mixed races, accepted Julie immediately. She said they treated her like a daughter and has always felt very close to them. Julie's parents, however, had always lived in a homogeneous neighborhood and their friends were white and Jewish. As a result, this relationship presented a problem to them, particularly to her father. He held many traditional beliefs, and although accepting religious differences was easier for him than racial ones, the combination of both made him very uncomfortable. Her mother, with time, became more supportive and was glad to see her daughter so happy.

The problems that Preston and Julie perceive deal more with others than with interpersonal ones. Both have struggled with what other people think. At times, they have felt uncomfortable with stares from strangers and in meeting new people until they sensed an acceptance. For themselves, they plan to get married within the next year or two. They both want children and agree that the children will be raised to maintain basic Jewish cultural traditions.

Questions to Consider

Preston and Julie have known each other for seven years. Why do you think they have waited so long to get married?

Do you think all groups of people in our society have an equal chance of getting married? What might lessen a person's chances of getting married?

Should everybody get married at some point in life? If so, why? If not, can a person lead a happy, fulfilling, and healthy life without getting married?

Preston and Julie come from different racial and religious backgrounds. Is this an important challenge for them to overcome, or can "love" conquer all? How significant are racial and religious differences when two people such as Preston and Julie love each other?

What impact do you perceive others (such as Julie's father, friends, or strangers) will have on the success or failure of the relationship between Preston and Julie?

With this chapter, the discussion shifts from family change and racial/ethnic/class variations in U.S. families to structures and processes in selecting intimate partners and creating marriages. Whenever the term *marriage* is used in this context, we are referring to officially recognized marriages between heterosexual couples. This is not to imply that other marriage-like relationships are not important; nor that marriage should not be allowed between same-sex couples; nor that other forms of long-term committed relationships should be viewed as deviant or alternative. We limit the term here only because we desire a starting point for considering how these institutional norms might be changing in contemporary U.S. society and for discussing the cultural context within which nonmarital romantic relationships (be they preludes to marriage or otherwise) develop today. In Chapter 7, we will consider these nonmarital relationships in greater detail.

This chapter will begin by examining the rates of marriage in the United States and consider why increasing numbers of young people choose not to marry or are disadvantaged in finding a marital partner. We will then ask the question "Why marriage?" We will also consider how our system of marriage differs from that of other societies or our own society in the past and what factors shape patterns of partner selection and choice under different cultural contexts. Finally, we will look at what factors lead to non-normative choices and the consequences of such choices.

*M*arriage Trends and Characteristics

What proportion of the population in the United States is currently married, and what are the specific marriage trends in the United States? In 2007, of the 222.6 million persons age 18 and over in the United States, 129.7 million, or 58.2 percent, were married.[1] The remainder were either widowed, divorced, legally separated, or never married.

The percentages of married persons differed considerably by sex, race, and Hispanic origin. Overall, males were slightly more likely to be married than were females (59.9 percent versus 56.7 percent, respectively). Asian Americans were the most likely group to be married (65 percent), followed closely by non-Hispanic whites (61 percent) and Hispanic Americans (57.3 percent). African Americans were significantly less likely to be married, with less than a majority (only 41.4 percent) currently married in 2007. Sex differences in marriage rates were minimal for Asians and Hispanics, but larger for non-Hispanic whites and, in particular, for African Americans. Among non-Hispanic whites, males were more likely to be currently married (62.9 percent versus 58.9 percent, respectively) as were African American males, although the difference was significantly greater (45.5 percent of males versus only 38.1 percent of females).

An examination of the percentages for never-married adults and those currently divorced reveals that the lower rate of marriage for African Americans is due largely to the fact that this group also has a high proportion never-married. Although differences in the proportion currently divorced and not remarried is small, over 40 percent of adult African Americans have *never* married, compared to only 20 percent of non-Hispanic whites. These race differences hold for both males and females.[2]

In terms of current marriage behavior for the population as a whole, a little more than 2.2 million marriages occurred in 2007, a **crude marriage rate** (number of marriages per 1,000 population) of 7.3.[3] It is important to keep in mind when interpreting this figure that two people are involved in every marriage, so a crude marriage

---

[1]U.S. Census Bureau, *The 2009 Statistical Abstract* "Table 55—Marital Status of the Population by Sex, Race and Hispanic Origin." http://www.2010census.biz/compendia/statab/cats/population/marital_status_and_living_arrangements.html.

[2]Ibid.

[3]U.S. Census Bureau, *The 2009 Statistical Abstract* "Table 123—Marriages and Divorces—Number and Rate by State." http://www.2010census.biz/compendia/statab/cats/births_deaths_marriages_divorces/marriages_and_divorces.html.

CROSS-CULTURAL *Perspective*

Marriage Regimes in Latin America

Latin America has undergone tremendous social, political, and economic changes over the last half of the 20th century. Although not uniformly experienced throughout the region, most countries have seen high levels of economic development interspersed with economic stagnation and restructuring, internal political conflicts, and advances in women's education and employment levels. Given these changes, especially those involving economic development and the increased employment and education of women, one would expect to find a decrease in both fertility and marriage rates as well as an increase in the age at marriage and the prevalence of informal consensual unions (cohabitations). In an examination of marriage and fertility behaviors throughout this region, Elizabeth Fussell and Alberto Palloni found the expected declines in fertility, but, surprisingly, these declines were not accompanied by declines in marriage or increases in age at marriage.

Throughout the last half of the twentieth century, Latin American countries have maintained three variations on a marriage regime characterized by high rates and early ages of union formation. The first variation is characteristic of Central America and the Caribbean nations (Cuba, the Dominican Republic, El Salvador, Guatemala, Honduras, Nicaragua, and Panama) and involves a high level of consensual unions rather than formal marriages. The second is characteristic of the Andean countries and some of upper South America (Bolivia, Colombia, Ecuador, Paraguay, Peru, and Venezuela) where there is a greater mix between consensual unions and formal marriages. Lastly, the third is characteristic of the more economically developed countries of Argentina, Brazil, Chile, Costa Rica, Mexico, and Uruguay where formal marriage rates are high and consensual unions less frequent. All three groups of countries share an early age at first union and an early age at marriage, although those countries with higher rates of consensual unions exhibit the earliest ages of first marriage. They attribute the differences between these groups to "regional similarities in colonial histories, population mixes of Europeans, Africans, and Native populations, and economic development..." (1203–1204).

Why have the marriage regimes of these countries not been responsive to economic development as was the case in Western and Northern Europe? The authors of this analysis point to similarities between the situation in Latin America and that found in Southern and Eastern Europe during the period of early industrialization. The reason why the later group of countries did not experience the "European demographic transition" (see Chapter 2) involving low marriage rates and an increased age at first marriage was because their production activities were not strongly linked to property rights and marriage was therefore not linked to the precondition of establishing economic independence. Like the Southern and Eastern European marriage regimes of the past, marriage and family ties are still critical to adaptation and survival in Latin America and this linkage is reinforced by strong values in these countries placed on *familism* (see Chapter 5). In spite of economic development and women's more productive economic roles, survival conditions in Latin America remain highly uncertain—for both the economically privileged and the disadvantaged. As a result, a basic survival strategy has evolved (often involving co-residence and economic cooperation between men and women in relationships) that takes advantage of family ties and the strong sense of loyalty attached to those ties. The family ties created through marriage, then, are critical to survival and enhance the economic value and profitability of getting married and doing so early in life.

Source: Elizabeth Fussell and Alberto Palloni, "Persistent Marriage Regimes in Changing Times," *Journal of Marriage and Family,* 66 (December 2004): 1201–1213.

rate of 7.3 really indicates that 14.6 out of every 1,000 people in the population entered into a marriage in the year 2007. It is also important to note that the base of this rate (the number in the denominator) includes individuals not eligible for marriage (children, youth, already married persons, and those not likely to marry such as the elderly). Thus, the crude marriage rate, although universally reported, is not a good measure to use when trying to assess the *likelihood* that adults will get married.

It is especially of limited value when looking at changes that have occurred over time in the tendency to marry because it will vary depending on changes in the age distribution of the population. For example, during periods of high birthrates (as experienced after World War II during the *baby boom*, see Chapter 10), the crude marriage rate will be artificially suppressed (it will underestimate the popularity and likelihood of marriage) because the population expands but the number of potential marriages does not because children and youth are not eligible for marriage. Thus, the denominator in the rate calculation increases, but the numerator (the number of marriages occurring in the year) cannot. Correspondingly, the crude rate will be artificially inflated (it will overestimate the popularity and likelihood of marriage) twenty to thirty years after any short-term increase in the birthrate (as was the case during the decades following the post–World War II baby boom) because there will be a rise in the number eligible for marriage (due to the earlier high birthrates) but no corresponding rise in the number of persons in the population. Thus, crude marriage rates will appear to go up even when the number of marriages among those eligible to marry does not change or even declines.

To correct for these misrepresentations, demographers have developed an alternative measure called the **general marriage rate.** This rate is based on the number of persons in the population who are eligible to get married in a given year and corrects for the fact that two people are involved in every marriage. It does this by using the same numerator (the number of marriages occurring in a given year) but restricting the denominator to include only unmarried women age 15 years and older. Although not a perfect indicator, it is less sensitive to changes over time in the age distribution in the population and does not have to be doubled to get an estimate of an individual's likelihood of getting married. In 2005, the general marriage rate was approximately 40.7.[4]

As can be seen in Figure 6.1 (page 240), the general marriage rate has varied over the past eighty-five years. These fluctuations have been reinforced by changing cultural orientations regarding marriage but have occurred primarily because of the influence of wars and changing economic conditions. The long-term trend, however, is toward continual decline.

Characteristically, the marriage rate has risen at the outset of a major war, declined during the course of the conflict, and increased sharply in the immediate postwar years. This was the pattern for World Wars I and II and probably also for the Civil War. The increase in the marriage rate during the World War II era remains unparalleled in the history of the United States. In 1945, the general marriage rate reached 105, an increase from eighty-two in 1940 and an unprecedented and yet unsurpassed peak. By 1950, the rate had returned to the pre–World War II level, dropping as rapidly as it had climbed. In contrast to pre- and postwar periods, economic recessions and depressions generally have had an inhibiting effect

---

[4]The general marriage rate is no longer calculated by the U.S. Census Bureau. Rates reported here were based on data reported in: The National Marriage Project, *The State of Our Unions 2007: The Social Health of Marriage in America.* http://marriage.rutgers.edu/Publications/SOOU/SOOU2007.pdf

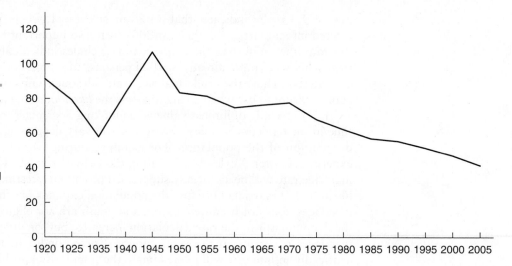

Figure 6.1

General Marriage Rates, 1920–2005

Source: For years prior to 1970: Yearly volumes of the *Statistical Abstract of the United States* prior to 1960. For 1970–2005: The National Marriage Project, *The State of Our Unions 2007: The Social Health of Marriage in America.* http://marriage.rutgers.edu/Publications/SOOU/SOOU2007.pdf

on marriage. In 1935, at the depth of the Depression, the general marriage rate plunged from about seventy-eight in 1925 to a low of fifty-seven. This period of decline in the rates was probably unprecedented in the United States except during the Civil War.

The gradual but steady decline in marriage rates from 1970 through 2005 also reflects changes in the economy but more in terms of a change in the importance of different sectors. With the decline of the industrial sector and an increase in the growth of the information and services sectors of the economy, there has been an increase in required training for economically viable positions and a radical increase in women's labor force participation. These changes have resulted in a delay in establishing the economic prerequisites for marriage (accumulating resources and establishing a stable source of economic support) and a decrease in women's dependence on marriage as a source of social status. As a result, both men and women have been delaying marriage more and more each year (thus reducing the marriage rates), and more women are choosing not to marry at all (discussed later). In addition to these structural factors, this long-term trend could be the result of a transformation in the meaning of marriage in modern society from an institution of obligation to one of voluntary association in the interest of achieving life goals and personal gratification and fulfillment.

Conversely to the changes in marriage rates, the percentage of those who have never been married has risen sharply since 1970. This increase is particularly apparent in the age groups in which most men and women have traditionally married. In the group age 20 to 24, for example, there has been more than a doubling of the number of never-married women (from 35.8 percent in 1970 to 76.4 percent in 2007) and a more than 50 percent increase in the number of never-married men (from 54.7 percent in 1970 to 86.9 percent in 2007).[5] The increase in the 25–29 age group is even more dramatic.

---

[5]U.S. Bureau of the Census, *Statistical Abstract of the United States:* 2001; U.S. Census Bureau, *The 2009 Statistical Abstract* "Table 55—Marital Status of the Population by Sex and Age: 2007." http://www.2010census.biz/compendia/statab/cats/population/marital_status_and_living_arrangements.html.

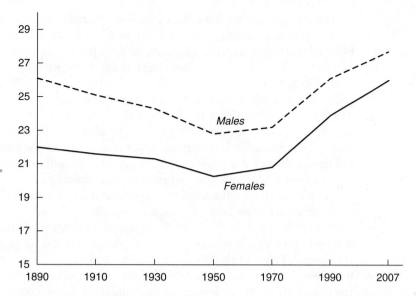

Figure 6.2

Median Age at First Marriage, by Sex: 1890–2007

Source: U.S. Bureau of the Census, Current Population http://www.census.gov/population/socdemo/hh-fam/ms2.csv

As might be expected, these changes reflect dramatic changes in the age at marriage for both men and women since the early 1950s. Historically, the United States has had a high age at marriage for men and a lower age at marriage for women. An examination of the trends shown in Figure 6.2 shows that the median age at first marriage and the age difference between males and females have changed considerably since the turn of the century. From 1890 until the 1950s, the trend in the United States was toward a younger age at marriage and a narrowing of the age difference between bride and groom at first marriage. In 1890, the median ages at first marriage were 26.1 years for males and 22.0 for females, an age difference of 4.1 years. In 1956, the median age at first marriage reached an all-time low: 22.5 for men and 20.1 for women. Since that time, there has been a gradual, though not continuous, increase in the median age at first marriage for both men and women. In the past twenty years, there has been more than a three-year increase in the median age at first marriage for both males and females. Today's median ages for first marriage (27.7 for males and 26 for females) approach the highest that have ever existed in the United States.

What explains this incredible increase in the median age at marriage in just several decades? Several factors appear to explain this trend. Young people are delaying marriage because they are spending more time in school, taking longer to find and establish themselves in careers, burdened with school loans and other forms of debt, and taking longer to accumulate assets to support a marriage and family. It could even be argued that it takes young people longer to find a partner and make a decision on whom to marry because the mechanisms for finding partners have broken down and the clarity of criteria for who is the best choice have become more complex and ambiguous.[6] Alternatively, young people may simply be less certain about marriage and less committed to it as a lifelong institution and, therefore, put off their decisions until they are more sure. The social acceptance of cohabitation as an alternative to early marriage has probably increased as a result of these new realities and likely has contributed to the delay of marriage as well.

---

[6]Ulrich Beck and Elisabeth Beck-Gernsheim, *The Normal Chaos of Love* (Cambridge, MA: Blackwell Press, 1995).

More significantly, does this increase in the median age at marriage, accompanied by a tremendous increase in cohabitation (see Chapter 7), mean simply a postponement of marriage (marriage delayed), or does it portend an increase in the proportion of people who will remain single their entire lives (marriage forgone)? An examination of U.S. cohorts of women born in the 1950s and 1960s suggests that marriage will remain nearly universal for American women.[7] Close to 90 percent were predicted to marry. Although both men and women are marrying later and cohabitation is common, results of the study support the idea that the U.S. pattern is for cohabitation to be a precursor to marriage rather than a permanent substitute. For all groups, the desirability of marriage remains high, yet the authors recognize that substantial variations will occur by race and educational attainment.

It is clear that as the median age at marriage increases, so does a longer period of singlehood. With later marriage comes an increased likelihood of remaining in the family home. In a 1995 study, national data revealed that 29 percent of never-married adult children lived with their parents (as did 13 percent of divorced adult children).[8] Thus, both delayed marriage and high divorce rates increase parents' long-term, day-to-day responsibility for their children. On the other hand, with later marriage and a longer period of singlehood comes the potential for an increased period of independent living away from the parental home. Some consequences of remaining single and living independently for a longer time, particularly for women, are that they are more likely to plan for employment, lower their expected family size, be more accepting of the employment of mothers, and be more nontraditional on sex roles than those who live with parents.[9]

Structural Constraints on Marriage Rates

As noted previously, there is significant variation in marriage rates and singlehood across race and ethnic groups in the United States. Most of these differences are best attributed to variations in the conditions that make marriage possible and profitable for individuals in different groups.[10] African Americans and Hispanics strongly endorse marriage and desire to get married,[11] but many find that the costs of marriage exceed the benefits due to poor economic conditions and the effects of the *marriage squeeze*.

The **marriage squeeze** describes the effects of an imbalance in the sex ratio, or the number of males in the population relative to the number of females. Any shortage of marriageable males (a low sex ratio) or shortage of females (a high sex ratio), for whatever reason, will produce a marriage squeeze. When a marriage squeeze exists, the marriage rates tend to decrease and the age at marriage may decrease for

---

[7]Joshua R. Goldstein and Catherine T. Kenney, "Marriage Delayed or Marriage Forgone: New Cohort Forecasts of First Marriage for U.S. Women," *American Sociological Review* 66 (August 2001): 506–519.

[8]Lynn White and Debra Peterson, "The Retreat from Marriage: Its Effect on Unmarried Children's Exchange with Parents," *Journal of Marriage and the Family* 57 (May 1995): 428–434.

[9]Linda J. Waite, Frances Kobrin Goldscheider, and Christina Witsberger, "Nonfamily Living and the Erosion of Traditional Family Orientation among Young Adults," *American Sociological Review* 51 (August 1986): 541–554.

[10]Julius Wilson, *The Truly Disadvantaged: The Inner City, the Underclass, and Public Policy* (Chicago, IL: University of Chicago Press, 1990).

[11]Richard A. Bulcroft and Kris A. Bulcroft, "Race Differences in Attitudinal and Motivational Factors in the Decision to Marry," *Journal of Marriage and the Family* 55 (1993): 338–356.

Most marriages are relatively age homogamous, which means that the partners are very similar in age. In the United States, when marriages are age exogamous, the most common pattern is for an older male to marry a younger female.

the less available gender. For example, one investigation of 111 countries showed that high sex ratios (an oversupply of men and a relative undersupply of women) were positively associated with the proportion of women who married and inversely associated with women's average age at marriage.[12] That is, the fewer the number of women relative to that of men, the higher the proportion who marry and the younger the age at which they do so.

When applied to the field of available marriage partners (also known as marriage markets in modern societies), the concept of sex ratios is expanded to denote not just a shortage of available partners but also conditions that lead to a shortage of *eligible* or *desirable* partners. Thus, not only will a shortage of men or a shortage of women vis-à-vis the other sex create a reduction in the marriage rate, but also any disproportionate decrease of men or women with desirable traits will produce the same effect. For example, low rates of marriage among African American women in previous decades was attributed not just to an imbalance in sex ratios at birth twenty to thirty years earlier and higher rates of mortality among young African American males but also to higher levels of imprisonment among African American men, higher levels of unemployment and underemployment, and lower levels of education relative to levels achieved by African American women.[13]

As will be noted in the discussion of the mating gradient later in this chapter, groups other than African American women also experience a marriage squeeze. For example, women at the top and men at the bottom of a class or professional hierarchy have lower marriage rates because of a lack of available partners with desirable qualities. This type of marriage squeeze exists not only in the United States but in other countries as well. High-caste women in India are a good illustration of this pattern.[14]

Age is the characteristic considered most often in examining the marriage squeeze. Consider the hypothetical population, where males age 27 typically marry females age 24. If the annual number of births decreases each year, 27-year-old males will be looking for brides among the smaller cohort (an age-specific group) of females born three years later. The males will be caught in a marriage squeeze because they will encounter a shortage of females. Conversely, if a population experiences a substantial increase in the annual number of births, the same process will operate, but the females will be caught in the marriage squeeze. That is, the male population born three years earlier will be smaller than the female population born three years later.

---

[12]Scott J. South, "Sex Ratios, Economic Power, and Women's Roles: A Theoretical Extension and Empirical Test," *Journal of Marriage and the Family* 50 (February 1988): 19–31.

[13]Wilson, *The Truly Disadvantaged.*

[14]Michael S. Billig, "The Marriage Squeeze on High-Caste Rajasthani Women," *The Journal of Asian Studies* 50 (May 1991): 341–360.

Crowder and Tolnay demonstrate how black–white intermarriage (discussed later in this chapter) also contributes to a marriage squeeze for black women.[15] Black males who intermarry reduce the likelihood that black women currently will be married or that they will make the transition to marriage. The preference of intermarried black men for women with high levels of education, income, and occupational prestige negatively affects the pool of economically attractive black males, especially for highly educated black women. Thus, there is a further squeeze on the marriage prospects for black women.

Similar effects of the marriage squeeze have been found in Israel and Brazil. In Israel, women born to cohorts that faced severe marriage squeezes were more likely to remain single and those who did marry were more likely to out-marry, that is, marry exogamously.[16] In Brazil, the marriage squeeze led to a rise in highly unstable informal (consensual union) marriages.

Variations in Marriage Rates

In the United States, marriage rates have a distinct seasonal pattern: more marriages typically occur in June, July, and August than in any other months. The seasonal low for marriage tends to occur in January, February, and March. Seasonal variations are also greatly affected by holidays, the beginning and ending of the school year, climatic conditions, and religious holy periods such as Lent.

Marriage rates also vary widely by day of the week. Over half of all marriages take place on Saturday, with Friday being the next most popular day and Tuesdays, Wednesdays, and Thursdays being the least popular days.

Marriages are reported by and subject to the laws of the state in which the ceremony is performed. Lenient marriage laws attract couples from out of state, particularly if the adjoining states have more restrictive laws. The major attractions are (1) laws that do not require a waiting period between the date of application and issuance of the license or between license issuance and the ceremony and (2) laws that do not require a medical examination or blood test. These factors have a two-pronged effect: They lower the marriage rates of the states from which the couples are drawn and raise the marriage rates of the states to which the couples are attracted.

Marriage rates in the United States (per 1,000 population) have consistently shown distinct differences by state, partly due to differences in policies and partly due to the cultural, political and social climate. One way to examine these variations is to focus on differences based on political orientations. If the definition and support of marriage as an institution is related to larger scale cultural and political conflicts, then we might expect differences in marriage rates between so-called "red states" (Republican leaning states) and "blue states"(Democratic leaning states). These political differences in voting patterns have been linked to larger cultural differences related to religion, traditionalism and modernity.

---

[15]Kyle D. Crowder and Stewart E. Tolnay, "A Marriage Squeeze for Black Women: The Role of Racial Intermarriage by Black Men," *Journal of Marriage and the Family* 62 (August 2000): 792–807.

[16]Haya Stier and Yossi Shavit, "Age at Marriage, Sex-Ratios, and Ethnic Heterogamy," *European Sociological Review* 10 (May 1994): 79–87; and Margaret E. Greene and Vijayendra Rao, "The Marriage Squeeze and the Rise in Informal Marriage in Brazil," *Social Biology* 42 (1995): 65–82.

In an analysis of these potential differences, the National Marriage Project reports that red states had significantly higher general marriage rates in 2005.[17] Some of the highest marriage rates are found in red states in the South, with Arkansas (77) and Alabama (54) leading the pack, and in the Mountain states of Idaho (66), Wyoming (60), and Utah (58). The lowest marriage rates, in contrast, are found in the blue states of the Northeast with Pennsylvania (24), New Jersey (27), Delaware (28), and Connecticut (28) at the bottom.

*P*urposes and Consequences of Marriage

Even though marriage rates have decreased and the number of unmarried adults has increased over the past several decades, marriage and marriage-like relationships are still very popular in the United States. Despite conflict, divorce, and a changing marital scene, most Americans marry or choose to live in monogamous, sexually based, and opposite-sex or same-sex primary relationships. Around the world, normative expectations include marriage as an appropriate and desirable state, although these norms are changing in many countries to include cohabitation. Most persons and groups in these societies fulfill these normative expectations despite the complex tasks of mastering partner-selection interactions, managing the rituals and ceremonies that accompany the act of marriage, and fulfilling the requirements of domestic life. But why? Let us examine some of the factors that lead people to marry.

Why Marry?

When examined cross-culturally, the reasons for and consequences of marriage for individuals and the broader society differ (see Chapter 1). These differences may have resulted in differences in the structures of marriage but have not appreciably diminished the significance of this institution. For example, one important reason for marriage in other societies and one that has been mentioned as a reason in contemporary U.S. society is to have children. In many societies, marriage is specifically an extension of the kinship and extended-family systems and serves such basic functions as procreation, passing on the family name, recruitment of laborers, and continuation of property. Consequently, the role of marriage in providing a context for having children and for establishing property relations between kinship groups and those children is a primary motivation for marriage. Indeed, in these societies, not having a child (or more specifically, not having a male child) is sufficient reason to end a marriage and replace a present wife with a new one.

In the United States, however, the nuclear family does not function as an economic production unit and the consideration of property transfer across generations can only be cited as a reason for marriage for a few among the elite and in some farming communities. Thus, even though most children are born to married couples (and most married couples want children), not having children is rarely sufficient reason to divorce and remarry. Conversely, not wanting or being unable to have children—an issue faced by men and women whose identities are less tied into having children or are either infertile or feel too old to have a child—is not sufficient reason for *not* marrying. So, what motivates us in contemporary U.S. society to marry?

---

[17]The National Marriage Project, *The State of Our Unions 2007: The Social Health of Marriage in America.* http://marriage.rutgers.edu/Publications/SOOU/SOOU2007.pdf.

TRANSNATIONAL FAMILIES

Risk and Ritual in British-Pakistani Arranged Marriages

Arranged marriages between Pakistanis living in the West and partners in Pakistan have been occurring for a long time. Such marriages are highly consistent with cultural traditions in Pakistan and have been adapted to help members of this ethnic community find partners when the pool of potential partners is small. However, the practice in Britain has become more widespread, complex, and risky in recent years as a result of new restrictions placed on immigration. In a study of this practice, Katharine Charsley shows how traditional rituals have been adapted to address the unique character and increased levels of risk involved in these truly transnational marriages. Of particular note is her documentation of how the traditional *nikah* (signing of the wedding contract) and the practice of the *rukhsati* (transition to the husband's home) have been extracted from the tripartite wedding traditions of the *menhdi, barat,* and *walima* and implemented in a variety of ways to manage the risks involved in these marriages.

In traditional wedding ceremonies in Pakistan, the *nikah* is usually, but not always, included as part of the *barat*—the second stage of the wedding when the groom's family visits the bride's family to celebrate and formalize the marital arrangement. The signing of the *nikah* is considered the equivalent of a legal marriage in Pakistan and is accepted as such by the British government when it takes place in Pakistan but not when it takes place in Britain. The *rukhsati* is traditionally the ending point in the *barat* and marks the bride's transition from her family home to her husband's. This tradition also includes the wedding night and the consummation of the marriage. It is followed immediately afterwards by the visit of the bride's family to the husband's family home—the *walima*. How then are these traditions extracted and modified because these marriages are occurring across borders?

One modification is to hold the *nikah* many months or even years prior to legally marrying in Britain. This practice is particularly practiced by brides living in Britain who are marrying grooms from Pakistan. By finalizing the marriage through the *nikah* but delaying the legal marriage, several advantages are gained, such as securing a good match but also giving the couple and their families time to get acquainted before proceeding to formalize the marriage. More importantly, the early signing of the *nikah* allows the British resident to secure a match without experiencing the risk of becoming an "immigration widow" should her new husband not be granted residency in Britain.

A second modification involves the delaying or modification of the *rukhsati*. Here couples marry in Pakistan by signing the *nikah*, but they wait until the spouse arrives in Britain before consummating the marriage. Like in the case of the *nikah*, much of the motivation for this practice can be found in the risk of having a visa application denied and becoming an immigration widow and a single parent. In addition, sexuality is considered a powerful force in the lives of Pakistanis and the long period of separation that would occur after the ritual was over, as couples waited for visas to be approved, was thought to be too difficult to endure. Finally, concerns over preserving the bride's virginity were also expressed as it was realized that a later Pakistani divorce might be needed should the husband not receive a visa.

Source: Katharine Charsley, "Risk and Ritual: The Protection of British Pakistani Women in Transnational Marriage," *Journal of Ethnic and Migration Studies*, 32 (September 2007): 1169–1187.

From a structure-functionalist perspective, marriage and cohabitation, operating within the context of the family system, continue to fulfill many functions attributed to the family in general. These family functions include basic personality formation, status attainment, nurturant socialization, tension management, replacement of members through reproduction, economic cooperation, stabilization of adult identity and behavior, and the like. Even though these functions do not require marriage, sexual exclusivity, or heterosexual exclusivity to be fulfilled, they are enhanced by a marital system premised on long-term committed relationships between consenting adults.

At a personal level, marriage in the United States and other modern Western societies serves many purposes and involves many positive as well as negative outcomes: a family of one's own, children, companionship, happiness, love, ego support, economic security, an approved sexual outlet, affection, escape, elimination of loneliness, pregnancy, and so on. The greater the extent to which the perceived needs of marriage are met and the fewer the alternatives to replacing unmet needs, the greater the likelihood of marriage and the continuation of marriage.

It is important to emphasize that the social and cultural context for marriage in the United States demonstrates a variety of forms other than the traditional monogamous, sexually exclusive, heterosexual, and lifelong marriage pattern for the fulfillment of societal functions and individuals' perceived needs. One familiar pattern that has emerged might be classified as **sequential or serial monogamy**: the marriage, divorce, remarriage, divorce pattern. Another involves the maintenance of the life-long marriage together with a satisfaction of sexual and emotional needs outside the conjugal relationship. A third is the emergence of **nonmarital cohabitation,** a relatively common practice today, involving two unmarried adults of the same or opposite sex sharing a common residence in a marriage-like relationship.

These newly emerging patterns may signal the reshaping of the marital institution, either in response to newly emerging societal needs (structure-functionalism) or in response to the restructuring of power relationships in society (social conflict theory). Alternatively, of course, they may signal a breakdown or weakening of marriage and marriage-like relationships in the face of growing individualism in society.[18] Given the continued strong attitudinal support for the idea of marriage, the fact that most people will still get married at some point in their lifetime, the high likelihood of remarriage after a divorce, and the desire among same-sex couples to participate in the institution of marriage (see Chapter 1), we believe these changes in marriage behavior are due to a reshaping rather than an abandonment of marriage. The answer, however, lies in the observation and analysis of these trends as they unfold.

Marital Status and Well-Being

One fundamental reason for the continuation of marriage as an institution might lie in its consequences for individual well-being. Robert Coombs, in reviewing more than 130 empirical studies conducted prior to 1990 on a number of well-being indices, found that married men and women generally are happier and less stressed than unmarried men and women (including those separated, divorced, or widowed).[19] This pattern was highly consistent and has been replicated in other studies done since 1990.[20] Studies of alcoholism, suicide, mortality (death), and morbidity (the relative incidence of disease); schizophrenia and other psychiatric problems; and self-reported happiness have supported the hypothesis that married

[18]David Popenoe, Jean Bethke Elshtain, and David Blankenhorn, eds., *Promises to Keep: Decline and Renewal of Marriage in America* (Lanham, MD: Rowman & Littlefield Publishers, Inc., 1996); and David Popenoe, "American Family Decline, 1960–1990: A Review and Appraisal," *Journal of Marriage and the Family* 55 (August 1993): 527–555.

[19]Robert H. Coombs, "Marital Status and Personal Well-Being: A Literature Review," *Family Relations* 40 (January 1991): 97–102.

[20]See Steven Stack and J. Ross Eshleman, "Marital Status and Happiness: A 17-Nation Survey," *Journal of Marriage and the Family* 60 (May 1998): 527–536; and Allan V. Horwitz, Helene Raskin White, and Sandra Howell-White, "Becoming Married and Mental Health: A Longitudinal Study of a Cohort of Young Adults," *Journal of Marriage and the Family* 58 (November 1996): 895–907.

individuals experience fewer emotional and health problems than their unmarried counterparts.

These findings should not lead us to assume that all married persons experience the same benefits, however. Research also shows that married respondents who are female, younger, lower in socioeconomic status, and nonwhite have significantly higher depression levels than their unmarried counterparts.[21] But, in general, marriage may serve to improve the financial situation, increase social networks that facilitate access to medical information and services, constrain risk-taking behavior, and act as a buffering mechanism in stressful situations.

These studies also need to be interpreted with caution since most were cross-sectional and many failed to fully account for sources of spuriousness (see Chapter 3). Such studies are often fraught with questions of causal validity. For example, it is reasonable to expect that individuals who are happier, healthier, wealthier, and without negative personality traits and habits are also more likely to get married and attract a more rewarding marital partner. As a result, when studies are done comparing married to nonmarried individuals, differences are found that were present even before those in the married group were married. Thus, marriage may not be the cause of these positive traits but the outcome of them. Without assessing these traits before and after marriage occurs (as can be done in longitudinal studies), the time priority of the cause cannot be clearly established.

Another question to ask when interpreting these studies is to what extent the effects are uniform across unmarried groups. Frequently in summarizing results, those who have never married are grouped together with those who are single for reasons of widowhood or divorce. Given the losses that occur to individuals for these latter reasons, it is not surprising that they experience many of the negative consequences attributed to not being married. However, it may not be their state of being unmarried that is responsible for these consequences as much as it is the state of their actually *having been* married. The loss of married status due to the death of a partner or divorce might be expected to reduce well-being.

One recent study that separated out the never-married singles and controlled for selection factors showed much smaller or nonexistent differences between those who were continuously unmarried over a two-year period and those who moved into a marital union.[22] Indeed, this study showed that over a two-year period, those who were married and those who were in cohabiting unions experienced a greater decrease in health and increase in depression than did those who remained continuously outside of any unions.

To the extent that marriage is beneficial, it has been suggested that marital and intimately bonded partners might provide companionship, interpersonal closeness, emotional gratification, and support to each other that serve to buffer them against physical and emotional pathology (a **marriage protection hypothesis**).[23] For example, married individuals are more likely to abstain from smoking, to drink moderately, to

---

[21]Shelia R. Cotton, "Marital Status and Mental Health Revisited: Examining the Importance of Risk Factors and Resources," *Family Relations* 48 (July 1999): 225–233.

[22]Wu Zheng and Randy Hart, "The Effects of Marital and Nonmarital Union Transition on Health," *Journal of Marriage and Family* 64 (May 2002): 420-432.

[23]Walter R. Gove, "Sex, Marital Status, and Mortality" *American Journal of Sociology* 79 (1973): 45–67; and Francis E. Kobrin and Gerry E. Hendershot, "Do Family Ties Reduce Mortality? Evidence from the United States, 1966–1968," *Journal of Marriage and the Family* 39 (1977): 737–745.

avoid risk-taking behavior, and to lead more stable, secure, and scheduled lives. One consequence of this marriage protection hypothesis is that married people live longer than unmarried people.

Another explanation as to why married women may be healthier than single women is referred to as the **safety net hypothesis** and is based on the idea that marriage increases the availability of economic resources needed to respond to negative life circumstances and stressor events when they occur.[24] Often married couples enjoy the benefits of two incomes and even in single-breadwinner marriages there are certain economies of scale that occur at home and at work that can enhance income and reduce expenditures. This economic "safety net" provides access to better housing, food, and services than a man or woman would otherwise have, resulting in a lower level of stress and a higher level of health.

The safety net hypothesis and the marriage protection hypotheses might actually work together in ways that make marriage even more consequential for some groups of people versus others. Research has shown that, for both men and women, income has a *moderating effect* on the relationship between marital status and mortality. That is to say, the effects of marital status on mortality are different, or moderated, by how much income the couple has. For those with high incomes, married individuals had only slightly lower mortality than single individuals, but for those with low incomes, the difference was much greater (with the highest mortality experienced by those who were both poor and single),[25] indicating that marriage was more protective (at least on this outcome measure) under conditions of greater risk and fewer resources to address those risks.

In addition to those with lower incomes, marriage and marriage-like relationships have been shown to be particularly rewarding for men. Research has clearly rejected (at least in terms of health outcomes) the popular folklore that marriage is a blessed state for women and a burdensome trap for men. In reality, men—more than women—receive mental health benefits from marriage. Women, more than men, provide emotional aid and other support in marriage. Even public opinion polls have shown that more married men are satisfied with their marriages than women. When asked, "Would you say that your marriage is very happy, pretty happy, or not too happy?" about two-thirds (67 percent) of the men said "very happy" compared to only 57 percent of the women.[26] Very few said "not too happy" (1 percent men and 4 percent women), but these figures must be considered carefully. Perhaps many people who would have responded "not too happy" were not in the study because of having been divorced.

The differences between married and unmarried people may be declining, however. Norval Glenn, using national survey data, demonstrated a substantial decline in the stability and quality of marital relationships as well as a decrease in the difference between married and nonmarried individuals in their levels of happiness.[27] It was suggested that these changes may relate to the increasingly similar circumstances

[24]Beth A. Hahn, "Marital Status and Women's Health: The Effect of Economic Marital Acquisitions," *Journal of Marriage and the Family* 55 (May 1993): 495–504.

[25]Richard G. Rogers, "Marriage, Sex, and Mortality," *Journal of Marriage and the Family* 57 (May 1995): 515–526.

[26]Floris W. Wood, ed., *An American Profile—Opinions and Behavior, 1972–1989* (Detroit: Gale Research, Inc., 1990), 239.

[27]Norval D. Glenn, "The Recent Trend in Marital Success in the United States," *Journal of Marriage and the Family* 53 (May 1991): 261–270.

Family Diversity

Age and the Desire to Marry

The study of marriage attitudes and behaviors as long overlooked a significant subgroup of American society—the aged. The omission of this group from consideration with respect to marriage attitudes and behaviors has been fueled by an almost exclusive reliance on studies of youth (e.g., the National Longitudinal Survey of Youth) for information about marriage attitudes and the intentional neglect of major surveys of marriage and family life using samples more inclusive of elderly (e.g., the National Survey of Families and Households) to include questions about marriage attitudes for people over the age of 35. One source of evidence that does exist for looking at these attitudes, however, is the General Social Survey (GSS).

In an analysis of GSS data on attitudes toward marriage, Jenna Mahay and Alisa Lewin note that rates of singlehood (due to never having married or having married but then divorced or widowed) have increased over the past several decades, and this is particularly true of the elderly. Although remarriage rates in the United States are high, there remains an increasing likelihood that these single people will choose not to marry again and many will not desire to do so. To help understand why this is the case, they asked whether or not the attitudes of the elderly were influenced by the same rational decision-making processes and the same profitability parameters that influence young people's attitudes. In other words, they were interested in whether or not marriage for this group is a "market place" activity where positive attitudes toward getting married are shaped by three factors: one's own marketability, the potential for profit to be found in the market place of potential partners, and access to the market. Based on this perspective, they then looked at the impacts of five factors that might influence marriage likelihoods as well as attitudes based on those likelihoods: personal resources, presence of children, experience of divorce, religious involvement, and demographic characteristic such as race and gender.

Their results showed that older single people are significantly less likely to want to get married than their younger counterparts and that this difference is not explained by any of the factors they looked at. Presence of children did explain some of the effect insofar as having children reduced the desire to marry. This effect could be due to the alternative sources of emotional and financial support provided by children, making marriage less of an exclusive choice for profitability in life; or, it could be due to the complications that having children present when considering adding a new partner to an existing family system. They conclude that in order to understand the decision-making process and attitude formation of the elderly toward marriage, it is important to examine the way that variables that affect younger people might have different effects later in life because their meaning in terms of profit is different. For example, when an older widowed woman remarries, she could put her deceased husbands retirement benefits in danger thus reducing the perceived profitability of marriage—even though her new husband would bring new resources. Other factors that are also important to consider are health and mobility and the value found in independence after having lived with a partner for many years. This might especially be the case among women.

Source: Jenna Mahay and Alisa C. Lewin, "Age and the Desire to Marry," *Journal of Family Issues*, 28 (2007): 706–723.

of being married and unmarried. A substantial proportion of unmarried persons, for example, have regular sexual relations without stigma. Also, given the ease with which divorce can be obtained by either spouse who wants it, marriage no longer provides the security it once did, financial or otherwise. In other words, the societal and personal functions that marriage has traditionally fulfilled may be increasingly found in contexts other than marriage.

This may be particularly true for women as the decreased difference between married and unmarried persons occurred primarily through an increase in the reported happiness of never-married males and a decrease in the reported happiness of married females. Thus, married men remained at about the same level of happiness, but married women have come to find their lives less happy than they did in the past. In the United States, for females at least, being single has a number of consequences that most might view as positive. For example, being single is associated with having a higher educational level, a higher median income, a higher occupational status, and in general a higher level of achievement.

Such a decrease in single/married differences is not universal, however. For example, in contemporary Japan, it was found that the levels of mortality experienced by single Japanese are staggeringly high in comparison with those of married Japanese.[28] Not only are discrimination and stigma associated with those who do not marry, but also unmarried individuals experience relatively high rates of dying and presumably much poorer health. For example, mortality data for the mid-1990s indicate that a 20-year-old Japanese man or woman who remains single can expect to live as much as fifteen years less than his or her married counterpart.

Systems of Partner Selection and Choice

A sizable volume of research has suggested that all societies have systems of norms and sometimes specific rules about who may marry whom and how intimate partners are selected. These norms are likely to vary from one culture to another and to differ for a first marriage and a remarriage, for males and females, for wealthy and poor people, and so forth. However, norms, rules, and controls appear in all societies.

On a continuum, these norms may vary from totally **arranged marriages,** at one extreme, to totally free choice of partners (**autonomous marriages**), at the other. When marriages are arranged, the couple has nothing to say about the matter. The selection is usually, but not always, made by parents or kin. The other extreme, totally free choice, is so rare that to discuss it would simply be conjecture. The United States is, however, one of the few societies of the world that approaches this end of the continuum. In its extreme form, parents and kin are not consulted and in some instances not even informed of the impending marriage.

Between these two extremes are various combinations of arranged/free-choice possibilities. Parents may arrange a marriage and give their son or daughter veto power. The sons or daughters may make their own selection and give the parents veto power. One of the persons to be married, usually the son and his parents, may select the bride. Regardless of the method of partner selection, every society has a set of norms that prescribes the appropriate procedure.

In traditional economies, the family generally is the chief and only source of employment for the selected partners; rather than establishing a new family, marriage is a means of providing for the continuity and stability of the existing family. Arranged marriage has the effect (function) of providing elders with control over younger family members and control over whom from the outside may enter and become part of the family unit. In addition, arranged marriage preserves family property, furthers political linkages, protects economic and status concerns, and keeps the family intact from one generation to another.

As a result, almost without exception, the chosen partners in an arranged marriage must share similar group identities. Racial/ethnic, religious, and particularly

---

[28]Noreen Goldman, "The Perils of Single Life in Contemporary Japan," *Journal of Marriage and the Family 55* (February 1993): 191–204.

economic statuses must be similar. Arranged marriage is not based on criteria such as romantic love, desire for children, loneliness, or sexual desire; rather, it will likely be based on factors such as a **dowry** (a set amount paid by the bride's family to the family of the groom) or the size of the **bride's price** (a set amount paid by the groom's family to the family of the bride), the reputation of the potential spouse's kin group, levirate and sororate obligations, and traditions of prescribed marriage arrangements.

A contemporary example of arranged marriage comes from Japan, where as recently as 1995, about 25 to 30 percent of all marriages were arranged.[29] Due to a "marriage drought" making it very difficult for young people to find desirable partners, professional "go-between services" modeled after the more traditional type of arranged marriage have arisen. The objective criteria for mate selection through an arranged marriage are based on family standing such as reputation, social rank, or lineage as well as the selected person's schooling, salary, or attractiveness. The match between the two persons must be that of equals to avoid embarrassment to either family.

Arranged marriages result in a commitment among the selected partners that is, in many instances, as binding as the marriage itself. Since the marriage exists primarily to fulfill social and economic needs, concerns such as incompatibility, love, and personal fulfillment are not relevant. As a result, divorce is practically unknown or occurs only infrequently. Instances in which marriages must be terminated frequently bring a great sense of shame and stigma to the entire family and kin group.

Evidence has suggested that, as traditional cultures are exposed to Western models of modernization and as they industrialize and adopt new technology from the outside world, marriage patterns will change. Namely, those segments of traditional cultures with the greatest exposure to outside influences tend to increasingly depart from an arranged-marriage pattern to free-choice or love-matched marriages, which we will discuss in greater detail in Chapter 7.

Patterns of Selection and Choice

The terms generally employed to describe the selection or choice of a primary intimate partner from among those who share similar characteristics are *endogamy* and *homogamy*. **Endogamy** describes marriages and relationships between individuals who belong to the same sociocultural group. This term is more frequently found in cross-cultural studies done by anthropologists looking at societies in which marriages are arranged and partners are selected by the group in consideration of the group's survival needs, power hierarchies, or relationships with other groups. **Homogamy** denotes likenesses or similarities among marital or relationship partners and tends to be used when discussing patterns of individual free choice in partners in autonomous partner selection systems. That people choose partners like themselves more often than could be attributed to chance is known as **assortive mating**. The "assorted" mates are matched on specific structural dimensions.

Most of us in the United States believe we are free to marry anyone we choose. But in the real world of partner choice, all kinds of restrictions exist. How free are you to choose someone of the same sex, someone already married, a child, a sibling, certain ethnic/racial groups, and so forth? Clearly, free choice is only "free" from within

---

[29]Kalman D. Applbaum, "Marriage with the Proper Stranger: Arranged Marriage in Metropolitan Japan," *Ethnology* 34 (Winter 1995): 37–51.

CROSS-CULTURAL *Perspective*

Arranged Marriage in China

Major changes are taking place in Chinese patterns of partner selection, moving dramatically from the arranged pattern to one of greater freedom and personal choice. In the past, marriages were predominantly arranged by parents or a third party. The party who made the arrangements (usually the bride's parents) would demand and receive substantial gifts from the family of the groom as a precondition for marriage. The nature of the betrothed's gifts (sometimes referred to as brideprice) included money or goods and often were used to prepare the bride's dowry. The dowry included any material possessions the bride brought with her into marriage, including clothes, jewelry, and land. Under the traditional system, the couple to be married usually did not have the chance to see each other before marriage.

Increasingly, however, young women are insisting on self-determination and love relationships.

Kejing provided interview data from two surveys of Chinese women from three age groups. It was found that the percentages of arranged marriages by year of marriage declined from 83 percent in 1946 to 38 percent in 1953 to 2 percent in 1986. The free choice of marriage partners increased from none in 1946 to 14 percent in 1953 to 22 percent in 1986. Yet, it is clear that parents continue to have a major influence on the decisions made for marriage. Riley notes that housing shortages, the continuing strong family ties, the proximity of younger and older generations, and the lack of dating culture all have contributed to the continuing decision-making cooperation between parents and children.

Dai Kejing, "The Life Experience and Status of Chinese Rural Women from Observation of Three Age Groups," *International Sociology* 6 (March 1991): 5–23; Nancy E. Riley, "Interwoven Lives: Parents, Marriage, and Guanxi in China," *Journal of Marriage and the Family* 56 (November 1994): 791–803.

---

selected, socially appropriate categories. And no society in the world leaves the selection of an intimate or marriage partner unregulated and indiscriminate.

Studies throughout the world have reported high rates of racial/ethnic, religious, class, educational, and age homogamy, even in autonomous partner-selection systems. Why is this so? One key factor relates to interacting with people who are socially and culturally similar. That is, the opportunities to meet people who are similar generally are greater than the opportunities to meet people who are different. A study of married and cohabiting couples in the Netherlands focused on five meeting settings (work, school, the neighborhood, common family networks, and voluntary associations) and five types of homogamy (age, education, class destinations, class origins, and religious background). The five settings accounted for a sizable portion of the places partners met. Schools provided the most forms of homogamy. Workplaces promoted homogamy with respect to class destinations. Neighborhoods and common family networks promoted religious homogamy. In short, mating requires meeting a pool of available partners shaped by various institutionally organized arrangements already sharing similar characteristics.[30]

The explanation for homogamy goes beyond a simple probability of meeting, however. Interpersonal dynamics also may be at play in explaining why people with

---

[30]Matthijs Kalmijn and Henk Flap, "Assortive Meeting and Mating: Unintended Consequences of Organized Settings for Partner Choice," *Social Forces* 79 (June 2001): 1289–1312.

similar traits tend to form long-term committed relationships with each other. This can be seen in studies showing that homogamy exists even along the dimension of more personological traits, such as among persons with anxiety disorders and alcohol or drug dependence.[31] Whether the choice is made by the persons themselves, by parents, by relatives, by delegated persons or groups, or by specific social agencies, however, it is important to keep in mind that it is always subject to regulation by social and cultural controls.

One should not be led into believing that endogamy and homogamy are the preferred or required norms in all respects. The most universal of all norms regarding marriage and sexual relationships—the incest taboo—is an exogamous norm. Exogamy describes marriages and relationships with persons outside of one's own sociocultural group. Thus, all marriages are exogamous in that they do not occur between members of the same nuclear family unit. The terms exogamy and heterogamy often are used interchangeably. However, exogamy focuses on institutional rules restricting in-group marriage and encouraging out-group marriage; whereas heterogamy focuses on any differences that arise as a result of free-choice of partner. In the sections that follow, we will refer to levels of homogamy and heterogamy rather than endogamy and exogamy. We do this because Western modern societies like the United States are closer to an autonomous—rather than an arranged—type of selection system.

Intermarriage

Another term that captures the idea of heterogamous choice or exogamy is **intermarriage**, or the marriage between individuals from different sociocultural groups. In the past this term, along with a similar term, *mixed marriage*, has carried with it negative connotations. When endogamous marriage norms exist in a society or among members of a particular sociocultural group, any marriage outside the group is considered deviant. Today, intermarriage exists with increasing frequency because endogamous norms are much weaker in a modern society premised on the idea of individual freedom and choice. Group boundaries are also more ambiguous, however, so in looking at this phenomenon we need to first ask how intermarriage is defined and who is included or excluded in determining whether a relationship is actually mixed or exogamous. We also need to consider how rates of intermarriage are influenced by reporting, particularly when using statistics of couples as opposed to individuals. Finally, we will look at what social and cultural factors are likely to foster or affect the likelihood of intermarriage.

Defining Intermarriage

How much of an age difference must there be between two people before their relationship is age exogamous? Is a marriage between a Methodist and a Lutheran (both Protestants) an interfaith marriage? At what point does any difference or characteristic determine homogamy or heterogamy, endogamy or exogamy?

Obviously, in any study or in any reporting of rates, some definition must be used to determine whom to include and exclude. In research, **operational definitions** are used; in other words, variables are defined according to the way they will be

---

[31]Jane D. McLeod, "Social and Psychological Bases of Homogamy for Common Psychiatric Disorders," *Journal of Marriage and the Family* 57 (February 1995): 201–214.

measured. As a result, an age difference of more than four years may be arbitrarily defined as age exogamous. Or an interracial/interethnic relationship may be defined as any in which the couple defines themselves as such, regardless of color or lineage. This problem of what is or is not an intermarriage is a serious one in determining rates and in comparing studies. Greater attention is devoted to this issue in dealing with specific social dimensions.

Reporting Intermarriage

Specifically, can intermarriage rates be influenced by the reporting of couples as opposed to individuals? Most published rates of mixed marriage (or intermarriage) are based on the total number of *marriages*. But some rates are interpreted as if they were based on the number of individuals who marry. An **intermarriage rate** refers to the percentage of marriages that are mixed relative to all marriages involving individuals in a specific category. It is a rate *per couple*. An **intermarriage rate for individuals** refers to the percentage of married *individuals* in a specific category who enter into mixed marriages.

To illustrate the difference in these rates, suppose there are ten couples, four that are black–white (*interracial*) and six that are white–white (*intraracial*). Is the intermarriage rate (or, in this case, interracial marriage rate) 40 percent, 25 percent, or 100 percent? Consider that four of the ten relationships (40 percent) are interracial (the rate for *couples*), but four of the sixteen white persons (25 percent) and four out of four blacks (100 percent) entered interracial relationships (the intermarriage rates for white and black *individuals*, respectively). Neither is necessarily better than the other, but it is important when conveying information, comparing studies, and trying to understand and explain intermarriage that one is clear about which rate is presented.

In addition to distinguishing rates between couples and individuals, it is also possible to distinguish a group's **actual intermarriage rate** from its *expected* rate. The *actual* intermarriage rate refers to those marriages that do take place. The **expected intermarriage rate** is the percentage of people who would have selected a mate outside their own group if they had chosen their marriage partners randomly; the rate is based on the frequency distribution of the particular groups in the population. The ratio between the two is important in determining if intermarriage rates are greater than could be expected to occur by chance or if partners had been chosen randomly. For example, if you lived in a community where there were only a few others with similar characteristics to your own, your expected intermarriage rate would be much higher than if you lived in a highly homogenous community where there were very few people with different characteristics than your own.

In a study of interfaith marriages, Norval Glenn illustrated the importance of the expected intermarriage rate. Based on the relative sizes of religious categories, he calculated that 68 percent of Protestants, 26 percent of Catholics, and only 2.3 percent of Jews could be expected to be homogamous with random mating. In actuality, as will be shown later, an overwhelming majority of Protestant, Catholic, and Jewish members marry homogamously.[32] Based on the comparison of these two rates, he was able to conclude that, clearly, assortive mating processes are operative for religious as well as most social groups. People marry homogamously in autonomous partner selection systems far more often than could be expected simply by chance or at random.

---

[32]Norval D. Glenn, "A Note on Estimating the Strength of Influences for Religious Endogamy," *Journal of Marriage and the Family* 46 (August 1984): 725–727.

Factors That Foster Intermarriage

Actual rates of homogamy (and, conversely, intermarriage) are influenced by various factors, many of which center around the normative eligibility rules for partner selection, premised on the interests of major sociocultural groups in society such as social class, religion, and race/ethnicity. However, apart from these normative rules there are non-normative factors that either favor homogamous marriages or lead to an increase in intermarriage rates. Consider, for example, factors such as group size, community heterogeneity, sex ratio, group controls, cultural similarities, the romantic love complex, and influences of certain psychological factors.

Group Size

The size of a group relative to that of the larger population is likely to influence the extent to which the actual intermarriage rate is larger or smaller than would be expected by chance. Generally, the larger the group of similar others, the lower its intermarriage rate; the smaller the group, the higher its likelihood of intermarriage. For example, in Utah, the heart of the Mormon population in the United States, marriages are highly homogamous on social traits. But in Florida as of the late 1970s, where Mormons constituted less than 1 percent of the population, research showed that about two-thirds of the Mormons living there had married non-Mormons.[33] That such a difference exists between the proportions of Mormons in Utah and Florida who marry outside their faith stems far less from differences in religious conviction than from the probability of meeting and interacting with persons from a Mormon background.

Heterogeneity

Peter Blau and others proposed that, in addition to group size, the degree of heterogeneity in the community will positively influence the rate of intermarriage.[34] The nature of the heterogeneity is important, however. On one hand, intermarriage is more likely to occur when people reside in communities with many persons who are different from them. On the other hand, evidence has supported the idea that inequality is antagonistic to homogamy.[35] Thus, a paradox exists. People in heterogeneous communities are more likely to meet, interact with, and marry persons different from themselves. Yet inequality in education and socioeconomic status exerts constraints on intermarriage and increases the desire for status homogamy. As a result, actual intermarriage rates are likely to be lower than would be expected by chance.

Sex Ratio

The sex ratio (number of males per 100 females) is likely to influence the rate of intermarriage. In a community or setting where one sex outnumbers the other, traditional barriers are crossed with increased frequency as the sex with greater numbers expands its limited pool of available homogamous partners by selecting

---

[33]Brent A. Barlow, "Notes on Mormon Interfaith Marriages," *The Family Coordinator* 26 (April 1977): 148.

[34]Peter M. Blau, Terry C. Blum, and Joseph E. Schwartz, "Heterogeneity and Intermarriage," *American Sociological Review* (February 1982): 45–62.

[35]Steven Rytina, Peter M. Blau, Terry Blum, and Joseph Schwartz, "Inequality and Intermarriage: A Paradox of Motive and Constraint," *Social Forces* 66 (March 1988): 645–675.

outside its own group. Obviously, the intermarriage rate will go up for both groups, but it will do so more rapidly for the group that is smaller (see example of white and black marriage rate calculations above).

Group Controls

Intermarriage rates are also likely to be influenced by the extent of social or group controls over the individuals involved. The Amish and Orthodox Jews, both religious minorities in the United States, maintain group sanctions through teachings and religious practices that discourage marriage with outsiders. Groups experience a loss of control over individual's partner choices, however, the more they interact with other groups and lose their cultural distinctiveness. Thus, as ethnic minorities attend public schools, work in diverse social environments, and identify with the new or larger society, the differences in language, dress, and traditional practices decrease. As a result, the likelihood of intermarriage increases.

Romantic Love Complex

Intermarriage rates also increase as a result of what might be called the romantic love complex: the idea that love is more important than group controls, cultural differences, and homogamous characteristics (see Chapter 7). Related to this complex is a personal choice ideal that suggests each person has the right to choose whom to marry with minimal interference from others. As a result, psychological factors come into play in individual's choices. As we will see in Chapter 7, many of these psychological factors tend to reinforce homogamous selection patterns with respect to social status characteristics, but others can also disrupt them. For example, factors such as rebellion against one's own group, feelings of alienation and emotional immaturity are likely to lead to nonhomogamous choices.

Dimensions and Consequences of Homogamy and Intermarriage

The discussion that follows will examine selected social/structural characteristics that affect interpersonal relations and the selection of a marriage partner. These characteristics include age, social class, religion, and race/ethnicity. Obviously, this list does not include all social structures relating to selection of a partner. However, discussion of these characteristics will clearly demonstrate the extent to which homogamous marriages are predominant in the United States. We will also consider the consequences of intermarriage across these different dimensions.

Age at Marriage

The age at which people marry is an important social/structural characteristic in most countries. It influences family/kin networks, birthrates, and educational advancement and, in turn, is influenced by social class, women's roles, occupational and educational opportunities, and countless other factors. For example, data from forty developing countries showed that a substantial proportion of women continue to marry as adolescents; however, women who attended extended secondary school were less likely to do so.[36] The general trend in age at marriage around the world—in countries

---

[36]Susheela Singh and Renee Samara, "Early Marriage among Women in Developing Countries," *International Family Planning Perspectives* 22 (December 1996): 148–157.

such as Ireland, Japan, Australia, and the United States—seems to be upward, representing a delay in or shift away from marriage.[37] What about the homogamy, or age similarity, factor?

Age Homogamy

Most couples are relatively homogamous in terms of the age at which they marry. Although in many countries a person is free to marry someone considerably older or younger, most often a single person selects someone from a closely related age group. In the United States, in 2007, the median age at first marriage was 27.7 for males and 26 for females, an age difference of only 1.7 years, although the difference was greater in earlier time periods.

Age homogamy is itself a function of age at marriage. Without exception across societies, the median age at marriage for grooms is always higher than that for brides. It is estimated that, in six out of seven marriages in the United States, the male is the same age as or older than his bride. For both types of age-heterogamous marriages (husband older as well as husband younger), when compared with age-homogamous marriages (operationally defined as plus or minus four years), a tendency exists for the age heterogamous marriages to be characterized by lower educational levels, multiple marriages, lower family incomes, and lower occupational statuses of the husbands.

Why the overwhelming likelihood that males will be older than females? Several explanations have been offered, including the male's slower physiological and psychological maturity compared to that of the female, the traditional responsibility of the husband to be the major breadwinner (which requires more preparation time), the slight excess of males through the early twenties, the mating gradient (described later in this chapter), and the continued subjugation of women. This last gender argument is consistent with the proposition that female–male marital age differences narrow as societies become more egalitarian.

One study found that age differences in marriage affected how long women live: that women married to younger men tended to live longer than expected, whereas women married to older men tended to die sooner than expected.[38] These results can be explained in two ways. One explanation suggests a mate-selection factor. That is, healthy and active women select or are selected by younger men and will live longer, whomever they marry. The second explanation bases women's longevity on the biology, psychology, and sociology of marital interaction. Combinations of genetic factors, interpersonal interactions, and social norms lead partners to develop similar activities, interests, appearances, emotional states, and so forth. The causal factor of age difference in marriage and longevity may be related to the literal chemistry that people create in close relationships.

A final question dealing with age homogamy is whether age differences affect the quality of marriage. Are age-dissimilar marriages problem-ridden and unstable? Most evidence suggests that they are not, but some contradictory evidence does exist. On

[37]James A. Schellenberg, "Patterns of Delayed Marriage: How Special Are the Irish," *Sociological Focus* 24 (February 1991): 1–11; Kenji Otani, "Time Distribution in the Process to Marriage and Pregnancy in Japan," *Population Studies* 45 (1991): 473–487; and Peter McDonald, "The Shift Away from Marriage among Young Australians," *Family Matters* 30 (December 1991): 50.

[38]Laurel Klinger-Vartabedian and Lauren Wispe, "Age Differences in Marriage and Female Longevity," *Journal of Marriage and the Family* 51 (February 1989): 195–202.

one hand, a review of age-dissimilar marriages[39] cited some research showing that marital satisfaction does not differ between age-heterogamous and age-homogamous couples and that age differences do not impact negatively on marital quality. On the other hand, research was cited that showed age-discrepant unions more susceptible to dissolution, especially if the wife is older. It appears that the longer a couple is married, the more the effects of age heterogamy diminish.

Social Status

Social class was discussed in Chapter 4. In terms of partner selection, what is the likelihood of choosing someone from within or outside one's own class? Class homogamy in U.S. society and around the world is a desirable social norm, particularly for higher-status parents in regard to their children. Whether mates are selected by the individuals themselves, by parents, or by someone else, conditions supporting similarity of marital partners along social class lines appear to be present across a wide range of societies.

Class Homogamy

Numerous studies in the past fifty years have found that both men and women marry persons within their own class with greater consistency than could be expected simply by chance. As early as 1918, an analysis of marriages in Philadelphia showed that intermarriage between men and women in the same industry was distinctly more common than chance expectancy, revealing something of a homogamous trend.[40]

Like occupational homogamy, educationally homogamous marriages occur more often than could be expected by chance. This is true not only in the United States but also around the world, as was revealed in an analysis of educational homogamy in sixty-five countries.[41] Educational homogamy varied considerably by country, but it did not do so linearly. When comparing the least developed countries with countries at an intermediate level of development, the level of educational homogamy increased as the level of economic development increased, but it decreased when the intermediate countries were compared with the most developed countries. This pattern likely reflects the more extreme cultural differences introduced through education during the early stages of societal development making potential partners across educational levels less compatible. In the more developed societal context, cultural values are less distinct across educational levels and outward status characteristics become less significant in partner choices. In the United States, educational homogamy is common among all groups but particularly for the least educated. According to research by Debra Blackwell and Daniel Lichter, those with less than a completed high school education are 53 times more likely to marry someone with a similar level of education. Those with professional or graduate degrees are also more likely to marry

[39]Felix M. Berardo, Jeffrey Appel, and Donna Berardo, "Age Dissimilar Marriages: Review and Assessment," *Journal of Aging Studies* 7 (1993): 93–106.

[40]D. M. Marvin, "Occupational Propinquity as a Factor in Mate Selection," *Publications of the American Statistical Association* 16 (1918–1919): 131–150.

[41]Jeroen Smits, Wout Ultee, and Jan Lammers, "Educational Homogamy in 65 Countries: An Explanation of Differences in Openness Using Country-Level Explanatory Variables," *American Sociological Review* 63 (April 1988): 264–285.

within their educational group, but only 16 times more likely than would be expected by chance.[42]

As we will discuss in Chapter 7 commonalities of meaning systems, values, and world views are key components to advancing the development of intimate relationships in modern societies. One reason why social class position (and especially education) exerts such a strong effect on partner choice is that it shapes socialization experiences and distinguishes between individuals in terms of their meaning and value systems. As a result, those from the same social class background will find each other more attractive. In addition, there will be strong influences from others in one's social class to marry homogamously in order to preserve group values and consolidate group resources. Finally, social exchange theory tells us that those with equal resources will be better able to sustain ongoing reciprocity and thereby find that long-term profits and feelings of equity are enhanced through homogamous marriage. Even with these social forces acting on individuals to promote homogamy along social class lines, differences between spouses still occur. If this is the case, what does a person of lower social class have to "trade" with someone of higher social status? The following discussion will examine some patterns of marriage across class lines.

Mesalliance

Marriage with a person of a lower social position has been termed **mesalliance**. Special cases of mesalliance are **hypergamy**, denoting the pattern wherein the female marries into a higher social stratum, and **hypogamy**, in which the female marries into a lower social stratum.

With particular reference to the United States, a number of writers have concluded that hypergamy is more prevalent than hypogamy; that is, women marry men of higher status more frequently than men marry women of higher status. On the basis of an exchange theory argument, the social advantages of hypergamy seem to exist primarily for low-status women. For equity to occur, this type of exchange would require that the woman be exceptional in those qualities defined as desirable by the culture into which she marries. Depending on the society, qualities in women that determine status might include shade of skin, facial and morphological features, and relative age.

Men in the United States rank physical attractiveness at or near the top among the qualities they desire in women. Women, on the other hand, appear to be concerned with the socioeconomic status of potential spouses.[43] Thus, it would be expected that a male who achieves status through his occupation will exchange his social rank for the beauty and personal qualities of a female. Certain ideas related to mesalliance have been confirmed. One is that when males marry outside their class, they more frequently marry down than up. And the higher the occupational stratum of the male, the more commonly he marries down. Conversely, when females marry outside of their class, they more frequently marry up than down.

---

[42]Debra L. Blackwell and Daniel T. Lichter, "Homogamy among Dating, Cohabiting and Married Couples," *The Sociological Quarterly*, 45 (June 2004): 719-737.

[43]Scott South, "Sociodemographic Differentials in Mate Selection Preferences," *Journal of Marriage and the Family* 53 (November 1991): 928–940; and Susan Sprecher, "The Importance to Males and Females of Physical Attractiveness, Earning Potential, and Expressiveness in Initial Attraction," *Sex Roles* 21 (1989): 591–607.

In brief, hypergamy is more prevalent than hypogamy. This notion extends to dating, as well, and is referred to as the mating gradient.

Mating Gradient

If, as stated, when persons marry outside their social class, men tend to marry down and women tend to marry up, then it can be assumed the same patterns occur prior to marriage. Thus, when men and women date or engage in intimate personal interaction, women seek men of similar or higher status and men seek women of similar or lower status. This tendency has been called the **mating gradient**. It is rooted in the notion that men at the top have a wider range of mate choice than do men at the bottom with the reverse being true for women; namely, women at the top have a more narrow range of choice than those at the bottom.

One interesting consequence of these choices is an excess number of unmarried men at the bottom of the socioeconomic ladder and an excess number of unmarried women at the top. Lower-status men must compete against other lower-status men as well as against higher-status men for the lower-status women. Conversely, the higher-status women compete against other higher-status women as well as those below them for the higher-status men. Thus, unmarried men are likely to be disproportionately of lower status, and unmarried women are likely to be disproportionately of higher status. For women, however, as will be shown later in the discussion on marriage, higher-status or professional women who are more economically independent increasingly choose not to marry (or remain married) in spite of the smaller pool of eligible men. The lower marriage rate among African American women seems to be related to the smaller pool of higher-status eligible men.

The mating gradient also seems to operate in dating on college campuses. For example, the freshman male and the senior female have the smallest choice of probable dating partners. The freshman girl is the choice of college males at any class ranking, whereas the freshman male must, to a greater extent, limit his choices to freshmen females. Among seniors, the situation is reversed: The male can select from any of the class rankings of females, whereas the female is more limited to senior and junior men.

Religion and Intermarriage

In the United States, religious homogamy is strong. The number of people who marry within their own religion is far greater than chance occurrence can explain. According to Blackwell and Lichter's estimates, all religious groups are significantly more likely to marry within their religious group than would be expected simply on the basis of chance. The most likely to marry homogamously were the "other" category that included Jews, Muslims, and other non-Catholic and non-Protestant religions. Those in the "other" category were 63 times more likely to marry within their group than outside of it. By contrast, Catholics were 6.1 times more likely to marry homogamously than heterogamously and Protestants were 4.1 times more likely to do so.[44]

Yet, in spite of high rates of homogamy, Kalmijn showed how the social boundary between people from Catholic and Protestant backgrounds has declined over

---

[44]Debra L. Blackwell and Daniel T. Lichter, "Homogamy among Dating, Cohabiting and Married Couples," *The Sociological Quarterly*, 45 (June 2004): 719–737.

Around the world, most couples who marry are of similar religious backgrounds. But interfaith marriages are increasing, particularly as partner selection moves toward personal choice and a criteria of being in love.

the course of this century, resulting in dramatic increases in Catholic/Protestant intermarriage.[45] It is Kalmijn's contention that education has become a more significant factor than religion in spouse selection.

It is interesting to note that homogamy is not the predominant pattern merely when the broad Protestant/Catholic/Jewish classification is used; it is also the predominant pattern among Protestant denominations as well. Protestants still marry other Protestants, as previous studies have shown, but they marry Protestants who share the same denominational affiliation (Lutheran, Methodist, Baptist, etc.). The ratio of mixed marriages does not vary much across denominational lines. Interfaith marriages are most frequent among those who are religiously less devout.

Defining Interfaith Marriage

Determining what is within one's religion can be an extremely complex problem. To even define, much less measure, an interfaith (mixed religious) marriage involves problems that few persons have satisfactorily resolved. For example, is a Methodist–Lutheran marriage an intra- or interfaith union? If a devout Catholic married a person reared in the Catholic tradition but presently indifferent to religion, would this be a mixed marriage? If an atheist married an agnostic, would their marriage be endogamous or exogamous? If a Protestant married a Catholic and then the Protestant converted to Catholicism, would this be an inter- or intrafaith marriage?

---

[45]Matthijs Kalmijn, "Shifting Boundaries: Trends in Religious and Educational Homogamy," *American Sociological Review* 56 (December 1991): 786–800.

How interfaith is defined influences the incidence as well as the consequences. Sander, for example, illustrated that the incidence of Catholic mixed marriage rates are much lower if current religion is used rather than religious upbringing.[46] Yet most studies of interreligious marriage in the United States are limited to three broad categories—Catholic, Protestant, and Jewish—with little differentiation between religious upbringing, intensity of religious belief, extent of religious activity, or differences within categorical groups.

For example, Catholics tend to be viewed as quite homogamous. In Judaism, even though definite differences regarding interfaith and intra-Jewish marriages have been found to exist among the three major branches—Orthodox, Conservative, and Reform—studies distinguish among them relatively infrequently. The same is true among some of the major denominations of Protestantism: Methodist, Presbyterian, Lutheran, Baptist, and the like. This lack of differentiation is very unfortunate, for even the most untrained persons in religious thought recognize differences in beliefs and practices *among* Protestant denominations, to say nothing of the differences *within* denominations.

One means for resolving these measurement ambiguities is to follow the example of Scott Myers[47] and redefine religious homogamy as either shared beliefs in the authority of religion in life (**religious authority homogamy**) or in terms of joint attendance (**shared religious practices**). Myers argues that these two measures will not only be highly correlated with denominational homogamy, but that they better reflect how and to what degree religious homogamy will impact marriage and family life.

Consequences of Interfaith Marriage

The general opposition to interfaith marriages stems from the widespread belief that they are highly unstable and create a multitude of problems that intrafaith marriages do not. Some empirical evidence has supported the belief that interreligious marriages are less satisfying and less stable than religiously homogamous marriages.[48] Those homogamous partners with no religious identification, however, are the least stable of all. Couples of the same denominational affiliation, as well as those who attend church frequently, are more likely to have happy, stable marriages than those whose religions are different or those who claim no religion. This relationship, however, has weakened over the past two decades due to a decline in religious authority and a rise in contemporary views of family life and work lives.[49]

Findings from these cross-sectional, homogamous/heterogamous comparisons must be interpreted cautiously, even if the reports are accurate. Marriages that were unhappy and have already ended in divorce do not contribute to unhappiness in the currently married population. Nevertheless, even taking this factor into account, it is likely that lower levels of happiness and slightly higher rates of divorce occur

---

[46]William Sander, "Catholicism and Intermarriage in the United States," *Journal of Marriage and the Family* 55 (November 1993): 1037–1041.

[47]Scott Myers, "Religious Homogamy and Marital Quality: Historical and Generational Patterns, 1980–1997," *Journal of Marriage and Family*, 68 (May 2006): 292–304.

[48]Evelyn L. Lehrer and Carmel U. Chiswick, "Religion as a Determinant of Marital Stability," *Demography* 30 (August 1993): 385–404; and Tim B. Heaton and Edith L. Pratt, "The Effects of Religious Homogamy on Marital Satisfaction and Stability," *Journal of Family Issues* 11 (June 1990): 191–207.

[49]Scott Myers, Religious Homogamy and Marital Quality: Historical and Generational Patterns, 1980–1997," *Journal of Marriage and Family*, 68 (May 2006): 292–304.

among interreligious marriages than among intrareligious, homogamous marriages. That the highest rates of divorce and marital instability occur among those with "no religion" underscores the importance of religion, whether inter- or intrafaith.

What about the children of interfaith marriages? It has been argued that these children, compared to children of homogamous marriages, are subjected to less intense and less consistent religious socialization, such that they are weakly religious themselves. In other words, the assertion is that interfaith marriages have a secularizing effect on the children.

For the most part, this assertion has not been found to be true. Larry Peterson, in studying over a thousand adult Catholics, claimed that, contrary to the secularization hypothesis, interfaith marriages have relatively inconsequential effects on religious commitment.[50] In this study, offspring from interfaith marriages did not consistently score lower on general religiosity measures than did offspring of homogamous marriages. Catholics who were the offspring of interfaith marriages and Catholics who formed them were as firmly committed to Christianity, in general, and Catholicism, in particular, as were Catholics in homogamous families.

In sum, the negative consequences often assumed of interfaith marriages regarding the success of the marriage and the secularization of the children do not have much empirical support.

Black-white intermarriages, while increasing, still constitute a very small proportion of all marriages. When they do occur, a disproportionate number of couples include a black male and a white female.

Race, Ethnicity, and Intermarriage

Of all the norms involving intermarriage, few are more widely held or rigorously enforced than those pertaining to race and ethnic origins. Despite scientific findings and the removal of legal barriers, the restrictions concerning interracial marriage still remain the most inflexible of all mate-selection boundaries.

The intermingling of people of different races and ethnic origins is nothing new in world affairs. Based on historical and biological evidence, the idea of a "pure race" or a "pure ethnic group" is totally inaccurate. Racial and ethnic mixture has been evident throughout recorded history; some evidence has suggested that racial/ethnic intermingling occurred even in prehistoric times. As there is no evidence to support the notion of a pure race, neither is there evidence to support the idea that racial/ethnic mixtures result in biologically inferior offspring. Biologically, there is nothing to prevent marriage of, or procreation between, persons of different races or ethnic groups.

Removal of the legal prohibition against interracial marriage in the United States came in 1967 when the U.S. Supreme Court struck down as unconstitutional a 1924 Virginia law forbidding

---

[50]Larry R. Peterson, "Interfaith Marriage and Religious Commitment among Catholics," *Journal of Marriage and the Family* 48 (November 1986): 725–735.

marriage between persons of different races. According to the Court, laws of this type violate rights guaranteed to all persons under the Fourteenth Amendment to the Constitution. Irrespective of the Supreme Court's decision declaring such laws unconstitutional, the social mores and the disfavor placed on interracial marriage by all major racial, religious, and ethnic groups were so strong in most areas that relatively few interracial marriages take place.

As recently as 1991, a Gallup poll revealed that 48 percent of the U.S. population approved, 42 percent disapproved, and 10 percent had no opinion. Blacks were more likely to approve than whites (70 percent to 44 percent), males were more likely to approve than females (52 to 44 percent), and people under 30 were more likely to approve than those over 50 (64 to 27 percent). People from the western United States and large cities as well as people who were well educated and who had no religious preference were likely to approve of intermarriage.[51] These attitudes have undergone considerable transformation in the subsequent fifteen years. In June of 2007, a similar poll revealed an approval rate of 77 percent and a disapproval rate of only 17 percent. Among non-Hispanic Whites the approval rate was 75 percent and among Blacks and Hispanics it was 85 percent or higher. In addition, earlier age differences have become less pronounced as 85 percent of those under 50 years old approve compared to 67 percent of those over 50.[52]

Although the trend over several decades has been toward greater approval of interracial marriage, the strength of the prohibition—particularly against black–white marriage—remains high. Interestingly, a major discrepancy exists between verbal approval of interracial marriage and its actual occurrence.

Frequency of Interracial/Interethnic Marriage

Determining the frequency of mixed or interracial/interethnic marriage is exceedingly difficult. As with religion, there is the matter of classification. If an African, Asian, or Native American is able to "pass" for white and marries a white American, is this an intermarriage or an endogamous marriage? Given the laws in various states, where a person who has one-eighth or one-sixteenth African blood is deemed black (an empirical impossibility), would it not be an intermarriage, regardless of which race the individual married? Even if a categorization could be precisely determined and agreed on, it could be argued that social sanctions against certain types of interracial/interethnic marriage are so severe in most parts of the United States that the reported number of such marriages would be less than the actual number.

Since 1960, the U.S. Census has been tabulated to show the number of husbands and wives who have the same or different racial backgrounds. This information, like all census information involving race, does not denote any clear-cut scientific definition of biological stock. Rather, it is based on self-identification by respondents.

Figure 6.3 (page 266) shows how interracial and interethnic marriage rates have changed over the past several decades. As can be seen in this chart, the rates of interracial and interethnic marriage have increased substantially since 1980 from 1.31 and 1.79 to 3.65 and 3.51, respectively. Rates for intermarriage between blacks and whites, however, have not changed much during the same period. The percentage of marriages involving a black husband and a white wife in 2004 was less than one half of a percent (.49). The percentage involving a white husband and a black wife were even lower at .21 percent.

---

[51]George Gallup, Jr., and Frank Newport, *The Gallup Poll Monthly* 311 (August 1991): 62.

[52]Joseph Carroll, "Most Americans Approve of Interracial Marriages," *Gallup News Service* (August 2007). http://www.gallup.com/poll/28417/Most-Americans-Approve-Interracial-Marriages.aspx.

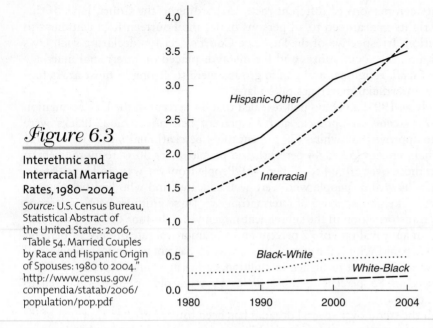

Figure 6.3

Interethnic and Interracial Marriage Rates, 1980–2004

Source: U.S. Census Bureau, Statistical Abstract of the United States: 2006, "Table 54. Married Couples by Race and Hispanic Origin of Spouses: 1980 to 2004." http://www.census.gov/compendia/statab/2006/population/pop.pdf

Thus, most interracial marriages in the United States do not occur between blacks and whites. Rather, intermarriages between Native American women and white men, Japanese American women and white men, and Filipino American women and white men are most common. Qian noted that during 1980–1990, intermarriage of whites occurred most frequently with Asian Americans, followed by Hispanics, and least frequently by African Americans.[53] Census figures on interracial marriages must be interpreted with caution because they are based on self-reports and, thus, devoid of reliability or validity checks; however, such data do provide a valuable source of information on frequency, the increase over time, and the husband–wife differential.

Interracial/interethnic marriages are sociologically important because they serve as an indicator of the relationship among various racial and ethnic groups. If full equality was achieved and social norms were favorable, the rate of interracial/interethnic marriage would be high. The very low rate of black–white intermarriage, for example, serves as a stark indicator of the separation of the races and the disapproval accorded to interracial marriage in the United States.

Male–Female Interracial Differences

As indicated, census data have shown that most interracial marriages in the United States occur between white men and Native American, Japanese, and Filipino women. However, many articles and books have addressed black–white intermarriage, finding that black males marry white females more frequently than white males marry black females. This black husband–white wife pattern has also been strongly supported by census data (see Figure 6.3).

---

[53] Zhenchao Qian, "Breaking the Racial Barriers: Variations in Interracial Marriage between 1980 and 1990," *Demography* 34 (May 1997): 263–276.

Same-Sex Marriage and Racial Justice Find Common Ground

news item

Not long into the oral argument before the California Supreme Court in March over whether gay and lesbian couples have a constitutional right to marry, Chief Justice Ronald M. George showed his hand.

Three times he quoted from the court's 1948 decision in *Perez v. Sharp* that struck down a state ban on interracial marriage, a high point in the history of a prestigious and influential court....

That was when Shannon P. Minter, a lawyer with the National Center for Lesbian Rights, knew things were looking good for his side. The chief justice seemed to be accepting arguments for same-sex marriage that were consciously rooted in the struggle for equal rights for blacks. Mr. Minter's optimism was vindicated on Thursday, when a majority of a divided court, citing Perez, found that same-sex couples had a constitutional right to marry....

Opponents of same-sex marriage say they are uncomfortable with the analogy to interracial marriage bans. "It's well suited to a sound-bite culture," said Monte Stewart, president of the Marriage Law Foundation, which supports traditional marriage.

"Sure, it works at the surface level," Mr. Stewart continued. "But it is actually defeated by the deeper reality of marriage itself. Marriage in its deep logic has nothing to do with race and everything to do with the union of a man and a woman...."

As divisive as Thursday's decision was, the Perez decision was a judicial earthquake. Six years would pass before the United States Supreme Court...ruled that racially segregated public schools violated the Constitution. Thirteen more years would pass before that court followed Perez in striking down bans on interracial marriage in *Loving v. Virginia* in 1967....

"The Perez case shaped the environment for the court, shaped the landscape in which it was ruling," said Suzanne Goldberg, a law professor at Columbia.... "This is the court that made history by rejecting bans on interracial marriage and did not see the sky fall."...

Therese M. Stewart, a lawyer for the City and County of San Francisco...asked the court whether it would have satisfied California's Constitution in 1948 to give interracial couples the same rights under a different name. "Say we called it 'transracial unions' instead of marriage," she said, in a mocking tone.

But Mr. Stewart, of the Marriage Law Foundation, said that the analogy to race discrimination should not hold and that gay and lesbian groups were using the debate over marriage to advance a political agenda.

"We understand," he said, "that there is a very different moral equivalence on the one hand between the white supremacist agenda and on the other advocating equal rights for gays and lesbians...."

The history of restrictions on interracial marriage can thus be read two ways. The Perez court can be said to have struck an early blow for equality. Or it can be said to have overridden the democratic process, imposing a decision that most of the country was not ready to embrace.

Jennifer C. Pizer, a lawyer with Lambda Legal, which represented gay and lesbian couples in the same-sex marriage case, said there were limits to the analogy with Perez. "We're talking about constitutional principles," Ms. Pizer said, "not social parallels." But she said Perez informed her side's approach and would continue to resonate.

Source: Adam Liptak, "Same Sex Marriage and Racial Justice Find Common Ground," *New York Times* (May 2008). http://www.nytimes.com/2008/05/17/us/17marriage.html?ex=1368763200&en=2641ea4aef9c25fd&ei=5124&partner=permalink&exprod=permalink.

There is a lack of consensus on the reasons for different incidences of interracial marriage by sex. Research attempts aimed at establishing a race/class exchange have failed to find consistent support.[54] For example, when education has been used as an

---

[54]Tim D. B. Heaton and Stan L. Albrecht, "The Changing Pattern of Interracial Marriage," *Social Biology* 43 (1996): 203–217.

indicator of class, highly educated black men are more likely to marry interracially. But this tendency is less true for highly educated black females and white males. Availability has also been ruled out as an answer, for the greater number of black females than black males would lead one to expect more intermarriage by black females.

Scott Coltrane and Randall Collins suggest[55] that one possible explanation for the sex difference among blacks may be that cultural ideals of beauty have been based on white standards. Images of thin young Caucasian models predominate in the media. Another explanation they suggest is that a particularly strong distinction exists between male and female cultures in the black community. Black women have a tradition of independence (not being very subservient to men), which may account both for their own lower rate of intermarriage and for the tendency of black males to seek wives elsewhere.

One could hypothesize as well that differential norms operate for white and black males in relation to females. For example, for both races, males are more likely than females to initiate partner selection and marriage. In addition, due to historical and socioeconomic differences, it may be more prestigious for a black male to initiate interaction with a white female than for a white male to initiate interaction with a black female. Other factors or explanations may be operative as well.

Success of Interracial/Interethnic Marriages

Do interracial and interethnic marriages succeed? A generally accepted view is that people who enter a racially or ethnically mixed marriage are more likely to get divorced. However, evidence supporting this view is conflicting. For example, data from Hawaii showed that interethnic (mixed) marriages more often resulted in divorce than intraethnic (within-group) marriages. However, a sizable portion of these intermarriages in Hawaii were between nonresidents. When the proportion of divorces among resident marriages was examined, intraethnic marriages were more at risk than interethnic marriages. Other mixed results came from an analysis of differing groups. Some cross-ethnic combinations appeared more at risk for divorce than others. For example, marriages in which the bride was from a higher income group than the groom were at a significantly greater risk for divorce than marriages in which the bride came from a lower income group than the groom.[56]

In sum, the success or failure of an interracial or interethnic marriage is not dependent solely on the fact that it is mixed; as with other marriages, success is influenced by age, religious beliefs, educational level, residence location, first marriage or remarriage, support of the parents and family, and many other factors. Recognizing that Hawaii may be a unique case, recognizing that interracial/interethnic marital success depends on which races or ethnic groups are intermarrying and the circumstances surrounding the marriage, and recognizing different methodological and research problems, findings should certainly lead one to seriously question the negative aspects of interracial/interethnic marriage per se as viewed by the couple themselves.

But what about the children of interracial and interethnic couples? Are they at risk for personality and adjustment problems?

Popular literature, often based on speculation or unrepresentative case histories, has been strongly biased toward the notion that offspring of cross-racial/cross-ethnic

---

[55]Scott Coltrane and Randall Collins, *Sociology of Marriage and the Family: Gender, Love, and Property*, 5th ed. (Belmont, CA: Wadsworth/Thompson Learning, 2001), 275.

[56]Fung Chu Ho and Ronald C. Johnson, "Intra-ethnic and Inter-ethnic Marriage and Divorce in Hawaii," *Social Biology* 37 (Spring/Summer 1990): 44–51.

marriages are likely to suffer from adjustment problems. Data from Hawaii and New Mexico, at least, have suggested that this literature is incorrect.[57] In these states, positive effects of bicultural socialization were found for intergroup contact and attitudes, language facility, and enjoyment of the culture of minority groups. In contrast to their single-heritage peers, students of mixed heritage did not have lower self-esteem or feel more alienated, nor did they experience greater stress.

Whether dealing with husband–wife, parent–child, or employer–employee relationships, the success of the relationship depends on the total situation and not merely on the fact that the partners have different skin colors or ethnic heritages. Interpersonal relationships of any sort are clearly affected by external forces. Parents, kin, neighbors, teachers, politicians, and society in general lend either support or opposition with varying degrees of pressure on the marriage, family, or job situation. Success is relative to the sociocultural context, extending far beyond the boundaries of any two persons—whether their skin color is alike or different.

---

[57]Walter G. Stephan and Cookie White Stephan, "Intermarriage: Effects on Personality, Adjustment, and Intergroup Relations in Two Samples of Students," *Journal of Marriage and the Family* 53 (February 1991): 241–250.

Summary

1. There are many ways of summarizing information about the prevalence, popularity, and probabilities of marriage in society. One can look at the proportion of the population that is currently in different marital statuses (married, divorced, separated, widowed, or never married) or at the rate of marriage (the *crude marriage rate* and the *general marriage rate*) in a given year. The general marriage rate is particularly useful for looking at changes in marriage behavior over time and is a reasonable measure of the changing popularity of marriage.

2. In 2007, less than 60 percent of the U.S. population over age 18 was married. In addition, there has been a decline in the general marriage rate since World War II, although the beginning of this decline marked what perhaps was the highest rate of marriage ever recorded in U.S. history. Much of this recent decline in the general marriage rate has occurred in conjunction with a corresponding increase in the age at marriage for men and women to levels comparable to those observed at the turn of the twentieth century.

3. There are few data to suggest that young people in the United States have rejected marriage. Instead, the evidence seems to point to a reduced marriage rate resulting from the delay of marriage until necessary life course tasks (e.g., education, training, employment stability) can be completed.

4. There are many forces that may play a role in explaining why people continue to get married. Marriage or some variation of marriage continues to fulfill many of the functional needs of society and may have taken on even greater personal significance in a modern society where enduring primary relationships outside of marriage are more difficult to find and maintain.

5. Marriage continues to provide many health and well-being benefits to individuals, although this observed effect is getting smaller in recent decades and may be spurious. It could be that healthier people are just more likely to get married or that most of the difference between married and nonmarried individuals exists because of the negative effects of divorce and widowhood rather than the decision to never get married.

6. There are structural conditions that result in some people having a lower likelihood of marriage. The term *marriage squeeze* is used to describe the effects of an imbalance in the sex ratio, or the number of males and females available for marriage. Based on age alone, this squeeze resulted in a shortage of women in the 1950s and a shortage of men in the 1980s. The marriage squeeze is particularly acute among black women.

7. The terms *homogamy* and *endogamy* refer to the extent of intermarriage among people who share similar characteristics. This chapter examined the nature of intermarriage and four normative structures surrounding the selection of intimate partners in the United States: age, social status, religion, and race/ethnicity.

8. Reporting and interpreting types of intermarriage are difficult. The boundaries of race/ethnicity, class, and religion are rarely clear-cut and precise. Rates for individuals often are confused with rates for marriages. Actual rates of intermarriage vary according to numerous social factors, such as group size, heterogeneity, sex ratio, controls over marriage, development of cultural similarities, romantic love complex, and influence of certain psychological factors.

9. Most couples in the United States are relatively homogamous in the age at which they marry. Since the turn of the twentieth century, the tendency has been for the male–female age difference at the time of marriage to narrow, and since the mid 1950s, the tendency has been for a delay in—that is, a later age at—marriage.

10. Mate-selection studies have concluded that marriages are highly endogamous by social class, more so than could be expected to occur simply by chance. When marriage occurs with someone from a lower social position (*mesalliance*), it may denote *hypergamy* or *hypogamy*. The general tendency for men to date and marry downward more frequently than upward has been termed the *mating gradient*.

11. Religious endogamy, although less rigid than racial/ethnic endogamy, remains an important factor in mate selection. There seems to be consensus that people who are religiously devout marry endogamously with greater frequency than those who are religiously less devout and that endogamous marriages have higher levels of happiness and slightly lower rates of divorce than interfaith marriages.

12. In the United States, racial/ethnic endogamous norms are more rigorously enforced than any others described in this chapter. Findings have suggested that black males marry white females more frequently than white males marry black females. Although the trend in interracial/interethnic marriage is upward, the incidence is low and the number will, in all probability, have little effect on racial integration.

13. In general, intermarriage of all types appears to be on the increase, but endogamous marriage continues to occur with a frequency far greater than could be expected to occur by chance alone.

14. As we have seen, most people get married at some point in their lives, but young people are delaying their marriages and living for extended periods of time independently in a single status. The next chapter examines the process of premarital relationship development as well as the dynamics of nonmarital relationships regardless of the intention to marry.

Key Terms and Topics

Crude marriage rate p. 237

General marriage rate p. 239

Marriage squeeze p. 242

Sequential or serial monogamy p. 247

Nonmarital cohabitation p. 247

Marriage protection hypothesis p. 248

Safety net hypothesis p. 249

Arranged marriage p. 251

Autonomous marriage p. 251

Dowry p. 252

Bride's price p. 252

Endogamy p. 252

Homogamy p. 252

Assortive mating p. 252

Intermarriage p. 254

Operational definitions p. 254

Intermarriage rate p. 255

Intermarriage rate for individuals p. 255

Actual intermarriage rate p. 255

Expected intermarriage rate p. 255

Age homogamy pp. 258–259

Class homogamy pp. 259–260

Mesalliance p. 260

Hypergamy p. 260

Hypogamy p. 260

Mating gradient p. 261

Interfaith marriage pp. 261–264

Religious authority homogamy p. 263

Shared religious practices p. 263

Race, ethnicity, and intermarriage pp. 264–269

Discussion Questions?

1. What do the statistics tell us about the popularity of marriage today, and how it has changed over the past hundred years? Discuss the meaning of different statistics and how some may misrepresent the state of marriage today.

2. Describe the *marriage squeeze*. What factors account for a shift from a shortage of women to a shortage of men and vice versa? Why is the marriage squeeze so significant for black women?

3. Do you think that marriage is good for you? What argument could you make against the idea that marriage is beneficial?

4. Differentiate between terms in the following pairs: *endogamy/exogamy* and *homogamy/heterogamy*. What is meant by *assortive mating*? What constitutes *intermarriage* or *mixed marriage*?

5. Discuss factors likely to increase the incidence of intermarriage in the United States. What factors operate most strongly to discourage or prohibit intermarriage?

6. What trends are likely to emerge regarding age at marriage, place of residence, social class, religion, and race/ethnicity? Why?

7. Discuss *hypergamy* and *hypogamy*—how likely each is to occur, why it occurs, and what consequences result from its occurrence.

8. Is the mating gradient a common phenomenon in your school? Why or why not? Is the basic pattern among college students likely to change in ten years?

9. To what extent is a social exchange theory adequate in explaining interclass and interracial marriages? What factors are offered in exchange (for example, between a black male and white female)? How are exceptions handled?

10. In regard to black–white interracial marriages: Why do they occur so infrequently? What explains the predominance of black husband–white wife marriages? Why is the reverse pattern uncommon? What objections to interracial marriages likely lack empirical support?

Further Readings

Azoulay, Katya Gibel. *Black, Jewish, and Interracial.* Durham, NC: Duke University Press, 1997.

A blending of personal, theoretical, and historical perspectives to explore what it means to be black, Jewish, and interracial.

Dalmage, Heather M. *Tripping the Color Line: Black-White Multiracial Families in a Racially Divided World.* New Brunswick, NJ: Rutgers University Press, 2000.

Through recorded interviews, the author incorporates the stories and ideas of black–white multiracial families showing how race permeates every aspect of life.

Hamon, Reann, and Ingoldsby, Bron B. *Mate Selection across Cultures.* Thousand Oaks, CA: Sage Publications, 2004.

A global perspective on the variation in mate selection practices in contemporary societies. Examines differences both within and across societies.

Lazarre, Jane. *Beyond the Whiteness of Whiteness.* Durham, NC: Duke University Press, 1997.

A white Jewish mother writes of her personal experiences in raising two biracial sons.

Root, Maria P.P. *Love's Revolution: Interracial Marriage.* Philadelphia: Temple University Press, 2001.

A look at trends, families, parents, children, and race as related to interracial relationships.

Rosenblatt, Paul C., Karis, Terri A., and Powell, Richard D. *Multiracial Couples: Black and White Voices.* Thousand Oaks, CA: Sage Publications, 1995.

Using a qualitative research design, the authors explore the interpersonal dynamics of twenty-one interracial couples in committed relationships.

Sollars, Werner, ed. *Interracialism: Black-White Intermarriages in American History, Literature and Law.* New York: Oxford University Press, 2000.

A series of essays covering the history of miscegenation, with a section on social theory and analysis of black–white intermarriage.

The National Marriage Project, *The State of Out Unions 2007: The Social Health of Marriage in America* (Piscataway, NJ: Rutgers University, 2007).

A comprehensive and easy-to-read review of the data on the state of marriage and family life in contemporary American society with commentary on the meaning of the statistics.

7

Premarital and Nonmarital Relationships

Josie Recommends Nonmarital Cohabitation

Josie is a 30-year-old undergraduate student at Wayne State University. She was raised in a devout Catholic family, got married at age 20, divorced at age 27, moved back to her parents' home for two years, and then moved in with Joe. Was that a good idea for her, and would she recommend it to others? In Josie's words:

"Cohabitation is definitely a good idea before you get married. You get a clearer idea about someone when you see them morning, noon, and night rather than on an occasional evening and weekend. In many ways I'm very traditional. I do all the housework and cooking but I want to work full-time when I finish school. Joe accepts that but he'd be just as happy with me in the traditional housewife role.

"I guess I'm very traditional in my commitment to Joe. I wouldn't even consider going out with or sleeping with anyone else, although I did go to bed with several men after my divorce. But now I'm really committed to Joe and would be badly hurt if he went out with someone else. I know he feels the same. I love him and know he loves me.

"We have thought about marriage but I don't believe that would change much. The only reason I can think of for marrying is that it might be a statement on the part of each of us of the trust we really have for each other. Sometimes I feel that my life is secondary to his, less important, since he's earning all the money. But I saved quite a bit from when I worked full-time before I went back to school. Since I have a merit scholarship and he pays for all the groceries, I don't see anything changing with marriage. I don't ask him for money now and don't think I would even if we were married.

"Joe's really a great guy. Unlike my ex-husband, we can talk openly about anything. For example, my ex-husband would never talk about sex—what I liked or how I felt—and he never seemed to hear me or give any expression of hearing. Now it's so different. For me, physical pleasure isn't enough. I must feel strongly about someone and be able to communicate and share openly with them.

"I really believe God led me to Joe. He's all I ever could want in a guy—warm, affectionate, expressive, willing to talk, caring. We might marry someday but he brings it up more than I do. I like living with him and don't see how marriage would improve anything. So for now, I'm happy with things as they are."

Questions to Consider

Josie got married at age 20. Do you think that this was a good idea? Why or why not?

Do you think that it is easier or harder today than in the past to make a choice about a long-term intimate partner—to know who would be the best choice, to have clear procedures to follow in your searching, to be certain about your choice, and so on? Explain.

Is cohabitation a marriage-like relationship? How are marriage and cohabitation different? For example, consider the division of household labor, sexual relationships, children, ending the relationship, and the like. Josie said that "cohabitation is definitely a good idea before you get married" and that she didn't "see how marriage could improve anything." Do you agree with either or both of these statements? Why or why not?

As discussed in Chapter 6, selection of an intimate partner is not simply a matter of preference or free choice. Despite the increases in freedom and opportunities available to people both young and old to choose anyone they please, many factors well beyond the control of the individual severely limit the number of eligible persons from whom to choose. The taboo on incest and the restrictions placed on age, sex, marital status, class, religion, and race/ethnicity in most societies (including our own) narrow considerably the "field of eligibles." In this chapter, we will further examine the sociocultural context within which partner selection and relationship development take place. We will then consider individual factors and interactional processes involved in interpersonal attraction and partner choice. Finally, we will examine the interactional dynamics involved in premarital and nonmarital relationships, such as dating and cohabitation, and look at the effects of premarital experiences such as cohabitation on later marriage.

Sociocultural Context of Nonmarital Relationships

Whether we are talking about relationships formed in the pursuit of marriage or for the satisfaction of more immediate needs and desires, it is important to consider the ways in which the social structure and the realm of cultural meaning systems impact not just our choices of partners but also the meanings we give to those relationships and the ways that we act within them. Early **filter theories of mate selection** recognized the ways that society defined our field of eligibles (acted as a filter) but then assumed that these forces gave way to individual need fulfillment or interactional processes of attraction to specific others within the field.[1] One exception was Ira

---

[1]Alan C. Kerckhoff and Kingsley E. Davis, "Value Consensus and Need Complementarity in Mate Selection," *American Sociological Review* 27 (1962): 295–303.

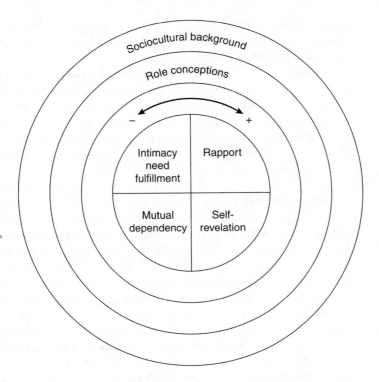

Figure 7.1

Reiss's Wheel Theory of Love

Source: From Family Systems in America, 3rd edition, by Reiss. © 1980. Reprinted with permission of Wadsworth, a division of Thomson Learning: www.thomsonrights.com. Fax 800-730-2215.

Reiss's **Wheel Theory of Love** (see Figure 7.1), which proposed that the process of attraction and relationship formation is never independent of sociocultural influences. As relationships progress to the most intimate stage of need fulfillment, they are rocked to and fro by increasing levels of interpersonal disclosure as well as by the constant influence of a context of social networks and cultural ideas. We believe this model is more informative of the process of partner choice and relationship dynamics.

All human societies have some socially approved and structured procedures to follow in getting married, particularly for the first time. As described earlier, when marriages are arranged, the process generally occurs between kin groups and all nonmarital, sexually intimate relationships between adults are highly restricted or regulated for the purpose of facilitating marriage arrangements. In more autonomous marriage systems, however, the procedures for selecting marital partners and moving the relationship toward marriage are contained in an institutionalized system of organizational contexts and norms for *individual* behavior during the process. In some autonomous marriage contexts, all nonmarital, sexually intimate relationships prior to marriage are also considered "premarital" and the processes of relationship formation and development are more institutionalized. In these contexts, individuals have clear guidelines defining with whom they should form relationships, how they should go about seeking relationship partners, how they should act in the process of developing their relationships, and what the status of their relationship is with respect to the end point of marriage. In other words, a clear **social script** (or set of procedural norms and expectations) exists to guide the behaviors of the actors in the process. Such a highly institutionalized system was developed during the transition from tradition to modernity in North America and Western Europe[2] and remnants of it can still be seen today in the rituals and norms associated with dating and courtship.

More recently, however, the advance of modernity has brought about a breakdown in these institutionalized organizations and norms in North America and Western Europe, introducing increased uncertainty into intimate relationships outside of marriage[3] with respect to the criteria for partner selection, the processes of meeting and initiating relationships, the appropriateness of behavior in the context of intimate relationships, the changing status of relationships over time, and the very purpose or goals of relationships.

In the nineteenth and early twentieth centuries, intrusions into nonmarital intimate relationships by parents and others (as in the system of chaperoning) were broadly accepted and young people clearly understood social categories of others from which to make partner choices (based on in-group identification), the rules for how to behave on "dates" or within the context of "courtship" and "engagement," and a system of symbols that denoted changes in the development of the relationship toward increasing degrees of intimacy and commitment (e.g., "going steady," "pinning," engagement rings, and so forth). In today's late modern society, however, the process has become much more individualized, flexible, personal, and ambiguous. The old norms and expectations continue to be transmitted through socialization processes, but they are far from universally accepted. As a result, the procedures are left up to the individuals involved to negotiate between them and there is an increased likelihood of misunderstandings due to different socialization experiences and a lack of consensus about social scripts. This lack of scripts has led to the popularity of recent publications about dating such as *The Rules*.[4]

The criteria for partner selection have also become more individualized and ambiguous. In a society in which the "expressive self" has emerged as more important than the "instrumental self,"[5] the criteria for partner choice have moved from traditional, outward status criteria (such as religion, social class, ethnicity, etc.) to less visible and more ambiguous criteria based on personality traits and the ability of the other to meet one's psychological needs. Since each person is unique and psychological needs and capacities are unclear, finding the best and most compatible partner has become the most significant issue in nonmarital relationships and a significant source of uncertainty and risk.

Another consequence of this emergence of the expressive self and the advance of modernity is that intimate relationships inside and outside of families have taken on increasing significance as a means for building one's personal biography over a greatly

---

[2]John R. Gillis, *For Better, For Worse: British Marriages, 1600 to the Present* (New York: Oxford University Press, 1985).

[3]Ulrich Beck and Elisabeth Beck-Gernsheim, *The Normal Chaos of Love* (Cambridge: Polity, 1995); Richard A. Bulcroft and Silvia K. Bartolic, "Risk in Relationships," in Harry T. Reis and Susan K. Sprecher (Eds.), *Encyclopedia of Human Relationships* (Thousand Oaks, CA: Sage Publications, 2009).

[4]Ellen Fein and Sherrie Shamoon, *The Rules: Time Tested Secrets for Capturing the Heart of Mr. Right* (Lebanon, IN: Warner Books, Inc., 1995). These authors have since published several other *Rules* books including one on the rules for marriage and one on the rules for online dating. They also have a website for purchasing their publications and DVDs.

[5]Marlis Buchmann and Manuel Eisner, "The Transition from the Utilitarian to the Expressive Self: 1900–1992," *Poetics* 25 (1997): 157–175.

news item

Hot but Virtuous Is an Unlikely Match for an Online Dating Service

The women who appear in Web ads for the dating site True.com almost certainly do not need to look online for a date.

The buxom and often barely dressed models, posing next to slogans like "It's nice to be naughty," are plastered across the Internet these days, and are hard to avoid on the social networking site MySpace.

In part because of its provocative ads, True.com…has seemingly come out of nowhere to become one of the most visited sites in the $700 million-a-year online dating industry, attracting 3.8 million people last month.

True's rise has been controversial. The company has riled competitors like Match.com and Yahoo Personals, which say that True's lowbrow advertisements clash with its high-minded lobbying and legal efforts. True, which conducts criminal background checks on its subscribers, is the primary force behind a two-year-old campaign to get state legislatures to require that social Web sites prominently disclose whether or not they perform such checks.…

"I want to make sure that our members have a wholesome environment for courtship," said Herb Vest, True's 63-year-old founder and chief executive.

Rivals dismiss the company's piety as a play for publicity.…

True joined the crowded online dating scene in 2004. To distinguish itself from the pack, it offered a range of personality and sexuality surveys. It also hired the data broker ChoicePoint to perform background checks on customers to ensure that they had no criminal record and were not married.

The company then tried to have laws passed in several states that would require other sites to conduct background checks or disclose that they do not.

Companies like Yahoo, Google and IAC/Inter ActiveCorp, which owns Match.com, lobbied against the proposal…. Markham Erickson, the group's executive director, said background checks were ineffective, partly because felons can easily circumvent them by providing false information. "Their initial sound bite sounds great, but once you get past that, you realize it's totally unworkable," he said.…

…David Evans, who writes Online Dating Insider…said the competition was upset with True because its ad blitz, which included text ads tied to dating-related search terms, is driving up advertising costs while harming the industry's reputation.

"They worked hard to overcome the stigma of providing these services," Mr. Evans said.…

Mr. Vest denies that his ads are exploitive or semi-pornographic. "We are very conscious of our reputation," he said. "Pornography brings perverts, and we do not want perverts on our site. On the other hand, you can state from me in bold letters that True is in favor of sex."

The site has also been criticized for generating random "winks"—the industry term for messages of interest from other members. Dan Consiglio, a 49-year-old engineer from Vancouver, Wash., said he received dozens of winks from women after signing up for True, and responded to many of them. He got only one response, from a woman who kindly informed him that she had not, in fact, winked at him.

Mr. Vest acknowledged that the service sends artificial winks, but he said users have the option to disable them and that they serve an important purpose. "We try getting people who otherwise might be very retiring or shy to meet each other and fall in love and have children," he said. "We are just trying to do our job as a matchmaker."

Source: Brad Stone, "Hot but Virtuous Is an Unlikely Match for an Online Dating Service," *New York Times*, March 19, 2007. http://www.nytimes.com/2007/03/19/technology/19true.html?ei=5090&en=2bf2b5ff6107fd0e&ex=1331956800&partner=rssuserland&emc=rss&pagewanted=print.

expanded life course. Unlike in premodern/preindustrial/precapitalist societies, we live much longer today and many will change their social context many times over their life course. Personal biography is no longer determined at birth and no longer stable over one's life. We must create and maintain our own identities and biographies and establishing long-term intimate relationships such as marriage has become one way of doing so.[6] Furthermore, the responsibility for one's individual happiness and fulfillment has shifted from the public realm of institutions to the private sphere of personal choice. One of the consequences of free choice is that if one chooses poorly, there is no one to blame but oneself. As a result, the personal stakes have been raised at the same time that the choice has become more problematic.

Complicating nonmarital relationships further is the increased variety of goals and objectives found among young adults forming relationships. For some, the purpose is to find a marriage partner. For others, however, less permanent arrangements are being sought. As a result, topics traditionally found in family courses and textbooks, such as mate selection or premarital relationships, are no longer sufficient. Instead of assuming that all nonmarital sexually intimate relationships are formed and are shaped by the overriding goal of choosing a marriage partner, we need to understand how individuals manage the goals of their relationship as well as the processes leading to the attainment of those goals.

How has this new cultural context affected relationship formation and development processes? Many young people today continue to maintain the goal of marriage partner selection in their sexually intimate relationships and often rely on traditional mechanisms for finding a partner and for developing their relationship along the lines defined by a cultural script. This relatively "safe" route is not possible for all, however, and many have to or want to negotiate their way outside of traditional institutional structures, thus assuming greater risks and uncertainties.

As Ulrich Beck has noted, the method for dealing with risks in a modern society is to apply rational principles to making choices.[7] We can see this approach today with the growing popularity of such rational means of partner selection as dating and matchmaking services and technologically sophisticated personals ads in which individuals can specify their own and the other's characteristics that they see as relevant to making a good match and, in some cases, have a computer program designed by "experts" make the best match for them.[8] Still, the task can become daunting and many people revert back to traditional criteria and means or make choices under conditions of only partial information and then hope for the best.[9] As we will discuss in Chapter 9 the risks and uncertainties involved in nonmarital relationships today may account for the increased elaboration of rituals (such as weddings and honeymoons) surrounding the transition to marriage.

The Social Construction of Love

A related complication to the process of partner selection and nonmarital relationship development in a modern society like ours is the highly developed cultural concept of love. **Love** is an elusive concept. We all talk about it, some experience it at first sight, and others claim they fell in it, made it, have it, or would like to find it. But what is this thing called love? The dictionary gives definitions such as an intensive affection for another person based on familial or personal ties, an attachment based on shared

---

[6]Kris Bulcroft, Linda Smeins, and Richard Bulcroft, *Romancing the Honeymoon: Consummating Marriage in Modern Society* (Thousand Oaks, CA: Sage Publications, 1999).

[7]Ulrich Beck, *Risk Society* (Beverly Hills, CA: Sage Publications, 1992).

[8]Richard Bulcroft, Kris Bulcroft, Karen Bradley, and Carl Simpson, "The Management and Production of Risk in Romantic Relationships: A Postmodern Paradox," *Journal of Family History* 25 (January 2000): 63–92.

[9]Bruno S. Frey and Reiner Eichenberger, "Marriage Paradoxes," *Rationality and Society* 8 (1996): 187–206.

experiences or interests, and an intense attraction to another person based largely on sexual desire. Love is also defined as a zero score in tennis, but it may be difficult to link this specifically to partner selection.

Social scientists view love as a multidimensional construct experienced by individuals in relationships but shaped and interpreted within the context of a culturally specific social construction. Four interrelated dimensions of love can be identified—emotional, cognitive, relational, and behavioral.

As an *emotion*, love is a particular state of physiological arousal attached to a disposition to act in particular ways toward the love object. Whether love is a primary emotion inherent in all humans or a set of other emotions (fear, satisfaction, etc.) interpreted as love given the situation within which they are felt (in the presence of a culturally appropriate love object in an appropriate situation),[10] it is clear that the emotional content and reactions that we have to those emotions are highly influenced by the dominant social constructions within the culture in which we live.[11]

As a *cognitive state*, love is a way of thinking about another person or some object. When our thoughts become preoccupied with another, we interpret this state as being in love. Our preoccupation may stem from an emotional reaction or it could be the result of perceived rewards or psychological needs. We also interpret each other's behaviors differently when we perceive another as a love object. On one hand, we show greater concern for those we love and we are more likely to give them the benefit of the doubt when their behaviors violate our expectations. On the other hand, we also hold different sets of expectations for others when we define our relationships as based on love.

Relationally, love can be defined as a strong or close attachment to another. The attachment can be a secure one in which the persons involved maintain independence at the same time that they have feelings of closeness or connectedness, or the attachment could be more anxious/ambivalent in which the persons involved desire to completely possess the other and/or be consumed by the other.

Finally, love is a construct that has many outward *behavioral* manifestations in which the failure to act in socially prescribed ways can indicate and create a condition of a lack of love (regardless of emotions, cognitions, or relationship conditions). For example, men sometimes believe they are showing their love for their wives by washing the car or keeping up the yard (not entirely unlike the knight of old who slew dragons for his damsel in distress). Is this *really* love? There is no answer to this question. What is important is how the other person interprets those behaviors.

As a social construction, the meaning of love has changed over time and across cultural contexts.[12] For the early Greeks, love could take several forms, two of which—*eros* and *agape*—were most significant. **Eros** captured the physical/emotional dimension tied to sexuality, whereas **agape** captured the spiritual/cognitive

---

[10]For a discussion of love as a primary emotion, see Theorore D. Kemper, "How Many Emotions Are There? Wedding the Social and the Autonomic Components," *American Journal of Sociology* (1987): 263–289. For a theory of love as a secondary emotion, see Steven Schachter, "The Interaction of Cognitive and Physiological Determinants of Emotional State," in L. Berkowitz, *Advances in Experimental Social Psychology*, Volume 1 (New York: Academic Press, 1964), 49–80.

[11]Bernard Murstein, *Love, Sex, and Marriage through the Ages* (New York: Springer Publishing Company, 1974).

[12]Ibid.

relationship dimension of rationality, intellectualism, and selfless duty to the other. These two dimensions were seen as exclusive of each other and limited to women and men, respectively.

In contrast, later Roman society saw love as more of a game (**amor ludens**) in which both men and women participated. Like the early Greeks, love was not tied to marriage between a man and a woman. Instead, it was seen as a basis for relationships outside the context of marriage. In stark contrast to the Roman concept of love, early Christian societies thought of love in a purely spiritual sense, with love between humans being an outward expression of love for God. Like the early Greeks and Romans, however, these societies also did not link love to marriage. The focus here was on community and love for neighbors (friend or foe).

The dawn of modernity saw yet another transformation of our concept of love. The Renaissance concept of **courtly love** was a complex multidimensional construct consisting of emotional, cognitive, and behavioral components. This was a concept carefully scripted through writings and other cultural forms. In many ways, it was the origin of our modern ideas about **romantic love** as something we can feel for anyone regardless of class or other social boundaries, as a powerful force in transforming our lives and overcoming obstacles, as an exclusive relationship that cannot exist with competition from other relationships, as an obsessive state of cognition, as possessive, and as a source of intense emotional feelings such as jealousy. Although love could exist within the context of marriage, it was neither restricted nor essential to it. It was only in the midmodern period of Victorian England that we see a clear linking of love and marriage.

What is love today? As Cancian points out, love has increasingly become an emotional experience tied to women.[13] She shows through an analysis of cultural expressions that love became increasingly *feminized* during the twentieth century, with women becoming more and more responsible for creating and maintaining love relationships, although Cancian believes that we are moving toward a more egalitarian state of what she calls **androgynous love**. Giddens notes a similar transformation in the modern cultural concept of love, although he focuses on the rational transformation of love relationships to relationships of greater equality (what he calls **confluent love**).[14]

From a more psychological perspective, we analyze relationships and make distinctions between **passionate love** (characterized by high levels of emotional intensity) and **companionate love** (characterized by more secure and trusting attachments). Although the former is important, relationships cannot sustain themselves for long in modern society without the development of the latter.[15] In addition to this distinction, others have also been offered; most notably, Lee's typology of six types of love based on historical conceptions and Steinberg's nine types based on the triangle dimensions of intimacy, passion, and commitment.[16]

[13]Francesca Cancian, *Love in America: Gender and Self-Development* (Cambridge, United Kingdom: Cambridge University Press, 1987).

[14]Anthony Giddens, *The Transformation of Intimacy: Sexuality, Love and Eroticism in Modern Societies* (Cambridge, United Kingdom: Polity Press, 1992).

[15]Ellen Bersheid and Elaine Walster, *Interpersonal Attraction* (Reading, MA: Addison-Wesley, 1969).

[16]John A. Lee, "Love-styles," in Robert J. Sternberg & Michael L. Barnes, *The Psychology of Love* (New Haven, CT: Yale University Press, 1988), 38–67; Robert J. Sternberg, "A Triangular Theory of Love," *Psychological Review* 93 (1986): 119–135.

CROSS-CULTURAL *Perspective*

Love and Emancipation in Vietnam

Not only have the meanings of love and its linkage to marriage changed over the centuries, but cultural discourses on love have also changed over shorter periods of time. One recent example is provided in an analysis of literature and official historical writings in Vietnam during the twentieth century by Harriet Phinney.

Prior to colonization by the French, Vietnam was a collectivistic and patriarchal society based on Confucianism where marriages were arranged for instrumental reasons, family concerns had greatest priority, and couples were expected to find intimacy and companionship only after they were married. With French colonization, romantic love ideals were introduced that cast the "old ways" as feudal and constraining on individual freedom and expression—especially the freedoms of women. These ideals were an essential element of two groups of writers in the early 1930s—the *Tho Moi* poets and the *Tu Luc Van Doan* (the Self Reliance Literature Group). The dominant themes expressed in the works of these writers involved a concern with the development of the self through exploration of feelings and a rejection of ideas linked to the Confucian ideal. The source of these new ideas about love, however, were linked to the cultural influences of the French colonists. As such, they became tied to "the colonial policy of 'racial diarchy'" (335) and reacted to and transformed by the Marxist revolutionaries rising to power at the time.

Thus, the rise of Marxist communism marks a second turning point in the cultural meanings of love in Vietnam. These revolutionaries sought to enhance the freedoms of individuals from traditional ways. They also sought to free the country from the evils of French colonialism and capitalism. Therefore, they actively sought to shape cultural expressions of love in a way that reinforced individual dedication to the new communist state. They did this by emphasizing the freedoms from traditional family and patriarchal constraints, but shifted the object of individual expressions of love from another individual to the state. During this time, individual expressions of love where presented as motivated by a desire to improve the conditions of the nation by contributing to the revolutionary movement. Women in particular were targeted as love was tied to motherhood—a motherhood of the state—and conjugal love was made possible by mutual love for the state. These ideals were formalized in the 1959 Law on Marriage and the Family, which legislated voluntary marriage, gender equality in marriage, and freedom from the interference of the extended family.

The third phase in this developing discourse occurred as a result of the failures of the socialist economic model and the economic reform movements of the 1980s (the *Doi Moi*). The key to this reform was a shift from "collective land use to a household economy based on the land rights of individuals and families" (346). As a result, the Law on Marriage and the Family was modified to increase the emphasis on strong marriages and strong parent-child bonds. State motherhood was replaced by biological motherhood and this tie became essential to family life. As Phinney concludes: "This contemporary configuration, despite its beneficent and progressive nature, ironically reduces female subjectivity by defining it is terms of maternal identity. Yet, at the same time, the *Doi Moi* discourse on maternal love retrieves a sense of individuality and self-expression inherent in the prerevolutionary discourses on romantic love and the romantic longings of post-revolutionary fiction...." (351).

Sources: Harriet M. Phinney, "Objects of Affection: Vietnamese Discourses on Love and Emancipation," *Positions* 16 (Fall 2008): 329–358.

Finally, Patricia Noller writes of the love that supports marriage and family. She reviews the literature that explores the emotional, cognitive, and behavioral aspects of both mature and immature love. In her words,

Given the evidence that love is socially constructed, however, and that love relationships occur in a social and cultural context, the cognitive aspect of love may be the most important determinant of the love experienced by those in love relationships. It seems that the emotional and behavioral aspects of love are both strongly affected by the ideas about love that have been accepted by the individuals concerned.[17]

In the context of partner selection, love has different meanings in arranged marriages than when the choice is made by the persons themselves. It is socially constructed.

*I*ndividualistic Factors in Partner Selection

With a decrease in kinship control over mate selection, particularly in Western societies, has come a freedom that has brought about an enormously complex process. This process clearly begins long before the first date. And for many, the selection process never ends, since, in the United States, it is possible to have more than one marriage partner (although legally, only one at a time). Most psychological and other individualistic theories explaining the choice of mate are based on a wide range of experiences, along with a variety of subconscious drives and needs.

Instinctive and Biological Theories

One of the oldest and perhaps most radical explanations of partner selection suggests that what guides a man to a woman (and vice versa) is instinct. Instinct is established by heredity and deals with unlearned behavior. Some sociologists would argue there is no such thing as human instinct, but many biologists and psychologists would counter that instinct is basic to human behavior.

As far as is known, no one has ever discovered any instinctive, unconscious, or purely biological determinant for mate selection. Evolutionary biologists have claimed, however, that biological predispositions do exist that channel our choices in a certain direction.[18] Of course, the fact that such predispositions are unconscious or innate makes them difficult to discover. In short, to attribute the selection of a mate to instinct, the unconscious, or even predispositions adds little more to understanding basic processes involved in mate choice than does attributing it to fate, spirits, or supernatural powers (sources, by the way, that some people acknowledge).

Parental Image Theory

Closely related to the instinct theory is the psychoanalytic idea of Sigmund Freud and his followers, which suggests that a person tends to fall in love with and marry a person similar to his or her opposite-sex parent. This, too, is generally a theory rooted in the unconscious.

According to the **Oedipus complex,** early in a male child's life, his mother becomes his first love object. But the presence of his father prohibits him from fulfilling his incestuous desire. As a result, the male infant develops an antagonism

---

[17]Patricia Noller, "What Is This Thing Called Love? Defining the Love That Supports Marriage and Family," *Personal Relationships* 3 (1996): 111–112.

[18]David M. Buss, *The Evolution of Desire: Strategies of Human Mating* (New York: Basic Books, 1994); and Mary Batten, *Sexual Strategies: How Females Choose Their Mates* (New York: G.P. Putnam's Sons, 1994).

toward his father for taking his love object from him. This, in turn, results in an unconscious desire to kill his father and marry his mother. The male infant's desire for his mother and fear of his father become so great that he develops a fear of castration, or, as Freud called it, *castration anxiety*—a fear that his father wants to emasculate him by removing his penis and testes. But since the father is also protective and helpful and respected by the mother, a great amount of ambivalence exists for the son, which is resolved only by a primary type of identification with his father. The Oedipus complex is, thus, temporarily resolved for the male, but the repressed love for his mother remains. By adolescence, when the male is free to fall in love, he selects a love object that possesses the qualities of his mother.

The opposite but parallel result occurs for the female. At an early age, the girl becomes aware that she does not have a male sexual organ and develops *penis envy*. Feeling castrated, her feelings are transformed into the desire to possess a penis, especially the father's. These feelings for the forbidden object remain repressed throughout childhood, but her love for her father, known as the **Electra complex**, culminates in marriage when she selects a mate with the qualities of her father. (Both the Oedipus complex and the Electra complex are discussed more fully in Chapter 11.)

Although it seems reasonable to believe that young people, in selecting partners, would be keenly aware of the qualities of their parents and the nature of their marriage, no clear evidence has supported the hypothesis that the boy seeks someone like his mother or that the girl seeks someone like her father. Even if such evidence did exist, this same hypothesis could be derived from other theories.

Complementary Needs Theory

The **complementary needs theory** of mate selection was developed and enhanced by Robert F. Winch about fifty years ago.[19] It was his belief that, although mate selection is homogamous with respect to numerous social characteristics—age, race/ethnicity, religion, residential propinquity, socioeconomic status, education, and previous marital status—when it comes to psychic level and individual motivation, mate selection tends to be complementary rather than homogamous. The idea grew out of a modified and simplified version of a need-scheme theory of motivation, but the needs tend to be complementary rather than similar.

For mate selection to take place on the basis of love—that is, due to complementary needs—it is understood that both man and woman must have some choice in the matter. The theory would not be operative in settings in which marriages are arranged (as by parents, marriage brokers, or others). Thus, love will likely be an important criterion only under cultural conditions in which (1) the choice of mates is voluntary, (2) the culture encourages premarital interaction between men and women, and (3) the marital friendship is culturally defined as a rich potential source of gratification. Because love is defined in terms of needs, the general hypothesis is that when people marry for love, their needs will be complementary.

---

[19]Robert F. Winch, Thomas Ktsanes, and Virginia Ktsanes, "The Theory of Complementary Needs in Mate Selection: An Analytic and Descriptive Study," *American Sociological Review* 19 (June 1954): 241–249; Robert F. Winch, "The Theory of Complementary Needs in Mate Selection: A Test of One Kind of Complementariness," *American Sociological Review* 20 (February 1955): 52–56; and Robert F. Winch, "The Theory of Complementary Needs in Mate Selection: Final Results on the Test of the General Hypothesis," *American Sociological Review* 20 (October 1955): 552–555.

Reports by Winch and his colleagues led to a constant flow of articles attempting to retest the complementary needs hypothesis. The results were basically negative, failing to provide empirical support for the idea that people tend to choose mates whose needs complement their own.

Various interpretations have been presented to explain why the complementary needs theory refutes popular opinion and fails to gain research support. Perhaps there are problems in the measurement of needs. Perhaps the basic theoretical considerations of the complementary needs theory are incorrect. Perhaps, like findings of endogamous factors presented in the previous chapter, needs also are more homogamous than heterogamous, more similar than different. Perhaps "likes do marry likes" rather than "opposites attract."

Any or all of these reasons may be correct. It is clear that relatively little empirical support exists for the theory of complementary needs, as originally formulated. In fact, most of the research that has attempted to explain mate selection on the basis of personality traits—whether similar, different, complementary, or some combination thereof—seems to have bogged down into a morass of conflicting results. Most findings have suggested the probable futility of further pursuits of personality matching. Perhaps instincts, drives, needs, complexes (including Oedipus ones), and personality traits all fail to find empirical support because they are based within persons rather than resulting from interactions. The cultural contexts and social situations in which these needs, drives, and traits are expressed are not considered.

*I*nteractional Processes in Partner Selection

Age, class, religion, and race/ethnicity are sociocultural factors that influence intimate partner selection. These variables indicate subgroup membership in society, subgroups that not only apply social pressures (through endogamy and exogamy norms), but also shape socialization experiences that determine social values and learned scripts (role expectations) for the desired behaviors of self and other in both nonmarital and marital relationships and determine what resources are available for use in exchange with others in forming and developing relationships. Thus, it is important to consider the ways that values, roles, and resources play a role in the interactional process through which relationships form and develop.

Value Theory

A **value theory** of mate selection suggests that interpersonal attraction is facilitated when persons share or perceive themselves as sharing similar value orientations. Values define what is good, beautiful, moral, or worthwhile. They are the criteria or conceptions used in evaluating things (including objects, ideas, acts, feelings, and events) as to their goodness, desirability, or merit. Values are not concrete goals of action but criteria by which goals are chosen.

A value theory of mate selection suggests that when persons share similar values, this in effect validates each person, thus promoting emotional satisfaction and enhancing the means of communication. When a value is directly attacked or is ignored under circumstances that normally call it to one's attention, those who hold the value are resentful. Because of this emotional aspect, it seems reasonable to expect that persons will seek informal social relations with others who uncritically accept their basic values and, thus, provide emotional security. Such compatible

Common values make interactions easier to sustain, create a sense of rapport, increase the perceived profitability of relationships, and encourage higher levels of personal disclosure in communication. These effects can lead to the development of long-term relationships.

companions are most likely those who feel the same way (share values) about things they feel are of major importance—be it smoking, abortion, the use of stem cells for research, pacifism, or whatever. This accounts for the tendency to marry homogamously and explains why friendships (*homophily*) and marriages involve people with similar social backgrounds.

The inverse is equally true. Persons from different backgrounds learn different values; interactions among such persons are less rewarding and will likely result in feelings of tension and dissatisfaction and little desire to continue the relationship. Suppose, for example, a woman places a high value on heterosexual dating, marriage, and sexual activity. Would she accept as a dating or marriage partner someone known to have engaged in homosexual activities? Value theory suggests (predicts) that she would not, and research has strongly supported this very example.[20]

Which values do people believe are important in selecting a marriage partner? Have these values changed and do they differ from one area of the country to another? A study was conducted in different time periods ranging from 1939 to 1996 in four different regions of the United States (and one Canadian sample) to assess the values students hold important in mate preferences.[21] Some key values included a dependent character, emotional stability and maturity, a desire for home and children, chastity, physical attractiveness, financial resources, education and intelligence, good homemaker, mutual attraction and love, and others.

One of the striking changes over time was the value both sexes placed on chastity. The cultural value attached to virginity declined between 1939 and 1977 but leveled off, or in Texas actually increased, since then. Physical attractiveness showed a steady climb for both sexes, a value reflected in actual behavior based on the tremendous growth in cosmetics, diet, and the cosmetic surgery industries. Both sexes, but especially men, showed a trend in the increasing importance of financial resources. Across the decades, men showed a curvilinear relationship in the importance they attach to mates who are good cooks and housekeepers, dropping between 1939 and 1967 and then increasing while women showed no change over time. Mutual attraction and love held first place in the most recent assessments, showing a steady increase over time for both sexes. For college students, marriage may be evolving to a more companionate form from a more institutional one.

[20]John D. Williams and Arthur P. Jacoby, "The Effects of Premarital Heterosexual and Homosexual Experience on Dating and Marriage Desirability," *Journal of Marriage and the Family* 51 (May 1989): 489–497.

[21]David M. Buss, Todd K. Shackelford, Lee A. Kirkpatrick, and Randy J. Larsen, "A Half Century of Mate Preferences: The Cultural Evolution of Values," *Journal of Marriage and Family* 63 (May 2001): 491–503.

Role Theory

Role theory, like value theory, appears to be conceptually more justifiable as an overall explanation of marital choice than any of the previous individualistic explanations. All social humans—or, more specifically, all marriageable persons—have expectations regarding their own behavior and also that of their respective partners. One perception of *role* (as described in the first chapter) refers to a set of social expectations appropriate to a given status: husband, wife, male, female, single, and the like. These expectations, implicit or explicit, have been internalized and serve to direct and influence personal behavior as well as the behavior desired in a prospective marriage partner. Basically, people tend to desire (internalize) the roles defined by the society, subculture, and family in which they live.

Roles and personality needs differ in a very important respect. With roles, the focus of attention is on behaviors and attitudes appropriate to situations, regardless of the individual, whereas with personality needs, the focus is on behaviors and attitudes characteristic of the individual, regardless of the situation. The difference is crucial. Roles focus on definitions, meanings, and social expectations. In regard to mate selection, individuals select one another on the basis of role consensus (agreement) or on the basis of courtship, marital, and family shared expectations as to their relationship and future activities.

Role consensus, widely used as an indicator of marital success or adjustment, has been applied relatively infrequently to partner selection. However, similar processes in partner selection are likely operative prior to marriage as they also are during marriage. When role discrepancies exist, marriage is unlikely to occur in the first place. Would a man who expects a wife to care for children, cook meals, and clean the house marry a woman who despises these activities? Or reciprocally, would this woman want to marry this man if that is what he expects?

In brief, the couple likely to marry is the male and female who share similar role definitions and expectations. This assumes, of course, that other forces—such as an existing marriage, age, parents, money, schooling, or other sociocultural factors—do not hinder or prevent it.

Exchange Theory

Exchange theory, as described in Chapter 3 and as mentioned in several instances in the current and previous chapters, involves the idea that some type of exchange is basic to the mate-selection process. Whether it is an exchange of athletic prowess for beauty or an exchange of sex for money, the central idea is that some type of transaction or bargaining is involved in the selection of an intimate partner.

Prior to 1940, a major contribution of Willard Waller's treatise on the family was his analysis of courtship conduct as bargaining and/or exploiting behavior. In his words, "When one marries he makes a number of different bargains. Everyone knows this and this knowledge affects the sentiment of love and the process of falling in love."[22]

Today it is doubtful that only he makes bargains or that "everyone knows this." But it is well established that bargaining or some type of social exchange takes place in partner selection and affects the process of falling in love. The difference between *bargaining* and *exchange* is that bargaining implies a certain purposive awareness of

---

[22]Willard Waller, *The Family: A Dynamic Interpretation* (New York: Cordon, 1938), 239.

the exchange of awards. Bargaining entails knowing what one has to offer and what the other person can get, whereas in a simple exchange, this awareness is not always readily apparent. What is apparent is that few people get something for nothing; partner selection is a process of social exchange.

Exchange theorists argue that the behavior of socialized persons is purposive, or goal oriented, and not random. Implicitly, this indicates that people repeat behaviors that are rewarded and avoid those that go unrewarded. Also, each party in a transaction will attempt to maximize gains and minimize costs. Over the long run, however, in view of the principle of reciprocity, actual exchanges tend to become equalized. If reciprocity does not exist—that is, nothing is given in return—the relationship will likely terminate. A key factor in exchange theory that may deter or delay termination of an inequitable exchange is the lack of an alternative to the current relationship. But if an alternative to the current relationship is perceived as superior to the present relationship, one of the partners will terminate the present relationship in favor of pursuing the more attractive alternative.

There are perhaps few areas in which social exchange appears more evident than in research on dating and partner selection. In dating, for example, the male may consider sexual intercourse as a desired goal and a highly valued reward. To achieve this reward, he may have to offer in exchange flattery ("My, how beautiful you look tonight"), commitment ("You are the only one I love"), goods ("I thought you might enjoy these flowers"), and services ("Let me get you a drink").

The social exchange approach to partner selection neither explains how interaction arises nor describes the larger social environment. Rather, it seeks to explain why certain behavioral outcomes take place.

Sequential Theories

Up to this point, it should be evident that, although single factors have been stressed as significant in the process of selecting an intimate partner, most explanations take into account factors implied in other explanations. Several writers have consciously and intentionally combined or placed in sequence selected single factors: roles, values, needs, exchanges, and the like. An example of this is seen in the stimulus-value-role (SVR) idea of Bernard Murstein.[23]

SVR theory holds that, in a relatively free-choice situation as exists in the United States, most couples pass through three stages before deciding to marry. In the *stimulus* stage, individuals may be drawn to one another based on the perception of qualities that might be attractive to the other person (physical attributes, voice, dress, reputation, social standing). Because initial movement is due primarily to noninteractional cues not dependent on interpersonal interaction, these are categorized as stimulus criteria.

If mutual stimulus attraction occurs between a man and a woman and they are both satisfied, they enter the second stage of *value comparison*. This stage involves the appraisal of value compatibility through verbal interaction. The couple may compare their attitudes toward life, politics, religion, abortion, nuclear energy, or the roles of men and women in society and in marriage. If, as they discuss these and other areas, they find that they have very similar value orientations, their feelings for one another are likely to develop.

---

[23]Bernard I. Murstein, "A Clarification and Extension of the SVR Theory of Dyadic Pairing," *Journal of Marriage and the Family* 49 (November 1987): 929–933.

The *role* stage requires the fulfillment of many tasks before the couple is ready to move into marriage. It is not enough to have similar values if each partner is dissatisfied with how the other is perceived in such roles as lover, companion, parent, and housekeeper. The partners must increasingly confide in each other and become more aware of each other's behavior. They must measure their own personal inadequacies and those of their partner. If the partners navigate the three stages successfully, they are likely to become a permanent pair (marry or cohabit), subject to such influences as parents, friends, job transfers, competition from more attractive partners, and so forth.

Numerous other sequential theories exist. However, all **sequential theories** of relationship development or partner selection tend to view the movement toward marriage or cohabitation as a series of changing criteria, stages, or patterned regularities. However, the progression to marriage may not be quite so orderly or simplistic. Many alternative pathways may exist that involve other partners, may involve getting into and out of a relationship with the same partner several times, or may involve factors totally separate from the personal and interactional exchanges generally involved in relationship developmental processes. Factors external to the person or couple (such as family/kin influences, socioeconomic conditions, community heterogeneity, and technological changes) are likely, from a sociological perspective at least, to be important factors or dimensions in understanding the process of changing one's status from single to married.

*P*remarital/Nonmarital Relationship Dynamics

In the United States, the partner-selection process, particularly for first marriages, is highly youth centered and competitive. It encompasses a wide range of social relationships prior to marriage, involving increasing degrees of commitment. Writers have used different terminology to describe this process, but generally it entails a series of stages that may include group activities, casual dating, hanging out, hooking up, being engaged, cohabiting, or some other type of classification indicating a more binding relationship or even a marriage commitment. The flexibility of the process provides that it can be followed once or many times prior to marriage, covering a timespan of days to years and including or omitting one or several stages.

One way of looking at this process is to compare it to a game, which has rules, goals, strategies, and counterstrategies.[24] The parameters of the game are determined by the culture and are likely to reflect functional role relationships in the society as well as structures of power, especially to the extent that they are organized around distinctions of gender. Even though playing the game is voluntary, it is probably more difficult to avoid playing than to play because the script provides at least initial guidelines that make behaviors predictable and thereby make interaction possible and more rewarding. In elementary school (or before), parents inquire about boyfriends or girlfriends. As children mature, parents, peers, and an internalized self-concept all encourage getting involved. The goals of the game may range from simple enjoyment to the seeking of affection and group approval or to finding a permanent partner.

---

[24]This idea is an expansion of Waller and Hill's "courtship bargains" and "courtship barter." See Willard Waller (revised by Reuben Hill), *The Family: A Dynamic Interpretation* (New York: Holt, Rinehart and Winston, 1951), 160–164.

Functional role positions and power differences between men and women in society have led to a double standard in the game played by heterosexual couples, in which females play by a different set of rules and set different goals than males. Traditionally at least, the social norm for the male in the United States implied that his basic goal in this game was to move the relationship toward sexual intimacy. Even before the first meeting or date, the key question was, Will she or won't she? The extent to which direct or rapid approaches were used to answer the question depended on a wide range of social and interpersonal factors: previous marriage, age, social class, income, religion, beauty, and friends. Factors of social exchange were also relevant: what he had to offer relative to what he wanted.

The traditional social norm for the female in the United States implied that her basic goal in the game was to move the relationship toward commitment. Even before the first date, key questions were, Will he ask me out again? or Is he a potential husband? To get the commitment, the female had the responsibility to regulate the progression of the intimacy goal of the male. To get intimacy (sex is a more accurate term, at this point), the male had to convince the female that she was not like all other women but was different, unique, and special.

These two norms worked reciprocally. Progress toward one called for progress toward the other. As commitment increased, intimacy increased and vice versa. Much of the communication in this game was likely to be in the form of nonverbal cues, signs, gestures, and other symbolic movements.

Suppose the rules were not followed: The male made no move toward intimacy or the female made no move to halt the intimacy or to get a commitment. The female, after one date, may have said to herself or others, What a nice guy; he really is a gentleman, or the like. Suppose after two, four, or eight dates, the male still made no move toward intimacy. Now the female was likely to ask questions such as, What's wrong with him? or What's wrong with me? Suppose the female made no move to stop or slow down the intimacy moves of the male, or suppose she made the initial move. The game may have continued but under a new set of less traditional rules and conditions.

What about today? Do these intimacy/commitment norms continue to exist? Let us begin by reviewing the "hooking up" and dating scene.

Hooking Up and Dating

Data from a nationally representative sample of a thousand college women and in-depth interviews with sixty-two women on college campuses suggest that "hooking up" is widespread. In contrast, dating, at least in a traditional sense, was infrequent.[25] **Hooking up** in this study referred to sex without commitment or even without affection. Often, hooking up occurred between persons who did not know one another very well and who had few expectations that the relationship would continue. A frequent feature of hooking up was that it occurred when both participants were drinking or drunk. The behaviors ranged from kissing to having sexual intercourse. Forty percent of these college women said they experienced a hookup and 10 percent said they did so more than six times.

[25]Norval Glenn and Elizabeth Marquardt, *Hooking up, Hanging out, and Hoping for Mr. Right: College Women on Dating and Mating Today* (New York: Institute for American Values, 2001).

Dating to these students carried various meanings. To most, it meant just "hanging out" with several guys such as going to a movie together or studying at the library. These activities were loosely organized and interest in one another was not made explicit. To others, it meant boyfriend–girlfriend relationships in which the persons agree they will not see other people. About half of the women in the national survey said they currently had a boyfriend but many of these did not "date" in the traditional sense. To another group, dating followed the traditional norm: Male invites female to go out, picks her up, and pays the bills. And even this type of dating was often related to a special occasion such as a fraternity–sorority event.

Even separate from the college scene, it appears that the traditional type of date may be a dying or dead event. Today, dating more likely involves students or young people "hanging out," congregating in groups, evolving into pairs while retaining allegiance to the group, sharing food or entertainment expenses, and engaging in less structured and less predetermined behaviors.

One consequence of changing partner-selection norms as well as the older age at marriage has been the emergence of new forms of partner connections other than hooking up, hanging out, or dating in the traditional sense. These include chat lines on the Internet and other types of computer-mediated romantic relationships, videotape selections, singles clubs, newspaper advertisements, and other informal opportunities for coming in contact or actually meeting.[26]

What are these people looking for in romantic partners? An analysis of published personals advertisements yielded various results.[27] Men, more than women, tended to focus on physical appearance or attractiveness, more casual relationships, and youth. Women, more than men, tended to focus on financial security, success, and longer-term relationships.

The fact that partner-selection preferences vary by sex, age, or marital status does not mean that some aspects of dating don't remain very similar. Laner and Ventrone found, as did other studies, that adults' scripts for dating maintain the traditional dominant–subordinate relationship between the sexes.[28] Despite claims to egalitarian attitudes and beliefs, dating interactions begin and appear to continue in a clearly nonegalitarian mode. When dating does take place, the man's control of the situation persists. He is more likely to pick her up, decide where to go, open the doors, and pay the bills. She is more likely to take extra preparation time, wait for the date to arrive, be the recipient of affectionate or sexual moves, and talk with friends about the date.

The reasons for hanging out or dating and the relationship goals desired influence the type of behaviors that will take place. In other words, it could be expected that persons who date for fun, something to do, status (being seen with the "right" person), or even hooking up would behave differently than those who date for reasons of

---

[26]Note, for example, Aaron C. Ahuvia and Mara B. Adelman, "Formal Intermediaries in the Marriage Market: A Typology and Review," *Journal of Marriage and the Family* 54 (May 1992): 452–463; and Erich R. Merkle and Rhonda A. Richardson, "Digital Dating and Virtual Relating: Conceptualizing Computer Mediated Romantic Relationships," *Family Relations* 49 (April 2000): 187–192.

[27]I.A. Greenlees and W.C. McGrew, "Sex and Age Differences in Preferences and Tactics of Mate Attraction: Analysis of Published Advertisements," *Ethnology and Sociobiology* 15 (1994): 59–72; and Frank N. Willis and Roger A. Carlson, "Singles Ads: Gender, Social Class, and Time," *Sex Roles* 29 (1993): 387–404.

[28]Mary Riege Laner and Nicole A. Ventrone, "Egalitarian Daters/Traditional Dates," *Journal of Family Issues* 19 (July 1998): 468–477.

TRANSNATIONAL FAMILIES

Outsourcing Family Formation through Planet-Love.com

The practice of "mail ordering" brides has been occurring for more than 200 years in the United States, but has increased in recent years due to the forces of economic globalization, increasing economic discrepancies between rich and poor nations, and the emergence and ubiquity of the internet. The U.S. Immigration and Naturalization Service (INS) estimated that in 1998, the number of marriages occurring to U.S. citizens as a result of the mail order bride business was between 4,000 and 6,000. Although this is a small proportion of all marriages, the high rates of violence, abuse and exploitation that takes place in these marriages make them of particular concern.

Previously, most mail order brides came from countries in Eastern Europe, Russia and Southeast Asia and tended to be of working class origins. As noted by Felicity Schaeffer-Grabiel, however, the growth of the Internet has significantly altered the complexion of the transnational market place for brides. In particular, recent decades have seen an increase in middle class and professional women from Latin America participating via more interactive websites, chat rooms, and "Vacation Romance" tours.

In a study involving the content analysis of websites and guidebooks, participant observations in chat rooms, and interviews with 40 men at Vacation Romance tours, Schaeffer-Grabiel shows how the international marketplace is being transformed in a way that makes questions about the "deviant" and exploitive nature of the mail order bride business more complex. Of particular note is her observation that men who participate in this marketplace do so as a way of preserving their "masculinity" as well as what they see is the integrity of the American family—both of which are seen as threatened by the advance of feminism and the feminization of manhood.

These men as well as the websites themselves express sentiments for a return to traditional "authentic" gender roles. They see this return as essential to preserving the American family. As Schaeffer-Grabiel puts it: "[These] men imagine themselves as the benevolent engineers who racially uplift the moral fabric of the national family by importing a superior *breed* of women" (337, emphasis added). Furthermore, they couch their motivations "in romantic ethics of chivalry and the saving of women" (338). They also expressed concerns about the authenticity of their identity in the modern world of U.S. society and the potential for women from more exotic locales to help produce that authenticity: "...women from developing nations embody the frontier of the future; their bodies and the products they represent promise spiritual vitality, a connectedness to nature, and access to a new, rejuvenated self" (339).

Given their more traditional upbringing and the lack of desirable partners in their own countries, middle-class and professional Latin American women willingly participate in this international exchange as they see the potential for profitability in forming marriages with the men on these sites. When they form such marriages, however, they find that in many cases the technological fantasies that attracted their new partner to seek them out on the Internet as sources of "authenticity" are themselves what was sought. As a result, they feel rejected, in spite of their more "passionate nature," in a relationship with someone whose individualistic and self-absorbed nature led them into this unique marketplace to begin with.

Sources: U.S. Citizenship and Immigration Services, Reports and Studies, "International Matchmaking Organizations: A Report to Congress" (February 1999); and Felicity Schaeffer-Grabiel, "Planet-Love.com: Cyberbrides in the Americas and the Transnational Routes of U.S. Masculinity," *Signs* 31 (2005): 331–356.

marriage or the selection of an exclusive partner. For example, emotional involvement, sexual intimacy, exclusivity of the relationship, paying patterns, and discussions of future plans will likely differ depending on the motive for dating. It follows that the person who is more emotionally involved and more committed to the relationship will likely be hurt more if the relationship ends. Finally, it will be likely that the person with the lower status or prestige will have less say (power) in what interactions and activities occur.

This idea parallels that of Waller more than sixty years ago in what he termed the *principle of least interest*.[29] He observed that seldom are both persons in a dating relationship equally interested in continuing the relationship. In cases in which both parties are not equally emotionally involved, if dating terminates it will be more traumatic for one person than for the other. Essentially, the **principle of least interest** says that the person who is less interested in continuing the dating relationship is in a position to dominate and possibly exploit the other party. Conversely, the person more interested is in a position to be dominated and used. Felmlee, for example, found research support for the idea that individuals who were less invested emotionally had more say (power) in their romantic relationships.[30]

Traditional norms have given men more power to dominate women. But when either individual rejects these traditional norms, the principle may suggest that inequality is a key factor involved in the breakup of relationships. If an imbalance or unequal interest exists, it may be difficult to continue and further develop the relationship. Consistent with exchange theory, when there is no perception of equity between what one receives relative to what one gives, the relationship is likely to end or result in a power imbalance where one person can dominate the other. (This principle, by the way, may apply not only to dating interactions but to friendships and marriages as well.)

In the process of selecting a romantic partner or mate, most people make the move from an uncommitted relationship to a relationship that involves some commitment to one another to the exclusion of others. These relationships may involve what is known as going steady or "my" girlfriend or boyfriend, implying an exclusive type of romantic or love attachment. For many, it leads to a formal engagement and/or to cohabitation.

Engagement

Engagement, in some form, has existed in almost every society in the world. Because marriage is seldom taken lightly, most societies have provided some social structure to instill an awareness in the couple and the community that the relationship is a serious one and that marriage will likely occur. In many societies, engagement is considered extremely important and much more binding than it is in the Western world today. Because engagement implies the final transition in the process of changing status from single to married and involves a transfer from dating availability to dating exclusiveness, various rituals are conducted and gifts are given to reinforce publicly and privately the importance of the relationship.

In the United States and in many other countries, an engagement ring serves the purpose of enabling the female to publicly and continuously display her symbol of commitment.

Engagement, with its accompanying ring, signifies to the female and to the public a commitment on the part of the male and a likely future wedding. The female indicates her commitment by accepting the ring but seldom gives one in return.

---

[29]Waller, *The Family*, 275.

[30]Diane H. Felmlee, "Who's on Top? Power in Romantic Relationships," *Sex Roles* 31 (1994): 275–295.

The ring, which involves a financial commitment on the part of the male (and sometimes on the part of the female), symbolizes the seriousness of the relationship and the intent of a forthcoming marriage. (To provide equality between the sexes, perhaps the time is near when the male will expect an engagement ring as well.)

Engagement, with or without a ring, provides the function of making the couple's plans public. In colonial days, the announcement was accomplished by the posting of **banns**. A number of days or weeks prior to the marriage, a public notice of intent to marry would be published, posted at key locations in the community, and announced in the churches. In the smaller folk-like, or gemeinschaft-like communities, characterized by a sense of solidarity and a common identity, the word traveled quickly and the community served as a key force in the binding of the relationship. In modern urbanized societies, formal newspaper announcements are one way to publicize the marriage or marriage plans of the couple. Many community newspapers publish a picture of the couple, of the bride-to-be, or of the bride herself.

Engagement serves many other purposes or functions for both the couple and society. For the couple, it provides a clear indication that marriage is about to occur. Due to the exclusive nature of the relationship, personal and interpersonal testing can continue with less threat from competitive forces. A more thorough awareness of value consensus or dissensus, marital-role expectations, and future aspirations can be examined. Of course, the fact that the traditional practice involves the female partner wearing the ring provided by the male suggests that gender-based power relations and conflicts may also be involved. Could the traditional script of a male giving an engagement ring to his fiancée and not the reverse symbolically represent and culturally reinforce the idea that men have more power in relationships, are expected to be "good providers" for their dependent female partners, and are establishing "ownership" over their partners who become their "property"? This is a difficult proposition to test empirically but one that conflict theorists would argue may nonetheless be valid and important as the practice of engagement may be a prologue to the more traditional gender roles that emerge later on in marriages and between new parents, even among couples with more egalitarian values and ideologies (see later chapters on marriage and parenthood).

In any case, engagement provides the final opportunity prior to the legal union for each person to understand himself or herself in relation to the other. It is likely that many couples view an engagement as a kind of trial marriage, including total sexual intimacy, the sharing of certain financial obligations, and, in many instances, living together, that is, in nonmarital cohabitation.

$\mathcal{N}$onmarital Cohabitation

Is it possible that selecting an intimate partner in the twenty-first century is not necessarily marriage oriented, is not limited to a single partner, is not always heterosexual, and does not stress permanence? Is it possible that a decrease in the sexual double standard will totally eliminate the male–female game described earlier? Is it possible that the premarital structures of dating, going steady, and engagement are significant only as historical phenomena? Or are the traditional mate-selection and marriage processes simply adapting and reconfiguring?

What some have argued has become an alternative to marriage and all would agree is an increasingly prevalent nonmarital arrangement is **nonmarital cohabitation,** also referred to as *living together, unmarried-couple households,* and *consensual* *unions.* This pattern is when two adults of the same or opposite sexes who are not married to each other, either by ceremony or by common law, occupy the same dwelling. The arrangement, among the young or the old, may or may not be marriage oriented; may be a long-range lifestyle or a short-term convenience; may or may not involve an intimate, unrestricted sexual union; may or may not include children; and may or may not be made known to parents by young people or perhaps to children by older people.

In order to understand these couples, a number of characteristics will be considered: their prevalence, how they differ from noncohabitants, consequences of their cohabitation, patterns among people who are elderly, and legal factors related to cohabitation.

Incidence and Prevalence of Cohabitation

To what extent are people in the United States living together in intimate heterosexual relationships without being married to one another? U.S. Census reports have provided some interesting data. The United States has witnessed a dramatic increase in the **prevalence** of cohabitation (in the number of unmarried heterosexual couples living together in a given year). In 2006, approximately 4.7 percent of all households were headed by cohabiting heterosexual couples and another 0.7 percent were headed by a member of a cohabiting same-sex couple.[31] Although only a small proportion of the total, this prevalence of heterosexual cohabitation also represented more than a 300 percent increase since 1980, and more than a 900 percent increase since 1970. As can be seen in Figure 7.2, this increase has been greatest for couples without children, but significant increases have also occurred for those with children under the age of 15. The prevalence of cohabitation was pretty much unchanged in the decades preceding 1970. In terms of **incidence** (the number of people in the population who have ever experienced a cohabiting union), the numbers are much more revealing of how common this practice is today. Using nationally representative data from the National Surveys of Family Growth, Kennedy and Bumpass estimate that the incidence of cohabitation among women between the ages of 19 and 44 increased from 45 percent in 1995 to 54 percent in 2002, and this substantial increase was seen in all age groups except for those between 19 and 24.[32] In terms of the percentage of all unions that were cohabitations rather than marriages, the numbers increased from 12 percent in 1995 to 15 percent in 2002. Finally, they estimated that 68 percent of all *first unions* formed between 1997 and 2001 were cohabiting unions rather than marriages and the incidence of cohabitation among those entering into marriages during this same period was 62 percent. Not surprisingly, these figures represent considerable increases in the incidence of cohabitation over the period from 1990 to 1994 when the corresponding percentages were 60 and 57 percent, respectively. Numbers for the incidence of cohabitation are much higher than those for the prevalence because

---

[31]U.S. Census Bureau, *The 2009 Statistical Abstract*, "Table 62—Unmarried-Partner Households by Sex of Partners: 2006." http://www.2010census.biz/compendia/statab/cats/population/households_families_group_quarters.html.

[32]Sheela Kennedy and Larry Bumpass, "Cohabitation and Children's Living Arrangements: New Estimates from the United States," *Demographic Research*, 19 (September 2008):1663–1692.

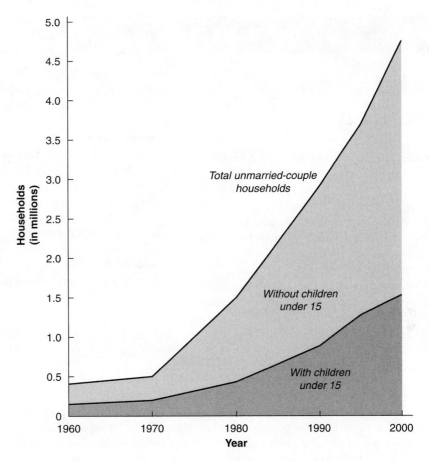

Figure 7.2

Unmarried-Couple
Households, by
Presence of Children
under 15 Years Old:
1960–2000

Source: U.S. Bureau of the
Census, Current Population
Reports, Series P20-537,
"America's Families and
Living Arrangements:
March 2000" (Washington,
DC: U.S. Government
Printing Office, 2000),
Table Uc3, p.1.

most cohabitations last two years or less before ending with either the dissolution of the relationship or the formalization of the relationship in marriage. Thus, at any given point, the percentage of couples currently in cohabitation will be low, but the percentage of individuals who have ever experienced cohabitation could be quite high.

Unmarried cohabitation is increasing not just in the United States but also in most Western nations (Sweden, Finland, Norway, Netherlands, France, Great Britain, Canada, and Australia). In Comparison to other OECD nations, the rate of cohabitation in the United States is relatively low compared to most of Western and Northern Europe and higher than most of Southern, Central, and Eastern Europe. Cohabitation in the United States in 2002 was considerably higher than in Japan.[33] In Sweden and Norway, nonmarital cohabitation is a civil status accepted by all and is an established institution.[34] In these two countries,

[33]Organization for Economic Co-operation and Development, OECD Family Database, "SF9: Cohabitation rate and prevalence of other forms of partnership." http://www.oecd.org/dataoecd/52/27/41920080.pdf.

[34]Natalie Rogoff Ramsoy, "Non-marital Cohabitation and Change in Norms: The Case of Norway," *Acta Sociologica* 36 (1994): 23–37.

CROSS-CULTURAL *Perspective*

Cohabitation in Sweden

Swedish partners are selected on the basis of love relationships with only minimal parental involvement in couple decision making; and an acceptable norm is to engage in nonmarital cohabitation. Nonmarital cohabitation is the lifestyle of couples who form consensual unions, or who live together but are not legally or officially married. In Sweden, these people are classified as living in "marriage-like relationships." It is estimated that, today, about one in four, or 25 percent, of Swedish couples live in this type of arrangement, and it is generally recognized that virtually all Swedes now cohabit before marriage. Trost notes that very few couples are against marriage and many view it as

something to come eventually. But marriage is not necessary for a couple to live together nor is it necessary for a "respectable" woman to have a child. For cohabitors, marriage is something they can switch over to whenever they want, if they ever do want.

Trost notes as well that increasing in incidence is the phenomenon of LAT (living apart together). This means that two persons constitute a couple under marriage-like conditions but they keep separate housing units. They may stay overnight for weekends or for other periods of time in either one's household. They see themselves as a married couple and might also be considered so by their social environment. He suggests that LAT will probably soon be regarded as a social institution.

See: Jan Trost, "Family Studies in Sweden," *Marriage and Family Review* 23 (1996): 723–743.

the concept of in or out of wedlock has lost most of its meaning for children because the government has taken steps to secure their future. Cohabiting couples have the same rights to subsidized housing as married couples. And homosexual unions have been granted the right to register their partnerships and celebrate them in civil ceremonies.

While cohabitation rates have been rising, marriage and remarriage rates have shown a corresponding decline over the last thirty years of the twentieth century. Larry Bumpass and others claimed that one trend offsets the other; that is, a decline in the marriage rate is offset by an increase in the cohabitation rate. The authors asserted that the increase in the proportion of unmarried young people should not be interpreted as an increase in singlehood, as traditionally regarded. Instead, young people are setting up housekeeping with partners at almost as early an age as they did before marriage rates declined. In this study, even though most cohabitants expected to marry, many disagreed about marriage. The picture that emerged was one of cohabitation as a family status but one in which levels of certainty about the relationship are lower than in marriage.[35]

Several factors may account for, or contribute to, this partial institutionalization of cohabitation. Perhaps the dramatic increase in the labor force participation of women provides a way to enjoy the benefits of couplehood without

---

[35]Larry L. Bumpass, James A. Sweet, and Andrew Cherlin, "The Role of Cohabitation in Declining Rates of Marriage," *Journal of Marriage and the Family* 53 (November 1991): 913–927; and Fjalar Finnas, "Entry into Consensual Unions and Marriages Among Finnish Women Born between 1938 and 1967," *Population Studies* 49 (1995): 57–70.

having to sacrifice their careers. Perhaps young couples feel financially unequipped to attain a lifestyle considered sufficient for marriage. Clarkberg finds, for example, that both men and women who are economically unstable are likely to cohabit.[36] Cohabitation may provide an attractive alternative for those who are in romantic relationships but lack the economic well-being required for marriage.

Who are these people who are choosing to cohabit in greater numbers? What may come as a surprise to those who have thought of cohabitation as a practice restricted to white, liberal, middle-class college students experimenting with alternative lifestyles are several demographic facts about the cohabiting population. As might be expected, of all households with two unrelated adults of the opposite sex, more than two-thirds involved younger couples. About 23.7 percent were under age 25 and 44 percent were ages 25 to 44. But cohabitation is not restricted to young people, as another 24.9 percent were 45 to 64, and 7.4 percent were 65 and over.[37]

In terms of family backgrounds, individuals whose mothers married young and were pregnant at marriage enter into cohabitational unions (and marriage) at a substantially higher rate than other individuals.[38] African Americans cohabit at rates only slightly higher than for non-Hispanic whites, although both groups cohabit more than Hispanics.[39] Finally, those with low education, and those lacking economic resources are more likely to cohabit than their counterparts and are also less likely to formalize their cohabiting unions in later marriage.[40]

Methodological Concerns in the Study of Cohabition

Before considering further the nature of cohabitations and their consequences for the individuals involved in them and later marriage, two methodological concerns need to be taken into consideration when doing research or interpreting research results comparing cohabiting to noncohabiting or married couples. The first involves an issue of *causal validity* and the other involves a concern with the variety of meanings cohabitations might have for those involved in them.

Selection versus Experience

Like many other marriage and family-related topics, researchers are unable to comply with the procedures of experimental design. In particular, it is impossible and

---

[36]Martin Clarkberg, "The Price of Partnering: The Role of Economic Well-Being in Young Adults' First Union Experiences," *Social Forces* 77 (March 1999): 945–968.

[37]U.S. Census Bureau, *The 2009 Statistical Abstract*, "Table 70—Nonfamily Households by Sex and Age of Householder: 2007." http://www.2010census.biz/compendia/statab/cats/population/households_families_group_quarters.html.

[38]Arland Thornton, "Influence of the Marital History of Parents on the Marital and Cohabitational Experiences of Children," *American Journal of Sociology* 96 (January 1991): 868–894; and William G. Axinn and Arland Thornton, "Mothers, Children, and Cohabitation: The Intergenerational Effects of Attitudes and Behavior," *American Sociological Review* 58 (April 1993): 233–246.

[39]Sheela Kennedy and Larry Bumpass, "Cohabitation and Children's Living Arrangements: New Estimates from the United States," *Demographic Research*, 19 (September 2008):1663–1692.

[40]Judith Seltzer, "Cohabitation and Family Change," in Marilyn Coleman and Lawrence Ganong, *Handbook of Contemporary Families: Considering the Past, Contemplating the Future* (Thousand Oaks, CA; Sage Publications, 2004).

unethical to randomly assign people into cohabitation and noncohabitation groups to see if the experience alters their outcomes in any way. Instead, we allow individuals to *self-select* themselves into the two groups. This introduces what is called **self-selection bias** into our studies. It is bias because people with similar characteristics or conditions of life will be similarly more likely to select cohabitation as an option and it could be those characteristics or conditions that make them more likely to cohabit that also determine their outcomes and not the cohabitation experience itself. For example, a very religious person with religious beliefs that prohibit cohabitation will be less likely to cohabit. Because religion also is a strong predictor of positive marital outcomes (such as marital quality and stability) regardless of cohabitation, the noncohabiting group will exhibit these same positive outcomes. Thus, the cohabitation group has more negative outcomes simply because there are more nonreligious people who are in it and not because the experience of cohabitation changed them or their life circumstances in any meaningful way.

Researchers refer to effects due to selection bias as **selection effects** and it is another way of saying that the cohabitation effect is *spurious* or noncausal (see Chapter 3). Selection effects can be dealt with in analyses by statistically controlling for (or holding constant) all variables that might lead to systematic selection bias. In the preceding example, a researcher could look at the religious and nonreligious groups separately to see if the cohabiting group still had more negative outcomes even when the individuals studied were the same on religiosity. Unfortunately, in most research on cohabitation, researchers use only partial and often inadequate control variables to account for selection effects.

There are two types of selection factors that need to be considered. First, the individuals may have background characteristics that place them at a *greater risk* of negative relationship outcomes anyway. For example, we know that cohabitors have less education, fewer economic resources, and are more likely to have children at the time of their marriage. All of these factors will place them at a higher risk of negative marital outcomes because they are conditions that increase stress in the relationship and limit the availability of resources to deal with that stress. Negative outcomes are more likely to occur for this group regardless of whether they cohabit—they just happen to choose cohabitation more often. In fact, they may choose cohabitation because they realize the potential impacts of their life circumstances on their likelihood of having a successful marriage.

Second, individuals who cohabit are more likely to hold unconventional attitudes and beliefs that could lead to lower-quality relationships and a greater likelihood of marital dissolution should they get married. This would be especially true of cohabitations that took place in the past when cohabitation was much less institutionalized and accepted. Indeed, there is some evidence that cohabitors experienced a higher risk of later marital divorce if their cohabitation occurred during an earlier time period, although more recent evidence has called this finding into question.[41]

---

[41]The initial finding of cohort differences was by Robert Schoen, "First Unions and the Stability of First Marriages," *Journal of Marriage and the Family* 54 (1992): 281–284. Counterevidence, however, is presented by Claire M. Kamp Dush, Catherine L. Cohan, and Paul Amato, "The Relationship between Cohabitation and Marital Quality and Stability: Change across Cohorts," *Journal of Marriage and the Family* 63 (August 2003): 539–549. See also Jay Teachman, "Premarital Sex, Premarital Cohabitation and the Risk of Subsequent Marital Dissolution among Women," *Journal of Marriage and the Family* 65 (May 2003): 444–455.

To the extent that sociocultural risk factors and unconventional attitudes can be controlled and initial differences eliminated, we can then determine whether cohabitation has a valid causal effect. If we still find differences between cohabitors and noncohabitors, then we are left with the conclusion that the *experience* of cohabiting somehow altered the individuals involved, the nature of their interactions, or their life circumstances and environment in a way that creates the difference. This true causal effect has been called the **experience effect**.

The possible *experience* effects of cohabitation on individuals and relationships could be attitudinal, behavioral, or situational. With respect to attitudes, since cohabitation has been a deviant or unconventional lifestyle, it could lead those cohabiting to look at themselves in a more deviant or unconventional manner. This could then lead them to adopt other deviant behaviors or even more unconventional attitudes and beliefs that could later undermine their relationship or their individual well-being. They wouldn't have become so deviant or unconventional if they hadn't cohabited, so cohabitation would be a true causal factor in their outcomes.

Another way that the cohabitation experience could affect later individual and relationship outcomes is by altering the patterns of interaction in a way that makes long-term relationship success less likely. Because cohabitation takes place under conditions of limited commitment, couples may develop processes of social exchange and conflict that are not conducive to long-term relationship success. For example, we know that cohabitors are less likely to combine their resources through income pooling and develop more egalitarian role relationships[42] that might raise expectations and put pressure on later marital relationships that tend to become more traditional. As a result, couples will become less satisfied and less stable. Weaker identity bonds may also develop between the couple because of the less certain nature of the relationship's duration.

Finally, the experience of cohabitation might alter the ecological conditions under which the relationship must adapt and maintain itself. For example, we know that cohabitors develop fewer and less close relationship ties to their families of orientation, perhaps because it is not a fully institutionalized practice like marriage. These ties can be important resources in times of stress or crisis and can foster increased satisfaction and stability in the relationship. If they do not develop as strongly among those who cohabit and these weaker ties persist even after a later marriage, then we can say that cohabitation was a cause of more negative outcomes. If the couple had not cohabited, they may have developed stronger family relationships and those relationships would promote high levels of satisfaction and stability.

These are just a few examples of how the experience of cohabitation might impact the relationship and the individuals in it. Unfortunately, in addition to the lack of adequate controls for selection effects, most research on cohabitation has focused mostly on outcomes and has not fully explored the causal process through which the cohabitation experience may have produced those outcomes.

---

[42]Judith Seltzer, "Cohabitation and Family Change."

Meanings of Cohabitation

With the variety of traits among cohabiting couples and the drastic changes that have taken place in the incidence and prevalence of cohabitation, it would not be surprising to find a variety of meanings attached to the cohabitation experience. Given the lack of consensus about its meaning, Judith Selzer argues that cohabitation should be considered to be an incomplete institution.[43] An **incomplete institution** is a set of practices and relationships that are increasingly accepted and engaged in by the population but that lacks clear role expectations to govern the behaviors of those engaged in it.[44]

In some of the earliest research and theorizing about cohabitation, a distinction was made among four types or purposes of cohabitation: (1) cohabitation as a relationship of convenience, (2) cohabitation as a "trial marriage," (3) cohabitation as a temporary alternative to marriage, and (4) cohabitation as a permanent alternative to marriage.[45] Today, the distinction most often drawn is between cohabitation as a *stage in the courtship process* and cohabitation as an *alternative lifestyle* to marriage. As a stage in the courtship process, cohabitation is either an opportunity to try out one's potential marriage partner (that is, a "trial marriage") or it is an opportunity to begin a marital relationship the couple has already committed to before formalization in marriage (that is, a "temporary alternative") so that other tasks seen as prerequisites can be accomplished first (such as completing one's education, getting established in a job, saving up for the wedding or honeymoon, completing military service, etc.). As an alternative lifestyle, cohabitation could simply be a way to stabilize sexual and economic relationships without any necessary connection to later marriage intentions (cohabitations of "convenience"), or it could represent a rejection of marriage as an institution or at least a rejection of marriage as an option for the individuals involved (a "permanent substitute").

To complicate matters further, the meanings of cohabitation can vary within the couple as well as over time for the same couple. About 20 percent of couples disagree about their long-term relationship goals and less than half of those couples who see their cohabitation as potentially leading to marriage actually do get married within three years of the start of their cohabitation.[46]

Why is it important to make distinctions about the meanings of cohabitation in research studies? The reason lies in the applicability of research results to our own lives and to informing social policy. If you are thinking of cohabiting as a stage of your courtship and wish to know how cohabitation might affect your later marriage chances, happiness, and stability, you wouldn't want to base your decision on research in which most of the couples were cohabiting for convenience or as a permanent substitute to marriage but then got married for perhaps less positive reasons (such as pressures from others, pregnancy, increased interdependency, etc.). Similarly, if we really want to know if cohabitation can have a positive effect on marriage decisions, then we should restrict our research to

---

[43]Judith Seltzer, "Cohabitation and Family Change."

[44]Andrew Cherlin, "Remarriage as an Incomplete Institution," *American Journal of Sociology* 84 (1978): 634–650.

[45]Ellen Macklin, "Nontraditional Family Forms: A Decade of Research," *Journal of Marriage and the Family* 42 (1980): 905–922.

[46]Judith Seltzer, "Cohabitation and Family Change."

those who practice cohabitation solely as a form of trial marriage. Unfortunately, most research on cohabitation is restricted to large data sets that were not designed to make such distinctions. Thus, the results of these studies need to be interpreted with caution.

Interactional Patterns and Outcomes in Cohabiting Relationships

Reviews of the cohabitation literature that compare cohabiting couples with married couples and noncohabiting-engaged or going-steady couples suggest various similarities and differences in both patterns of interaction and individual consequences or outcomes.

One important area of difference involves gender-role attitudes and behaviors. Cohabiting couples have more liberal gender role attitudes and a greater proportion of these households are two-earner households.[47] Cohabitors are also more likely than married couples to keep their financial affairs separate and not to engage in homeownership. In regard to housework, national data show that women spend more time than men doing housework, but the gender gap is widest among married persons. Married women spend more time doing housework than female cohabitors who spend more time than never-married females.[48] Men's housework time is very similar for cohabitors, those in a marriage relationship, and those never married. Divorced and widowed men, however, do substantially more household work (such as cooking, cleaning, and laundry) than any other group of men. This study suggested that the division of labor between cohabitors may be closer to that of married persons than single ones, but in other areas such as number of children, employment, school enrollment, and homeownership, cohabitors more closely resemble single persons.

Given low levels of participation in housework among men in cohabiting unions (comparable to levels of men in marriages) and the more egalitarian gender role attitudes found among cohabiting couples, it should not be surprising to find that cohabiting relationships have lower levels of perceived fairness and relationship satisfaction. In a longitudinal analysis of both waves of the National Survey of Families and Households, cohabitors were found to experience greater declines over a five- to seven-year period in both perceived relationship fairness and happiness than did married individuals after controlling for a variety of factors

In most Western nations, a dramatic increase has occurred in nonmarital cohabitation (living together while not officially married). In many ways these couples resemble married ones, but cohabitors are more likely to keep their finances separate, express lower levels of commitment to the relationship, and break up more readily.

---

[47]Ibid.

[48]Scott J. South and Glenna Spitze, "Housework in Marital and Nonmarital Households," *American Sociological Review* 59 (June 1994): 327–347.

(including gender, duration, education, presence of a child, and initial levels of relationship fairness and happiness), although changes in communication and disagreements were more similar between the two groups.[49]

It appears that cohabiting couples tend to mirror the society around them and engage in sexual behavior characteristic of other couples their age. Although most cohabitors believe in sexual freedom within the relationship, most also voluntarily restrict their sexual activity as evidence of their commitment to the relationship. They do, however, have intercourse significantly more frequently than either married couples or unmarried noncohabitants.

On a more negative note, cohabitors were found to differ considerably from dating couples in "hitting without a license."[50] Young adult cohabitors exceeded daters in rates and levels of partner abuse. They were nearly twice as likely as daters to be physically abusive toward their partners. DeMaris, who studied the impact of violence on ending the cohabiting relationship, found that intense male violence raised the likelihood of separation, whereas violence by women retarded the transition to marriage.[51]

Differences between cohabiting and noncohabiting couples exist along other dimensions as well. For example, Nock found that in addition to lower levels of happiness with their relationship, cohabitors expressed lower levels of commitment and had poorer relationships with parents than comparable married persons.[52] He argues that the poorer quality of cohabiting relationships stems largely from the absence of institutional norms related to cohabitation. As might be expected due to their lower levels of commitment, cohabitations also have much higher rates of dissolution. Although cohabitations may have higher dissolution rates than marriages, however, one should not get the idea that all these relationships are unstable. The survival of them appears to depend on equal power sharing. Cohabitors are more likely to remain together under conditions of equality.

With respect to the consequences and outcomes of cohabitation for the individuals involved, a number of studies have shown that, after controlling for selection factors, cohabitation yields the same types of health benefits as marriage but to a lesser degree.[53] Similar results came from other studies of national samples in Canada, Sweden, and elsewhere.[54] A seventeen-nation study of marital status and happiness revealed higher levels of happiness among married couples

[49]Kevin B. Skinner, Stephen J. Bahr, D. Russell Crane, and Vaughn R. A. Call, "Cohabitation, Marriage, and Remarriage: A Comparison of Relationship Quality over Time," *Journal of Family Issues* 23 (2002): 74–90.

[50]Lynn Magdol, Terrie E. Moffitt, and Phil A. Silva, "Hitting without a License: Testing Explanations for Differences in Partner Abuse between Young Adult Daters and Cohabitors," *Journal of Marriage and the Family* 60 (February 1998): 41–55.

[51]Alfred DeMaris, "The Influence of Intimate Violence on Transitions out of Cohabitation," *Journal of Marriage and the Family* 63 (February 2001): 235–246.

[52]Steven L. Nock, "A Comparison of Marriages and Cohabiting Relationships," *Journal of Family Issues* 16 (January 1995): 53–76.

[53]Kathleen A. Lamb, Gary R. Lee, and Alfred DeMaris, "Union Formation and Depression: Selection and Relationship Effects," *Journal of Marriage and the Family* 65 (2003): 953–962; Hyoun K. Kim and Patrick C. Henry, "The Relationship between Marriage and Psychological Well-Being: A Longitudinal Analysis," *Journal of Family Issues* 23 (November 2002): 885–911.

[54]Zheng Wu, Margaret J. Penning, Michael S. Pollard, and Randy Hart, "'In Sickness and in Health': Does Cohabitation Count?" *Journal of Family Issues* 24 (September 2003): 811–838; Zheng Wu and Randy Hart, "The Effects of Marital and Nonmarital Union Transition on Health," *Journal of Marriage and the Family* 64 (May 2002): 420–432.

Family Diversity

Diversity in Cohabitation Experiences

In order to understand how cohabitation impacts individuals and couples, it is important to first understand the motivations and conditions leading up to the decision to cohabit. Julie Phillips and Megan Sweeney set out to explore the importance of motivations by examining race and ethnic differences in the effects of cohabitation on later marital stability. Using a sub-sample of the National Survey of Family Growth (NSFG) consisting of over 4,500 non-Hispanic white, non-Hispanic black and Mexican American women who married for the first time sometime after 1975, they predicted different effects of cohabitation on later marriage between these groups on the basis of presuppositions about differences in why each group chooses to cohabit.

In terms of the incidence of cohabitation, the rates for non-Hispanic whites and blacks were nearly identical and both rates were considerably higher than those found for Mexican Americans. In addition, 80 percent or more of all three groups of women who were cohabiting did so with only one person—their eventual marital partner. In terms of the effects of cohabitation on later divorce, they found that cohabitation had a negative effect on the stability of white women's marriages but not on the stability of black or Mexican American women's marriages. In fact, there was some evidence than the effect of cohabitation on the later marriage of foreign-born Mexican Americans is actually positive.

Although they did not control for sexual activity (an important "selection" factor that explains the negative effects of cohabitation on later marriage), they were able to show that non-Hispanic whites who cohabited with more than one other partner or with someone other than their eventual marital partner had higher risks of divorce than those who cohabited with just their eventual marital partner.

These findings are consistent with the hypothesis that much, if not all, of the negative effect of cohabitation on marriage is due to having multiple sex partners rather than the cohabitation experience itself.

The authors interpret their results as suggesting that non-Hispanic whites cohabit for different reasons than the other two groups. In particular, they speculate that the more negative effects of cohabitation for this group come about because non-Hispanic white women choose cohabitation because they are unsure that their partner is the one they want to marry (cohabitation as "trial marriage"); whereas, among the other two groups, cohabitation is entered into with relatively more certainty about and commitment to their partner (cohabitation as a substitute for marriage). As a result, when non-Hispanic whites eventually marry, more of them do so because of social pressures or factors other than commitment and this puts their marriages at risk.

Although this attention to the issue of "intent" is important, these results could be interpreted in other ways. First, it could be that non-Hispanic whites experience more pressure to marry their cohabiting partner because cohabitation (and especially long-term cohabitation) is less normative in the white community. Blacks and Hispanics, on the other hand, have a longer history and broader social acceptance of cohabitation. As a result, those cohabitations that develop into marriages will generally be stronger ones not influenced by outside pressures. A second possible explanation for these differences in effects could be the higher levels of sexual activity found among non-Hispanic blacks. As a result, cohabitation should be less of a proxy for sexual behavior in this group and therefore have less of an impact on later marital outcomes.

Source: Julie A. Phillips and Megan M. Sweeney, "Premarital Cohabitation and Marital Disruption Among White, Black, and Mexican American Women," *Journal of Marriage and Family*, 67 (May 2005): 296–314.

than among cohabitors, who were happier than other categories of single persons.[55] Although both married persons and cohabitors had a live-in partner, marriage was 3.4 times more closely associated with the variance in happiness than was cohabitation.

Researchers have also shown that those who cohabit have a lower desire to marry and a reduced likelihood of ever getting married. Susan Brown, using two waves of national data, found that cohabitors were about as likely to formalize their unions as they were to dissolve them. In the first year, approximately 20 percent of cohabitors married and 15 percent separated. Within two years, one-quarter married. For many couples, however, cohabitation serves as a permanent alternative to legal marriage.[56]

This reduced likelihood of marriage is not uniform across all social groups, however. Manning and Smock observe that black cohabitors are less likely than white cohabitors to formalize their unions through marriage, although the presence of children was found to increase the chances of marrying a cohabiting partner for both blacks and whites.[57] In Britain as well, conceptions resulting in a live birth were found to be a key factor in promoting marriage. Younger women from poorer economic backgrounds were more likely to continue to cohabit after becoming pregnant, as were those who had behavioral or emotional problems as adolescents.[58]

It is unclear whether the reduced likelihood to marry is due to the cohabitation experience or was present beforehand. An analysis using longitudinal data from the National Survey of Families and Households has suggested the former. Single persons who were cohabiting during the first wave of data collection were found to perceive marriage as less beneficial and more costly and to have lower marriage intentions and expectations than their noncohabiting counterparts five to seven years later. These lower perceptions, intentions, and expectations in turn predicted a lower likelihood of getting married in the later time period.[59]

Cohabitation and Marital Quality and Stability

Does establishing an unmarried-couple household provide a basis for a successful long-term relationship or even make for a better marriage? Is cohabitation a good trial for marriage? Or does cohabitation place couples at a greater risk of later marital dissolution? The answers to these questions remains mixed.

Several studies of both small and large national data sets in the United States and Canada over the past several decades have found that couples who cohabited before marriage report lower-quality marriages, lower commitment to the institution of marriage, more individualistic views of marriage, and greater likelihood of divorce

---

[55]Steven Stack and J. Ross Eshleman, "Marital Status and Happiness," *Journal of Marriage and the Family* 60 (May 1998): 527–536.

[56]Susan L. Brown, "Union Transitions among Cohabitors: The Significance of Relationship Assessments and Expectations," *Journal of Marriage and the Family* 62 (August 2000): 833–846.

[57]Wendy D. Manning and Pamela J. Smock, "Why Marry? Race and the Transition to Marriage among Cohabitors," *Demography* 32 (November 1995): 509–520.

[58]Ann Berrington, "Entry into Parenthood and the Outcome of Cohabiting Partnerships in Britain," *Journal of Marriage and the Family* 63 (February 2001): 80–96.

[59]Sandra L. McGinnis, "Cohabiting, Dating, and Perceived Costs of Marriage: A Model of Marriage Entry," *Journal of Marriage and the Family* 65 (February 2003): 105–116.

than couples who did not cohabit.[60] Similar results have been found in other countries as well. In Sweden, a national sample of nearly five thousand women found that those who cohabited premaritally had almost 80 percent higher marital dissolution rates than those who did not.[61] However, with an increase in marital duration came a decrease in the difference of dissolution rates between premarital cohabitors and noncohabitors, with no differences found among those whose marriages remained intact for eight years.

Why, in all these studies from many countries, is there a consistent finding of lower-quality relationships, less happiness, and higher dissolution rates among previous cohabitors who later married? Some evidence exists that this may be at least partly due to self-selection. In a recent longitudinal analysis of the National Survey of Families and Households, individuals were matched on important background characteristics and, although differences between previous cohabitors and noncohabitors were found consistent with previous studies, all couples showed a similar decline in companionship, sexual interaction, satisfaction, and commitment and an increase in conflict over the five- to seven-year time span of this study.[62] In another analysis of the same data set using a different set of control variables, no difference was found in the degree of change in perceived relationship fairness and satisfaction between married couples who had cohabited before marriage and those who had not.[63] In yet another study using the National Longitudinal Survey of Youth (1979–1998), cohabitation effects were accounted for by ethnicity, religion, and prior levels of delinquency.[64]

In what may be one of the most comprehensive studies to date that used a sample of over six thousand women from the National Survey of Family Growth, Jay Teachman found that the effects of cohabitation on the likelihood of marital dissolution were completely accounted for by the number and variety of sexual partners a woman had prior to marriage. Having sex only with one's future marriage partner or cohabiting with him and him alone before marriage did not increase the risk of later marital dissolution. Having sex with more than one's future spouse, however, did increase the risk of divorce and the risk increased further with each additional partner. This effect occurred regardless of whether the woman cohabited, indicating

---

[60]There are many studies showing the negative effects of cohabitation on later marital quality and stability, but the size of these effects varies greatly and often is dependent on the quality of the study and the control variables used in the analysis. For a review, see Pamela Smock, "Cohabitation in the United States: An Appraisal of Research Themes, Findings, and Implications," *Annual Review of Sociology* 26 (2000): 1–20. Some recent studies include Claire M. Kamp Dush, Catherine L. Cohan, and Paul Amato, "The Relationship between Cohabitation and Marital Quality and Stability: Change across Cohorts," *Journal of Marriage and the Family* 63 (August 2003): 539–549; and Catherine L. Cohan and Stacey Kleinbaum, "Toward a Greater Understanding of the Cohabitation Effect: Premarital Cohabitation and Marital Communication," *Journal of Marriage and the Family* 64 (February 2002):180–192. See also Elizabeth Thompson and Ugo Colella, "Cohabitation and Marital Stability: Quality or Commitment?" *Journal of Marriage and the Family* 54 (May 1992): 259–267.

[61]Neal G. Bennett, Ann Klimas Blanc, and David E. Bloom, "Commitment and the Modern Union: Assessing the Link between Premarital Cohabitation and Subsequent Marital Stability," *American Sociological Review* 53 (February 1988): 127–138.

[62]Laura Stafford, Susan L. Kline, and Caroline T. Rankin, "Married Individuals, Cohabitors, and Cohabitors Who Marry: A Longitudinal Study of Relational and Individual Well-Being," *Journal of Social and Personal Relationships* 21 (April, 2004): 231–248.

[63]Skinner, Bahr, Crane, and Call, "Cohabitation, Marriage, and Remarriage."

[64]LaKeesha N. Woods and Robert E. Emery, "The Cohabitation Effects on Divorce: Causation or Selection?" *Journal of Divorce and Remarriage* 37 (2002): 101–119.

that the cohabitation effect is most likely spurious (at least for women) and is due instead to the fact that women who cohabit are more likely to have had multiple sexual partners before marriage.[65]

In addition to these studies that controlled for important selection factors, another study of 136 couples using data from interactional observations done prior to marriage and then again ten months after marriage demonstrated the importance of distinguishing between the meanings or types of cohabitation. These researchers divided their sample into three groups: noncohabitors, cohabitors who began their cohabitation after their engagement, and cohabitors who started cohabiting before being engaged. After controlling for selection factors, they found that the only group difference was for the latter group. Those who cohabited before engagement had more negative interactions, less personal commitment, lower relationship quality, and lower confidence in their relationship. Those who cohabited only after becoming engaged did not differ from the noncohabiting group.[66]

Finally, it is suggested that cohabitation may be so different from marriage in its structure and expectations that what happens during cohabitation is not especially useful in predicting the quality of the marriage that may follow.[67] Whatever the reasons, existing data do not support the contentions that cohabitation serves as an effective training ground or trial for marriage or that it results in improved marital quality or stability.

---

[65]Teachman, "Premarital Sex, Premarital Cohabitation and the Risk of Subsequent Marital Dissolution Among Women."

[66]Galena H. Kline, Scott M. Stanley, Howard J. Markman, P. Antonio Olmos-Gallo, Michelle St. Peters, Sarah W. Whitton, and Lydia M. Prado, "Timing Is Everything: Pre-Engagement Cohabitation and Increased Risk of Poor Marital Outcomes," *Journal of Family Psychology* 18 (June 2004): 311–318.

[67]Lee A. Lillard, Michael J. Brein, and Linda J. Waite, "Pre-Marital Cohabitation and Subsequent Marital Dissolution: Is It Self-Selection?" *Demography* 32 (August 1995): 437–457.

Summary

1. In looking at nonmarital and premarital relationships, it is important to consider the ongoing influence of the cultural context. In late modern society, the choice of partners, the process of relationship development, and the long-term outcomes of relationships are highly ambiguous and create uncertainty and risk. This ambiguity has come about because of an increased emphasis on the expressive self, the need to match on personality traits rather than social status, and the breakdown in institutional regulation of nonmarital and premarital relationships.

2. The concept of love is important in late modern societies as it captures the primary criteria for relationships. Love is a socially constructed concept, however, with emotional, cognitive, relational, and behavioral components.

3. A range of explanations addresses who selects whom and why. At one extreme are individualistic explanations, which are rooted in instinct, genetic similarity, needs, drives, parental images, and complementary needs. In contrast are sociocultural explanations, which are rooted in norms, values, roles, and social exchanges.

4. Sociocultural explanations operate at a more conscious level, are more readily testable, and have greater research support than individualistic explanations. One sociocultural theory suggests that interpersonal attraction is facilitated when persons share or perceive themselves as sharing similar value orientations.

5. Related to sharing values is sharing roles—the internalized, learned, social expectations as to what attitudes and behaviors are appropriate or inappropriate in the selection of a partner. In brief, the couple likely to cohabit or marry involves a male and female who share similar role definitions and expectations.

6. Exchange theorists view partner selection as a bargaining or social exchange process. The choice of a partner is based on the selection of persons who share equivalent resources; each has something to offer that is desired by the other.

7. Some writers see the selection of a partner as the result of several of the preceding processes operating simultaneously or sequentially. One explanation involves a three-stage chronological sequence of stimulus, value, and role (SVR).

8. The partner-selection process is the means by which an individual changes status from single to married. The process involves all sorts of rules and roles applicable to male–female interaction. Generally, various types of hanging out, hooking up, or dating fulfill a variety of purposes, many of which lead to increasing degrees of intimacy and commitment, such as engagement or cohabitation.

9. Unmarried cohabitation is an increasingly popular lifestyle choice in the United States and much of the Western world. In the United States, the numbers have increased dramatically for those with and without children under the age of 15 as well as among all age groups including the elderly.

10. Even though unmarried people who cohabit enjoy many of the same positive relationship benefits that married people enjoy, cohabitation does not serve as a successful trial for marriage. Whether it is bad for marriage remains an open question. There is evidence to suggest that self-selection bias accounts for many of the negative effects observed and that premarital sexual experiences are more predictive of negative marital outcomes than is cohabitation.

Although the male–female sexual relationship generally is an important dimension of intimate relationships, only minimal attention was given to it in this and the previous chapter. Nonmarital sexual relationships throughout the world are analyzed and described in the chapter that follows. Marital sexuality will be discussed in Chapter 8.

Key Terms and Topics

Discussion Questions

1. How certain do you feel about the type of person you would be best off choosing as a long-term partner? In what ways would you say there is uncertainty in the process of meeting people, dating them, and knowing where your relationship stands at any given point in time? In what ways are relationships risky these days?

2. Talk to fellow students of the opposite sex about what they think love is. Compare their ideas about love to your own. Are they the same or different? How?

3. To what extent is partner selection likely to be a result of instincts, innate drives, parental images, and complementary needs? Consider your personal experience.

4. In spite of the logical and rational basis of the theory of complementary needs, why is there so little empirical support for it?

5. What values are most important to you? Could you marry someone who did not share these values? Why?

6. List a number of role expectations that you hold for yourself and your partner. Have a dating partner do the same. (Examples: "I expect the male to do the laundry." "Both the husband and wife should be employed full time.") On a rating scale of 1 to 5, indicate whether you agree or disagree with one another's expectations. Compare and discuss the results.

7. To what extent is the portrayal of the male–female game in the mate-selection process accurate? Has the game changed over the years? If so, how and why?

8. How do you select intimate partners? Do you or have you been involved in hooking up, hanging out, or dating? What does each mean to you? What different expectations for behavior are attached to each?

9. Recall your own past intimate relationships or those of your friends. Is the principle of least interest applicable? How was it manifested?

10. What explains the increase in cohabitation as well as its seemingly negative relationship to marital satisfaction and stability? How is cohabitation similar to and different from marriage?

11. Explain the difference between selection and experience effects with respect to the effects of cohabitation on later marital quality and stability. Why do selection effects indicate that the effect of cohabitation on later marriage is spurious?

Further Readings

Booth, Alan, and Crouter, Ann C., eds. *Just Living Together: Implications of Cohabitation on Families, Children, and Social Policy*. Mahwah, NJ: Lawrence Erlbaum Associates, Inc. 2002.

Based on presentations from a national symposium, the book looks at the foundations for and the impact of cohabitation.

Bulcroft, Kris, Smeins, Linda, and Bulcroft, Richard. *Romancing the Honeymoon: Consummating Marriage in Modern Society*. Thousand Oaks, CA: Sage Publications, Inc., 1999.

A multidisciplinary examination of the custom of honeymooning, integrating cultural theory across a variety of methodological approaches.

Harvey, John H., and Wenzel, Amy. *Close Romantic Relationships: Maintenance and Enhancement*. Mahwah, NJ: Lawrence Erlbaum Associates, Inc., 2001.

An account of why close relationships are or are not maintained and the manner in which these principles can be applied to current social issues.

Honeycutt, James M., and Cantrill, James G. *Cognition, Communication, and Romantic Relationships*. Mahwah, NJ: Lawrence Erlbaum Associates, Inc., 2001.

An extended analysis of the role that memory, communication, and social cognition play in the development or termination of romantic relationships.

Nazio, Tiziana. *Cohabitation, Family and Society* (New York:L Routledge, 2008).

An analysis of data on cohabitation from the Family and Fertility Survey conducted in six European countries, this book looks at the cultural diffusion process by which cohabitation became the norm in some countries but not in others.

Seltzer, Judith. "Families Formed Outside of Marriage," *Journal of Marriage and the Family* 62 (November 2000): 1247–1268.

One of the decade-review articles that provides an overview of cohabitation and childbearing outside of marriage.

Thornton, Arland, Axinn, William G. and Xie, Yu, *Marriage and Cohabitation*. (Chicago: The University of Chicago Press, 2007).

Using data from the Intergenerational Panel Study of Parents and Children (IPS), this book examines the intergenerational factors that predict cohabitation versus marriage.

Waite, Linda J., ed. *The Ties That Bind: Perspectives on Marriage and Cohabitation*. Hawthorne, NY: Aldine de Gruter, 2000.

A volume of nineteen articles that assesses the scientific evidence about the causes of trends in marriage and other forms of intimate unions, including cohabitation.

chapter 8

Sexuality and Nonmarital Relationships

Case Example

High-Risk Behavior—One Rape, Eight Pregnancies, and Two Children

Andrea is a 29-year-old mother of two young children, ages 3 and 4. She has a master's degree in social science and is employed full time. She is currently married but separated from her husband. Prior to the birth of her two children, she had experienced a rape, five abortions, and a miscarriage.

The rape, a very traumatic experience, occurred at age 12. She was walking home from school with a boyfriend who was one year older. He wanted to kiss her but she refused. So, behind a church, he held a broken glass pop bottle to her neck, removed her clothes, and forcibly raped her. She recalls how he called her black and ugly and told her that no one would ever want to marry her. Arriving home badly battered, she told her mother that two high school girls jumped her. Not until age 21 did she reveal the rape experience to anyone.

At age 15, Andrea began having intercourse on a regular basis. Her first pregnancy occurred at age 16 by an older boy she was "sleeping with" regularly and felt she loved. She had the pregnancy terminated at a local clinic. The same year, she got pregnant again by another boyfriend and miscarried. Then she met Eugene, whom she dated for two years. She got pregnant again and wanted to keep the child but Eugene insisted she get an abortion. In her words, "I really loved him and felt sex was the way to keep him. I wanted him so badly I even let him sodomize me, which was worse than the rape. I was so humiliated. He became more abusive and violent, so four months later, I had no choice but to break off our relationship.

"At age 18, I became involved with the man (let's call him Vic) who is now my husband. With him, I had three abortions, two at his insistence. I really wanted a child but knew I couldn't make it as a single mother and continue my schooling. Vic offered no support at all and wasn't willing to marry me. Several times we broke off our relationship but would get back together.

"At age 25, I got pregnant again. I was extremely depressed and wanted to commit suicide. I had earlier made a promise to God that I would never have another abortion. Vic wanted me back so I said only if he married me. So, five months into my pregnancy, I married him. Three months after my son was born, I was pregnant again and, following a very difficult pregnancy, gave birth to my daughter. Again, my worst nightmares were being realized. We were in trouble financially since I wasn't working. I didn't want to accept food stamps (but had to) and our marriage declined even more. For a long time, Vic had been sleeping on the couch. Recently, when my 3-year-old daughter told me how daddy rubbed himself against her, I knew we had to separate.

"Looking back over all my sexual experiences, I can say that until my marriage, I never really enjoyed sex. It was something you do to please (and keep) a man. I didn't even know girls could have an orgasm until I was 18 and read about it in a magazine. Now I can really enjoy sex. I'm currently seeing a 67-year-old married attorney who really is kind to me. He buys me things, pays for my day care, and tells me he loves me. I never had that happen before. I know that I was adequate as a student, and am adequate as an employee, and as a mother. Now, for the first time, I am beginning to feel adequate as a woman: pretty, wanted, and loved."

Questions to Consider

How would you explain Andrea's high-risk sexual behavior? Given her situation, how realistic were the decisions she made to have abortions, to give birth to two children, and to leave her husband?

What is the relationship, if any, between the need for acceptance and one's sense of self-worth with sexual permissiveness?

ew topics draw as much widespread attention and occupy as much thought as matters relating to sex, as both a social and a personal phenomenon. The significance of sex in modern life is evidenced by the recent controversies centering around AIDS, abortion, gays in the military and in particular professions, sexual affairs among government officials, sex education in the public schools, pornography, distribution of contraceptives to adolescents, and general concern over gender identity and male–female roles, to mention a few.

Many distinctions can be made in classifying sexual relationships. A sexual relationship may involve persons of the same sex (homosexuality) or of opposite sexes (heterosexuality). It may involve persons who are not married but whose relationship is marriage oriented (premarital) or persons who are not married and to whom marriage is not a factor (nonmarital). It may involve a husband and wife (marital). Married persons may have a sexual relationship with partners other than their spouses (extramarital), perhaps involving a sexual exchange of married partners ("swinging"). A sexual relationship may involve divorced or widowed persons who were once married but are currently socially and legally single (postmarital).

Ira Reiss, in a sociological analysis of **human sexuality,** defined *sexuality* as erotic and genital responses produced by the cultural scripts of a society.[1] He suggested that sexuality is universal in that, in all societies, it is viewed as important and in need of societal regulation of some sort. The basic reason for the importance of sex is that *sexual scripts* often encompass the elements of physical pleasure and self-disclosure. These are crucial elements in forming relationships in a society, sexual or otherwise.

Human sexuality, within and outside of marriage, was brought into the public arena with the publication of the Kinsey studies in 1948 and 1953.[2] These landmark publications set the stage for making sexuality a legitimate area of research and also provided a wealth of information, making sexuality a legitimate subject for popular discussion as well.

How do Kinsey's findings compare with research done since then? This may be a difficult question to answer, since recent research in the area of human sexuality has been limited. One of the consequences of the political and religious atmosphere of the 1980s and 1990s was to severely restrict funds as well as to define investigations into sexuality as off-limits. Even a proposed $18 million project that had been peer-reviewed, as well as approved and funded by the National Institutes of Health (NIH), was retracted when a few conservative legislators objected to sex research as part of a "conspiracy of the liberal left and the organized homosexual community."[3]

Social Regulation of Sexual Relationships

All societies have social norms that grant approval to certain sexual behaviors and disapproval to others. Perhaps the most universal taboo on sexual behavior relates to incest; the most universal approval is granted to sexual behavior in marriage. Clearly, no society grants unrestricted sexual liberties; all societies control sexuality. How is this done?

First, basic social institutions are key components in controlling human sexual expression. The *family* has played a primary role in the regulation and control of sexual conduct through the socialization process, controlling who marries whom and providing negative sanctions when sexual norms are violated.

Around the world, *religion* has mandated what persons are legitimate sexual partners and what behaviors are acceptable. In the United States, for example, certain churches embody a procreation orientation toward sex. Acts that have no reproductive value—such as masturbation, sodomy (anal, oral, bestiality), and

---

[1]Ira L. Reiss, *Journey into Sexuality. An Exploratory Voyage* (Englewood Cliffs, NJ: Prentice-Hall, 1986), 37.

[2]Alfred C. Kinsey, Wardell B. Pomeroy, Clyde E. Martin, and Paul H. Gebhard, *Sexual Behavior in the Human Female* (Philadelphia: W. B. Saunders, 1953); and Alfred C. Kinsey, Wardell B. Pomeroy, and Clyde E. Martin, *Sexual Behavior in the Human Male* (Philadelphia: W.B. Saunders, 1948).

[3]J. Richard Udry, "The Politics of Sex Research," *The Journal of Sex Research* 30 (May 1993): 103–110.

CROSS-CULTURAL *Perspective*

Sex and Sexuality in Contemporary Arab Society

Sexuality in contemporary Arabia cannot be easily disentangled from ideas of biological sex and gender and is deeply connected to *Qur'anic* beliefs and practices and masculine interpretations of Islamic law (*Shari'a*). Women are defined by *not* being men, and both genders are defined relative to their sexuality. As Fez University Professor Abdessamad Dialmy states it, Arab culture is a "phallocracy" where men are dominant and "penetrative," while women are submissive and "receptive." This linkage, and the nature of sexual relationships it implies, is encoded through the *Qur'anic* concept for sex—*Farj*—which translates as vagina. It is also expressed through cultural practices such as the veiling of women, the defloration of virgins, and male and female circumcision. These practices symbolically reinforce notions of manhood as penetrative and "unveiled" as well as prescriptions for woman to be nonsexual, passive, and controlled. Ironically, women are also seen as having strong sexual desire that requires men to be more virulent in order to maintain their satisfaction and loyalty.

Many of these beliefs have been undergoing change. Due to an increased standard of living, female education and employment, cultural diffusion of ideas from the West regarding sexual consumerism, unemployment, and housing shortages, there has been an increasing delay in marriage and a major growth in the single population. As a result, it has become more difficult to constrain sexual behaviors to the confines of marriage and for the purpose of procreation. Rates of nonmarital sexuality are high for Arab males, although a strong double standard exists as indicated by low rates among women. Prostitution, while condemned, typically is overlooked, and older institutional practices of *visitation marriage* and *Shi'a*

marriage have been revised to accommodate new realities. Visitation marriage is described as a "softened" form of polygyny where men take on additional wives informally and in secret. Shi'a marriage involves relationships not recognized by the state. Traditionally permanent, long-term relationships, Shi'a marriages have become temporary and accommodate relationships prohibited for economic or religious reasons. They symbolize resistance to modern states and are used to consolidate loyalty among members of radical groups. They are also used to legitimate the practice of "sex tourism" among Arabs from wealthy oil-rich nations seeking sex with women from poorer Arab nations in exchange for a "bride price."

Contemporary Arab society is a society in transition with respect to sexuality. Although there is a freeing of sexual relations from traditional marriage, many of the older customs related to sexuality—such as male and female circumcision and honor crimes justifying the killing of a woman for sex outside of marriage—still persist. There also is still a strong opposition to sex education and the use of condoms insofar as these practices symbolically challenge Islamic beliefs about sex and sexuality. Finally, Arab cultural notions of masculinity as related to sexual virility have intersected with modern sex and reproductive technologies (specifically the growth of pharmaceuticals for male sexual dysfunction) to create a new problem—perceived sexual impotence among men and the growing use of erectile dysfunction drugs. The Arab world has an unusually high level of reported erectile dysfunction and an unusually high use of drugs such as Viagra to boost sexual performance. This high use of ED drugs is perceived to be a threat by Egyptian women who fear that it will lead their husbands to seek out affairs or even take on additional wives, which would threaten the stability of their marriage or their autonomy within it.

Source: Abdessamad Dialmy, "Sexuality in Contemporary Arab Society," *Social Analysis*, 49 (Summer 2005), 16–33.

homosexuality—are taboo and sinful, as are activities that threaten the family unit, such as incest and adultery. *Education* often is assigned a regulatory role in defining, clarifying, and teaching what sexual conduct is appropriate. Even the *workplace* may establish boundaries and restrictions on sexual expression through dress and behavioral codes, such as sexual harassment rules.

Beyond the role of institutions, sexual expression is regulated and controlled through social norms, social statuses and roles, and social sanctions. Sexual expectations, as well as rights and privileges, differ for males and females; for adults and children; in public and private places; for married people and single ones; for grandparents and grandchildren; or for heterosexuals and homosexuals. Laws may be established that punish the prostitute, the distributor of child pornography, or the rapist. Violators of approved behavior may face public shame, ridicule, fines, imprisonment, physical and/or mental torture, and even death. In brief, sexual expression is highly regulated in a variety of ways in every society in the world.

Biological versus Sociological Approaches to Sexual Behavior

Are we genetically predisposed to have sexual drives and needs, to seek out sexual partners of a specific sex, and to be socially and sexually competitive? Are our sexual interests and behaviors biologically determined? Or are we carefully taught what is erotic, how to suppress or act on our sexual impulses or drives, and what sexual behavior is deviant or appropriate? **Biological theories** tend to focus on and emphasize the innate, genetic, hormonal, and physiological factors involved in human (and animal) sexuality. **Social theories** tend to focus on socialization and social control factors involved in human sexual behavior.

The debate about nature versus nurture regarding sexual needs, interests, and behaviors has been long-standing. Perhaps the debate is both futile and unnecessary. Is it not possible, and likely, that nature and nurture work in concert? There are crucial biological differences between the sexes, and these co-act with social factors to promote variations in interest and behavior. This is the position taken by John and Janice Baldwin, who show that several biological factors tilt males and females in different directions related to sexual interest.[4]

This position eliminates the dichotomous "either nature or nurture" argument but does not address the question as to which one contributes more. Can most sexual behaviors and their variations be credited to biological theories? Do behaviors differ cross-nationally, over time, or even between the sexes because of genetics, hormone levels, anatomical factors, or innate physiological predispositions?

Today, few would dismiss hormonal, testosterone, or other anatomical or chemical changes as irrelevant to one's sexual drives and needs. For example, a longitudinal three-year study of boys 12 and 13 years of age linked normal changes in testosterone with changes in sexual behavior.[5] Increases in testosterone were associated with coital initiation and the rising incidence of sexual behaviors.

On the other hand, a considerable body of evidence exists that demonstrates that men and women appear very similar in their needs, drives, and responses.

---

[4]John D. Baldwin and Janice I. Baldwin, "Gender Differences in Sexual Interest," *Archives of Sexual Behavior* 26 (1997): 181–210.

[5]C. Halpern, J. Udry, and C. Suchindran, "Monthly Measures of Salivary Testosterone Predict Sexual Activity in Adolescent Males," *Archives of Sexual Behavior* 27 (1998): 445–465.

Research findings of Masters and Johnson, about forty years ago, indicated that women have as definite an orgasm as men and that, in general, women have a greater potential for sexual responsiveness than men, since women tend to respond faster, more intensely, and longer to sexual stimulation. Aside from obvious anatomical variants, men and women are homogeneous in their physiologic responses to sexual stimuli.[6]

Kinsey had come to the same conclusion almost fifteen years earlier when he reported:

> The anatomic structures, which are most essential to sexual response and orgasm, are nearly identical in the human male and female. The differences are relatively few. They are associated with the different functions of the sexes in reproductive processes but they are of no great significance in the origins and development of sexual response and orgasm. If females and males differ sexually in any basic way, those differences must originate in some other aspect of the biology or psychology of the two sexes.[7] Ideas such as these led most social scientists, including family scholars, to ignore or overlook biological explanations of family or sexual behavior.[8] Biological components, while necessary, were not sufficient to explain or predict values and behaviors. And besides, are not biological factors believed to be the business of the biologist, whose theories will not affect the sociologist? J. Richard Udry, a sociologist at the University of North Carolina, did not believe so. With colleagues, he explored the interplay between biological predispositions and sociological models of adolescent sexuality and argued that biological components could not be ignored.[9]

Udry examined the hormonal changes of puberty, commonly regarded as the foundation for sexual behavior, for evidence of their role in adolescent sexual behavior. He stated that, since adolescents mature at different rates and at different ages, some will be more predisposed to sexual activity than others. The inclusion of a hormone measure with the social control measures would make the sociological models not wrong but rather more complete. Udry tested a biosocial theory that combines elements of social science with a biological model of hormonal dispositions.

What Udry found was evidence of strong biological as well as sociological effects on coitus with more moderate effects on subjective (thoughts and feelings) sexual variables. Social controls acted to suppress the effects of hormones on behavior. Udry concluded that a biosocial model of sexual behavior produces results that are more convincing than either a sociological or biological model alone. He urged caution, however, in applying his results only to early adolescence and not to coital transitions occurring earlier or later.

---

[6]William H. Masters and Virginia E. Johnson, *Human Sexual Response* (Boston: Little, Brown, 1966), Chapter 17 and p. 285.

[7]Kinsey, Pomeroy, Martin, and Gebhard, *Sexual Behavior in the Human Female*, 593.

[8]Note, for example, Alan Booth, Karen Carver, and Douglas A. Granger, "Biosocial Perspectives on the Family," *Journal of Marriage and the Family* 62 (November 2000): 1018–1034.

[9]J. Richard Udry, "Biological Predispositions and Social Control in Adolescent Sexual Behavior," *American Sociological Review* 53 (October 1988): 709–722. See also Carolyn Tucker Halpern, J. Richard Udry, Benjamin Campbell, Chirayath Suchindran, and George A. Mason, "Testosterone and Religiosity as Predictors of Sexual Attitudes and Activity among Adolescent Males: A Biosocial Model," *Journal of Biosocial Science* 26 (1994): 217–234.

Male and female sexual behaviors in adolescence or adulthood go beyond hormonal and biological factors to include social and technological ones. For example, male–female differences are thought to have been weakened by the feminist movement (which sought gender equality), the development of contraception (which eliminated much of the fear of pregnancy), and the Industrial Revolution (which gave women greater economic opportunities). But behavior differences by gender are still very evident in U.S. society.

The Social Dimensions of Sexuality

Laumann and others[10] look at three theoretical traditions to construct a more comprehensive theory of the social dimensions of human sexuality. These include a social network theory, a choice theory, and a scripting theory. These three theories are not mutually exclusive. They tend to focus on different but interrelated questions about sexual activity. The first two will be described very briefly with a more extensive analysis given to scripting theory.

Social Network Theory

Social network theory focuses on the sexual dyad embedded within larger networks of social relationships. Sexual activity involves two or more persons either explicitly or implicitly (such as with sexual fantasy or masturbation). These persons seek out other persons in their network of *eligibles* who are of relatively equal status. The principle of least interest, described in the previous chapter, comes into play as well in the dyadic sexual relationship. If the partners are not of similar status or do not have something equal to offer, one can extract or demand from the other person something greater than he or she is ordinarily willing to provide.

The two or more persons in a relationship are themselves part of a larger social network involving parents and friends that encompasses the norms and values of a larger social community, subculture, and culture. People connected to the sexual dyad imply pressures to engage in or refrain from engaging in various activities. Even formal organizations such as schools or Planned Parenthood contribute to and influence such things as sexual knowledge or contraceptive availability. Certainly the mass media, religious and political groups, and other sources in society have an impact on sexual dyads and their behaviors. In brief, network theory implies that sexual partnerships are social relationships that do not exist in a vacuum.

The importance of neighborhood characteristics on adolescent sexual behavior is an important extension of this social network theory. In particular, the concept of community *collective efficacy* (introduced in Chapter 4) reflects social network effects. As measured by Christopher Browning and his colleagues, in a study using representative data from the Project on Human Development in Chicago, this concept refers to the degree to which residents viewed their neighborhood as "close knit" and mutually supportive, as a place where the parents of children's friendship groups knew each other and looked out for each others'

---

[10]Edward O. Laumann, John Gagnon, Robert T. Michael, and Stuart Michaels, *The Social Organization of Sexuality* (Chicago: University of Chicago Press, 1994), 3–24.

children, and as a place where the residents were people that children could "look up to." Their analysis revealed that high levels of community collective efficacy significantly reduced the likelihood that children in the neighborhood would engage in sexual intercourse with more than one partner during the previous three-year time period. This effect held generally for all adolescents in their study (between the ages of 12 and 16), but was even stronger among older adolescents in their early teens.[11]

Choice Theory

Choice theory focuses on sexual decision making and how individuals choose what to do. Sexually, as in economics, people have choices that require certain resources to get the "goods" or rewards. The necessary resources may include time, money, physical energy, attractiveness, or available partners. Because resources are limited, choices must be made. In making these choices, certain goals must exist. The goals may be for physical pleasure, emotional satisfaction, marriage, having children, maintaining a good reputation, or something else.

Goals influence the amount and types of resources to use in reaching them. Seeking a long-term relationship will require different resources of time, money, and energy than seeking a "one-night stand." Both entail costs in order to gain the rewards. Both have the potential to produce desirable and/or undesirable by-products. Desirable ones may be a happier person, sexual satisfaction, or a committed partner, whereas negative ones may be an unwanted pregnancy, a sexually transmitted disease, or guilt. In concurrence with social exchange theory, individuals make decisions about sexual behavior on the basis of a weighing of these potential rewards and costs.

Generally, the more information one has about the outcome, the wiser will be the choice. But, unfortunately, choices are always made under varying degrees of information and certainty. Individuals often make decisions not in their best interest because they lack sufficient information to make choices that will best allow them to meet their goals. Making the best choice also requires the individual to calculate the correct probabilities of obtaining desired outcomes and avoiding potential costs. Thus, there is considerable room for variability in choice across individuals with similar goals under the same structures of rewards and costs. We may be accustomed to thinking of these choices as private and personal, but network theory reminds us that other persons are involved. The partner is making choices as well that will affect the outcome, and personal or relationship outcomes can have consequences at a collective or societal level: STDs, welfare costs, family reputations, and so forth. As a result, others will attempt to influence our perceptions of alternatives, actual rewards and costs, and assessments of outcomes in a way that maximizes their own outcomes.

In sum, choice theory involves sexual decision making. It demands choices based on the goals we have in mind and the resources available to meet them. All choices have consequences, positive or negative, that influence us personally, our partner in a dyadic relationship, our social groups and networks, and even the society at large.

---

[11]Christopher R. Browning, Lori A. Burrington, Tama Leventhal, and Jeanne Brooks-Gunn, "Neighborhood Structural Inequality, Collective Efficacy, and Sexual Risk Behavior among Urban Youth," *Journal of Health and Social Behavior*, 49 (September 2008): 269–285.

news item

Chinese City Is Chilly to a Sex Theme Park

BEIJING — Sex in China has a long and varied history, as evidenced by accounts of carnal excess in "The Plum in the Golden Vase," a Ming-era classic, and more recent tales of Mao's insatiable appetite.

But an attempt to open the first sex theme park in China was quashed by local officials over the weekend, well before construction was completed.

Officials in the sprawling city of Chongqing, where Love Land was being built, recently became incensed over the risqué nature of the park and ordered its destruction, according to a report published Sunday in the Chongqing Evening News, a state-run newspaper...

Photographs on the Internet showed workers on Saturday pulling down a pair of white plastic legs and hips that appear to be the bottom half of a giant female mannequin towering over the park entrance. The mannequin is wearing a red G-string.

The park manager, Lu Xiaoqing, had planned to have on hand naked human sculptures, giant models of genitals, sex technique "workshops" and a photography exhibition about the history of sex, according to China Daily. The displays would have included lessons on safe sex and the proper use of condoms.

Mr. Lu told China Daily that the park was being built "for the good of the public." Love Land would be useful for sex education, he said, and help adults "enjoy a harmonious sex life." He added, "Sex is a taboo subject in China, but people really need to have more access to information about it..."

Officials could not be reached for comment late Monday afternoon.

Chinese approach sex with an attitude that seems alternately more prudish and more open than that of Westerners.

The government, for example, regularly censors movies and other works of art that are deemed to have overly graphic depictions of sex...Parents rarely talk to their children about sex.

On the other hand, prostitution, while officially illegal, is practiced openly, with full-service "massage parlors" and "hair salons" found everywhere. Officials and businessmen have a propensity to take and support a mistress as a sign of success in their careers.

Source: Edward Wong, *New York Times*, May 19, 2009.

Sexual Script Theory and Sexualization

Scripting theory explains sexual content: what we perceive to be sexual and how we construct our ideas, thoughts, and fantasies. It is assumed that human beings have no biological instincts about how to act sexually; thus, behaviors must be learned through a process of sexual socialization—that is, sexualization.

Sexualization is the process by which persons learn of and internalize their sexual self-concepts, values, attitudes, and behaviors. It is a process that begins at birth and continues into adulthood and old age. Details of the socialization process, with regard to sexuality, gender, violence, and other factors, are described in Chapter 11 At this point, attention will focus specifically on the learning and development of sexual knowledge, attitudes, and values. These aspects of sexualization are vital to understanding sexual behavior.

Symbolic interaction theory posits that people become sexual beings through social interaction. Even though there is an important biological and hormonal basis to sexual development, simply having female or male genitals does not guarantee that one's gender identity or preferences will follow anatomical makeup. This is evidenced in transvestism (dressing in the clothing of the opposite sex), transsexualism (feeling trapped in the body of the wrong sex), and homosexuality (preference for same-sex relationships). That behaviors differ in spite of genetic similarities is

Sexual socialization is a process that begins at birth and continues into adulthood and old age. Social responses to child sexual play influence the meanings internalized—the sexual scripts—about what is appropriate sexual behavior.

evidenced as well in the wide range of acceptable or nonacceptable attitudes and behaviors that exist among persons in general: sexual abstinence, fellatio, masturbation, sodomy, voyeurism, rape, experimentation with sexual positions, and so forth.

Symbolic interaction theory posits as well that sexual behavior can be understood only in terms of internalized symbolic meanings. This suggests that the definition of the situation and the meaning given to a certain behavior are basic to understanding that behavior or lack of behavior. If premarital coitus is defined as sinful, if masturbation is believed to cause insanity, and if homosexuality is perceived as perverted, these meanings will have a major but not absolute influence on whether the behavior occurs and also how. That is, definitions, attitudes, meanings, values, and other internalized mental processes predispose behavior.

These ideas, basic to a symbolic interaction frame of reference, parallel the ideas of William Simon and John Gagnon. They conceptualized the outcome of what is here termed *sexualization* in terms of **sexual scripts.**[12] Like a script for a play or movie, a sexual script provides an overall blueprint of what sexuality is and how it is practiced. The sexual script designates the *who*, *what*, *when*, *where*, and *why* of sexuality.

Scripts are the plans that people have in their heads. The sexual script defines *whom* one has sex with. Sex is not allowed with certain categories of people, but others are on the "approved" list. The script defines *what* sexual behaviors are right or wrong, appropriate or inappropriate. While kissing or masturbation may be on the approved list, anal sex or beastiality may not. The script includes the *when* and *where* of sex. Is it appropriate only at night in a bedroom? Is it also appropriate at noon in an automobile? And, finally, the script includes the *why* issue. Is sex for fun, intimacy, reducing tension, procreation, or some other reason?

One's sexual script is the internalized notions of these who, what, when, where, and why questions. It is learned in interaction with others and contains notions of the society, subculture, reference groups, and significant others in which one is a member and with whom one interacts. In interaction with others, individuals build their scripts, those cognitive schemes that affect their actual conduct.

The process by which one's sexual script is formulated tends to illustrate the importance of adult socialization in contrast to the Freudian emphasis on the early years. At puberty, a young person may be largely ignorant of adult sexuality. Adolescence is a period when adult sexual scripts become formulated, experienced, and modified. Simon and Gagnon argued that, for behavior to occur, something

---

[12]William Simon and John H. Gagnon, "Sexual Scripts: Permanence and Change," *Archives of Sexual Behavior* 15 (1986): 97–120. For a more detailed discussion of sexual scripts, see William Simon and John H. Gagnon, "A Sexual Script Approach," in James H. Geer and William T. O'Donohue, *Theories of Human Sexuality* (New York: Plenum Press, 1987), Chapter 13, 363–383.

resembling scripting must occur on three distinct levels: cultural scenarios, interpersonal scripts, and intrapsychic scripts.[13]

Cultural scenarios are the instructional guides that exist at the level of collective life. The enactment of virtually any role reflects the institutions, groups, and social context in which one was born and raised and currently functions. The mass media, including movies, television, and magazines, have profound real-life effects in the formation of sexual scripts.[14] **Interpersonal scripts** transform the person trained in cultural scenarios and general social roles to context-specific behavior. What one does is influenced by the responses of others. These cultural scenarios and interpersonal scripts result in **intrapsychic scripting,** an internal dialogue, a world of fantasy, or in interaction terms—a personal self that is in reality a social self. The private world of individual wishes and desires is bound to social life. All sexual behavior includes these three levels of scripting.

One illustration of scripting theory is seen in an attempt to understand female topless behavior on Australian public beaches.[15] Female students at a university in Sydney, half of whom had gone topless on the beach, were asked a series of questions about their behavior. There was universal agreement about toplessness not being appropriate when walking off the beach area. Scripts differed considerably between the women who had gone topless and those who had not. Those who had gone topless focused on the natural aspect of sunbathing and the sense of personal freedom, believed that the behavior was not sexual or exhibitionist, believed that the community as well as their peers and significant others approved of the behavior, and had higher self-esteem and higher body image. Those who had not gone topless perceived it as being too embarrassing and had a more negative body image.

It would seem that differences in sexual attitudes and behaviors cross-nationally, as well as changes over time, can be explained less by physiological or biological factors than by the scripts that predominate at any given time or place. If national data from Finland are any indicator of what is happening in the Western world, sexual satisfaction is increasing greatly, particularly among women. Scripts such as being sexually unreserved, a nonreligious orientation, sexual assertiveness, considering sexuality important in life, and acceptance of many-sided (versatile) sexual techniques were simply a few of the factors (scripts) that correlated with finding sexual intercourse pleasurable.[16]

Sexual Orientation

One aspect of sexuality that has been at the center of the debate over biological versus social influences is that of *sexual orientation*. **Sexual orientation** is defined as "an enduring emotional, romantic, sexual or affectional attraction to another person."[17] Although it is perceived by many in society to be a discrete dichotomous concept

---

[13]Simon and Gagnon, "Sexual Scripts," 98–104.

[14]Note, for example, Laura M. Carpenter, "From Girls into Women: Scripts for Sexuality and Romance in *Seventeen Magazine*, 1974–1994," *The Journal of Sex Research* 35 (May 1998): 158–168.

[15]Edward Herold, Bruna Corbesi, and John Collins, "Psychosocial Aspects of Female Topless Behavior on Australian Beaches, *The Journal of Sex Research* 31 (1994): 133–142.

[16]Elina Haavio-Mannila and Osmo Kontula, "Correlates of Increased Sexual Satisfaction," *Archives of Sexual Behavior* 26 (1997): 399–419.

[17]American Psychological Association, *Answers to Your Questions about Sexual Orientation and Homosexuality*. Retrieved from www.apa.org/pubinfo/answers.html, 2005.

referring to an exclusive attraction either to the opposite sex (**heterosexual**) or the same sex (**homosexual**), research has shown that sexual orientation exists on a continuum with many people exhibiting a primary but not exclusive orientation to one sex or the other and others identifying themselves as having an attraction to both sexes equally (**bisexual**).[18]

A key element of this definition is the idea of it being an *enduring* attraction or a *preference* and not just incidental engagement in sexual behavior of one type or the other.[19] The best estimate (based on the most representative sample) of the number of people admitting to a same-sex experience sometime after the age of 18 is about 5 percent for men and 4 percent for women. The actual number of men and women who identify themselves as having a same-sex (**gay** or **lesbian,** respectively) or bisexual orientation, however, is only 2.8 percent for men and 1.4 percent for women.[20] Furthermore, many experience a shift in sexual orientation over their life course, although such shifts are less likely to occur after the age of 17.[21] Thus, a same-sex orientation becomes part of one's sexual identity but is not a necessary outcome of having experienced isolated incidences of sexual relations with someone of the same sex.

Where does this sexual identity originate from? Again quoting from the American Psychological Association website, "Sexual orientation is most likely the result of a complex interaction of environmental, cognitive and biological factors...shaped at an early age."[22] Recent studies of identical twins versus fraternal twins and adopted sibling pairs suggest the strong biological component of sexual orientation[23] and one study of gay fathers and their sons showed little evidence of socialization into a same-sex orientation.[24] Given this strong biological component (especially for men) and the fact that sexual orientation appears to be shaped at an early age regardless of its source, it would not be fair to say that sexual orientation is a choice. There is also no convincing evidence from unbiased studies to document that sexual orientation can be changed in adulthood.

Sexual orientation is an important variable in the study of families. Although the American Psychological Association no longer classifies homosexuality as a mental disorder, the heterosexist culture that led to that diagnosis continues to treat homosexuality as deviant. As such, the coming-out process of homosexual youth in families is likely to generate conflict and the processes of partner selection and relationship formation will likely be different. Once relationships are formed, they then

---

[18]P.C.R. Rust, "Bisexuality: The State of the Union," in J.R. Helman and C.M. Davis, *Annual Review of Sex Research*, Volume 12 (Allentown, PA: The Society for the Scientific Study of Sexuality, 2003), 180–240.

[19]L. Ellis and M.A. Ames, "Neurohormonal Functioning and Sexual Orientation: A Theory of Homosexuality-Heterosexuality," *Psychological Bulletin* 101 (1987): 223–258.

[20]R. Michael, J. Gagnon, E. Laumann, and G. Kolata, *Sex in America: A Definitive Survey* (Boston: Little, Brown, 1994).

[21]G. Ramafedi, M. Resnick, R. Blum, and L. Harris, "Demography of Sexual Orientation in Adolescents," *Pediatrics* 89 (1992): 714–721.

[22]American Psychological Association, *Answers to Your Questions about Sexual Orientation and Homosexuality.*

[23]J.M. Bailey and R.C. Pillard, "A Genetic Study of Male Sexual Orientation," *Archives of General Psychiatry* 48 (1991): 1089–1096; and J.M. Bailey, R.C. Pillard, M.C. Neale, and Y. Agyei, "Heritable Factors Influence Sexual Orientation in Women," *Archives of General Psychiatry* 50 (1993): 217–223.

[24]J.M. Bailey, D. Bobrow, M. Wolfe, and S. Mikach, "Sexual Orientation of Adult Sons of Gay Fathers," *Developmental Psychology* 31 (1995): 124–129.

must weather a more hostile and less supportive social context, which should in turn produce greater stress. Finally, the resolution of such major issues as same-sex marriage and adoption may depend on gaining a fuller understanding of what homosexuality is and how it affects us, our relationships, and society in general.

Heteronormativity

The debate over the meaning of sexual orientation and the cultural tendency to divide the world of sexuality into two opposing "orientations"—heterosexual and homosexual—has led a number of scholars to examine how the definition of *homosexuality* contributes to the meaning of *heterosexuality* itself and how the meaning of heterosexuality more generally combines with other systems of meaning (e.g., the meaning of being a man versus being a woman) to produce a broader ideological system.[25] These scholars attempt to show how our beliefs about sexuality are *constructed* through a process whereby some behaviors are negatively sanctioned as deviant in order to clarify the boundaries of what is acceptable across a wider range of behaviors and relationships. For example, by defining homosexuality as deviant and denying homosexuals certain rights or protections from being harmed by others, society reinforces the idea that sex is for procreation and should occur within the context of a family consisting of two biological parents. It also reinforces the idea that there is a *natural* difference between men and women that is tied to their roles in the sex act and the power relations implied by those roles. Thus, how we define what is appropriate in terms of sexuality and sexual behavior is closely tied to our ideas of what is appropriate behavior for men versus women as well as ideas about what makes up a *true* family. The term **heteronormativity**, then, is intended to convey a social process whereby the rules or scripts for acceptable social behavior are constructed by labeling unacceptable behaviors and attaching negative images and sanctions to those labels. Like all social processes, heteronormativity is shaped by controlling interests such that our beliefs about what constitutes appropriate sexual behavior will be consistent with other intersecting belief systems—gender, family, race, and so on. One of the goals of sociology, then, should be the *deconstruction* of these definitions, or the critical examination of how social definitions of sexual orientation reflect the interests of dominant groups in society and contribute to existing inequalities.

Although the deconstruction of heteronormativity has been a particular concern of queer theory, cultural beliefs, rules and scripts about sexuality and sexual behavior extend beyond the simple heterosexual–homosexual distinction. Ramona Faith Oswald, Libby Balter Blume, and Stephen Marks highlight three sets of oppositions found in contemporary ideas of heterosexuality: the "gender binary," the "sexuality binary," and the "family binary."[26] The **gender binary** consists in a belief that men and women are naturally different from each other and this difference defines not

---

[25]For a discussion of the concept of heteronormativity, see: Chrys Ingraham, "The Heterosexual Imaginary: Feminist Sociology and Theories of Gender," in Steven Siedman, ed. *Queer Theory/Sociology* (Cambridge, MA: Blackwell, 1996): 168–193.

[26]Ramona Faith Oswald, Libby Balter Blume, and Stephen R. Marks, "Decentering Heteronormativity: A Model for Family Studies," in Vern L. Bengston, Alan C. Acock, Katherine R. Allen, Peggye Dilworth-Anderson, and David M. Klein, *Sourcebook of Family Theory and Research* (Thousand Oaks, CA: Sage Publications, 2005), 143–166.

TRANSNATIONAL FAMILIES

British Transient Heterosexuality in Dubai

With increasing numbers of young single people moving to other parts of the world in search of education and employment in a global economy, a question arises about how these individuals construct identity. It was this problem that led Katie Walsh to Dubai, United Arab Emirates, where she would conduct an ethnographic study of British expatriates. However, as she became integrated into this community—especially among her own 24–35 year old age group—she discovered another important challenge faced by transnationals in this particular context: an environment of relatively free and unbridled sexuality.

As a Muslim country, Dubai places considerable restrictions on the public displays of sexuality but also allows its transnational citizens (80 percent of the population) to operate freely within the context of private locations such as bars and nightclubs. It was here that Walsh did most of her ethnographic work. What she found was that high levels of casual sexual relations with multiple partners were the norm in this age group of expatriates. Based on an examination of her own experiences and feelings as well as those she observed around her, she found the "foreignness" of the place and its exotic character created an opportunity to be free of the conventional heteronormativity found back home in Britain. Both men and women reported wanting to escape from the commitment constraints of long-term relationships that came with the practice of sexuality in Britain. They didn't want to become "trapped" in a relationship but they also wanted sexual experiences. Thus, they participated in "transient heterosexuality" in a foreign location where the setting was carefully controlled by club owners to keep out sex trade workers and natives and where the rules of life and sexuality were temporarily "suspended."

This "sexual performance" was not simply motivated by uncontrolled sexual desire nor was it always rewarding. Most did not move to Dubai for sex. Rather, they were there for education or work. What they encountered was a highly transient culture where the establishment of long-term relationships was difficult. As a result, many saw more anonymous sexual relations as less risky insofar as they avoided the development of fragile intimacies and helped negate the potential loneliness that can come from seeking intimacies that don't materialize. Even so, the young people living in Dubai experienced considerable ambivalence about their sexual performances. Many of the longer term residents would refer to highly active newcomers as "freshers" and mock them because they did not yet understand how their promiscuous behaviors would become predictable, boring, and superficial. At the same time, however, they were engaging in similar activities themselves. Walsh also notes how this transient sexuality was not as free from gender inequalities as many women thought it was. She noted how women continued to spend more and work more than men on their appearance, how many still saw marriage as a goal in terms of potential status attainment, and many acted within their sexual relationships with men in a way that denied their own intimacy needs and catered to the idea of a nonemotional, nonintimate male partner.

Source: Katie Walsh, "'It got very debauched, very Dubai!' Heterosexual Intimacy Amongst Single British Expatriates," *Social and Cultural Geography*, 8 (August 2007): 507–533.

only the nature and purpose of sexuality but also sustains other inequalities that exist based on gender. The **sexuality binary** contrasts "natural" sex with "unnatural" sex and attempts to constrain sexual behavior to heterosexual intercourse. This belief that heterosexual intercourse is natural while other sex acts are not often is sustained by references of biological and physiological differences between men and women. The "naturalness" of heterosexual intercourse ties into a larger belief that sex should be oriented toward procreation and that other forms of sex are deviant. Finally, the **family binary** involves a contrast between "real" families defined by the presence of a father and a mother and "pseudo" families defined by undesirable conditions such as single parenting and cohabitation. The sustaining of this distinction privileges certain groups over others (e.g., whites vs. blacks) and is tied to the beliefs that the genders are fundamentally different from each other and that heterosexual intercourse is natural while other forms of sexual behavior are not.

A key point made by Oswald and her colleagues is that individuals' behaviors are not over-determined by heteronormativity. Although we make decisions about sexual behavior and identity in a context that is more or less heteronormative, we also actively construct our own identity and meaning systems. By "doing gender," "doing sexuality," and "doing families" in alternative ways we can break down artificial binaries and the systems of inequality and oppression attached to them.

Nonmarital Sexual Behavior

Family Antecedents of Sexual Behavior

Antecedents of sexual behavior are factors that precede or occur prior to a given sexual activity. These include biological antecedents, such as age and sexual maturation; psychological antecedents, such as cognitive and emotional development; and social antecedents, such as family, peers, religion, and cultural norms. Although we tend to assume that sexual behavior is private and personal, it is shaped by social/cultural factors. Even the community context of racially segregated neighborhood environments, labor force participation of women, population composition, and family planning service availability were found to affect the likelihood of sexual activity.[27] The primary focus in this section, however, will be on family and parental actions.

Families and parents are considered central in forming sexual attitudes and behaviors, in providing role models, in promoting a healthy social and economic environment, and in teaching appropriate standards of sexual conduct.

The importance of family structure per se, however, varies. In Great Britain, for example, family environments characterized by parent–child arguing, parental divorce or separation, and a family history of nonmarital fertility were all found to be related to premarital conception.[28] In contrast, several studies using U.S. national longitudinal data suggest that family structures, such as growing up in step-, cohabiting, or lesbian families, prolonged exposure to a single-mother family, or prolonged absence of a biological father, do not significantly influence adolescents' sexual initiation for either black or white women.[29]

Simple logic would indicate that a major antecedent factor in explaining adolescent sexual behavior is parental influence in the sexual socialization process. For example, is it not logical to assume that individuals brought up in sexually

---

[27]John O.G. Billy, Karin L. Brewster, and William R. Grady, "Contextual Effects on the Sexual Behavior of Adolescent Women," *Journal of Marriage and the Family* 56 (May 1994): 387–404; and Karin L. Brewster, "Race Differences in Sexual Activity among Adolescent Women: The Role of Neighborhood Characteristics," *American Sociological Review* 59 (June 1994): 408–424.

[28]Stephen T. Russell, "Life Course Antecedents of Premarital Conception in Great Britain," *Journal of Marriage and the Family* 56 (May 1994): 480–492.

[29]Erin Calhoun Davis and Lisa V. Friel, "Adolescent Sexuality: Disentangling the Effects of Family Structure and Family Context," *Journal of Marriage and Family* 63 (August 2001): 669–681; and Lawrence L. Wu and Elizabeth Thom-son, "Race Differences in Family Experience and Early Sexual Initiation: Dynamic Models of Family Structure and Family Change," *Journal of Marriage and Family* 63 (August 2001): 682–696.

conservative homes will have less premarital heterosexual involvement than those from more liberal home environments? Children who grow up in homes in which parents do not openly display affection, have a rigid and concerned attitude toward nudity, never discuss sex openly, and never have books or pamphlets available on sexual subjects should demonstrate conservative behavior and have little sexual involvement.

Data from two independent studies that included teenagers and their mothers, however, suggest a different reality. These studies showed that neither parental attitude toward premarital sex nor parent–child communication about sex and contraception affected teenagers' subsequent sexual and contraception behavior.[30] Teens who communicated little with their mothers were as likely to use effective birth control as were those who communicated well. Authors of both studies suggested that family communication does not count for very much in terms of either sexual behavior or contraceptive use. One reason may be that parental communication about sex and contraception generally is too vague or too limited to have an impact. It is possible as well that the quality of the parent–child relationship decreases as a result of teenagers' sexual activity or that parents (mothers) are more likely to talk with their children about sex *after* the fact (a time-order issue).

What about the related issue of parental discipline? Are adolescents from homes with very strict discipline and rules about dating sexually conservative, and are those from homes with few rules and lenient discipline sexually permissive?

Survey data from several thousand adolescents (ages 15 to 18) and their parents were analyzed to determine how parental discipline was related to the sexual permissiveness of their children.[31] As just hypothesized, sexual permissiveness was highest among adolescents who viewed their parents as not being strict or not having rules about dating. But, interestingly, adolescents who experienced very strict parental discipline and many dating rules were more permissive than those with moderate parental strictness and rules. In other words, a *curvilinear* relationship was found showing that both strict and lenient disciplinary patterns resulted in higher levels of sexual permissiveness. The lowest level of permissiveness was among adolescents with moderately strict parents.

How might the preceding findings be explained? First, perhaps children do not interpret the presence or absence of sexual behavior on the part of parents as being particularly relevant to their own sexual needs and experiences. Second, perhaps parental disciplinary behavior is a consequence of adolescent permissiveness. That is, if parents suspect that their teenager is engaging in sexual intercourse, they may impose more dating rules. Third, although parents may be extremely influential in general socialization, they may be less influential in sexual socialization than significant others outside the home, particularly peers.

---

[30]Susan F. Newcomer and J. Richard Udry, "Parent–Child Communication and Adolescent Sexual Behavior," *Family Planning Perspectives* 17 (July/August 1985): 169–174; and Frank F. Furstenberg, Jr., Roberta Herceg-Baron, Judy Shea, and David Webb, "Family Communication and Teenagers' Contraceptive Use," *Family Planning Perspectives* 16 (July/August 1984): 163–170. See also Monica A. Longmore, Wendy D. Manning, and Peggy C. Giordano, "Preadolescent Parenting Strategies and Teens' Dating and Sexual Initiation: A Longitudinal Analysis," *Journal of Marriage and Family* 63 (May 2001): 322–335.

[31]Brent C. Miller, J. Kelly McCoy, Terrance D. Olson, and Christopher M. Wallace, "Parental Discipline and Control Attempts in Relation to Adolescent Sexual Attitudes and Behavior," *Journal of Marriage and the Family* 18 (August 1986): 503–512.

Nonfamily Influences on Sexual Behavior

The role of nonfamily relationships in shaping sexual behavior may be particularly important during the period of adolescence and may account for the general lack of clear evidence for family effects. According to **reference group theory** (the symbolic interaction frame of reference), individuals continuously form and reform their self-concepts and corresponding behavioral expectations based on the reactions they receive from a subset of others in their network of social relationships. In childhood, that network is largely restricted to parents and other family members. During adolescence, however, the child's social networks expand and new *reference groups* are formed whose reactions may take on greater importance than those of parents.

Support for this theory comes from a study of Hispanic adolescents.[32] Family measures of parent–child communication and parental warmth were not related to Hispanic adolescent sexual involvement. However, peer influences were. Perceived peer sexual behavior was a significant predictor of adolescent sexual expression for both males and females, but strongest for males. Attitude toward nonmarital sex was also found to be significantly related to young Hispanic teens' sexual behavior, when controlled for age. Consistent with reference group theory, peers were chosen ahead of parents as referents for judging the correctness of sexual involvement for Hispanic youth.

Further support for reference group theory can be found in studies showing a relationship between deviant behavior and sexual behavior in adolescence. A nationally representative sample of young Americans revealed that, even when controlling for important risk factors (family intactness, school context, biological maturity, and sociodemographic characteristics), the reported prior use of cigarettes, alcohol, marijuana, and illicit drugs greatly increases the risk of early sexual activity for adolescent males and females.[33] The higher the stage of drug involvement and the earlier the reported onset of drug use, the greater the probability of early sex.

This finding is highly consistent with more recent data from high school students in Alabama, New York, and Puerto Rico comparing four groups of teenagers in various levels of sexual involvement.[34] The most active group, those who had multiple partners, were most likely to smoke, use alcohol and marijuana, have friends who had

One of the strongest predictors of adolescent sexual promiscuity is the level of other problematic or deviant behaviors engaged in. Sexual scripts are just one other constraint against which adolescents can assert their independence.

---

[32]F. Scott Christopher, Diane C. Johnson, and Mark W. Roosa, "Family, Individual, and Social Correlates of Early Hispanic Adolescent Sexual Expression," *The Journal of Sex Research* 30 (February 1993): 54–61.

[33]Emily Rosenbaum and Denise B. Kandel, "Early Onset of Adolescent Sexual Behavior and Drug Involvement," *Journal of Marriage and the Family* 52 (August 1990): 783–798.

[34]Daniel J. Whitaker, Kim S. Miller, and Leslie F. Clark, "Reconceptualizing Adolescent Sexual Behavior: Beyond Did They or Didn't They?" *Family Planning Perspectives* 32 (May/June 2000): 111–117.

had sex, have been pregnant themselves or made someone pregnant, be in poorer psychological health, engage in riskier peer behaviors, and have weaker ties to family, school, and church. In both of these studies, it is unlikely that smoking, alcohol, and drug use were the direct causes of sexual behavior. Rather, it is more likely that sexual behavior is part of a set of nonconforming behaviors promoted and positively reacted to by deviant peers who form a reference group for each other.

Relevance of Formal Sex Education

Formal **sex education**—that is, education dealing with the general area of sexuality in a structured context of classes, seminars, workshops, clinics, and the like—is, in general, supported by the public. Disagreement exists over what is appropriate content, who should teach it, whether to include moral values, and so forth.

Consider, for example, the topic of abortion, currently an emotionally charged issue in the United States. Should objective information on the prevalence, techniques, safety, and psychological consequences of abortion be taught to adolescents? Should it be taught by physicians, nurses, clergy, sex educators, social scientists, or others? Should this information be presented, regardless of whether it contradicts the moral and religious values and beliefs of adolescents or their parents?

Although some will argue that the need for services and information related to pregnancy prevention and safe abortion cannot be denied, others will argue that to teach or demand abstinence—or in any case, safe sex—eliminates any need for abortion or abortion education in the first place. A study of adolescent knowledge and attitudes about abortion revealed a lack of accurate knowledge. Most adolescents described abortion as medically dangerous, emotionally damaging, and widely illegal, despite much published evidence to the contrary.[35]

One might say, So what? Should information be presented that contradicts value and belief systems? Is ignorance better than knowledge? Or is false information that fits one's value system better than truth that contradicts it?

One argument against formal sex education, irrespective of topic, asserts that it should be taught in the home. However, many parents find it difficult to communicate openly and freely about sexuality and birth control with their children. Even when parents have accurate knowledge and make conscientious efforts to encourage sexual discussion and effective contraceptive behavior, emotional factors in the parent–child relationship may make such discussion difficult. Sexually active teenagers, who are likely to think their parents want them to be sexually inactive, are not likely to discuss experiences such as masturbation, oral/genital sex, and intercourse with their parents. Neither are they likely to go to their parents for contraceptive information or devices. Numerous legislative efforts to require clinics and agencies to inform parents of their adolescents' inquiries about contraception and abortion may make matters worse. Specifically, such efforts may have the unintended consequence of more unwanted pregnancies and sexually transmitted diseases rather than the intended consequence of improving parent–child communication.

Several key questions concerning formal sex education programs and clinics include: Does sex education lead the sexually inactive to become active? Does adolescents' knowledge increase? Are diseases and pregnancies prevented? In short, does sex education make any difference at all?

---

[35]Rebecca Stone and Cynthia Waszak, "Adolescent Knowledge and Attitudes about Abortion," *Family Planning Perspectives* 24 (March/April 1992): 52–57.

The results from evaluation research studies of formal programs are mixed, at best. Few programs lead to the negative consequences feared or the positive consequences hoped for. With support from the World Health Organization, forty-seven evaluation intervention studies were reviewed to assess the effects of HIV/AIDS and sexuality education on young people's sexual behavior.[36] Twenty-five of the forty-seven studies reported that sexuality education neither increased nor decreased sexual activity and attendant rates of pregnancy and sexually transmitted diseases (STDs). Seventeen reported that education delayed the onset of sexual activity, reduced the number of sex partners or reduced unplanned pregnancy and STD rates. Only three studies found increases in sexual behavior associated with sexuality education. Hence, the argument that sex education promotes promiscuity or earlier sexual activity has little support, either in the United States or around the world. Formal classes, school-based clinics, or sex education programs seldom influence sexual activity. In fact, a large proportion of teenagers initiate coitus before they have entered high school or participated in any sex education programs.

Sex education does, however, influence knowledge and behavior regarding contraceptives. Sexually active teenagers who had formal instruction reported knowing how to use more methods of contraception and using them more effectively than adolescents who had no instruction.[37] Also, sexually active women who had sex education were less likely to become pregnant than those who did not. The availability of contraceptives per se and the taking of a sex education class does not appear, however, to have much influence on adolescent sexual behavior. What does seem clear however, is that a sex education program that focuses exclusively on a single topic or approach—abstinence, pregnancy prevention, a "just say no" theme—is likely to be ineffective.[38]

$\mathcal{P}$remarital Sexual Intercourse

Premarital sexual intercourse is defined as coitus involving at least one partner who is single and has not been previously married. *Premarital* denotes that the person has never been married, not that the relationship is confined to the person one will marry.

First sexual intercourse in the United States most often occurs within a hooking-up or dating relationship, is a spontaneous and unplanned event, and seldom includes the use of contraceptives. It often is looked on as a major life transition and an event that most people remember. However, it is not always a pleasurable experience, especially for females. Data from more than 1,600 college students who had had sexual intercourse revealed that men reported experiencing more pleasure and less guilt than women.[39] Both sexes reported more pleasure and less guilt when sex occurred in a

---

[36]Anne Grunseit, Susan Kippax, Peter Aggleton, Mariella Baldo, and Gary Slutkin, "Sexuality Education and Young People's Sexual Behavior: A Review of Studies," *Journal of Adolescent Research* 12 (October 1997): 421–453.

[37]Marvin Eisen, Gail L. Zellman, and Alfred L. McAlister, "Evaluating the Impact of a Theory-Based Sexuality and Contraceptive Education Program," *Family Planning Perspectives* 22 (November/December 1990): 261–271; and Mark A. Schuster, Robert M. Bell, Sandra H. Berry, and David E. Kanouse, "Impact of a High School Condom Availability Program on Sexual Attitudes and Behaviors," *Family Planning Perspectives* 30 (March/April 1998): 67–72.

[38]F. Scott Christopher and Mark W. Roosa, "An Evaluation of an Adolescent Pregnancy Prevention Program: Is 'Just Say No' Enough," *Family Relations* 39 (January 1990): 68–72; and Mark W. Roosa and F. Scott Christopher, "Evaluation of an Abstinence-Only Adolescent Pregnancy Prevention Program: A Replication," *Family Relations* 39 (October 1990): 363–367.

[39]Susan Sprecher, Anita Barbee, and Pepper Schwartz, "Was It Good for You Too?: Gender Differences in First Sexual Intercourse Experiences," *The Journal of Sex Research* 32 (1995): 3–15.

close relationship than in a casual one. A pleasurable reaction for women was associated with a continuing involvement in the relationship.

Cross-culturally, it appears that many societies permit or even encourage premarital sexual relationships, particularly for males. The taboo that falls primarily on females is more a precaution against childbearing out of wedlock than a moral sanction. Using a global perspective, the crucial question, particularly for females, may not be whether premarital intercourse is permitted but whether unmarried motherhood is allowed. It is likely that a female's commitment to norms of chastity lessens as a separation of premarital intercourse from pregnancy becomes possible. Thus, if contraceptives, sterilization, abortion, and other social arrangements exist to prevent or terminate a pregnancy, sexual permissiveness will increase (prior to, apart from, or within a marriage).

Premarital **sexual permissiveness** will also increase as a couple approaches marriage or even a commitment to the relationship. The most conservative behaviors can be expected on a first meeting or date; behavior becomes increasingly permissive as the couple moves from hanging out or casual dating to a more serious commitment to the relationship, and eventually toward nonmarital cohabitation or marriage. Because marriage is the context of the greatest approval or legitimization of coitus, it can be expected that the more exclusive the relationship (the more marriage-like), the more permissive the sexual behavior.

Evidence for an increase in permissiveness with an increase in commitment has existed for decades. For example, when women were asked about their first intercourse experience, data from the 1995 National Survey of Family Growth showed that only 3 percent of women had their first intercourse with a man they had just met. About three of five women (61 percent) were "going steady" with the man they had intercourse with the first time and an additional one in five were engaged or married to him. About 12 percent of all women were married when they had their first intercourse.[40]

Evidence from undergraduate college students revealed that, whether the behavior was heavy petting, sexual intercourse, or oral/genital sex, the percentage of people who agreed each behavior was acceptable increased with each relationship stage.[41] That is, each behavior had the lowest level of acceptability when the relationship constituted dating with no particular affection; acceptability increased with dating and being in love, dating one person only, and engagement. Although practically no females and only 1 to 3 percent of males agreed that any of the three behaviors were acceptable in dating where there was no particular affection, more than three-fourths of all respondents agreed that all three behaviors were acceptable during engagement.

Changes in Premarital Sexual Activity

Many social forces in the contemporary United States have led to behavioral changes regarding premarital coitus and have the potential for producing further changes. In the past few decades, the birth control pill and numerous other means of contraception became readily available and acceptable for personal use among a large number of unmarried college women. Sexual candor became increasingly legitimized in the mass media, even by one of the most conservative media: television. The arrival of

---

[40]National Center for Health Statistics, "Fertility, Family Planning, and Women's Health: New Data From the 1995 National Survey of Family Growth," *Vital and Health Statistics* (Hyattsville, MD: Public Health Service, 1992–1995, May 1997), Series 23, no. 19, p. 5.

[41]John P. Roche and Thomas W. Ramsbey, "Premarital Sexuality: A Five-Year Follow-Up Study of Attitudes and Behavior by Dating Stage," *Adolescence* 28 (Spring 1993): 67–80.

Family Diversity

Sex, Love and Intimacy in the Lives of Gay Men

Cultural and scientific thinking about the lives of gay men tend to focus on their sexual practices without consideration of how these practices take on meaning in the heteronormative context of modern society. In an attempt to more fully develop our understanding of these men and their sexuality, Sean Slavin and his colleagues (HIV educators and researchers in Australia) undertook an exploratory study of how gay men perceive their sexuality and how sexuality is linked to their views on love and relationships and their marginalized position in society. A dominant theme they found in their qualitative interviews with 38 gay men was one of a struggle to make sense of their sex lives in light of a perceived distinction or "binary" between sex and love. There interviews revealed that gay men, not unlike heterosexuals, want all three—sex, love and long-term relationships—but in having been denied the opportunities to openly establish the latter and to participate in institutions that make sex and love commensurable experiences (such as marriage), they have developed much stronger ideas of separation between these relationship goals.

This separation has in turn led to a gay culture that is highly accepting of casual sex and gay individuals who experience high levels of ambivalence about their sexual behaviors. There is both a strong desire for intimacy, caring, and love in their sexual relationships as well as a strong rejection of the heteronormative romantic ideal that links these ideas together. As a result, many of the men they interviewed felt a sense of dissatisfaction in their casual sexual relationships as well as a sense of inadequacy in their less exciting love relationships. These feelings and desires may lie behind the low levels of condom use and high levels of sexual risk taking that put gay men at an increased risk of HIV infection and AIDs.

On a positive note, some of the men talked about how their casual sexual encounters often involved high levels of caring without having to make long-term commitments, suggesting the emergence of an alternative framework to the heteronormative one that casts sex and love as normalized in hierarchical marriage. Based on his analysis of these interviews, Slavin concludes:

> The findings in this study present two challenges.... The first challenge is to sex researchers,...not to reduce the complexity of gay desire to questions of sexual practice. The second is...not to ignore the difficulties that arise for many gay men attempting to find and build sexually and emotionally fulfilling relationships...gay men must continue the struggle to have their relationships recognized by the law and wider society, but they must seek recognition for the relationships they have, not the ones that are ideal or acceptable (e.g., gay marriage)." (94)

Source: Sean Slavin, "'Instinctively, I'm Not Just a Sexual Beast': The Complexity of Intimacy Among Australian Gay Men," *Sexualities*, 12 (2009), 79–96.

the Internet brought with it easy access to sexual chat with total strangers and an abundance of pornographic material. Social forces such as these have led to increased rejection of many traditional values, resulting in many changes in the sexual behavior of never-married people.

An analysis of premarital sexual behavior and attitudes over an extensive range of years—1965, 1970, 1975, 1980, and 1985—revealed a continued but asymptotic increase in reported premarital sexual behavior among both men and women.[42] Namely, the increase continued but at a slower rate over time; the rate in change in frequency of premarital coitus was much greater before 1980 than after. The reported change in the percentage of college males engaging in premarital sexual activity increased by

---

[42]Ira E. Robinson, Ken Ziss, Bill Ganza, and Edward Robinson, "Twenty Years of the Sexual Revolution, 1965–1985: An Update," *Journal of Marriage and the Family* 53 (February 1991): 216–220.

12.3 percent between 1965 and 1980; the increase for college females over the same period was 35 percent. Between 1980 and 1985, however, the rate of increase was a mere 2 percent for males, whereas for females the rate actually decreased a half percent.

Data on teenagers suggest an actual decline in the 1990s in the percentage reporting sexual intercourse (see Figure 8.1). Figures from several sources based on the National Survey of Family Growth[43] indicate that about 68 percent of males and 49 percent of females ages 15 to 19 reported they had ever had sexual intercourse as of 1995. For males, this was down from 76 percent in 1988, an increase from the 66 percent in 1979. For females, this was down from the 51 percent in 1988, an increase from the 41 percent in 1976. While the authors suggest caution, it appears that the long-term increase in sexual activity among teenagers may have ended, at least temporarily.

As might be expected, levels of sexual activity increased with age. While overall, 52 percent of females and 56 percent of males had ever had sexual intercourse at the time of the survey, by age 19, 71 percent of women and 85 percent of men had had intercourse. At all ages, the proportion of sexually experienced was higher among males than females, blacks than whites, those living with one parent than with two, and those with mothers who had not finished high school than those who did. Sixty-nine percent of adolescent women reported that their first experience was voluntary and wanted, 24 percent said it was voluntary but unwanted, and 7 percent said it was nonvoluntary.

The determination as to whether a sexual conservatism has returned depends on the nature of premarital sex considered. If premarital sex refers to intercourse and heavy

Figure 8.1

Percent of Females and Males Ages 15 to 19 Who Have Ever Had Sexual Intercourse by Year of Survey: United States, 1971–1995

Source: National Center for Health Statistics, "Sexual Activity and Contracepetive Practices among Teenagers in the United States: 1988 and 1955," *Vital and Health Statistics* (Hyattsville, MD: Public Health Service, April 2001), Series 23, no. 21, p. 9.

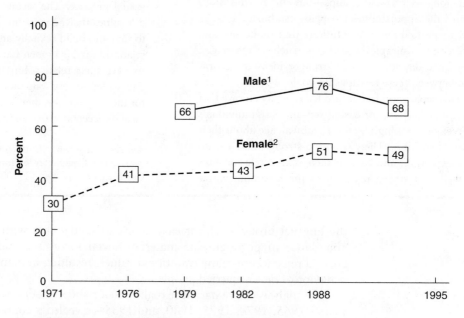

[1]Never-married metropolitan males ages 17–19 years
[2]Never-married females ages 15–19 years

[43]Susheela Singh and Jacqueline E. Darroch, "Trends in Sexual Activity among Adolescent American Women: 1982–1995," *Family Planning Perspectives* 31 (September/October 1999): 212–219; and Leighton Ku, Freya L. Sonenstein, Laura D. Lindberg, Carolyn H. Bradner, Scott Borgess, and Joseph H. Pleck, "Understanding Changes in Sexual Activity among Young Metropolitan Men: 1979–1995," *Family Planning Perspectives* 30 (November/December 1998): 256–262.

petting, there has been no return to conservatism. That is, increases in both have occurred over a twenty-year period (albeit at diminishing rates), along with a decline in negative attitudes toward premarital sex. When promiscuity (casual sexual relationships with numerous partners) is considered, a more conservative pattern emerges. Compared to the 1970s and 1980s, a greater percentage of both males and females today consider promiscuity immoral or sinful. The offense is still considerably more serious for the female: the double standard has not disappeared. The so-called sexual revolution in the United States over the past two or three decades was real, but it was restricted to premarital heterosexual relations. Attitudes toward extramarital and homosexual relations and, as noted earlier, promiscuity have remained distinctly restrictive.

In the past two decades, a new and serious health epidemic, involving an STD now widely known as AIDS, appeared on the world scene. A United Nations Report indicated that, as of the end of 2007, an estimated 33 million people worldwide (2 million of them children under the age of 15) were living with HIV/AIDS.[44] This represents about .9 percent of the global population between the ages of 15 and 49 and this percentage has changed little since it peaked in 2000. This leveling off in the rate is a reflection primarily of more effective programs in sub-Saharan Africa where rates have mostly declined. Globally, new cases of AIDS in 2007 amounted to 2.7 million, less than the 3 million new cases reported in 2001. Finally, AIDS has continued to become more equally distributed between men and women, with 50 percent of all cases around the world being found among women.

According to the U.S. Centers for Disease Control, more than 983,000 persons were infected with AIDS in the United States and its dependencies through the end of 2006.[45] More than 80 percent of all individuals living with AIDS in the United States were male. Among men with AIDS, 54.3 percent of cases were acquired by male-to-male sexual contact, with another 20.6 percent coming from injection drug use and 6.3 percent coming from high-risk heterosexual contact. In contrast, among women living with AIDS in 2006, most (44.4 percent) acquired the infection through high-risk heterosexual contract, with injection drug use the second most common means of contracting AIDS (35.3 percent) followed by the receipt of blood transfusion, blood components or tissue (27.5 percent). Forces such as these can be expected to restrict or modify the sexual activities of people of all ages, including adolescents and adults in the United States.

High-Risk Sexual Behavior and AIDS

Many infected persons are under age 25, yet young people continue to engage in high-risk sexual behavior—which basically refers to sex with multiple partners and a failure to protect themselves or their partners against sexually transmitted diseases and/or unwanted pregnancies. These behaviors are most common among men, younger people, and the unmarried.[46]

---

[44]Joint United Nations Programme on HIV/AIDS (UNAIDS), *Report on the Global HIV/AIDS Epidemic*, 2008.

[45]U.S. Census Bureau, *The 2009 Statistical Abstract*, "Table 177 - Reported AIDS Cases for Adults and Adolescents, by Transmission Category and Sex: Cumulative Through 2006." http://www.2010census.biz/compendia/statab/cats/health_nutrition.html.

[46]M. Margaret Dolcini, Joseph A. Catania, Thomas J. Coates, Ron Stall, Esther S. Hudes, John H. Gagnon, and Lance M. Pollack, "Demographic Characteristics of Heterosexuals with Multiple Partners: The National AIDS Behavioral Surveys," *Family Planning Perspectives* 25 (September/October 1993): 208–214.

A sample of college students at a midwestern university revealed that 80 percent of heterosexual males and 73 percent of heterosexual females were sexually experienced, defined as having had either penile/vaginal or penile/anal intercourse at some time in their lives.[47] About one-fifth of both the men and the women had engaged in anal intercourse. Males reported more sexual partners than females (an average of 8.0 for males and 6.1 for females). Over one-third of the respondents who had engaged in vaginal or anal intercourse during the previous year used either no form of protection from STDs or no method of contraception for pregnancy protection. These high levels of sexual activity, the tendency toward multiple partners, and the nonuse or inconsistent use of condoms and contraception are well-documented antecedents to unplanned pregnancy and contraction of STDs.

What kinds of factors are associated with sexual risk-taking among adolescents? A sample of several thousand midwestern sexually active teenagers comparing high risk-takers (multiple partners with rare or no use of contraception) with low risk-takers (one partner and regular use of contraceptives) revealed significant differences between the two groups.[48] For females and males, the high risk-takers had lower GPAs, more frequent alcohol consumption, lower levels of parental monitoring, a lack of communication with mothers about birth control, more frequent contemplation of suicide, a much greater history of sexual and physical abuse, and more troubled relationships with their parents.

How great is the risk of AIDS for groups other than teenagers? Nationally representative data from over 3,000 men revealed that, overall, a very small proportion of the male population is engaging in sexual conduct that involves a high risk of AIDS transmission.[49] Only 2 percent of sexually active men age 20 to 39 had had any same-gender sexual activity during the last ten years, about one-fifth of never-married and formerly married men had four or more partners over an eighteen-month period, and two-thirds of the never-married and one-third of the formerly married did not have any coitus in the four weeks preceding the interview.

Concern about HIV and other sexually transmitted diseases appears to have changed patterns of contraceptive use among unmarried women. Data from national samples in 1982, 1988, and 1995 revealed significant declines in pill and diaphragm use and an increase in reliance on condom use, especially among women under age 25, black and Hispanic, or unmarried.[50] In contrast, there was little change in condom use among married couples.

Nationally representative data from some 8,500 American women revealed that nearly one-third of sexually experienced unmarried women changed their

---

[47]June M. Reinisch, Craig A. Hill, Stephanie A. Sanders, and Mary Ziemba-Davis, "High-Risk Sexual Behavior at a Midwestern University: A Confirmatory Survey," *Family Planning Perspectives* 27 (March/April 1995): 79–82.

[48]Tom Luster and Stephen A. Small, "Factors Associated with Sexual Risk-Taking Behaviors among Adolescents," *Journal of Marriage and the Family* 56 (August 1994): 622–632. Note also Daniel F. Perkins, Tom Luster, Francisco A. Villarruel, and Stephen Small, "An Ecological, Risk-Factor Examination of Adolescents' Sexual Activity in Three Ethnic Groups," *Journal of Marriage and the Family* 60 (August 1998): 660–673.

[49]John O.G. Billy, Koray Tanfer, William R. Grady, and Daniel H. Klepinger, "The Sexual Behavior of Men in the United States," *Family Planning Perspectives* 25 (March/April 1993): 52–60.

[50]Linda J. Piccinino and William D. Mosher, "Trends in Contraceptive Use in the United States: 1982–1995," *Family Planning Perspectives* 30 (January/February 1998): 4–10.

sexual behavior in response to the threat of AIDS.[51] The most common change was to limit their number of sexual partners to one. This may explain as well why most women perceived their risk of developing AIDS to be low; 80 percent claimed they had little or no chance of becoming infected with the human immunodeficiency virus (HIV) that causes AIDS. The same report revealed that, although American women in general are well informed about AIDS, misinformation persists, especially among African American, Hispanic American, and low-income women.

---

[51]J.W. McNally and W.D. Mosher, "Digest," *Family Planning Perspectives* 23 (September/October 1991): 234–235.

Summary

1. Human sexual activity is regulated through social institutions, social norms, and a wide range of social sanctions.

2. Male–female and cross-national differences in premarital sexual attitudes and behaviors generally have been attributed by sociologists to the social context and the nature of socialization and social control factors. However, a number of researchers have explored the interplay between biological predispositions and sociological models of human sexuality.

3. Three theoretical traditions assist in constructing a more comprehensive theory of the social dimensions of human sexuality: a social network theory, a choice theory, and a scripting theory.

4. Scripting theory and sexualization explain the process by which people acquire their sexual self-concepts, values, attitudes, and behaviors. These meanings and definitions make up individuals' sexual scripts, designating the *who, what, when, where,* and *why* of sexuality.

5. One important aspect of human sexuality in which biological versus social factors have been debated is sexual orientation. Sexual orientation is an aspect of identity and isn't an either/or characteristic. Most people are either predominantly heterosexual or predominantly homosexual in orientation, but many fall in between and some identify as more clearly bisexual.

6. Studies of the origins of sexual orientation reveal a complex interplay of biological and environmental factors, although biology seems to be a major contributor and both types of effects appear to occur early in life leaving individuals with little choice in their sexual orientation.

7. Family antecedents to sexual behavior include parenting behaviors. However, neither parental attitudes nor parent–child communication appear to affect teenagers' subsequent sexual and contraceptive behavior. Parental discipline appears to have a curvilinear effect; both the most restrictive and permissive disciplinary patterns result in greater permissiveness.

8. Formal means of sex education seldom result in the type of positive consequences desired or the negative consequences feared. The decision to engage in sexual activity is not influenced by sex education classes, but sex education appears to have some effect on contraceptive knowledge and its effective use.

9. Adolescent heterosexual intercourse has attracted widespread research attention. Major changes have taken place in the sexual behavior of never-married individuals. These changes have been most pronounced for females, moving toward increased permissiveness; male–female differences have lessened, but the double standard has not been eliminated.

10. In spite of a fear of AIDS, data have suggested that many people continue to engage in high-risk behaviors, meaning multiple partners and no protection. Others have moved toward increased selectivity of sexual partners and greater condom use (but not abstention from sexual activity).

This chapter examined sexual relationships in the context of nonmarital relationships. Whether the context is nonmarital, marital, or extramarital, each is significant to interaction among intimate partners. Continuing within a partner selection and marital life course sequence, attention is directed in the next chapter to marital structures and processes.

Key Terms and Topics

Human sexuality p. 313
Social regulation of sexual relationships pp. 313–315
Biological theories p. 315
Social theories p. 315
Social network theory p. 317
Choice theory p. 318
Scripting theory p. 319
Sexualization p. 319
Sexual scripts p. 320
Cultural scenarios p. 321
Interpersonal scripts p. 321
Intrapsychic scripting p. 321
Sexual orientation p. 321
Heterosexual p. 322

Homosexual p. 322
Bisexual p. 322
Gay p. 322
Lesbian p. 322
Heteronormativity p. 323
Gender binary p. 323
Sexual binary p. 324
Family binary p. 324
Reference group theory p. 327
Sex education p. 328
Premarital sexual intercourse p. 329
Sexual permissiveness p. 330
Changes in premarital sexual activity pp. 330–333
High risk sexual behavior and AIDS pp. 333–335

Discussion Questions

1. All societies control sexual activities. Why? How?
2. Which is more important to understanding sexual behavior: (a) biological needs, drives, hormones, and the like; (b) social norms, values, attitudes, and so on; or (c) social controls and sanctions? Explain.
3. Are males and females inherently different in sexual socialization? If so, in what ways does society contribute to the difference?
4. Consider your own sexual script—with whom, what, where, when, why, and so forth. What factors are most influential in your script?
5. Examine the relationship between attitudes and behavior: what you believe versus what you do or have done. For you, how accurate is the idea that behavior often exceeds the acceptable belief/value script, which in turn modifies the belief or value?
6. In what ways is one's sexual orientation likely to impact one's family and romantic relationships?

How does discrimination and prejudice against gays and lesbians play a role in these effects?
7. What explains the finding that parental attitudes and parent–child communication seem to have little effect on adolescent sexual behavior and contraceptive usage?
8. Discuss the impact, if any, of sex education on adolescents' sexual attitudes, sexual behavior, and contraceptive usage. Should topics be taught (nonmarital sexuality, abortion, homosexuality) that may run counter to individuals' religious or moral values? Why?
9. What changes in sexual behavior have occurred over the past few decades? What accounts for these changes? Why have the changes been greater for females than males?
10. What explains the continuation of high-risk behaviors? Discuss the impact of AIDS on sexual behavior.

Further Readings

Christopher, F. Scott. *To Dance the Dance: A Symbolic Interactionist Exploration of Premarital Sexuality.* Mahwah, NJ: Lawrence Erlbaum Associates, Inc., 2001.

Symbolic interactionism is used to develop a model that integrates the research on premarital sexuality over the past four decades.

Christopher, F. Scott, and Sprecher, Susan. "Sexuality in Marriage, Dating, and Other Relationships: A Decade Review," *Journal of Marriage and the Family* 62 (November 2000): 999–1017.

A decade-review article covering sexuality inside and outside of marriage, including sexual coercion and aggression in dating.

Dalin, Liu, Ng, Man Lun, Zhou, Li Ping, and Haeberle, Erwin J. *Sexual Behavior in Modern China*. New York: The Continuum Publishing Co., 1997.

An extensive nationwide survey of the sexual behavior of 20,000 men and women in China.

Gagnon, John H. and Simon, William. *Sexual Conduct: The Social Sources of Human Sexuality*. Hawthorne, NY: Al-dine de Gruyter (expanded edition), 2002.

Using social script theory, the authors trace the ways that sexuality is learned and fits into different expressions of behavior.

Kamen, Paula. *Her Way: Young Women Remake the Sexual Revolution*. New York: New York University, 2000.

Based primarily on interviews with young women, the author provides a chronicle of a new generation of women considering their sex lives and the broad menu of choices they have.

Laumann, Edward O., Gagnon, John H., Michael, Robert T., and Michaels, Stuart. *The Social Organization of Sexuality: Sexual Practices in the United States*. Chicago: University of Chicago Press, 1994.

A comprehensive survey of sexual behavior based on a probability sample of 3,432 American women and men age 18–59.

Richardson, Diane. *Rethinking Sexuality*. London: Sage, 2000.

A critical examination of debates attached to conceptualizing sexuality as a site of knowledge and politics.

Schwartz, Pepper, and Rutter, Virginia. *The Gender of Sexuality*. Thousand Oaks, CA: Pine Forge Press, 1998.

A concise, well-written paperback presenting a sociological analysis that combines the topics of gender and human sexuality.

Weiderman, Michael W. and Whitley, Jr., Bernard E. *Handbook for Conducting Research on Human Sexuality*. Mahwah, NJ: Lawrence Erlbaum Associates, Inc., 2002.

A multidisciplinary examination of methodological issues inherent in conducting human sexuality research.

part IV

Life Course Conditions and Changes in Families

chapter 9

The Marital System

Fifty-Plus Years of Marriage and Family Life

Jim and Effie have experienced fifty-seven years of married life. They, more than any couple I have ever known, fit my image of a model marriage/family. Much to my pleasure, they consented to be interviewed.

Jim is a husband, father, grandfather, retired farmer, retired postal worker, and part-time Amish tour guide in Lancaster County, Pennsylvania. Effie is a wife, mother, grandmother, homemaker, and quilter. Together, they raised three children and today have six grandchildren. In addition, they took in the daughter—from birth until three months—of a mother who had cancer. For eight summers, they took in fresh-air inner-city children from New York City. Literally hundreds of friends of their children, family members, church and community people, and guests from throughout the world can testify to delicious home-cooked meals by Effie and visits or assistance of every kind from Jim.

Jim and Effie went to different high schools but were active in the same youth groups and church/community choral groups. She married at age 19, he at age 21. Effie had completed one year of college and had planned to major in home economics. She dropped out to get married, commenting that in the 1940s it was unheard of for a farmer's wife to get a college degree. Jim, being the only son, was expected to take over the family farm. His home became their home and is where they live today.

And their marriage? What did they find so special in each other? Jim spoke of the sparkle that Effie had in her eyes, her neatness, her devotion to their children, and her homemaking skills. He spoke with pride of her quilting accomplishments (at this writing she had completed about 130 quilts by herself—most of which she has given to family and friends). She has won many honors and is a recognized quilting authority in eastern Pennsylvania. Effie spoke of Jim's tolerance and understanding, his compassion, his sense of humor, and how they enjoy doing things together, such as gardening, singing, attending community concerts, and spending time with their children and grandchildren.

Neither Jim nor Effie ever doubted or questioned their love for one another. They mentioned some very difficult times, both financially and in trying to fulfill professional obligations that put tremendous pressure on their marriage and on their children. They spoke of some of their differences, such as how he enjoyed travel and she didn't and how he liked baseball and she tolerated it. Effie felt she was always the one more focused on saving money while Jim was more willing to spend and, if need be, borrow. They mentioned times when they got upset and raised their voices but never lost their tempers with one another.

Jim and Effie took their marriage vows to love until death as a sacred oath and commitment. Both viewed the other as understanding, tolerant, compassionate, and forgiving. Both spoke of their Christian values and their attempt to exhibit daily these values toward each other and everyone else with whom they come in contact. The church family, as they call it, has always been a priority in their lives and this is expressed through their kind words, hospital visits, volunteer work, providing meals and assistance as needed, and literally loving their neighbors as themselves.

Questions to Consider

What is your perception of a "model" marriage? Based on the information given about Jim and Effie, how do they conform to this model?

How important are factors such as marriage vows, age at marriage, equity in decision making, employment, income, or religion in having a marriage last fifty years or more?

Do you think the same things that helped Jim and Effie maintain their marriage for so long would also work today in making a successful and enduring marriage?

*I*n the previous three chapters, we examined marriage behavior, partner selection, and relationship dynamics in nonmarital and premarital relationships. Following a life-course model, we now will look at relationship dynamics in the context of marriage and marriage-like relationships. After an examination of the process of making the transition into marriage, we will discuss the nature of the division of labor between spouses, the principles of power and decision making in marriage, changes in sexual behavior over the course of marriage, and the concepts of marital quality and stability. We will then conclude this chapter with a look at same-sex relationships.

Transition to Marriage

In today's late modern society, the transition into marriage tends to be marked by large elaborate weddings and extended honeymoons in exotic locations. But did such customs always mark the transition and do they serve any purpose or function

news item

Poor Economy Is Taking a Toll on Wedding Bell$

Love will find a way. It always does.

Wedding season is in full swing, and not even a seriously dismal economy can douse the flames of true love. It can, however, tame the cost of the blaze...

Many...couples are finding creative ways to pare their costly visions for the big day. In some cases, they're moving the dates up and shrinking the guest list, while others are choosing faraway venues that ensure a turnout of only family and dear friends—and a much lower price tag...

Sometimes couples are opting to skip the guests' favors,...Others are cutting back on bar provisions or food.

And...young women [are] finding ways to skirt the expense of a gown, sometimes ordering bridesmaids' dresses in white or ivory and saving many hundreds of dollars.

Eloping, with Company

...Joe Ritt...owns The Wedding Travel Registry Inc., which arranges destination wedding/honeymoon packages. He says business is "way up" in his niche of the $80 billion wedding industry...

Typically, the guest list looks the same; only the address of the events is different. Much different: think Cancun or Milan or Montego Bay. The bottom line is that exotic settings notwithstanding, the attendance will still be a lot smaller.

"They know that people aren't going to answer positively in the same numbers as they would if it were at a venue nearby," Ritt said.

The idea appears to be catching on.

"Destinations are picking up," said Richard Markel, director of the 1,000-member Association for Wedding Professionals International.

Along with the benefit of a lower-cost wedding, the approach provides the option of having a reception later, which usually is a lower-key affair that calls for lighter staffing and much less expense, he said.

Going to Court

Another alternative many couples are choosing is heading to the courthouse for the nuptial formalities—quick, simple and extremely affordable...

The downtown Joliet courthouse offers wedding services six days a week. You don't even need an appointment, but couples need to bring along a marriage license, after a waiting period of at least a day, and $10 cash for the judge's fee.

As of May 20, the courthouse had seen 300 couples come in to be married this year, a call center spokeswoman said. The total for all of 2008 was 401...

Ever After

Wherever they take place, weddings aren't going to disappear into the sunset anytime soon. The Naperville area is bucking the trend toward fewer nuptials, but elsewhere, it's often a matter of a dream deferred.

"From a national level, the number of weddings has decreased, I'm going to guess, 5 percent," Markel said.

Usually there are 2.2 million weddings in the U.S. each year, and for 2009, events look to be down about 100,000. Markel predicted that those postponements will translate to a boom of about that many additional ceremonies in 2010, but expect the bells and whistles to be fewer.

"The wedding itself will not go away. They may get more frugal and more sharp-penciled about who they invite," he said. "So those second cousins may not get an invitation."

Many still will find the creamy, heavyweight envelope in the mailbox with the customary six to eight weeks' lead time.

"You're still going to see the majority of brides getting married when they want, where they want," Markel said. "The wedding industry is not bulletproof, it's not recession-proof, but it's resistant."

Source: Susan Frick Carlman, *The Naperville Sun*, May 27, 2009. http://www.suburbanchicagonews.com/napervillesun/news/1592474,Down-economy-weddings_na052709.article.

today? Historical research suggests that although large weddings took place as far back as the Middle Ages, the purpose of these weddings was quite different and the practice itself was not uniform over time.[1] As for honeymoons, this custom has even more recent origins.[2]

The big wedding of the Middle Ages was more of a community event than one conducted for the benefit of the couple. The institution of marriage was at the center of the fabric of agrarian societies, so community members were keenly interested in recognizing marriages when they occurred and reinforcing social norms and community responsibilities through rituals such as the wedding. With the beginning of modernity and industrialization, changes in the custom began to emerge, however. The early Puritans of the seventeenth century attempted to ban such extravagances, but their efforts were resisted. Nevertheless, over time the community significance of the wedding began to fade. The seventeenth and eighteenth centuries saw the emergence of the **bidden wedding** in which the expenses were paid for by the guests who were recruited from surrounding areas by young men called *bidders*. Many guests were not closely acquainted with the newlyweds and came from different communities. Weddings were still very public events, as evidenced by traditions such as **rough music** (loud music played on the wedding night to annoy the couple) and the intrusion of wedding guests into the wedding chamber on the wedding night, but the community solidarity functions of the ritual were being lost. With time, the earlier sensibilities of the Puritans took hold and, by the Victorian era, the sanctity of marriage as an event for the newlyweds took precedence over the interests of the community. Consistent with the shift to a modern society with its emphasis on the individual, weddings became smaller, private affairs and expectations for privacy on the wedding night were strong. It wasn't until the affluence of the post–World War II years that big weddings began to reemerge but for perhaps very different reasons.

Prior to the late nineteenth century, once the wedding ended, couples quickly resumed their daily tasks. There was little time or need for any extended honeymoon. Communities provided some leeway in public expectations during the first year of marriage, but the idea of the couple "getting away" for an extended period of privacy was unheard of. Elites prior to this time may have embarked on the **wedding tour**, but this custom was less about the couple and more about the need to foster network connections to kin living in faraway places.

The modern **honeymoon** of today found its origins in the wedding tour, but it evolved well beyond a simple kinship solidarity function. During the late nineteenth and early twentieth centuries, a few but growing number of couples began taking honeymoons in natural locations with relatively primitive accommodations that allowed them to practice gendered domestic roles based on the separation of public and private spheres (husband as provider and wife as caregiver). The focal actor in the honeymoon was the husband. By the middle of the twentieth century, however,

---

[1]John R. Gillis, *For Better, For Worse: British Marriages, 1600 to the Present* (New York: Oxford University Press, 1985).

[2]See Kris Bulcroft, Linda Smeins, and Richard Bulcroft, *Romancing the Honeymoon: Consummating Marriage in Modern Society* (Thousand Oaks, CA: Sage Publications, 1999); and Kris A. Bulcroft, Richard A. Bulcroft, Linda Smeins, and Helen Cranage, "The Social Construction of the American Honeymoon Experience, 1880–1995," *Journal of Family History*, 22 (1997): 462–490.

things had changed considerably. Couples were still taking honeymoons in natural locations, but the practice had spread and the nature of the experience had changed. The establishment of the first honeymoon resort marks this shift in the honeymoon experience. No longer did couples practice domestic roles. The resort took care of their day-to-day needs. Instead, they were expected to explore each other's personality and find interpersonal compatibility. This new emphasis was also marked by the emergence of marriage experts who advised anxious couples about the honeymoon and wedding night. At the same time, the honeymoon became a bride-centered event, much like the nature of love had evolved during this same time (see Chapter 8). Finally, with the increased elaboration and planning that came about in response to these anxieties and a growing affluence in society, the exotic honeymoon of today emerged. Today couples go away, not to discover their interpersonal compatibility, but as an escape from the highly rationalized world in which they must live. It is a highly constructed and managed fantasy experience where little can go wrong and satisfaction is largely assured.

Both the wedding and the honeymoon have become symbols of the couple's status through consumption, sources of recognition from an increasingly diffuse "community," and markers in their extended personal life biographies. What were once rituals that served functions for the community have now become rituals that serve the individuals involved by alleviating uncertainties about life in a modern world. By celebrating the transition to marriage with such elaborate and orchestrated rituals, the couple is able to project an image of themselves to others, place a "book-mark" in their life histories, and receive assurances that they have made the right choice and that their marriage has promise for the future.

The modern honeymoon experience of today is a relatively recent invention. The idea of a honeymoon located in a natural environment where the couple's everyday needs are taken care of found its first expression in the first honeymoon resort "The Farm" in the Poconos Mountains of Pennsylvania.

Division of Labor in Marriage

One of the foremost tasks that needs to be accomplished in the early stages of marriage, and one that is often negotiated and renegotiated throughout marriage, is the establishment of a mutually acceptable division of labor. Marital couples, often for the first time in their relationship, must decide how they will meet their mutual instrumental and emotional needs. They need to decide who will do the shopping, cooking, washing up, housecleaning, yard care, car maintenance, finances, and so on. They also have to make decisions about who will work for pay outside the home and, if they choose to have children, who will be primarily responsible for child care and child rearing. These decisions are not easy ones because individual choices have implications for societal functioning, the conflict between interest groups, individual identity, and levels of costs and rewards in the marriage.

Traditionally, few roles of women have held a higher priority than that of wife and homemaker. In contrast, for men, work generally is defined in terms of labor force employment, not in terms of housework and child care. Traditionally, at least in terms of recent history, husbands and fathers were not responsible for any substantial amount of housework or child care. The husband's responsibility to the family was to provide economic support through paid employment. In terms of role differentiation, the male held primary responsibility for relationships and needs external to the family; the female held responsibility for relationships and needs internal to the family. In terms of exchange, the husband exchanged his work and economic services for the wife's companionship and household services.

Are these traditional ideas changing? Some observers would say "yes, but not much." In 2007, 38.4 percent of married women with a husband present did not work outside the home, although rates of employment were higher for married women with older children in the home.[3] There is also, as you will see, little question that wives continue to hold the primary responsibility for housework and child care and that the pace of change has been both slow and minimal. Nevertheless, men's behavior appears to be changing. There is currently no major trend toward full-time male homemakers, but there is increased participation of men in household and child-care tasks, as revealed in studies of dual-employed and dual-career marriages.

Meanings of Housework and the Homemaker Role

The full-time homemaker has been relatively neglected by social scientists as a central topic for research. The attention granted women in paid employment has clearly overshadowed that given to women who are *not* in the paid labor force. No set qualifications exist for the role of homemaker. Factors such as age, education, skills, hours, and productivity are basically ignored in job performance, as are benefits such as sick days and bonuses. The role of **homemaker** generally is categorized as a low-status position, earning both low prestige and low economic value. Research findings of Bird and Ross suggest that **housework** is more routine than

---

[3]U.S. Census Bureau, *The 2009 Statistical Abstract*, "Table 578: Employment Status of Women by Marital Status and Presence and Age of Children." http://www.2010census.biz/compendia/statab/cats/labor_force_employment_earnings.html.

With or without children, in paid employment or as homemakers, studies show that women perform most of the household and child-care tasks. Cross-nationally, women are more likely to do the cleaning, laundry, dishes, and meal preparation, whereas men do repairs and yard work.

paid work, is the least fulfilling of any type of work examined, and provided the least recognition for work well done.[4] "I'm only a housewife" is a phrase that captures the sentiment of many women.

The fact is that homemakers perform tasks that are economically valuable to society and would be costly for a family to purchase. At times, the homemaker serves as cook, baker, waitress, teacher, sexual partner, seamstress, housekeeper, bookkeeper, secretary, chauffeur, nurse, therapist, tutor, counselor, hostess, and recreation director. Exactly what is the productive value of housework and of being a homemaker? Specific data are difficult to obtain, because payroll checks and dollar expenditures seldom document homemakers' efforts. But the cost of purchasing all the services mentioned would be extremely expensive. Certainly, the work a woman does contributes to the family economy and, thus, to the society's total economic output. Without the services performed by the full-time homemaker, the family's standard of living would be lowered drastically.

Although research has tended to present the homemaker's status as negative (low prestige, heavy workload, no salary or fringe benefits), it should not be overlooked that many women find satisfaction in the performance of this role. The job

[4]Chloe E. Bird and Catherine E. Ross, "Houseworkers and Paid Workers: Qualities of the Work and Effects on Personal Control," *Journal of Marriage and the Family* 55 (November 1993): 913–925.

is not competitive. The work schedule is highly flexible. The position may even be one of choice. Some women prefer housekeeping to other types of work. Some women define their highest contribution as service to their husbands and children.

A report from national surveys conducted by the Survey Research Center at the University of Michigan indicated that, as of 1980, 50 percent of homemakers had a positive opinion of housework and 44 percent had a neutral or ambivalent opinion.[5] Only 6 percent perceived housework as negative. Positive views were inversely related to level of education; that is, homemakers with more formal education were less likely to respond positively to housework. Educated women were also most likely to want careers. The group least likely to favor housework was college-educated, young wives.

Have the attitudes of homemakers changed over the past few decades? Apparently they have, but not entirely in the direction one might assume. National surveys of homemakers from 1972 to 1986 revealed that they were increasingly likely to hold traditional attitudes regarding marital roles, mothers' employment outside the home, sexuality, and abortion.[6] Attitudes of part-time workers/homemakers were very similar to those of full-time homemakers. But a widening attitudinal gap was found between women who were full-time homemakers versus full-time workers. The latter group was younger, better educated, had fewer children, and had more income than the homemakers. Even when the survey controlled for these differences, attitudes differed sharply on topics such as abortion for married women and the effects of mothers' employment on children.

Gender Differences in Housework

How much are men or husbands involved in household and child-care tasks and how much work do homemakers do compared to employed wives? It appears that women in most countries, even when employed, do most of the housework and child care, with the gender gap widest among married persons.[7] Women who are employed spend less time doing household work than homemakers do and husbands spend some additional time doing housework when their wives work outside the home, but equality exists only as an ideal, not in actual practice.

This lack of equality in the gendered division of household labor is, however, changing. Time-diary data from representative samples of American adults show that the difference between women and men in the average hours spent on housework has narrowed since 1965,[8] although most of the convergence was due to a steep decline in women's hours of housework rather than a sharp increase in men's hours. In 1965, women spent about 30 hours doing unpaid housework, dropping to

---

[5]Alfreda P. Iglehart, "Wives, Work, and Social Change: What About the Housewives?" *Social Service Review* 54 (September 1980): 317–330.

[6]Jennifer Glass, "Housewives and Employed Wives: Demographic and Attitudinal Change, 1972–1986," *Journal of Marriage and the Family* 54 (August 1992): 559–569. Note also Karen A. Schroeder, Linda L. Blood, and Diane Maluso, "An Intergenerational Analysis of Expectations for Women's Career and Family Roles," *Sex Roles* 26 (1992): 273–291.

[7]Scott J. South and Glenna Spitze, "Housework in Marital and Nonmarital Households," *American Sociological Review* 59 (June 1994): 327–347; and David H. Demo and Alan C. Acock, "Family Diversity and the Division of Labor: How Much Have Things Really Changed," *Family Relations* 42 (July 1993): 323–331.

[8]Suzanne M. Bianchi, Melissa A. Milkie, Liana C. Sayer, and John P. Robinson, "Is Anyone Doing the Housework? Trends in the Gender Division of Household Labor." *Social Forces* 79 (September 2000): 191–228.

about 24 hours in 1975, 20 hours in 1985, and 17.5 hours by 1995 (a decrease of 12.5 hours). In contrast, men's hours went from 5 in 1965, to 7 in 1975, to 10 in 1985, and leveled off at that level in 1995 (an increase of about 5 hours). Put another way, in 1965, women spent about six times as much time on housework as men. By 1995, the difference was less than twice as much. The sharp decrease for women was due primarily to compositional shifts: increased labor force participation, later marriage, and fewer children. This "undone" labor is likely made up with a greater reliance in the service economy (like take-out meals) and a general devaluation of housework so that sheets no longer need to be ironed, more clothes are wrinkle-free, and dishes can be stored in the dishwasher.

Husband–wife differences appear to exist not only in the United States but also throughout the world, even in the Scandinavian countries, generally perceived to have greater gender equality. As reported by women, the percentage contributed to total housework by their husbands was 24.7 percent in Sweden, 19.3 percent in Norway, 20.5 percent in Canada, and 22.6 percent in Australia.[9] Men reported figures about 5 percent higher than did women in each of these countries. The results, whether reported by wives or husbands, suggest that from 75 to 80 percent of the housework is done by women.

Why do men around the world contribute such a small proportion of their time to housework? Why does there appear to be a division of labor along instrumental and expressive dimensions in families? We have already noted and dismissed the structure-functionalist argument that a male–female/instrumental–expressive division of labor in groups is necessary and natural (see Chapter 3). Groups can function adequately with a single leader fulfilling both instrumental and expressive functions and men and women have shown equal potential for fulfilling tasks of either type.

From a conflict and feminist perspective, the unequal division of housework serves as a prime example of how unequal opportunities for men and women and patriarchal gender ideologies can affect family role organization. Women as homemakers augment the power of men in the broader society by freeing them to concentrate on resource-yielding work roles and creating dependencies on them. The fact that female homemakers are discouraged and excluded from paid employment and an opportunity to support themselves reinforces their dependence on their husbands. The family remains a primary arena in which men exercise their patriarchal power over women's labor. Note, however, that from this perspective the source of the family inequality lies in the dominant culture that discourages women from working outside the home and the structures of inequality in the workplace and not necessarily in the sexist intentions of husbands. Thus, change in the household division of labor in families is highly contingent on more fundamental changes in the structure of the society.

At the micro level, social exchange theorists discount the importance of ideologies as they argue that the division of labor is the outcome of a free negotiation between husbands and wives in which the balance of resources determines who does the less rewarding and less rewarded tasks. As we will discuss in the next section, the balance of resources determines who has power in the relationship and power allows one to secure the more rewarding and rewarded roles. The unequal assignment of roles, in turn, further reinforces the difference in available resources. Of course, many of the most effective types of resources (money, prestige, information) used in

---

[9]Janeen Baxter, "Gender Equality and Participation in Housework: A Cross-National Perspective," *Journal of Comparative Family Studies* 28 (Autumn 1997): 220–247.

TRANSNATIONAL FAMILIES

Bindis and Headsets: Global Indianness and the Family

Growth in the information technology industry worldwide has had profound effects on India and, in particular, Indian women. In India and the United States, images abound of an attractive Indian woman adorned with traditional Indian clothing and jewelry wearing a headset symbolizing her place as an educated and employed professional in the global technology industry. These images are more than symbolic as they reflect the high level of involvement of Indian women in this modern workforce.

The symbolic juxtaposition of traditional clothing and adornments with modern devices, however, does suggest a potential dilemma for Indian-born and educated women. This dilemma involves the formation of identity and the shaping of family and work conditions through which we create identity. As Smitha Radhakrishnan discovered through her ethnographic research and interviews with hundreds of IT professional women in the Silicon Valley and in Bangalore, India, these women feel a strong need to balance their career and family lives in a manner that is consistent with the notion of "global Indianness."

The challenge of balancing work and family life for these women takes on added meaning because of the contradictions that arise in the meaning of those careers with respect to national identity, individual identity, and family identity. The advancement of Indian trained men and women in technology fields has been a source of pride in India and has contributed to increases in standards of living there. The advancement of women has had particular significance insofar as it coincided with an increased recognition in the Western world of the physical attractiveness of Indian women. Thus, women who succeed in IT contribute to nationhood and feel a strong responsibility to do so. A contradiction arises in this responsibility, however,

as Indian nationhood means the endorsement of values that often run counter to emerging individual identities of independence and autonomy that provide much of the drive to invest in careers and succeed. For example, the Indian national identity is highly intertwined with notions of patriarchy, extended family controls, and motherhood. Endorsing these values and altering their work and family lives to be consistent with them is not easy.

Many of the women had experienced positive outcomes in their personal and family lives as a result of the respect (and income) they gained from their careers. For many, careers had bought greater input into family decisions, greater personal freedom within their marriages, greater ability to disperse economic resources to enhance their extended families' lives in India, and greater respect from their husbands and children. They also saw the importance of maintaining their careers in terms of the potential positive consequences for their children, which would then further contribute to the identity of India in the world economy. Nevertheless, many also chose to cut back or leave the workforce entirely after having children in order to fulfill their responsibilities as "Indian" women.

Thus, the balancing act between work and family life faced by Indian women participating as workers in a global economy is similar to that faced by other women in the United States, but it is also complicated by the mixed positive and negative implications of Indian women's career successes for notions of Indian nationhood. Through continued participation and success in this workforce, they are actively transforming the meaning of Indianness to one of *Global Indianness* where values on individualism and autonomy are tempered by and integrated with family and parenting values.

Source: Smitha Radhakrishnan, "Examining the 'Global' Indian Middle Class: Gender and Culture in the Silicon Valley/Bangalore Circuit," *Journal of Intercultural Studies,* 29 (February 2008), 7–20.

bargaining can be obtained only through participation in economic roles outside the family, a possibility limited by more macro social processes.

Other scholars, from the symbolic interactionist perspective, argue that men's reluctance to do family work is because they associate it with "women's work" and, thus, is inconsistent with their identities as men and a threat to their masculinity.

Arrighi and Maume claim that this is directly linked to the organization of the workplace.[10] Because men tend to define themselves by their control and autonomy in the workplace, threats to that identity as men are met with strong resistance to assume a more feminine identity by doing more "women's work" at home. For similar reasons, women may be reluctant to give up their homemaker roles or may find it difficult to let housework go undone due to their socialized identities as women and the feeling rules associated with those identities.[11] As Hochschild notes, these feeling rules amount to negative emotional responses felt by women when internalized role expectations are not met in the areas of housework, nurturance, and child care.

Where do these identities and expectations come from? As we will discuss in Chapter 11, we learn expectations by watching others in similar positions to the ones we eventually occupy and watching the reactions of others to those in these positions during childhood. As a result, early childhood socialization experiences in the area of housework are likely to be instructive. In a series of analyses of a large intergenerational longitudinal data set, Mick Cunningham showed that both parental attitudes and division of labor during childhood and adolescence are predictive of the children's attitudes and levels of participation in household labor in their later marriages. Although mothers' attitudes are more important than fathers' attitudes in predicting more egalitarian attitudes in their children later in adulthood, the fathers' participation in household labor and the mothers' participation in work outside the home both positively predict a more equal division of labor in the later marriages of their sons and daughters.[12] In addition, the role of children in the performance of household tasks should not be overlooked. Studies suggest that children's contribution to housework is minimal but they do increasing amounts of housework as they get older and their contributions are based on gender. Daughters do more than sons, a gender gap that increases during high school, and children in larger families and one-parent households do more than those in smaller families and two-parent households.[13]

Factors that increased the husband's proportionate contribution to housework were the wife having greater resources, the wife having less traditional values, the husband having greater time availability, the wife having less time availability, and an increase in child-care demands. In other words, the average woman does most of everything, but the average husband's involvement is influenced by employment schedules, time availability, relative resources, and role ideology.[14]

---

[10]Barbara A. Arrighi and David J. Maume, Jr., "Workplace Subordination and Men's Avoidance of Housework," *Journal of Family Issues* 21 (May 2000): 464–487.

[11]Arlie Hochschild, *The Second Shift: Working Parents and the Revolution at Home* (New York: Viking, 1989).

[12]Mick Cunningham, "Parental Influences on the Gendered Division of Housework," *American Sociological Review* 66 (April 2001): 184–203; and Mick Cunningham, "The Influence of Parental Attitudes and Behaviors on Children's Attitudes toward Gender and Household Labor in Early Adulthood," *Journal of Marriage and Family* 63 (February 2001): 111–122.

[13]Constance T. Gager, Teresa M. Cooney, and Kathleen Thiede Call, "The Effects of Family Characteristics and Time Use on Teenagers' Household Labor," *Journal of Marriage and the Family* 61 (November 1999): 982–994; and Glenna Spitze and Russell Ward, "Household Labor in Intergenerational Households," *Journal of Marriage and the Family* 57 (May 1995): 355–361.

[14]Harriet B. Presser, "Employment Schedules among Dual-Earner Spouses and the Division of Household Labor by Gender," *American Sociological Review* 59 (June 1994): 348–364; and April Brayfield, "Juggling Jobs and Kids: The Impact of Employment Schedules on Fathers' Caring for Children," *Journal of Marriage and the Family* 57 (May 1995): 321–332.

Perceptions of Fairness

As indicated, based on the number of hours spent on household tasks, objective equality between husbands and wives does not exist. But are these differences perceived as unfair or unjust? Several studies, including a decade review of research on household labor, suggest that for many women they are not.[15] Although married women perform the majority of household labor, relatively few women felt that this arrangement was unfair. This was especially true among women holding traditional gender attitudes. Nontraditional women were more likely to perceive such inequalities as unfair. A relative deprivation theory suggests that gender ideology functions as a moderator variable between objective inequality and perceived inequality. Furthermore, wives' perceptions of the fairness of the division of labor are better predictors of marital conflict than the actual extent of inequality. Perceived unfairness has also been found to be positively related to psychological distress for mothers and negatively related to marital quality for mothers and fathers.[16]

Now the question becomes, Why do some women perceive such an objectively unfair division of labor as fair? Thompson as well as others[17] encouraged family scholars to apply the framework of distributive justice (note the social exchange theory in Chapter 3) to understand this situation. The **distributive justice framework** suggests that wives will perceive the allocation of family work as fair if they (1) perceive some alternative *valued outcomes* (feeling appreciated, serving loved ones, confirming their sense of proper gender roles), (2) choose an alternative *comparison referent* (comparing their husband's involvement to that of other men rather to themselves, comparing the value of their unpaid and invisible work to that of paid work), or (3) can construct a *justification* (a mutual decision of how things will be done, or excuses such as "men are incompetent at domestic labor" or "wives have a greater need for a clean house than men"). According to this framework, women with more egalitarian ideologies will be more likely to value equality over other outcomes, compare themselves to their husbands rather than to other women, and be less likely to find justifications for inequalities. As a result, they are also more likely to perceive actual inequalities as unfair.

Finally, we might ask how an unequal division of labor affects marriages and the individuals in them. The literature in general suggests that, when wives' and husbands' views of marriage are compared, "his" marriage is considerably better than "her" marriage.[18] Jessie Bernard stated this most explicitly by reporting that

---

[15]Scott Coltrane, "Research on Household Labor: Modeling and Measuring the Social Embeddedness of Routine Family Work," *Journal of Marriage and the Family* 62 (November 2000): 1208–1233; and Theodore N. Greenstein, "Gender Ideology and Perceptions of the Fairness of the Division of Household Labor: Effects on Marital Quality," *Social Forces* 74 (March 1996): 1029–1042.

[16]Patricia Voydanoff and Brenda W. Donnelly, "The Intersection of Time in Activities and Perceived Unfairness in Relation to Psychological Distress and Marital Quality," *Journal of Marriage and the Family* 61 (August 1999): 739–751.

[17]Linda Thompson, "Family Work: Women's Sense of Fairness," *Journal of Family Issues* 12 (June 1991): 181–196; and Alan J. Hawkins, Christina M. Marshall, and Kathryn M. Meiners, "Exploring Wives' Sense of Fairness about Family Work," *Journal of Family Issues* 16 (November 1995): 693–721.

[18]Jessie Bernard, *The Future of Marriage* (New Haven: Yale University Press, 1982), 26–53.

CROSS-CULTURAL *Perspective*

Division of Housework in Urban and Rural China

According to American researchers, Zai Zai Lu, David Maume, and Marcia Bellas, traditional Chinese culture holds to the motto "Men dominate the outside; women dominate the inside." As they note, however, the establishment of the Peoples Republic of China in 1949 and the subsequent Great Leap Forward in 1958 has altered the ideological and material conditions of life in Chinese families. Thus, the question arises as to whether or not these transformations of Chinese society have significantly altered the roles of men and women in families. Although others have attempted to answer this same question in the past, they have usually been small studies involving higher status professional families in urban settings. Lu, Maume, and Bellas base their analysis on a large representative study of eight provinces in China (the 1991 Household Survey of the China health and Nutrition Study) consisting of both urban and rural villages, towns and cities.

One of the most significant changes that have occurred in China over the past 50 years has been the large increase in the participation of women in the paid labor force. This increase has occurred among urban and rural women alike. Given this change in resource earning among women one would expect that corresponding changes in the division of household work would also take place as women have less time to devout to the household and are at a greater bargaining advantage when negotiating household work activities with their husbands. In general, the results of this study support such a resulting change in household work in China. Wives who work more hours (in rural settings) or who work at all (in urban settings) have husbands who participate more in household labor. For rural couples, waged employment in particular affects the division of household labor. When rural husbands have waged jobs (instead of or in addition to farming) their household labor decreases. When rural wives hold waged employment positions, their husbands' household labor goes up. Higher levels of education also increase husbands' household labor, especially in rural areas where education is a proxy for more progressive attitudes.

Not only do time considerations and cultural beliefs explain the change in household labor among men, but also the resource differences that result from employment. Among urban couples, the more the wife makes in income relative to her husband, the more work he does around the house. Finally, there is evidence to suggest that the presence of children in the household—especially younger and older daughters and daughters-in-law—tends to reinforce more traditional roles, at least in urban settings.

Source: Zai Zai Lu, David J. Maume, and Marcia Bellas, "Chinese Husband's Participation in Household Labor," *Journal of Comparative Family Studies*, 31 (March 2001), 191–215.

more wives than husbands expressed marital frustration and dissatisfaction, negative feelings, and marital problems; considered their marriages unhappy; regretted getting married; sought marital counseling; initiated divorce proceedings; felt they were going to have a nervous breakdown; had more feelings of inadequacy in marriage; and blamed themselves for their own lack of general adjustment. Bernard described housework as menial labor, isolating, and a dead-end job with no chance of promotion. According to Bernard, "In truth, being a housewife makes women sick."[19]

---

[19]Ibid., 48.

Given these findings, one must ask about women who are employed outside the home: Are they more satisfied than homemakers are? Evidence from six large national surveys consistently failed to support the hypothesis that women with jobs outside the home are happier and more satisfied with their lives than full-time homemakers.[20] Working outside the home and being a full-time homemaker were both found to have benefits and costs. The net result was that no consistent or significant differences were found in patterns of life satisfaction between the two groups. Constance Shehan, as well, surveyed employed wives and homemakers and found no significant difference between the two groups in feelings of depression, health, anxiety, or life satisfaction. The majority of respondents in both groups were "well off" psychologically.[21]

Employed Women and Marriage

As noted in Chapter 2, both the number and proportion of females in the paid labor force (especially women with children) have increased dramatically over the past three decades. The implications of these trends for both the economic system and the family system are dramatic. Today's economy is highly dependent on the tasks performed and roles fulfilled by women. And the fact that the majority of the female labor force is married raises questions about dual incomes, dual careers, fertility, child rearing, and various other marital and family factors.

The effects of female employment on marriage, intimate partnerships, and other relationships are significant and vary considerably, depending on whether the woman's employment is full time or part time, on whether she has preschool children, on her age and the age of her husband, on their stage in the lifecycle, and on many other factors.

Considerable shifts in power in the husband–wife relationship seem to occur when the wife is employed. In general, the wife's power tends to increase when she is employed. (See the following section on Power and Decision Making.) Thus, as the wife becomes employed she gains income, independence, and new contacts (resources) that increase her contribution to the marriage. This increase in power among employed wives appears not only in the United States but also cross-culturally.

One hidden consequence of this shift in power is witnessed in spousal violence. Female employment per se has little effect on men's violence toward their wives but appears to be conditioned by the employment status of the partner. When their male partners are also employed, women's labor force participation has been found to lower the risk of abuse. But when their male partners are not employed, a substantial increase in risk of spousal abuse occurs.[22] The symbolic meaning of wife employment reflects the economic insecurity of unemployed men leading to efforts to coercively control their female partners.

---

[20]James D. Wright, "Are Working Women Really More Satisfied? Evidence from Several National Surveys," *Journal of Marriage and the Family* 40 (May 1978): 301–313. See also Myra Marx Ferree, "Class, Housework, and Happiness: Women's Work and Life Satisfaction," *Sex Roles* 11 (1984): 1057–1074.

[21]Constance L. Shehan, "Wives' Work and Psychological Well-Being: An Extension of Gove's Social Role Theory of Depression," *Sex Roles* 11 (1984): 881–899.

[22]Ross MacMillan and Rosemary Gartner, "When She Brings Home the Bacon: Labor-Force Participation and the Risk of Spousal Violence against Women," *Journal of Marriage and the Family* 61 (November 1999): 947–958.

Employment of mothers affects far more than wages, children, and marriage. It affects the women as well. In one study, paid employment was found to have a substantial liberalizing effect on women's roles and responsibilities but only a small effect on their support of feminist positions (support for the Equal Rights Amendment, approval of legalized abortion, approval of sexual behavior between consenting adults, etc.).[23] Employed mothers were likely to enjoy their activities and relationships with children, reveal positive feelings about themselves, and project an image of stability and confidence. In brief, employment can, and often does, have a positive effect on self-esteem and a personal sense of worth.

Scott South revealed that the impact of wives' employment on marital dissolution has increased over the past thirty years. He suggests three societal changes that might account for this increasingly destabilizing impact of wives' employment on marriage: (1) the development of institutional supports for unmarried mothers; (2) a reduced tendency for working wives to adopt traditional gender roles that otherwise temper the effect of their economic independence; and (3) the growing exposure of working women to spousal alternatives concomitant with declines in workplace sex segregation.[24]

One factor that modifies the effect of wife employment on marriage is nontraditional gender ideologies held by women. Greenstein found that hours employed per week did not have a significant effect on a marriage if the wife held traditional gender ideologies, but it has a strong negative effect on marital stability for nontraditional women.[25] As shown earlier in this chapter, husbands tend not to share equally in the division of household labor. This is not perceived as a major problem for women who hold traditional gender ideologies. Nontraditional women, however, have normative expectations of an egalitarian relationship, and the inequality of the division of household labor seems to manifest itself in a decrease in marital satisfaction, increase in marital conflict, and ultimately in an increased probability of marital disruption.

Another factor that negates the negative impact of wife employment on marriage is the extent to which the family experiences accommodate the wife's employment. The marriage is improved when a woman has her husband's support of her working and has some freedom from child-rearing responsibilities.[26] An increase in family size is yet another factor that modifies the effect of wife employment on marriage. National data analyzed by Rogers[27] showed that when family size increases, mothers' full-time employment is associated with greater marital happiness and lower marital conflict. Mothers' contributions to the family coffers are likely to ease feelings of economic strain and increase marital quality.

The most important conclusion from a review of twenty-seven studies, spanning over thirty years and exploring the relationship between employment status

---

[23]Eric Plutzer, "Work Life, Family Life, and Women's Support of Feminism," *American Sociological Review* 53 (August 1988): 640–649.

[24]Scott J. South, "Time-Dependent Effects of Wives' Employment on Marital Dissolution," *American Sociological Review* 66 (April 2001): 226–245.

[25]Theodore N. Greenstein, "Gender Ideology, Marital Disruption, and the Employment of Married Women," *Journal of Marriage and the Family* 57 (February 1995): 31–42.

[26]Dana Vannoy and William W. Philliber, "Wife's Employment and Quality of Marriage," *Journal of Marriage and the Family* 54 (May 1992): 387–398.

[27]Stacy J. Rogers, "Mothers' Work Hours and Marital Quality: Variations by Family Structure and Family Size," *Journal of Marriage and the Family* 58 (August 1996): 606–617.

CROSS-CULTURAL *Perspective*

Gender Roles in Great Britain and Saudi Arabia

The role of the media in reinforcing traditional gender roles has long been recognized in family sociology. Media presentations are shaped by a combination of forces such as the values of those who control the media message, the dominant ideologies that resonate with the target population, and the lived realities of the target population. Most studies in the past in Western societies such as the United States have shown that media advertising messages have been gender biased and have tended to portray men in active, dominant and instrumental roles while women are relegated to images of submissiveness, domesticity, and physical ornamentation. More recent studies in the United States have shown some shift towards more equality in gender roles, although it has been more toward portraying women roles that combine traditional male and female activities and characteristics more so than portraying men in traditionally feminine activities and realms.

Thus, during a period when economic forces were transforming women's lived realities and creating more equality between spouses, media advertising was a primarily constraining force reinforcing traditional roles. As gender relations began to change, however, media messages followed. But what about the role of the media in a society where patriarchy norms are still exceptionally strong and where state and religious controls constrain women's activities to the domestic sphere and prevent women from participating in public life? In such a context, could advertising on television—a particularly Western medium of communication—actually have more of a liberating effect on gender roles? Do the Western source of the message and the nature of Western products' appeal and marketability lead to advertising that overrides the dominant patriarchal culture; or are these message reshaped to find legitimacy from those in power by reinforcing traditional beliefs about gender roles?

A study by Atif Nassif and Barrie Gunter provide some insights into this question. In an analysis of 164 television advertisements broadcast over a six-month period on the most popular channels in Great Britain (ITV1) and Saudi Arabia (Channel One), they found little gender bias or traditional stereotyping in the former, but considerable amounts in the latter setting. In terms of male-female differences, Saudi Arabian television is significantly more likely to use males in "lead character" roles in advertising, to cast males in leisure roles and women in household roles, to show women in domestic settings and men in outdoor settings, and to use women in the advertising of domestic and personal care products. Thus, Western advertisers appear to modify their messages to fit with the dominant patriarchal culture. There was also some evidence, however, that change may be occurring insofar as women were significantly more prominent in lead roles in advertising aimed at younger age groups.

Source: Atif Nassif and Barrie Gunter, "Gender Representation in Television Advertisements in Britain and Saudi Arabia," *Sex Roles*, 58 (2008), 752–760.

and marital adjustment, was that the wife's employment status alone appears to have little or no effect on marital adjustment.[28] A finding such as this challenges the common beliefs that employment of wives per se places the marital relationship in jeopardy or that women's rising employment levels have increased their economic independence and greatly reduced the desirability of marriage.

---

[28]Drake S. Smith, "Wife Employment and Marital Adjustment: A Cumulation of Results," *Family Relations* 34 (October 1985): 483–490. Note also Valerie Kincade Oppenheimer, "Women's Employment and the Gain to Marriage: The Specialization and Trading Model," *Annual Review of Sociology* 23 (1997): 431–453.

$\mathcal{P}$ower in Conjugal and Intimate Relationships

Another important aspect of the marital system (a conjugal relationship) and of other intimate relationships is the power positions of the partners—as individuals and in relation to each other. **Power** is the ability to influence others and affect their behavior in spite of their resistance. Power is often measured by determining who makes certain decisions or who performs certain tasks, although rarely do such measure assess the degree of resistance involved.

Power involves the crucial dimensions of **authority** and **influence**. Social norms determine who has authority, in that the culture designates the positions that have the legitimate and prescribed power (authority). In some societies, authority is invested in the husband (patriarchy); in others, it rests with the oldest male in an extended-family situation; and in others, authority goes to the mother-in-law (matriarchy). Other family members can influence—that is, exert pressure on—the person with authority. Evidence of such influence may indicate family members' power in the family system even though they do not have authority. One must be careful not to assume, however, that such indirect influence is a necessary indicator of power because the person in authority may not care much about the outcome and thereby *allow* the influence to occur.

The domestic arena is one in which women, wives, and mothers are not likely to be as passive and powerless as often described or believed. Domestic power—the ability to impose one's will on decisions concerning sexual relations, household tasks, and the lives of children—frequently departs from male ideals. In a study of domestic power in southern Spain, for example, an anthropologist showed that working-class women often united with their mothers to prevail in domestic decision making, despite opposition from their husbands.[29] In fact, the statement has been made that male dominance in the lower classes is mythical.

How can this be explained or understood? Where and how do women get power in contexts of male dominance and patriarchal norms? The following section will examine some characteristics of conjugal power and the key theories that explain it.

Characteristics of Power

Several decades ago, Mary Rogers[30] made several key points about power that are equally relevant today:

1. Power is a capacity or an ability to influence others, not the exercise of that ability. Ability does not denote social action. The perceived or real ability to influence can affect outcomes even when the exercise of that ability is not undertaken.
2. An individual's power must be viewed relative to specific social systems and the positions (statuses) a person occupies within a given social system. Note that power is not inherent within a person. Power must be viewed in dynamic terms; one must note that the power of individuals to influence others is linked to the

---

[29]David D. Gilmore, "Men and Women in Southern Spain: 'Domestic Power' Revisited," *American Anthropologist* 92 (December 1990): 953–970.

[30]Mary F. Rogers, "Instrumental and Infra-Resources: The Base of Power," *American Journal of Sociology* 79 (May 1974): 1418–1433.

social statuses and social roles they occupy and perform within special social systems.

3. If power is an ability to influence others, resources are the primary determinants of that ability. A resource is "any attribute, circumstance, or possession that increases the ability of its holder to influence a person or group."[31] Attributes might include age, sex, race, health, and level of energy; circumstances might include location, friendships or acquaintances, flexibility, and access to information; possessions might include money, land, property, goods, and so on.

The contention is that persons with greater resources have an advantage over individuals without those resources. In a social exchange perspective, they can bargain with others from a position of strength, exchanging their resources for the other person's compliance.

Rebecca Warner and others made a strong case for broadening the conceptualization of resources to include selected features of family and kinship structures (family organization).[32] For example, wives will have more power in marriages in societies with nuclear—rather than extended—family structures and in societies with matrilateral rather than patrilateral customs of residence and descent. This power will derive from a lack of or enhanced access, respectively, to others who can provide resources that can be used in bargaining with one's spouse, an increase or reduction in dependency on one's spouse, or both. Ethnographic data on more than one hundred nonindustrial societies provided support for these propositions, highlighting the fact that organizational resources may be as important as material and personal resources in understanding conjugal power.

Power and Decision Making in Intimate Relationships

One of the ways in which power has traditionally been measured is to determine which spouse or partner makes the major decisions and how decision-making patterns vary by area of concern. One of the most widely cited studies and one that served to stimulate many others was done in the late 1950s by Robert Blood and Donald Wolfe.[33] In an attempt to measure the balance of power between husbands and wives, they interviewed 731 city wives in metropolitan Detroit. Blood and Wolfe selected eight situations that they felt would include both masculine as well as feminine decisions about the family as a whole. The wives' answers to the eight situations revealed that two decisions were primarily the husband's province (his job and car), two were primarily the wife's province (her work and food), and all the others (decisions about insurance, vacations, residence, and physician choice) were joint decisions in the sense of having more same responses. Even the wife's working turned out to be quite a middling decision from the standpoint of the mean score, leaving only decisions about food expenditures predominantly to the wife.

Blood and Wolfe's theoretical explanation of why husbands and wives make certain decisions individually rather than together is based on resource availability. That is, the source of authority and power lies in the comparative resources each

---

[31]Ibid., 1425.

[32]Rebecca L. Warner, Gary R. Lee, and Janet Lee, "Social Organization, Spousal Resources, and Marital Power: A Cross-Cultural Study," *Journal of Marriage and the Family* 48 (February 1986): 121–128.

[33]Robert O. Blood, Jr. and Donald M. Wolfe, *Husbands and Wives: The Dynamics of Marital Living* (Glencoe, IL: The Free Press, 1960), 20.

news item

Wives "Submit Graciously" to Your Husbands

The New York Times (June 10, 1998) reported that the Southern Baptist Convention amended its essential statement of beliefs to include a declaration that a woman should "submit herself graciously" to her husband's leadership and that a husband should "provide for, protect and lead his family."

The amendment, a 250-word declaration on family life, was adopted at the Baptists' annual meeting in Salt Lake City as an addition to the denomination's basic theological statement of beliefs and the Baptist Faith and Message. Because the Southern Baptist Convention is a creedless organization, no Baptist is required to agree with the Faith and Message statement. But the statement is nonetheless important. It stands as a central theological proclamation for the denomination, and Southern

Baptist ministers are expected to agree with it.

Not all clergy or church members agree, however. For example, *The Charlotte Observer* (September 26, 1998) noted that after 153 years, Raleigh, North Carolina's oldest Baptist church broke away from the Southern Baptist Convention in part because of this "submitting graciously" call. Churchgoers said they could no longer tolerate "authoritarian trends" within the 15.6 million member denomination. This followed earlier grievances with the conservative convention, such as a resolution against the ordination of women and a 1997 measure calling for a boycott of the Walt Disney Company.

Source: Gustav Niebuhr, "Southern Baptists declare wife should submit to her husband," *The New York Times*, June 10, 1998; Associated Press, "First Baptist in Raleigh quits convention," *The Charlotte Observer*, September 26, 1998.

spouse has available. The balance of power is weighted toward the partner who has the greatest resources, as perceived by the other partner.

Resource Theory Issues

A number of writers have questioned the theoretical accuracy of explaining power based on resources. The **resource theory** (in reality, a proposition rather than a theory) contends that the more partners control resources of value to themselves and their mates, the greater the relative power. Data on this subject have shown some mixed and inconsistent results. To understand why requires examining this issue more closely.

The resource theory provides the conceptual core around which many later studies have been built. Over the past several decades, a number of authors have stressed that power is not based merely on comparative resources but also on the cultural context of norms within which spouses bargain for power. Hyman Rodman, for example, developed a **cultural resource theory** that takes into account the comparative contributions of both husband and wife and the cultural context in which the interaction occurs.[34] For example, in certain societies, it is the upper- and middle-status groups (the highest income, educational, and occupational groups) that first accept norms of marital egalitarianism. This, in effect, diminishes the impact of resources on power in marital settings.

This differentiation of a basic resource theory from a cultural resource theory sheds some light on understanding variations in power between men and women

---

[34]Hyman Rodman, "Marital Power in France, Greece, Yugoslavia, and the United States: A Cross-National Discussion," *Journal of Marriage and the Family* 29 (May 1967): 320–324; and Hyman Rodman, "Marital Power and the Theory of Resources in Cultural Context," *Journal of Comparative Family Studies* 3 (Spring 1972): 50–69.

and between social classes, various groups, and even countries. One example that focused on this differentiation was a study of dual-career couples in which half the wives earned at least one-third more than their husbands and half the husbands earned at least one-third more than their wives.[35] Consistent with resource theory, spouses who earned more viewed their careers as more important and had more say at home than spouses who earned less. Consistent with cultural resource theory, men overall had more say in financial matters, took less responsibility for the children and the household, and saw their own careers as more important than their wives' careers. Thus, even though resources had significant effects on the wives who had them (those who earned more than their husbands), these women were still more likely to say they would move to another location on their husbands' behalf.

Other studies have drawn similar conclusions. Mark Rank found that increments in wives' resources correlated positively with wives' influence, supporting the theory of resources argument.[36] But increments in husbands' resources correlated negatively with husbands' influence, thus not supporting the argument that greater resources lead to greater influence and power. The explanation is that as husbands gain higher levels of income, education, and occupational prestige, they come in contact with egalitarian norms regarding spousal relations. In brief, as both husbands and wives gain resources, women become less economically dependent on their spouses while men become socialized into an egalitarian ethic.

Another cautionary note on accepting the theory of resources per se or without qualifications comes from Karen Pyke.[37] It is her contention that women's market work (employment) is not considered a resource in some marriages and, hence, does not have a positive effect on marital power. Why? Consistent with a symbolic interactionist perspective, it is necessary to examine the meanings couples give to the material and structural conditions of their lives. Thus, a woman married to a man who views her employment as a threat rather than as a gift will derive less power from her employment. Likewise, the extent to which a woman views her own paid or unpaid labor as a gift or a burden will also affect her marital power.

Pike's research gave support to these ideas, in that men who were denied a sense of occupational success were less likely to view their wives' market work as a gift; some wives, sensitive to their husbands' feelings of failure, responded by not resisting their husbands' dominance in order to "balance" the husbands' low self-esteem. Pike's research suggests that any explanation of marital power must reflect the gender of the actors and the gendered meanings these actors give to the powering process.

This argument is supported as well by Tichenor, who examined marriages in which the wives earned more than their husbands and/or worked in a higher-status occupation.[38] She contends that resource and exchange theory breaks down when women bring more money and status to the marital relationship. Instead, the balance of marital power is more closely related to gender than to income or status. In other words, in the case of married women, greater resources in terms of income and occupational status do not, per se, result in more power within the marriage.

[35]Janice M. Steil and Karen Weltman, "Marital Inequality: The Importance of Resources, Personal Attributes, and Social Norms on Career Valuing and the Allocation of Domestic Responsibilities," *Sex Roles* 24 (1991): 161–179.

[36]Mark R. Rank, "Determinants of Conjugal Influence in Wives' Employment Decision Making," *Journal of Marriage and the Family* 44 (August 1982): 591–604.

[37]Karen D. Pyke, "Women's Employment as a Gift or Burden? Marital Power Across Marriage, Divorce, and Remarriage," *Gender and Society* 8 (March 1994): 73–91.

[38]Veronica Jaris Tichenor, "Status and Income as Gendered Resources: The Case of Marital Power," *Journal of Marriage and the Family* 61 (August 1999): 638–650.

Egalitarian Ethic

Joint decision making, sharing marital power, perceptions of both self and partner doing a fair share of family work, and a feeling of equity appear to be positively related to marital and relationship satisfaction. This is particularly true of husbands who hold less traditional gender-role attitudes.[39] Husbands who were more progressive (less traditional) were found to show increases in reported positive marital quality. Increases in egalitarianism were also found to be associated with declines in reports of negative aspects of the marriage (problems, disagreements, divorce proneness). The pattern was different, however, for women. Wives who held nontraditional gender-role attitudes reported increases in negative aspects of the marriage (less happiness, more disagreements, more problems). In contemporary marriages, stress is lessened when husbands, with their wives, have attitudes that support role sharing and gender equality.

Perhaps feminists lead the way in stressing an **egalitarian ethic**. Feminists have demonstrated the problematic nature of marital and family life for women and have provided an awareness of how traditionally structured marriage requires an overwhelming cost to women in financial, emotional, and physical dimensions. Given the incongruence between the ideology and practice of marital equality, a key question may be whether a feminist ideology of full equality is compatible with marriage.

A partial answer comes from a study of feminist heterosexual marriages.[40] Rather than rejecting marriage, these feminist couples considered revitalizing the relationship by promoting a *vigilance to equality*. Some of the important aspects of this process included (1) the partners critiquing gender injustices in their relationship (an ongoing dialogue of gender expectations); (2) participation in public acts of equality (different names, common financial decisions); (3) the husband's support of the wife's activity (her career); (4) reflective assessment (monitoring of the contributions of each); and (5) emotional involvement (openness about feelings). The study suggests that feminist women need not forgo relationships with men but can expect men to assume feminist beliefs and, with women, strive to enact them.

Findings such as these have lent support to social exchange theories and equity models suggesting that personal happiness, the highest levels of marital satisfaction, and the lowest levels of depression occur when individuals, men and women, believe their partners contribute a fair share to housework and child care and perceive equity in the exchange. For many married persons, particularly wives, a perception of an inequitable balance of marital power is a serious problem.

What conclusions can be drawn about an egalitarian ethic and partners' well-being? Steil,[41] in a summary of the empirical evidence, suggests the following:

1. A wife's dominance in decision making, which is relatively rare, is associated with the lowest level of satisfaction for both partners.
2. A husband's dominance in decision making may be more frequently associated with satisfaction for husbands than for wives.
3. Equal sharing may be associated with the highest level of satisfaction for wives.
4. When measures other than marital satisfaction are considered, relative equality is most beneficial for relationships.

---

[39]Paul R. Amato and Alan Booth, "Changes in Gender Role Attitudes and Perceived Marital Quality," *American Sociological Review* 60 (February 1995): 58–66.

[40]Karen R. Blaisure and Katherine R. Allen, "Feminists and the Ideology and Practice of Marital Equality," *Journal of Marriage and the Family* 57 (February 1995): 5–19.

[41]Janice M. Steil, *Marital Equality: Its Relationship to Well-Being of Husbands and Wives* (Thousand Oaks, CA: Sage, 1997), 39.

Steil goes on to say that relatively equal relationships are characterized by more mutually supportive communication, less manipulative forms of influence, and greater sexual and marital satisfaction for both partners than are relationships in which either one of the partners is dominant.

Marital Quality

The literature on marital quality and the quality of marriage-like relationships is prolific.[42] Many attempts have been made to assess the quality of relationships, using such concepts as *adjustment*, *success*, *satisfaction*, *stability*, *happiness*, *well-being*, *consensus*, *cohesion*, *adaptation*, *integration*, *role strain*, and the like. Sometimes these terms are used interchangeably; at other times, each denotes something different. The terms are also used in a psychological sense, describing the state of one of the partners, or they are used in a social/psychological sense, referring to the state of the relationship. They are used also in a sociological sense, referring to the state of the group or system. In addition, the terms refer to the achievement of a goal or a dynamic process of making changes. All the concepts emphasize a dimension that contrasts with maladjustment, dissatisfaction, instability, and unhappiness.

Assessing Marital Quality

From the introductory statement, it should be clear that marital quality, marital adjustment, and marital well-being are varied concepts that lack a general consensus of definition. **Marital quality or adjustment** is essentially a relative agreement by husband

This couple, known to the author, has been married more than forty years. The quality of a marriage is based on a wide variety of factors. These include satisfaction with the relationship, agreement on issues such as finances and friends, enjoying doing things together and exchanging ideas, and affectionate expressions of love and support.

---

[42]See Norval D. Glenn, "Quantitative Research on Marital Quality in the 1980s: A Critical Review," *Journal of Marriage and the Family* 52 (November 1990): 818–831; and Thomas N. Bradbury, Frank D. Fincham, and Steven R. H. Beach, "Research on the Nature and Determinants of Marital Satisfaction: A Decade in Review," *Journal of Marriage and the Family* 62 (November 2000): 964–980.

and wife as to what issues are important, the sharing of similar tasks and activities, and the demonstration of affection for one another. **Marital success**, as distinguished from *marital quality*, generally refers to the achievement of one or more goals: permanence, companionship, fulfilling expectations of the community, and so forth. **Marital happiness or satisfaction**, distinguished from both *adjustment* and *success*, is an individual emotional response. Although marital happiness is an individual phenomenon, marital quality, success, and adjustment are dyadic achievements or states of the marriage or the relationship. Yet a fourth concept is that of **marital stability**, or the likelihood of a marriage ending in separation or divorce. This concept will be further explored in the next section on *marital commitment*.

Assessment of the quality of marriage and intimate relationships began in earnest in the late 1920s. Each decade since then, an extensive body of literature has been accumulated in an effort to predict marital success and determine factors, psychological and social, associated with marital quality or adjustment.

About forty years ago, Jessie Bernard included the quality of the relationship as one of three major dimensions of marital *adjustment*. Namely, marital adjustment is determined by:

1. The degree or nature of the *differences* between or among the parties involved
2. The degree or nature of the *communication* between or among the parties
3. The *quality of the relationship* between or among the parties (positive or negative, friendly or hostile)[43]

Differences may be a matter of degree, or they may be categorical (no flexibility, no leeway). Often matters of principle are categorical and, thus, the most difficult to resolve. On the one hand, statements such as "We will never miss Mass" and beliefs such as "Oral sex is wrong," if taken categorically, do not permit flexibility in dealing with a mate or spouse who feels differently. On the other hand, differences of degree permit give and take, bargaining, and negotiation. The point is that differences, as well as the nature and extent of those differences, affect dyadic or interpersonal adjustment.

The second dimension, communication, necessitates interaction. Few people would doubt or question the importance of communication to successful relationships of any kind. Yet communication is an extremely complex factor in marital relationships: It may be verbal or nonverbal, it may be explicit or tacit, it may clarify or mislead, or it may draw relationships closer together or tear them apart. To not talk at all, to talk constantly, to order, to nag, to scold, to praise—each may convey a certain message.

A review of research over the past twenty years revealed strong support for the relationship between communication and marital satisfaction.[44] This relationship held true for both the content and the process of communication. Findings consistently replicated were that couples with higher rates of self-disclosure and expressions of love, support, and affection tended also to experience greater satisfaction. Research on process variables suggested that positive forms of nonverbal communication—such as

---

[43]Jessie Bernard, "The Adjustment of Married Mates," in *Handbook of Marriage and the Family*, ed. Harold T. Christen-sen (Chicago: Rand McNally, 1964), 690.

[44]Patricia Noller and Mary Anne Fitzpatrick, "Marital Communication in the Eighties," *Journal of Marriage and the Family* 52 (November 1990): 832–843; and W. Kim Halford, Kurt Hahlweg, and Michael Dunne, "The Cross-Cultural Consistency of Marital Communication Associated with Marital Distress," *Journal of Marriage and the Family* 52 (May 1990): 487–500.

laughter, voice tone, touch, and body position—were found more frequently in happy couples. Nondistressed couples were more likely to show good listening skills and clarity of speech and to positively interpret their partners' behavior.

The quality of the relationship was Bernard's third major dimension of adjustment. She used the term *quality*, however, not as an overall assessment of the relationship, but as a specific dimension or characteristic of the interactions between spouses. Spouses who are friendly and loving are not necessarily well adjusted to marriage, but such qualities make accommodation easier. Making sacrifices or changing plans is easier when spouses have love and genuine concern for one another. If the relationship is affectionate, results will be far different than if it is hostile or distancing (as in intimacy avoidance, conflict avoidance, or angry withdrawal).[45]

Perhaps a fourth dimension can be added to the differences, communication, and quality of the relationship mentioned by Bernard. This fourth dimension is that of *social support* and the influence of *social networks*. No couple is an island unto itself, separate from family, friends, and a social context. Findings suggest that social networks are influential in marital relationships and the conjugal adjustment of both heterosexual and homosexual couples.[46] Even after several decades of marriage, relationship-specific support from in-laws, other relatives, and friends was found to lead to increased marital success and the quality of the relationship.

Today, one of the most widely used measures of marital quality or interpersonal adjustment is the Dyadic Adjustment Scale developed by Graham Spanier.[47] Based on a review of all existing conceptualizations and scales prior to it (including Bernard's), this scale consists of thirty-two items centering around four basic components: dyadic satisfaction, dyadic cohesion, dyadic consensus, and affectional expression.

- *Satisfaction* is measured by asking questions about happiness and regrets in the relationship.
- *Cohesion* focuses on whether the spouses do things together and exchange ideas.
- *Consensus* measures the extent of agreement on issues such as finances, friends, religious matters, and household tasks.
- *Affectional expression* refers to the degree of affection, sexual relations, and love expressed between spouses.

This scale, however, has been criticized for confusing causes with outcomes and for potential bias.[48] Are cohesion, consensus, and affectional expression indicators of

---

[45]Linda J. Roberts, "Fire and Ice in Marital Communication: Hostile and Distancing Behaviors as Predictors of Marital Distress," *Journal of Marriage and the Family* 62 (August 2000): 693–707.

[46]Chalandra M. Bryant and Rand D. Conger, "Marital Success and Domains of Social Support in Long-Term Relationships: Does the Influence of Network Members Ever End?" *Journal of Marriage and the Family* 61 (May 1999): 437–450; Danielle Julian, Elise Chartrand, and Jean Begin, "Social Networks, Structural Interdependence, and Conjugal Adjustment in Heterosexual, Gay, and Lesbian Couples," *Journal of Marriage and the Family* 61 (May 1999): 516–530; Diane H. Felmlee, "No Couple Is an Island: A Social Network Perspective on Dyadic Stability," *Social Forces* 79 (June 2001): 1259–1287; and Chalandra M. Bryant, Rand D. Conger, and Jennifer M. Meehan, "The Influence of In-Laws on Change in Marital Stability," *Journal of Marriage and Family* 63 (August 2001): 614–626.

[47]Graham B. Spanier, "Measuring Dyadic Adjustment: New Scales for Assessing the Quality of Marriage and Similar Dyads," *Journal of Marriage and the Family* 38 (February 1976): 15–28; and Graham B. Spanier and Linda Thompson, "A Confirmatory Analysis of the Dyadic Adjustment Scale," *Journal of Marriage and the Family* 44 (August 1982): 731–738.

[48]Frank D. Fincham and Thomas N. Bradbury, "The Assessment of Marital Quality: A Reevaluation," *Journal of Marriage and the Family* 49 (1987): 797–809.

marital quality or conditions of the relationship that *predict* whether or not a marriage works successfully and is satisfying to the partners involved? For example, do couples have to do things together for it to be a "good" marriage? Can couples who disagree or have conflict with one another actually have a better marriage than those who never have any conflicts? To Fincham and Bradbury, these are empirical questions and we should not assume that high levels of consensus, cohesion, and affection expression are necessary for all marriages to be successful and satisfying. To do so would be to incorporate our own biases into the measure. The issue of consensus or conflict in marriage is a good case in point.

As couples interact, as they define and redefine their relationship with one another, and as they perform daily activities and fulfill role expectations, conflict is inevitable. These conflicts, when ongoing and unresolved, are likely to be linked to dissatisfaction with, or even the ending of, the relationship. And marital conflicts that result in anger and violence can be harmful, not only to the couple themselves but to the children as well. For example, mothers' and fathers' verbal and physical anger expressions were found to be associated with the presence of an anger organization in children.[49] Children exposed to anger-based conflict between parents showed more frequent and more deviant anger expressions than children not exposed to these parental anger-based conflicts.

If conflicts are inevitable, however, the question is not how to eliminate conflict but how to manage it in a way that is mutually satisfactory to both marital partners. In a chapter entitled "Marital Conflict as a Positive Force," John Scanzoni argued that, in order to understand the dynamics of husband–wife interaction, the first step is to throw out the notion that equilibrium or stability is a necessary ideal, and the second step is to throw out the idea that conflict is by nature bad or unhealthy within marriage.[50]

Conflict brings into the open the issues that one or both partners consider unjust or inequitable. When such issues are presented, negotiated, and resolved in a way that is satisfactory to both partners, the outcome may be a new, more positive level of marital adjustment or solidarity. In contrast, failure to engage in conflict when injustice is perceived may result in a less beneficial, less rewarding situation for both marital partners and may actually increase the chances for dissolution of the marriage.

Thus, a lack of conflict in marriage is not necessarily an indicator for relationship health or quality. It could also be argued that high levels of cohesion and affectional expression are also not necessary for a quality marriage. Individuals may have different levels of comfort and expectations with respect to their marital interactions. What is important for defining a high-quality marriage is to identify dimensions of interaction that allow couples to achieve their relationship goals, maintain their relationship over time, and have a personal sense of satisfaction or happiness with their relationship. With respect to this latter criterion, it is conceivable that every marriage will have its own criteria for what constitutes quality because the individuals involved will have different sets of expectations. Thus, any assessment of marital quality or adjustment must incorporate the perceptions of the individuals involved. To the extent that individuals are satisfied with their marriage because their outcomes equal or exceed

---

[49]Jennifer M. Jenkins, "Marital Conflict and Children's Emotions: The Development of an Anger Organization," *Journal of Marriage and the Family* 62 (August 2000): 723–736.

[50]John Scanzoni, *Sexual Bargaining: Power Politics in the American Marriage*, 2nd ed. (Chicago: The University of Chicago Press, 1982), 61–102. Note also Suzanne M. Retzinger, *Violent Emotions: Shame and Rage in Marital Quarrels* (Newbury Park, CA: Sage, 1991).

their expectations, then measures of marital satisfaction would seem to be an important criterion for judging the quality of a marriage.

Furthermore, the expectations that individuals use to evaluate their relationship satisfaction will usually be tempered by an assessment of what they have to give in the relationship and the situation in which they find themselves. Jessie Bernard made such a point when she suggested that a criterion be set up in terms not of the best *imaginable* relationship but of the best *possible* one.[51] Thus, a marriage may be successful to the extent that it provides the highest satisfaction possible, not imaginable. Thibaut and Kelley[52] provide a concept for capturing this process—*comparison level*. A **comparison level** is a criterion or standard that individuals develop for what constitutes the maximum profit they can expect in any given situation or relationship. Because all social exchange requires that one give something of equal or greater value in return for rewards received from the other, we come to learn that we shouldn't expect unlimited rewards. We can only get back a level roughly equal to our ability to reward the other. We develop these expectations from previous and ongoing interactions and through the observations of others who have similar levels of resources to our own. We are happy or satisfied with our relationship when the rewards we are receiving are at or above our comparison level, but when the level of rewards falls below our comparison level, we become dissatisfied. Thus, even low-quality relationships can be satisfying and high-quality relationships can be dissatisfying.

Finally, we might ask whether or not marital quality and satisfaction are personological traits that individuals bring to their marriages or the product of interactional experiences. Johnson and Booth[53] explored the individual versus dyadic nature of marital quality. Is marital quality based more on personal factors or more on dyadic properties of the relationship? Using data from a national sample, they concluded that marital quality is largely a product of the dyadic relationship environment. This conclusion was based on an analysis of persons in two successive unions coupled with data on marital quality over time for those with the same partner. Johnson and Booth found that quality was less changed for the latter group indicating that although some individuals carry personal characteristics from one marriage to the next that bear on marital quality many of these qualities are malleable and altered by the marriage itself.

Marital Quality between Generations

In Chapter 1, it was noted that some scholars claim that marriage is in a state of decline and is an institution in decay. Given the popularity of marriage and marriage-like relationships, the institution of marriage, while exhibiting many changes, remains popular. But what about the quality of marital relationships? Has the quality of marriage declined over previous decades?

Rogers and Amato looked at two generations representing distinct marriage cohorts: married individuals from the original sample who were between 20 and 35 years of age in 1980 and married individuals from the offspring sample who

---

[51]Bernard, "The Adjustment of Married Mates," 732.

[52]John W. Thibaut and Harold H. Kelly, *Interpersonal Relations: A Theory of Interdependence* (New York: Wiley, 1978).

[53]David R. Johnson and Alan Booth, "Marital Quality: A Product of the Dyadic Environment or Individual Factors," *Social Forces* 76 (March 1998): 883–904.

Family Diversity

When Women Earn More in African American Families

African American women have a long history of employment outside the home and, combined with historically high rates of male unemployment, they have also made significantly greater relative contributions to household income than their white counterparts. Much of this history can be attributed to the post-slavery period when African American women were better able to find domestic and manufacturing employment in urban areas in the North, while a lack of transferable skills and high levels of discrimination in hiring left them without as viable employment opportunities. At the same time, African American men have a pattern of contributing more toward household work, but those contributions are inconsistent with black women's beliefs that men should be the economic providers in families and tend to lead to lower levels of marital satisfaction. Given these historical patterns, Holly Furdyna and her colleagues set out to examine how income disparities between men and women might impact African American women differently than they impact white women.

Using a single item indicator of marital happiness, they were able to show that, for white women only, when the wife earned as much as or more than her husband, she was significantly less likely to be happy with her marriage, although this negative effect was reversed when she held more progressive beliefs about men and women's economic roles in marriage and when economic need in the family was high. For African American women, on the other hand, earning more had no effect on her marital happiness regardless of financial need or conservative gender role attitudes. African American women who were very religious, however, did experience less happiness when they were making more income than their husbands. The authors attribute the lack of income disparity effects on African American women to the possibility that African American women are hyper-aware of how their greater income earning may cause their husbands more distress due to their disadvantaged position in society and thus temper any negative evaluations of their marriage when their husbands fail to fulfill role expectations for income provision. They also note the more precarious position of African American women who must negotiate their marriages in a context where their marriage market is poor while their husband has a greater pool of alternative relationships available to him should he decide to leave the marriage.

Source: Holly E. Furdyna, M. Belinda Tucker, and Angela D. James, "Relative Spousal Earnings and Marital Happiness Among African American and White Women," *Journal of Marriage and Family*, 70 (May 2008), 332–344.

---

were between 20 and 35 years of age in 1992.[54] Controlling for gender, race, duration of marriage, and marriage order, significant differences existed between the two cohorts in three of five dimensions of marital quality. The younger cohort reported lower levels of marital interaction and higher levels of marital conflict and marital problems. Declines were apparent for both husbands and wives. Interestingly, this younger cohort did not report lower levels of marital happiness or divorce proneness in that commitment to the idea of a lifelong marriage appeared to be stronger in the younger cohort. These changes are accounted for by changes in economic resources, work and family demands, wives' gender role attitudes, and cohabitation prior to marriage. The writers conclude that such findings suggest that young married people may be committed to salvaging their marriages and that reports of increased marital tensions and difficulties reflect not the struggles of an

---

[54]Stacy J. Rogers and Paul R. Amato, "Is Marital Quality Declining? The Evidence from Two Generations," *Social Forces* 75 (March 1997): 1089–1100. Note also Paul R. Amato and Alan Booth, *A Generation at Risk: Growing up in an Era of Family Upheaval* (Cambridge, MA: Harvard University Press, 1997).

outmoded social institution but the inherent difficulties in adapting marriage to a rapidly changing social climate.

Marital Quality over the Life Course

What happens to marriages and marital quality over long periods of time? Most studies have sought answers to this question by comparing groups at different points in the life course or at different stages of the family lifecycle (a cross-sectional approach). That is, newlyweds have been compared with families that have pre-school children, who in turn have been compared with families that have adolescents in the home, and so forth.

One unique exception to this cross-sectional approach took place at the Institute of Human Development at the University of California in Berkeley.[55] This study used a longitudinal approach. Seventeen couples, who had been married for fifty to sixty-nine years, were the survivors of an original study of 250 couples, who were first studied in 1928 and 1929 and then interviewed again from time to time over the following years. In all of the surviving marriages, partners had both shared and separate interests and had both a commitment to the marriage and an acceptance of each other. Husbands tended to be more satisfied with their marriages than were wives. Of the authors' model of six types of very long-term marriages, the greatest number exhibited a U-shaped or a curvilinear pattern, that is, starting at a high level of affect and satisfaction, dipping during the years of having young children until the children left, and increasing in the later years to a point as high as at the beginning. All of the other couples were categorized as stable (positive, neutral, or negative), and no couples showed a continuous increase or a continuous decline in marital satisfaction. (Any such couples may have previously divorced.)

Numerous other studies have attempted to discover how families manage their lives, what explains their relative successes and failures, and how their relationships change over time. One study asked 1,140 families, "What makes families work?" and analyzed results using a seven-stage, family life-cycle model.[56] This study confirmed the findings of other studies,[57] namely, that satisfaction with marriage and family life tends to decrease over the early stages of the lifecycle and then increase over later stages. The data, when plotted, form a U-shaped curve (see Figure 9.1). Specifically, from young couples without children (stage 1) to families with preschool-age children (stage 2) to families with school-age children (stage 3) to families with adolescents in the home (stage 4), there was a decline in family satisfaction for both husbands and wives. The decline continued for wives through the launching period (stage 5), but satisfaction increased slightly for husbands at this time. A sharp increase in family satisfaction occurred at the "empty nest" stage (stage 6), and satisfaction increased more or remained high through retirement (stage 7).

Some explanations for the dramatic increase in satisfaction found following the launching stage and into the later years may result from the relaxation of sex

---

[55]Sylvia Weishaus and Dorothy Field, "A Half Century of Marriage: Continuity or Change?" *Journal of Marriage and the Family* 50 (August 1988): 763–774.

[56]David H. Olson, Hamilton I. McCubbin, and Associates, *Families: What Makes Them Work* (Beverly Hills, CA: Sage, 1983).

[57]David M. Lawson, "Love Attitude and Marital Adjustment in the Family Life Cycle," *Sociological Spectrum* 8 (1988): 391–406. Canadian data as well show a curvilinear relationship. See Eugene Lupri and James Frideres, "The Quality of Marriage and the Passage of Time: Marital Satisfaction Over the Family Life Cycle," *Canadian Journal of Sociology* 6 (1981): 283–305.

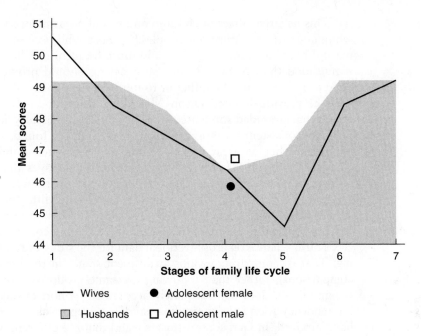

Figure 9.1

Satisfaction by Stage of Family Life Cycle

Source: David H. Olson, Hamilton I. McCubbin, and Associates, *Families: What Makes Them Work* (Beverly Hills, CA: Sage, 1983), figure 10.5, p. 181. Reprinted by permission of Sage Publications, Inc., and David H. Olson.

roles, the time couples have to spend together, and the sense of belonging. After the children leave home, women feel freer to look for work and organizational roles outside the home, and men find themselves with decreased financial responsibility and more ability to be passive and dependent. Russell Ward suggests that the quality of marital relationships in the later years is quite high, that time spent together and perceived fairness in the relationship are enhanced, whereas arguments are relatively infrequent.[58] For both men and women, the quality of the longer-term marriages is said to revolve around intimacy, interdependence, and a sense of companionship.

Studies of the effect that having children has on the marital happiness of parents are highly consistent in their results. Overwhelming evidence has documented that, in U.S. society, the presence of children in the family lowers marital happiness for the parents. Glenn and McLanahan, in conducting their own national surveys and in reviewing many others, found no evidence for distinctly positive effects and strong evidence for negative effects that children have on marital quality.[59] Given this highly consistent evidence, they suggested it is ironic that most people want to have and do have children. What's more, this phenomenon may serve as an example of the social function of ignorance; that is, people are motivated to perform the essential functions of reproduction and child care by the false belief that the psychological rewards of having children outweigh the costs or penalties. Perhaps there are perceptions of rewards, but research has not found them among the elements of marital satisfaction.

---

[58]Russell A. Ward, "Marital Happiness and Household Equity in Later Life," *Journal of Marriage and the Family* 55 (May 1993): 427–438.

[59]Norval D. Glenn and Sara McLanahan, "Children and Marital Happiness: A Further Specification of the Relationship," *Journal of Marriage and the Family* 44 (February 1982): 63–72.

This negative effect of children on marital adjustment seems to appear for both white and African American couples.[60] Those who became parents reported lower marital happiness, more tension, and more frequent conflicts after the transition to parenthood than before. Results such as this should provide caution in having a child to reduce marital conflict or to improve the quality of a marriage.

The previously cited Olson–McCubbin study in *Families*, as well as other research, has provided some precautionary notes to the lifecycle data presented. First, whereas consistent variation from stage to stage is found, the amount of change may be neither as great nor as significant as is often implied in textbooks such as this. For example, adding data from those marriages that had dissolved would reduce the increase in satisfaction reported by most studies.

Second, although male–female, husband–wife differences are found in most studies, these differences tend to be overplayed. Often the sex differences were even less pronounced than were differences across the life course.

Third, reliance on cross-sectional data for the study of trends can be very misleading. That is, comparing groups at different stages in the life course (cross-sectional comparisons), rather than following the same group over time and through stages (longitudinal), does not adequately account for cohort effects, social desirability, or the tendency found in longitudinal studies to report as happy those marriages that have survived. In fact, several studies claim that the differences in marital success between midterm and long-term marriages are largely cohort differences and an artifact of cross-sectional analysis.[61] Using a cohort type of analysis (people born within a specific time period), evidence fails to support the widespread belief that marriages tend to improve at midterm and that the later years of marriage are the golden ones. That is, the higher level of marital quality in late-term than in midterm marriages shown by cross-cultural studies apparently results largely from cohort differences in marital success.

Marital Commitment and Stability

Whether or not a person stays in a relationship and works to keep the relationship viable is a reflection of his or her level of commitment. At a psychological level, **commitment** is a motivation or desire to maintain a belief, behavior, or relationship. This definition makes good intuitive sense because it refers to a state of the mind that we can all experience directly, but it does not provide any guidance as to where this motivation derives from. Michael Johnson[62] has provided an alternative conceptualization that is more valuable for understanding commitment in marriage. He distinguishes among three types of commitment—*personal*, *structural*, and *moral*.

---

[60]Susan E. Crohan, "Marital Quality and Conflict across the Transition to Parenthood in African American and White Couples," *Journal of Marriage and the Family* 58 (November 1996): 933–944.

[61]Norval D. Glenn, "The Course of Marital Success and Failure in Five American 10-Year Marriage Cohorts," *Journal of Marriage and the Family* 60 (August 1998): 569–576; and Jody VanLaningham, David R. Johnson, and Paul Amato, "Marital Happiness, Marital Duration, and the U-Shaped Curve: Evidence from a Five-Wave Panel Study," *Social Forces* 78 (June 2001): 1313–1341.

[62]Michael P. Johnson, "Personal, Moral, and Structural Commitment to Relationships: Experiences of Choice and Constraint," in Jeffrey M. Adams and Warren H. Jones, *Handbook of Interpersonal Commitment and Relationship Stability* (New York: Kluwer Academic/Plenum, 1999): 73–87.

Personal commitment is a desire to stay in a relationship because it is highly rewarding—that is, because one *wants to stay*. It is largely determined by the quality of the relationship and one's level of marital satisfaction and happiness with the relationship. **Structural commitment** is a desire to stay in a relationship because one has few alternative sources of rewards and/or the costs of leaving the relationship are very high—that is, because one *has to stay*. The term **barriers to dissolution** refers to conditions that create high structural commitment (low alternatives and high costs of leaving). When individuals stay in unhappy marriages "for the sake of the children" or because they could not survive on their own, then they have high barriers to dissolution (high structural commitment). When divorce laws are highly punitive, the barriers to dissolution also are high. Finally, **moral commitment** refers to a desire to stay in a relationship, not because it is rewarding or because one cannot leave, but because it is the right thing to do—that is, because one *ought to stay*. Moral commitment may come about because of identity concerns ("I gave my word and cannot be true to myself if I ended the relationship") or from strong belief systems.

Commitment is important in relationships because it not only determines the likelihood of dissolution but also affects how individuals assess the profitability of their relationship.[63] When commitment is high, individuals tend to ignore alternatives and are willing to absorb costs without leaving. When commitment is low, however, individuals tend to make more active comparisons of their relationship to alternative relationship possibilities (that is, they "shop around") and are, therefore, more likely to leave the relationship for one that appears more potentially rewarding. Thus, when commitment is low, marital stability is also low.

When individuals make such comparisons of their relationship to other possibilities, they utilize what Thibaut and Kelley[64] refer to as a **comparison level for alternatives**. This comparison level refers to the maximum expected profit to be gained from participating in an alternative behavior or relationship. It increases with the perceived potential for rewards (and the probability of obtaining those rewards) and decreases with the perceived costs of ending one's current relationship. If the perceived rewards of one's own relationship exceed those of the comparison level for alternatives, then the rational choice is to stay. If, however, the level of rewards in one's own relationship falls below the comparison level for alternatives, then the rational choice is to leave in favor of the alternative.

The distinction between marital quality and stability, then, is an important one to make. Generally, these two variables will be positively correlated (high quality–high stability; low quality–low stability). There are two other possibilities, however. One that may occur with some frequency is a condition of low quality and high stability. In this case, a spouse is not receiving very high levels of rewards but has few alternatives and/or perceives many barriers to dissolution (low comparison level for alternatives). This type of marriage Levinger called an "empty shell" marriage.[65] This may be one reason why many women stay in abusive relationships. A second

---

[63]Carol E. Rusbult, J. Weiselquist, C. A. Foster, and B. S. Witcher, "Commitment and Trust in Close Relationships: An Interdependence Analysis," in Jeffrey M. Adams and Warren H. Jones, *Handbook of Interpersonal Commitment and Relationship Stability* (New York: Kluwer Academic/Plenum, 1999): 427–449.

[64]John W. Thibaut and Harold H. Kelly, *Interpersonal Relations: A Theory of Interdependence.*

[65]George Levinger, "A Social Exchange View on the Dissolution of Pair Relationships," in R.L. Burgess and Ted L. Huston, *Social Exchange in Developing Relationships* (New York: Academic Press, 1979): 169–193.

possibility is a condition of high quality and low stability. Although this condition is less likely, it is nonetheless possible. Here the relationship is generally satisfying, but the alternatives are so high and the barriers so low (a high comparison level for alternatives) that the level of rewards in one's own marriage cannot "measure up" and one might choose to leave to pursue greater profits in the alternative. Some situations that may produce this outcome would include, among others, a highly imbalanced sex ratio, very high levels of unattached potential partners with high levels of resources, no-fault divorce laws, a very low degree of economic or emotional dependency, and the lack of children in the relationship.

Richard Udry suggested that the dimension of **marital alternatives** appears to be a better predictor of marital disruption than are measures of satisfaction.[66] Using longitudinal data of married couples from sixteen U.S. urban areas, he measured the respondents' perceptions of marital alternatives, that is, how much better or worse they would be without their present spouse and how easily that spouse could be replaced with one of comparable quality. In the ensuing year or two after these resources were measured, couples in which spouses were rated high in marital alternatives had several times the disruption rate of those rated low in alternatives.

This observation perhaps gives a clearer idea of why many unhappy marriages remain intact: the spouses have no or few alternatives, or, as suggested by exchange theory, the existing alternatives have costs that exceed their benefits. Data have shown that about 7 percent of intact marriages are stable but unhappy. Age, lack of prior marital experience, commitment to marriage as an institution, low social activity, lack of control over one's life, dependency, and belief that divorce would detract from happiness are all factors that predict stability in unhappy marriages.[67]

Sex and Marriage

Social norms regarding sex make coitus between husbands and wives the one totally approved type of heterosexual activity in every society in the world. Few would deny the importance of sexual intercourse in marriage. It is the one factor that, normatively at least, differentiates the marital relationship from any other social relationship.

According to a Kinsey Institute report in 1953, the frequency of marital coitus decreased with age, dropping from an average of 3.7 times per week during the teens to about 2.7 at the age of 30, 1.4 at the age of 40, and 0.8 at the age of 60.[68] Male and female estimates were highly comparable, although females tended to estimate the frequency of marital coitus higher than males did. The incidence and frequency of marital coitus reached their maximums in the first year or two after marriage. From that point, levels steadily dropped into minimum frequencies in the oldest age groups. No other activity among females showed such a steady decline with advancing age.

Kinsey also found a common gender difference in patterns of desired sexual activity over time. Many husbands reported that, early in marriage, they wanted

---

[66]J. Richard Udry, "Marital Alternatives and Marital Disruption," *Journal of Marriage and the Family* 43 (November 1981): 889–897.

[67]Tim B. Heaton and Stan L. Albrecht, "Stable Unhappy Marriages," *Journal of Marriage and the Family* 53 (August 1991): 747–758.

[68]Alfred C. Kinsey, Wardell B. Pomeroy, Clyde E. Martin, and Paul H. Gebhard, *Sexual Behavior in the Human Female* (Philadelphia: W. B. Saunders, 1953), 77.

coitus more often than their wives, and young married females reported that they would be satisfied with lower coital rates than their husbands wanted. But in the later years of marriage, many of the older females expressed the wish to have coitus more frequently than their husbands desired. Over the years, most females became less inhibited and developed an interest in sexual relations that they might then maintain until they were in their fifties or sixties.[69]

Data reported in Chapter 8 showed an increase over several decades in nonmarital sexual permissiveness, so might one expect an increase in sexual activity within marriage, both in frequency and in the type of behaviors that occur? Why? For one, the availability of reliable contraception and abortion may decrease anxiety over an unintended pregnancy and, therefore, relax some of the constraints on sexual expression. In addition, the portrayal of sex in the mass media; the availability of sex videos and cybersex on the computer to be viewed and done in the privacy of one's home; the developing emphasis on women's rights to personal fulfillment; the shift from the traditional passive sexual role to more assertive behavior among women; and the viewing of sex itself as a natural, less taboo topic may all serve to decrease inhibitions and modify sexual frequencies and acceptable behaviors. Yet more recent data from a large national survey (see Figure 9.2) shows that the rates reported by Kinsey are not so different from those reported today.

Marital Sexual Activity Over the Life Course

The first year of marriage is clearly the time of most frequent marital coitus. After the first year, everything that happens to a couple—children, jobs, commuting, housework, financial worries, familiarity, fatigue, and perhaps even the aging process—combines to reduce intercourse frequency, whereas nothing leads to increase it.

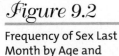

Figure 9.2

Frequency of Sex Last Month by Age and Marital Status

Source: Vaughn Call, Susan Sprecher, and Pepper Schwartz, "The Incidence and Frequency of Marital Sex in a National Sample," *Journal of Marriage and the Family* 57 (August 1995): 646. Copyrighted 1995 by the National Council on Family Relations, 3989 Central Ave, NE, Suite 550, Minneapolis, MN 55421. Reprinted by permission.

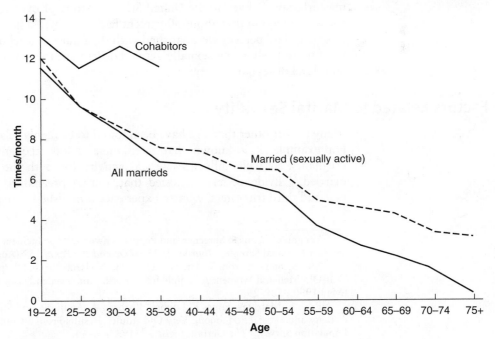

69Ibid., 353.

Figure 9.2 shows the frequency of sexual intercourse by age for all marrieds, the sexually active marrieds, and cohabitors. For all married couples, the frequency has a steady decline with age. More specifically, the average times a young married couple ages 19 to 24 had sex was 11.7 times a month. This drops to 8.5 times for those ages 30 to 34, 5.5 times at ages 50 to 54, and 2.4 times for those 65 to 69. Cohabiting relationships, according to the authors, are definitely "sexy relationships."[70] They reported having sex an average of eleven to thirteen times a month, but sample sizes were too small to provide estimates for those over age 35. This higher rate of sexual intercourse was explained, at least in part, by their more permissive values, including the justification of sex without marriage.

Several factors were said to contribute to the decline in sexual intercourse over time, including biological aging, diminished health, and habituation to sex. Age was the single most important factor associated with a declining sexual frequency. The second most important predictor was marital happiness. The higher the overall happiness, the more sex the couple had. The writers say that, unfortunately, their results don't reveal whether couples became unhappy with the marriage and then had less sex or whether their reduced sex had consequences for marital happiness. This issue will be discussed later.

Other factors were found to have a modest effect on sexual intercourse frequency: a pregnancy, the presence of children, and sterilization (which increased frequency). Those who had cohabited before marriage or those in their second or later marriage had intercourse more frequently than those who had not experienced these events.

The discussion of declining coital frequency with age should not be interpreted to mean that sex becomes unimportant in marriage after ages 40 or 70. In fact, results from more than 1,500 randomly chosen men and women in Sweden, who were between 60 and 80 years old, revealed that 61 percent of the total group expressed their sexuality through intercourse, mutual sexual stimulation (other than intercourse), and masturbation.[71] Even in the United States, a study of over 1,200 older adults (mean age = 77.3) found that about 30 percent had participated in sexual activity in the past month and 67 percent were satisfied with their current level of sexual activity.[72] Men were more likely to be sexually active but less apt than women to be satisfied with their level of sexual activity.

Factors Related to Marital Sexuality

Many factors other than age have been found to be highly related to marital sexuality. For example, it is known that intercourse is less frequent during menstruation. Pregnancy, as well, influences sexual activity for both the married and the non-married.[73] Evidence has suggested that, during pregnancy, particularly during the first and third trimesters, women experience diminished sexual desire, frequency, and

---

[70]Vaughn Call, Susan Sprecher, and Pepper Schwartz, "The Incidence and Frequency of Marital Sex in a National Sample," *Journal of Marriage and the Family* 57 (August 1995): 646.

[71]Maj-Briht Bergstrom-Walan and Helle H. Nielsen, "Sexual Expression among 60- to 80-Year-Old Men and Women: A Sample from Stockholm, Sweden," *The Journal of Sex Research* 27 (May 1990): 289–295.

[72]Ruth E. Matthias, James E. Lubben, Kathryn A. Atchison, and Stuart O. Schweitzer, "Sexual Activity and Satisfaction among Very Old Adults: Results From a Community-Dwelling Medicare Population Survey," *The Gerontologist* 37 (1997): 6–14.

[73]Lennart Y. Bogren, "Changes in Sexuality to Women and Men During Pregnancy," *Archives of Sexual Behavior* 20 (1991): 35–45.

satisfaction. For men, diminished sexual desire and decrease in sexual satisfaction seem to exist only during the third trimester of the partner's pregnancy.

Earlier studies support the hypothesis that intercourse is related to stress within the marriage. The more severe the marital strain, the lower the frequency of marital coitus. Other earlier research has suggested that coital frequency increases with the amount of education of the wife, is higher among women who work in paid employment (highest among career-motivated women), and is positively associated with the effectiveness of contraception.

Contraception Usage

Regarding contraception, it is of interest to note that a national survey of women, ages 15 to 45, showed a long-term trend in the United States toward convergence of contraceptive usage among the major religious groups.[74] About 77 percent of married Protestant women and 75 percent of married Catholic women used some type of contraception or practiced some type of pregnancy control. Among women who used contraceptives, Protestants were the most likely to use female sterilization (30 percent, compared to 18 percent Catholic and 12 percent Jewish). Catholic women were the most likely to use the pill (34 percent, compared to 28 percent Protestant and 14 percent Jewish). Jewish women were most likely to use a diaphragm (26 percent, compared to 5 percent Protestant and 7 percent Catholic) or a condom (23 percent, compared to 13 percent Protestant and 18 percent Catholic).

Class-Related Differences

Although certain female/male and Catholic/non-Catholic differences appear to be decreasing, marital sexual activities still vary considerably in numerous respects, such as social class. Contrary to the notion that people of the lower social classes are less sexually inhibited, people from the middle and upper classes are more likely to have intercourse in total nudity, use a variety of positions in intercourse, and engage in oral/genital contact. Although social stratification literature has suggested that working-class people have increasingly adopted middle-class values and behaviors, Martin Weinberg and Colin Williams found that social class is still an important determinant of sexual behavior.[75] Compared to the lower and working classes, middle-class men and women start their sexual activities at a later age, are more likely to enjoy their first sexual experiences, and are more likely to react positively to masturbation.

Sexual Adjustment in Marriage

Sexual adjustment has been highlighted by certain writers as the keystone to marital adjustment. However, it is highly unlikely that adjustment of any sort is a dichotomous, either/or phenomenon. Within any marriage, sex is better or worse at certain times or in various situations. Also, to assume that frequency of intercourse, attainment of female orgasm, or lack of inhibition is equal to sexual adjustment is both misleading and false. It is very difficult to separate sex from the complex interaction

---

[74]Calvin Goldscheider and William D. Mosher, "Patterns of Contraceptive Use in the United States: The Importance of Religious Factors," *Studies in Family Planning* 22 (March/April 1991): 102–115.

[75]Martin S. Weinberg and Colin J. Williams, "Sexual Embourgeoisment? Social Class and Sexual Activity: 1938–1970," *American Sociological Review* 45 (February 1980): 33–48.

Coitus, or sexual intercourse—although not confined to marriage, cohabiting, or sexually exclusive partners—is an expected behavior between people in such relationships. The frequency of intercourse among couples tends to decrease with age and duration of the relationship; nonetheless, sex remains important throughout the life course.

of variables that constitutes married life. Sexual adjustment may be one indicator of general marital adjustment, but it is doubtful that having a good sex life by itself will maintain an otherwise poor relationship. Dissatisfaction in marriage is likely to be reflected in the frequency and performance of marital coitus, and conflict in sexual coitus may be symptomatic of other tensions within the marital relationship.

In a national sample of over 6,000 married couples, Donnelly wanted to determine if sexually inactive marriages were less happy and stable than those with sexual activity.[76] It was determined that 16 percent of the marriages had been sexually inactive during the month prior to the interview, indicating that such marriages are not uncommon. It was also determined that these couples were not in happy, stable marriages in which the partners simply did not have sex. The lack of sexual activity appeared to be associated with the existence of other problems in the relationship and may indeed be a danger signal for many marriages.

The relationship between sexual activity in marriage and marital satisfaction is one of two prominent discourses about marital sex discovered by Snikka Elliott and Debra Umberson.[77] In qualitative interviews with over thirty couples (sixty-two separate interviews with husbands and wives) who were married for between 8 and 52 years, they found a commonly expressed theme that "sex is a gauge of marital

[76]Denise A. Donnelly, "Sexually Inactive Marriages," *The Journal of Sex Research* 30 (May 1993): 171–179.

[77]Sinikka Elliott and Debra Umberson, "The Performance of Desire: Gender and Sexual Negotiation in Long-Term Marriages," *Journal of Marriage and Family*, 70 (May 2008): 391–406.

well-being."[78] They found this discourse alongside another that would appear to challenge the potential for happiness in their marriages—that men are inherently more sexual than women. If the latter is true, then there would be much tension in marriage leading to an inevitable decline in satisfaction.

In order to reconcile these two discourses, they found that married couples engaged in considerable *emotional work* around sex. **Emotional work** consists of activities or behaviors engaged in by actors to manage their own emotions and/or those of their partner in a way that facilitates the relationship. This type of work often requires changes to identities or the enactment of behaviors that run counter to one's own self-conception. An example of this work among these couples involved wives' attempts to consciously increase their interest in sex and mens' attempts to decrease their interests.

They also found that this "double standard" in perceived sexual interest affected negotiations in other areas of the relationship. In particular, men utilized participation in housework as a strategy for increasing levels of sexual activity and women participated in this exchange, seeing their husbands' housework activity as "earning" them greater levels of sex.

Thus, while on the one hand a discourse of gender differences in sexual interest gives women more negotiating power vis-à-vis the principle of least interest, on the other hand it requires them to put more emotional work into their relationship which, for employed women in particular, only adds to their domestic burdens and created resentment in many of the women in this study.

Extramarital Sex

The terms **extramarital sex** and *adultery* are defined as sexual intercourse between a man and a woman, at least one of whom is married at the time to someone else. Almost without exception in the United States, adultery is legally punishable. And although actual prosecution is rare, the moral condemnation that accompanies extramarital coitus is, in general, much stronger than that directed at coitus among nonmarrieds.

Around the world, there is much greater concern for the extramarital behavior of the wife than that of the husband. Most societies permit or condone extramarital coitus for the male if he is reasonably circumspect about it and if he does not carry it to extremes that would break up his home, lead to the neglect of his family, outrage his in-laws, stir up public scandal, or start difficulties with the husband or other relatives of the women with whom he has relationships.[79] Such extramarital activity is much less frequently permitted or condoned for the female.

Even though a double standard exists in the United States, it is far less pronounced than in many countries, many of which permit considerable freedom for the male yet place harsh restrictions on the female. For example, prior to World War II, Japan was considered a "man's world." Japanese husbands were permitted to engage in sexual contact outside of marriage but infidelity by wives was condemned as a crime. Since World War II, social and economic conditions for Japanese women have improved, radically changing the situation. However, the sexual freedom of women has not approached that of men. Even today, Japanese men openly seem to enjoy more sexual freedom than do U.S. and probably European men.

---

[78]Ibid., 403.
[79]Kinsey, *Sexual Behavior in the Human Female*, 414.

Incidence of and Attitudes toward Extramarital Sex

What factors account for, or are highly related to, extramarital coitus? Of all the factors that Kinsey examined, religious devoutness, more than any other factor, affected the incidence of extramarital coitus, particularly for females. The lowest incidence of extramarital coitus occurred among people who were most devoutly religious, and this was true of all Protestant, Jewish, and Catholic groups in the sample.[80]

More recent data from a National Survey of Women suggest that religion continues to have a significant influence on sexual exclusivity.[81] Women who belonged to a religious group other than a mainstream Protestant or Catholic group or who belonged to no religious group at all were twice as likely to have a secondary sex partner as women with a mainstream religious affiliation. Other factors from the same study that appear to decrease the likelihood of sexual exclusivity for married women included a previous history of multiple sex partners, having cohabited prior to marriage, and having more education than their partner. Black and Hispanic women were less sexually exclusive than their white counterparts. Other national representative survey data reveal a higher likelihood of sexual infidelity among those with stronger sexual interests, more permissive sexual values, lower subjective satisfaction with their union, weaker sexual ties to their partner, and greater sexual opportunities.[82]

Chien Liu shows that the duration of marriage affects the likelihood of extramarital sexual relationships with consideration by gender.[83] For women, the likelihood of sexual infidelity decreases with marital duration. For men, the relationship between extramarital sex and marital duration is convex (U-shaped). That is, over the course of marriage, the likelihood of extramarital sex for men decreases until about the eighteenth anniversary and increases continually thereafter. One of his explanations for this gender difference over time married is that men, middle age and older, are experiencing less marital sex and also see less of a threat that their wives will sanction them, due to the wives' heavy investments in their marriage and their declining prospects for remarriage. He adds, however, that this theoretical explanation needs to be examined more fully.

Extramarital sex is a behavior that, in the United States, at least, is seldom looked upon favorably. In 1990, when one national opinion survey asked about a married person having sexual relations with someone other than the marriage partner, 78 percent said it was "always wrong" (up from 70 percent in 1980) and an additional 13 percent said it was "almost always wrong." Only 2 percent said it was "not wrong at all."[84] The respondents' estimates for the incidence of extramarital activity ranged from 25 to 50 percent for men, and 15 to 35 percent for women. But national data from the 1990s showed the figures to be lower than the estimated minimums: 22.7 percent for men and 11.6 percent for women.[85]

---

[80]Kinsey, *Sexual Behavior in the Human Female*, 424.

[81]Renata Forste and Koray Tanfer, "Sexual Exclusivity among Dating, Cohabiting, and Married Women," *Journal of Marriage and the Family* 58 (February 1996): 33–47.

[82]Judith Treas and Deirdre Giesen, "Sexual Infidelity among Married and Cohabiting Americans," *Journal of Marriage and the Family* 62 (February 2000): 48–60.

[83]Chien Liu, "A Theory of Marital Sex Life," *Journal of Marriage and the Family* 62 (May 2000): 363–374.

[84]Floris W. Wood, ed., *An American Profile—Opinions and Behavior. 1972–1989* (Detroit: Gale Research, Inc., 1990), 603.

[85]Michael W. Wiederman, "Extramarital Sex: Prevalence and Correlates in a National Survey," *The Journal of Sex Research* 34 (1997): 167–174.

Justifications for extramarital relationships were found to relate to a number of dimensions, including sexual, emotional, and extrinsic.[86] Sexual dimensions, which men more commonly cited as justifications, included sexual excitement, sexual curiosity, novelty or variety, and sexual enjoyment. Emotional dimensions, which women more commonly mentioned, included romantic love, getting love and affection, intellectual sharing, understanding, companionship, ego-bolstering, aspects of enhancing self-esteem, and respect. Extrinsic dimensions included career advancement and "getting even" with the spouse.

Variations in extramarital sex by one spouse include those in which both spouses participate: swinging, consensual adultery, mate swapping, comarital sexual behavior, or group sexual activities. While these involve a single standard of sexual permissiveness, they do not find widespread acceptance, and it is doubtful they will ever approach the frequency of extramarital sexual relationships engaged in by one of the marital partners. These extramarital encounters, however, differ from adultery in their nonsecrecy and openness between partners.

Same-Sex Relationships

Although the number of same-sex couple households in the population is extremely small (less than 1 million),[87] it is nonetheless a significant number deserving of further study. In addition, recent debates about same-sex marriage and adoption make it very important that we understand more fully the nature of these relationships. Unfortunately, data on same-sex couples are scarce and the methodological problems that arise in studying these couples are substantial. Lawrence Kurdek has undertaken one of the better longitudinal studies of gay and lesbian couples[88] and has reviewed some of the better studies done by others.[89] Therefore, we will rely on his review for a brief overview of what we know about gay and lesbian relationships.

Before presenting data on same-sex relationships, however, it is important to consider some of the factors that might be important in shaping their intereactions. Obviously, the first difference is that these couples are not influenced by the same cross-gender dynamics that affect heterosexual couples. For example, the power differences that exist between men and women in the broader society and that filter into heterosexual marriages are not present in same-sex couples. Socialization differences based on gender are also lacking, such as different styles of communication and conflict and different attitudes and values with respect to relationships. Same-sex couples also must interact and maintain their relationships without the benefits of institutional recognition and under less supportive and sometimes hostile conditions. Levels of support are likely to be more problematic, normative guidelines will be lacking, environmental risks will be greater, and the community context of

---

[86]Shirley P. Glass and Thomas L. Wright, "Justifications for Extramarital Relationships: The Association between Attitudes, Behaviors, and Gender," *The Journal of Sex Research* 29 (August 1992): 361–387.

[87]Lawrence A. Kurdeck, "Gay Men and Lesbians: The Family Context," in Marilyn Coleman and Lawrence H. Ganong, *Handbook of Contemporary Families: Considering the Past, Contemplating the Future* (Thousand Oaks, CA: Sage Publications, 2004)

[88]For a description of this study, see Lawrence A. Kurdeck, "Relationship Outcomes and Their Predictors: Longitudinal Evidence from Heterosexual Married, Gay Cohabiting, and Lesbian Cohabiting Couples," *Journal of Marriage and the Family* 60 (1998): 553–568.

[89]Lawrence A. Kurdeck, "Gay Men and Lesbians: The Family Context."

relationship alternatives is likely to be different. As a result, it would not be surprising to find significant differences between same-sex couples and those in heterosexual marriages and even cohabitations.

It is also important to note that there is likely to be variation across same-sex couples. In particular, there should be some systematic variation between gay male couples and lesbian couples based on gender differences in socialization and social position. It would be a serious mistake, however, to classify same-sex couples within these two types as the same. Just as there is tremendous variation among heterosexual couples, there will be variation among gay male couples and among lesbian couples. In fact, this expected variation is a point of caution in reviewing the research on these couples because most studies have used only small and nonrepresentative samples (usually young, white, and middle class). Keeping these cautions in mind, what can we say about same-sex relationships?

The most significant conclusion that we can draw is that same-sex couples do not look very different from heterosexual couples. Gay and lesbian couples use special names for each other to refer to their relationship status (such as "lover" or "partner"), engage in rituals such as ring exchanges and commitment ceremonies to symbolically represent their relationships status, and pool their resources. Areas where they differ the most from heterosexual couples include their division of labor and power structures, their orientations and behaviors regarding closeness and autonomy, their sexual relationships, and their support networks.

Same-sex couples, especially lesbian couples, are more likely than heterosexual couples to divide household chores equally, although they do divide up tasks rationally based on individual skills and preferences and, as in heterosexual relationships, there is a tendency for there to be less sharing over time as these relationships progress. In fact, there is evidence that partners in lesbian couples will actually "unlearn" skills so as to facilitate a more equal division of labor. Similarly to the equality found in the division of labor among same-sex couples, these couples (again, especially same-sex female couples) are also more likely to hold and comply with an ethic of equality of power in their relationships. Same-sex couples are also more comfortable with closeness but have more openness and autonomy in their relationships. With respect to gendered and sexual behavior, there is no evidence of same-sex couples taking on traditional male–female identities or sexual roles. All evidence points to the butch–femme identity pairing (where one partner assumes the identity of a man and the other assumes the identity of a woman) as being a myth, or at least an identity pairing of previous times, and same-sex couples do not typically adopt active and passive roles in their sexual relationships. Finally, with respect to social support networks, same-sex couples often have fewer family members to rely on and tend to place more reliance on friends (especially same-sex friends) than do heterosexual couples.

Summary

1. The large wedding and elaborate honeymoon of today are unique in terms of their functions and forms. The large wedding of the distant past was a community event whereas today's weddings serve more of a personal relationship function. The honeymoon has more recent origins and also serves the needs of the individuals involved. Both are rituals that may have arisen from the increased uncertainty of interpersonal relationships in a modern society.

2. Deciding on a mutually agreeable division of household and outside work responsibilities is an important task of the transition to marriage and one that must be renegotiated throughout the life of a marriage. Although the homemaker role may have many rewards, it is generally underrewarded and underappreciated. Outside work roles, on the other hand, bring more rewards and greater independence. As a result, higher levels of equality in the participation of spouses in household tasks generally improve evaluations of the marriage, although this effect will be less significant for those with traditional ideologies and identities.

3. An important and widely researched area of marriage has addressed the power positions of husband and wife or intimate partners as individuals and in relation to each other. *Power* is the ability to influence others and affect their behavior in spite of their resistance. Power includes the crucial dimensions of authority (legitimized power) and influence.

4. Studies of decision-making outcomes have indicated that certain decisions are made primarily by the husband, others primarily by the wife, and others jointly. Who makes which decision has been widely explained by a theory of resources: the person with the most resources—information, education, income, and so forth—makes the decision.

5. Resource theory per se has been viewed as inadequate. Thus, a theory of comparative resources or a cultural resource theory has been developed and tested. It recognizes that resources are important but understood only in the context of the dominant values of a society or culture.

6. As with conjugal power, many attempts have been made to measure marital quality. Although there is no general consensus as to what *quality* means, definitions generally include characteristics such as high levels of husband–wife agreement and sharing of activities, tasks, and affection. Because individuals hold different sets of expectations with respect to their marriages and have different goals in their marriages, however, the best measures may be comparisons of outcomes to goals or subjective assessments of how satisfied the partners are with their relationship. The concept of comparison level is use to help capture the idea that individuals have different standards of profitability for their relationships.

7. When marital quality, adjustment, and satisfaction are examined throughout the lifecycle or life course, satisfaction appears to be highest at the beginning of marriage and lowest when the family has teenagers. Studies have indicated a curvilinear (U-shaped) relationship throughout the marital life course; the beginning and the end of marriage are the points of highest satisfaction. A cohort type of analysis, however, calls this finding into question.

8. Marital commitment and marital stability are distinct aspects of relationships. A person could have a low-quality marriage but still be committed or have a stable relationship. Alternatively, a person could have a high-quality marriage but have low commitment and stability. The reason is that there are three different sources or types of commitment—personal, structural, and moral. The former is more closely tied to the quality of the relationship and one's satisfaction in the relationship, whereas the latter two are based on social constraints or personal convictions. As a result, a number of writers have suggested that marital alternatives may be a better predictor of marital disruption than are measures of adjustment or satisfaction. The concept of comparison level for alternatives is used to help capture the idea that individuals have different alternative sources of rewards available to them and compare their relationship rewards to those alternatives. When alternatives are perceived as having greater costs than benefits (a low comparison level for alternatives), many unhappy marriages are likely to remain intact.

9. Studies have indicated that the incidence and frequency of marital coitus reach their maximums in the first year or two after marriage, with a steady decline from that time on. As with nonmarital coitus, marital coitus rates have shown an increase over the past several decades.

10. Not all heterosexual coitus of married persons occurs among spouses. Extramarital coitus appears to be widespread, with major differences between males and females and across cultures.

11. Although research on same-sex relationships is limited, the few quality studies that have been done show few differences between these couples and those in heterosexual relationships. When differences are found, they tend to be in areas of closeness, autonomy, support networks, equality in the division of labor and power.

Many families include only the marital system, but most include children living with a marital couple or with a single parent. As we have seen, the presence of children can have a profound impact on the marriage system. Given these potential impacts and differences and changes in the value societies place on having children, it will come as little surprise that fertility decisions vary across societies as well as across individuals and over time in the same society. Chapter 10 examines patterns of fertility, decision making with respect to having children, and the impacts of family size on marital and family functioning. Chapter 11 examines the process by which families socialize children.

Key Terms and Topics

bidden wedding p. 342
rough music p. 342
wedding tour p. 342
honeymoon p. 342
homemaker p. 344
housework p. 344
gender differences in housework pp. 346–349
perceptions of fairness pp. 350–352
distributive justice framework p. 350
employed women and marriage pp. 352–354
power p. 355
authority p. 355
influence p. 355
characteristics of power pp. 355–356
power and decision making in intimate
    relationships p. 356
resource theory p. 357
cultural resource theory p. 357
egalitarian ethic p. 359
marital quality or adjustment p. 360
marital success p. 361

marital happiness or satisfaction p. 361
marital stability p. 361
comparison level p. 364
marital quality between generations pp. 364–366
marital quality over the life course pp. 366–368
commitment p. 368
personal commitment p. 369
structural commitment p. 369
barriers to dissolution p. 369
moral commitment p. 369
comparison level for alternatives p. 369
marital alternatives p. 370
factors related to marital sexual activity
    pp. 372–373
contraception usage p. 373
sexual adjustment in marriage p. 373
emotional work p. 375
extramarital sex p. 375
incidence of and attitudes toward extramarital
    sex pp. 376–377
same-sex relationships pp. 377–378

Discussion Questions

1. If big weddings and elaborate honeymoons no longer have functions for either the community or the relationship, why are they so popular today?
2. If many women report finding happiness with their roles as homemakers, why is the division of labor such a major issue of conflict in marriages?
3. Compare the conflict perspective with the exchange and symbolic intereactionist perspectives on the division of labor in marriage. What would each perspective say is the key to creating equality in the division of labor and in power relations in marriage?
4. Differentiate among the terms *power*, *authority*, and *influence*. How can women and other groups in subordinate positions obtain power?
5. What is your theory of conjugal power? In what (if any) instances does the person with the greatest resources not have the most power? In what (if any) instances does the person with few resources still have a high degree of power?
6. Define the *egalitarian ethic* and discuss its relationship to satisfaction in marriage. What might this

suggest about the quality of relationships in highly patriarchal countries?
7. Discuss the concept of *marital quality*. What is it? Can it be measured or determined? How? Why do some couples rated low on marital quality remain together?
8. Think of older and younger couples you know and select two or three at different stages of life that seem to have the most ideal marriages or relationships. What factors tend to make those relationships ideal? Do the same features exist in each? Give examples.
9. What explains the curvilinear relationship between marital adjustment and the family lifecycle or family life course?
10. Think of older and younger couples you know and think about what keeps them together. To what extent do they differ on personal, structural, and moral commitment levels?
11. In what ways is marital coitus likely to be influenced by length of time married, age, the media,

employment of husband and/or wife, religion, number and/or residency status of children, and the like? What explains changes that have taken place?

12. What constitutes good sexual adjustment in marriage? Is it possible to have good sexual adjustment and poor marital adjustment? Is the opposite possible? Why?

13. What are the arguments for and against extramarital sex and "swinging"? Are these activities inherently disruptive to marriage? Can they ever benefit or improve marriage? Why?

14. Why do you think same-sex couples differ from heterosexual couples along the dimensions of closeness, openness, autonomy, and equality in the division of labor and power?

Further Readings

Booth, Alan, Crouter, Ann C., and Clements, Mari, eds. *Couples in Conflict*. Mahwah, NJ: Lawrence Erlbaum Associates, 2001.

Seventeen chapters share the general theme of couples in conflict and ways our society can work to minimize destructive conflict or enhance couples' ability to constructively handle it.

Braithwaite, Dawn, and Baxter, Leslie. *Engaging Theories in Family Communication: Multiple Perspectives*. Thousand Oaks, CA: Sage Publications, 2005.

A communications expert looks at family communication.

Hackstaff, Karla B. *Marriage in a Culture of Divorce*. Philadelphia: Temple University Press, 1999.

An investigation of two generations of married couples exploring changes in how people talked about, constructed, and interpreted divorce in the context of marriage.

Popenoe, David, Elshtain, Jean Bethke, and Blankenhorn, David, eds. *Promises to Keep: Decline and Renewal of Marriage in America*. Lanham, MD: Rowman & Littlefield Publishers, Inc., 1996.

A collection of thirteen articles that suggests marriage in the United States is in trouble and the time has come for U.S. society to change course.

Schwartz, Pepper. *Peer Marriage: How Love between Equals Really Works*. New York: The Free Press, 1994.

In-depth interviews with people in egalitarian marriages reveal how true equality is possible but only by a radical departure from traditional marriage patterns.

Shirley, Karen J. *Resilient Marriages: From Alcoholism and Adversity to Relationship Growth*. Lanham, MD: Rowman and Littlefield Publishers, 2000.

An exploration of relational repair of couples in long-term marriages who have weathered the crisis of alcoholism and sobriety.

Steil, Janice M. *Marital Equality: Its Relationship to Well-Being of Husbands and Wives*. Thousand Oaks: CA: Sage, 1997.

A book about equality among heterosexual marriages and the historical evolution of "gender justice."

Veroff, Joseph, Douvan, Elizabeth, and Hatchett, Shirley J. *Marital Instability: A Social and Behavioral Study of the Early Years*. Westport, CT: Praeger, 1995.

A study of the major factors that make for commitment, stability, and happiness in married couples over the first four years.

Whyte, Martin King, ed. *Marriage in America: A Communitarian Perspective*. Lanham, MD: Rowman and Littlefield Publishers, 2000.

This edited volume of essays presents a wide range of viewpoints probing the extent to which existing policies and practices support or undermine marriage.

chapter 10

Parenthood and Fertility

Growing Up in Large Families

Stewart and Joyce have been married forty-five years. They have two adult children, both graduates of North Carolina State University, married, and successful in their careers. They have one granddaughter and one grandson, both of whom are their pride and joy. Stewart was the twelfth of fourteen children and Joyce was the youngest of twelve children. What was it like for them to grow up in large families?

Stewart and Joyce expressed many similar childhood experiences. Both lived on farms and each had their specific tasks or chores to perform, including carrying wood and coal and helping with farm chores. Both indicated they didn't have much but always had plenty to eat and felt they were very similar to other families in the community. Neither home had electricity and none of the parents owned or drove an automobile. Both had mothers who would discipline the children but fathers who would perform any needed spankings. Both had mothers who would serve three meals a day and families that would eat meals together, sitting on benches around one long table. Both, being younger siblings, felt closer, and even today feel closer, to their younger brothers and sisters than to the older ones.

Joyce, being the youngest, felt she got more privileges than the others. She liked having lots of brothers and sisters because there was always someone around to help her. She had special memories of how her older brothers, who had jobs away from home, would come home on weekends and give her money or how her mother would make her new dresses from colorfully designed cotton feed sacks. She shared how she had wanted a hair permanent but not having any money, picked blackberries to pay for it. What she missed most was not having a grandmother like the other kids had.

Stewart, too, felt he got some special privileges—but not like his kid brother, who lived like a king and got whatever he wanted. He, too, has special memories of working beside and learning from his dad who was a skilled carpenter. Since his grandpa gave the land his school was built on, he and his brothers and sisters only had to walk one-fourth of a mile to school and would walk home each day for lunch.

Today, both Stewart and Joyce keep in close touch with their siblings. Joyce remembers all their birthdays and Stewart says he remembers certain ones. Joyce's siblings, their spouses, and her nephews and nieces get together twice a year, once in June and again in December, at which time they give a Christmas present to the person whose name they had drawn earlier. Stewart's family gets together every May. Does either have any regrets in having so many siblings? None whatsoever. Neither would have wanted it any other way.

Questions to Consider

What would you consider a "large" family? Why? How do you account for the significant decrease in the number of children desired and the actual number born?

What are some of the advantages and disadvantages of Stewart and Joyce having many siblings? Do these same factors exist today?

Is there any significance to being a boy or girl, last-born of twelve or third-to-last of fourteen? Would things have been different for them if they had been first-born or third-born? Why?

*I*n all societies, children have considerable instrumental and/or emotional value and in most societies the responsibility for reproduction and the subsequent socialization of children into adult roles lies in the realm of marriage and the family institution. However, although marriage is often seen as a prerequisite to bearing children, it is important to note that this is not always the case. Similarly, it also is not always the case that the family is responsible for early socialization.

In this chapter, we will examine the value of children across different types of societies and, more specifically, in modern Western societies such as the United States. We will also explore the meaning that having children has for their parents. Both of these factors enter into the motivation to have children and help determine the number of children born in a society at any given point in time and the typical size of families in those societies. We will then look at fertility patterns across societies and within U.S. society. We will examine how birthrates have changed over time, changing patterns in childfree or childless marriages, and the phenomenon of young and unwed parenthood. Finally, we will consider the positive and negative consequences that result from having children, as well as the effects of having multiple children, on parents and the children themselves. Issues of parenting behaviors and socialization of children will be discussed in Chapter 11.

*T*he Value of Children

In most countries, married couples in general and women in particular face considerable social pressures to become parents. In the United States and other highly industrialized countries, these cultural and social pressures appear to have decreased over recent years, as evidenced by the delay in first pregnancies; the increased ability to control conceptions and births; the decline in birthrates; the movement of increasing numbers of women into the labor force; the increasing preference for limiting family size to two-children or fewer. Of course, many unplanned conceptions result from sexual acts that were recreational rather than procreative, or coerced rather than voluntary. These unplanned and often undesired pregnancies lead to personal and social concerns over terminating the pregnancy or having the child and raising it alone or placing it for adoption.

In spite of unplanned pregnancies, a decreasing birthrate, a decrease in the average family size, and an increase in childless marriages (all discussed later in this chapter), men and women continue to want and voluntarily have children. Given the number of both married and single persons who want to adopt, the legal battles of child custody following divorce, and even the numerous incidents of child snatching (the abduction of a child by one parent from another), it must be assumed that children are valued.

Although children are significant to men and women around the world, the number of children and their value are changing. In pre-industrial societies, values of pronatalism prevailed. **Pronatalism** was a belief that having children (and many children) was highly desirable. But what was the source of that desire and does it still exist in modern societies like the United States? S. Phillip Morgan and Rosalind Berkowitz King suggest three factors that sustain high fertility rates and that should encourage pronatalism.[1]

To be certain, some of the desire for children is *biological.* Species cannot survive without their genetic material being passed down across generations through reproduction. The translation of genetic material into behaviors, however, is neither a direct nor a deterministic process. Genetic material produces physiological conditions (e.g., the presence of certain hormones and neurotransmitters) that make some activities and external conditions more pleasurable than others. In terms of reproduction, the most obvious activity that sustains the drive to reproduce is sexual stimulation. A second is more complex and involves the physiological responses that occur as a result of altruism toward close kin and, in particular, interactions with infants. Third, having children might produce a positive emotional response insofar as this condition reflects and reinforces one's power and status—conditions that enhance the survival of one's children.

Thus, those who are driven to engage in sexual relations and who have strong positive emotional experiences in response to pregnancy will be most successful at producing children who survive into adulthood, where they can reproduce the subsequent generation. As a result, their drive and predisposition to respond positively to pregnancy and parent–child interaction will also survive into later generations and find expression in cultural values such pronatalism. None of these forces "determines" fertility rates. Rather, they *predispose* individuals to reproduce. These predispositions, however, can and are often constrained and sometimes redirected given current environmental conditions.

A second factor that promotes pronatalism is the *institutional consequences* of high fertility. Both the addition of new members through childbirth and the dependencies of women on men created as a result of repeat pregnancies can have consequences

---

[1]S. Phillip Morgan and Rosalind Berkowitz King, "Why Have Children in the 21st Century? Biological Predisposition, Social Coercion, Rational Choice," *European Journal of Population*, 17 (2001): 3–20.

TRANSNATIONAL FAMILIES

Globalization and the Value of Children in Latin America

In an historical analysis of family life and childhood in Latin America, Elizabeth Kuznesof argues that modernization and globalization forces have contributed to a disruption of functional kinship relationships of the past, the perception of childhood conditions as problematic, and a distorted view that the family system has broken down in recent decades. Previously functional kinship relations have become challenged by growing inequalities due to globalization that have made mutual aid giving to kin across social status boundaries less feasible. Perceptions of childhood as being problematic and in need of social control has come about because of global processes shaping a narrow definition of what childhood involves without considering the unique context that Latin American children find themselves in and the relationship between their street activities and family adaptability. Finally, the perception that the family is in disrepair is reinforced by the failure of children other than those of the wealthy to fulfill Western ideas of what childhood should be about—namely, a period of dependency, nurturance, protection, play and education.

Children in Latin America have long been considered marginal and need of social control when judged through Western eyes. Much of this perception stems from the historically high numbers of children in the population (30–50 percent of the population in the eighteenth century and more than 50 percent in the late twentieth century were under the age of 20), high historical "illegitimacy" rates (30–60 percent between the sixteenth and twentieth century), and an expectation that children should be living Western-like lives in stable nuclear family units. In more recent decades, these perceptions have been reinforced by the growth in homelessness and street families throughout Latin America due to the inequalities brought about in the globalization process.

Although there is certainly a need to help those in need, it is also incorrect to over-state the problem of childhood in Latin America. Children in this context live a "nurturing childhood" rather than the "nurtured childhood" of their Western counterparts. This nurturing quality of their experience reveals their value. In societies that are highly matricentric and where single mothers exist in high numbers among the popular classes, children are brought up as active contributors to family well-being. Thus, their childhoods need to be understood in a different light. Street children are many times living in a family context and their spells on the streets are often limited based on circumstances having to do with family adaptations occurring at home. For the most part, they are not "problems" in need of "control." Unfortunately, globalization is a process that leads to the development of a single set of concepts for understanding the world – a set of concepts that reinforces the globalization process itself. As a result, the value of children and the needs of children in more peripheral countries often are misunderstood and go unaddressed.

Source: Elizabeth A. Kusnesof, "The House, The Street, Global Society: Latin American Families and Childhood in the Twenty-First Century," *Journal of Social History,* 38 (Summer 2005): 859–872.

for societies and the institutional arrangements within them (e.g., gender roles and gender stratification). For example, when children have high economic value through their ability to contribute to production activities (as in early agricultural societies), levels of pronatalism and fertility should be high. Societies should also encourage fertility when cultural and political boundaries are threatened. Increasing fertility will increase the availability of future warriors as well as help preserve cultural values over generations by creating cohesive communities of similar minded people. Since fertility also has consequences for the dependency of women on men and the power differences that result, pronatalism and fertility should also be responsive to the system of gender stratification in a society.

Finally, children have reward-cost consequences for individuals and these consequences should motivate parents to have more or fewer children, especially in societies where institutional controls over reproduction are not strong. When the profitability of having children for individuals and couples is high, the desire for children and the expression of positive attitudes toward having children should also be high. Thus, having children is a *rational choice* process. When children cost little to have (economically, socially, and emotionally) and when they have much to contribute, individuals and couples will desire to have more children—or at least lack a strong desire to limit their reproduction. When having children exacts more costs (both direct and opportunity costs—such as reduced opportunities for employment or promotion at work), fertility rates will be lower and support for cultural norms of pronatalism will be weaker.

One example of how rational choice operates in child bearing decisions is **uncertainty reduction theory**.[2] The assumption of this theory states that throughout the world, people seek to reduce uncertainty. Children are of value insofar as they can provide security (increasing certainty) when parents face divorce, widowhood, and financial insecurity. Thus, when there are no societal provisions for providing for the elderly other than through family ties, fertility rates and pronatalism should be strong. If infant and childhood mortality is also high, these effects will be even stronger as parents will attempt to increase their chances that a child will survive into adulthood by having more children.

What do these forces tell us about pronatalism in modern societies like the United States? You would think that fertility would be lower and pronatalism would be weakened in modern societies for a number of reasons.

First, women in modern societies have greater control over their sex lives and their potential fertility outcomes due to the combined effects of greater gender equality and advancement in reproductive technologies (e.g., birth control and abortion). Evolutionary perspectives assert that a gender difference exists in men's and women's interests in procreation, an assertion known as **parental investment theory**.[3] This theory argues that it is in males' interest to maximize their sexual behavior with the "fittest" of the females of the species. The more children produced with females possessing traits signifying health and the predisposition to nurture children, the greater their chances of having more of their offspring survive into adulthood and be successful reproducers themselves. Females of the species, however, will be more interested in limiting their fertility so as to invest more of their psychological, emotional, and physical resources in nurturing each child and assuring their survival. Thus, an increase in females' power in society should reduce the number of children each produces but there should still be a strong desire to have some children.

Second, industrialization and modern capitalism have brought about a fundamental transformation in the value of children for economic production and loosened the control of men over dominant gender ideologies. Since children have less production value, the society has less interest in promoting high levels of procreation. Some degree of fertility will still be promoted, however, so as to produce a workforce for sustained economic activity and growth over time. The loosening of men's control over dominant ideologies should undercut the

---

[2]Debra Friedman, Michael Hechter, and Satoshi Kanazawa, "A Theory of the Value of Children," *Demography* 31 (August 1994): 375–401.

[3]See David C. Geary, "Evolution of Paternal Investment," in D.M. Buss, ed., *The Handbook of Evolutionary Psychology* (Hoboken, NJ: John Wiley & Sons, 2005): 483–505.

strength of pronatalistic norms insofar as those norms promote a dependency condition of women on men—although technological advances and the emergence of child care and other related institutions have reduced the dependencies created in child bearing considerably.

Finally, pronatalism norms should be weakened as a function of modernity as individuals are given freedom to make their own choices and are more likely to resist normative pressures to have children. Under these cultural conditions, fertility will be more of a rational choice and less a function of normative compliance. To be sure, norms have not ceased to exist in modern societies and gendered ideologies still play an important role in encouraging women to be mothers. As feminist scholars[4] have pointed out, pronatalism is alive and well in contemporary Western societies but has taken a more insidious form as child bearing and motherhood have become synonymous with the concept of womanhood to such an extent that a failure to become a mother takes on meaning as a failure to be a woman.

Fertility Behaviors

For whatever reasons, married couples in the United States want, have or expect to have children sometime in their life course. *When* they have those children and *how many* they have, however, suggest a different type of pronatalism, one that focuses on the positive personal outcomes (for self, couple and child) of having only one or two children rather than on the value of children from an economic, political of cultural perspective. This new form of pronatalism is reflected in the results of a 2007 Gallup poll[5] in which 56 percent of Americans said it was best to have two or fewer children, 34 percent said three or more and 9 percent were undecided. The importance of having at least one and preferably two children was reflected in the fact that only 1 percent said that no child was preferred and only 3 percent preferred one child. The average of all responses indicated that the ideal family size in the United States is 2.5 children. This is much lower than it was in the more distant past but is virtually unchanged since the early 1970s when, like many other aspects of family life, public opinion shifted radically toward a smaller family model. But these are just opinions and expectations, what about the actual rates of child bearing?

Birthrates are one of the best-documented series of descriptive social data available today. In 2009, the U.S. Census Bureau estimated that there were 4.27 million births in the United States in 2006, a rate of 14.2 *births per thousand population*, one of the lowest rates in the past 60 years.[6] Of course, birth rates don't tell us

---

[4]See: Elaine May, *Barren in the Promised Land: Childless Americans and the Pursuit of Happiness* (New York: Basic Books, 1995); Ann Phoenix, Anne Woollett, and Eva Lloyd, eds. *Motherhood: Meanings, Practices and Ideologies.* (Newbury Park, CA: Sage, 1991); Carolyn Morell, "Saying No: Women's Experiences with Reproductive Refusal," *Feminism and Psychology*, 10 (2000), 313–322; and Rosemary Gillespie, "Contextualizing Voluntary Childlessness within a Postmodern Model of Reproduction: Implications for Health and Social Needs," *Critical Social Policy*, 21 (2001): 139–159.

[5]Joseph Caroll, "Americans: 2.5 Children Is 'Ideal' Family Size," Gallop News Service, June 26, 2007. http://www.gallup.com/poll/27973/Americans-25-Children-Ideal-Family-Size.aspx.

[6]Department of Health and Human Services, *National Vital Statistics Reports*, vol. 50, no. 5, "Births: Final Data for 2000" (Hyattsville, MD: National Center for Health Statistics, April 17, 2001), Tables 1, 10, 15, and 16, pp. 27, 40, and 45; and U.S. Census Bureau, *The 2009 Statistical Abstract*, "Table 77—Live Births, Deaths, Marriages, and Divorces." http://www.2010census.biz/compendia/statab/cats/births_deaths_marriages_divorces.html.

CROSS-CULTURAL *Perspective*

Population Control and the "Missing Girls" of China

In China, with over 1.2 billion people, population growth is a major concern. This led to the institution of what is now widely known as the one-child policy. The Chinese government not only tells couples that they must practice birth control; it also often tells them what type of contraceptive they must use. For example, one government announcement was that a woman with one child should use an IUD, that a couple with two children should have one partner sterilized, and that a woman with an unauthorized pregnancy should undergo an abortion.

The one-child policy has had both positive and negative effects. Some positive effects mentioned include a higher standard of living, increased social development that eliminates the patriarchal/feudal clan system and the inferior position of women, enhanced quality of life, and increased social assistance. Some negative effects include social and psychological pressures associated with having only one son or daughter, an increased incidence of divorce, and an unbalanced sex ratio. The sex ratio at birth appears to have increased from 105 before 1970 to about 114 in the 1990s, well above the biologically normal level of 105 to 106 boys at birth per 100 girls. A study by Greenhalgh and Li of three villages in 1993 suggests that during the period of strong enforcement between 1988 and 1993, the sex ratio in these villages for first births was 133, for second births 172, and for third and higher births was 1,100.

Studies of the "missing girls" of China tend to focus on three explanations: female infanticide, an underreporting of births of girls, and gender-specific abortion. *Female infanticide*, a traditional practice in China, may have accounted for the high sex ratios of cohorts prior to the 1950s but does not appear to be a significant factor today. The second explanation, the *underreporting of female births*, appears to be related to the incidence of adoption. Adoption (which often goes unreported) increased greatly during the 1980s, with female adoptions outnumbering males by three to one. This may account for half of the "missing girls" in China in the late 1980s. The third explanation, *gender-specific abortion*, seems to be the major reason for the escalation in the proportion of young females missing in China.

See: Susan Greenhalgh and Jiali Li, "Engendering Reproductive Policy and Practice in Peasant China: For a Feminist Demography of Reproduction," *Signs: Journal of Women in Culture and Society* 20 (Spring 1995): 601–641; Sten Johansson and Ola Nygren, "The Missing Girls of China: A New Demographic Account," *Population and Development Review* 17 (March 1991): 35–51.

much about the likelihood that a woman of child bearing age will give birth because they are sensitive to changes in the proportion of the population that are outside of child bearing age (0–15 and 45 and older) and they include men as well as women in the denominator. Therefore, a second measure is more sensitive to the child bearing patterns of women—the **fertility rate.** In 2009, the U.S. Census Bureau estimated that in 2006 the number of *births per 1,000 women between 15 and 44* in the population was 68.5, a slight and unexpected increase over the year 2005 of almost two per 1,000 after more than a decade of more or less constant rates between 64 and 66.[7]

Rates of birth in 2006 varied widely by demographic characteristics. By region of the country, they were below the national average in the Northeast and most of the

[7]U.S. Census Bureau, *The 2009 Statistical Abstract*, "Table 78—Live Births, Birth Rates, and Fertility Rates by Hispanic Origin Status." http://www.2010census.biz/compendia/statab/cats/births_deaths_marriages_divorces.html.

Midwest, Atlantic States, and Northwest; and above the national average in the South and Southwest.[8] By state, they ranged from a high of 21.0 in Utah to below 11 in Vermont (10.4), Maine (10.7), and New Hampshire (10.9). These variations are consistent with those found in previous years. Given these regional differences in rates it would be no surprise to find that birth rates are high among those of the Mormon faith (many of whom live in high fertility states of Utah and Idaho), among Hispanics (accounting for high rates in New Mexico, Arizona, California, and Texas), and among Christian conservatives (accounting for high rates in the Southern states).

As can be seen in Figure 10.1, the number of births per year and fertility rates in the United States vary widely over time as well. For example, in 1930, the fertility rate was about 85 per 1,000 women between 15 and 44. This rate decreased to below 80 during the Depression years (1930–1940), and then rose steeply after WWII to a peak rate of over 120 in 1956, a period known as the **baby boom.** This postwar spurt in annual births did not represent a return to the large families of the nineteenth century. Rather, the boom was a movement away from singlehood, childless marriage, and one-child families. Only a minor part of the baby boom can be attributed to an increase in the number of families having three or more births. The rate then fell precipitously to the low 60s in 1975, where it stayed steady or increased slightly through 2005.

Looking at the numbers of births during this same time period, the pattern closely follows that of the fertility rate until the period of 1975 through 2007. Unlike the fertility rate during this time, the number of live births has been spiraling upward, a phenomenon referred to as the **baby boomlet** or the **baby boom echo.** Since the fertility rate remained relatively flat during this period, the rise in births cannot be attributed to an increase in either the proportion of women giving birth or the number of births per woman. Instead, it is a reflection of the fact that 25–35

Live Births and Fertility Rates: 1930–2005

Source: Department of Health and Human Services, *National Vital Statistics Reports,* vol. 50, no. 5, "Births: Final Data for 2000" (Hyattsville, MD: National Center for Health Statistics, February 12, 2002), Figure 1, p. 4.

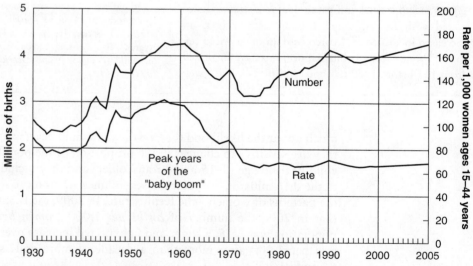

Note: Beginning with 1959, trend lines are based on registered live births; trend lines for 1930–59 are based on live births adjusted for underregistration.

---

[8]U.S. Census Bureau, *The 2009 Statistical Abstract,* "Table 81—Live Births by State and Island Areas: 2006." http://www.2010census.biz/compendia/statab/cats/births_deaths_marriages_divorces.html.

years after the baby boom began, the girls born during that boom moved into their peak child bearing ages, creating a sudden increase in the numbers of births. In other words, there were more women in the population who could have a child even though the likelihood of doing so among this group and the number of children each woman was giving birth to remained the same.

The baby boom was a post–World War II event that upset what had been a century-long decline in the U.S. fertility rate. Theories as to its cause include increases in normative pressure on women to have children, the disruption and dislocation brought about by the war, postwar economic prosperity, and the long-term psychological effects of growing up during the Depression.

One final measure that is useful for examining child bearing behaviors and their causes and consequences is to look at the *total fertility rate* (TFR). The **total fertility rate** is an estimate of how many births each woman of child bearing age in the population in a given year would experience in her lifetime if her child bearing followed the same age pattern present in the population in that year. In other words, it assumes that a 20-year-old woman in the population in 2008 will have a likelihood of giving birth in 2009 (when she would turn 21) that is the same as the observed fertility rate for 21-year-olds in 2008. In 2010 (when she would turn 22), her likelihood of giving birth (either a first or later birth) is assumed to be the same as the observed fertility rate for 22-year-olds in 2008. Using these series of **age-specific fertility rates** applied to the age weighted distribution of women in the population in any given year, it is possible to predict how many children the women in the population are likely to bear in their lifetimes. There are obviously some important and not necessarily valid assumptions being made in these estimates, but the TFR has proven a useful tool for understanding long term trends in fertility.

In the United States, the total fertility rate for 2006 was estimated to be 2.10.[9] This rate is considered to be close to "replace" the population through natural reproductive means (i.e., without in-migration). Since only women can give birth, two are required by every woman in order to replace herself and one man in the population after they have died. Given that sex ratios are not exactly 50/50 and a small proportion of women are physiologically unable to have children, fertile women in the population need to average slightly more than two (2.11) in order to replace the population (the **replacement threshold**). How do U.S. fertility rates and patterns compare to other countries in the West? Figure 10.2 shows a long-term trend in total fertility among European countries that has led to considerable concern among politicians and policy makers. Although there has been some leveling off in the pattern, total fertility rates were moderately below replacement for 25 of the 39 countries measured and extremely below replacement for 10 or more of the countries. As shown in Figure 10.3, the lowest total fertility rates can be found in Southern, Central, and Eastern Europe. Such declines in total fertility have led to calls for a "new pronatalism" that puts normative pressure on women to have more children.[10] Others, however, advise caution and argue that a more comprehensive solution is required.[11]

---

[9]U.S. Census Bureau, *The 2009 Statistical Abstract*, "Table 82—Total Fertility Rate by Race and Hispanic Origin." http://www.2010census.biz/compendia/statab/cats/births_deaths_marriages_divorces.html.

[10]European Commission, *The Demographic Future of Europe—From Challenge to Opportunity*, Communication of 12 October 2006 [COM(2006) 571]. http://ec.europa.eu/employment_social/news/2006/oct/demography_en_pdf.

[11]Jonathan Grant and Stijn Hoorens, "Does the Commission's Report Adequately Address the Key Issues of the Demographic Future of Europe," *Vienna Yearbook of Population* (2007): 13–17.

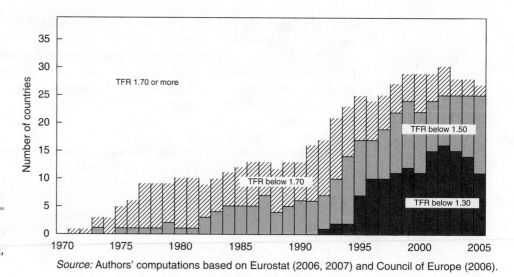

Figure 10.2

Number of European Countries with a Period TFR below 1.7, 1.5, and 1.3, 1970–2005

Source: Authors' computations based on Eurostat (2006, 2007) and Council of Europe (2006).

Overall, compared to European countries, the United States has a relatively high total fertility rate, although its rate of decline over the past fifty years was greater than any of the other countries studied (see Figure 10.3). Why has this decline in fertility occurred and what does it mean for these societies?

It is clear that over the past few decades there has been a trend to delay first births. In particular, women with college degrees have experienced dramatic

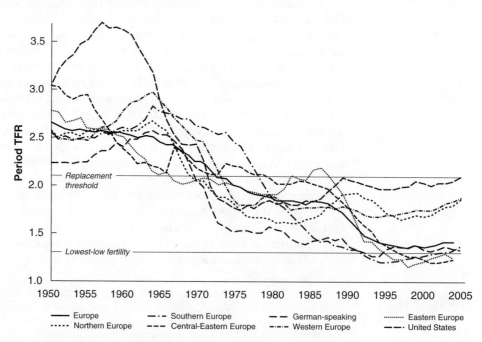

Figure 10.3

Period Total Fertility Rate in Major Regions of Europe and in the United States, 1950–2006

Source: Authors' computations based on Eurostat (2006, 2007), Council of Europe (2006), Festy (1979), Chesnais (1986) and national statistical data.

shifts toward postponing marriage and child bearing as they pursued careers and as changes occurred in the availability of child care.[12] Around the world, women who delay child bearing have fewer children and are significantly better off economically than average-age child bearers. For example, in Japan, which has one of the lowest fertility rates in the world, the decline over the past two decades has been attributed not to contraceptive use but to the postponement of marriage.[13] The mean age at which Japanese women marry—about 27 years—is among the highest in the world and the proportion who likely will never marry has tripled in the past thirty years. Both delayed marriage and nonmarriage reduce fertility rates.

Delayed marriage and child bearing is part of a larger process in Western modern societies linked to changing institutional interrelationships (e.g., between education, work, and family life), a breakdown of institutional controls over behavior and a focus on individual need fulfillment. In pre-modern society, individuals' lives were shaped largely by the institutional structures within which they lived their lives. Behaviors were shaped by the needs of the collective. In modern societies, individuals need to find a rationale for their behaviors, one that has a rational connection to desired goals or "ends." One important goal in life is individual development for its own sake. Modern society values the individual and therefore the development of his or her psychological and emotional capacities.

On the one hand, these changes have led to men and women delaying or even foregoing child bearing in the interest of advancing their own careers, marriages and general well-being. These delays have had a negative effect on total fertility rates. On the other hand, these changes have led to a new kind of pronatalism, one that sees women's individual self-fulfillment as linked to child bearing/child rearing roles and that advocates limitations on the numbers of children one gives birth to in order to maximize the outcomes for those children. As a result, fertility rates are sustained, albeit at drastically reduced levels.

As for the consequences of reduced fertility rates, Tomas Frejka and Tomas Sobotka note that, at the societal level, they could be extensive and severe.[14] Low total fertility is a precursor to a distorted age distribution in the population with an increase in the proportion of dependent elderly and a reduction in the proportion of younger workers to support them and maintain economic vitality and growth. In the shorter term, attempts to augment the work force through liberal immigration policies can also have negative consequences in terms of political unrest, increased social problems, and concerns about national identity and culture. Fortunately, these trends in total fertility may be short lived, especially in the developing areas of Europe that are undergoing considerable social transformation. Once these transitions are complete, a return to replacement fertility is likely to occur.

---

[12]Ronald R. Rindfuss, S. Philip Morgan, and Kate Offutt, "Education and the Changing Age Pattern of American Fertility, 1963–1989," *Demography* 33 (August 1996): 277–290.

[13]Naohiro Ogawa and Robert D. Retherford, "The Resumption of Fertility Decline in Japan: 1973–1992," *Population and Development Review* 19 (December 1993): 703–741.

[14]Tomas Frejka and Tomas Sobotka, "Overview Chapter 1: Fertility in Europe: Diverse, Delayed and Below Replacement," *Demographic Research*, 19 (July 2008): 15–46.

news item

Birth Rate Crisis Hits Central Europe

Population levels across many parts of the developed world are declining, but this is particularly noticeable in former Eastern Bloc states where the number of children being born has plummeted within a generation.

The exception is Slovakia, where a bundle arrives every day with a postmark from the 1970s. Former Czechoslovak leader Gustav Husak keeps sending gifts. During his regime, cheap flats, long maternity leave and, for want of a politer word, sheer boredom, produced a baby boom. And his major boom is reproducing a minor baby boom today.

The girls conceived in the tall panel houses of the Petrzalka suburb of Bratislava, or beneath the weeping willows along the shores of the Danube, have reached the age of peak fertility. Slovakia is suddenly the only country in Central Europe where births outnumber deaths...As populations plunge throughout the region, the plucky Slovaks are proudly producing offspring...

Something to Do

Boris Vano, from the Slovak Demographic Research Centre is less impressed by the numbers. "In 1974, 100,000 babies were born in Slovakia—now barely 50,000 a year," he laments. And when the boom girls have had their baby—two if we are lucky—he foresees Slovakia slipping back into the same, shrinking population straits as the rest of Central Europe.

In the 1970s, his counterpart in Prague Jan Hartl explains, couples married on average after only three months of acquaintance. The girl was 22 and usually pregnant. Those marriages may not have survived, but their copious young are now delaying conception until their early thirties. They have access to an arsenal of contraceptives their parents could not have dreamt of. Under Communism, abortion was the most commonly available method...

Another irony in Europe's formerly communist countries was that the crushing of popular resistance under the tank tracks often ended in the maternity ward. In Hungary, after the failed 1956 revolution, in Czechoslovakia after the Prague Spring in 1968 and in Poland after martial law in 1981, the birth rate rose spectacularly. It was as if the youth, frustrated in their desire for greater political freedom, took consolation in their desire for one another.

Baby Incentives

In Warsaw, Families Minister Joanna Kluzik Rostkowska is watching the calendar. The final baby boom generation of the communist years, the class of 1983, is just beginning to think of procreation. Her conservative government is looking for ways to encourage them. "Our research proves that Polish women still want to have babies," she explains. But they also want to carry on working. So she has drawn up a package of measures, including increased maternity and paternity leave, tax breaks for businesses, flexibility for the self-employed, and enabling workplaces to establish kindergartens and nurseries in the hope that her compatriots can be persuaded back into bed. It is a model which appears to have succeeded in France, where the population is increasing by a quarter of a million a year.

Elsewhere in Warsaw, demographer Krystyna Iglicka says it cannot be done in Poland. She has studied the French statistics in detail, and says the only women having lots of children in France today are immigrants. "And we don't let our immigrants stay long enough."

Poland has a growing labour shortage, as its young and skilled workers flood west, to countries like Britain and Ireland. And the latest research shows they plan to stay longer than they originally thought. The Polish babies of the future may be born in Dublin, and Darlington...

Source: Nick Thorpe, "Birth rate crisis hits Central Europe," BBC News, Poland. http://news.bbc.co.uk/2/hi/programmes/from_our_own_correspondent/6929516.stm.

Social Consequences of Parenthood

In trying to understand recent declines in fertility, it is also useful to understand how fertility affects parents' lives. As noted earlier, child bearing is something of a rational choice in modern societies and many men and women will have to have some expectations for how having a child will affect their well-being in order to make the best choice. What types of social consequences of parenthood have been documented in the research literature? For one, parenthood changes both the employment patterns as well as wages of both men and women.

For men, notions of fatherhood suggest opposite effects of having children on work activities.[15] On the one hand, studies document that fathers are more likely to be employed and to work more hours than their male counterparts who do not have children. On the other hand, with the growing prevalence of married women sharing the provider role, many younger more egalitarian fathers are sacrificing work time outside the home in order to contribute more time to their families and children. In other words, a "good provider" model suggests that fathers work more than nonfathers, while the "involved father" model suggests fatherhood encourages men to work less. For women, the majority of ever-married women have jobs prior to pregnancy, but most leave these jobs as the pregnancy progresses. In studies by Linda Waite and others, only one in five women remained employed in the month that her child was born.[16] Many of these mothers returned to work, but by two years after the birth, their rate of employment was only about 60 percent of what it was prior to childbirth. Wages as well are affected by the presence of children. Even after controlling for part-time employment, a negative effect on women's pay remains.

Another consequence of parenting relates to psychological effects. Parents were found to report higher levels of psychological distress and anger than parents without children.[17] Children increased anger more for mothers than fathers, and each additional child in the household increased the lever of anger. Two major types of stressors included economic strains and the strain associated with child care. Mothers had the highest levels of both distress and anger because of economic inequality and the inequitable distribution of parental responsibilities.

A third consequence of parenthood, at least in the short run, relates to marital stability. In Chapter 9, data were presented that showed how marital satisfaction drops with the presence of children. Data will be presented later in this chapter that show how couples without children have higher levels of marital adjustment than couples with children. In contrast, studies from both New Zealand and the United

---

[15]Gayle Kaufman and Peter Uhlenberg, "The Influence of Parenthood on the Work Effort of Married Men and Women," *Social Forces* 78 (March 2000): 931–949.

[16]Linda J. Waite, Gus W. Haggstrom, and David E. Kanouse, "Changes in the Employment Activities of New Parents," *American Sociological Review* 50 (April 1985): 263–272; and Young-Hee Yoon and Linda J. Waite, "Converging Employment Patterns of Black, White, and Hispanic Women: Return to Work after First Birth," *Journal of Marriage and the Family* 56 (February 1994): 209–217.

[17]Chloe E. Bird, "Gender Differences in the Social and Economic Burdens of Parenting and Psychological Distress," *Journal of Marriage and the Family* 59 (November 1977): 809–823; and Catherine E. Ross and Marieke Van Willigen, "Gender, Parenthood, and Anger," *Journal of Marriage and the Family* 58 (August 1996): 572–584.

States have shown the strong, positive effects of firstborn and preschool children on the marital *stability* of young adults. It was estimated that, by the time the first child reached age 2, more than 20 percent of the parents would have been divorced or separated if the child had not been born compared with actual disruption rates of 5 to 8 percent.[18] The presence of preschool children in the family acts as a protective factor that reduces risk of family breakdown.

Lynn White and Alan Booth referred to this factor as the **braking hypothesis.** They suggested that although having children does not prevent divorce, doing so might cause couples to approach the divorce decision more slowly.[19] These researchers also found that new parents were significantly less likely to divorce over a three-year period than those who remained childless, again in contrast to the persistent negative correlation between the presence of children and marital happiness. The explanation for these seemingly inconsistent findings was not that persons in more stable marriages have children (a selectivity argument), and it was only partially based on the argument that a new baby causes major negative changes in marital structure. Rather, White and Booth focused on a differential propensity to divorce. Childless couples, they suggested, value marital happiness more than parents. The result is a greater willingness of childless couples to divorce when unhappy. Whatever the reason, fewer divorces seem to occur among couples with very young children.

Childless/Childfree Marriages

For many years, the myth existed that, because of a so-called maternal instinct, all women wanted children. This myth of maternal instinct even went one step further and assumed that, once children were born, the mother would instinctively love and care for them. As a result, women who did not bear children in their lifetime were considered physically or psychologically defective.

These assumptions were quickly disproved when statistics, research reports, newspaper accounts, and gossip networks revealed the widespread termination of pregnancies through legal and illegal abortions, the frequency of mothers abusing and even killing their children, the discovery that some women didn't want children, and that those who never had children—in or out of marriage—did not suffer physical or emotional damage. These and other factors tended to dispel the notion of the biological linkage between being female and having a natural desire for and love of children. Living without children came to be seen as more of a lifestyle choice than a deficit. As a result, many scholars argued for a change in the terminology used to refer to these women. Instead of labeling them childless, a less pejorative term would be childfree. Nevertheless, as noted previously, only 1 percent of the American public felt as though no children was a desired number.

In contrast to these ideals as expressed on general social surveys, the actual childless rate is considerably higher than 1 percent. In 2006, 20 percent of

---

[18]David M. Fergusson, L. John Horwood, and Michael Lloyd, "The Effect of Preschool Children on Family Stability," *Journal of Marriage and the Family* 52 (May 1990): 531–538; and Linda J. Waite, Gus Haggstrom, and David E. Kanouse, "The Consequences of Parenthood for the Marital Stability of Young Adults," *American Sociological Review* 50 (December 1985): 850–857.

[19]Lynn K. White and Alan Booth, "The Transition to Parenthood and Marital Quality," *Journal of Family Issues* 6 (December 1985): 435–449.

Family Diversity

Reproductive Technologies

Today, families are faced with choices related to conception, pregnancy, and birth unlike ever before in history. Note some of these choices made possible by technology.

New *contraceptives* pose problems and choices for both men and women. Cost, access, safety, side effects, ethical issues, or legality may limit their choices. What about the use of a *morning-after pill*, a preventive measure that requires no preplanning? How about *Norplant*, a hormonal implant that can be effective for up to five years? What about contraceptive *vaccines* that use physiological processes (immune responses) to regulate fertility? What about a *vasectomy* for the male or a *tubal ligation* for the female that disrupts the passage through which sperm or eggs travel? Should research continue on the use of *spermicides, condoms, pills, foams, jellies, creams, cervical caps, diaphragms, IUDs*, or other methods that may prevent pregnancy, STD transmission, or both?

If a pregnancy has occurred, then come choices related to continuing or terminating it. *Abortion* has stirred up the most controversy among religious groups and legal analysts but is performed widely around the world. France was one of the first countries to have approved the drug *RU486* that induces a miscarriage up to eight weeks following a pregnancy. Should these procedures or drugs be made available to all women, no women, or select groups of women such as those who can afford it, those with a health risk, those made pregnant by rape or incest, or those

pregnancies that medical technologies have determined to be defective? Social factors to consider are many: the quality of the life of the mother, child, or marriage, the "wantedness" of the pregnancy, financial considerations, and the like.

Then, of course, there are the technologies available for *in vitro fertilization*: commonly known as the "test-tube baby" procedure. A woman's egg or eggs are surgically removed, a partner's sperm is produced by masturbation, and the egg and sperm are combined in a dish. If fertilization occurs, the resulting embryo is inserted into the woman's uterus and if it implants in the uterine wall a pregnancy will begin. This technology, separating the pregnancy from intercourse, is especially useful for same-sex couples or for the impregnation of a *surrogate* mother who is acting on behalf of another woman or couple.

Other new reproductive technologies focus on the *preservation of human embryos*. Today, embryo freezing is offered in many in vitro fertilization clinics and is said to be established as a routine component. But its availability does not rule out ethical issues such as those surrounding the death or divorce of one or both of the parents, the use of the embryos by others, and the identity of the persons making such decisions.

This list of reproductive technologies is not meant to be comprehensive. In fact, given the advances in medical and biological research, new ones may be available by the time this is read. It does provide new considerations and possibilities for the planning of families and for parenthood.

---

women between the ages of 40 and 44, a point marking the end of a woman's fecundity, were childless. This number was double what it was in 1980.[20] Historically, however, childless rates have been as high or higher, ranging from 18 percent in 1880 to 22 percent in 1940.[21] Two problems with using this rate are that it may not reflect rates for current young women and it doesn't tell us whether or not these women were childless by choice. Nevertheless, the rate is substantial.

---

[20]Jane Lawler Dye, Fertility of American Women: 2006, *Current Population Reports* (P20–558) Washington, DC: U. S. Census Bureau, August 2008.

[21]S. Morgan, "Late Nineteenth- and Early Twentieth Century Childlessness. *American Journal of Sociology*, 97 (1991): 779–807.

According to research done over the past few decades, the most important demographic predictors of childlessness have been found to be:

- *Lack of fecundity*—Some people are unable to have children.
- *Marital status*—Never-married people are more likely to be childless than people who are or have been married.
- *Age*—As people grow older, they are less likely to have children.
- *Labor force participation*—People who are working or temporarily unemployed are less likely to have children.
- *Education*—The higher the level of education attained, the greater the likelihood of childlessness.
- *Race/ethnicity*—Asian Americans and American Indians are less likely to be childless than members of other racial/ethnic groups.[22]

Voluntary Childlessness

In reviewing the reasons given by women for not having children, Sharon Houseknecht[23] reminds us that individuals interpret their own motives within the dominant cultural narratives of the time. In her review, she found several reasons given, rank ordered as follows: (1) more freedom and fulfillment, (2) greater marital quality, (3) career and monetary considerations, (4) concern about population growth (women) and dislike of children (men), (5) early socialization experiences and doubts about ability to parent (women), (6) concern about childbirth and recovery (women), and (7) concern about raising children under unstable or negative world conditions (women). Rosemary Gillespie[24] adds, based on her more recent research, that most of voluntarily childless women made active choices, usually early in life and as a function of a rejection of motherhood as a life course option. Many did not find children "appealing," although there was a tendency for these women to be involved in some capacity—usually through occupations—with children. Among men, the predominant reasons given for not having children reflected early and strong socialization into a traditional masculine role focused more on financial success and less on children and family life.[25]

Parenthood not only seems to interfere with personal happiness and freedoms, it seems also to interfere with marriage and family life. As noted previously in several chapters, children impose a strain on marriage. Does this suggest that couples without children have higher levels of health and marital adjustment and satisfaction than couples with children?

Apparently it does. When voluntarily childless wives, undecided wives, and postponing wives were compared with mothers, the results from one study were that all three groups of childless wives had higher mean levels of marital satisfaction than mothers.[26] Most available evidence shows that the consequences of voluntary childlessness to persons or marriages are more positive than negative.

---

[22]Cardell K. Jacobsen, Tim B. Heaton, and Karen M. Taylor, "Childlessness among American Women," *Social Biology* 35 (1988): 186–197.

[23]Sharon K. Houseknecht, "Voluntary Childlessness," in M.P. Sussman and S.K. Steinmetz, eds. *Handbook of Marriage and the Family* (New York: Plenum Press, 1987): 369–395.

[24]Rosemary Gillespie, "When No Means No: Disbelief and Deviance as Discourses of Voluntary Childlessness," *Women's Studies International Forum*, 23 (2000): 223–234.

[25]Patricia Lunneborg, *Chosen Lives of Childfree Men* (Westport, CT: Bergin and Garvey, 1999).

[26]Karen A. Polonko, John Scanzoni, and Jay D. Teachman, "Childlessness and Marital Satisfaction," *Journal of Family Issues* 3 (December 1982): 545–573.

Involuntary Childlessness

What about women or couples who want children but can't have them? Infertility has been estimated to affect approximately 15 percent of couples, or one in seven, in the United States. Studies of infertile couples with a desire for children have revealed high levels of stress.[27] Infertility is a major negative life event that has deleterious effects on both women's and men's subjective well-being. Infertility would seem especially relevant for sexual and marriage issues, but its strongest impact may be on global well-being. That is, frustrations over infertility spill over into other domains, including work, finances, and social life, producing strained relationships with coworkers, friends, and family.

It would appear that, for couples of child bearing age, the choice to have or not to have children and the ability to carry out that choice may be one of the most significant factors in the satisfaction or dissatisfaction that results from being childless. In other words, there's a big difference between being able to have children but choosing not to and wanting to have children but not being able to. People who remain childless by choice are more likely to be satisfied with that result than those who remain childless by fate.

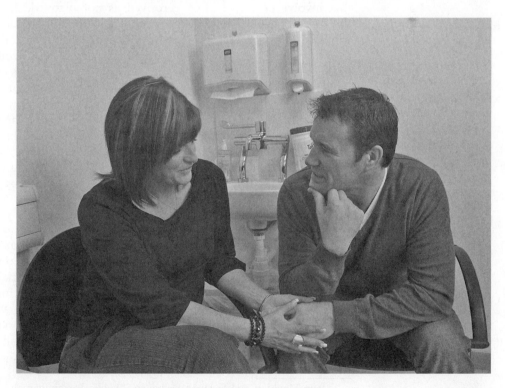

More couples are choosing to remain childfree as a lifestyle choice, but others are without children even though they have a strong desire to have them. The physical, emotional and financial costs of fertility treatments can be significant, but the desire to have children is often greater.

[27]Margaret V. Pepe and T. Jean Byrne, "Women's Perceptions of Immediate and Long-Term Effects of Failed Infertility Treatment on Marital and Sexual Satisfaction," *Family Relations* 40 (July 1991): 303–309; and Antonia Abbey, Frank M. Andrews, and L. Jill Halman, "Infertility and Subjective Well-Being: The Mediating Roles of Self-Esteem, Internal Control, and Interpersonal Conflict," *Journal of Marriage and the Family* 54 (May 1992): 408–417.

The reproductive technology available today can decrease the number of people who are involuntarily childless. Until recently, women and couples who were involuntarily childless and wished to comply with societal norms would resort to adoption. But the decline in the availability of infants for adoption has led many infertile women to seek alternative solutions, such as artificial insemination with the sperm of the husband (AIH); artificial insemination with the sperm of an anonymous donor (AID); in-vitro fertilization, in which an artificial environment outside the living organism is used; and surrogate motherhood, in which another woman is used to conceive, carry, and give birth to a child. These alternative methods of reproduction have led to heated debates over their social, legal, and moral implications.

Young and Unwed Parenthood

To be married young (generally in one's adolescence or teens), to be a young parent (to have a child as a teenager), and to be an unwed parent (to have a child apart from marriage, regardless of age) are three interrelated social structural patterns that involve processes often perceived as not planned, desired, or preferred. All three result in social consequences defined as difficult and negative.

It is estimated that at least 40 percent of all births in the United States result from unplanned conception and about 23 percent of all conceptions end in abortion. These figures suggest that the majority of pregnancies among U.S. women are unplanned. A survey of U.S. adults indicated great concern about these unplanned pregnancies, which generally are perceived to be highly prevalent among unmarried adolescents and present a very serious problem, particularly to this age group.[28] A decline in moral standards, a lack of education, and barriers to contraceptive access were cited by about 88 percent of the respondents as contributing to the problem. Our attention is directed more specifically to the related issues of **young parenthood** and **unwed parenthood**.

Concerns about Young Parenthood

Why do teenagers get pregnant and become young parents? One source reported that, of teen girls who do become pregnant, 26 percent obtain abortions, 22 percent marry before childbirth, and 52 percent have out-of-wedlock births.[29] The choice of what to do with an unplanned pregnancy is seldom easy for anyone, but particularly difficult for a female who is young and unmarried. White teenage girls are more likely than their black counterparts to end a pregnancy through abortion.[30] Placing a child for adoption traditionally has been and still is less of a choice for

---

[28]Jane Mauldon and Suzanne Delbanco, "Public Perceptions about Unplanned Pregnancy," *Family Planning Perspectives* 29 (January/February 1997): 25–29.

[29]Elizabeth C. Cooksey, "Factors in the Resolution of Adolescent Premarital Pregnancies," *Demography* 27 (May 1990): 207–218; and J. Richard Udry, Judith Kovenock, and Naomi M. Morris, "Early Predictors of Nonmarital First Pregnancy and Abortion," *Family Planning Perspectives* 28 (May/June 1996): 113–116.

[30]Naomi B. Farber, "The Process of Pregnancy Resolution among Adolescent Mothers," *Adolescence* 26 (Fall 1991): 697–716; and Christine A. Bachrach, Kathy Shepherd Stolley, and Kathryn A. London, "Relinquishment of Premarital Births: Evidence from National Survey Data," *Family Planning Perspectives* 24 (January/February 1992): 27–32.

Concern about young and unwed parenthood tends to focus on the mother, but fathers are affected as well. Most of the pregnancies are not intended, but the birth of the child carries with it tremendous educational, social and economic costs.

young black women than young white women, but both are less likely to place a child for adoption than was the case prior to the 1980s. Marriage is also declining as an option for both black and white teenage girls, but blacks are still more likely to become single mothers. Family members and other significant adults are very important to teens in the decision-making process. The input that parents have is strongly affected by their level of education; for example, highly educated parents are more likely to recommend abortion for their teens.

Despite his obvious involvement in the pregnancy, the male is studied far less frequently and is assigned a less deviant label than the female. Data from a nationally representative U.S. survey[31] of teenage fathers showed that one-third of those who were responsible for a nonmarital conception married within twelve months of conception, and half the young men lived with their child shortly after the birth. Young black men were more likely to have been responsible for a nonmarital first birth than were males of other racial and ethnic backgrounds, but only 15 percent of black teenage boys lived with their first children compared with 48 percent of Hispanics, 58 percent of disadvantaged whites, and 77 percent of nondisadvantaged whites.

One national study concluded that adolescent child bearing is more an unintended result of risky behaviors than a result of rational choice. About 85 percent of adolescent respondents who had a child outside of marriage had no intention to do so.[32] Another study of teenage pregnancies found that 92 percent of those conceived premarital (unwed) and half of those conceived in marriage (by teenagers) were unintended.[33] Startling evidence explained this high incidence of unplanned teenage pregnancies: only one in three sexually active young women used contraceptives and only one in two of these relied on the most effective methods. The two most common reasons for not using contraceptives were the failure to anticipate intercourse and the belief that pregnancy risk was small. Explanations from other studies for the high rate of teenage pregnancy included a lower social class, ethnicity (African American or Hispanic American), an early age at first sex, and sexual abuse by a boyfriend.[34]

[31]William Marsiglio, "Young Nonresident Biological Fathers," *Marriage and Family Review* 20 (1995): 325–348.

[32]Katherine Trent and Kyle Crowder, "Adolescent Birth Intentions, Social Disadvantage, and Behavioral Outcomes," *Journal of Marriage and the Family* 59 (August 1997): 523–535.

[33]James Trussell, "Teenage Pregnancy in the United States," *Family Planning Perspectives* 20 (November/December 1988): 262–272.

[34]Mark W. Roosa, Jenn-Yun Tein, Cindy Reinholtz, and Patricia Jo Angelini, "The Relationship of Childhood Sexual Abuse to Teenage Pregnancy," *Journal of Marriage and the Family* 59 (February 1997): 119–130.

Both an intragenerational and an intergenerational pattern appear to exist for both teenage marriage and child bearing. In several articles, Patricia East has shown that younger sisters and younger brothers (intragenerational) of pregnant teenagers are affected negatively by their older sister's pregnancy.[35] When compared to never-pregnant older siblings, the younger siblings of pregnant teenagers are more accepting of adolescent child bearing, perceive younger ages as appropriate for first intercourse, see school and career as less important, have lower self-esteem, and engage in more problem behaviors such as drug use, smoking, partying, and skipping school. The younger sisters of these child bearing teens themselves become vulnerable to early parenthood.

In terms of intergenerational patterns of child bearing, studies in both the United States and Great Britain found that the daughters of both white and black teen mothers faced significantly higher risks of teen child bearing than the daughters of older mothers.[36] It should be noted that although most daughters of teen mothers didn't have a teen birth, they were at greater risk of having a birth in their teens.

It is clear that U.S. teenagers are far more likely to become pregnant than comparable women in other developed countries. Charles Westoff found that the teenage pregnancy rates in six other Western countries—Canada, England and Wales, Finland, the Netherlands, Norway, and Sweden—ranged from only 13 to 53 percent of the U.S. rate.[37] Teenagers in the United States appeared no more likely than their Canadian or European contemporaries to marry or engage in intercourse, but they seemed less likely to practice contraception.

Why are U.S. teenagers so different, even when compared to teens from countries very similar to the United States, such as Canada and Great Britain? Westoff suggested that U.S. teenagers may not have the same access to contraceptives that teens from other countries have, may face different costs in family-planning services than teens from countries with national health care systems, may comprise a large underclass of ethnic diversity and unequal income distribution that alienates them from middle-class values, may be greater risk takers, and may have an ambivalence toward sexuality. That is, although sex saturates American television programs, movies, and advertisements, the media fail to communicate responsible attitudes about it; for the most part, birth control for teenagers is a taboo subject.

High rates of teenage pregnancy and young parenthood have tremendous costs: educational, social, and economic consequences for the individuals involved and for society at large. One way to determine the impact or cost of being a young parent is to compare adolescents who relinquish (place for adoption) their children to those who raise them. Sources suggest that, when background and other characteristics are controlled, young girls who relinquished their babies are more likely to complete

---

[35]Patricia L. East, "Do Adolescent Pregnancy and Childbearing Affect Younger Siblings?" *Family Planning Perspectives* 28 (July/August 1996): 148–153; and Patricia L. East, "The Younger Sisters of Childbearing Adolescents: Their Attitudes, Expectations, and Behaviors," *Child Development* 67 (1996): 267–282.

[36]Joan R. Kahn and Kay E. Anderson, "Intergenerational Patterns of Teenage Fertility," *Demography* 29 (February 1992): 39–57; and Jennifer Manlove, "Early Motherhood in an Intergenerational Perspective: The Experiences of a British Cohort," *Journal of Marriage and the Family* 59 (May 1997): 263–279.

[37]Charles F. Westoff, "Unintended Pregnancy in America and Abroad," *Family Planning Perspectives* 20 (November/December 1988): 254–261; and S. Philip Morgan, "Characteristic Features of Modern American Fertility," *Population and Development Review* 11(1996): 30–31.

CROSS-CULTURAL *Perspective*

Births in Sweden

Sweden, in a dramatic contrast to overpopulation growth, has concerns over a low birthrate. This concern was a major factor in the formulation of their family leave policy, which grants up to fifteen months' leave from employment to parents of newborns. Swedes have a high regard for children and view having children as something that should be encouraged. Parental leave is believed to improve a couple's chance of having children by helping them combine parental and employment roles.

Given the high rate of nonmarital cohabitation in Sweden, is the rate of children born by a not-married mother high? Is this a significant social problem? The answer is yes to the first question and no to the second. Trost claims that 65 percent of first children are born to a not-married mother. Yet, evidence shows that only 2 or 3 percent of these children are born to a truly single mother. The vast majority are born to a cohabiting unit. He says that in Sweden and Denmark, the old connection between marital status and childbirth has disappeared.

Despite high rates of cohabitation, fertility control has given Swedish women a low unplanned pregnancy rate and a higher age of first child bearing. And even if the pregnancy rate were not low, the characterization and stigma would not occur. The term *illegitimacy* was dropped in Sweden in 1917 and the concept of children born out of wedlock was dropped from all Swedish legislation in the early 1970s. Virtually no Swedish child lives in absolute economic deprivation or poverty (in contrast to about one in five children in the United States). Compared to other European countries, Swedish children enjoy better physical health, and the relationships between parents and children are good.

See: Jan Trost, "Family Studies in Sweden," *Marriage and Family Review* 23 (1996): 728.

vocational training, have higher educational aspirations, and are less involved in sexual risk-taking behaviors.[38] They are more likely to delay marriage, be employed six and twelve months after the birth, and live in higher-income households. Young parents who choose to raise their children are more likely to become pregnant again sooner and to resolve subsequent pregnancies by abortion. It was noted that adolescents who relinquished their children expressed more sorrow and regret in the short run, but this did not translate into psychological difficulties over the course of the first two years postpartum. In brief, those who placed their child for adoption did not suffer more negative psychological consequences than those who raised their children and they experienced far more numerous positive social consequences.

Young parenthood also magnifies the general issues surrounding parenthood that have been discussed thus far. When compared to women in the 20- to 35-year-old age group, teenage mothers are most likely to postpone prenatal care, have children of low birthweight, and experience a higher rate of infant mortality.[39] Even when controlling for family background by comparing teenage mothers with sisters

---

[38]Brenda W. Donnelly and Patricia Voydanoff, "Parenting versus Placing for Adoption: Consequence for Adolescent Mothers," *Family Relations* 45 (October 1996): 427–434; and Steven D. McLaughlin, Diane L. Minninen, and Linda D. Wingers, "Do Adolescents Who Relinquish Their Children Fare Better or Worse Than Those Who Raise Them?" *Family Planning Perspectives* 20 (January/February 1988): 25–32.

[39]Steven L. Nock, "The Consequences of Premarital Fatherhood," *American Sociological Review* 63 (April 1998): 250–263.

who were not mothers, teen mothers were less likely to finish high school, attend college, or be married. They were more likely to be poor and on public assistance.[40]

Among teenage boys, Nock illustrated that few never-married fathers live with their children, are less likely to marry, and more likely to cohabit.[41] Compared to their peers who did not father children before marriage, they were found to leave school earlier, have lower earnings, work fewer weeks per year, and be more likely to live in poverty. These factors clearly hamper young fathers' abilities to contribute financially to the support of their partners and children. In sum, all information on unwed parenthood has suggested that a double standard is much more obvious for the consequences of pregnancy that result from sexual behavior than for sexual behavior per se.

Although teenage parenthood is often associated in the public's mind with single-parent, female-headed families, the vast majority of mothers 15 to 19 years of age do not live alone with their children. Rather, over 90 percent live with their husbands or other relatives.[42] Whites are more likely than African Americans or Asian Americans to marry and establish their own nuclear households (although they are at high risk of divorcing and later forming single-parent households). African Americans and Mexican Americans are more likely than whites to "double up" in extended households. These extended households serve as a major resource, both financially and emotionally. Support is often given in the form of free room and board and partly or wholly subsidized child care. This assistance can significantly alter the life chances of the young mother, enhancing her prospects of educational achievement and economic advancement.

Concerns about Unwed Parenthood

Apart from the justified concern about teenage child bearing, should unwed parenthood among those from other age groups be of concern? To answer this question, let us first examine how prevalent it is (the rates of birth outside marriage), followed by an examination of a "so what" or "who cares" question (the consequences of birth outside marriage).

Rates of Birth Outside Marriage

At the very time that birthrates in general are steadily declining or leveling off, the birthrates outside marriage are showing a dramatic increase. The *number* of births to unmarried women was approaching 1.75 million in 2007 (see Figure 10.4), which represented a 700 percent increase since 1940. The number of unmarried births showed particularly steep increases between 1980 and 1990 and between 2000 and 2007. This pattern of change is also reflected in the unmarried birth rate (over 50 per 1,000 unmarried women 15–44 in 2007) and the percent of all births to unmarried women (almost 40 percent).

---

[40]H.A. Hein, L.F. Burmeister, and K.A. Papke, "The Relationship of Unwed Status to Infant Mortality," *Obstetrics and Gynecology* 76 (1990): 763; and Richard A. Davis, "Adolescent Pregnancy and Infant Mortality: Isolating the Effects of Race," *Adolescence* 92 (Winter 1988): 899–908.

[41]Saul D. Hoffman, E. Michael Foster, and Frank F. Furstenberg Jr., "Reevaluating the Costs of Teenage Childbearing," *Demography* 30 (February 1993): 1–13.

[42]Katherine Trent and Sharon L. Harlan, "Teenage Mothers in Nuclear and Extended Households," *Journal of Family Issues* 15 (June 1994): 309–337.

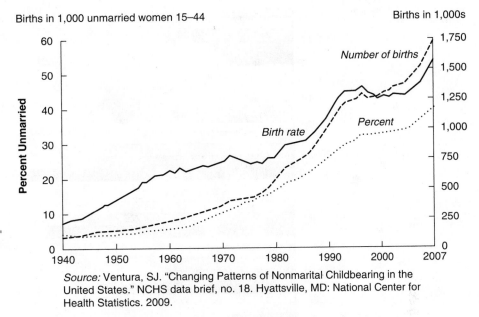

Births in 1,000 unmarried women 15–44

Births in 1,000s

Number of births

Birth rate

Percent

Figure 10.4

Number of Births, Birth Rate, and Percentage of Births to Unmarried Women: United States, 1940–2007

Source: Ventura, SJ. "Changing Patterns of Nonmarital Childbearing in the United States." NCHS data brief, no. 18. Hyattsville, MD: National Center for Health Statistics. 2009.

Although it would have been reasonable in the past to assume that most of these increases in births to unmarried women were the result of increased teenage child bearing, this is not the case in more recent decades. A comparison of age-group specific birth rates for unmarried women at points of significant change since 1980 (see Figure 10.5 on page 406) shows that the steep increase in these births between 1980 and 1995 occurred for all age groups between 15 and 39. Between 1995 and 2002, however, the birth rate to unmarried women between 15 and 17 *decreased* substantially and then leveled off between 2002 and 2006. The rate for 18-19 year olds also showed a similar pattern, although the initial decline was less and there was a slight increase between 2002 and 2006. For the three age groups between 20 and 34, however, the rate of unmarried child birth increased in all three time periods and has been particularly significant between 1980 and 1995 and between 2002 and 2006. As a result of these changes, the profile of unmarried child bearing has changed dramatically. As can be seen in Figure 10.6 (page 406), in 1970, 50 percent of births to unmarried mothers occurred among those less than 20 years old and another 42 percent among those between 20 and 29. By the year 2007, however, only 23 percent of births to unmarried mothers occurred among those under the age of 20, while 60 percent occurred among those between the ages of 20 and 29.

Why do these older, single women become mothers? One obvious factor is the steep increases in cohabitation discussed in Chapter 7, but attitudes and perceptions about relationships today also play a major role. In a comparison of single women who became mothers with married women who became mothers (all of whom were at least 25 years old), it was revealed that both groups accepted motherhood as a fundamental part of their own womanhood. Single mothers, however, had a greater ambivalence toward marriage and how they viewed relationships with men. The composite picture that emerged was a combination of an idealized image of what marriage should be, with an unwillingness to accept compromise as an essential relationship strategy.[43]

---

[43]Judith M. Siegel, "Looking for Mr. Right? Older Single Women Who Become Mothers," *Journal of Family Issues* 16 (March 1995): 194–211.

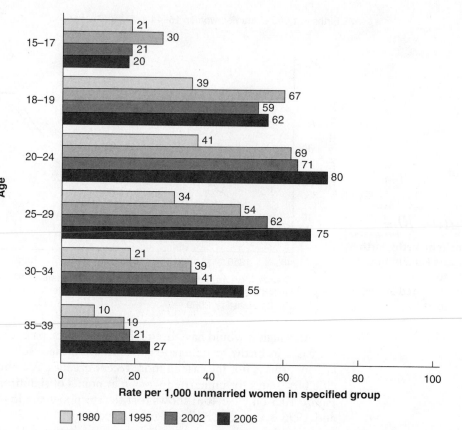

Figure 10.5

Birth Rates for Unmarried Women by Age, 1980, 1995, 2002, 2006

Source: Ventura, SJ. "Changing Patterns of Nonmarital Childbearing in the United States." NCHS data brief, no. 18. Hyattsville, MD: National Center for Health Statistics. 2009.

This trend among older single women toward separating marriage and child bearing may suggest fewer problems than among teenagers who lack emotional maturity, drop out of school, and have no child-rearing skills. Yet, data suggest this positive interpretation may be true only for women who are white, 25 years old or older, did not begin having children as teenagers, or are cohabiting.[44] The economic situation of older single mothers was closer to that of teen mothers than that of married child bearers the same ages.

In addition to age differences, the rate and percentage of births to unmarried mothers also vary dramatically by racial and ethnic category. As can be seen in Table 10.1, in 2007 the rate (number per 1,000) of births to black unmarried mothers was more than twice that of non-Hispanic white mothers (72 versus 32 per thousand). This difference, however, is down from what it was in 1990 when births among black unmarried mothers were almost four times greater than they were among whites. This is due to both an increase in unmarried parenthood among whites during this time period and a significant decrease among blacks. Hispanics have also added significantly to the increases in unmarried parenthood between 1990 and 2007. The unmarried childbirth rate for Hispanics increased from 90 per

---

[44]E. Michael Foster, Damon Jones, and Saul D. Hoffman, "The Economic Impact of Nonmarital Childbearing: How are Older, Single Mothers Faring," *Journal of Marriage and the Family* 60 (February 1998): 163–174.

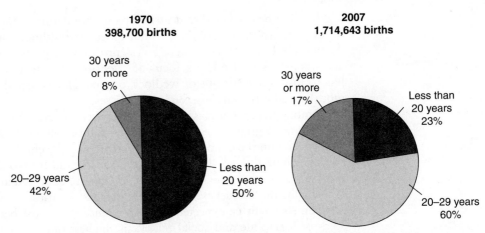

1970
398,700 births

2007
1,714,643 births

Figure 10.6

Distribution of
Nonmarital Births by
Age, 1970 and 2007

Source: Ventura, SJ. "Changing Patterns of Nonmarital Childbearing in the United States."
NCHS data brief, no. 18. Hyattsville, MD: National Center for Health Statistics. 2009.

thousand to 106 per thousand during this time period. Asians showed the lowest levels of unmarried child bearing at all times where data were available, although there has been an increase for this group as well from 21 in 2000 to 26 in 2007.

How does one explain these race and ethnic group discrepancies? A key factor in understanding the wide variation in births among racial and ethnic groups lies in differential social norms pertaining to sex, pregnancy, and cohabitation. For example, among many Asian American groups, sexual norms are very restrictive, leading to few unwed parents. Religious norms play a major role for groups such as the Amish, Mormon, and selected Hispanic subcultures. Cohabitation norms, such as exist in Scandinavian countries, show that many children are born outside of a marriage but often in a two-parent household. Other norms relating to the acceptability and availability of contraception or abortion enter the picture. Many of these factors are closely linked to the socioeconomic and class status of the child, family, and community.

Table 10.1

Births to Unmarried Women, by Race and Age of Mother: 1990–2005

Race and Age	YEAR				
	1990	1995	2000	2005	2007
Total rate (number per 1,000)	44	44	44	48	52
Non-Hispanic White	24	28	28	30	32
Black	91	75	71	68	72
Hispanic	90	89	87	100	106
Asian[a]	—	—	21	25	26

[a]No data is available on unmarried birth rates for Asians and Pacific Islanders in 1990 or 1995.

Sources: U.S. Census Bureau, *The 2009 Statistical Abstract*, "Table 84—Births to Unmarried Women by Race, Hispanic Origin, and Age of Mother." http://www.2010census.biz/compendia/statab/cats/births_deaths_marriages_divorces.html; and Ventura S.J. *Changing Patterns of Nonmarital Childbearing in the United States.* NCHS data brief, no 18. Hyattsville, MD: National Center for Health Statistics. 2009. http://www.cdc.gov/nchs/data/databriefs/db18.htm#citation.

It might be predicted that unwed parenthood among the lower classes would be of less concern to society than would unwed parenthood among the higher classes. Among the lower classes, there is less property to protect and inherit, and lineage and family honor are less a focus of attention; therefore, lower-class families have less to lose if a birth out of wedlock occurs. The expected result of this would be more unwed births among the lower classes.

Among the higher classes, where property control and family name are at stake to a greater degree, unwed parenthood would likely bring different results, including pressure on the couple to marry, to turn over the child to an adoption agency, or to leave home to bear the child. Or the birth could be avoided altogether via abortion, which is more accessible to people who are educated and financially able.

Finally, the frequency of unwed parenthood varies widely from one country to another. As might be expected given differences that exist between countries in other areas of family life and social policy, the highest rates of unmarried parenthood are found among the countries of Northern Europe. As can be seen in Figure 10.7 the

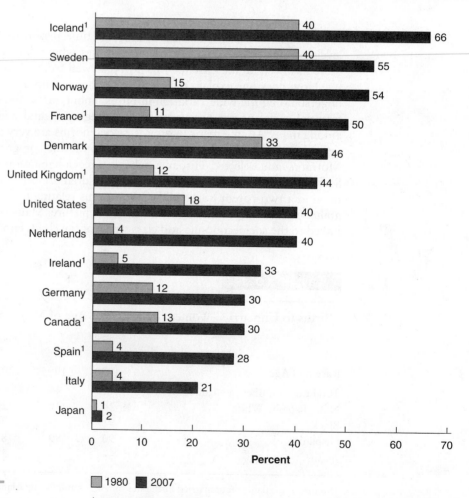

Figure 10.7

Percentage of Births to Unmarried Women, Selected Countries, 1980 and 2007

■ 1980   ■ 2007

[1]Listed data are for 2006.

Source: Ventura, SJ. "Changing Patterns of Nonmarital Childbearing in the United States." NCHS data brief, no. 18. Hyattsville, MD: National Center for Health Statistics. 2009.

percent of births to unmarried women were highest in Iceland, Sweden, and Norway. France, Denmark, the United Kingdom, and the Netherlands also had levels of unmarried child bearing that were as high, or higher, than the United States. As noted earlier with respect to Sweden, however, in many of these countries (especially those in Northern Europe) *unmarried* is not necessarily the same as *single parenthood*. High cohabitation rates, longer term and more stable cohabitations, and greater legal standing of cohabiting unions lead to births by couples who may be legally unwed but are in two-parent, marriage-like circumstances. In contrast, two predominantly Catholic countries in Southern Europe—Spain and Italy—had much lower rates of unwed parenthood; and, in Japan, unmarried parenthood is still pretty much nonexistent. With the exception of Japan, all Western countries experienced very substantial increases in the percentage of births to unmarried mothers, both in terms of absolute numbers as well as in terms of percentage increases. Most notably, countries such as France, the Netherlands, Ireland, Spain, and Italy experienced a greater than 500 percent increase in the percentage of births to unmarried mothers between 1980 and 2007.

The concern over these births varies widely from country to country as well. Some countries such as Sweden no longer have a concept such as "illegitimacy," and children born in or out of wedlock receive equal status and privilege. In the United States, however, the unwed parent and her child often are stigmatized and do not, in large part, enjoy the approval and congratulations granted to the married parent and the child born into a conjugal family unit.

It appears that marriage bestows legitimacy on parenthood more than on sex. That is, most societies are more concerned with births separate from a marriage than with sexual intercourse outside marriage. This greater concern for unwed parenthood than for unwed intercourse may be the key to understanding the emphasis and attention given to the mother and the relative lack of attention given to the father.

Consequences of Birth Outside Marriage

Now the questions "So what?" or "Who cares?" Does it really make a difference that in the United States more than 1.3 million births each year occur outside of wedlock? Do these children have more social, economic, and health problems than children born in wedlock? Is the presence of both male and female parents essential to the growth and development of a child? Does the unmarried mother face increased emotional and economic difficulties that seriously affect both her and her child?

Being born outside of wedlock does have an impact on the child, the parent, and society. Data clearly support negative and long-lasting repercussions of teenage and/or unwed child bearing. Young and unwed parents are less educated than their contemporaries; they are also often limited to less prestigious jobs and, in the case of women, to more dead-end jobs. Society, in general, may offer little toleration to the young unwed mother who wishes to keep her child as her own, but among lower-class strata, where the commitment to the norm of legal marriage is less stringent, greater toleration is likely. It has been demonstrated that living in a socioeconomically distressed neighborhood increases young women's risk of premarital child bearing. The behavior of peers and the more tolerant attitudes toward unmarried parenthood in distressed communities contributes significantly to the timing of child bearing.[45]

---

[45]Scott J. South and Eric P. Baumer, "Deciphering Community and Race Effects on Adolescent Premarital Childbearing," *Social Forces* 78 (June 2000): 1379–1408.

Despite a decrease in the degree of stigma attached to birth out of wedlock and the proliferation of services and programs for these children and their mothers, children born to young and unwed mothers do not begin life on equal footing with children born to an older person or married couple. These disadvantages persist beyond infancy. A national longitudinal study of early motherhood found that when compared to other children, children of teen mothers scored more poorly on tests of academic skill and were more likely to be retained in school, to initiate early sexual activity, and to display problem behaviors such as truancy and fighting.[46] A comparison of least successful children with most successful children, both from low-income mothers, revealed that the mothers of successful children achieved more years of education, were more likely to be employed, had fewer children on average, tended to live in a more desirable neighborhood, and were more likely to be living with a male partner.[47]

Family Size and Related Factors

In addition to decisions to have a child, individuals and couples are faced with decisions about how many children to have, how much time they should wait before having another child, and what sex of child they prefer. There is considerable folklore (or wisdom) regarding these matters, and researchers have been attempting to assess how much of this folk knowledge is valid and how much is fiction or myth.

Effects of Family Size on Members

The first *truth* to be examined is the notion that only children suffer deficiencies because they don't grow up with siblings. There are good sociological reasons to question this notion, however, as the number of interactions, the probability of disagreements, and the likelihood of receiving personal attention are influenced by the number of members in the group. The same factors hold true within a family system. One-child families are conducive to certain patterns of life that differ from two-, three-, and four-child families.

One-Child Families

One-child families have, in general, not been viewed in positive terms for either parents or children. The only child has been described as spoiled, selfish, overly dependent, maladjusted, and lonely. Parents of an only child have been described as selfish, self-centered, immature, cold, and abnormal. National surveys over the past thirty years have consistently shown a majority of respondents indicating that being an only child is a disadvantage. As noted earlier in this chapter, very few people say they want to have just one child or that the ideal number of children for a family is

---

[46]Judith A. Levine, Harold Pollack, and Maureen E. Comfort, "Academic and Behavioral Outcomes among the Children of Young Mothers," *Journal of Marriage and Family* 63 (May 2001): 355–369.

[47]Tom Luster, Laura Bates, Hiram Fitzgerald, Marcia Vanderbelt, and Judith Peck Key, "Factors Related to Successful Outcomes among Preschool Children Born to Low-Income Adolescent Mothers," *Journal of Marriage and the Family* 62 (February 2000): 133–146.

Traditionally, families with six or eight children were common among families in the United States. Today, a large family is more likely to result from the marriages of fewer children and the inclusions of spouses and grandchildren as part of the primary family network.

one. The popular stereotype of the unhappy, maladjusted only child and the view that a one-child family is neither a preferred nor a desirable family size calls for an empirical look at this small family.

In looking at only children as adults, data from seven U.S. national surveys were used to establish the effects of having a number of siblings on eight dimensions of well-being.[48] Without exception, all the effects of having siblings were negative, or, stated differently, all the effects of being an only child were positive. Only children were more likely to say they were very happy, find life exciting, see their health as excellent, and get satisfaction from where they live, from their nonworking activities, from their family life, from their friendships, and from their physical condition. The evidence most clearly contradicted the popular stereotype of the unhappy, maladjusted only child.

Similar results came from Judith Blake, who concluded that research findings on the only child do not support the negative stereotypes that still persist about singletons.[49] She claimed that only children are intellectually superior, have no obvious personality defects, tend to count themselves happy, and are satisfied with important aspects of life, notably jobs and health. Single children have increased problems with health and achievement only when they come from a broken family with its attendant loss of income or when mothers were young enough at birth to continue child bearing but, due to difficulties of their own, failed to do so. When parental background is controlled, only children do better than children from any other family size.

Additional Siblings and Achievement Levels

Is a bigger family better? Does increasing the number of siblings improve school performance and achievement? Precise answers to these questions come from Judith Blake, who analyzed numerous national data sets, all of which showed that an increased number of siblings had negative effects on both child and adult achievement outcomes. For example, the larger the family, the fewer the years of completed schooling. Even after controlling for major parental background differences such as

[48]Norval D. Glenn and Sue Keir Hoppe, "Only Children as Adults," *Journal of Family Issues* 5 (September 1984): 363–382.

[49]Judith Blake, "Number of Siblings and Personality," *Family Planning Perspectives* 23 (November/December 1991): 272–274; and *Family Size and Achievement* (Berkeley: University of California Press, 1989).

race and age, there was approximately a two-year difference in educational attainment of children between small and large families.

Why does increased family size negatively affect educational performance and graduation rates? Both Blake and Downey propose a **resource dilution hypothesis** that, in effect, suggests a dilution of familial resources available to children in large families and a concentration of such resources in small ones.[50] Downey, for example, in analyzing data from a national sample of nearly 25,000 eighth graders, found that parental *interpersonal resources* (frequency of talk, educational expectations, knowing their children's friends, and knowing their friends' parents) were all negatively affected by having additional children. Parental *economic resources* (having a computer; having other educational objects—a place to study, newspapers and magazines, an encyclopedia and atlas, more than fifty books, calculators; money saved for college; cultural classes in art, music, dance; and cultural activities of art, science, and history museums) were all negatively related to additional children.

Although the availability of parental resources was found to decrease as sibship size increased, so did school performance (grades as well as standardized math and reading test scores) decrease as sibship size increased. And surprisingly, even when children in large families had the same level of parental resources available as their counterparts in smaller families, they accrued less benefit from them. Having more children comes at a price, even if you can afford them. And according to Blake, the idea that the older children in large families function as parents to the younger ones assumes too much about sibling goodwill and maturity. Youngsters are not adults and are seldom the emotional and intellectual equivalent of parents.

Large Families

Perception of a family as "large" or "small" is relative. Today in the United States, the family with four or more children will likely be viewed as large. But in many other countries and perhaps in the United States at the turn of the century, having four children would lead to a reaction such as "only four?" Family size is certainly relative to cultural context.

Regardless of what is considered a large or small family, a small family is small for one of two primary reasons: Either the parents wanted a small family and achieved their desired size, or they wanted a large family but were unable to attain it. In both cases, there is a low probability of having unwanted children. In contrast, a large family is such because the parents achieved the size they desired or because they had more children than they in fact wanted. The probability is, therefore, greater that large families include unplanned, unwanted, or unloved children; last-born children are more likely to be unwanted than first- or middle-born children.

A substantial body of evidence has been compiled concerning the relationship between family size or number of children and factors such as discipline, child abuse and neglect, delinquency, and health. One review of family size effects showed that, in large families, child rearing was more rule ridden and less individualized, corporal

---

[50]Blake, *Family Size and Achievement*, 10–12; and Douglas B. Downey, "When Bigger Is Not Better: Family Size, Parental Resources, and Children's Educational Performance," *American Sociological Review* 60 (October 1995): 746–761.

punishment was more prevalent, and resources such as time and money were more limited.[51] Persons from small families tended to have higher IQs and greater levels of academic achievement and occupational performance. Large families also produced more delinquents and alcoholics. In regard to health, in large families, perinatal (surrounding birth) morbidity and mortality rates were higher, and mothers were at greater risk of several physical diseases.

In the words of the authors:

> Women who have many children more frequently develop hypertension, stress symptoms, gall bladder disease, diabetes, and postpartum depression. Women with many children are at higher risk for cancer to the cervix, digestion organs, and peritoneum, but are at less risk for breast cancer....Fathers of large families are at greater risk of hypertension and peptic ulcers.[52]

Are there no positive effects of having many siblings or coming from a large family? For example, are not children from large families more sociable, personable, friendly, warm, affiliative, and less aloof?

Apparently not. Several national surveys found no relationship between sibling number and sociability or being affiliative as an adult (or perhaps at any age).[53] Although a number of studies found no effects, positive or negative, associated with family size, very few studies substantiated positive effects associated with large families. The consequences of large family size, as with most social structural variables, tend to vary by factors such as educational level, social class, and religious subculture.

Birth Order and Sibling Relationships

Birth order (sibling position) has a major influence on a wide variety of behavioral and attitudinal phenomena. Research has shown that, in general, first-borns tend to be intellectual achievers and have high levels of self-esteem. Female first-borns, in particular, tend to be more religious, more sexually conservative, more traditionally oriented toward feminine roles, and more likely to associate with adults.

Last-born or youngest children, like only children, tend to be more sexually permissive, more likely to engage in social activities, more likely to visit with friends frequently, more likely to make use of the media, and consistently less traditional. Explanations for these differences have often focused on the older child being a role model for the younger, having more responsibility for other children, and receiving less attention as siblings enter the scene.[54]

Even middle-born children appear to differ from first-borns and last-borns. An analysis of a national sample of several thousand adolescent males found middle-borns

---

[51]Mazie Earle Wagner, Herman J.P. Schubert, and Daniel S.P. Schubert, "Family Size Effects: A Review," *The Journal of Genetic Psychology* 146 (March 1985): 65–78.

[52]Ibid., p. 72.

[53]Judith Blake, Barbra Richardson, and Jennifer Bhattacharya, "Number of Siblings and Sociability," *Journal of Marriage and the Family* 53 (May 1991): 271–283.

[54]Note, for example, Joseph Lee Rodgers, David C. Rowe, and David F. Harris, "Sibling Differences in Adolescent Sexual Behavior: Inferring Process Models from Family Composition Patterns," *Journal of Marriage and the Family* 54 (February 1992): 142–152.

to have significantly lower levels of self-esteem than first- or last-borns.[55] A one or three-year spacing between siblings was more positive for children's self-esteem than a two-year spacing, as was having female siblings as opposed to male or both male and female siblings. The explanation of a lower self-assessment of middle-born children may be based on a theory that first- and last-born children have a uniqueness that facilitates recognition and attention by parents and siblings. Middle children lack this inherent uniqueness.

Freeze and others suggest a word of caution on the effects of birth order, particularly as related to social attitudes. It is their contention, supported by their research evidence, that gender, class, or race are better predictors of social attitudes than is birth order. They find no support for a universal influence of birth order across time and cultures that firstborn adults are more conservative, supportive of authority, or "tough-minded" than laterborns.[56]

Having siblings, however, regardless of birth order, cannot be ignored. It is clear that siblings have a major impact on one's socialization, on each other as friends and companions, and on parents. Some aspects of sibling relationships are relatively constant, such as companionship and emotional support, while others, such as specific types of caretaking and sibling rivalry, stand out as unique to specific stages in the lifecycle. Sibling relationships are unique in their duration, their common genetic and social heritage, and their common early experiences with the family.

In an era of frequent remarriages and the formation of many stepsibling and halfsibling relationships, one might question if these relationships differ from full sibling relationships in adulthood. National survey data have revealed that they do.[57] On the one hand, individuals define *stepsiblings* as real kin and maintain these relationships into adulthood. On the other hand, sibling relationships are prioritized, with full siblings reporting significantly more contact with one another than with stepsiblings. Contact with both full and stepsiblings was facilitated by factors such as geographical proximity and being young and female. Having no full siblings also encouraged contact with step- and half siblings.

Sex Control

What will be the consequences for parents when they can increasingly control whether to have a boy or a girl (**sex control**)? The day is at hand when parents can choose the sex of their child using either of two basic procedures: (1) by controlling the type of sperm that will fertilize the egg or (2) by prenatally determining the sex of an embryo and then aborting it if it is of the undesired sex.[58] Amniocentesis and ultrasound photography are becoming low-risk, routine ways to both diagnose the health of fetuses already conceived and confirming their sex

---

[55]Thomas Ewin Smith, "Sex and Sibling Structure: Interaction Effects upon the Accuracy of Adolescent Perceptions of Parental Orientations," *Journal of Marriage and the Family* 46 (November 1984): 901–907.

[56]Jeremy Freese, Brian Powell, and Lala Carr Steelman, "Rebel Without a Cause or Effect: Birth Order and Social Attitudes," *American Sociological Review* 64 (April 1999): 207–231.

[57]Lynn K. White and Agnes Riedmann, "When the Brady Bunch Grows Up: Step/Half- and Full-sibling," *Journal of Marriage and the Family* 54 (February 1992): 197–208; and Lawrence Ganong and Marilyn Coleman, "An Exploratory Study of Stepsibling Subsystems," *Journal of Divorce and Remarriage* 19 (1993): 125–141.

[58]Elizabeth Moen, "Sex Selective Eugenic Abortions: Prospects in China and India," *Issues in Reproductive and Genetic Engineering* 4 (1991): 231–249; and Alison Dundes Renteln, "Sex Selection and Reproductive Freedom," *Women's Studies International Forum* 15 (1992): 405–426.

The one-child policy in China has been successful at reducing population growth through reduced fertility by providing incentives to families that have just one child. The strong preference for boys and the need for child labor in rural areas, however, has made implementing this policy difficult and resulted in some unintended negative consequences.

months before birth occurs. In brief, it is no longer unrealistic to foresee the ability to guarantee the reproduction of offspring of the chosen sex.

Of course, there is more to this issue than technology. Debate surrounds the general issue of controlling life, as evidenced by the controversy over abortion and surrogate motherhood as well as various types of genetic research and engineering. Traditional views hold that life is God-given and should not be manipulated by humans, for any purpose. Other views hold that knowledge about and abilities to control life should be used to improve and sustain the human condition. The controversy is likely to increase as techniques such as sex control become more prevalent. But the fact is, the technology exists.

Will techniques such as sex control result in an unbalanced sex ratio, as appears to have occurred under the one-child policy in China where males are preferred? It has been estimated that choosing the sex of the child will increase the proportion of male births by 7 to 10 percent. Also, a series of research reports has indicated that boys are preferred over girls in much of Africa, Asia, and the Middle East; among the Swiss, Belgians, and Italians in Europe; and among Jews and Catholics in the United States. If this excess of males were to occur, would it increase the number of males who never marry due to a "marriage squeeze," would it delay their age at marriage, would it force an increase in homosexuality and prostitution, or would it even force the introduction of polyandry?

Would a consequence of choosing the sex of a child be a reduction in the birth rate? Parents would not have to bear additional children in order to have one or another of a particular sex. Studies have indicated that the desire for more children is closely correlated with the number of sons.

Would a consequence of sex control be an increased proportion of first-born males? Some of the consequences of birth order have already been shown. The overall result may be children who have more friends, are more conservative, or are more eminent scholars.

Finally, would a consequence of choosing a boy or a girl be improved family relationships because births of the undesired sex were avoided? Would there be fewer resented or rejected children, or would gender-role confusion be eliminated? Regardless of choice, having female children does seem to affect support for feminism and more egalitarian views. In studies in both the United States and Canada, women in both countries and men in Canada were more likely to recognize gender inequality, to support a more feminist ideology, and to hold more egalitarian views if they had female children.[59] Family structure, in terms of the gender of children, affects the attitudes and behaviors of parents and children.

[59]Rebecca L. Warner, "Does the Sex of Your Child Matter? Support for Feminism among Women and Men in the United States and Canada," *Journal of Marriage and the Family* 53 (November 1991): 1051–1056.

news item

Sons Preferred over Daughters: Is Sex Selection Ethical?

An International Gallup Poll, as reported in *The Gallup Poll Monthly* (November 1997), revealed that, with few exceptions, boys are preferred over girls. Respondents from sixteen countries were asked "Suppose you could have only one child, would you prefer that it be a boy or a girl?" Thailand led the list in wanting a boy with 44 percent responding accordingly. Twenty-seven percent preferred a girl, with 29 percent giving no preference. Thailand was followed by France (41 percent boy; 31 percent girl), India (40 percent versus 27 percent), and Columbia (35 percent versus 27 percent).

In the United States, 42 percent of those surveyed gave no preference, but among those who did, boys were favored by a twelve-point margin, 35 percent to 23 percent. Other countries preferring boys over girls included Great Britain (31 to 26 percent), Mexico (31 to 24 percent), Taiwan (29 to 9 percent), Canada (26 to 16 percent), Hungary (25 to 12 percent), Guatemala (23 to 13 percent), Germany (21 to 19 percent), and Singapore (19 to 11 percent). Spain and Ireland gave a preference for girls over boys by 7 percent and 4 percent, respectively.

It is one thing to prefer one sex or the other, but how ethical is it to use certain methods that are currently available to achieve that preference? The chairman of the ethics committee of the American Society for Reproductive Medicine said that it is sometimes acceptable for couples to choose the sex of their children by selecting either male or female embryos and discarding the rest (*New York Times* September 28, 2001, p. A14). Couples would have to undergo in vitro fertilization and their embryos would be examined in the first few days. The embryo selection method, called preimplantation genetic diagnosis, has been available for about a decade but was reserved almost exclusively for couples at risk for having babies with certain genetic diseases. The same method, however, can be used for sex selection, as it is simple to see if the embryo is male with an X and Y chromosome or female with two X chromosomes. Earlier, the same society had issued a statement saying it was ethical to use a sperm-sorting technique for sex selection.

Source: Gallup Poll News Service, "Family Values Differ Sharply Around the World," *1997 Global Study of Family Values*, November 7, 1997. http://www.gallup.com/poll/9871/1997-global-study-family-values.aspx#1; Gina Kolata, "Fertility Ethics Authority Approves Sex Selection," *The New York Times*, September 28, 2001."

Summary

1. The value of having children and lots of them is called pronatalism. In most societies, pronatalism is a strongly held belief supported by biological drives, institutional concerns, and/or rational calculations of the profitability of children for individual life outcomes. In modern societies, however, pronatalism in the sense of "more is better" has been undermined by the ability to control sexual drives and the potential for child bearing that can result; the reduced value that children have for the sustenance of economic, political, and social relationships; and the greater freedom given to individuals to decide for themselves. Nevertheless, pronatalism still exists today in these societies and is tied to women's identities.

2. Most couples want and have children. Birthrates vary during wars and periods of economic depression and prosperity. Over the past few decades, women have delayed their first births; the consequences of this delay are having fewer children and being better-off economically.

3. The consequences of parenthood can be understood only in a social context. Many negative aspects in the lives of children have been attributed to family changes such as divorce, single parenthood, and maternal employment. However, to suggest that the family *causes* these negative aspects would be to exaggerate. Without doubt, parenthood does have significant consequences for employment patterns and marital satisfaction.

4. Some couples have no children by choice; for instance, some women choose career paths and marital styles that reject mothering and parenthood. Childless couples appear to have higher levels of health and marital satisfaction than couples with children. However, involuntarily childless couples experience negative effects on their well-being. Many infertile couples turn to adoption or alternative means of conceiving and/or having children, such as surrogate motherhood and artificial insemination.

5. Young parenthood and unwed parenthood are issues of specific concern, for both parents and children. The number of births outside of marriage is increasing sharply. The greatest increases are not among teenagers, but among women in their twenties. Young parents often are at a disadvantage in terms of marriage, education, income, employment, and training in general. Being born to unwed parents hinders a child's ability to get started on an equal footing with children born in wedlock and to avoid disadvantages after infancy, as well.

6. Family size influences the emotional and intellectual development of children. Research has supported the *dilution hypothesis*, which suggests a dilution of familial resources available to children in large families and a concentration of such resources in small families. Most of the negative stereotypes about small families and only children have little, if any, research support.

7. As with family size, order of birth also influences children's development. First-borns appear more tradition oriented, less sexually permissive, and more achievement oriented. Later-born children also differ in a variety of ways.

8. Some evidence has suggested that people in many countries prefer male children. Perhaps within the near future, parents will be able to choose to have a child of one sex or the other. This ability in sex control could result in dramatic changes in the sex ratio, in birthrates, and in family relationships in general.

This chapter covered a range of topics dealing with parents and parenthood: its value, young and unwed parenthood, birthrates, family size, birth order, and so forth. Chapter 11 will continue with the parenthood issue but focus more specifically on parent–child interaction, socialization patterns, and gender-role differences.

Key Terms and Topics

Value of children pp. 384–388

Pronatalism p. 385

Uncertainty reduction theory p. 387

Parental investment theory p. 387

Birthrates p. 388

Fertility rate p. 389

Baby boom p. 390

Baby boomlet/baby boom echo p. 390

Total fertility rate p. 391

Age-specific fertility rate p. 391

Replacement threshold p. 391

Braking hypothesis p. 396

Childless/childfree marriages pp. 396–400

Voluntary childlessness p. 398

Involuntary childlessness pp. 399–400

Young parenthood p. 400

Unwed parenthood p. 400

Rates of birth outside marriage pp. 404–409

Consequences of birth outside marriage pp. 409–410

Effects of family size on members pp. 410–413

One-child families pp. 410–411

Resource dilution hypothesis p. 412

Large families pp. 412–413

Birth order and sibling relationships pp. 413–414

Sex control p. 414

Discussion Questions

1. What factors help explain variation in levels of pronatalism and fertility across types of societies? How is pronatalism related to gender relationships and gender stratification in societies?
2. How have birthrates changed in the United States over the past century? What factors explain fluctuations in these rates over time?
3. How does having a child affect the lives of individuals and couples? How do these effects help explain why women and men choose not to have any children? What do you think about the reasons given by men and women who decide not to have a child?
4. How do strong pronatalism norms impact women who choose not to have children and those who cannot have children?
5. A number of states have passed legislation that requires Planned Parenthood and similar clinics to notify parents when their teenage children have requested contraceptive or abortion information. What will likely be some of the consequences of this type of action?
6. Discuss the implications of the slogan "stop at two" in regard to family size. Why two? What if everyone had two children? What means should be used to accomplish this goal, if it is perceived as desirable?
7. Itemize the advantages and disadvantages of growing up in large and small families. What are the consequences of being an only child? What types of factors are likely to influence the size of a family?
8. Discuss the implications of being an oldest, middle, or youngest child. Does child spacing affect the impact of birth order on an individual? How?
9. If the sex of the fetus could be determined accurately within a few weeks following pregnancy, what effect, if any, would this have on birthrates? Would most parents in the United States choose to have boys or girls or have no preference? What about in other countries, particularly outside the Western world?

Further Readings

Blankenhorn, David. *Fatherless America: Confronting Our Most Urgent Social Problem*. New York: Basic Books, 1995.

  The founder and president of the Institute for Family Values argues for reinstituting marriage, which would in turn reestablish fathers as responsible husbands and providers.

Blomquist, Barbara Taylor. *Insight into Adoption*. Springfield, IL: Charles C. Thomas, 2001.

  A factual glimpse into the world of adoption with some challenges directed toward parents.

Booth, Alan, and Crouter, Ann C., eds. *Men in Families: Why Do They Get Involved? What Differences Does It Make?* Mahwah, NJ: Lawrence Erlbaum Associates, 1998.

  A series of essays based on presentations at a national symposium on men in families.

Demo, David H., and Cox, Martha J. "Families with Young Children: A Review of Research in the 1990s," *Journal of Marriage and the Family* 62 (November 2000): 876–895; Marsiglio, William, Amato, Paul, Day, Randal D., and Lamb, Michael E. "Scholarship on Fatherhood in the 1990s and Beyond," *Journal of Marriage and the Family* 62 (November 2000): 1173–1191; and Arendell,

Terry, "Conceiving and Investigating Motherhood: The Decade's Scholarship," *Journal of Marriage and the Family* 62 (November 2000): 1192–1207.

  Three-decade review articles dealing with research in the 1990s on young children, fatherhood, and motherhood.

Fenwick, Lynda Beck. *Private Choices, Public Consequences: Reproductive Technology and the New Ethics of Conception, Pregnancy, and Family*. New York: Dutton, 1998.

  Accounts are presented of persons faced with intimate decisions, public concerns, and the dilemmas resulting from genetic knowledge.

LaRossa, Ralph, *The Modernization of Fatherhood: A Social and Political History*. Chicago: The University of Chicago Press, 1997.

  An explicit historical analysis of how American fatherhood was reshaped during the 1920s and 1930s into the modernized form that we see idealized today.

Peters, H. Elizabeth, Peterson, Gary W., Steinmetz, Suzanne K., and Day, Randall, eds. *Fatherhood: Research Interventions and Policies*. New York: The Haworth Press, Inc., 2000.

A series of articles covering fathers historically, in intact families and as single parents, with a concluding section on interventions and policies.

Simon, Rita J. *Abortion: Statutes, Policies, and Public Attitudes the World Over.* Westport, CT: Praeger, 1998.

Data are presented on the current grounds for abortion in 189 countries and linked to public opinion and population policies.

Westman, Jack, ed. *Parenthood in America: Undervalued, Underpaid, Under Seige.* Madison: The University of Wisconsin Press, 2001.

Parenthood is viewed as a way of life, a career, that includes the home, the community, workplace, and society at large.

Wu, Lawrence, and Wolfe, Barbara, eds. *Out of Wedlock: Causes and Consequences of Nonmarital Fertility.* New York: Russell Sage, 2001.

An investigation of the state of research in the United States and in other countries concerning nonmarital fertility.

chapter 11

Parenting Roles and Child Socialization

Case Example

Resocializing a Child Who Has Been Severely Deprived

I could write volumes about this foster child we've raised. When he came to us, he was 2 years and 4 months old and was really a basket case. I had read about children from deprived backgrounds, but I had never seen one. It was really a cultural shock for all of us.

The child didn't seem to know what people were for. He could ignore a person like he ignored a piece of furniture. He apparently had never had any interpersonal relations with another human. He did not want anybody near him and he was only 2 years old. Our way was to hold our children, cuddle them, tell them bedtime stories, and carry them around. The older children played with him, but he had no idea what they were doing. Everything terrified him. It was a lot more than "I miss my mother." In fact, he did not know the words *mama*, *daddy*. He didn't miss anybody 'cause he didn't know what anybody was for. He had no language in that he didn't understand like our 2-year-olds understood everything. He had no understanding of the difference between *yes, go ahead and do it* and *no, you can't do that. No* was a concept he never heard.

Apparently, he never sat at a table and ate a meal. He was more like an animal. I really hate using that word when we are talking about humans. But you could not sit him at a table; he didn't know what it was for. I recall the first breakfast we had—that he had with us. He drank orange juice for as long as I gave it to him. Like he had four or five glasses of orange juice. He gobbled up toast and ate huge bowls of cereal. First I thought, "Gee, the kid is starved." But then I realized that he ate like that probably because that's his pattern. You eat all you could get when you

421

could get it because you didn't know where the next meal was coming from. But we ate three times a day. It was years, and I mean years, before he could really sit at the table with us, eat a meal, and then leave without creating a major disturbance. By major, I mean he thought he could get his jollies by just sweeping everything off the table or grabbing the table and making things spill or taking his own food and throwing it around. You would think that in a few weeks this will all go away. But it didn't, and we started bringing him around to psychologists, and the agency was very helpful. He was seen by neurologists and psychologists and he had EEGs, intelligence tests, and all of the support that seemed to be available in the community. They would all just say that, as far as they could see, he had no brain damage; his intelligence was maybe below normal.

For a long time, he was as rigid as a door. He would not bend an inch. Like here's an example of what I mean. At our house, the children play outside in the summer. We have playground equipment in the backyard, and the children have bikes. I raised a bunch of kids who really love the outdoors. But I don't think he had ever been outside his little apartment or whatever it was they lived in. So, I would put him outside in the morning, and his hands would go up to his eyes like he couldn't stand the light. I'd stay out there with him, but unless I was holding his hand, he would spin right around and go into the house again. So I'd take him out and put him outside again. We actually had to physically hold him out there. You could not walk him. You couldn't put him in the sandbox. He didn't know what a sandbox was for. He didn't know what toys were for. He had no idea what you did with a toy. We had to very patiently teach him all of this.

Eventually, he began to show that it was becoming important to him that he start pleasing us. But now, this didn't happen until he was almost school age. Prior to that, he couldn't care less whether he pleased us or pleased anybody else. He had not been socialized that way, and I think that kind of socialization happens really early. I'm even more aware of it with my own grandchildren. They're sensitive. They cry if they are corrected. He never cried.

Questions to Consider

To what extent is personality developed or fixed by the first two or three years of life?

As with the boy described in this case, is it likely or possible that early damage cannot be totally corrected, or can anyone be resocialized?

What is your theory of socialization or explanation of what is important in rearing a child? How is it applicable to the case cited? How do you explain this boy's antisocial behavior and the ineffectiveness of spanking?

Chapter 10 examined selected structural arrangements of the family system: norms and values surrounding parenthood, young parenthood, unwed parenthood, birthrates, effects of large or small families, birth order, and the like. In this chapter, we will examine the meaning of good parenting, the nature of parenting roles, the dynamics of parent–child relationships, and some of the major theories of how children learn and develop. We will conclude with a discussion of the challenges of single parenting and the strategies used by single parents to effectively bring about positive results in their children.

Models of Good Parenting

What makes for good parenting? When things go wrong with children and youth in society, one of the first places that people look is to the family—and to the parents in particular. But is this fair? Certainly child outcomes are influenced by more than family experiences and parental approaches to parenting. When children are released into the world, they encounter many forces on their behaviors. Although parents can give them the psychological and social skills they need to negotiate their social environments, many times they lack sufficient economic, social, and cultural capital to do so successfully (see Chapter 2 for a discussion of different forms of capital). In addition, it is not always clear what skills and traits children will need to succeed nor what parenting approaches will work best in different social environments. Indeed, studies of criminal behavior and other negative outcomes tend to show that the power of more temporally proximate or immediate causes to predict outcomes is greater than the power of early childhood predictors.

There is a tendency to apply a single white, middle class, Western set of standards for what constitutes good parenting, but this ignores the fact that good parenting is defined by the context into which children are socialized. For example, hunting and gathering societies might encourage children to make it on their own and not to be overnurtured or overprotected because they will need to be self-reliant and adaptive to new circumstances as adults. In agricultural societies, however, the emphasis might be more on conformity, cooperation, and long-term planning insofar as these traits fit better in a more stable intergenerational economic system. In modern industrial societies, success is determined by flexibility, assertiveness, individualism, and psychological and emotional development. As a result, good parenting is protective and nurturing but also facilitative of exploration and independent decision making. The goals of parenting in modern industrial societies focus more on the development of the psychological and emotional capacities needed to adapt and succeed.

Parenting goals and the effectiveness of different parenting strategies will also vary within different segments of the same society. Recall from Chapter 4 the different parenting styles employed by blue-collar versus-white collar workers. Not only did these parents perceive the world into which they were socializing their children differently, but they also reflected the nature of their own occupational environments in their parenting styles, as the substantive complexity of their work shaped their cognitive flexibility which, in turn, altered their parenting behaviors. For which world should these parents be preparing their children, and what is their potential for doing so? Most will prepare their children for the world they know. Although many will want their children to succeed beyond their own status in life, their own capabilities and understandings of the world will often limit their use of parenting techniques that would make such upward mobility a reality.

Finally, children are part of a larger family system that is trying to adapt to its immediate surroundings. As a result, parental influence goes beyond intentional "parenting practices" and is shaped by family strategies for survival. How much freedom parents give their children outside the home, for example, can be limited by the level of risk involved in the environment or can be increased as a function of the family's need for economic resources brought in by children's outside street activities or by crowded home conditions and the need to provide space and resources for younger children.[1] How much freedom parents give children inside the home might be limited by crowded conditions or by the need to maintain control in a situation of parental absence due to work (see discussion of single parenting at the end of this chapter).

Motherhood and Fatherhood

The starting point for understanding parenting involves an understanding of what it means to be a mother or a father. There are some who believe children need both a mother and father because men and women have different characteristics and capacities that shape their interactional styles with the child and meet different developmental needs. In particular, it has been asserted that mothers naturally are more caring, nurturing, warm, accepting, self-sacrificing, moral, and capable of providing physical care while men are more controlling, detached, rational, and capable of teaching respect and task-accomplishment skills. Given these assumed differences, it would follow that mothering roles are distinct from fathering roles. Whereas mothers should be the primary caregivers and nurturers, fathers should have more remote roles as disciplinarians and teachers and their emotional roles more limited to that of playmates and advisors. But all of this hinges on the notion that these differences are "natural" and that mothers are incapable of "fathering" while fathers are incapable of "mothering."

The notion of inherited parenting traits can be traced to the evolutionary perspective of **parental investment theory**. According to parental investment theory,[2] the reproductive strategy that best increases the likelihood that the female's genetic material will be passed on through her offspring is to limit her fertility and do all she can to protect and nurture the child to adulthood. Thus, females will have a genetic predisposition to take on these roles when they have children. Males, on the other hand, increase their ability to pass on their genetic material by limiting their involvement with children and instead investing their resources in providing for and protecting the females with whom they have children. As a result, they do not develop the predispositions and physiological capacities needed to be primary caregivers and instead develop predispositions and traits that seem more rugged and counter to those required for nurturance and primary care of children.

A closely related **ethological perspective** also casts women in the role of primary caregivers by virtue of their ability to establish strong attachment bonds with dependent infants. According to this theory,[3] the process is more physical than genetic as women are the early providers of satisfaction for infants' basic physical needs (especially nutrition). This satisfaction of need then enhances the attachment bond and makes them more responsive to their children and makes their children more attentive to their proximity cues. Traditionally, this theory has held that children need a strong bond with a single parent in order to develop normally.

---

[1]Elizabeth A. Kusnesof, "The House, The Street, Global Society: Latin American Families and Childhood in the Twenty-First Century," *Journal of Social History*, 38 (Summer 2005): 859–872.

[2]See David C. Geary, *Male, Female: The Evolution of Human Sex Differences* (Washington, DC: American Psychological Association, 1998).

[3]John Bowlby, *Maternal Care and Mental Health* (World Health Organisation, 14, 1951).

news item

Breastfeeding the New Vacuum Cleaner?

If you have not yet heard the chatter about Hanna Rosin's article in *The Atlantic* this month, you will. Called "The Case Against Breast-Feeding," Rosin examines how nursing became gospel, a measure of committed mothering, and asks whether the science behind the belief that "Breast is Best" is really as definitive as we all seem to believe.

A mother who breast-fed three children...Rosin always believed she was protecting her children's health by feeding them this way. She'd heard that breast-feeding is credited with increasing intelligence and immunity and lowering risk of allergies and obesity. The first time she really questioned that was last year, while nursing her infant in her pediatrician's waiting room. As she writes:

I noticed a 2001 issue of the *Journal of the American Medical Association* open to an article about breast-feeding: "Conclusions: There are inconsistent associations among breastfeeding, its duration, and the risk of being overweight in young children." Inconsistent? There I was, sitting half-naked in public for the tenth time that day, the hundredth time that month, the millionth time in my life—and the associations were inconsistent?...That night, I did what any sleep-deprived, slightly paranoid mother of a newborn would do. I...sat up and read dozens of studies examining breast-feeding's association with allergies, obesity, leukemia, mother-infant bonding, intelligence, and all the Dr. Sears highlights. *[Dr. Sears is a contributor to* Parenting *and* Baby Talk *magazines.]*

After a couple of hours, the basic pattern became obvious: the medical literature looks nothing like the popular literature. It shows that breast-feeding is probably, maybe, a little better; but it is far from the stampede of evidence that Sears describes....So how is it that every mother I know has become a breast-feeding fascist?

Rosin spends pages parsing the medical literature...and then goes on to examine the downside to breast-feeding; not for all women, but for many. Using an analogy that is already generating sparks in the blogosphere, she wonders if "it was not the vacuum that was keeping me and my 21st-century sisters down, but another sucking sound."

It is impossible, she writes, to do meaningful, full-time, wage-earning work while feeding a baby only breast milk for the first six months...:

...Breast-feeding exclusively is...a serious time commitment that pretty much guarantees that you will not work in any meaningful way....This is why, when people say that breast-feeding is "free," I want to hit them with a two-by-four. It's only free if a woman's time is worth nothing...

And if your goal is an equal marriage, she says... breast-feeding doesn't help there, either. She writes...of an acquaintance who was physically able to nurse but chose not to: She just felt that breast-feeding would set up an unequal dynamic in her marriage—one in which the mother, who was responsible for the very sustenance of the infant, would naturally become responsible for everything else as well...

I caught up with Rosin...and she said the response to her article so far was what she had expected—an email box filled with personal stories of women thanking her for writing it, and an Internet full of women calling her "a loser, saying I have a bad marriage, telling me I'm a bad mother and saying I'm wrong."

What does it say about modern mothers, she wonders, that such energy is spent judging how other women feed their children? What are we reflecting about ourselves when we so readily apply the word "selfish" to any Mom who doesn't do things our way?...

"We are in a time of incredibly intensive parenting," she said, "Why now, when women have less time and more opportunity than ever before?...There is more being debated when we talk about breastfeeding than just breast-feeding."

Source: Lisa Belkin, *The New York Times*, March 16, 2009. http://parenting.blogs.nytimes.com/2009/03/16/is-breastfeeding-the-new-vacuum-cleaner/?pagemode=print.

Are these assumptions accurate? There is considerable evidence to refute the validity of these two theories. First, there is considerable evidence in the historical and anthropological record that men have taken on primary caregiver roles in parenting and women have taken on more instrumental roles. Furthermore, the types of roles taken on by mothers and fathers seem highly responsive to the levels of gender inequality in the society.[4] When men and women are more equal, fathers have higher levels of involvement in parenting. Second, the assumptions that females will only be interested in their children and that males are incapable of providing nurturance have also been challenged based on studies of animal behavior. Females of various species have been found to engage in "strategic philandering" as a means of fertility backup, gaining diverse paternity for their offspring, and manipulating male interest.[5] Males of some species have also been shown to engage in high levels of nurturance of offspring when there is an excess of males relative to females in the vicinity or there is a large number of offspring raised by females.[6] Finally, studies of couples who consciously attempted to have the father as fully involved in primary caregiving and nurturance as the mother have shown that not only are fathers capable of being full-time primary caregivers, but their children develop equally strong and healthy attachments to both parents in such situations.[7]

Parenting Styles and Child Outcomes

How parents relate to their children can have significant impacts on them when they become adults. These impacts can be either direct or indirect. For example, parents' patterns of responding to their child can affect the nature of attachment bonds which will not only affect the effectiveness of later attempts at socialization and control but will also have long-term effects on the child's later adult relationships.[8] In addition, certain parenting behaviors have been shown to be more effective in helping children adapt successfully to their environments and thereby lowering their levels of problem behavior.

Parent–Child Attachment

Attachment theory posits that children develop a sense of emotional security or insecurity early in life based on how their parents react to them in social situations. These feelings of security or insecurity then create a working model for the child that it uses when initiating relationships with others. Attachment theorists distinguish between four types of attachment based on levels of emotional comfort with proximity to an attachment object and levels of emotional discomfort or distress with distance from the attachment object. As a result of early childhood experiences (prior to

---

[4]Scott Coltrane, "Fathering: Paradoxes, Contradictions, and Dilemmas," in Marilyn Coleman and Lawrence H. Ganong, eds., *Handbook of Contemporary Families: Considering the Past, Contemplating the Future* (Thousand Oaks, CA: Sage Publications, 2004).

[5]Sarah Hrdy, *Mother Nature: A History of Mothers, Infants and Natural Selection* (New York: Pantheon, 1999).

[6]Barbara B. Smuts and David J. Gubernick, "Male-Infant Relationships in Non-Human Primates: Paternal Investment or Mating Effort?" in B.S. Hewlett, ed., *Father-Child Relations. Cultural and Biosocial Contexts.* (New York: Aldine de Gruyter, 1992): 1–30; For a critical review of the evidence for evolutionary explanations of behavior (including parenting), see David J. Buller, Adapting Minds: Evolutionary Psychology and the Persistent Quest for Human Nature (Cambridge, MA: MIT Press, 2005).

[7]Diane Ehrensaft, *Parenting Together: Men and Women Sharing the Care of Their Children* (Champaign, IL: University of Illinois Press, 1990).

[8]See Kim Bartholomew, K., A.J.Z. Henderson, and Donald G. Dutton, "Insecure Attachment and Abusive Intimate Relationships," in C. Clulow, ed., *Attachment and Couple Work: Applying the 'Secure Base' Concept in Research and Practise* (London: Routledge, 2001); and R. C. Fraley and Phillip R. Shaver, "Adult Romantic Attachment: Theoretical Developments, Emerging Controversies, and Unanswered Questions," *Review of General Psychology*, 4 (2000): 132–154.

1 year of age), but also later experiences, children can develop an attachment style that is either *secure*, *insecure-resistant*, *insecure-avoidant*, or *disorganized*.[9]

In **secure attachment** styles, individuals feel comfortable with both proximity and some distance, although too much distance (outside the range of eye contact and rapid access to parent) causes distress. This type of attachment is considered best insofar as it allows for closeness and intimacy, but also emboldens the child to explore his or her environment to more effectively learn about and act independently in the world without exposure to the risks that would come about from too much distance from the parent. In contrast, individuals with **insecure-resistant attachment** styles are uncomfortable with proximity and have a strong desire for distance. Such attachment style is maladaptive in that it exposes offspring to greater environmental risks, reduces learning through parental modeling (the child is less aware and influenced by the behaviors of his or her parents), and is not conducive to the development of intimate relationships in later childhood and into adulthood. An **insecure-avoidant attachment** style is also considered less adaptive but for different reasons. Here, the individual has a strong desire for closeness but is uncomfortable with any distance for fear of losing the attachment figure. When separation does occur, however, they react to reunion with the attachment figure with anger. This style is less conducive to exploratory behaviors and the learning and independence that results, and it is a model that leads to poorer intimate relationships later in life. Individuals with insecure-avoidant attachment styles tend to be overly clingy and controlling partners who have higher levels of emotional volatility. Finally, those with a **disorganized attachment** style are neither desiring of closeness nor distressed by distance. These individuals experience a high level of approach-avoidance anxiety in close relationships.

A secure attachment style is developed when parents are not overly anxious about the child, encourage both closeness and distance, and display high degrees of warmth, supportiveness, consistency, and responsiveness to the child's needs and communicative acts. Parents who synchronize their reactions to the child's emotional states are more likely to develop secure attachment styles in their children. Of course, parenting is not a one-directional process as children affect parents by their behaviors. Thus, a child's temperament plays a major role in the parents' ability to respond in ways that encourage secure attachments.

Parenting Styles

Over three decades ago, child psychologist Diane Baumrind[10] proposed that **parenting styles** could be broken down into three general types—authoritative, authoritarian, and laissez-faire—based on the degree to which parents expected or demanded behavioral standards from their children and the degree to which parents were supportive and responsive to their children's needs. Since it was initially formulated, this typology has been further elaborated into four types of parenting styles: authoritative, authoritarian, permissive/indulgent and indifferent/uninvolved.[11]

---

[9]Jude Cassidy and Phillip R. Shaver, eds., *Handbook of Attachment: Theory, Research, and Clinical Applications*, 2nd Edition (Guilford Press, 2008);

[10]Diane Baumrind, "The Development of Instrumental Competence through Socialization," in A.D. Pick, ed., *Minnesota Symposium on Child Psychology*, 7 (1973): 3–46.

[11]Martin Pinquart and Rainer K. Silbereisn, "Influences of Parents and Siblings on the Development of Children and Adolescents," in Vern L. Bengtson, Alan C. Acock, Katherine R. Allen, Peggye Dilworth-Anderson, and David M. Klein, eds., *Sourcebook of Family Theory and Research* (Thousand Oaks, CA: Sage Publications, 2005): 367–392.

CROSS-CULTURAL *Perspective*

Traditional Child Rearing in the Kibbutz

The kibbutz has been and continues to be extremely child centered. Children represent the future. Traditionally, child rearing followed a collective pattern from infancy to adulthood. In that context, the infant was born of a kibbutz couple who generally married just before or soon after the first child was born. This was done in accordance with the laws of Israel and gave the child legal rights. On return from the hospital, the infant was placed in the infant house. During the first year of the infant's life, his or her mother came to this house to breastfeed the infant as long as she physically could. Young fathers participated at this period in bottle feeding and diapering. In a radical departure from child rearing in most of the world, neither infants nor any older children lived with or were directly supported by biological fathers and mothers. The socialization and education of kibbutz children were functions of nurses and teachers.

During the first year, the general pattern of child care emerged. Most of the child's time was spent with peers in the children's house. In the afternoon, two or three hours could be spent with parents in their flat or room, meeting with other families, or engaging in some joint activity. On the Sabbath, only the essential chores were performed, and children of all ages spent much time with their parents. In addition to these hourly and Sabbath visits, the child frequently saw the parents while they worked or by attending the weekly assembly of the kibbutz. Thus, parents were extremely important in the life of the child but were, in a sense, junior partners.

For the most part, training occurred separate from the residence of the parents. For the first year, the infant was in the nursery. The child was then moved to a toddler's house, each of which had approximately two nurses and eight children. This was where toilet training, learning to feed oneself, and learning to interact with agemates occurred. When the children reached the age of 2 or 3, a nursery teacher replaced one of the nurses. By the fourth or fifth birthday, the children moved into the kindergarten. This involved a different building, sometimes a new nurse and teacher, and an enlargement of the original group to approximately sixteen members. This enlarged group remained together as a unit until age 12 and the completion of sixth grade. At this point, they entered high schools, where for the first time they encountered male educational teachers and began to work directly in the kibbutz economy. Their work varied from one to three hours per day, depending on age, and was done in one of the economic branches under the supervision of adults (not parents). Upon completion of high school, the students were expected to live outside the kibbutz for approximately one year. Membership in the kibbutz followed this experience.

Even though the children did not sleep with, did not have their physical needs addressed by, were not taught social, book, or economic skills by, and were not—for the most part—disciplined or socialized by their parents, most writers stress the importance of parents in the development of the child. Parents serve as the object of identification and provide a certain security and love not obtained from others.

Source: Bruno Bettleheim, *The Children of the Dream*, Simon and Shuster, 2001; Daniel Gavron, *The Kibbutz: Awakening from Utopia*, Rowman & Littlefield, Lanham, 2000.

The **authoritative style** involves high levels of expectations and demandingness but also involves high levels of support and responsiveness. Parents using this style are more focused on the child's needs and development than in simply maintaining control. They establish clear and consistent guidelines for behavior but bring about conformity to those guidelines through reasoning and positive reinforcement (see later section on social learning theory) rather than through punishment. They are also willing to make exceptions to rules or change the rules based on their assessment of their child's developmental state and needs. This parenting style has been shown to be the most effective of the four in bringing about more positive developmental outcomes and reducing problem behavior in children throughout childhood and adolescence.

Parents employing an **authoritarian style** are similar to authoritative parents insofar as they exhibit high levels of expectation and demandingness. The difference for these parents is in their level of supportiveness and responsiveness and the degree to which they are child centered rather than parent centered. Authoritarian parents lay down many rules and strictly and consistently enforce those rules using punishment techniques but do not discuss with the child the reasons for the rules or instill in them a set of principles they can use to regulate their own behaviors based on situational circumstances. These parents tend to promote high levels of conformity to rules in general, but they also have children more responsive to the presence or absence of authority figures when faced with dilemmas of how to act in situations. Conformity to rules is higher when an authority figure is present, but in the absence of such a figure (and the potential for punishment they represent) these children (in childhood and later adulthood) are more likely to break the rules and make choices more in their own self-interest.

Finally, the **permissive/indulgent style** and the **indifferent/uninvolved style** of parenting are both characterized by low levels of expectations and demand, the difference between them being the level of supportiveness and responsiveness shown toward the child. Permissive/indulgent parents are likely to make their children their friends and confidents. Such a condition fosters a strong emotional bond between the parent and the child, but does not provide sufficient guidance and control over the child's behaviors. Indifferent/uninvolved parents, on the other hand, provide neither guidance and control nor support and responsiveness. Children growing up under this style of parenting have little incentive to act in a prosocial manner and they experience the most negative developmental outcomes.

Although the categorization of parents into one of these four types of parenting styles has been widely practiced in research on parenting outcomes, such typologies may oversimplify and ignore the possibility that the separate dimensions of supportiveness, responsiveness, expectations, demandingness, use of reasoning, and use of punishment may interact in unique ways in different circumstances to produce positive or negative outcomes in children. For example, research has shown that the use of physical punishment is more effective in contexts where other parents use the same technique.[12] This typology also ignores the impacts of other dimensions of parenting that have been shown to produce positive outcomes in children and adolescents such as parental involvement, parental consistency, monitoring and supervision (as opposed to control), parental rejection, and the use of harsh discipline.

Corporal Punishment

Corporal punishment refers to the use of physical force (including spanking) for the purpose of correction or control of a person's behavior. To spank is deeply rooted in the legal and religious traditions of American culture. Although the prevalence of spanking varies by sex (boys more than girls), age of children (preschool more than older), sex of parent (mothers more than fathers), marital status (unmarried mothers more than married ones), social class (more common among the lower classes), religious beliefs (more common among those with conservative scriptural beliefs), race (blacks more than whites), and region of the country (most common in the South), most parents (90 to 95 percent) claim to have spanked their children and most

---

[12]Ronald L. Simons, Kuei-Hsiu Lin, Leslie C. Gordon, Gene H. Brody, Velma Murry, and Rand Conger, "Community Differences in the Association between Parenting Practices and Child Conduct Problems." *Journal of Marriage and the Family* 64 (2002): 331–45.

parents (75 to 85 percent) approve of spanking and believe it is necessary in order to discipline a child.[13]

But with what effects? Does spanking improve the mental health and well-being of children and adolescents or lead to aggression and psychological disorders? Does it lead to conformity and tolerance of others or result in adolescent delinquency and adult abusiveness? A literature review can perhaps find evidence for any or all of the above. Is it corporal punishment per se that produces (causes) specific outcomes, or do parental intents and social contexts modify the results?

Support for the latter position was revealed in a study that examined the impact of "harsh corporal punishment" and quality of parental involvement on adolescent aggressiveness, delinquency, and psychological well-being.[14] Basically, the results indicated that it was not corporal punishment per se that predicted negative adolescent outcomes but the disregard, inconsistency, and uninvolvement of parents that increases a child's risk for problem behaviors. Corporal punishment in a context of parental support and involvement did not have a detrimental impact. In different contexts, however, it often results in physical injury to the child, feelings of anger, defiance, and rejection, psychological disturbances, aggressive action, and delinquent behaviors.

Closely related to the context is the meaning or perception attributed to corporal punishment. Data gathered from black and white youth in a poor southern community suggested that physical punishment was associated with children's psychological adjustment only if the punishment was seen (perceived) as a form of caretaker rejection.[15] Consistent with an interactional perspective, it may be less corporal punishment per se than the context in which it takes place and the perceptions (meanings) attached to it.

The high prevalence of physical punishment, much of which is outside a context of love and parental involvement, led Murray Straus to recommend that its elimination should become a public health agenda because it presents a serious threat to the well-being of American children.[16] Not only is corporal punishment associated with the subsequent aggressiveness of children but also evidence suggests that, later in life, this aggression includes physical assault on spouses.[17] Other research supports the

[13]Jean Giles-Sims, Murray A. Straus, and David B. Sugarman, "Child, Maternal, and Family Characteristics Associated with Spanking," *Family Relations* 44 (April 1995): 170–176; Clifton P. Flynn, "To Spank or Not to Spank: The Effect of Situation and Age of Child on Support for Corporal Punishment," *Journal of Family Violence* 13 (1988): 21–37; Clifton P. Flynn, "Regional Differences in Spanking Experiences and Attitudes: A Comparison of Northeastern and Southern College Students," *Journal of Family Violence* 11(1996): 59–80; Randall D. Day, Gary W. Peterson, and Coleen McCracken, "Predicting Spanking of Younger and Older Children by Mothers and Fathers," *Journal of Marriage and the Family* 60 (February 1998): 79–94; and Christopher G. Ellison, John P. Bartkowski, and Michelle L. Segal, "Conservative Protestantism and the Parental Use of Corporal Punishment," *Social Forces* 74 (March 1996): 1003–1028.

[14]Ronald L. Simons, Christine Johnson, and Rand D. Conger, "Harsh Corporal Punishment versus Quality of Parental Involvement as an Explanation of Adolescent Maladjustment," *Journal of Marriage and the Family* 56 (August 1994): 591–607.

[15]Ronald P. Rohner, Shana L. Bourque, and Carlos A. Elordi, "Children's Perceptions of Corporal Punishment, Caretaker Acceptance, and Psychological Adjustment in a Poor, Biracial Southern Community," *Journal of Marriage and the Family* 58 (November 1996): 842–852.

[16]Murray A. Straus, *Beating the Devil Out of Them; Corporal Punishment by Parents and Its Effects on Children* (Boston: Lexington/Macmillan, 1994); Straus, Murray A., Emily M. Douglas, and Rose Anne Medeiros, *The Primordial Violence: Corporal Punishment by Parents, Cognitive Development, and Crime* (Walnut Creek, CA: Alta Mira Press, In Press).

[17]Murray A. Straus and Carrie L. Yodanis, "Corporal Punishment in Adolescence and Physical Assaults on Spouses in Later Life: What Accounts for the Link," *Journal of Marriage and the Family* 58 (November 1996): 825–841; and Steven P. Swinford, Alfred DeMaris, Stephen A. Cernkovich, and Peggy C. Giordano, "Harsh Physical Discipline in Childhood and Violence in Later Romantic Involvements: The Mediating Role of Problem Behaviors," *Journal of Marriage and the Family* 62 (May 2000): 508–519.

TRANSNATIONAL FAMILIES

Parenting Across the Mexico–U.S. Border

Although sending one or both parents to the United States and splitting families up for short periods of time has long been a strategy among immigrants, recent immigration patterns between Mexico and the United States have resulted in more long term and somewhat "normalized" separations. Three reasons for this involve the temporary work opportunities made available to Mexican laborers, the proximity of Mexico to the United States, and the large number of undocumented immigrants who don't want to expose their children to the dangers of illegal border crossings. In an ethnographic and qualitative interview study of 21 mother and 22 fathers living in the United States with children still resident in Mexico, Joanna Dreby shows how these parents manage their parenting roles and identities and the extent to which gender differences in parenting exist in these transnational families.

On the one hand, Dreby shows that expected gender differences in parenting do not appear in this transnational context. Specifically, both fathers and mothers in her study were equally likely to keep in touch with their children through frequent and regular telephone contact; were equally likely to discontinue contact because they established new relationships in the United States or had children with a new partner in the United States; and were equally likely to see their parenting role as one of providing for their children's financial needs by sending money or gifts.

On the other hand, there were some important differences, many due to differences in circumstances. When fathers migrated they tended to do so either alone—leaving their children in the care of their wife, or with their spouse—leaving their children with their maternal grandmother. The former group of fathers typically made frequent return trips to Mexico as seasonal laborers and had done so for many years. These fathers expressed a greater sense of significance in maintaining contact with their children. The temporary separations made them more involved and invested parents. Their contact and involvement with their children, however, was very much subject to their distant relationships with their wives. In the married couple group, most were unconcerned about the care their children were receiving back in Mexico in their grandparents' home. They felt that their children were getting quality care (if not getting a bit spoiled) and they anticipated returning in a few years with greater accumulated wealth to improve their children's lives. Single Mexican mothers living in the United States, however, expressed the greatest level of distress and often experienced a loss of contact with their children because they had to leave them with their ex-husband who limited their contacts and refused their gifts for the children.

Some of the biggest gender differences in parenting had to do with the importance of instrumental versus emotional providing roles of mothers and fathers. Fathers often lost contact with their children because they felt guilty about their inability to provide financial support. Mothers expressed greater emotional distress about leaving their children behind in Mexico and felt more like they were abandoning their children as events kept them from maintaining high levels of contact.

Source: Joanna Dreby, "Honor and Virtue: Mexican Parenting in the Transnational Context," *Gender and Society*, 20 (2006): 32–59.

conclusion that corporal punishment significantly contributes to both psychological distress and depression among youth and even to committing animal cruelty as preteens and teenagers.[18]

In brief, the development of self-esteem, sound mental health or well-being, or any other aspect of internalizing definitions of the self must be viewed in a sociocultural context. Because everyone learns in interaction with others, attention must be

---

[18]Heather A. Turner and David Finkelhor, "Corporal Punishment as a Stressor among Youth," *Journal of Marriage and the Family* 58 (February 1996): 155–166; and Clifton P. Flynn, "Exploring the Link between Corporal Punishment and Children's Cruelty to Animals," *Journal of Marriage and the Family* 61 (November 1999): 971–981.

paid to *culturally prescribed meanings* of socialization behaviors as well as to *social structural variations* in which the socialization occurs.

Theories of Socialization

Socialization refers to the lifelong process by which people learn the ways of a given society and culture and develop into participants capable of operating in that society. A number of relatively comprehensive theories have been developed to explain various aspects of this process. Reviewing several of these theories can illustrate the ways in which different assumptions and conceptual frameworks lead to differing ways of understanding the process by which you and I become social beings.

Learning/Behaviorist Frame of Reference

Learning theory—also recognized as *reinforcement theory, stimulus/response theory,* and *behaviorism*—assumes the same concepts and principles that apply to lower animals also apply to humans. Thus, it is logical and rational to spend time in the laboratory experimenting with rats, cats, dogs, pigeons, monkeys, and other animals to learn more about humans. Although there are many variations of learning theory, as with the theories that follow, basic assumptions and common lines of agreement do exist.

Learning, or socialization, as applied to the newborn infant, involves changes in behavior that result from experience. (This is opposed to changes in behavior that result from physiological maturation or biological conditions.) Learning involves conditioning that may include classical conditioning or instrumental (operant) conditioning.

Classical conditioning links a response to a known stimulus. Many people are familiar with Pavlov's dog experiment, which provides a good example of classical conditioning. The hungry dog, placed in a soundproof room, heard a tuning fork prior to receiving meat. After repetition of the pattern, the dog began to salivate as soon as the tuning fork sounded, prior to receiving—and even *without* receiving—the meat. The tuning fork, a conditioned stimulus, produced the response, salivation. In the classical conditioning experiment, the focus of attention is largely on the stimulus. If conditioning works with dogs, the same principle should hold true with infants upon hearing their mothers' voices or approaching footsteps. The voice or footstep stimulus, with repeated occurrences, should elicit a response from the child.

Instrumental conditioning, or what Skinner called **operant conditioning**, places the focus of attention on the response. The response is not related to any known stimuli; rather, it functions in an instrumental fashion. One learns to make a certain response on the basis of the consequences that the response produces. It is the response, rather than the stimulus, that correlates with reinforcement. Return to the example of the hungry dog. Under classical conditioning, the dog salivated upon hearing the tuning fork, the stimulus. Under operant conditioning, the hungry dog would sniff, paw, and chew whatever was around. If, upon pawing, the dog opened a door behind which was food, the sniffing and chewing would soon decrease and the pawing on the door would occur whenever food was desired. Thus, instrumental conditioning is a response followed by a reward (reinforcement).

How does this apply to an infant? Suppose the infant utters sounds such as "da-da-da." Father, who is convinced the child is saying "Daddy," rewards him or her by picking up, feeding, or rocking the child. As a result, the infant uses the response ("da-da-da") all day long. The infant has learned to make a certain response on the basis of the consequence or result the response has produced; hence, the response is correlated with reinforcement.

These same general principles—refined by behaviorists with reference to intermittent reinforcement, partial reinforcement, negative and positive reinforcement, discrimination of stimuli, differentiation of response, behavior modification, and the like—apply in learning any kind of behavior. Socialization results from stimulus/ response conditioning and from positive and negative reinforcements and punishments. Individuals adopt behaviors that bring about positive rewards (**positive reinforcement**) and avoid engaging in behaviors that bring negative consequences (**punishment**). They also adopt behaviors that bring about the termination of negative conditions—a kind of reward (**negative reinforcement**). In fact, negative reinforcement is an important part of the **coercion theory** of parent-child interaction.[19] This theory explains how a parent and child can get trapped in cycles of escalating negative behaviors and how these cycles can then contribute to the development of antisocial behavior. When a child makes a request for something and is refused, it often escalates the emotional intensity of the request. If the parent responds with an increasingly negative refusal, the child will often further escalate its demand behavior. As this series of *aversive* behaviors continues to escalate, eventually the parent ends the episode. By this time, whether or not the parent gives in to the initial request becomes irrelevant. The entire cycle of interaction is reinforced by the fact that the parent stopped being aversive as a result of the child's continued escalation of demand behaviors—a more positive condition than what existed during the conflict.

The conditioning stimuli (classical conditioning) and the consequences of responses (operant conditioning) are both *external* to the animal or human. Within the learning theory/behaviorist framework, symbols, language, reasoning, internalized meanings, and other internal processes play a minimal role. This is in sharp contrast to the symbolic interaction framework (introduced in the first chapter and discussed further in this section), in which socialized beings can create their own stimuli and responses, can define and categorize, can distinguish between self and others, can separate inner and outer sensations, and can take the role of the other. As a result, the behaviorist approach to socialization is accepted with considerable reservation by most sociologists, to whom the self, roles, reference groups, symbolic processes, and meanings *internal* to the individual are viewed as central to understanding human behavior. Although learning theory has been extremely illuminating in research with animals and infants, it has been less successful in explaining social situations, group norms, and the learning of language itself.

Psychoanalytic Frame of Reference

Classic psychoanalytic theory, developed by Sigmund Freud and his adherents, stresses the importance of biological drives and unconscious processes. This theory is in sharp contrast to the behaviorist theory just described.

The process of socialization, according to this framework, consists of a number of precise though overlapping stages of development. What happens at these stages, from birth to age 5 or 6, although unconscious, becomes relatively fixed and permanent. These stages are referred to as the *oral*, *anal*, and *phallic* stages, followed later by a period of *latency* and then a *genital* phase. Attention

---

[19]Gary R. Peterson, "The Aggressive Child: Victim and Architect of a Coercive System," in E.J. Marsh, E.A. Hammerlynck and L.C. Handy, eds., *Behavior Modification and Families* (New York: Brunner/Mazel, 1976): 267–316.

Same sex parents present a challenge to the psychoanalytic perspective. Research to date shows no significant deficit and no abnormal personality traits among children raised by same-sex parents.

is focused on three principal erogenous zones—the mouth, the anus, and the genitals—which are the regions of the body where excitatory processes tend to become focalized and where tensions can be removed by some action such as stroking or sucking. These regions are of extreme importance in the socialization process because they are the first important sources of irritating excitations with which the baby has to contend and upon which the first pleasurable experiences occur.

The first stage of development, the **oral stage**, occurs during the first year of the child's life. The earliest erotic gratifications come from the mouth, and as a result, the child forms strong emotional attachments to the mother, who supplies the source of food, warmth, and sucking. During the first year, the child is narcissistic; self-gratification is derived via the oral source, namely, the mouth. The mouth's functions include taking in, holding on, biting, spitting out, and closing—all prototypes for ways of adjusting to painful or disturbing states. These functions serve as models for adaptations in later life.

The **anal stage** of development follows and overlaps with the oral stage. This phase is so called because the child experiences pleasure in excretion and because toilet training may become a major problem. At this point, two functions become central: retention and elimination. Because the mother is still the predominant figure in the child's life, her methods of training the child and her attitudes about such matters as defecation, cleanliness, and control are said to determine the impact that toilet training will have on the development of the person. Carried to the extreme, the mother who praises the child for a large bowel movement may produce adolescents or adults who will be motivated to produce or create things to please others or to please themselves, as they once made feces to please their mothers. On the other hand, if the mother is very strict and punitive, the child may intentionally soil himself or herself and, as an adolescent or adult, be messy, irresponsible, disorderly, wasteful, and extravagant.

The **phallic stage** is the period of growth during which the child is preoccupied with the genitals. Prior to this stage, the first love object of both the boy and girl is the mother. But in the phallic stage, the sexual urge increases, the boy's love for his mother becomes more intense, and the result is jealousy of the father, who is seen as the boy's rival. The boy's attachment to his mother is widely known as the Oedipus complex. Concurrently, the boy becomes fearful that his father will remove his (the boy's) genitals and develops a fear known as castration anxiety. This anxiety increases on observation of the female, who has, in his unconscious mind, already been castrated. A similar or reverse process is in operation for the female. She forms an attachment to her father, the Electra complex, but has mixed feelings for him because he possesses something that she does not have. The result is penis envy. According to traditional Freudian psychology, penis envy is the key to feminine psychology. Located in this phenomenon are the roots of male dominance and female submissiveness, male superiority and female inferiority.

The oral, anal, and phallic stages taken together are called the pregenital period and occur in the first five or six years of one's life. These are the important years during which basic personality patterns are established and fixed. Following this time, for the next five or six years until the onset of puberty, the male and female egos go through a **latency phase**, during which the erotic desires of children are repressed and they form attachments to the parent of the same sex.

Finally, with the arrival of puberty, the **genital phase** of development begins. This period is less a stage than the final working out of the previous ones, particularly the oral, anal, and phallic stages that occurred during the pregenital period. During the genital phase, group activities, marriage, establishing a home, and developing vocational responsibilities and adult interests become the focus of attention. Given the importance of the early years, one can readily understand why factors such as bottle- or breast-feeding, nursing on a regular or self-demand time schedule, weaning abruptly or gradually, bowel training early or late, bladder training early or late, punishment or nonpunishment for toilet accidents, and sleeping alone or with one's mother serve as crucial developments to the Freudian psychoanalyst.

Freudian claims regarding the importance of infant training to personality adjustment have received mixed empirical support. What support exists has, in general, been derived from clinical studies of emotionally disturbed individuals. Other studies have shown different results. For example, one attempt to test empirically the crucial role of infant discipline in character formation and personality adjustment was published about fifty years ago and has since become a somewhat classic article on the subject.[20] That study set up a series of null hypotheses concerning the relationship of specific infant disciplines to subsequent personality adjustments. The general hypothesis was that the personality adjustment and traits of children who had undergone varying infant-training experiences would not differ significantly from each other. These infant-training experiences included the self-demand feeding schedule, gradual weaning, late bowel training, and similar factors. The results supported the null hypothesis; that is, there were no significant differences in the personality adjustments of children who had undergone varying infant-training experiences. Such practices as breast-feeding, gradual weaning, demand schedule, bowel training, and bladder training, which have been so emphasized in the psychoanalytic literature, were almost completely insignificant in terms of their relationship to personality adjustment.

---

[20]William H. Sewall, "Infant Training and the Personality of the Child," *The American Journal of Sociology* 58 (September 1952): 150–159.

Child Development Frames of Reference: Erikson and Piaget

The ideas of Erik Erikson and Jean Piaget are also of interest in dealing with the socialization issue. Like Freud, both focused primarily on stages of development. Unlike Freud, both extended their stages beyond the early years and placed more importance on social structure and reasoning.

Erik Erikson, one of Freud's students, was a psychoanalyst who saw socialization as a lifelong process, beginning at birth and continuing into old age. Erikson is well known for developing his theory of the eight stages of human development.[21] Each stage constitutes a crisis brought on by physiological changes and the constantly changing social situation.

In infancy (the first year), the crisis centers around *trust versus mistrust*. In early childhood (the first two to three years), the issue centers around *autonomy versus shame and doubt*. The play stage (age 4 or 5) involves the issue of *initiative versus guilt*. From school age up to adolescence, the issue is *industry versus inferiority*.

In adolescence, the issue is *identity versus role confusion*. **Identity**, the focal concern of Erikson, is defined as being able to achieve a sense of continuity about one's past, present, and future. Young adulthood, another major turning point in life, involves the issue of *intimacy versus isolation*. In young adulthood and middle age, the issue is *generativity versus stagnation*. Old age, the last stage of development, is a time of reflection and evaluation and focuses on the issue of *integrity versus despair*.

In sum, Erikson sees the social order as resulting from and being in harmony with these eight stages of development. As people work out solutions to these developmental concerns, those solutions become institutionalized in the culture.

Jean Piaget, a Swiss social psychologist, spent more than thirty years observing and studying the development of intellectual functions and logic in children.[22] His work has stimulated an interest in maturational stages of development and in the importance of cognition in human development. Differing dramatically from supporters of the learning and psychoanalytic frames of reference, Piaget characterized development as an ability to reason abstractly, to think about hypothetical situations in a logical way, and to organize rules (which he called *operations*) into complex, higher-order structures. For instance, children are able to invent ideas and behaviors they have never witnessed or had reinforced.

Piaget asserted that there are four major stages of intellectual development:

1. *Sensorimotor*—0 to 18 months old
2. *Preoperational*—18 months to 7 years old
3. *Concrete operational*—7 to 12 years old
4. *Formal operational*—12 years old and up

The stages are continuous; each is built on and is derived from the earlier one.

The **sensorimotor stage** is characterized by children's physical understanding of themselves and the world. Unlearned responses, such as sucking and closing one's fist, become repetitive, but at first the child performs them with no intent, purpose, or interest in the effect this behavior has on the environment. Later in this first stage, activities become more intentional. The **preoperational stage** involves language and its acquisition. Objects are treated as symbolic of things other than themselves. For example, a doll may be treated as a baby, or a stick may be treated as a gun or a sword. At this stage, overt actions and the meanings of objects and

---

[21]Erik K. Erikson, *Childhood and Society*, 2nd ed. (New York: Norton, 1963), Chapter 7.

[22]Jean Piaget and Barbara Inhelder, *The Psychology of the Child* (New York: Basic, 1969); and Jean Piaget, *The Construction of Reality in the Child* (New York: Basic, 1954).

Child development experts such as Erikson and Piaget saw cognitive development and the ability to reason beginning in children at a very early age. Socializing agents such as parents, siblings, grandparents, and others are essential to this process.

events are manipulated, but the child has difficulty seeing the point of view of another child or adult.

During the **concrete operational stage**, children learn to manipulate the tools of their culture and also learn that mass remains constant in spite of changes in form. They learn to understand cause and effect, to classify objects, to consider the viewpoints of others, and to differentiate between dreams and reality. By approximately age twelve, the child enters the adult world and the stage of formal operations. The **formal operational stage** is characterized by the ability to think in terms of abstract concepts, theories, and general principles. Alternate solutions to problems can be formulated, and hypothetical propositions can be formulated and answered. Preoccupation with thought is the principal component of this stage of development.

Piaget's insights into cognitive development are unsurpassed. His stages take into account both social and psychological phenomena. Like Freud, Piaget had a specific conception of the goals of maturity and adulthood. Also like Freud, Piaget believed that the child passes through stages. But whereas Freud emphasized emotional maturity and the unconscious as extremely important, Piaget emphasized reasoning and consciousness. And whereas Freud focused on bodily zones, Piaget focused on the quality of reasoning.

The frames of reference covered up to this point can be summarized by suggesting that the learning theorists are concerned with overt behavior, the Freudians with motives and emotions (often unconscious and rooted early in childhood), and the child developmentalists with motor skills, thought, reasoning processes, and conflicts. The symbolic interaction frame of reference, discussed next, shares many assumptions of Erikson and Piaget in the importance given to language, reasoning, and societal influences.

Symbolic Interaction Frame of Reference

Contrasting considerably with the learning and psychoanalytic frames of reference is the symbolic interaction frame of reference. Within this framework, the first five years of life are considered important, but it is not believed that personality becomes fixed; rather, socialization is a lifelong process. Although mothers are important figures, so too are fathers, siblings, grandparents, teachers, and many others perceived as significant to the child or adult.

To understand socialization as explained within a symbolic interaction frame of reference, it is necessary to review the basic assumptions and meanings of key concepts such as *social self*, *significant others*, and *reference group*.

Basic Assumptions

As summarized in the first chapter, the interactionist frame of reference, when applied to the study of the family and to an understanding of socialization, is based on several basic assumptions. Four basic assumptions of symbolic interactionism were delineated by Sheldon Stryker several decades ago.[23]

Stryker's first assumption is that *humans must be studied on their own level.* Symbolic interactionism is antireductionistic. If one wants to understand socialization, infant development, and parent–child relationships among humans, then one must study humans and not infer their behavior from the study of nonhuman or infrahuman forms of life.

The basic difference between *human* and *infrahuman* is not simply a matter of *degree* but one of *kind.* The evolutionary process involves quantitative differences among species, not merely qualitative ones. Human/nonhuman differences include language, symbols, meanings, gestures, and related processes.

Thus, to understand a person's social development and behavior, relatively little can be gained by observing chimpanzees, dogs, pigeons, or rats. Social life—unlike biological, physiological life or any nonhuman form—involves sharing meanings and communicating symbolically. Using language and gestures, human beings can correspond with one another, relaying intentions and meanings.

This assumption is in direct contrast with the behaviorist assumption, which suggests that humans can best be understood by studying forms of life other than human. Psychologists who assume the difference between humans and animals is one of degree can explain and control those who do not share meanings or communicate with one another at a symbolic level: infants, isolated children, and people who are extremely psychotic, severely retarded, brain damaged, or aphasic. To the interactionist, the possession of language enables humans alone to deal with events in terms of the past, present, or future and to imagine objects or events that may be remote in space or entirely nonexistent.

Saying the lower animals do not have culture may summarize the differences between socialized human beings and the lower animals (or between human families and nonhuman families). They have no system of beliefs, values, and ideas shared and symbolically transmitted among the group. Animals have no familial, educational, religious, political, or economic institutions. They have no foreign languages, art, literature, Supreme Being to pray to, or a philosophy that gives life meaning. They have no sets of moral codes, norms, or ideologies. In short, they are not human.

Similarities between the animal and human worlds often are stressed, but equal emphasis should be given to understanding and focusing on the differences. Recognizing these differences, symbolic interactionists assume one must

---

[23]Sheldon Stryker, "The International and Situational Approaches," in *Handbook of Marriage and the Family*, ed. by Harold T. Christensen (Chicago: Rand McNally, 1964): 134–136; and Sheldon Stryker, "Symbolic Interaction Theory: A Review and Some Suggestions for Comparative Family Research," *Journal of Comparative Family Studies* 3 (Spring 1972): 17–32.

study humans to understand humans. Thus, very little can be learned about socialization—of any people in any lifestyle or social class—by studying nonhuman forms.

Stryker's second assumption is that the *most fruitful approach to social behavior is through the analysis of society.* One can best understand the behavior of a husband, wife, or child through a study and an analysis of the society and subculture of which they are a part. Personal behavior is not exclusively or even primarily an individual phenomenon but is predominantly a social one. The assumption is not made that society is the ultimate reality, nor that society has some metaphysical priority over the individual, nor that cultural determinism explains all behavior. Neither biogenic nor psychogenic factors are excluded as important in explaining or understanding behavior. However, these factors are not salient variables.

Being born into a given society means that the language one speaks, how one defines situations, and the appropriateness or inappropriateness one assigns to any activity are learned within that social and cultural context. Thus, the behavior of a couple from the rural Philippines, who would not be seen holding hands in public, versus the behavior of a U.S. couple, kissing and caressing in a public park, can only be understood by analyzing the society in which each of these behaviors takes place.

Stryker's third assumption is that the *human infant at birth is asocial.* Original nature lacks organization. Thus, the infant is neither social nor antisocial (as with original sin in certain religions or the id in the psychoanalytic scheme). The "equipment" with which newborns enter life does, however, give them the potential for social development.

Society and the specific social context in which a behavior occurs determine whether that behavior is social or antisocial. A newborn infant does not cry all night to punish or displease parents, nor does he or she sleep all night to please them. Only after these expectations become internalized do social and antisocial acts take on meaning. Although the newborn infant has impulses, as does any biological organism, these impulses are not channeled or directed toward any specific ends. But, having the potential for social development, the human infant can, with time and training, organize these impulses and channel them in specific directions. This process, by which the newborn infant becomes a social being, is the main concern of social psychologists, who are interested in the process of socialization, and of family sociologists, who are interested in child rearing.

Stryker's final assumption is that *a socialized human being* (meaning one who can communicate symbolically and share meanings) *is an actor as well as a reactor.* This does not mean merely that one person acts and another reacts. Socialized human beings do not simply respond to stimuli from the external environment. Rather, humans respond to a symbolic environment that involves both responses to interpreted as well as anticipated stimuli. Humans can talk to themselves, think through alternative courses of action, feel guilty over past behaviors, and dream of future possibilities.

That humans are actors as well as reactors suggests that investigators cannot understand behavior only by studying the external environment and external forces; they must see the world from the viewpoint of the subject of their investigation. Humans not only respond to stimuli but also select and interpret them. As a result, it becomes crucial and essential that this interpretation and meaning be known. It is this final assumption of Stryker's that most precisely differentiates symbolic interactionists from positivists in sociology, and behaviorists in psychology.

The assumption that humans are both actors and reactors suggests that humans alone can take the roles of others; that is, they can view the world from perspectives of other people. Thus, one can put oneself "in someone else's shoes," feeling sad over the misfortune of a friend or sharing the joys of one's children. A professor can take the role of the student and anticipate his or her response to a three-hour lecture or a certain type of exam without giving either the lecture or the exam. A wife can anticipate the response of her husband to an embrace or to inviting friends to dinner. The predictions of the professor and the wife may be inaccurate, but the perception and meaning or definition attached to the situation will influence and direct behavior. In short, a person's behavior is not simply a response to others but also is a self-stimulating response: a response to internal symbolic productions.

Development of a Social Self

Self is the key concept in understanding socialization and personality. Self, although often defined in psychological and personal terms, is a social phenomenon. Self is developed in interaction with others. The process of socialization, a primary concern of child rearing and that which makes humans social beings, is the development of a social self: the organization of internalized roles.

A woman may occupy the statuses of wife, mother, sister, student, executive, Methodist, and many others. Each status has expectations (roles) assigned to it. A person must know how each role is related to the others, and all these roles must be organized and integrated into some reasonable, consistent unity. This organization of internalized roles is the **social self**.

This organization and internalization of roles occurs in interaction with others; the social self is never fixed, static, or in a final state. George Herbert Mead used the term *self* to mean simply that persons are the object of their own activities; they can act toward themselves as they act toward others.[24] Thus, one can talk to oneself or feel proud, ashamed, or guilty of oneself.

Who one is, how she or he feels, what she or he wants, and so on constitute the social self. One's social self consists of self-concepts, self-perceptions, and definitions of self-worth and self-esteem. **Personality** then, consists of these definitions of self with the predisposition to act and behave consistently. The person who is convinced she is not capable of passing the exam, not attractive enough to meet that special person, or not able to fulfill the expectations of a job may position herself for failure. A self-fulfilling prophecy may become operative. That is, the person will fail at the very thing she "knew" would bring failure. The opposite is equally true. Believing that one can do something increases the probability that one *will* do it.

These self-concepts and senses of self-worth develop in interaction with others. Such feelings and values do not exist at birth but must be internalized; that is, they must be learned. It does not take much imagination to assess the central role that a spouse, sibling, parent, grandparent, friend, teacher, or classmate—that is, family and nonfamily members alike—may play in the development of the social self and in influencing one's self-esteem and sense of worth. In turn, low self-esteem becomes a strong factor in poor school performance and feelings of depression and anxiety.

Significant Others and Reference Groups

Significant others and reference groups are of central importance in understanding the development of the child and modification of the social self. Not all persons or groups are of equal importance to individuals. Certain persons and groups—again, in processes of interaction—come to be perceived as more important, as more significant, and as sources of reference. These persons and groups

---

[24]George Herbert Mead, *Mind, Self and Society* (Chicago: University of Chicago Press, 1934).

news item

Experts Dispute Bush on Gay-Adoption Issue

Are children worse off being raised by gay or lesbian couples than by heterosexual parents? Responding on Thursday to a question about gay adoption, President Bush suggested that they were. "Studies have shown," Mr. Bush said in an interview with *The New York Times*, "that the ideal is where a child is raised in a married family with a man and a woman."

But experts say there is no scientific evidence that children raised by gay couples do any worse—socially, academically or emotionally—than their peers raised in more traditional households.

The experts, who cross the political spectrum, say studies have shown that on average, children raised by two married heterosexual parents fare better on a number of measures, including school performance, than those raised by single parents or by parents who are living together but are unmarred.

But, said Dr. Judith Stacey, a professor of sociology at New York University, "There is not a single legitimate scholar out there who argues that growing up with gay parents is somehow bad for children."

Dr. Stacey, who published a critical review of studies on the subject in 2001 and has argued in favor of allowing adoption by gays, added, "The debate among scientists is all about how good the studies we have really are."

"You can't force families to participate, and there aren't that many of them out there to start with," said Dr. J. Michael Bailey, a professor of psychology at Northwestern University who has studied gay men raising boys. "There is also a strong volunteer bias: the families who want to participate might be much more open about sexual orientation" and eager to report positive outcomes, Dr. Bailey said.

Critics of the studies have more often charged that it is the researchers who are biased, failing to probe aggressively enough to find differences.

"In many of these studies, they simply aren't asking hard questions," said Lynn Wardle, a law professor at Brigham Young University who has argued against adoption by gay couples. The researchers, Professor Wardle said, ask the families about the children's self-esteem, "about whether they have friends—soft and fuzzy questions—but not about sexual behavior, sexually transmitted disease and drug use."

One undisputed reality for children raised by gay parents is that they tend to face teasing, discrimination, and bullying in the schoolyard because of who their parents are. That many of these children can navigate such nastiness, on top of the usual social and emotional squalls of growing up, and still be found as well adjusted as their peers on standard psychological tests is remarkable in itself, some researchers say.

As the political debate over same-sex parents becomes more contentious, the quality of the research appears to be getting better, some social scientists say. Last month psychologists at the University of Virginia and the University of Arizona published a study of 44 adolescents from all over the country being raised in female same-sex households.

The families, with a variety of income levels, were drawn from a huge, continuing national family survey. The survey was random, and therefore unaffected by the sort of volunteer bias created when, say, families with good stories to tell respond to advertisements placed by investigators. In addition, the interviews were conducted by a team of government researchers who were interested in a wide array of social and demographic factors, all but eliminating the researcher bias that some critics point to.

The survey's results, published in the journal Child Development, confirmed some previous findings: the 44 girls and boys were typical American teenagers, the researchers found, no more confused or moody than a comparison group of 44 peers from similar but traditional families. "They even reported being more involved at school, in clubs, after-school activities, things like that," said the report's senior author, Dr. Charlotte Patterson, a professor of psychology at the University of Virginia. "I have no idea what that means, but we sure didn't expect it."

Source: www.nytimes.com/2005/01/29/politics/29marry.html? ei=507&en=c0cf490e3f6b. Copyright © 2005 by The New York Times Co. Reprinted with permission.

with which one psychologically identifies are termed, respectively, **significant others** and **reference groups**.

To most infants and young children, Mother is a significant person, that is, an object of emotional involvement, especially in the child's development. Note that *Mother*, in terms of interaction and involvement, is a social, not a biological, concept. As a result, an adoptive parent, foster parent, grandparent, or other person— male or female—can fulfill the expectations (roles) of Mother. And Mother (socially or biologically) is not the only significant other. Fathers, siblings, peers, teachers, athletes, and movie stars are all important people with whom one psychologically identifies. To do so is to attempt to conform to the expectations one perceives these people have of oneself. An attempt is made to please and receive approval from those others who are significant.

As children or adults interact with other people, they will become interested in some and attached to others; it follows that they will share certain expectations and behaviors with those people. Significant others are perceived as role models. Personal behavior and thinking are patterned on the conduct of these persons. Uncle Pete the pilot or Marcia the teacher, as a significant other, may each play a decisive part in the socialization and development of one's social self. A sister or brother, a boyfriend or girlfriend, or a television figure may become a role model, a significant other, and thus a person with whom one psychologically identifies.

In addition to persons viewed as significant, groups (real or imaginary) are used as frames of reference with which a person psychologically identifies. These groups, generally termed *reference groups*, are any from which individuals seek acceptance or that they use as a source of comparison. A church, a club, or a company may serve as a point of reference in making comparisons or contrasts, especially in forming judgments about oneself. In some instances, a person may attempt to gain membership or acceptance in the group, although this is not always the case. These groups, like significant others, serve as standards for conduct, as bases for self-evaluation, and as sources of attitude formation.

To most adolescents, peers rather than parents are key reference groups. Peers— who understand the adolescent and share his or her world—become a reference point for sizing up problems, strivings, and ambitions. Including peers as a source of reference may help one understand why the values of adolescents appear more like those of similar-age youth than those of parents.

Peers as a source of reference may also help one understand that behavior defined as deviant by parents may be given social approval by peers. Using drugs or alcohol, engaging in sexual intercourse, dating interracially, adopting a particular political stance, and the like may be conforming behavior to peers. The antisocial behavior of adolescents, as viewed by parents, may simply mean that the adolescent is "in step with a different drummer" (peers).

Socialization Stages and Interaction Processes

The importance of the early years cannot be denied. Very early experiences provide infants with their first sense of self, other people, and social relationships. The mother usually becomes the first, primary, and most significant other. Scolding, slapping, pampering, or praising may not be crucial per se, but their repetitive nature leads to internalization of a sense of self-worth and an image of oneself. Although the mother is crucial in the development of these images, so are the father, siblings, other kin, and friends. Although the mother may carry out most infant care, the socialization experiences of many infants include interaction with members of the nuclear family, extended family, and others.

Mead's Stages of Observation

In the development of the self, Mead postulated that children go through three continuous *stages of observation*: preparatory, play, and game.[25] In the **preparatory stage**, children do not have the ability to view their own behavior. Actions of others are imitated. As described under the learning frame of reference and also under the interaction frame of reference, certain sounds, such as "da-da-da," bring attention and response from others. This operant conditioning leads the child to repeat and learn the sounds.

The second stage, overlapping with and continuing the preparatory stage, is the **play stage**. At this point, children take roles of others; that is, they play at being whom they observe. A child may sweep the floor, put on a hat, or pretend to read a book. Elkin and Handel described a four-year-old "playing Daddy" who put on his hat and coat, said "goodbye," and walked out the front door, only to return a few minutes later because he did not know what to do next.[26]

Later, children enter the **game stage**. At this point, they do not merely play or take the roles of others; they now participate in games involving an organization of roles and the development of self. At this point, they have to recognize the expected behaviors of everyone else, which involves responding to the expectations of several other people at the same time. This mental construct is termed the **generalized other**. In Mead's famous example of the baseball game,

> the child must have the responses of each position involved in his own position. He must know what everyone else is going to do in order to carry out his own play. He has to take all of these roles. They do not all have to be present in consciousness at the same time, but at some moments he has to have three or four individuals present in his own attitude, such as the one who is going to throw the ball, the one who is going to catch it, and so on. These responses must be, in some degree, present in his own makeup.[27]

The concept of generalized other enables one to understand how given individuals may be consistent in their behavior even though they move in varying social environments. People learn to see themselves from the standpoints of multiple others who are either physically or symbolically present.

In light of this perspective of socialization, it should be recognized that any behavior results less from drives and needs, unconscious processes, and biological characteristics than from interaction processes and internalized meanings of self and others. As a result, the behavior appropriate to whites or blacks, royalty or outcasts, Jews or gentiles, or males or females is dependent less on skin color, genital makeup, and other biological facts than on the internalized meanings and definitions that result from interaction with others. These interactions, viewed in their broadest context, include schools, peers, the mass media, and all involvement of daily living.

Socialization in Adolescence and Beyond

Most books on socialization, most chapters on child rearing, and the greatest public interest in both topics generally focus on the young child. Perhaps this is readily understandable, since, to the newborn child, the entire world is new. Even the most common and routine events must be learned. But if socialization involves learning roles and the ways of a given society and culture and leads to the development of members

---

[25]Mead, *Mind, Self and Society*, 150.
[26]Elkin and Handel, *The Child and Society*, 57.
[27]Mead, *Mind, Self and Society*, 151.

Family Diversity

Preparing and Protecting Adolescents in Minority Communities

Cultural values and ecological contexts play a significant role in the strategies minority parents use to monitor and control their adolescent children's activities inside and outside the home. Both Hispanic Americans and African Americans must face more hostile and less certain external environments, both from deviant subcultures as well as from social control agents. The likelihood that minority adolescents will be arrested for a minor crime or for just being in the wrong place and the wrong time is much higher than it is for Anglo Americans. Although a police officer might choose to advise a white teen's parents of his or her misbehavior rather than make an arrest, a minority teen is more likely to be arrested. As a result, patterns of independence giving to adolescents outside the home are higher among whites than they are for the other two groups of parents. Differences exist, however, between Hispanic Americans and African Americans when it comes to independence giving both inside and outside the home.

Among Hispanic Americans two dominant cultural themes are familism and patriarchy and these themes affect how Hispanic parents relate to their sons and daughters. Although daughters are highly restricted both inside and outside the home early in adolescence, sons are given much more freedom outside the home. In later adolescence, however, girls are given more freedom outside the home (perhaps to establish new families), while more restrictions are placed on boys outside activities (perhaps to prepare them for their roles as family leaders). Among African American parents, cultural values placed on collectivism and community parenting combined with high risks of teenage pregnancy for girls likely lead to a reverse pattern. These parents give girls more freedoms outside the home early in adolescence and boys less. With age, however, the activities of girls are more closely monitored and more strictly controlled; whereas, the boys are released to engage in activities more freely outside the home.

Source: Richard A. Bulcroft, Dianne Cyr Carmody, and Kris A. Bulcroft, "Patterns of Parental Independence Giving to Adolescents: Variations by Race, Age, and Gender of Child. *Journal of Marriage and the Family,* 58 (1996): 866–883.

who are capable of operating in society, then how can anyone argue that socialization is complete after five or six years of life? Particularly in a rapidly changing society, such as exists in the United States, persons are newcomers to unfamiliar events almost daily. Without a doubt, early socialization experiences will have a major influence and impact on the types of events and experiences that are acceptable or unacceptable. But socialization is a continuous process. What's more, learning experiences after the early years mean not only incorporating the new but also discarding much of the old.

Adolescence is a period of active engagement in sex-role identification, learning the norms and expectations of the opposite sex, participating in new and different types of social activities, gaining insights and skills for the future occupational world, attempting to become emancipated from parents, and developing a new sense of self-reliance. Parents continue to be important agents of socialization, but their influence declines during the adolescent years while peer influence increases. An analysis of data collected annually over a four-year period of boys, girls, and their parents revealed that ineffective parenting during late childhood predicted increases in affiliation with deviant peers and involvement in delinquent behavior during adolescence.[28] Improvements in parenting during adolescence decreased delinquency indirectly by reducing affiliation with deviant peers.

---

[28]Ronald L. Simons, Wei Chao, Rand D. Conger, and Glen H. Elder, "Quality of Parenting as Mediator of the Effect of Childhood Deviance on Adolescent Friendship Choices and Delinquency: A Growth Curve Analysis," *Journal of Marriage and Family* 63 (February 2001): 63–79.

Furstenberg, in providing a critical commentary on adolescent research in the 1990s, indicated that the vast majority of studies of youth are focused on the problematic features of adolescence and explicitly on problem behavior.[29] Considerable attention was devoted to changes in the settings in which adolescents spent time: at home, with peers, in school, in the community, and at work. Time spent outside the household increases at the expense of family time, meaning that direct parental supervision declines, whereas contact with peers increases.

During the teen years, these settings of home, peers, school, community, as well as the influence of the media are powerful and pervading socializing forces. A life course perspective on socialization emphasizes the interdependence of life histories and the potential for both continuity and change. For example, an examination of daughters' gender ideology provides support for the childhood socialization theory but also points to the importance of the daughters' own status achievement.[30] That is, there is an intergenerational transmission of gender and work role identity as well as the daughter's own life experiences.

Even though socialization does not end at adolescence, research interest in this topic declines. In regard to persons ages 20 through 60, a mythical assumption seems to exist, namely, that socialization to new roles, tasks, and activities either does not exist or is unnecessary. The social self, it seems, is believed to be relatively stable or even fixed in these adult years; thus, adult socialization is not an exciting or vital area for research. One exception is the topic of people at retirement; literature has made reference to the need for resocialization to new lifestyles associated with aging and people who are aged.

Gender Identity and Sex-Role Socialization

Confusion often exists over concepts such as *sex*, *sex roles*, *gender roles*, and *gender identity*. Precisely, one's sex, regardless of behavior, refers to the biological condition of being male or female. **Sex roles**, therefore, refer to the expectations associated with being biologically of one sex or the other. *Gender*, in contrast to sex, is the umbrella term that refers to the totality of being male or female, masculine or feminine. **Gender roles** are, thus, the expectations associated with being masculine or feminine, which may or may not correspond precisely with one's sex. A statement such as, *he* (biological male) acts *feminine* (gender expectation), is one example of how sex and gender can be differentiated. **Gender identity** refers to the way one defines or perceives oneself in terms of one's sex—as male or female, as masculine or feminine, or as heterosexual, bisexual, or homosexual.

Does the sexual orientation of the parents matter in the formation of sexual or gender identity? For example, opponents of lesbian or gay parental rights claim that children raised by parents with these sexual orientations are at a higher risk for a variety of negative outcomes: confusion over their gender and sexual identities, becoming homosexual themselves, being molested, being more prone to delinquency, substance abuse, teen pregnancy, suicide, or dropping out of school, suffering greater risks of depression and other emotional difficulties, and not having only one "real" father or mother, among others. Stacey and Biblarz question these claims and conclude that social science research provides no grounds for

---

[29]Frank F. Furstenberg, "The Sociology of Adolescence and Youth in the 1990s: A Critical Commentary," *Journal of Marriage and the Family* 62 (November 2000): 896–910.

[30]Phyllis Moen, Mary Ann Erickson, and Donna Dempster-McClain, "Their Mother's Daughters? The Intergenerational Transmission of Gender Attitudes in a World of Changing Roles," *Journal of Marriage and the Family* 59 (May 1997): 281–293.

taking sexual orientation into account in the political distribution of family rights and responsibilities.[31] They suggest that homophobia and discrimination are the chief reasons why parental sexual orientation matters at all in the raising of children or in their developing sexual preferences and behaviors.

Sexual or gender identity formation is a developmental process but one that does not always move through stages in an orderly sequence. For example, one study of more than 400 lesbians and bisexual women noted that these women experienced periods of ambivalence during which they wondered about their sexual identities as well as periods during which they had no particular sexual identity. Bisexual-identified women became aware of their homosexual feelings and questioned their heterosexual identities at older ages than lesbian-identified women. Identities changed as a result of available social constructs, the sociopolitical landscape, and their own positions on that landscape.[32]

Female–Male Differences

There is no denying that normatively, attitudinally, behaviorally, and physically, males and females differ. Anthropologists have provided clear evidence that, from a worldwide perspective, certain activities—such as hunting, trapping, herding, and fishing—are predominantly the province of men. Other activities—such as care of infants and children, grinding grain, carrying water, gathering herbs, and preserving food—are predominantly the province of women.

These divisions are found both in the most primitive as well as the most egalitarian societies. Even in Finland and Sweden, where sex roles are deemphasized and a parental leave policy has been designed to eliminate the traditional gender-based division of labor, it is mostly wives and mothers who feed the family, shop for and wash the clothes, and serve as primary caregivers for the children.[33] Likewise, in the Israeli kibbutz, which was founded on sex-egalitarian terms, most of the men are in agricultural and industrial roles and most of the women are in service and educational roles. Similar household and child-care patterns exist today in mainland China, even though the overwhelming majority of women are employed outside the home.

Not only do females and males differ in behaviors, but gender differences exist as well in value orientations. A national representative sample of U.S. adolescents found support for females being (1) more likely than males to express concern and responsibility for the well-being of others, (2) less likely than males to accept materialism and competition, and (3) more likely than males to indicate that finding purpose and meaning in life is extremely important.[34] In spite of major changes in gender-role attitudes and young women's occupational aspirations between the mid-1970s and early 1990s, these value differences persisted.

Beyond these sex-based task and value differences, who would deny that physical differences exist between males and females? Probably no one. But who would

[31]Judith Stacey and Timothy J. Biblarz, "(How) Does the Sexual Orientation of Parents Matter," *American Sociological Review* 66 (April 2001): 159–183.

[32]Paula C. Rust, "'Coming Out' in the Age of Social Constructionsism: Sexual Identity Formation among Lesbian and Bisexual Women," *Gender and Society* 7 (March 1993): 50–77. Note also Frederick L. Whitam, Christopher Daskalos, Curt G. Sobolewski, and Peter Padilla, "The Emergence of Lesbian Sexuality and Identity Cross-Culturally: Brazil, Peru, the Philippines, and the United States," *Archives of Sexual Behavior* 27 (1998): 31–56.

[33]Linda Haas, "Gender Equality and Social Policy," *Journal of Family Issues* 11 (December 1990): 401–423.

[34]Ann M. Beutel and Margaret Mooney Marini, "Gender and Values," *American Sociological Review* 60 (June 1995): 436–448.

argue that differences in the behavior of males and females are innate, biological, or anatomical? Probably some people would, others wouldn't be so sure, and still others would deny it forcefully. Maybe all three groups are partially correct.

For centuries, it was assumed that sex-based differences in behavior were inborn or natural. Females had maternal instincts and were submissive; males were aggressive and dominant. More recently, certain social scientists—particularly anthropologists, who discovered societies in which men are passive and women are domineering—have questioned any relevance of biological factors in behavior. They have argued that all behavior is learned. While these authors tend to lean more toward the latter position, the most accurate answer, as was described in Chapter 8, probably lies between the two positions and is far more complex than suggested by a nature/nurture, biology/culture argument.

It had been argued (and tested) that, regardless of the extent of actual inborn differences between the sexes, the *belief* that they are innate provides a major ideological justification for a system of stratification by sex. Because men/husbands are in the advantageous power position, it could be expected that they would believe in innate, inborn sex roles more than women/wives. Research has found this to be true. Within a marriage, however, disagreement about the origin of sex roles was reduced by the mutual influence that husbands' and wives' beliefs had on each other, resulting in more similar beliefs.[35]

The biological argument is deeply rooted in a number of theories of socialization, including the psychoanalytic frame of reference discussed earlier in this chapter. This view is further enhanced by research into hormones (such as progesterone and estrogen secreted by the ovaries in females and testosterone and the androgens secreted by the testes in males) that initiate sexual differentiation in the fetus and that later, at puberty, activate the reproductive system and the development of secondary sex characteristics. Research has shown that if a female fetus is given testosterone, she will develop malelike genitalia. If a male is castrated (testes removed) prior to puberty, he will not develop secondary sex characteristics such as a beard. But do hormones determine or predict behavior?

The strength of cultural factors is overwhelming in understanding gender identity and sex-role socialization. One prime example comes from cross-cultural data that have shown great diversity in the attitudes, values, and behavior of both men and women. Margaret Mead's classic study of three primitive tribes in New Guinea found both men and women among the Arapesh to be cooperative, mild-mannered, gentle, and unaggressive (sex-typed "feminine" behavior). Among the Mundugumor, both men and women were hostile, aggressive, combative, individualistic, and unresponsive (sex-typed "masculine" behavior). Among the Tchambuli, the typical sex roles found in Western cultures were reversed: women were dominant, powerful, and impersonal; men were emotionally dependent and less responsible.[36]

If it can be assumed that the biological makeups and hormonal balances of men and women in these tribes and men and women in the Western world are similar, then how can these differences be explained? It is not necessary to have been in New Guinea in the 1930s to note the strength of cultural factors in gender differences and sex-role socialization. Data from students in the 1990s, for example, showed that the attitudes

---

[35]John Mirowsky and Catherine E. Ross, "Belief in Innate Sex Roles: Sex Stratification versus Interpersonal Influence in Marriage," *Journal of Marriage and the Family* 49 (August 1987): 527–540.

[36]Margaret Mead, *Sex and Temperament in Three Primitive Societies* (New York: Mentor, 1950). Originally published in 1935 by Morrow.

CROSS-CULTURAL *Perspective*

Matrilineage among the Khasi Tribe in India

The Khasi tribe resides as the dominant ethnic group in the hill country of Meghalaya in northeastern India. As reported in *The Chicago Tribune* (April 7, 1996), for centuries the Khasis have had a matrilineal society in which property and the family name pass from mother to daughter. In the past, the remote hill kingdom was often under attack from other tribes, and Khasi warriors would spend months away from home, traversing the rugged territory to defend their borders. Women ran the family, looked after their villages, and carried out the religious and traditional rites of the tribe.

The result was that the women acquired a status and independence that would be the envy of women in the West. Today, women run many businesses in Shillong, the state capital, and in the home they play a vital role in domestic decision making. In Khasi households, the birth of a girl is greeted with joy and many families invest more in the education of their daughters than in

their sons. In rural areas, some boys never go to school, while their sisters may be educated to university level.

Traditionally, the only male who held any importance in family matters was the maternal uncle, the brother of the mother of the house. On marriage, the Khasi husband went to live in the house of his wife's family and had to defer to the authority of his mother-in-law.

A major concern for the tribe today centers around the estimated 30 percent of Khasi women who marry outsiders. These women take the names of their husbands and their property goes with them. One member stated that "the Khasi matrilineal system does not meet the needs of the modern world. What Khasi man will work hard for his entire life to establish a business knowing that it will pass on to his daughter and son-in-law?" Yet for generations the Khasi men have done just that.

As a result, an unlikely alliance of radical women and young men are challenging the tribal traditions. Many urban Khasi women believe that the matrilineal system has destroyed the confidence of their menfolk, and that the time has come to replace it with the patrilineal system found in the rest of the world.

Nick Haslam, "Reluctant Rulers: Matrilineal Tribe Tries to Shape Up its Men," *The Chicago Tribune*, April, 1996.

---

toward appropriate roles for men and women were strongly affected by fraternity and sorority membership, by race and ethnicity, and by religious affiliation.[37]

Another and even more convincing line of research came from studies of *hermaphrodites* (persons who possess complete, or almost complete, sets of both male and female genitalia and reproductive organs). During most of the twentieth century, in the United States (and elsewhere) such babies were usually surgically "corrected" while quite young, based on a medical "guess" as to which sex was the predominant one. Sometimes the individual's chromosomal sex (X–X or Y–Y) did not match the surgeon's guess, though this unknown fact usually did not "matter" to the individual because socialization proved stronger than biology. For instance, biological females "defined" and reared as males had fantasies typical of males, enjoyed sports assigned generally to males, and fell in love with girls. Biological males defined and reared as females had an interest in mothering, preferred marriage over career, and were oriented toward dolls and domestic tasks.[38] Thus, when socialization

---

[37]Ilsa L. Lottes and Peter J. Kuriloff, "Sexual Socialization Differences by Gender, Greek Membership, Ethnicity, and Religious Background," *Psychology of Women* Quarterly 18 (1994): 203–219.

[38]John Money, *Sex Research: New Developments* (New York: Holt, Rinehart and Winston, 1965). See also John Money, "Sex Assignment in Anatomically Intersexed Infants," in M.A. Watson, ed. *Readings in Sociology* (Dubuque, IA: Kendall/Hunt, 1984).

contradicts biological, hormonal, or genetic factors, learned and interactional experiences prove to be powerful determinants of current gender roles.

Sex-Role Socialization

Socialization to sex (female/male) and gender (masculine/feminine) roles follows the basic socialization processes described earlier in this chapter. Socialization to anything, including sex roles, begins at birth and continues throughout one's lifetime. If the sex of the fetus was not known before birth, the very first question most parents want an answer to is, "Is it a girl or a boy?" Following the moment of sex determination, different-colored blankets are assigned to girls and boys in the hospital nursery and they are treated differently from then on. From birth, socialization as to appropriate roles for males and females constitutes one of life's most important learning experiences. In interaction with others as well as in words, deeds, films, and books, the child is taught what behavior is appropriate for each sex.

Even for adolescents, the home continues as a key source of sex-role socialization and sex-typing.[39] His-and-her tasks are evident in who does inside chores and who does outside chores. Mothers share more time with daughters in meal preparation, household labor, and family-care activities. In contrast, fathers share more time with their sons in activities involving the home, yard, car, and pet maintenance. Intergenerational continuity of stereotypical gender roles is perpetuated in North American home life.

Sex-typing isn't confined to the home and doesn't end in adolescence. For example, a content analysis of the top ten self-help books on the *New York Times* best-seller list over ten years (1988–1998) revealed that the four best-selling books (including *Men Are from Mars, Women Are from Venus*) contained advice for both sexes to behave consistently with traditional gender socialization.[40] In general, these books indicated that women should define themselves in relationship to male partners and that female independence and assertiveness may jeopardize these relationships.

Sex-typed behaviors are taught so effectively that, by adulthood, even within the same occupation, employed men more than employed women (1) are concerned about income, job security, and advancement into administration; (2) want to avoid being supervised; (3) are more likely to seek self-employment and/or autonomy in the work setting; and (4) value the opportunity to exercise leadership. Women more than men (1) want to work with and help people; (2) prefer part-time and employee status; and (3) emphasize the use of special occupational skills.[41]

If it is assumed that the workplace, parents, and others are influential in sex-role socialization, one can predict a continuation of sex-role stereotyping in this and future decades. For example, throughout the school years, the educational system continues to stereotype males and females. Textbooks, achievement tests, athletic emphases, vocational counseling, and parental and peer pressures all tend

---

[39]John F. Peters, "Gender Socialization of Adolescents in the Home: Research and Discussion," *Adolescence* 29 (Winter 1994): 913–934; and Susan D. Witt, "Parental Influence on Children's Socialization to Gender Roles," *Adolescence* 32 (Summer 1997): 253–259.

[40]Toni Schindler Zimmerman, Kristen E. Holm, and Shelley A. Haddock, "A Decade of Advice for Women and Men in the Best-Selling Self-Help Literature," *Family Relations* 50 (April 2001): 122–133.

[41]Michael Betz and Lenahan O'Connell, "Work Orientations of Males and Females: Exploring the Gender Socialization Approach," *Sociological Inquiry* 59 (August 1989): 318–329.

From birth, girls are taught to be and act feminine and boys to be and act masculine. With changing adult roles, however, these differences are becoming less distinct.

to reinforce stereotypical expectations and behaviors. Beyond school, the mass media, governmental policies, religious and work worlds, and most social institutions tend quite consistently to stress appropriate and clearly different behaviors for women and men.

In the socialization of males and females, empirical evidence has documented a continuation of sex-role stereotyping and gender segregation in spite of tremendous shifts in sex-role attitudes and gender ideology.[42] Current conceptions of femaleness and maleness have marked similarities to earlier conceptions. A contemporary view of men as aggressive, work-minded, and capable of leadership is remarkably similar to that presented in earlier research. Current conceptions of femaleness, stressing sensitivity, affection, and consciousness of appearance, are also similar to earlier stereotypes of women. In spite of shifts in attitudes, socialization to sex/gender roles continues to emphasize differentiation between males and females, concentrating on the perpetuation of traditional expectations and behaviors for each sex.

Single Parenting

As shown in the previous chapters, marriage has become less common in recent decades and births to unwed mothers have been escalating. As a result of these trends as well as high levels of divorce, more children are living and being socialized in a one-parent household. According to *The 2009 Statistical Abstract of the United States*,[43] nearly 22 million children under age 18 did not live with two parents. This amounted to about 30 percent of all children. This included 21 percent of non-Hispanic white children, 60 percent of black children, and 30 percent of children of Hispanic-origin. Most of these children lived with their mothers only (26 percent of children were

---

[42]Karin L. Brewster and Irene Padavic, "Changes in Gender-Ideology, 1977–1996: The Contributions of Intracohort Change and Population Turnover," *Journal of Marriage and the Family* 62 (May 2000): 477–487.

[43]U.S. Census Bureau, *The 2009 Statistical Abstract* "Table 68—Children Under 18 Years Old by Presence of Parents," http://www.2010census.biz/compendia/statab/cats/population/households_families_group_quarters.html

living with their mother only and 3 percent with their father only). The remaining children (3.5 percent) did not live with either parent. The majority of these lived with other relatives, however.

The number of children in a single-parent context and in poverty is quite dramatic when children's actual living arrangements are examined over an extended period rather than considered for a given year or at a single point in time. In one study examining a set of life tables built from twenty-five waves of longitudinal data, Rank and Hirschi show that 34 percent of America's children between ages 1 and 17 will spend at least one year below the poverty level.[44] During these seventeen years of childhood, 69 percent of black children, 81 percent of children in nonmarried households, and 63 percent of children whose head of household had fewer than twelve years of education will be touched by poverty.

Of all white single mothers, more than one-half are divorced (53 percent) and nearly one-fifth are married but with a spouse absent (18 percent). Thus, most white children under age 18 come from two-parent households but, as a result of divorce or an absent parent, find themselves in one-parent contexts. The proportion of white single mothers who never married increased between 2000 and 2007 from about 20 to 24 percent.

Black children, in contrast, are much more likely to be born into single-parent situations because their mothers have never married (62 percent). Less than one-fifth of black children enter one-parent situations because of divorce (17 percent). Although white one-parent families typically result from divorce and black one-parent families typically result from never-married parents, Hispanic-origin one-parent families result from several circumstances: divorce (26 percent), married but absent fathers (29 percent), and never-married mothers (42 percent).

Among all three racial/ethnic groups, relatively few one-parent situations (about 4.0 percent) result from widowhood; this might be expected, since widowhood most often occurs when mothers are older and their children are no longer under age 18. In sum, several trends—the increase in births to unmarried women, the frequency of divorce, and the number of married couples with a spouse absent—seem to ensure that the vast majority of children born in the 1990s and 2000s will experience one-parent living arrangements.

As could be expected, most literature on single-parent households has dealt with the mother/child unit. What's more, rather than consider the mother who is present, this literature has considered the father who is absent. Thus, it seems the real topic has been the fatherless family.

To avoid this oversight, the following sections will consider these two single-parent situations: the mother/child family (the father-absent family) and the father/child family (the mother-absent family).

Mothers as Single Parents

The greatest concern among single mothering tends to focus on African American children because about half live in mother-only households. This concern is heightened by (1) the widely held view that every child needs a father or his social equivalent, (2) the financial plight of female-headed families, and (3) the welfare expenditures that go to support these families.

---

[44]Mark R. Rank and Thomas A. Hirschi, "The Economic Risk of Childhood in America: Estimating the Probability of Poverty across the Formative Years," *Journal of Marriage and the Family* 61 (November 1999): 1058–1067.

Sara McLanahan and Karen Booth addressed issues such as these in an essay focusing on problems, prospects, and politics in mother-only families.[45] When compared with two-parent families, the authors found that mother-only families were much more likely to be poor, to have higher levels of stress, and to have lower levels of social integration. Economic insecurity, the authors suggested, was high in mother-only families because of low earning capacity, lack of child support from nonresidential parents, and meager public benefits. The authors also found evidence of negative intergenerational consequences. Children living in mother-only families were more likely to be poor in adulthood than children who lived with both parents. Children living with single mothers were also more likely to become single parents themselves.

How well mother-only families manage seems to be closely linked to their living arrangements. The poorest households are those in which mother-only families live alone, followed closely by those in which two related single mothers and their families (typically a mother and her daughter) double up. Single mothers who live in married-couple households (such as with the mother's parents) fare better from an economic perspective. And data suggest that single mothers cohabiting with unrelated males where income is fully shared do best of all and appear to differ little from the average-income household of a young married couple with children.[46] Findings such as these tend to support the argument of Bumpass and Raley that definitions of single-parent families should be based on living arrangements rather than on the marital status of the parent.[47] A growing proportion of premarital births into assumed single-parent families, in fact, occur in two-parent cohabiting families.

Patterns of assistance to single mothers vary by race and kin networks. One nationally representative sample confirmed that single mothers have better access to kin than married mothers have and that kin access is better among blacks than among whites.[48] In this sample, black mothers were more likely to reside with their kin, more likely to have free child care provided by kinfolk (most often grandmothers), and more likely to receive at least one-half of their income from individuals other than husbands. Even though these informal support networks were especially important for black mothers, they seldom provided support adequate enough to fully compensate for the costs of single motherhood.

As stated before, the children of mother-only households are themselves more likely to be poor and to be single parents. What other consequences do they face? A simple comparison of two-parent and one-parent families documents many differences. Children who grow up in single-parent families are less likely to complete high school and attend college[49] and more likely to smoke cigarettes, use drugs, and have sexual intercourse.[50] Children from the two groups also differ on many other dimensions.

---

[45]Sara McLanahan and Karen Booth, "Mother-Only Families: Problems, Prospects, and Politics," *Journal of Marriage and the Family* 51 (August 1989): 557–580.

[46]Anne E. Winkler, "The Living Arrangements of Single Mothers with Dependent Children: An Added Perspective," *The American Journal of Economics and Sociology* 52 (January 1995): 1–18.

[47]Larry L. Bumpass and R. Kelly Raley, "Redefining Single-Parent Families: Cohabitation and Changing Family Reality," *Demography* 32 (February 1995): 97–109.

[48]Dennis P. Hogan, Ling-Xin Hao, and William L. Parish, "Race, Kin Networks, and Assistance to Mother-Headed Families," *Social Forces* 68 (March 1990): 797–812; and Sara McLanahan and Gary Sandefur, *Growing up with a Single Parent* (Cambridge, MA: Harvard University Press, 1994).

[49]Nan Marie Astone and Sara S. McLanahan, "Family Structure, Parental Practices and High School Completion," *American Sociological Review* 56 (June 1991): 309–320.

[50]Robert L. Flewelling and Karl E. Bauman, "Family Structure as a Predictor of Initial Substance Use and Sexual Intercourse in Early Adolescence," *Journal of Marriage and the Family* 52 (February 1990): 171–181.

What are the findings when factors such as socioeconomic status are controlled? That is, are the differences among children due more to family structure (one parent or two) or to social class (level of poverty)?

Two decades ago, Barbara Cashion reviewed the social-psychological research pertaining to female-headed families published over a decade and concluded that children in mother-only families are likely to have good emotional adjustment, high levels of self-esteem (except when they are stigmatized), intellectual development comparable to that of others in the same socioeconomic status, and a rate of juvenile delinquency comparable to that of others in the same socioeconomic status.[51] Major problems in mother-only families stem from *poverty* and *stigma*. Poverty, as a general social problem, may be associated with the child's problems in school and juvenile delinquency, as well as the mother's poor attitude about her own situation and her sense of not being in control. The stigma of being without a father causes lowered self-esteem in children; they may also be labeled or defined problematic even in situations where problems are minimal or nonexistent. Overall, Cashion concluded that the majority of single-female-headed families, when not plagued by poverty, raise children comparable to those from two-parent families.

Fathers as Single Parents

The father/child family, like the mother/child family, is a result of widowhood, divorce, separation, nonmarriage, and, more recently, single-parent adoption. While only 3.2 percent of all children under age 18 live with their fathers only, that

Increasing numbers of children in the United States are being raised in single parent households, many in conditions of poverty. Research shows that these children often suffer disadvantage due to their poor economic situation.

---

[51]Barbara G. Cashion, "Female-Headed Families: Effects on Children and Clinical Implications," *Journal of Marital and Family Therapy* (April 1982): 77–85.

number increased from 1970. This increase is likely to continue as a result of more divorced fathers who desire to continue parenting, greater economic resources available to fathers than to mothers, and more favorable opinions of single fathers.

Research on fathers as single parents has been relatively infrequent and generally limited to small nonprobability samples. Yet father/child studies may prove to be more insightful than mother/child studies in light of the extreme importance placed on the mother as the key agent of socialization. Can men "mother"?

This question was posed by Barbara Risman, who surveyed fathers about their experiences as homemakers, the nature of the father–child relationship, and their overall role satisfaction.[52] Risman's major finding was that most men felt comfortable and competent as single parents, regardless of the reason for custody or their financial status. This was true even though four out of five single fathers had no outside housekeeping help, either paid or volunteer. These men felt very close to and very affectionate toward their children, were glad to be fathers, and had little trouble fulfilling either the instrumental or expressive functions of single parenthood. Clearly, successful mothering is not an exclusively female skill. Men *can* "mother."

Similar support for men as single parents came from a study that examined whether significant differences exist between children reared in single-mother and single-father families. Factors examined included self-perception, self-esteem, social competencies, and the frequency and severity of reported behavioral problems. The historical assumption that single mothers are more effective parents than single fathers was not supported.[53] In a number of ways, fathers who maintain families alone are better situated than their female counterparts. Single-parent fathers typically have higher levels of education, are in the labor force, and, as shown earlier, are better situated economically.

Do males do better in single-father households and females do better in single-mother households? That is, are there advantages to living with the same-sex parent in single-parent households? Apparently not. In a national study of several thousand eighth graders living in mother-only and father-only homes, of thirty-five social-psychological and educational outcomes, not even one revealed significant benefits from living with the same-sex parent as contrasted with the opposite-sex parent.[54] This research casts doubt on the advocacy of same-sex custody determinations.

Overview of Single Parenthood

Can any conclusions be drawn from the data available? It does seem clear that, just as growing up in a two-parent family does not guarantee that children will be happy, well-adjusted, and well-behaved, growing up in a one-parent family does not ensure the opposite. But neither can the findings be understood to imply that the absence of a father or mother has no effect whatsoever. Single parents assess their options, and mothers in particular make choices that allow them to forge

---

[52]Barbara J. Risman, "Can Men 'Mother'? Life as a Single Father," *Family Relations* 35 (January 1986): 95–102. Note also: Geoffrey L. Greif, "Lone Fathers in the United States: An Overview and Practice Implications," *British Journal of Social Work* 22 (1992): 565–574.

[53]A. Reuben Schnayer and R. Robert Orr, "A Comparison of Children Living in Single Mother and Single Father Families," *Journal of Divorce* 12 (1989): 171–184.

[54]Douglas B. Downey and Brian Powell, "Do Children in Single-Parent Households Fare Better Than Living with Same-Sex Parents?" *Journal of Marriage and the Family* 55 (February 1993): 55–71; and Brian Powell and Douglas B. Downey, "Living in Single-Parent Households: An Investigation of the Same-Sex Hypothesis," *American Sociological Review* 62 (August 1997): 521–539.

meaningful lives despite harsh economic conditions in which they and their children find themselves.[55]

Single parents have definite limitations on the time and energy to do various tasks. Children in single-parent families are assumed to have more responsibility than children in two-parent families and to engage in more chores, regardless of gender stereotype. Single parents are often forced to exhibit both masculine and feminine behaviors, which may tend to socialize their children in more nontraditional and flexible gender-role values and behaviors.

[55]Robin L. Jarrett, "Living Poor: Family Life among Single Parent, African-American Women," *Social Problems* 41 (February 1994): 30–49.

Summary

1. Specifying what constitutes "good parenting" requires and examination of the context within which parenting occurs and for which parents are preparing children for adult roles. It is also important to consider that in many contexts, intentional parenting is difficult to disassociate from family adaptation and from the roles children often play in contributing to that adaptation to difficult environments.

2. In order to understand parenting, one must first understand potential differences between men and women in their predispositions and capacities to parent. Although evolutionary theories propose such differences, most of the research shows than men can be good "mothers" and women can be good "fathers."

3. One of the basic outcomes of good parenting in modern societies is the establishment of s secure attachment style in children. Children with secure attachment styles are better able to establish close intimate relationships throughout their lives and are better prepared for learning.

4. Psychologists and sociologists distinguish between four types of parenting styles: authoritative, authoritarian, permissive/indulgent, and indifferent/uninvolved. Child outcomes are maximized by authoritative parenting, which consists of high levels of expectations and demand for behavioral standards combined with high levels of warmth and supportiveness.

5. Several frames of reference were examined to explain various aspects of socialization: a learning/behaviorist theory, a psychoanalytic theory, two theories of child development, and a symbolic interaction theory.

6. Learning (reinforcement) theory assumes the same concepts and principles that apply to lower animal forms apply to humans. The conditioning processes may be classical or operant. Child rearing and socialization processes result from conditioning and positive or negative reinforcements.

7. Classic psychoanalytic theory contrasts sharply with behaviorist theory. Internal drives and unconscious processes are of central importance. Socialization takes place according to precise though overlapping stages of development. These include the oral, anal, and phallic stages, followed later by a period of latency and a genital phase. What happens in these early stages, from birth to age 5 or 6, although unconscious, becomes relatively fixed and permanent, serving as the basis for responses in later life.

8. Child development theories focus on the individual and the manner in which motor skills, thought, and reasoning develop. Erikson described eight stages of human development, each constituting a crisis brought on by changing social situations as the individual moves from infancy through old age. Piaget focused more on the cognitive development of the child and described four major stages of intellectual development.

9. Symbolic interaction theory contrasts greatly with the theories already described. Infants are not born social; they develop through interaction with other persons. As interaction occurs, meanings are internalized and organized, and the self develops. The social self enables people to consciously and purposively represent to themselves what they wish to represent to others.

10. A social being can take the role of others, can interpret and define, and can have and use symbols. In interaction with others, the child learns to define herself or himself and the world in certain ways. These definitions and meanings, in turn, predispose the child to behave in ways consistent with these self-concepts. *Interaction*, the *social self*, *significant others*, *reference groups*, and the *generalized other* are concepts basic to the socialization process.

11. Socialization does not end at any given age; it is a lifelong process. For teens, school and peer groups serve as important sources of reference, interaction, and identity.

12. *Sex/gender identity* and *sex/gender roles* refer to one's identity and the expectations associated with being male or female. Male–female differences are universal. Debate continues over the extent to which sex and gender roles have their roots in biology, culture, or a combination of the two.

13. Sex-role socialization follows the principles of any type of socialization. In interaction with others, children learn about gender/sex roles very early in their lives. These roles are heavily reinforced in schools, the media, the workplace, and the home. Although some change in attitudes toward sex roles has taken place, current conceptions of femaleness and maleness fit earlier stereotypes and highly traditional expectations.

Chapter 10 on the parental system and this chapter on parent–child interaction follow a life course sequence that generally but not always follows marriage. Chapter 12 will continue this time sequence by turning to families in the middle and later years.

Key Terms and Topics

Discussion Questions

1. What makes for good parenting?
2. What do you think about the idea that women can "father" and men can "mother" at equal levels?
3. What factors are most important in the development of stable, healthy adults? Why?
4. Contrast the learning/behaviorist, psychoanalytic, child development, and symbolic interaction frames of reference in regard to how each defines *socialization*. What contributions does each theory make? What drawbacks does each have?

5. Interview three mothers or fathers of preschool children. Find out whether they toilet trained their children early, breast-fed or bottle-fed them, and whether they believe it made any difference; what means of punishment they have used; what role the father plays in child rearing; how other children assist or hinder the socialization process; and so forth. What similarities link the parents' answers?

6. In what ways and areas are you being socialized? To what extent are you a victim of early childhood experiences, perhaps a father-absent family, a lower-class background, or a home with marital conflict? When will you be fully socialized? Why?

7. What influence did early adolescence, dating, friendship relationships, siblings, and teenage experiences have on your personality? To what extent is your personality today a product of your early (as opposed to more recent) socialization experiences?

8. Is a marriage with no sex- or gender-role differentiation (androgyny) possible? Explain and give examples.

9. To what extent does one's biological sex determine one's behavior? Could you be socialized to think and act like someone of the opposite sex? Why?

10. In spite of the women's movement, the increasing number of women entering the paid workforce, decreasing family size, and so forth, why do school materials, the mass media, and the work world continue to differentiate and segregate people by sex?

Further Readings

Barber, Nigel. *Why Parents Matter: Parental Investment and Child Outcomes*. Westport, CT: Bergin and Garvey, 2000.

An argument is presented that parents are preparing children to succeed in the world in which they find themselves, as opposed to supporting their dreams for the future.

Booth, Alan, and Crouter, Ann C., eds. *Does It Take a Village? Community Effects on Children, Adolescents, and Families*. Mahwah, NJ: Lawrence Erlbaum, 2001.

A focus on the mechanisms that link community characteristics to the functioning of individuals and families within them.

Coltrane, Scott. *Gender and Families*. Thousand Oaks, CA: Sage Publications, 1998.

Using images from popular culture, the book explores how families and gender are inseparably linked.

Danziger, Sheldon, and Waldfogel, Jane, eds. *Securing the Future: Investing in Children from Birth to College*. New York: Russell Sage Foundation, 2000.

An interdisciplinary team of scholars looks at factors that bear on a child's development.

Handel, Gerald, ed. *Childhood Socialization*. 2nd ed. Hawthorne, NY: Aldine de Gruyter, 2002.

An excellent source showing the process of transformation of newborns into social persons capable of interaction with others.

Hill, Shirley A. *African American Children: Socialization and Development of Families*. Thousand Oaks, CA: Sage Publications, 1999.

A focus on how slavery, race, and the African American culture influence the ways parents socialize their children.

Hrdy, Sarah, *Mother Nature: A History of Mothers, Infants and Natural Selection* (New York: Pantheon, 1999).

An excellent critical look at the foundations of evolutionary theories and research on motherhood and fatherhood.

Julia, Maria, ed. *Constructing Gender: Multicultural Perspectives in Working with Women*. Belmont, CT: Wadsworth, 2000.

A look at how the socialization of women differs among ethnic groups, with chapters on African American, Amish, Arab, Hispanic, Jewish, Native American, and other groups.

Power, Thomas George. *Play and Exploration in Children and Animals*. Mahwah, NJ: Lawrence Erlbaum Associates, 2000.

An interdisciplinary review of comparative and evolutionary studies of many different types of play.

Roche, Jeremy, and Tucker, Stanley, eds. *Youth in Society: Contemporary Theory, Policy and Practice*. Thousand Oaks, CA: Sage Publications, 1997.

A series of twenty-seven readings to encourage thinking about the changing and diverse lives and priorities of young people.

Straus, Murray A., Emily M. Douglas, and Rose Anne Medeiros, *The Primordial Violence: Corporal Punishment by Parents, Cognitive Development, and Crime* (Walnut Creek, CA: Alta Mira Press, In Press)

A comprehensive look at corporal punishment in child rearing and its consequences in the United States and around the world. Straus makes the argument that corporal punishment is violence and a major social problem, and that ending it is one of the most important steps to achieving a less violent world.

chapter 12

The Aging Family

An African American Widow and Grandmother

Phyllis has been a widow for four years. She and her husband had been married thirty-eight years and had five children; today, at age 60, Phyllis is the proud grandmother of eight grandchildren. She is currently employed as a special education teacher. Following are thoughts she shared.

"It was very hard for me around the time of my husband's death. He had been making some visits to the doctor but one day when he asked me to take off work to go with him, I feared something serious. The doctor explained he had leukemia and estimated he had six months to a year to live. Eight months later he died. At that same time, I was providing care to my mother who had Alzheimer's disease. Thank goodness for the support and help from my children. With work and all that was happening at home, the time was very stressful.

"Adjusting to his absence has been difficult. What I miss most are the little things he'd do for me—fix breakfast, warm my car, or surprise me with small gifts. I miss the walks we'd take together, his companionship, and would you believe even the squabbles we'd have over things in the news. Of course we had our differences, but these don't appear so important now.

"I enjoy being a grandmother. Three of my grandchildren are staying with me now and I see all eight of them at least three times a week. You ask, what is my role or responsibility as a grandmother? I guess to just give them love and do what your heart tells you to. I only give advice when asked. Four of my five children are boys, and I'm fortunate that I'm close to my daughters-in-law. We do lots of things together as a family like going on outings. I like when the grandchildren call and I always try to find time for them, even with helping with their homework.

"I think about retirement in a few years but wonder if I'll be ready. I know that when I retire I'll do volunteer work. Even now, I'm very active in church. For me, life is good. I believe life is what you make it. If you want happiness, you can find it in the smallest things. If you carry a smile, cheer will follow. I've known for a long time that if you treat people the way you want to be treated and if you try to make someone happy, what you put out comes back."

Questions to Consider

Do you see any relationship between Phyllis as a widow and as a grandmother and her upcoming retirement?

What are the responsibilities or roles of a grandparent? Explain. Should grandparents discipline their grandchildren and give advice to them—or to their parents?

Chapters 10 and 11 examined selected aspects of families with children. But marriage and family life do not end when children enter adolescence or in later adolescence, when the children leave home for marriage, employment, school, or some other reason. Family structure, interactions, and lifestyles change considerably at this period of the family life cycle: the second half. A prime example of this change was shown in Chapter 9, regarding marital satisfaction over the lifecycle. Several studies indicated increasing disenchantment and decreasing satisfaction throughout the years of parenting, followed by increasing satisfaction in the later years, after the children have left home.

This chapter will examine two major periods in the life course: the middle years, from approximately age 40 to retirement, and the later years, from approximately age 60 or 65. This examination will include general descriptions of families at these periods; specific consideration will be given to grandparents, retirement, socialization of people who are aged, and social conditions and problems faced by this group.

Postparental Period: The Middle Years

In order to describe the experience of the period after children leave home, a number of phrases have been used. Among these are the *empty-nest* period, the *launching stage*, the period of *contracting family size*, and the term used here, the **postparental period.**

Technically, the term *postparental* is a misnomer, for parents do not stop being parents or become ex-parents after their children leave home. Postparental suggests that, at this time, the children are now legally and socially recognized as adults and assume greater independence from their parents as well as greater personal autonomy and responsibility. They are, in effect, ready to be "launched" from the family.

Aquilino notes that in young adulthood, home leaving acts as a signal to parents that their child is entering a new stage in the life course, and the transition appears the greatest power to shake up earlier styles of relating.[1] As might be expected,

---

[1]William S. Aquilino, "From Adolescent to Young Adult: A Prospective Study of Parent–Child Relations during the Transition to Adulthood," *Journal of Marriage and the Family* 59 (August 1997): 670–686.

parental control lessens and shared leisure time declines. What was not anticipated was the finding that parents do not feel as emotionally close to children who have left. The quality of the relationship with adult children improves when their children enter roles such as marriage and full-time employment that parents have occupied for years.

For many families, the postparental period may include episodes of child "reentry" into the parental home. But essentially, this period is characterized by the return of the conjugal family to a two-person, married-couple household and of many nuclear one-parent families to a one-person household. The periods of family life from this point until the death of one or both parents can be classified as:

1. Families launching their oldest children—parents ages 45 to 54
2. Families of preretirement—parents ages 55 to 64
3. "Young/old" retired families—parents ages 64 to 74
4. "Old/old" families in the later years—parents ages 75 and older

The following section examines families in the middle years, as they launch their children and approach retirement, when the parents are approximately 45 to 65 years old.

Marital Status and Coresidence in the Middle Years

Marital Status

According to *The 2009 Statistical Abstract of the United States*, in 2007, 66.3 percent of men and 65 percent of women between the ages of 45 and 54 were married with a spouse present (see row 2 of Table 12.1). These proportions are lower than they were in 2000 (the numbers in parentheses) and, for men, they are considerably lower than the proportion in this category in the 55–64 age group, where 74 percent of men were married with a spouse present compared to 62.7 percent of women. These data reflect the shift in marriage and divorce behaviors over previous decades (see Chapters 6 and 14) and indicate a need to increase our understanding of

Table 12.1

Marital Status of Men and Women, Ages 45 to 64: March 2007
(Percent Distribution—2000 Figures in Parentheses)

	AGE OF MEN		AGE OF WOMEN	
MARITAL STATUS	45–54	55–64	45–54	55–64
Never married	13.6(9.5)%	6.8(5.5)%	10.3(8.6)%	6.6(4.9)%
Married, spouse present	66.3(72.8)%	74.1(76.0)%	65.0(66.3)%	62.7(64.7)%
Married, spouse absent	2.0(3.5)%	1.3(3.1)%	1.2(4.0)%	1.0(3.3)%
Widowed	1.0(0.9)%	2.2(2.9)%	3.0(3.9)%	9.0(11.8)%
Separated or divorced	17.0(13.3)%	15.6(12.5)%	20.5(17.2)%	20.6(15.3)%
Total	100.0(100.0)%	100.0(100.0)%	100.0(100.0)%	100.0(100.0)%

Source: U.S. Census Bureau, *The 2009 Statistical Abstract*, "Table 56—Marital Status of the Population by Sex and Age: 2007," http://www.2010census.biz/compendia/statab/cats/population/marital_status_and_living_arrangements.html.

nonmarital and premarital behaviors among these two age groups and not assume that people between 45 and 64 are going to be married.

As noted above, the decline in the proportion married is a reflection of changes in marriage and divorce behavior over the previous decades. These changes are reflected in increases in the proportion never married and in the proportion currently unmarried due to separation or divorce (rows 1 and 5 in Table 12.1). These proportions have increased for both men and women since 2000 and are greater in the more recent cohort (the 45–54 year old group). For those who are married in mid-life, the period after the children leave home lasts longer than any other in the marital life course. Interestingly, this phenomenon is unique to families of the twentieth century. In 1900, the average man married at age 26, had his last (fifth) child at age 36, saw that last child marry at age 59, and lost his spouse at age 57. A woman married at age 22, had her last child at 32, lost her spouse at 53, and saw her last child married at 55.[2] The result for both sexes was no postparental period, since the average couple died two years before their last child was expected to marry.

In contrast today, both sexes marry in their mid-twenties, have their last child in their early thirties, see their last child launched in their mid- to late forties, but do not lose their spouse until the mid- or late seventies. The result is a postparental period of twenty-five to thirty years. Although couples are marrying at a later age, they have fewer children and, thus, gain an earlier release from child rearing. These factors, combined with longer life expectancies for both sexes, give the average couple several decades together prior to retirement or the death of one spouse.

Coresidence

Coresidence refers to adult children living in the same household as their parents. Demographic indicators show that more young adults reside with their parents now than they did a few years ago. Although more than four-fifths of young adults leave home by age 23, the parental home is nevertheless the primary residence for most of the transition to adulthood. Even during the ages 21 to 23, parental living accounts for more than 40 percent of all residential experience.[3]

Women tend to leave home earlier than men, but for men in particular, the trend toward earlier leaving has been reversed with more cohorts leaving later. Compared to the past, young people in both the United States and Canada are more likely to leave to achieve independent living and less likely to leave for reasons of marriage. Single-parent families, stepparent families, instability in the home, and all forms of nontraditional families increase the probability of both men and women leaving to achieve independent living. The same is true for household density: crowding is a positive incentive to leave home. Nest leaving and the process of the transition to adult and independent status involve not merely the children but parental/home conditions as well.[4]

---

[2]Figures are taken from Paul C. Glick, "The Life Cycle of the Family," *Marriage and Family Living* 17 (1955): 3–9.

[3]Arland Thornton, Linda Young-DeMarco, and Frances Goldscheider, "Leaving the Parental Nest: The Experience of a Young White Cohort in the 1980s," *Journal of Marriage and the Family* 55 (February 1993): 216–229.

[4]Nicholas Buck and Jacqueline Scott, "She's Leaving Home: But Why? An Analysis of Young People Leaving the Parental Home," *Journal of Marriage and the Family* 55 (November 1993): 863–874; and Frances K. Goldscheider and Calvin Goldscheider, "The Effects of Childhood Family Structure on Leaving and Returning Home," *Journal of Marriage and the Family* 60 (August 1998): 745–756.

As might be expected, coresident young adults give, receive, and perceive more support from their parents than nonresident children.[5] Less expected was the finding that these coresiding young adults report significantly lower affective relationships with their parents. Coresidence was found to be a more positive experience when children were older, in school, and employed. Young adults who delay leaving home and have coresidence with parents until at least age 21 were shown to obtain a substantially higher education at every level through college graduation than those who leave earlier.

What about "boomerang kids," those who leave and return? Returning home in young adulthood has increased from a rare event to one experienced by nearly half of all those leaving home. One article suggested that the leaving home transition has become more renewable, less of a one-way street, and more like circular migration.[6] These young adults who left home to attend school, to take a job, to cohabit, or simply to be independent had higher probabilities of returning home than those who left to get married.

A study done in Canada found that parents are willing to accept one or two returns home, but that a pattern of bouncing back and forth strains family relationships, thus diminishing the marital satisfaction of parents.[7] Adult children who leave and return do so for a variety of reasons: following a job loss or divorce or separation; unwed motherhood; or when other hardships, particularly economic, arise. Consistent with findings from the previous U.S. study cited, both nonfamily living and cohabitation lead to much higher return rates than marriage. The parents' characteristics—such as health, marital, and employment status—have little bearing on whether their children return in either middle or later life. Returning home, in direct contrast to leaving home, is not an event constrained by age. Rather, the child's needs and situations are more important predictors of coresidence.[8]

The effect of either children or parents returning to the family in the middle years is to modify the nature of the postparental period. Namely, either event will delay return of the family to the single-householder or two-person-household unit.

Significance of the Middle Years

What is the significance of being a quadragenarian (ages 40 through 49)? To many couples, the middle years are the "prime of life." Business and professional men, in particular, are likely to hold their top positions, women are likely in the paid labor force, and total family income is at its peak. For example, in 2007, the median income of families where the householder was between the ages of 45

[5]Lynn K. White and Stacy J. Rogers, "Strong Support But Uneasy Relationships: Coresidence and Adult Children's Relationships with Their Parents," *Journal of Marriage and the Family* 59 (February 1997): 62–76; and Lynn White and Naomi Lacy, "The Effects of Age at Home Leaving and Pathways from Home on Educational Attainment," *Journal of Marriage and the Family* 59 (November 1997): 982–995.

[6]Frances Goldscheider, Calvin Goldscheider, Patricia St. Clair, and James Hodges, "Changes in Returning Home in the United States, 1925–1985," *Social Forces* 78 (December 1999): 695–728.

[7]Barbara A. Mitchell and Ellen M. Gee, "Boomerang Kids and Midlife Parental Marital Satisfaction," *Family Relations* 45 (October 1996): 442–448.

[8]Russell Ward, John Logan, and Glenna Spitze, "The Influence of Parent and Child Needs on Coresidence in Middle and Later Life," *Journal of Marriage and the Family* 54 (February 1992): 209–221; and Richard A. Settersten Jr., "A Time to Leave Home and a Time Never to Return? Age Constraints on the Living Arrangements of Young Adults," *Social Forces* 76 (June 1998): 1373–1400.

and 54, was $75,692, considerably higher than family incomes for younger householders between 15 and 24 ($31,471) as well as for families of older householders 65 and over ($39,649).[9]

Debate exists over whether the middle years are, in fact, the prime of life, as family income data suggest, or a period of great stress and even depression. The middle years bring many physical and emotional changes, which may create confusion and anxiety. The individual who saw himself as a "ladies' man" at 20 or 30 may, at 40, need to convince himself of his virility. The woman who loses her ability to "make men look twice" may have similar doubts about her attractiveness and sexuality. What's more, menopause brings on the loss of reproductive capacity and other emotional changes, which may challenge the woman's self-perception. Children growing up, leaving home, and getting married will likely stir emotions of both parents, who see their families changing and themselves aging.

The middle years are also filled with pressures to be successful and get ahead. For many people, "it's now or never." During this time, the prestigious position one wants to attain, the book he or she wants to write, the children he or she wants to have, or the stardom he or she yearns for may become a reality or simply remain a dream, never to be fulfilled. Supporting a comfortable lifestyle, paying for things such as college tuition and weddings, and planning for retirement add to economic pressures. Thus, the argument can be made that the middle years are rough—physically, socially, emotionally, and economically.

The opposite argument suggests that the middle years are a period of life when things are brightest. Income is highest, leisure time is greatest, child-bearing responsibility is past, and opportunities exist as never before. Which view is correct—or is it possible that both are?

Two decades ago, Michael Farrell and Stanley Rosenberg addressed this issue, comparing 300 men entering middle age to men in their late twenties. Contrary to their expectations, they did not find evidence of a universal mid-life crisis or signs of increased alienation or social disconnection.[10] The exception was among men in the lowest socioeconomic class. Men who were unskilled laborers gave evidence of personal disorganization and psychopathology as they approached middle age. Lower-middle-class men (skilled workers, clerical workers, small businessmen) showed a remarkable ability to ignore, distort, or deny information that challenged their world views. Professionals and middle-class executives exhibited neither denial patterns nor identity problems but reported satisfaction with work, family, and position in the community.

What about women? Do they find the postparental period of the family life course traumatic and unhappy? Not according to two psychologists who studied 700 women between young adulthood and old age.[11] Women in their early fifties rated their quality of life as higher than younger or older women. This was their prime of life, a time of good health combined with greater autonomy and relational security.

The notion of the **empty-nest syndrome** as a period of depression, identity crisis, role loss, and lowered sense of well-being for females has little research support. The

---

[9]U.S. Bureau of the Census Bureau, Current Population Reports, *The 2009 Statistical Abstract*, Series P60–213, "Table 676—Money Income Of Families—Distribution by Family Characteristics and Income Level: 2006. Money Income in the United States: 2000" (Washington, DC: U.S. Government Printing Office, September 2001), Table 4. http://www.2010census.biz/compendia/statab/cats/income_expenditures_poverty_wealth/family_income.html.

[10]Michael P. Farrell and Stanley D. Rosenberg, *Men at Midlife* (Boston: Auburn House, 1981).

[11]Valory Mitchell and Ravenna Helson, "Woman's Prime of Life," *Psychology of Women Quarterly* 14 (1990): 451–470.

Rules for a Good Marriage

When the kids leave home, there will be nothing left to keep your marriage together.

Most parents have pangs of sadness when the kids are finally gone, moments when the house seems impossibly quiet but you can make your marriage flourish in the new freedom. When your kids move out, keep your life full and your relationship central. Decide what you and your husband can do now that you couldn't before. Celebrate! You've succeeded in raising independent adults and now you have the opportunity to decide what to do next. Will you get more involved in town politics or social work? Go out to dinner more often? Whatever it is, make sure it's something you both enjoy as you rediscover each other.

Every guy has a mid-life crisis—any day, your spouse will drive off in a new red sports car. It's true that men sometimes do crazy things when they reach a certain age. You may feel like snickering at some of their attempts to regain their lost youth, like the balding executive who tries to get a wig. Such drastic changes are fortunately far from commonplace, but psychologists say that most of us will go through a period of midlife reevaluation. Actually as people move into their 40s, 50s, and beyond, their perspectives shift. Careers may plateau or take off in unexpected new directions. The first serious health problem may come along, or a parent may die and spur you to rethink your priorities. All of these are natural, inevitable transitions, and the best approach to dealing with them is to learn what you can and follow where they lead you. Fortunately, most people do: Not only are these course corrections good for us as individuals, they also seem to invigorate our relationships. People in their 40s and 50s feel they have more control over their work, their finances, and their marriages. Instead of worrying about his issues, focus on whether you're ripe for reinvention

yourself. Rediscover your priorities, and above all, don't feel you're being selfish by pursuing your passion: What's good for you is good for your marriage, too.

One day you fear the two of you will just realize you've grown apart and fallen out of love. The fable is that some couples just drift apart as their personalities change or their interests diverge. But experts say if you look closely at most happy twosomes, you'll be amazed at how little they actually have in common. She could spend every spare hour crafting, and he might be the world's most ardent sports fan…Yet they've discovered ways to be themselves and together at the same time: That means sometimes she reads on the sofa to keep him company while he watches a cricket match…In fact, experts say, shared interests or even similar temperaments are no assurance of marital longevity.

A marriage doesn't run on feelings—it thrives because both spouses work hard on it…We need to give long-term partners credit for their marriages. These couples have probably worked their way through hundreds of disagreements, illnesses, financial problems, kids' issues, maybe even an affair. They survive because they understand that they are a team, and they work to find ways to come together, whether in a crisis or in good times. The truth is, we all change constantly, and that's a blessing. But make sure you and your husband are checking in regularly with each other, and that all the little marital compromises and negotiations are making you both feel happy and involved in each other's evolving lives. That way, you can grow together, rather than apart, and, if anything, feel more in love than ever.

Source: Daily Mirror, "Rules for a good marriage" May 26, 2009, http://www.dailymirror.lk/DM_BLOG/Sections/frmNewsDetailVie w.aspx?ARTID=49938 © 2008 Wijeya Newspapers Ltd.

extent to which it occurs at all may vary by factors such as socioeconomic level and employment status. Dolores Borland hypothesized that, if an empty-nest syndrome does occur, it may occur to a greater degree in a particular cohort of white middle-class women because of the unique set of social circumstances in which they live and the unique set of family values and social norms concerning women's so-called proper roles.[12] Specifically, these women dedicate their lives selflessly to their families' needs

---

[12]Dolores Cabic Borland, "A Cohort Analysis Approach to the Empty-Nest Syndrome Among Three Ethnic Groups of Women: A Theoretical Position," *Journal of Marriage and the Family* 44 (February 1982): 117–129.

and believe that to be feminine and happy is to be married and a mother. Lower- and upper-socioeconomic status women, Borland argued, are less likely to experience this syndrome. The former have had to work throughout their lives to help support their families, and the latter have developed other community roles, have the resources to find parental-role substitutes, and have smaller families, which lead them to the empty-nest stage at a younger age.

What about marital status and well-being in the middle years? Results from respondents 51 to 61 years old indicate that married women are less likely to report symptoms of depression than their unmarried counterparts.[13] As might be expected, unhappily married respondents are much more likely to be depressed than those who report higher levels of marital satisfaction. The health benefits of marriage are greater for men than for women, for the married than the unmarried, for those more affluent and educated, and for those who are employed.

A study of the passage of U.S. women through thirteen years of mid-life demonstrated a significant diversity in the occurrence of life events as well as in their sequencing and spacing.[14] A large portion of these women experienced no transitions, at least with respect to marriage and the presence of children in the home. Two events, however, had detectable and important effects on their employment patterns and economic well-being: the launching of the last child and marital dissolution.

These two events were found to have opposite effects. The empty-nest transition (launching the last child) increased both labor market involvement and economic well-being, while marital dissolution (divorce and widowhood) decreased well-being. The sequence of these events made a difference, as well. If marital dissolution occurred first, the woman suffered a reduction in income while maintaining custody of the child. Recovery from this situation was difficult, even when benefits of an empty-nest transition were forthcoming. If the empty nest occurred first, the woman benefited economically as long as her marriage was kept intact.

The absence of children symbolizes the mother's new independence. Once the children are gone, many mothers form new nonfamilial relationships to fill the void. Many women in this age category become more active in civic and religious affairs, and an increasing number of wives and mothers become employed. This is also the time period when parents become grandparents.

Grandparent Status

Grandparenting has become a middle-age as well as an old-age phenomenon, given the potential of being a grandparent for three or four decades of life. With the majority of men and women in U.S. society marrying in their mid-twenties and with many of them having children within the first year or two of marriage, parents may become grandparents in their forties. The rocking chair and the cane-carrying grandfather images seem grossly inappropriate. The reduction in family size, closer spacing of children, and women having their last children at a younger age have

[13]John R. Earle, Mark H. Smith, Catherine T. Harris, and Charles F. Longino Jr., "Women, Marital Status, and Symptoms of Depression in a Midlife National Sample," *Journal of Women and Aging* 10 (1998): 41–55.

[14]Ken R. Smith and Phyllis Moen, "Passage through Midlife: Women's Changing Family Roles and Economic Well-Being," *The Sociological Quarterly* 29 (1988): 503–524. Note also Phyllis Moen, "Transition in Mid-Life: Women's Work and Family Roles in the 1970s," *Journal of Marriage and the Family* 53 (February 1991): 135–150.

made the transition into grandparenthood a distinct status of the middle years, separate from one's own parenting years.

An extensive demographic profile of grandparents suggested that grandparenthood is a near universal experience.[15] Most grandparents have, on average, five to six grandchildren. Close to two-thirds of women experience the birth of great-grandchildren. An increase in longevity led to a reversal in the timing of grandparenthood and widowhood, in that today's parents enjoy a lengthy empty-nest period and will experience grandparenthood well before the death of their partner. Black women are particularly prone to enter grandparenthood early (about nine years earlier than white men). Compared to past generations, many more of today's grandmothers are employed and, thus, less able to care for grandchildren during work hours.

Two key demographic changes have shaped modern grandparenthood in U.S. society: increased life expectancy and changed fertility patterns. Because more people reach old age, more people experience grandparenthood as well as great- and great-great-grandparenthood. Consistent with grandparents, great-grandparents revealed in interviews that most found the role significant and emotionally fulfilling, providing a sense of personal and familial renewal and a diversion to their lives, as well as serving as a mark of longevity.[16]

It has been suggested that the grandparent role represents a double bind.[17] On the one hand, grandparents are helpful and supportive, act warmly toward their grandchildren, and serve as resources for knowledge of family heritage and affective bonds. On the other hand, grandparents often interfere in child rearing and provide children and grandchildren with unwelcomed advice.

Perhaps this double bind illustrates the "roleless role" idea and the confusion that centers around the appropriate expectations for grandparents. The kinship status of the grandparent includes role expectations to provide nurturance, assistance, and support to children and grandchildren. At the same time, no clear normative expectations exist as to specific rights, duties, and obligations, or at what point assistance becomes interference. Perhaps grandparents, particularly middle-class ones, must construct roles for themselves as baby-sitters, surrogate parents, gift givers, crisis interveners, and the like. In contrast to middle-class grandparents, lower-class grandparents appear far more integrated into daily family life. The lower-class maternal grandmother frequently parents (socializes and nurtures) her grandchildren, engages in regular interaction, and feels a sense of obligation far more than simple contact between generations.

Grandparenthood appears to have different meanings for grandmothers and grandfathers. Sometimes, the grandparent role is depicted as maternal, with women, rather than men, feeling greater responsibility to their grandchildren. One study, for example, concluded that the grandfather role was more affectionate than functional.[18] For both black and white older men, levels of association with grandchildren and help exchanged were low; expressions of closeness and getting along were more characteristic of the relationship than interaction. The same study found greater centrality of the

---

[15]Maximiliane F. Szinovacz, "Grandparents Today: A Demographic Profile," *The Gerontologist* 38 (1998): 37–52.

[16]Kenneth J. Doka and Mary Ellen Mertz, "The Meaning and Significance of Great-Grandparenthood," *The Gerontologist* 28 (1988): 192–197.

[17]Jeanne L. Thomas, "The Grandparent Role: A Double Bind," *International Journal of Aging and Human Development* 31 (1990): 169–177.

[18]Vira R. Kivett, "Centrality of the Grandfather Role among Older Rural Black and White Men," Journal of Gerontology 46 (1991): S250–S258.

Throughout most of the world, grandparents serve as a valuable family resource to their children and grandchildren. Grandparents can fulfill many roles: custodians of family history, mediators in family conflicts, friends, gift givers, child-care providers, significant others, and even playmates.

grandfather role among black than white men, as demonstrated by association with grandchildren, help given, feelings of closeness, and perceptions of getting along with grandchildren. These racial differences were said to be based on cultural distinctiveness and not a function of economic or structural factors.

In contrast to grandfathers, grandmothers are likely to have high levels of interaction with and provide mutual assistance to grandchildren. Grandmothers are more likely than grandfathers to be regular providers of child care. National data of a youth cohort, for example, showed that over one-half of young mothers with children relied on relatives for child care when they were employed, and the primary relative was the grandmother.[19] The number of hours of child care provided per week by grandmothers was substantial, even though one-third of these middle-aged grandmothers were also employed. Like employed husbands and wives who juggled their work schedules to care for children, grandmothers and their children also juggled their work schedules to provide child care.

One underlying assumption of these patterns is that a relative, particularly the grandmother, is more emotionally committed to the child and will provide more loving care than nonrelatives. However, this caregiving often can produce stress and hardship for the grandparents, particularly grandmothers. It was found that being relatively young, caring for a grandchild with psychological and/or physical problems, caring for grandchildren over a long period of time, having low family cohesion, and lacking supports or resources were all associated with grandparent stress.

---

[19]Harriet B. Presser, "Some Economic Complexities of Child Care Provided by Grandmothers," *Journal of Marriage and the Family* 51 (August 1989): 581–591. Note also Margaret Platt Jendrik, "Grandparents Who Parent Their Grandchildren: Effects on Lifestyle," *Journal of Marriage and the Family* 55 (August 1993): 609–621.

A grandchild's behavior problems made the largest impact on the grandmother, decreasing her grandparenting satisfaction.[20]

Stepgrandparents

Given the frequency of divorce and remarriage, stepgrandparents are taking on new significance. Grandparenthood has been described as a "roleless role," but that description is even more apt for the grandparent by marriage rather than birth. Unlike grandparents, stepgrandparents have no biological tie and a shorter relationship time with newly acquired grandchildren. Thus, children have greater contact, more social involvement in personal and social roles, and stronger relationships with grandparents than stepgrandparents.[21]

Grandparent Rights

Divorce and remarriage patterns affect not only stepgrandparents, they also have a major impact on grandparents. Many grandparents experience frustration in having infrequent interaction and even maintaining contact with their grandchildren, particularly when the grandchildren reside with the former son- or daughter-in-law rather than with the son or daughter.

These frustrations have prompted a relatively new and increasingly frequent phenomenon, specifically, legal cases involving grandparent/grandchild visitation rights.[22] All fifty states now statutorily provide an avenue by which grandparents can petition the courts for visitation with their grandchildren over a parent's objections. Such visitation laws allow grandparents to petition for the opportunity to visit with a grandchild following the child's adoption by a stepparent, to visit with a grandchild who has been adopted by strangers, to visit with a child who has been surrendered to an agency for adoption, and to force visitation with a grandchild living with his or her married parents in an intact home over the objection of those parents.

$\mathscr{F}$amilies of Later Life and People Who Are Aged

Growth of the Elderly Population

Since the turn of the century, one of the more significant changes in family and marital relationships has been life expectancy. People are living longer and more people are alive, both of which have increased the number of older persons in the United States today (see Figure 12.1 on page 470). An early marriage age, the absence of divorce, and a longer life have combined to increase the length of marriage, the number of generations of family living, and the kin network.

---

[20]Roberta G. Sands and Robin S. Goldberg-Glen, "Factors Associated with Stress among Grandparents Raising their Grandchildren," *Family Relations* 49 (January 2000): 97–105; and Bonita F. Bowers and Barbara J. Myers, "Grandmothers Providing Care for Grandchildren: Consequences of Various Levels of Caregiving," *Family Relations* 48 (July 1999): 303–311.

[21]Carolyn S. Henry, Cindi Penor Ceglian, and Diane L. Ostrander, "The Transition to Stepgrandparenthood," *Journal of Divorce and Remarriage* 19 (1993): 25–44; and Carolyn S. Henry, Cindi Penor Ceglian, and D. Wayne Matthews, "The Role Behaviors, Role Meanings, and Grandmothering Styles of Grandmothers and Stepgrandmothers: Perceptions of the Middle Generation," *Journal of Divorce and Remarriage* 17 (1992): 1–22.

[22]Edward M. Burns, "Grandparent Visitation Rights: Is It Time for the Pendulum to Fall?" *Family Law Quarterly* 25 (Spring 1991): 59–81.

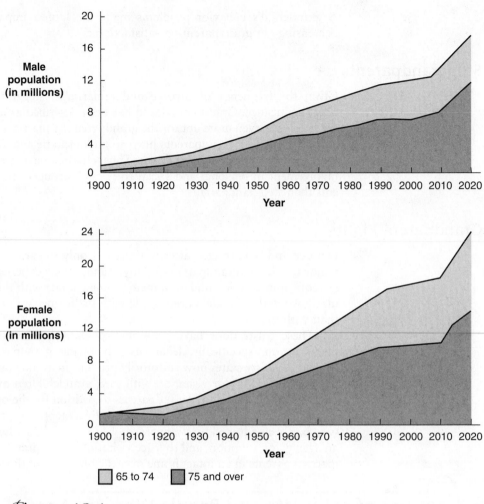

Figure 12.1

Growth of Population, Age 65 and Older: 1900–2020
Source: U.S. Bureau of the Census, *Current Population Reports.*

A person born in 2005 can expect to live 77.8 years. For white males, the life expectancy is 75.7 years and for white females, 80.8 years.[23] Life expectancies for black males and females—69.5 and 76.5, respectively—are considerably lower than those for whites. People who reach age 65 can expect to live, on average, another 18.7 years (17.2 for white men; 20.0 for white women; 15.2 for black men; and 18.7 for black women). Even people who reach the age of 100 can expect to live 2.6 more years. Thus, each additional year you live increases the length of time you can expect to live.

There has been relatively little increase in the **life expectancy** of older persons since the turn of the century. In 1900, the person who reached age 65 could expect to live until age 76.9. In 2005, the person who reached age 65 could expect to live until age 83.7, or seven years longer than his or her counterpart of a century ago.

[23]U.S. Census Bureau, *The 2009 Statistical Abstract*, "Table 103—Expectation of Life and Expected Deaths by Race, Sex, and Age," http://www.2010census.biz/compendia/statab/cats/births_deaths_marriages_divorces/life_expectancy.html.

CROSS-CULTURAL *Perspective*

The "Long-Living" Abkhasians of the Republic of Georgia

The Abkhasians, who live in a rough mountainous region in the Republic of Georgia, are said to have a disproportionate number of people who live to be over 100 years old and some who live to be 120. Many scientists, however, have questioned the authenticity of these ages. Nevertheless, whether they are 70 or 107, how does one account for their good eyesight, having their own teeth, little loss of hearing, few, if any, cases of mental illness or cancer, rare hospitalization, and their longevity?

Some accounts attribute these factors to their work habits and their physical daily labor as herders and farmers, to their taking walks of more than two miles a day, and to swimming in the mountain streams. Others claim they are due to their diet and the value they attach to staying slim, eating lots of fruits and vegetables, and consuming few fatty substances.

Explanations of longevity related to family life focus on (1) the family status accorded to them and (2) their sex practices. As to family status, Abkhasians are said to gain status throughout the life course with no self-devaluation and few abrupt changes in their lives. The old are granted certain rights and privileges not accorded to the young. They feel needed by their children and grandchildren and enjoy secure roles and statuses in extended families.

As to their sexual practices, the norms of the culture call for sexual relations to be postponed until after 30, the traditional age at marriage. Writings suggest it was even considered unmanly for a new husband to exercise his sexual rights on his wedding night. Sex was a pleasure to be regulated for the sake of one's health, and like a good wine, to get better with age. Reports exist of Abkhasian men fathering children at the age of 100.

Adapted from: Harold G. Cox, *Later Life: The Realities of Aging*, 4th ed. (Upper Saddle River, NJ: Prentice-Hall, 1996), pp. 70–74.

Significantly, more people are living longer as fewer die in infancy and childhood. In the 1990s, approximately 74 percent of men and 85 percent of women in the 65-year-old cohort reached age 65.[24] Near the turn of the century, only 39 percent of men and 44 percent of women reached age 65. Thus, there has only been a relatively small increase in life expectancy, but more people are living longer.

By 2010, approximately 40.2 million U.S. citizens will be age 65 and over.[25] This group comprises 13 percent of the population of the United States, and its size has been expanding far more rapidly than the nation's population as a whole. While the number of U.S. citizens in 2010 will have increased by about 35 percent since 1970, the number of people age 65 and over will have increased by more than 65 percent. The continual increase in the over-65 age group has not been due to an increase in the **lifespan** (the biological age limit) but rather to an increase in the number of people living. If birthrates decline or remain stable, people over 65 will likely constitute an even larger proportion of the U.S. population for decades to come.

[24]U.S. Bureau of the Census, *Statistical Abstract of the United States, 2001*, 121st ed. (Washington, DC: U.S. Government Printing Office, 2001), no. 97, p. 73; and U.S. Census Bureau, *The 2009 Statistical Abstract*, "Table 101—Average Number of Years of Life Remaining by Sex and Age," http://www.2010census.biz/compendia/statab/cats/births_deaths_marriages_divorces/life_expectancy.html.

[25]U.S. Census Bureau, *The 2009 Statistical Abstract*, 24 U.S. Bureau of the Census, Current Population Reports, Series P20-537, "Table 10—Resident Population Projections by Sex and Age. America's Families and Living Arrangements: March 2000," http://www.2010census.biz/compendia/statab/cats/population/estimates_and_projections_by_age_sex_raceethnicity.html. (Washington, DC: U.S. Government Printing Office, June 2001), Table 5, p. 11.

Throughout history, older persons have played significant roles. Men, in particular, have often received increased status, prestige, and deference with age. However, in the United States and apparently in modernized societies in general, old age does not bring increased prestige and status but rather negative perceptions and definitions. Frequently, old age is defined as a time of dependency and declining productivity and vitality. Elderly persons' socioeconomic status is generally determined by their achievements earlier in life; if the achievements were limited and provisions for these later years were inadequate, opportunities for a full, meaningful life will be limited.

Social gerontology, the study of older persons and the aging process, and the closely related field of the sociology of aging have both been concerned with the social definition of who is thought to be old; their interaction patterns and behaviors; the expectations imposed on them; their age, sex, place of residence, and other demographic factors; as well as the problems and needs they have. Within this framework, the family of later life has taken on particular significance when one studies these and other factors of concern to people who are aged.

Marital Status in the Later Years

Later-life families are characterized by continuity and change as they experience marriage, divorce, widowhood, remarriage, grandparenthood, sibling relationships, and family caregiving. In 2007, there were an estimated 15.4 million men and 20.6 million women in the United States who were 65 years old and over. Nearly 75.4 percent of the men and 64.5 percent of the women age 65 and over were married.[26]

A relatively small percentage of men and women 65 and over were never married or divorced (less than 4 percent and less than 10 percent, respectively). However, among these age groups, widowed status becomes increasingly frequent. Less than 14 percent of men ages 65 and over were widowers, but 42 percent of women ages 65 and over were widows. These numbers reflect the longer life expectancy of women.

Married couples comprise a high proportion of this over-65 group. Of those couples in first marriages, most had previously celebrated silver wedding anniversaries (twenty-five years), and many had celebrated or would soon celebrate golden anniversaries (fifty years). Over time, these couples have shared many joys and weathered many crises. One rarely reads about divorce or incompatibility among these couples, but such problems do exist. Even when they are unhappy in their marriages, the experiences of their years, the lives and activities of their children, and perhaps the lack of realistic alternatives to the marriage keep the older couple together.

Marital and family relationships are often proclaimed to be the primary sources of social involvement, companionship, fulfillment, and happiness for elderly people. Existing studies have suggested that marriage has a positive effect on psychological well-being among elderly people (particularly when compared to people who are divorced and widowed)[27] and, as shown earlier, that marital satisfaction may be higher for married elderly people than for married people in the intermediate stages of the family life course.

What about the elderly who never married or are divorced (see Figure 12.2)? How important are families to them? Studies have shown that geographic proximity to siblings, particularly same-sex siblings, exerts a positive influence on life satisfaction

---

[26]U.S. Census Bureau, *The 2009 Statistical Abstract*, "Table 33—Persons 65 Years Old and Over—Characteristics by Sex," http://www.2010census.biz/compendia/statab/cats/population/elderly_racial_and_hispanic_origin_population_profiles.html.

[27]Walter R. Gove and Hee-Choon Shin, "The Psychological Well-Being of Divorced and Widowed Men and Women," *Journal of Family Issues* 10 (March 1989): 122–144.

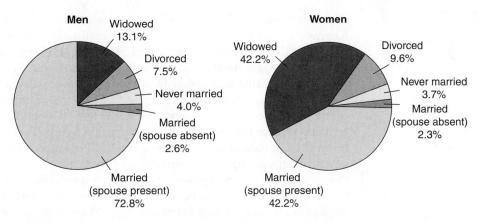

Figure 12.2

Percentage of Persons Age 65 and Older, by Marital Status and Sex: 2007

Source: U.S. Census Bureau, *The 2009 Statistical Abstract.* "Table 33—Persons 65 Years and Older—Characteristics by sex." http://2010Census.biz/compendia/stafab/cut/population/elderly_racial_hispanic_origin_population_profiles.html.

and well-being.[28] Women's ties and emotional attachments with siblings are more involved than those of men. And respondents whose highest-contact sibling is a sister talk on the phone more often than those whose highest-contact sibling is a brother. Overall, personal contact with siblings is greater for the single than all other marital status groups. This greater contact with siblings by single persons is not because of greater emotional commitment to them but is more likely an outcome of having fewer competing relationships.

Interestingly, one hedge against loneliness for the unmarried was found to be dating.[29] Older women derived increased prestige and status rewards from dating, and older men stressed the importance of dating as a means for self-disclosure. For most persons, greater emphasis was placed on the compassionate nature of such relationships than as a means for marriage. As one 73-year-old woman stated:

> It was a lot harder when my boyfriend, Ted, died than when my husband of forty years passed away. I needed Ted in a way I never needed my husband. Ted and I spent so much time together; he was all I had. And at my age I know it will be hard to find someone else... but, well, let's face it; how many men want a seventy-three-year-old woman?[30]

Intergenerational Relationships

Intergenerational relationships encompass a wide variety of interaction patterns between family members of different generations. Chapters 10 and 11 focused primarily on the generations of young children and their parents. This chapter focuses

[28]Ingrid Arnet Connidis and Lori D. Campbell, "Closeness, Confiding, and Contact among Siblings in Middle and Late Adulthood," *Journal of Family Issues* 16 (November 1995): 722–745; and Lynn White, "Sibling Relationships over the Life Course: A Panel Analysis," *Journal of Marriage and Family* 63 (May 2001): 555–568.

[29]Kris Bulcroft and Margaret O'Connor, "The Importance of Dating Relationships on Quality of Life for Older Persons," *Family Relations* 35 (July 1986): 397–401; and Richard A. Bulcroft and Kris A. Bulcroft, "The Nature and Functions of Dating in Later Life," *Research on Aging* 13 (June 1991): 244–260.

[30]Ibid., 401.

more on parents (adult children) and their parents. Parents in these middle years have sometimes been referred to as the **"sandwich generation,"** squeezed between the demands and needs of their children and those of their aging parents.

In the Burgess Award Lecture to the National Council on Family Relations, Vern Bengtson suggested that rather than "family decline" and a breakup of the nuclear family, family multigenerational relations will be more important in the twenty-first century for three reasons.[31] One, these are and will be longer years of shared lives between generations as a result of population aging. Two, grandparents and other kin will be in increasing importance in fulfilling family functions. And, three, inter-generational solidarity has a strength and resilience that continues over time. Due to changes in family structure such as divorce and stepfamily relationships, these multi-generational relations will be increasingly diverse and perhaps more important than nuclear family ties for well-being and support over the course of peoples lives.

A review of U.S. studies using national probability samples of adult children and their parents pointed to a number of conclusions.[32] Adult children and their parents enjoy frequent contact, are emotionally close to each other, and provide each other with emotional support and advice. They do not routinely provide each other with practical or financial assistance. These parents with sufficient resources provide young adult children with financial support to launch them into independent adulthood. Changes in the family, such as an increase in divorce, have marked consequences for adult parent–child relations. For example, divorced fathers are

Members of the "sandwich generation" may find themselves caring for their young grandchildren as well as their elderly parents. Family members—particularly wives, mothers, and daughters—serve as caregivers and primary sources of support and affection for both the young and the old.

---

[31]Vern L. Bengtson, "Beyond the Nuclear Family: The Increasing Importance of Multigenerational Bonds," *Journal of Marriage and Family* 63 (February 2001): 1–16.

[32]Diane N. Lye, "Adult Child–Parent Relationships," *Annual Review of Sociology* 22 (1996): 79–102.

less likely to be in contact with their children, less emotionally close to them, and less likely to be involved in exchange of assistance.

It appears that African Americans are less likely than whites to be involved in adult parent–child exchanges. African American kin networks may be more extensive than those of whites, but they are less likely to exchange resources. Blacks do, however, have higher filial (parent–child) responsibility expectations than whites. This suggests a cultural difference between the races, in that aged blacks regard assistance from children as more normative than do aged white parents.[33]

Who is likely to provide a disproportionate amount of this support, particularly to older parents? As one might guess, significant differences exist by gender. Daughters, far more than daughters-in-law, not only provide more support than sons, but also do so for different reasons.[34] Daughters are most motivated to provide support by intergenerational affection and altruism. Sons, on the other hand, are more motivated by principles of obligation, familiarity, and self-interest. They contribute to the support of their parents more out of an expectation of financial reward implicit in the endorsement of intergenerational inheritance than out of sentiment. Affection is a stronger predictor of support when mothers are the recipients, and inheritance is a more salient predictor when fathers are the recipients of care. Regardless of motives, the notion that adult children abandon their elderly relatives or fail to meet their needs is basically a myth.

A second myth appears to be that high levels of conflict exist among generations who live together. Certain circumstances, such as financial dependency and unemployment, seem to increase parent–child conflict, but episodes of open disagreement and arguing occur much less often than episodes of enjoyable leisure time. Coresidency results in surprisingly low levels of conflict between parents and their resident adult children.[35] Even the parents' health and dependency are not related to parent–child conflict. Most parents and adult children, including those who live together, get along quite harmoniously.

A third myth relates to intergenerational patterns of wealth. Many people believe that baby boomers (described in Chapter 10) may be the first generation to do worse than their parents. An analysis of surveys conducted by the Federal Reserve Board to assess the wealth ownership and expenditures of U.S. families revealed otherwise. Baby boomers had more accumulated wealth as young adults than their parents had at all stages of the life course and were more likely to be upwardly mobile than their parents.[36]

What about people who are elderly and childless? The value of children to their elderly parents in providing emotional, material, financial, and other support has

---

[33]Gary R. Lee, Chuck W. Peek, and Raymond T. Coward, "Race Differences in Filial Responsibility Expectations among Older Persons," *Journal of Marriage and the Family* 60 (May 1998): 404–412.

[34]Merril Silverstein, Tonya M. Parrott, and Vern L. Bengston, "Factors That Predispose Middle-Aged Sons and Daughters to Provide Social Support to Older Persons," *Journal of Marriage and the Family* 57 (May 1995): 465–475; and Sally K. Gallagher and Naomi Gerstel, "Connections and Constraints: The Effects of Children on Caregiving," Journal of Marriage and Family 63 (February 2001): 265–275.

[35]William S. Aquilino and Khalil R. Supple, "Parent–Child Relations and Parent's Satisfaction with Living Arrangements When Adult Children Live at Home," Journal of Marriage and the Family 53 (February 1991): 13–27; and William S. Aquilino, "From Adolescent to Young Adult: A Prospective Study of Parent–Child Relations during the Transition to Adulthood," *Journal of Marriage and the Family* 59 (August 1997): 670–686.

[36]Lisa A. Keister and Natalia Deeb-Sossa, "Are Baby Boomers Richer Than Their Parents? Intergenerational Patterns of Wealth Ownership in the United States," *Journal of Marriage and Family* 63 (May 2001): 569–579.

Family Diversity

African-American Elder Fraud and Adult Child Advocates

A growing problem in American society involves the financial victimization of the elderly—especially poor minority elderly—by lending agencies, home refinance companies, home repair contractors and others. When the elderly are victimized their adult children often times become their only source of help and support. As a result, the burdens that fall to the "sandwich" generation of caring for one's own children as well as one's parents grow even larger. Since financial fraud schemes are disproportionately perpetrated against low income minorities and women are at the center of family life in African American families, this situation reflects "a 'quadruple whammy' constituted by race, class, gender, and age." (162–163).

In order to gain a better understanding of how this problem affects adult child advocates and the ways they respond, two African American woman therapists and consultants—S. Alease Ferguson and Toni C. King—undertook a review of cases that they encountered in their practice. Noting that adult child advocates frequently become victims themselves once they enter the cycle of legal proceedings to assist their parents, they wanted to know how their involvement affected their feelings, perceptions, and actions in ways that reflected their position in multiple systems of oppression.

When asked why they got involved in advocating for their parents, the women in their case studies said that they were "compelled" to get involved because of their bonds of love and family loyalty. At another level, however, they also expressed moral outrage over the victimization of those who are disadvantaged. This sense of outrage was linked to their own status as minority women and the discrimination and victimization they had suffered in their own lives. With respect to emotional reactions, the women in their case studies also expressed two levels of reaction. At a personal level they felt rage and outrage over their parents' victimization. They had spent most of their lives protecting their children against the risks of neighborhood environments and had not anticipated risk stemming from what they had seen as the legitimate financial sector. The authors describe their personal emotional reactions as "root shock" or the traumatization of one's "emotional ecosystem." Many of the women used terms reflecting the aggressive and predatory nature of those responsible for their parents' victimization and often times these terms were also reflective of men's violence against women.

At a secondary level, these women also directed their outrage against their community which they saw as betraying them by allowing for these predatory practices to occur. Such feelings were often exacerbated by a legal system that discredited their accounts of the situation, rejected their requests for help and sometimes even threatened legal and financial actions against them as advocates. This reaction often times led them to develop a stronger race, gender and class consciousness leading to engagement in cooperative actions to fight against the system.

The women in these case studies were not just victims, however. In confronting their parents' situations, they experienced a transformative developmental event. Many were able to transform their rage into constructive action and instead of silencing themselves, they developed an "active" and "passionate" voice through which they were able to articulate the conditions of their parents' victimization and effectively advocate on their behalf. They were then able to transfer this new found capacity into other areas of their lives.

Source: S. Alease Ferguson and Toni C. King, "Taking Up Our Elders' Burdens as Our Own: African American Women against Elder Financial Fraud," *NWSA Journal,* 18 (Summer 2006): 148–169.

been widely asserted and empirically supported. However, one study of childless elderly people demonstrated levels of well-being that matched and sometimes exceeded those of elderly parents.[37] The childless group was more financially secure (see Chapter 10 on childless couples) and in better health; parents, however, tended to be surrounded by a greater number of friends and have more general satisfaction

---

[37]Judith Rempel, "Childless Elderly: What Are They Missing?" *Journal of Marriage and the Family* 47 (May 1985): 343–348.

with life. By and large, this study and others showed that people who are elderly, whether parents or childless, are very satisfied with family, friendships, and life. They are less satisfied with health and income, two problems that will be discussed later in this chapter.

Living Arrangements among the Elderly

As persons reach and pass the age of 65, an increasing number retire, suffer decreases in income, and experience the loss of spouses and siblings. Where do people of this age category live? Are they institutionalized? Do they live with children? Do they live alone? Living arrangements depend greatly on the sex to which one is referring.

In 2006, 64.9 percent of those 65 and older lived in family households,[38] 32.3 percent were the householder, another 23 percent were the spouse of the householder, 5.6 percent were living in the household of one of their children, and 4 percent were living with another relative or in the family household of a nonrelative. Clearly, this distribution reflects the nuclear nature of the American family. It is also evident that a sizable population of the elderly live in nonfamily situations (30 percent in nonfamily households and 5.1 percent in group quarters). In total, 27.5 percent lived alone.

Many older people who do not live with spouses live with children or other relatives. A situation of this nature may be a matter of choice or of necessity. When parents and children elect to live together, the arrangements frequently work out to the satisfaction of both.

The pattern of the elderly living with children or other relatives was found to vary by ethnicity. Japanese and Chinese Americans are more likely than their white counterparts to live in extended-family households, particularly in their never-married children's homes.[39] This appears to be greatly influenced by the traditional value of filial responsibility. Living with *never married* children or other relatives is attributed more to specific adaptive strategies of old age than to the continuation of a cultural tradition. While the impact of immigrant culture on elderly living arrangements is significantly reduced through acculturation, even those born in the United States adhere to the cultural traditions of children having an obligation to assist and care for their aging parents.

Another living arrangement that is frequently satisfactory is for the aging parents and the married children to have separate but geographically close residences, which supports maintaining close relationships. Many parents prefer to be independent and want their children to allow them to remain so. This arrangement permits both generations to give favors or suggestions with fewer threatening feelings. In addition, parents and children can share interests and lifestyles without having the constant physical presence of one another. Unfortunately, census data are not available on the number or percentage of persons in the later years who maintain residences separate from but close to their children.

As of the mid-1990s, about 1.4 million (4 percent) of the population of men and women 65 years of age and over lived in long-term care institutions, primarily nursing

---

[38]U.S. Census Bureau, *The 2009 Statistical Abstract*, "Table 34—Persons 65 Years Old and Over—Living Arrangements and Disability Status: 2006," http://www.2010census.biz/compendia/statab/cats/population/elderly_racial_and_hispanic_origin_population_profiles.html.

[39]Yoshinori Kamo and Min Zhou, "Living Arrangements of Elderly Chinese and Japanese in the United States," *Journal of Marriage and the Family* 56 (August 1994): 544–558; and John R. Logan, Fuqin Bian, and Yanjie Bian, "Tradition and Change in the Urban Chinese Family: The Case of Living Arrangements," *Social Forces* 76 (March 1998): 851–882.

homes.[40] The nursing home residents are predominately women (75 percent), 75 years old and over (82 percent), white (89 percent), and widowed (66 percent). At the time of admission, most nursing home residents rely primarily on Medicaid (38 percent). This was followed by private insurance, own income, or family support (32 percent), Medicare (26 percent), and other government assistance or charity (4 percent). As might be expected, entrance into a nursing home increases sharply with age, and it is estimated that about 20 percent of all persons 85 years of age and older live in institutions, and over a lifetime, about one in four persons will spend some time in an institution.

Figures such as these have supported the idea that (1) most people who are elderly are not in nursing homes or long-term care institutions, and (2) most elderly are not abandoned by their families. Even those people who are institutionalized are disproportionately drawn from those who are childless, widowed, and living alone.

Common Problems of People Who Are Aged

Health and Care

As already suggested, people who are aged have definite problems, one of which is health and care. During these later years, a disproportionate number of people are isolated, disabled, sick, or in poor health. Some type of health problem almost invariably accompanies old age. Sometimes hospitalization is required, which raises a range of issues: medical payments, visiting patterns, care for the residence of the hospitalized, and, on occasion, legal matters.

Research confirmed the preference for and the importance of family members and adult children, particularly daughters, as caregivers for noninstitutionalized elderly people. Daughters serve as caregivers to dependent mothers and self-sufficient elderly mothers, as well.

Findings such as these have led many to question the popular notion that families today are less willing than those of the past to care for their elderly and perhaps impaired family members. This notion, referred to as the myth of abandonment, has received little scientific support; indeed, there is much evidence to the contrary. National surveys show that informal caregiving by families is the dominant mode, by far, of providing care to people who are aged. And this care goes beyond simply performing tasks such as personal care (bathing, eating, toileting), mobility (from room to room or in and out of chairs or beds), or daily living tasks (shopping, cleaning, cooking). It includes concern for older family members' safety, comfort, autonomy, and emotional needs as well as providing them with companionship and affection.[41]

Are caregiving tasks such as these a burden, and does caregiving produce stress? Common logic would suggest they are and it does, and an abundance of literature documents the physical, emotional, financial, and interpersonal costs experienced by family members caring for parents with a disability. Exchange theory, too, suggests that if an elderly infirm parent requires much and can return little, stress will be high.

Family caregiving does not seem to extend to multigenerational families. A study of four-generational families found that ties extended only to aging parents

---

[40]Achintya N. Dey, "Characteristics of Elderly Nursing Home Residents: Data from the 1995 National Nursing Home Survey" (Hyattsville, MD: National Center for Health Statistics, July 2, 1997), no. 289, pp. 1–7.

[41]Kathleen W. Piercy, "Theorizing about Family Caregiving: The Role of Responsibility," *Journal of Marriage and the Family* 60 (February 1998): 109–118.

TRANSNATIONAL FAMILIES

Living Alone among Elderly Chinese in Canada

Although Canada has the youngest population among G8 countries (only 13 percent are 65 or older), a large proportion of the elderly are ethnic Chinese. Because of liberal immigration policies and a strong cultural belief in multiculturalism, Canada has experienced high levels of immigration in recent decades, especially from Hong Kong and mainland China. As a result 25.8 percent of all visible minorities in Canada in 2001 were Chinese and 10 percent of this group was 65 years old or older. Given the strong filial responsibility norms in Chinese cultural heritage and the fact that many of these Chinese immigrants arrived in Canada as a result of being sponsored by relatives or reunited with families who had immigrated in previous years, the question arises as to whether or not these elderly are living in families or living alone. This was the question researched by Daniel Lai and Wendy Leonenko using data on 660 single Chinese Canadians 65 and older from a study titled: Health and well Being of Older Chinese in Canada.

This study found a high proportion of single Chinese Canadian elderly were living alone (about 40 percent). When they examined predictors of living alone among this group, they found that the status was a preferable one in that it was more likely to occur when respondents had the financial means and physical capabilities to do so. These findings are consistent with other studies of Chinese Canadian elderly which have found a strong preference for NOT living with children. Although some of this preference may be due to acculturation, only two of the cultural variables in their study—not being religious and years lived in Canada—predicted living alone. The other measures (such as language proficiency and responses on a traditional Chinese beliefs scale) did not predict this living status. They conclude that acculturation is a complex process where home country beliefs are often mixed with adopted country beliefs.

Source: Daniel W. Lai and Wendy L. Leonenko, "Correlates of Living Along among Single Elderly Chinese Immigrants in Canada," *International Journal of Aging and Human Development*, 65 (2007): 121–148.

who cared for their now-adult children.[42] Consistent with other studies, the closest relationships were between mothers and daughters. In some families, such ties extended to three generations, but beyond two generations was a rarity. Ties weaken as the family line lengthens. Three- and four-generation families often have large numbers of members, but close ties among them are few. In most cases, the arrangement could not be called an extended-family caregiving system.

Children's Problems

A second difficulty is a reversal of the common theme that elderly parents place stress and burden on their adult offspring. That is, do adult children's problems affect the well-being of their elderly parents?

Evidence has suggested that they do. A small U.S. sample and a national survey of elderly people in Canada demonstrated that parents whose adult children have marital, mental, physical, or stress-related problems experience greater depression than parents whose children do not have these problems.[43] Grandmothers (grandfathers

---

[42]Martha Baum and Mary Page, "Caregiving and Multigenerational Families," *The Gerontologist* 31 (1991): 762–769.

[43]Karl Pillemer and J. Jill Suitor, "Will I Ever Escape My Child's Problems? Effects of Adult Children's Problems on Elderly Parents," *Journal of Marriage and the Family* 53 (August 1991): 585–594; and Edie Jo Hall and E. Mark Cummings, "The Effects of Marital and Parent–Child Conflicts on Other Family Members: Grandmothers and Grown Children," *Family Relations* 46 (April 1997): 135–143.

were not studied) experienced negative reactions to family conflict and, while not directly threatened, they did feel empathy and concern. While health status, described earlier, appears to be the most powerful predictor of distress in the elderly, their children's major problems have a direct and profound effect, as well.

Income and Standard of Living

In economic terms, people who are aged remain a sizable segment of the U.S. poor, particularly people who do not live in family households. Yet in 2007, the percentage of elderly people living below the poverty level was 9.6 percent, about one-third of what it was in 1970.[44] Social Security, retirement plans, tax allowances, and other benefits have succeeded in reducing poverty for the segment of the population over age 65.

An examination of economic hardship across the life course showed that despite low income and high medical needs, America's elderly enjoy lower levels of economic hardship than any other adult age group. Most age group differences in economic hardship were found to be attributable to differences in the presence of children in the home, in resources such as home ownership and medical insurance, and in behaviors such as moderation and thrift. Older age groups are less likely to have children in the home and more likely to own homes, have medical insurance, and live more temperate and thrifty lifestyles. These factors, combined with the success of government programs such as Social Security and Medicare, reduce the economic hardship of America's elderly.[45]

For those elderly persons who do not enjoy improved economic status, the poverty rate varies dramatically by race, sex, and marital status. As of 2006, African Americans (black females, in particular) and Hispanic Americans had a poverty rate two and one-half times that of white persons in the 65 and over age category (7.0 percent for non-Hispanic whites; 12.0 percent for Asian and Pacific Islanders; 19.4 percent for Hispanics; and 22.7 percent for blacks).[46] Marriage generally protects elderly people from poverty; thus, elderly people who were widowed or divorced all had poverty rates significantly higher than those of married people. And among this age group, nonmarried categories included women predominantly.

Despite gender inequality, overall, the quality of life of elderly people in the United States has improved dramatically, particularly when compared to children. A growing number of elderly are demanding and getting what they want in terms of government services and support, whereas the needs of many children are being ignored. As of 2007, whereas one in ten persons (9.6 percent) age 65 and over in the United States was below the poverty level, nearly one in six children under age 18 (17.4 percent) were so listed, the highest of all age groups. By race/ethnicity, this included 10 percent of non-Hispanic white children, 26.9 percent of Hispanic children, and 33.4 percent of black children.[47] This contrast in economic well-being

[44]U.S. Census Bureau, *The 2009 Statistical Abstract*, "Table 33—Persons 65 Years Old and Over—Characteristics by Sex," http://www.2010census.biz/compendia/statab/cats/population/elderly_racial_and_hispanic_origin_population_profiles.html.

[45]John Mirowsky and Catherine E. Ross, "Economic Hardship across the Life Course," *American Sociological Review* 64 (August 1999): 548–569.

[46]U.S. Census Bureau, *The 2009 Statistical Abstract*, "Table 691—Persons Below Poverty Level by Selected Characteristics: 2006," http://www.2010census.biz/compendia/statab/cats/income_expenditures_poverty_wealth.html.

[47]U.S. Census Bureau, *The 2009 Statistical Abstract*, "Table 691—Persons Below Poverty Level by Selected Characteristics: 2006," http://www.2010census.biz/compendia/statab/cats/income_expenditures_poverty_wealth.html.

between the elderly and preschool-age children and those under age 18 can be partly attributed to the expansion of Social Security and noncash benefits, such as Medicare. The politics of this contrast reveal the power of special-interest groups, as determined by wealth and size. Children don't vote, nor do they have much financial clout.

Abuse and Neglect

A fourth problem facing the elderly is abuse and neglect. This may be one of the newest social problems in the United States, in that little or no information prior to the late 1970s was published about domestic mistreatment of the elderly in their homes by relatives or other domestic caregivers. (This issue is examined more thoroughly in the next chapter.)

Extreme caution must be taken in categorizing people who are aged as a homogeneous population. To be sure, dependency, sickness, isolation, and abuse occur frequently among elderly people. Nonetheless, a sizable proportion of these people have few health problems, carry on active lives with families and friends, and continue to make major economic and social contributions to their communities and society.

Socialization in Later Life

Tremendous emphasis has been given to children and youth in socialization literature, and consequently the resocialization needs of the aged have largely been ignored and overshadowed. In contrast to people who are aged, children receive much of their socialization within the family and from peers, schools, jobs, and the community. But what socializing agents direct the aged? Where is the training for retirement? Where is the training for widowhood? Where is the training to prepare for illness and death? Where is the training regarding the narrowing of social relationships?

Intimacy and familiarity characterize the family system and make it highly suitable for fulfilling many of the needs, services, and interaction patterns of the individual members. Even when the family system is absent or when persons have no living kin, older people tend to substitute for missing relatives by converting close friends into quasi-kin.[48] Fictive kin for the elderly serve in much the same way as the fictive kin described in Chapter 4 among families in poverty. These nonrelatives serve as meaningful kin components of their social networks and as a valuable resource in meeting specific needs of elderly people.

It should be noted that family factors do not operate independently of the culture in which families exist. To avoid having people who are aged become "socially disabled," there must be congruence between the cultural goals and structural opportunities that society provides. The effectiveness of the family as a resource is largely contingent on the values and services of the larger society: job opportunities, leisure-time activities, health care, clarity of roles, perception of the aged as fulfilling valuable functions, and socializing and resocializing opportunities appropriate to the later stage of the lifecycle.

---

[48]Hazel MacRae, "Fictive Kin as a Component of the Social Networks of Older People," *Research on Aging* 14 (June 1992): 226–247.

Retirement

One major issue in retirement involves resocializing men and women to new roles and lifestyles. Traditionally, men assumed the major economic responsibility for their families, and their lives revolved around work/employment roles. Thus, it followed that the literature on retirement focused heavily on men. Women's retirement was less studied because it was not perceived to constitute a salient social issue. With the dramatic increase in the labor force employment of women and the growing proportion of women retirees, studies of retirement and its effects on both sexes are appearing with increasing frequency.[49]

Take, for example, the effect of retirement on housework. Continuing employment of the wife after the husband retired led men to take on more household responsibilities. Retirement of the wife was shown to lead to a reduction in the husband's time with female chores. That is, the wife again takes charge of "her" domain.[50]

One study of 1,530 retired residents of Washington State found that retirement was not materially different for women than for men.[51] The idea that retirement is less stressful for women was not supported. In fact, women reported somewhat

Many persons in retirement and their later years continue to lead highly productive lives. Those in good health and with sufficient incomes are most likely to express satisfaction with retirement and enjoy engaging in activities.

[49]Kathleen F. Slevin and C. Ray Wingrove, "Women in Retirement: A Review and Critique of Empirical Research Since 1976," *Sociological Quarterly* 65 (February 1995): 1–21.

[50]Maximiliane E. Szinovacz, "Changes in Housework after Retirement: A Panel Analysis," *Journal of Marriage and the Family* 62 (February 2000): 78–92.

[51]Karen Seccombe and Gary L. Lee, "Gender Differences in Retirement Satisfaction and Its Antecedents," *Research on Aging* 8 (September 1986): 426–440.

lower levels of satisfaction with retirement than men. Reasons given include their lower incomes and, if they were widowed or divorced, their lower probability of getting married. Regardless of gender, people in good health and those with high incomes were most likely to express satisfaction with retirement.

Retirement may have a greater influence on marital quality than previously believed. One national study found that leaving a high-stress job improves marital quality. Lower marital quality results from factors that signify gender-role reversals (such as the need for a retired man to do more household work while his wife continues to work), from poor health, and from reduced social support.[52] One of the most troubling areas was the division of labor within and outside the household. With most wives being younger than their husbands and, thus, remaining in the labor force, husbands increasingly find themselves retiring while their wives continue to work. Husband's resistance to housework, coupled with their wives occupational success, lowered marital quality.

Regardless of the reasons for retirement, it seems likely that it will require major role readjustments for both sexes. Health, income, status, and feelings of self-worth often tend to decrease at the time of retirement. Being married appears to be a major buffer for a variety of these problems. Spouses provide one another with a great deal of social support. One national survey provided evidence that when approaching retirement, marriage has powerful and pervasive health benefits.[53] Being divorced or widowed increases the risk of an adverse health effect and decreases one's available network of family caregivers. Marriage not only reduces the chance of death but reduces the mortality risk among those who are married. In short, health and other problems are compounded upon the death of a spouse.

Dying and Death

Death is an inescapable event, one that will occur within all family and kin networks. Certainly, the loss of those one loves most intensely—parent, spouse, child, or other family member—causes tremendous pain. Few relationships are more intimate and few groups more primary than those of marriages and families.

The death of a parent adversely affects marital relationships as well as the physical and psychological well-being of adult children.[54] Bereaved children suffer a decline in social support from their partners and an increase (or at least the perception of an increase) in the partner's negative behaviors. They and their partners may also experience a significant increase in psychological distress, heightened alcohol consumption, and a decline in physical health status. These individuals for whom relationships with parents were salient and positive prior to the parents' death were more adversely affected. The loss of a parental relationship characterized by negativity (a difficult family history) sometimes led to an improvement in an adult child's well-being. But for most, psychological distress was very apparent in the first few months following the death of a parent, with healing effects apparent later.

---

[52]Scott M. Myers and Alan Booth, "Men's Retirement and Marital Quality," *Journal of Family Issues* 17 (May 1996): 336–357.

[53]Amy Mehraban Pienta, Mark D. Hayward, and Kristi Rahrig Jenkins, "Health Consequences of Marriage for the Retirement Years," *Journal of Family Issues* 21 (July 2000): 559–586.

[54]Debra Umberson, "Marriage as Support or Strain? Marital Quality Following the Death of a Parent," *Journal of Marriage and the Family* 57 (August 1995): 709–723; and Debra Umberson and Meichu D. Chen, "Effects of a Parent's Death on Adult Children: Relationship Salience and Reaction to Loss," *American Sociological Review* 59 (February 1994): 152–168.

The circumstances surrounding the death of a friend, child, or spouse frequently require major decisions by family members:

- Should dying family members be assured the right to die with dignity and to determine the time, place, and manner of their death?
- Should **euthanasia** (the deliberate ending of a loved one's life to spare that person from the suffering that goes with an incurable and agonizing disease) be permitted?
- If permitted, should euthanasia be passive (not preventing death through means of life-support systems) or active (causing death by poisoning, strangling, shooting)?
- What about funeral and burial decisions—how, where, payment, and so forth?
- What about the disbursement of personal effects, the carrying out of a will, and the settlement of an estate?
- If a long-term illness preceded the death, are care and its cost the sole responsibility of the family?
- If the family cannot care for or pay, does the church, community, state, or someone else bear the responsibility?

The list of questions that surround dying and death could go on and on.

In the United States, as well as in most cultures, the immediate family and the immediate kin network are the major sources of decision making and social support. With the help of relatives, bedridden persons can live outside institutions. Elderly people turn first to their families for help, then to friends and neighbors, and, as a last resort, to bureaucratic organizations. It is not surprising that surveys indicate that most people would prefer to die at home.

Movements in health care make family/kin interaction with the terminally ill or dying patient more possible. One plan, called **hospice,** is a therapeutic environment for the terminally ill, designed from the patient's point of view. The goals of hospice care are to provide a good quality of life for the dying patient and to help the patient and the family to deal with the upcoming death. Emphasis is put on the care of the patient rather than on curing the disease or extending life. Control of pain (physical, mental, social, and spiritual) is stressed. Although hospice services are available in inpatient settings, most of these services are provided in the patient's home or place of residence.

Unlike a regular hospital, which stresses privacy, a hospice program emphasizes interaction with staff, family, and friends. Hours of visits are unlimited, and interaction is permitted with young children and grandchildren. When medical facilities are needed, they involve a team of medical, nursing, psychiatric, and religious people plus social workers and family members, as appropriate. The concern in a hospice is on increasing the quality of the last days of life and on making humane care synonymous with good medical practice.

The significance of family ties takes on an added dimension when one looks at the relationship between marital status and mortality.[55] Mortality is lower for married persons than unmarried ones and lower for people with children than for those without children. These findings suggest that protection against death itself may be afforded by different kinds of social ties, particularly marital, parental, and kin ties. Losing these ties is likely behind some of the difficulties of the widow or widower.

---

[55]Cathleen D. Zick and Ken R. Smith, "Marital Transitions, Poverty, and Gender Differences in Mortality," *Journal of Marriage and the Family* 53 (May 1991): 327–336; and Richard G. Rogers, "Marriage, Sex, and Mortality," *Journal of Marriage and the Family* 57 (May 1995): 515–526.

Widows and Widowers

Being a widow or widower is not unique to older people, but **widowhood** is disproportionately represented among people older than age 65 (see Figure 12.2 on page 473). Facing the loss of a spouse and making the shift from a married to a widowed status may present extreme emotional and financial difficulties.

Society compounds the difficulty of adjusting to the widowed status by placing an unstated taboo on the discussion of death between husband and wife or parents and children while they are alive. As a result, the widow or widower often is unprepared for the decisions that need to be made following the death of a spouse.

Even if discussions preceded the death, the likelihood is great that loneliness, social isolation, and a need for major readjustments in living patterns will result. One study compared the adjustment process for women who lost a spouse through death and those who had experienced divorce.[56] It was found that widowhood was more distressing and disruptive of identity than divorce. Unlike those divorced, most widows would likely have continued to live with their spouses if death had not intervened. The loss of a spouse by death involved more positive evaluations of the deceased and with time the husband became an "unusually good man." Divorce had quite the opposite effect. The adjustment process, however, was similar for both the widows and divorcees in terms of the impact of the identity process on psychological distress.

Readjustment may be less difficult if widowhood follows a major illness or some type of major role change on the part of the spouse. Adjustment to widowhood is often best when a person has already established some personal autonomy, close continuing friendships, a realistic philosophy of life, economic security, and meaningful personal interests.

One problem believed to be widespread among elderly persons and particularly among the widowed is that of social isolation and loneliness. *Social isolation* is the objective condition of having few contacts with family, friends, or both. *Loneliness* is a subjective condition that includes feelings of emptiness, aimlessness, and lack of companionship. Life history data from a Dutch survey of nearly 3,400 older adults showed that those currently not living with a partner are lonelier than those with a partner.[57] Furthermore, loneliness increased with the number of union dissolutions experienced and decreased with the time elapsed since the last dissolution. Time does not "heal all wounds," as those who lost a partner felt more lonely than those who never had a partner. The loss of a partner was more detrimental for males than for females.

The extreme outcome of conditions of loneliness is demonstrated by the frequency of suicide. Suicide rates of people who are widowed are consistently higher than those of people who are married, at any age group; the rate of completed suicides is significantly higher for males than for females.

Rosemary Blieszner, in viewing widowhood from a socialist–feminist perspective, writes that in some respects, women who have been dependent on and subordinate to

---

[56]David S. DeGarmo and Gay C. Kitson, "Identity Relevance and Disruption as Predictors of Psychological Distress for Widowed and Divorced Women," *Journal of Marriage and the Family* 58 (November 1996): 983–997.

[57]Arnold Peters and Art C. Liefbroer, "Beyond Marital Status: Partner History and Well-Being in Old Age," *Journal of Marriage and the Family* 59 (August 1997): 687–699.

CROSS-CULTURAL *Perspective*

Marriage Dissolution and Mortality in Sweden

In a study of 44,000 deaths in Sweden, Orjan Hemstrom sought to (1) analyze the long-term effect of marriage dissolution for mortality risk and (2) examine whether the mortality risk is different for men and women.

Data were gathered by linking the deaths that occurred in the total census population from 1981 to 1986 with information obtained in the 1960, 1970, and 1980 censuses. Information in the census made it possible to distinguish six marital status groups: (a) married to the same spouse as in 1970, (b) remarried, (c) cohabiting, with the marriage dissolved between 1970 and 1980, now living with a new partner, (d) separated, (e) widowed, and (f) divorced.

The answer to the first inquiry was that previously married individuals, whether separated, divorced, cohabiting, or remarried, had higher mortality risks than those who stayed married with the same spouse. When age was controlled, the excess mortality was highest for the divorced and lowest for the remarried. Those co-habiting had a somewhat higher mortality risk than those who remarried.

The answer to the second inquiry about gender differences was clear. Men who were separated, widowed, or divorced had higher relative mortality ratios than corresponding women. Divorced men had the highest mortality risks. The author suggests that these findings indicate men are more dependent on marriage than women.

The study shows that marriage dissolution is causally related to mortality. One explanation for this included a stress hypothesis: Marriage dissolution is a major, stressful life event that influences survival chances, most often negatively, later in life. In contrast, marriage is usually a positive and desired feature of social life that has a favorable impact on survival chances.

Source: Orjan Hemstrom, "Is Marriage Dissolution Linked to Differences in Mortality Risks for Men and Women?" *Journal of Marriage and the Family* 58 (May 1996): 366–378.

men over the life course have an edge over men in bereavement.[58] Widowed women are adept at housekeeping and kinkeeping, whereas widowed men are inexperienced at these tasks and more susceptible to dependence on others. On the other hand, widows are less likely to have adequate financial resources, since they may have neither the savings, pension benefits, skills, nor work experiences more common to men.

Some widows and widowers remarry, but the chances of remarriage are, of course, higher for widowers than for widows. In one study, age was found to be the single most important factor in the remarriage of widows; the younger the age, the greater the likelihood of remarriage. For widowers, age was not significant. Older widowers did not have higher remarriage rates than younger widowers, despite the greater availability of potential marriage partners.[59] The sex ratio of unmarried men per one hundred unmarried women (about 87 for all age groups over 15) becomes extremely unbalanced in the later years. In 2007, the ratio of unmarried males age 65 and over to unmarried females age 65 and over was 44.3, or less than one unmarried man for every two unmarried women. Social programs to encourage remarriage among widows and widowers would not be successful given the unbalanced sex ratio,

---

[58]Rosemary Blieszner, "A Socialist–Feminist Perspective on Widowhood," *Journal of Aging Studies* 7 (1993): 171–182.

[59]Ken R. Smith, Cathleen D. Zick, and Greg J. Duncan, "Remarriage Patterns among Recent Widows and Widowers," *Demography* 28 (August 1991): 361–374.

at least not in a monogamous system. The problem is further compounded in U.S. society by the norm that suggests that women should marry men of their own age or older. The remarriage problem for widowers is less severe, since there are both an excess of women their own age and social approval for marriage to women younger than themselves.

Summary

1. This chapter examined two major periods of the lifecycle: the middle years, from approximately age 40 to retirement, and the later years, from approximately age 60 or 65 until the end of the life course.

2. The postparental period—those middle years after the departure of children and prior to retirement—is one in which most men and women are still married, with small percentages of single, widowed, and divorced people. This is one of the longest periods of the marital lifecycle, covering, on average, a span of twenty to twenty-five years.

3. The significance of the middle years appears to differ somewhat for men and women. Although family income approaches its peak, there is mixed evidence as to the extent to which this period of life is bright or difficult. Conventional wisdom supports the concepts of a mid-life crisis or transition for men and an "empty-nest" syndrome for women. The existence of a "crisis" in mid-life seems to have little research support.

4. Grandparenting has become a middle-age and an old-age phenomenon. Grandparent appears to be a positive status for most respondents, although the roles are seldom clearly defined and tend to vary considerably by social class and cultural context.

5. In the United States, about three-fourths of the men but only about two in five of the women over age 65 are married. Marriage in the later years is perceived as favorable, compared to marriage in preceding periods of the life course. Most of the men and women of this age are living in families or in geographical proximity to their children. Relatively few older people are in long-term care institutions, such as nursing homes.

6. The problems facing elderly people are many, but this chapter focused briefly on four: health and care, children's problems, income and standard of living, and abuse and neglect. Most health problems are handled in the home rather than hospitals, with primary care coming from spouses or children. Income drops in old age, but most families cope quite well. Abuse and neglect, relatively new social problems, are discussed more fully in the next chapter.

7. Retirement, widowhood, and changing relationships create a need for resocialization of people who are elderly to new roles and definitions of self in relation to society.

8. Dying and death are processes of major importance and significance to family members. Family members offer support systems both to the dying person as well as to one another following death. Recognition of this support seems to be encouraging movements such as hospice, which treats terminally ill and dying patients in home settings and in family-focused medical settings.

9. The widow or widower is not unique to the aged family, but is disproportionately represented among persons over age 65. Women in this age group are more likely to be widows than any other marital status. With the unbalanced sex ratio, remarriage is unlikely for most older women.

This chapter examined selected factors relating to the postparental periods: middle years, retirement, and old age. Conflict, crisis, and marital disorganization, although present at these periods of the life course, are not confined to these periods. Chapter 13 explores social patterns surrounding crisis and disorganization, with a particular focus on abuse and violence among intimates.

Key Terms and Topics

Postparental period p. 460

Marital status and coresidence in the middle years p. 461

Empty-nest syndrome p. 464

Families of later life and people who are aged p. 469

Growth of the elderly population p. 469

Life expectancy p. 470

Lifespan p. 471

Social gerontology p. 472

Marital status in the later years p. 472

Intergenerational relationships p. 473

"Sandwich generation" p. 474

Discussion Questions

1. What is unique about the middle years, or the post-parental period? How is the period of adjustment different for women and men?
2. Discuss the mid-life transition and the empty-nest syndrome. Do they exist, and if so how serious are they? How might sex-role socialization patterns affect the middle years for men versus women?
3. Discuss changes in the grandparent role over the past thirty years. How might the grandparent status differ by class and subculture? What roles do step-parents and great-grandparents play?
4. How true is the argument "You can't teach an old dog new tricks" when applied to the socialization or resocialization of the middle-aged or aged couple?
5. Health, children's problems, money, and abuse are problems facing people who are aged. What other problems exist? What types of social programs, tax structures, and social policies might lessen the negative impact of these problems?
6. Discuss changes in husband/wife roles that are likely to accompany illness, retirement, grandparenthood, remarriage, and so forth. How can resocialization be facilitated?
7. What are the implications of retirement at age 70, 60, or 50? Note marital status and male/female differences in adjustment patterns after retirement.
8. Should dying family members be assured the right to die with dignity and be allowed to determine the time, place, and manner of their death? Should active or passive euthanasia be supported? Why?
9. What advantages or disadvantages does the widow or widower have if living alone, if living with kin, if living in a private home with someone other than kin, or if living in an institution? What types of conditions make one situation more favorable than another?
10. Invite several persons over age 75 to your class or to a discussion group to address such topics as the empty-nest syndrome, grandparenthood, retirement, widowhood, and facing death. Examine the significance of having children and their importance as systems of support.

Further Readings

Allen, Katherine R., Blieszner, Rosemary, and Roberto, Karen A. "Families in the Middle and Later Years: A Review and Critique of Research in the 1990s," *Journal of Marriage and the Family* 62 (November 2000): 911–926.

A decade-review article examining more than 900 articles on family gerontology published in the 1990s.

Bengtson, Vern L., Kim, Kyong-Dong, Myers, George C., and Eun, Ki-Soo, eds. *Aging in East and West: Families, States, and the Elderly.* New York: Springer Publishing Co., 2000.

A comparative analysis of developments among six Eastern and Western nations concerning population aging and its consequences.

Dailey, Nancy. *When Baby Boom Women Retire.* Westport, CT: Praeger, 1998.

An examination of three structural variables impacting the future retirement of baby boom women: population aging, women's labor force participation, and retirement income sources.

Goldscheider, Frances K., and Goldscheider, Calvin. *The Changing Transition to Adulthood: Leaving and Returning Home.* Thousand Oaks, CA: Sage Publications, Inc., 1999.

A look at the changing patterns of leaving home, including the timing of departure, the routes taken, and the frequent returns.

Kornhaber, Arthur. *Contemporary Grandparenting.* Thousand Oaks, CA: Sage Publications, 1996.

A synthesis of the current knowledge about grandparents and their role in families and society.

Lopata, Helena Znaniecka. *Current Widowhood: Myths and Realities.* Thousand Oaks, CA: Sage Publications, 1996.

An examination of two major themes of widowhood: how changes in society influence it and the myths and assumptions surrounding widowhood.

Mills, Terry L., ed. "Grandparent–Grandchild Relationships," *Journal of Family Issues* 22 (May and July 2001): Part I, pp. 403–534 and Part II, pp. 541–679.

Approximately twelve articles in two special issues are devoted to grandparenthood and grandparents' involvement with young and adult grandchildren.

Nadeau, Janice Winchester. *Families Making Sense of Death.* Thousand Oaks, CA: Sage Publications, 1998.

Family grief is seen as a process of family meaning-making based on multigenerational grieving families.

Phillipson, Chris, Bernard, Miriam, Phillips, Judith, and Ogg, Sim. *The Family and Community Life of Old People.* New York: Routledge, 2001.

An investigation into the changes in the social and family networks of older people living in three urban areas of England.

Maximiliane E. Szinovacz and Adam Davey, eds., *Caregiving Contexts: Cultural, Familial, and Societal Implications* (New York: Springer Publishing, 2008).

A review of studies examining families caring for elderly parents as affected by three contexts: cultural values and beliefs, family circumstances, and sociopolitical forces.

Williams, Angie, and Nussbaum, Jon F. *Intergenerational Communication across the Life Span.* Mahwah, NJ: Lawrence Erlbaum, 2001.

A developmental view of communication, with Part II devoted to intergenerational relationship communication within and beyond the family.

chapter 13

Family Stress and Violence

Twenty Years of Domestic Abuse

Delores, age 46, was married for twenty-one years until she divorced her husband several years ago. She has three adult children and, in her words, two and one-half grandchildren. Except for the first year of married life, she suffered from verbal, emotional, and physical abuse by her husband.

"When we got married, I really loved my husband. He had a good job with an auto company so money was not an issue. I looked forward to starting a family and having a home we could call our own. As for having a family, I found myself pregnant one month after our wedding. After five years of marriage, we purchased a home.

"Six months after our son was born, I experienced being hit for the first time. My husband came home and made a comment about the floor not being mopped. An argument escalated until, in anger, he struck me. I was shocked, went and picked up the baby, and headed for my mother's home. Only when I got to her place did I start crying. I guess I was very naive, because at that time I didn't perceive it as abuse.

"As was the case on numerous occasions over the years, I'd leave him and, for a variety of reasons, go back with him. The abuse wasn't regular but I could never predict when it was coming. My husband, who never was very affectionate, needed to be in complete control. He drank but his hitting me was seldom due to his drinking. I could never please him. Over time, after hearing how stupid I was, how I wasn't worth anything, and that no one would want me, I lost a sense of who I was. I came to believe that maybe his womanizing, drinking, hitting me, and so forth were really my fault.

"The final blow, literally, came several years ago. The children and I had left him for seven months. He convinced me that he was a changed person, was going to church, and would operate under a budget. That was important because, even with a good paycheck, more and more of it was going for alcohol and other women. So, I returned to him. I knew he was under tremendous pressure at work, so I tried to do the best I could. But one day dinner wasn't ready or fixed properly or something. In the kitchen he threw a pot, which was followed by him hitting me in the eye with his fist. I bled profusely and rushed to a hospital with broken bones in my face and a fear of losing my eyesight. They asked if I had been in a car accident. When told that my husband did it, they called the police who wanted to know if I wanted to press charges. I knew that if I did, he would be put in jail and lose his job, which meant no income or food for the children. So I refused to file charges. That experience convinced me I had to get out or he would eventually kill me. I prayed like I never prayed before and with the help of Legal Aid, got a divorce. The church and my parents were my primary means of support and the source of me keeping my sanity.

"If it was only me, I think I might have done things differently. Today, when I see how the effects of domestic abuse have carried over to my children, it really hurts. My son has not married and my youngest daughter says she fears any kind of commitment. My oldest daughter, who has two children, postponed marriage. My ex-husband has remarried and I understand he beats his new wife too. For the past six years, I've been with a wonderful man but we have been burned so badly over our lifetime, both of us are hesitant about getting into another marriage."

Questions to Consider

Delores was married for twenty-one years and abused for twenty of them. Why didn't she leave? Why do abused wives stay?

Delores came to believe she was at fault for her abuse. Explain how many abused wives come to this conclusion.

Could most abuse be decreased or even eliminated if husbands or wives would conform to their partners' wishes and perform their roles more effectively?

*I*n the preceding chapters, marriages and families have been examined throughout the life course. Clearly, no period in life is without the potential for interpersonal stress and violence. Earlier chapters addressed social conflict, lower levels of marital satisfaction ten to fifteen years into marriage, role conflicts, and the like. Each chapter referred to some event or process that produces strain, stress, various degrees of crisis, or the potential for violence.

If observations about the American family are to be believed, this institution and the interpersonal relationships within it have been in a state of decline for the past several hundred years. Preachers, teachers, philosophers, political leaders, commentators, and others—regardless of the generation in which they lived— have recorded their beliefs that parental authority was becoming more lax, that sexual taboos were weakening, that spouses were rebelling against one another, and so forth. These beliefs usually were contrasted to values and behaviors of the "old days," when authority was respected, when sexual taboos were observed, when spouses were more understanding and tolerant, and when violence and abuse were rare.

That each generation makes reference to weakness and decline may indicate dissatisfaction with present events, whatever those events may be, or it may indicate that actual conditions are never equal to the ideal. In either case, intimate relationships and family life have seldom been perfect—for couples, families, or the marital and family system. At any given time over the life course within every society, stressful events produce crises and the need for family reorganization. The first section of this chapter examines social stresses on the family.

$\mathcal{S}$ocial Stresses on Families

In a widely quoted article written forty-five years ago, Reuben Hill spoke of **stressor events,** or crisis-provoking events.[1] These are *sources* of stress and situations for which families have little or no preparation. Stressor events are never the same for different families but vary in the power with which they strike and the hardships that accompany them. *Hardships* are complications in a crisis-precipitating event that demand of the family competencies that the event itself may have temporarily paralyzed or made unavailable.

Stress as used by Pauline Boss means "pressure or tension in the family system—a disturbance in the steady state of the family."[2] Stress is an *outcome*, or the degree of family disruption that results from particular events. With change comes disturbance and pressure—stress. Stress is normal, inevitable, and even desirable at times. The family's level of stress results from events or situations that have potential to cause change.

Why do different families respond so differently to particular events or circumstances? For example, why is a pregnancy a blessing to some and a curse to others? Why is a geographical move a thrilling event to some family members and a severe disruption to others? Why do unemployment, divorce, or deaths severely cripple some persons while others seem to take them in stride? A key to answering questions such as these is to look at mediating factors between the source (event) and the outcome (level of stress).

ABCX Model of Stress

Hill provided a simple but powerful model in what today is widely referred to as the **ABCX model** of stress. According to this model, A (the event) interacts with B (the family's crisis-meeting resources), which interacts with C (the meaning or definition the family makes of the event) to produce X (the crisis).[3] This sequence may be stated as a formula:

$$A + (B + C) = X$$

---

[1]Reuben Hill, "Social Stresses on the Family," *Social Casework* 39 (February/March 1958), 139–150.

[2]Pauline Boss, *Family Stress Management: A Contextual Approach* (Thousand Oaks, CA: Sage Publications, Inc., 2nd ed., 2002), 16.

[3]Hill, "Social Stresses on the Family," 141.

The two key dimensions in the formula are B and C. If both are adequate, the level of stress will be low or nonexistent. If one or both are inadequate, the level of stress will be high. Consider this ABCX formulation more closely.

Stressor events (A) may come from a wide variety of sources, both within and outside the family. The consequences of the events are likely to differ considerably, depending on their source. For example, a general principle in sociology is that certain events outside a group, such as war, a flood, or depression, tend to solidify the group. Thus, although stressful, certain external events may tend to unify the family into a more cohesive unit, rather than leading or contributing to its breakdown. Also, the same events may not be defined as critically stressful when other persons are in the same situation or worse. For example, it is disappointing to professional researchers to have their writings rejected by editors of journals. The pain may be less severe if the researchers recognize that a given publication has a 90 percent rejection rate. To know that many others submitted articles and were rejected, did not get their research funded, lost their homes, had premature births, or were unemployed often makes events appear less critical. It helps to know that others share similar misfortunes.

Events within the family that are defined as stressful may be more disruptive because they arise from troubles that reflect poorly on the family's internal adequacy. These events may be nonsupport, mental breakdown, violence, suicide, or alcoholism, among others. The range of events, either within or outside the family, that disturb the family's role patterns is numerous. These events involve losses of persons, jobs, or incomes—as well as additions. The arrival of a child, grandmother, or mother-in-law may be as disruptive as the loss of any of the three. Gaining sudden fame or fortune may be as disruptive as losing either. Any sudden change in family status or a conflict among family members in the conceptions of their roles may produce further family crisis.

It should be noted that not all events or changes, regardless of whether they come from within the family or outside it, are stressor events. For example, research has shown that major life changes and role transitions (job loss, divorce, retirement, widowhood, first marriage, first child, and so forth), often assumed to be stressor events, actually relieve stress when prior role stress is very high.[4] That is, life-transition events were found to be nonproblematic or even beneficial to mental health when preceded by chronic role problems—a case in which new stress is actually relief from existing stress.

What factors make for crisis-proneness and freedom from crisis-proneness? The explanation lies in B and C in the formula presented earlier. That is, to what extent do families have resources to meet the event (factor B), and to what extent do families define the event as a crisis (factor C)? Crisis-meeting resources (factor B) may include family adaptability, family roles, kin-support systems, money income, insurance, friends, religious beliefs, education, good health, and the like. Problem families often do not have adequate resources with which to handle stressor events.

The extent to which the family defines the event as a crisis (factor C) reflects their value system and previous experience in meeting crisis. Consistent with an interactionist frame of reference, this definition of the event refers to the meaning attached to it, the appraisal or the interpretation as to its seriousness, and the perception of the event as *enabling* (making other things possible) or *disabling* (weakening or destroying possibilities).

---

[4]Blair Wheaton, "Life Transitions, Role Histories, and Mental Health," *American Sociological Review* 55 (April 1990), 209–223.

TRANSNATIONAL FAMILIES

Domestic Violence in the Indian Diaspora

Due to their traditional patriarchal cultural heritage, the tentative nature or their ethnic communities in the host country, and issues of cultural identity in a foreign land, recent immigrants from Eastern countries to the United States, or any other Western country, face the prospects of escalated levels of domestic violence. In an essay exploring domestic violence in one such community—the Indian diaspora in New York City—Margaret Abraham demonstrates the various structural and cultural conditions that foster domestic violence among this population.

The fourth highest foreign born population in the United States, one factor that plays an important part in understanding life among this group is their history of immigration. As a result of immigration policies in the 1960s, a major wave of Indian professionals came to the United States and established themselves as a "model minority" whose identity and status was established by setting themselves off against other minorities, especially African Americans. In particular, the retention and elaboration of the centrality of family in Indian culture helped this group better distinguish themselves and find a better match with the dominant culture.

As later immigrants inflated this initial population by way of subsequent sponsorship and family reunification programs, the population became more "mixed" and put pressure on the community to maintain its model minority status. As a result, issues of cultural identity are highly salient, creating pressures to conform to traditional Indian family structure and processes—including patriarchal power hierarchies and gender roles. There is also pressure on individuals not to undermine community status by exposing private problems such as domestic violence in public.

A final aspect of immigration history concerns the impacts of the terrorist attacks on 9-11 on policies in the United States that made deportation of foreign born residents easier to effect. These policies further silenced women who were experiencing domestic violence for fear that expressing their condition would expose them to potential deportation or might threaten the deportation of other family members.

As a partial consequence of their desire to maintain cultural identity and status, many of the Indian diaspora seek partners in India through arranged marriages—either men seeking brides in India or women seeking husbands in India. This practice also increased risk of violence against women in families. Often times brides were sought in India because they were assumed to subscribe more strongly to traditional gender roles even though they were coming from areas of India where gender roles have been undergoing changes for decades. As a result, there is in increased likelihood of conflict over gendered expectations in marriage that could lead to the use of violence as a perceived legitimate means for enforcing the wife's responsibilities. The closed nature of the diaspora community and the condition of community threat reinforces such reasoning and practice.

Further conflicts due to failures to meet expectations can come about because the couple have little time to get to know each other and may not be compatible on other grounds. When conflicts between spouses do occur, the wife often has little recourse because she is often isolated from her own family back in India, depends on her husband or sponsors to maintain her residency status in the United States, and frequently has few alternatives for living independently in a foreign country.

Source: Margaret Abraham, "Domestic Violence and the Indian Diaspora in the United States," *Indian Journal of Gender Studies*, 12 (2005): 427–454.

Crisis-proneness (X)—that is, the level or degree of stress—is, therefore, a function of both a deficiency in family organization resources (factor B) and the tendency to define hardships as crisis-producing (factor C). These two factors combine into one concept: family inadequacy or family adequacy.

Variations of the ABCX Model

Hamilton McCubbin and others, in an attempt to build on Hill's ABCX model, proposed a *double-ABCX model*, which differentiates the precrisis and postcrisis variables and adds the idea of a pileup of demands.[5] This pileup of demands acknowledges that other life stressors and strains affect the family prior to and following a crisis-producing event. The model becomes a longitudinal one, and the factors of time plus the accumulation of demands differentiate the precrisis from the postcrisis situation. The initial stressor event becomes a double-A by separating the changes that occur regardless of the initial stressor from changes that result from the family's efforts to cope with the hardships of the situation. The resources become a double-B by differentiating resources already available to the family from coping resources strengthened or developed in response to the crisis situation. The perception and meaning become a double-C by likewise differentiating the definition prior to the event of how stressful it may be from the postcrisis perceptions of the level of stress. Combining the precrisis and postcrisis ABC factors leads to family adaptation (or maladaptation) as a possible outcome.

Alexis Walker made a case for expanding the ABCX model of stress and crisis to incorporate new dimensions, recognizing that:

1. All levels of the social system are interdependent.
2. Stress occurs in a unique and influential sociocultural context.[6]

The interdependence of levels incorporates individual factors with dyadic, family, nonfamily, and community levels. That is, levels more macro than individuals and families need to be incorporated into the model. Individual resources may be very different from family, community, and societal resources. Definitions or perceptions may vary among members of a family. Whose definition or perception is most important? If members don't agree, will the crisis be unresolvable?

The sociohistorical context recognizes how perceptions of stressful circumstances and resources available vary considerably over time. Different contexts and the unique perspectives and resources related to a given context need to be recognized.

One illustration of how developments in the wider society affect stress is seen in an examination of economic pressures and marital instability in the Czech Republic.[7] In the early 1990s, Czechoslovak communism collapsed, consumer price subsidies were lifted, and many families were in serious economic trouble and caught between price inflation and wage controls. These economic pressures made both husbands and wives irritable and their tension exacerbated problem behaviors such as drinking and fighting. These problems in turn generated hostility between the spouses and increased marital instability. These findings are consistent with results of U.S. research that show changes in the economy and economic pressures affecting family (and marital) stress levels.

Another factor to consider is how stress in one area or from one source spills over into other areas. An article on the "contagion" of stress across multiple roles documented that home-to-work stress occurs more strongly among men than women and that both men and women reduce their involvements in stressful home situations following a stressful day at work.[8] Wives, in particular, modified their housework efforts to compensate for the work stresses of their spouses. Stresses in

---

[5]Hamilton I. McCubbin and Joan M. Patterson, "Family Adaptation to Crisis," *Family Stress, Coping, and Social Support*, ed. Hamilton I. McCubbin et al. (Springfield, IL: Charles C. Thomas, 1982), 44–46.

[6]Alexis J. Walker, "Reconceptualizing Family Stress," *Journal of Marriage and the Family* 47 (November 1985), 827–837.

[7]Joseph Hraba, Frederick O. Lorenz, and Zdenka Pechacova, "Family Stress during the Czech Transformation," *Journal of Marriage and the Family* 62 (May 2000), 520–531.

[8]Niall Bolger, Anita DeLongis, Ronald C. Kessler, and Elaine Wethington, "The Contagion of Stress across Multiple Roles," *Journal of Marriage and the Family* 51 (February 1989), 175–183.

one area, such as work, affect stresses in other areas, such as home. What's more, stresses experienced by one spouse or partner affect stresses in the other.

While the list of stressor events, family problems, and conflict situations in relationships and families may seem infinite, this chapter will focus on only one: violence. A number of other potentially stressful events were discussed in some detail in prior chapters, including AIDS, abortion, incest, mobility, commuter marriages, dual-career situations, sexual and racial inequality, poverty, intermarriage, conjugal decision making, parenthood, father/mother absence, mid-life crisis, widowhood, death, and aging. Other issues—including separation, divorce, and stepchildren—are discussed in Chapter 14.

Violence in Families and among Intimates

Over the past four decades, research on family violence has grown exponentially, despite the fact that evidence has not indicated an increase in levels of family violence.[9] The terms *family violence* and *violence among intimates* are used to refer to any act carried out with the intention of causing physical harm to legally related individuals or those in close primary relationships. This broad definition includes acts such as spanking a disobedient child, raping a lover, and murdering a spouse. Many people (readers included) are not aware that they are more likely to be physically assaulted, beaten, raped, or killed in their own homes at the hands of loved ones than in any other place or by anyone else in society.[10]

Consider the following:

Pictures of missing children on cards and milk cartons seldom document that children are more likely to be kidnapped by their own parents than by strangers.

Most people believe that marriage is based on love and respect, yet more than half of all couples report physical violence by a partner at some time during their marriage.

Nearly one out of every four murder victims in the United States is killed by a member of his or her own family; this is also the case in Africa, Great Britain, and Denmark.[11]

It should be noted that violence, while frequent in most societies, is not an inevitable consequence of family life. David Levinson, for example, after examining violence cross-culturally, found that sixteen societies of the ninety in his sample were relatively free of family violence.[12] Hunter-gatherers (Ona, Andamans, Siriono, Bushman), for example, rarely mistreated their children and were overrepresented among the societies without family violence.

According to Levinson:

In general, in societies without family violence, husbands and wives share all domestic decision making, wives have some control over the fruits of family labor, wives can divorce their husbands as easily as their husbands can divorce

---

[9]Murray A. Straus, "Sociological Research and Social Policy: The Case of Family Violence," *Sociological Forum* 7 (1992), 211–237.

[10]Richard J. Gelles and Murray A. Straus, *Intimate Violence* (New York: Simon and Schuster, 1988), 18.

[11]Richard J. Gelles, *Family Violence* (Beverly Hills: Sage, 1979), 11.

[12]David Levinson, *Family Violence in Cross-Cultural Perspective* (Newbury Park, CA: Sage, 1989), 102–107.

CROSS-CULTURAL *Perspective*

Domestic Violence and Contraceptive Use in India

The use of violence by men to control their partners is a common occurrence in parts of India—especially in Northern India's lower caste communities. According to Lyndsey Wilson-Williams, domestic violence is supported by patriarchal norms and justified when a wife refuses to obey her husband or to meet his expectations. A majority of both men and women support these norms. Given that contraceptives give women greater autonomy in controlling their own fertility and make possible sexual relations outside of marriage without the fear of pregnancy, it is of little surprise that domestic violence and contraceptive use are closely linked. These authors note consistent research findings across countries with high rates of domestic violence that show a link between experiencing violence and low levels of contraceptive use and high fertility and unwanted pregnancies. To understand this link more fully, they conducted focus groups with 64 Hindi women from lower socioeconomic status areas in Northern India.

The women in these focus groups reported two major reasons for why violence occurs in Indian marriages. The first had to do with the husband's inability to fulfill his provider role due to economic circumstances. In this case violence is used to compensate for

his lack of economic bases for fulfilling power expectations. The second involved a logic that casts women as needing supervision and discipline to bring about the fulfillment of their duties in the family. Those duties apply primarily to activities inside the household, so a wife's movements outside the home often justify the husband's use of violence. It is also a wife's duty to comply with her husband's sexual demands and fertility desires. Since secret contraceptive use was seen as a deliberate attempt to circumvent the husband's right to control fertility, these women saw the husband's use of violence in these circumstances as also justified. Interestingly, when violence was used by husbands in the context of disagreements, it was also seen as a consequence of the wife's inability to fulfill her duties as a pacifier.

Finally, these women noted that often times husbands' behaviors are themselves controlled by a system of power hierarchy where mothers-in-law effect control over their daughters-in-law by encouraging the husband to use violence to correct behaviors, by distorting information to lead the husband to believe that the wife needs disciplining, or by using violence themselves as proxies for their sons. In the end, fertility control was a strong motivating force behind the abuse of wives in India as a result of strong pressures by parents and relatives of husbands to have many children, especially males.

Source: Lyndsey Wilson-Williams, Sanjay Juvekar, and Karen Andes, "Domestic Violence and Contraceptive Use in a Rural Indian Village," *Violence Against Women*, 14 (October 2008): 1181–1198.

them, marriage is monogamous, there is no premarital sex double standard, divorce is relatively infrequent, husbands and wives sleep together, men resolve disputes with other men peacefully, and intervention in wife beating incidents tends to be immediate.[13]

The central conclusion reached from these findings is that family violence does not occur in societies in which family life is characterized by cooperation, commitment, sharing, and equality. In contrast, family violence is more common in societies in which men control women's lives, violent resolution to conflicts is acceptable, and mothers bear the major responsibility for child rearing.

Precise data on conjugal and parental abuse and violence in the United States and other world societies are difficult to obtain. Not only do violence and abuse occur behind closed doors, hidden from public view, but they also may not be perceived as

---

[13]Ibid., 103.

improper. Spouse shoving, child spanking, and sibling fighting may be defined as normative, appropriate, and even necessary marital and family behaviors.

Myths of Family Violence

In a chapter entitled "People Other Than Us: Public Perceptions of Family Violence," Richard Gelles and Murray Straus revealed a number of stereotypes about abusive partners and families.[14] Stereotypes about the nature and causes of domestic violence often are more pieces of conventional wisdom than facts or truths. In effect, they are myths. The perpetuation of these myths serves a very significant function: Violence is attributed to "other people" (namely, mentally disturbed, unbalanced people) rather than acknowledged as an outgrowth of the very structures of society and family.

Consider the following seven myths:

Myth 1—The family is nonviolent. This double-sided myth relates to the one just cited above. One view is that family violence is rare, and the other view is that an increase in violence is of epidemic proportions. The range of estimates, from thousands to millions, suggests that no one really knows how much violence exists in families. The conclusion drawn is that the problem is not a problem at all.

Myth 2—Abusers are aliens, and victims are innocents. The stereotype is that the abuser is mentally disturbed, psychologically unbalanced, or even psychotic, whereas the victim is a defenseless innocent. Not wanting to see their own behavior or that of friends or relatives as improper, people envision family violence as committed by horrible persons against innocent people. Gelles and Straus suggested that, in fact, only about 10 percent of abusive incidents are caused by mental illness.

Myth 3—Abuse is confined to poor, minority families. Research has found that intimate violence is more likely to occur in lower-income and minority households, but it is not confined to them. Violence cuts across all classes and races; the poor have a greater likelihood of being violent and also run the risk of being over-represented in official statistics. Attributing violence to poor and minority families is another way of seeing others as violent and one's own behavior as normal.

Myth 4—Alcohol and drugs are the real causes of violence in the home. A high association has been shown between violence and alcohol and drug use. But does it follow that violence will end when the drinking/drug problem is eliminated? Are alcohol or drugs actually the cause of the violence? Evidence has disputed the claim that alcohol causes violence and has supported the claim that certain drugs rarely are associated with violence; in fact, some drugs produce a euphoric effect, reducing the level of violence. In short, curing or eliminating an alcohol or drug problem will not eliminate domestic violence.

Myth 5—Children who are abused grow up to be abusers. Again, this myth has some truth in that abused children tend to be abusive adults, but all abused children do not grow up to be abusive. Stith and others, for example, found a weak to moderate relationship between growing up in an abusive family and becoming involved in a violent marital relationship.[15] This relationship was

---

[14]Gelles and Straus, *Intimate Violence*, Chapter 2, 37–51.

[15]Sandra M. Stith, Karen H. Rosen, Kimberly A. Middleton, Amy L. Busch, Kirsten Lundeberg, and Russell P. Carlton, "The Intergenerational Transmission of Spouse Abuse: A Meta-Analysis," *Journal of Marriage and the Family* 62 (August 2000), 640–654.

stronger for men becoming a perpetrator of spouse abuse and for women becoming a victim of spouse abuse. But the claim that people who are abused are preprogrammed to be abusers has not been supported.

Myth 6—Battered women like being hit. This myth is rooted in misunderstanding as to why abused women stay in abusive situations and whether battered women provoke the abuse and thus desire to be beaten. The dynamics of family violence and the social position of women in U.S. society destroy this myth. The reality is that abused women do not have the resources (including healthy self-esteem) to get out of abusive situations. And the longer they stay, the harder it is to leave.

Myth 7—Violence and love are incompatible. Many battered spouses have strong loving feelings for their partners, and most battered children continue to love their parents. Unlike violence in the streets, violence in the home includes bonds of love, attachment, and affection.

Gelles and Straus concluded the discussion of myths by stating:

> It is not only the myths that have to be abandoned, but the social function that they serve. The greatest function served by the seven myths we have discussed is that collectively they serve as a smoke screen that blinds us to our own potential for violence. Moreover, when our explanations focus on "kinds of people" (mentally disturbed, poor, alcoholics, drug abusers, etc.) we blind ourselves to the structural properties of the family as a social institution that makes it our most violent institution with the exception of the military in time of war.[16]

Causes of Family Violence

Why is there so much violence in the family? Many theories have been advanced to explain interpersonal violence in general, and family violence more specifically. Some theories, as noted, place the cause within the individual, attributing violent behavior to psychopathologies and alcohol and drug use. Other theories are social/psychological in nature and attribute violence to social learning, exchange, and interaction. A third group of theories is sociocultural and attributes violence to societal resources, conflict systems, and the larger culture. Feminist scholars argue that domestic violence is rooted in gender and power and represents men's active attempts to maintain dominance and control over women.

This third group of theories helps us understand, for example, why there is a higher incidence of black-on-black violence as well as more violence toward black women than white women.[17] A *structural-cultural theory* looks at structurally induced economic problems (including unemployment and underemployment) as an important variable affecting black men's ability to enact traditional male roles in the family. A *feminist theory* indicates that incompatibilities in income, education, and occupational prestige between men and women give men greater power and control.[18] Violence is a social practice that enables men to

---

[16]Gelles and Straus, *Intimate Violence*, Chapter 2, 51.

[17]Robert L. Hampton and Richard J. Gelles, "Violence toward Black Women in a Nationally Representative Sample of Black Families," *Journal of Comparative Family Studies* 25 (Spring 1994), 105–119.

[18]Kristin L. Anderson, "Gender, Status, and Domestic Violence: An Integration of Feminist and Family Violence Approaches," *Journal of Marriage and the Family* 59 (August 1997), 655–669.

Family Diversity

Perceptions of Domestic Violence among American Indians

According to Melissa Tehee and Cynthia Willis Esqueda, American Indians experience the highest rate of intimate violence of any other race or ethnic group in the United States—more than twice the rate for African Americans. In fact, they note, the term "Indian love" has become synonymous with abuse. This high rate of domestic violence, however, is a more recent phenomenon and a deviation from American Indian traditional culture which safeguarded women through the enforcement of community sanctions. These community controls were unraveled by the effects of Europeans who systematically disrupted American Indian traditions and communities and in the process undermined the power of American Indian women and increased their vulnerability. These effects were further exacerbated by the emergence of a dominant stereotype of American Indian women as both strong and helpless at the same time. Given this cultural and historical context and the high levels of violence experienced, these two researchers set out to examine whether American Indian women have developed unique perceptions of intimate violence by interviewing 20 American Indian women and 20 European American women and comparing their responses.

The results of their study show that American Indian women are more likely to reserve their definition of abuse to physical acts, whereas European American women are more likely to include emotional and verbal acts as abuse. They are also more likely to see violence in their relationships as stemming from disagreements (common couple violence) rather than being the result of attempts to control (patriarchal terrorism). Third, American Indian women are more likely to see their abusive situation as the result of their partner's experiences of abuse as a child or their own experiences of abuse earlier in life. Even though internal factors play a role in their abusive situation, they are also more likely to see their partner's behaviors as the result of external situations such as poverty and unemployment rather than internal or dispositional factors. Finally, these women saw the legal system as ineffectual in abuse situations and were significantly less likely to call the police in the case of any violence short of that which produced significant physical harm. Although these perceptions are the result of their experiences, they also play a role in the continuation of high rates of abuse in this community.

Source: Melissa Tehee and Cynthia Willis Esqueda, "American Indian and European American Women's Perceptions of Domestic Violence," *Journal of Family Violence,* 23 (2008): 25–35.

express a masculine identity. Note that masculinity and femininity, according to feminists, are not individual traits but relational social constructs created through social practice.

Murray Straus and Christine Smith presented five social factors that converge to cause the high rates of intrafamily violence:

1. *Intrafamily conflict*—An irony of family life is that many of the same characteristics that contribute to intimacy and love among family members also contribute to conflict.
2. *Male dominance in family and society*—Given the concept of the husband as head of the family and the domination of men in U.S. society, force is a key resource in resolving conflict.
3. *Cultural norms permitting family violence*—Parents have a legal right and arguably a moral obligation to spank or slap their children.
4. *Family socialization in violence*—Children's early and continuing experience with violence between parents or by parents provides role models and a specific script in training for future violence.

5. *Pervasiveness of violence in society*—In American society, socially legitimate violence includes physical punishment by teachers, force by police, widespread ownership of guns, the death penalty, military force against governments, violent acts on television and in the movies, and so forth. Violence in one area of life spills over into other spheres of life.[19]

It is clear that violence begets violence and that aggression is transmitted across generations. Parents who yell frequently are the ones most likely to hit frequently, and both verbal and physical violence appear to be transgenerational.[20] Fortunately, most people are able to break out of this intergenerational cycle of abuse, but this does not negate the increased probability of yelling at children, spanking children, or hitting a partner if family violence was a pattern in one's childhood.

Child Abuse and Violence

Throughout the history of the world, children have been subject to a range of abuses and cruelties, including sexual abuse, beatings, and abandonment (infants left to die). Today, only isolated incidents of abandonment are reported, but cases of physical and sexual abuse are quite common.

Hitting children to punish them is legal in every state in the United States; in contrast, in Sweden, a parent can be imprisoned for striking a child. Parents in the United States tend to view corporal punishment (striking and spanking) as an acceptable and appropriate means of discipline. Traditionally, this "privilege" of spanking was even extended to schoolteachers and administrators as a means of inflicting punishment and maintaining discipline. The guideline commonly followed was "Spare the rod and spoil the child."

In most nations, including the United States, **corporal punishment** is central to the discipline of children and the socialization process. Almost all parents and the majority of teachers believe that physical punishment is an appropriate and effective form of discipline. Straus found that over 90 percent of parents of children ages 3 and 4 in the United States used physical punishment to correct behavior.[21] The most common forms include spanking, slapping, and grabbing and shoving a child with more force than is needed. Hitting a child with an object is also legally permissible and widespread if done by someone in a custodial relationship to the child.

What are the effects of physical punishment? Straus hypothesized that physical punishment by parents and teachers may produce conformity in the immediate situation, but in the long run it increases the probability of deviance, including delinquency in adolescence and wife beating, child abuse, and crime outside the family (robbery, assault, and homicide) in adulthood.[22] Studies have not proven that physical punishment *causes* these problems but that there is a spillover effect.

A **cultural spillover theory** suggests that violence in one sphere of life tends to engender violence in other spheres. The more a society uses force to attain socially

---

[19]Murray A. Straus and Christine Smith, "Family Patterns and Primary Prevention of Family Violence," in Murray A. Straus and Richard J. Gelles, eds. *Physical Violence in American Families* (New Brunswick, NJ: Transaction, 1990), 512–521.

[20]David Hemenway, Sara Solnick, and Jennifer Carter, "Child-Rearing Violence," *Child Abuse and Neglect* 18 (1994): 1011–1020; and Diana Doumas, Galya Margolin, and Richard S. John, "The Intergenerational Transmission of Aggression across Three Generations," *Journal of Family Violence* 9 (1994), 157–175.

[21]Murray A. Straus, "Discipline and Deviance: Physical Punishment of Children and Violence and Other Crime in Adulthood," *Social Problems* 38 (May 1991), 136.

[22]Ibid., 133–152.

CROSS-CULTURAL *Perspective*

Child Abuse in Sweden

In reviewing numerous research on children, Linda Haas reports that levels of sexual and physical abuse appear to be low in Sweden. For example, in 1991, 440 cases of sexual crimes against children were reported in which the perpetrators were family members, which is a rate of about 2 per 10,000 children. Reported cases in the United States were at a much higher rate of 25 per 1,000.

Haas reports on another study that asked college students about their parents' disciplinary practices.

About two-thirds of Swedish males and slightly over half of Swedish females had never been spanked by their parents. This compares to about 11 percent of American males and 15 percent of American females who have never been spanked. Only 11 percent of Swedes believe that corporal punishment is necessary in child rearing, compared to 84 percent of Americans who believe that to be true. It should be noted that a law passed in 1979 made it illegal for Swedish parents to spank their children or treat them in a humiliating way.

See: Linda Haas, "Family Policy in Sweden," *Journal of Family and Economic Issues* 17 (Spring 1996): 78–79.

desired ends (maintaining order in schools, deferring criminals, defending itself from foreign enemies), the greater the tendency for those engaged in illegitimate behavior to also use force in attaining their ends. Straus conceded he could not prove the theory, but that empirical findings were almost entirely consistent with it: there is a linkage between physical punishment of children and crime in society and support for Straus' assertion that physical punishment may produce conformity in the short term but creates or exacerbates deviance in the long term.

An eighteen-year longitudinal study in New Zealand provides some additional support for Straus's assertions. The authors found that young people reporting exposure to harsh or abusive treatment during childhood had elevated roles of juvenile offending, alcohol abuse/dependence, and mental health problems.[23] Although we need to be cautious in equating spanking or physical punishment used to correct behavior with harsh or abusive treatment, the distance between the two often is unclear. The context of a loving and supportive parent and the meanings attached to it by both parent and child need to be considered.

Violence toward children is found in all social classes and among families across the full spectrum of income. However, violence toward children, especially severe violence, is more likely to occur in households at or below the poverty line. Based on a national probability sample of over 6,000 households, Gelles reported that the incidence of overall violence was 4 percent higher among households with poverty-level incomes than among households with higher incomes. Severe violence (high probability of causing an injury) was 46 percent higher and very severe violence (such as burning, threatening with or using a knife or gun) was 100 percent higher among the poverty-level households.[24] Child abuse tends to increase as unemployment increases.[25] Factors such as poverty and unemployment are stressor events that

---

[23]David M. Fergusson and Michael T. Lynskey, "Physical Punishment/Maltreatment during Childhood and Adjustment in Young Adulthood," *Child Abuse and Neglect* 21 (1997), 617–636.

[24]Richard J. Gelles, "Poverty and Violence toward Children," *American Behavioral Scientist* 35 (January/February 1992), 258–274.

[25]Loring Jones, "Unemployment and Child Abuse," *Families in Society: The Journal of Contemporary Human Services* 71 (December 1990), 579–586.

influence family functioning, as exhibited in the greater abuse of children.

Is there an epidemic of child abuse in the United States? Does the number of children who are abused increase each year? Apparently, no. Straus and Gelles compared the rate of physical abuse of children from a 1975 study with the rates from a 1985 replication.[26] Both studies showed high incidences of severe physical violence against children; however, the 1985 rate of physical child abuse (as measured by the number of children who were kicked, punched, bitten, beaten up, or attacked with a knife or gun) was 47 percent lower than the 1975 rate.

These declines in levels of child abuse are reported to be consistent with other changes that have occurred in the family and society over the past decade and these changes most likely served to reduce violence in the home. Changes in *family structure*—such as increased age at marriage and the birth of the first child, the decline in the number of children per family, and the decreased number of unwanted children—are all related to lower rates of child abuse. Changes in the *economy*—for instance, lower rates of unemployment and inflation—also likely reduced the frequency of child abuse. The growth of new and innovative *treatment programs*, social services, and therapy approaches has probably helped to reduce intrafamily violence, as well. And finally, deterrence in the form of legal *sanctions* and the perceived high probability of getting caught and punished serve as reminders that abusive behavior is inappropriate behavior.

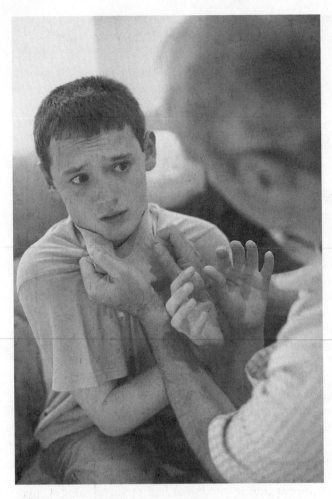

In contrast to Sweden, where it is illegal to spank children or treat them in a humiliating way, in the United States, many parents view corporal punishment as an acceptable and appropriate means of discipline. Because physical punishment usually occurs "behind closed doors" most cases of child abuse are never discovered.

Child Sexual Abuse

The child abuser, the victim, and the type of abuse all vary by gender and by the type of biological relationship. This seems to be particularly true with **child sexual abuse**.[27] Children are assumed incapable of consenting to sex with an adult because they lack the power to decline involvement and often do not understand to what they are consenting. Sexual abuse generally includes elements of force, manipulation, or coercion.

In a national survey of adults and their history of childhood sexual abuse, 27 percent of the women and 16 percent of the men reported being abused.[28] The me-

[26]Murray A. Straus and Richard J. Gelles, "Societal Change and Change in Family Violence from 1975 to 1985 as Revealed by Two National Surveys," *Journal of Marriage and the Family* 48 (August 1986), 465–479; and Gelles and Straus, *Intimate Violence*, 109–114.

[27]For a review of research see Richard J. Gelles and Jon R. Conte, "Domestic Violence and Sexual Abuse of Children: A Review of Research in the Eighties," *Journal of Marriage and the Family* 52 (November 1990), 1045–1058.

[28]David Finkelhor, Gerald Hotaling, I. A. Lewis, and Christine Smith, "Sexual Abuse in a National Survey of Adult Men and Women: Prevalence, Characteristics, and Risk Factors," *Child Abuse and Neglect* 14 (1990), 19–28.

dian age of abuse was slightly under ten. Boys were more likely to have been abused by strangers, whereas girls were more likely to have been abused by family members.

Another source, representing several thousand cases of child sexual abuse, revealed that nonbiologically related caregivers (stepparents, adoptive parents, foster parents, baby-sitters, institutions) were substantially overrepresented, and biologically related caregivers (parents, siblings, grandparents) were substantially underrepresented in reports of child sexual abuse.[29] The numbers of male perpetrators greatly surpassed those of female perpetrators in all situations: three times as many biological fathers as mothers, nearly five times as many male baby-sitters as female, and more than twenty times as many males as females in other caregiver roles (stepparents, parents' paramours or lovers, institutional staff).

The consequences of child sexual abuse appear to be severe and long lasting. Compared to those not abused, both females and males who were sexually abused as children were found to show greater evidence of sexual disturbance or dysfunction, homosexual experiences in adolescence or adulthood, depression, alcohol abuse, and even suicidal ideas.[30] Child sexual abuse was found to be a significant predictor of a woman's educational attainment and annual earnings.[31] National data show that sexual contact with an adult during childhood increases the likelihood of engaging in an active and risky sexual career in adolescence and adulthood. Victims have sex at earlier ages, have more partners, are more likely to bear children before they turn 19, and are more likely to experience sexually transmitted infections and forced sex.[32]

Parent Abuse and Violence

Violence between parents and children is reciprocal. That is, children not only are victims of violence but are perpetrators as well. Many cases of parental abuse of children go unnoticed and unreported, but assaulted parents, who are generally more powerful than their children, may go to great lengths to conceal being abused by them. Acts of severe violence, such as a child killing a parent, may get publicity, but cases of hitting and biting or making threats are likely to remain unnoticed by outsiders.

Perhaps at this point, a note should be added about children who are violent, not only to parents, but to animals. Clifton Flynn notes that this has been an ignored area of study but is a serious antisocial behavior by children and adolescents, is a relatively common childhood occurrence, is related to interpersonal violence, and is connected to and may be a marker of family violence.[33] Violence against animals may signify a troubled child and/or a dysfunctional family. Studies have shown that children who are cruel to animals are more likely to engage in aggressive and violent behavior toward others.

[29]Leslie Margolin and John L. Craft, "Child Sexual Abuse by Caretakers," *Family Relations* 38 (October 1989), 450–455.

[30]Joseph H. Beitchman, Kenneth J. Zucker, Jane E. Hood, Granville A. DaCosta, Donna Akman, and Erika Cassavia, "A Review of the Long-Term Effects of Child Sexual Abuse," *Child Abuse and Neglect* 16 (1992), 101–118; and Tom Luster and Stephen A. Small, "Sexual Abuse History and Problems in Adolescence: Exploring the Effects of Moderating Variables," *Journal of Marriage and the Family* 59 (February 1997), 131–142.

[31]Batya Hyman, "The Economic Consequences of Child Sexual Abuse for Adult Lesbian Women," *Journal of Marriage and the Family* 62 (February 2000), 199–211.

[32]Christopher R. Browning and Edward O. Laumann, "Sexual Contact between Children and Adults: A Life Course Perspective," *American Sociological Review* 62 (August 1997), 540–560.

[33]Clifton P. Flynn, "Why Family Professionals Can No Longer Ignore Violence toward Animals," *Family Relations* 49 (January 2000), 87–95.

Wife and Female Partner Abuse and Violence

Much research has focused on wives, but interestingly, findings have consistently shown that physical aggression is at least twice as common among cohabiting couples as it is among married couples. During a given year, about thirty-five out of every one hundred cohabiting couples experience physical aggression, compared to fifteen out of every one hundred married couples.[34] And much of this physical aggression is directed at women, many of whom believe their partners have the right to slap them or shove them under certain conditions. And as women begin to believe their male partners have this right, men learn that violence against their female partners is acceptable.

Michael Johnson argues that there are two distinct forms of violence against women.[35] One he calls **common couple violence**. This involves conflict between couples with an occasional outburst of violence from either husbands or wives. The other he calls **patriarchal terrorism**. As noted earlier, from a feminist perspective this is a product of patriarchal traditions of men's right to control "their" women (wives), not only by a systematic use of violence but by economic subordination, threats, isolation, and other control factors. This pattern of violence often is referred to as wife beating, wife battery, and battered women. Johnson notes that patriarchal terrorism escalates (increases in frequency and intensity over time), whereas common couple violence does not. Common couple violence is an intermittent response to the occasional conflicts of everyday life, motivated by a need to control in the specific situation, but not a more general need to be in charge of the relationship.

Violence against women, as is much family violence, is not always viewed as improper or deviant. One article was even titled "If violence is domestic, does it really count?"[36] This view had much historical precedence. As recently as the late nineteenth century in Great Britain and the United States, it was considered a necessary aspect of a husband's marital obligation to control and chastise his wife through the use of physical force. The husband, as the dominant ruler and head, was expected to use whatever means necessary to obtain obedience and control. Most physical abuse and violence toward wives and female partners does not take the form of beating; rather, throwing things, shoving, pushing, grabbing, slapping, and hitting are more common. To be sure, however, many women are seriously hurt by their partners. Nursing research reported that male intimate partners abused 8 percent of women in prenatal and primary care settings and approximately 20 percent of women in emergency room settings.[37] Approximately 8 percent of women were physically abused while pregnant, and an additional 15 percent were beaten prior to the pregnancy.

Female physical abuse is not uniformly distributed in all major social and demographic groups. Sociodemographic risk factors associated with wife abuse include low income, unemployment, and race; wife abuse is particularly common among blacks who have low incomes and high levels of unemployment. Wife abuse

---

[34]Jan E. Stets, "Cohabiting and Marital Aggression: The Role of Social Isolation," *Journal of Marriage and the Family* 53 (August 1991), 669–680.

[35]Michael P. Johnson, "Patriarchal Terrorism and Common Couple Violence: Two Forms of Violence against Women," *Journal of Marriage and the Family* 57 (May 1995): 283–294.

[36]Sharon Wofford Mihalic and Delbert Elliott, "If Violence Is Domestic, Does It Really Count?" *Journal of Family Violence* 12 (1997), 293–311.

[37]Jacquelyn C. Campbell, "A Review of Nursing Research on Battering," in Carolyn M. Sampselle, *Violence against Women: Nursing Research, Education, and Practice Issues* (New York: Hemisphere Publishing Corp., 1992), 69–81.

Some violence against women is an intermittent response to the occasional conflicts of everyday life. However, patriarchal traditions of men's superiority over women lend support to men using any means to maintain their dominant position, including partner abuse and wife beating.

is also more prevalent among people who are nonreligious, divorced or separated, and under age 30.[38]

What are the consequences of abuse to women? Studies suggest that both verbal and physical abuse have significant direct effects on depression, marital dissatisfaction, and relationship dissolution. One national study showed that physical aggression, and to a lesser extent, verbal conflict, predicted union disruption and marital dissolution.[39] Other research revealed that victimized women's marital experiences were characterized by less satisfaction and less stability but moderated by relationship efficacy and perceived intimacy and spousal support.[40] That is, the negative consequences were less severe if wives attributed their husbands' negative behavior to a cause other than the husband and did not see him as selfishly motivated or intentionally engaged in the negative behavior. The occurrence of negative, humiliating events was a strong predictor of depression in women.

The questions raised about changes in rates of child abuse must also be raised about wife or spouse abuse: is there an epidemic of wife abuse in the United States? Are more women abused each year? And again, the answer is apparently no. The same Straus/Gelles studies mentioned earlier, comparing violence rates in 1975 and 1985, showed that wife beating (as measured by the number who were kicked, punched, hit with an object, bitten, beaten up, or attacked with a knife or gun) decreased by 27 percent over these ten years.[41] Interestingly, similar severe assaults by wives on husbands decreased only 4.3 percent. Even if these rates indicated actual reductions, the number of wives beaten each year in the United States is staggering: 1.5 million. Quite often, these women stay in their abusive situations. The logical question is, *why?*

Some answers to this question are offered in the family diversity insert on abused wives. Most answers suggest that wives who are highly dependent on marriage are less able to discourage, avoid, leave, or put an end to abuse than women in marriages where the balance of resources between husband and wife is more nearly equal. Dependent wives lack both alternatives to marriage and resources within marriage to negotiate change. Other answers focus on the psychological strategies

[38]Michael D. Smith, "Sociodemographic Risk Factors in Wife Abuse: Results from a Survey on Toronto Women," *Canadian Journal of Sociology* 15 (1990), 39–58.

[39]Alfred DeMaris, "Till Discord Do Us Part: The Role of Physical and Verbal Conflict in Union Disruption," *Journal of Marriage and the Family* 62 (August 2000), 683–692.

[40]Ileana Arias, Carolyn M. Lyons, and Amy E. Street, "Individual and Marital Consequences of Victimization: Moderating Effects of Relationship Efficacy and Spouse Support," *Journal of Family Violence* 12 (1997), 193–210.

[41]Straus and Gelles, "Societal Change and Change in Family Violence," 465–479; and Gelles and Straus, *Intimate Violence*, 109.

women use to help them perceive their relationship in a positive light or convince themselves of their obligation to stay. In sum, these two variables—no resources or alternatives, and the perception of and the meaning attached to the relationship—seem to fit the B and C in the ABCX model and explain why many abused women remain with their partners.

Of those abused wives who leave, a number turn to shelters, which are short-term refuges from violent relationships. Again, within the context of the ABCX model, shelters represent an important community resource for many abused wives. Surprisingly, one national study found that having enlisted the help of shelters, lawyers, or therapists was related to greater fear of future abuse.[42] The authors suggest that these extreme actions may set in motion the wheels of the criminal justice system, resulting in formal sanctions applied to the husband. The victim's apprehension regarding his possible retribution may be an understandable consequence of such actions.

Rape among Intimates

Sexual abuse and rape by a spouse or by intimate partners is another common form of violence inflicted on women. The husband who forces sexual intercourse (technically, marital rape, although legally not usually recognized as such) is seldom viewed as a rapist by his wife, who may blame herself for the incident. That women blame themselves or learn to accept forced sexual intercourse by someone they know and have loved may be why so little attention has been devoted to this issue.

Rape, simply defined, is forced sex without consent. Legal definitions generally involve three separate factors: (1) sexual intercourse, involving vaginal, anal, or oral penetration; (2) force or threat of force; and (3) nonconsent of the victim. Until recently, marital rape and *rape among intimates* has been ignored in the marital/family literature. It has been brought to light as a feminist issue: Rape is a mechanism for maintaining male control and domination and a violent means of inducing fear in women and reinforcing their subordination to men.[43]

Diana Russell indicated that the 1980s was a decade of tremendous achievement in changing state laws regarding rape.[44] In 1980, only three states had completely abolished the marital rape exception and three others had partially stricken it. As of 1990, sixteen states allow the prosecution of husbands for raping their wives, without exception. In another twenty-six states, husbands can be prosecuted for raping their wives in some circumstances but are totally exempt in others. Some examples of exemptions include if a rape is imposed by force but without additional violence, such as a threat with a weapon; if nonforceful rape is imposed when a wife is mentally or physically helpless and cannot give her consent; and if the victim does not report the rape within a specified time period. In the remaining eight states (Kentucky, Missouri, New Mexico, North Carolina, Oklahoma, South Carolina, South Dakota, and Utah), a husband cannot be prosecuted for raping his wife unless the couple is living apart, is legally separated, or have filed for divorce. Yet Russell reported that one out of every seven women in her study who had ever been married reported at least one and sometimes many experiences of rape by her husband.[45]

---

[42]Alfred DeMaris and Steven Swinford, "Female Victims of Spousal Violence: Factors Influencing Their Level of Fearfulness," *Family Relations* 45 (January 1996), 98–106.

[43]Patricia L. N. Donat and John D'Emilio, "A Feminist Redefinition of Rape and Sexual Assault: Historical Foundations and Change," *Journal of Social Issues* 48 (1992), 9–22.

[44]Diana E. H. Russell, Rape in Marriage (Bloomington: Indiana University Press, 1990), 23.

[45]Ibid., 57.

Why Do Abused Women and Wives Stay?

If a woman or a wife is in an abusive relationship, why doesn't she leave? This question is based on an underlying assumption that the decision to stay or leave is a rational one and that realistic alternatives to staying exist. Pamela Choice and Leanne Lamke use a conceptual approach to understanding the stay/leave decision.[46] They draw upon four theories developed by others. These include:

1. A theory of *learned helplessness*. Here a woman comes to believe there is nothing she can do to change her situation, so she stops trying. Her efforts do not affect the outcome or change the situation, so why bother.

2. *Psychological entrapment*. Here a woman typically invests time, energy, and emotional involvement to attain the goal of a nonviolent relationship. She may believe that if only she would try harder, the relationship would improve. She may feel that too much has already been invested to quit. Remaining committed to the relationship and having invested so much in it results in psychological entrapment.

3. *An investment model*. Here a woman weighs the relative costs and benefits. Central to this model are concepts such as satisfaction, quality of alternatives, and irretrievable investments. Satisfaction refers to all the good things about the partner and how positive she feels about the relationship. Quality of alternatives are the forces that pull her away and enable her to leave the current relationship. And investments refer to the ways individuals become bound to their partners based on what has been put into the relationship—time, self-disclosure, friendship, and the like.

4. *Reasoned action and/or planned behavior*. This theory assumes people are quite rational and make systematic use of the information available to them. Here the decision is fully under her control. The implications of the decision to leave or stay are considered before an actual decision is made. The opinions of family members and friends are considered. According to this approach, a woman will be more likely to leave if (a) she views leaving as having a positive outcome, (b) she perceives leaving within her control, and (c) her significant others want her to leave and she wants to comply with their wishes.

They suggest that these four approaches can be combined into a single framework, and a stay/leave decision will revolve around two central questions women must ask themselves. One, will I be better off outside of this relationship? And, two, can I do it? Taken together, the authors argue that satisfaction, irretrievable investments, and quality of alternatives are critical factors contributing to whether a woman will be better off and whether she can do it.

Husband and Male Partner Abuse and Violence

The abuse of husbands and male partners by women has received far less attention than the abuse of females. One writer noted the following:

1. Less empirical data exist on relationship violence committed by women.
2. Feminists, in particular, fear that drawing attention to battered husbands will impede attempts to battle the more serious problem of wife abuse.

---

[46]Pamela Choice and Leanne K. Lamke, "A Conceptual Approach to Understanding Abused Women's Stay/Leave Decisions," *Journal of Family Issues* 18 (May 1997), 290–314.

3. Men are reluctant to acknowledge they have been beaten by their wives, given traditional social values about male–female relationships.

4. Women's abuse is more visible, given the greater severity of physical damage they suffer.[47]

Yet research has consistently shown that men and women engage in comparable amounts of violence. Straus and Gelles found this to be true. They state that "assaults by women on their male partners occur at about the same rate as assaults by men on their female partners, and women initiate such violence about as often as men."[48] The high rate within marriage may be explained by recognizing that many assaults by wives are acts of retaliation or self-defense, that implicit cultural norms tolerate or even accept marital violence, and that marriages involve a high degree of frustration. Wives, in comparison to husbands, are relatively powerless, yet some women have learned through training since childhood that violence toward their husband or male partner is appropriate.

Mutual Abuse and Violence in Couples

Wife/female abuse and husband/male abuse have been treated separately here, yet it needs to be emphasized that *mutual* abuse is more common than either form alone. This is true not only for physical abuse but for verbal/symbolic aggression as well. Again, men and women engage in about equal amounts of verbal/symbolic aggression against their partners.[49]

Disparity between husbands and wives in recall of violence is evident. Women typically report more violence in intimate relationships than men.[50] Spouses report more violence by their partners than they are willing to acknowledge by themselves. Also, spouses are more likely to report their own victimization rather than their use of violence.

Disparity by gender exists as well in the effects of domestic violence. While men and women report similar rates of domestic violence, as both victims and perpetrators, the violence is more frightening and undermining of female well-being than male well-being. Data from samples in both the United States and Canada showed that females exhibited higher depressions and anxiety scores than their male counterparts regardless of whether they were victims or nonvictims of either physical or psychological violence.[51] In general, violence has greater adverse effects on a sense of

---

[47]Clifton P. Flynn, "Relationship Violence by Women: Issues and Implications," *Family Relations* 39 (April 1990), 194–198.

[48]Murray A. Straus and Richard J. Gelles, *Physical Violence in American Families* (New Brunswick, NJ: Transaction, 1990), 110.

[49]Murray A. Straus and Stephen Sweet, "Verbal/Symbolic Aggression in Couples: Incidence Rates and Relationships to Personal Characteristics," *Journal of Marriage and the Family* 54 (May 1992), 346–357.

[50]Alfred DeMaris, Meredith D. Pugh, and Erika Harman, "Sex Differences in the Accuracy of Recall of Witnesses of Portrayed Dyadic Violence," *Journal of Marriage and the Family* 54 (May 1992), 335–345.

[51]Elaine Grandin, Eugene Lupri, and Merlin B. Brinkerhoff, "Couple Violence and Psychological Distress," *Canadian Journal of Public Health* 89 (January–February 1998), 43–47; and Debra Umberson, Kristin Anderson, Jennifer Glick, and Adam Shapiro, "Domestic Violence, Personal Control, and Gender," *Journal of Marriage and the Family* 60 (May 1998), 442–452.

personal control and is more detrimental to the self-perceptions and well-being of women than to those of men.

Violence between spouses or intimate partners affects persons other than those directly abused. Specifically, children who witness parents being abused may be vulnerable to a variety of behavioral and emotional difficulties. A national panel of married couples revealed that parents' marital violence was associated with divorce, reports of abusive behavior, and alcohol/drug problems, and that these variables, in turn, were associated with several offspring problems.[52] These included poorer parent–child relationships, lower psychological well-being as seen in lower self-esteem, less satisfaction with life, and more violence in the offsprings' own relationships.

Findings such as these are consistent with a *learned helplessness* model of wife abuse, which suggests that seeing one's mother in a helpless situation transmits the message that women are helpless to control their own lives. This message promotes depression in women, who are most likely to identify with the victim/mother. In contrast, men who witness parental violence might be more likely to identify with the aggressor/father and thus avoid depression. These men, in turn, are more likely to be abusive husbands themselves.

Sibling Abuse and Violence

The most frequent and accepted form of violence within families occurs between siblings. Parent interviews from the Straus and Gelles studies, mentioned previously, revealed that 40 percent of children had hit a brother or sister with an object during the preceding year and 82 percent had engaged in some form of violence against a sibling.

Sibling violence usually is explained in terms of sibling rivalry or jealousy. Supposedly, one sibling resents something the other has: parental attention, privileges, clothes, objects, and the like. Differences may also center around limited resources: use of the computer, bathroom, or telephone, what TV show to watch, or who gets the remaining candy bar. These resentments and differences may become aggravated when parents intervene and insist that the children share or make a decision that favors one over the other. Reacting abusively toward a sibling, who is more one's equal in terms of size and age, is both more equitable and more acceptable than reacting abusively toward one's parents. (Although, as noted earlier in this chapter, parent abuse occurs as well.)

Sometimes sibling discord revolves around the division of labor in the family. Siblings normally compete in avoiding undesirable tasks or chores, such as doing dishes, cleaning rooms, sweeping walks, and so on. Age differences may aggravate the situation if younger children are assigned fewer chores. In short, exchange theory is operative, and perceived inequalities lead to conflict. Obviously, not all inequity leads to abuse or violence, but fighting or throwing objects is a common reaction of many children. When one child is outmatched, parental intervention may be warranted in stopping the fight, protecting the younger sibling, and perhaps punishing the older sibling. Unfortunately, doing so may exacerbate the general problem of competition among siblings.

---

[52]Cosandra McNeal and Paul R. Amato, "Parents' Marital Violence: Long-Term Consequences for Children," *Journal of Family Issues* 19 (March 1998), 123–139.

A substantial problem exists with spouse and parent-child abuse at all stages of the life course. Many older persons are abused not only physically but also from neglect or from verbal threats and humiliation.

Elder Abuse and Violence

The battered elderly parent (as noted in Chapter 12) is increasingly prevalent in the literature of aging, with a consensus among these writers that a substantial problem exists. The variety and severity of mistreatment ranges from passive neglect (unintentionally ignored, forgotten) to active neglect (financial exploitation; withholding medicine, food, assistance) and from verbal or emotional abuse (name-calling, threatening, humiliating) to physical abuse (slapping, pushing, injuring). Abuse may take the form of tying the elderly parent to a bed or chair, excessive use of medication or other drugs to keep the parent more manageable, battering with fists or objects to enforce particular behaviors, and nearly any conceivable activity.

Elderly persons who are abused generally are frail, mentally or physically disabled, female, and living with the person responsible for mistreatment. A commonly cited cause of the abuse is the caregiver becoming overtaxed by the requirements of caring for the elderly adult, which often leads to despair, anger, resentment, or violence in the caregiver. In some instances, the abuse clearly is malicious and intentional; in other instances, caregivers have serious emotional and dependency problems and do not deliberately intend to abuse but are unable to control their behavior.

Violence among Other Intimates

Abuse and violence may be part of a relationship long before people marry and have children. One key example centers around friendships and intimates involved in the mate-selection process. Most studies of the courtship processes of dating, going steady, and becoming engaged have portrayed these events in a context of love, attraction, affection, mutual disclosure, and increasing closeness and commitment as the relationship moves toward increasing exclusivity and marriage. Other recent studies, however, have suggested that violence and sexual exploitation are the dark side of courtship,[53] and that dating violence is very prevalent.

---

[53]Sally A. Lloyd, "The Darkside of Courtship: Violence and Sexual Exploitation," *Family Relations* 40 (January 1991), 14–20.

news item

Aging Well: Awareness Key to Stopping Elder Abuse

Elder abuse can happen to anyone, though certain factors can make a person more vulnerable. These include illness, frailty, physical disability, mental impairment and living with or depending on a person with a history of mental illness, hostility or alcohol or drug abuse. While some abuse occurs in long-term living facilities, the vast majority of cases involve abuse in the home by family members, old or "new" friends or service providers in a position of trust, according to the American Psychological Association.

Although there are extreme cases of elder abuse, most situations are more subtle, making the difference between interpersonal stress and abuse sometimes difficult to discern. Some elder abuse may be a continuation of marital or family violence that has taken place during many years or the result of stress triggered by lifestyle adjustments and the difficulty of caring for an increasingly dependent older person, the association notes.

Reporting Abuse

There are many warning signs of elder abuse, such as slap or pressure marks or certain kinds of burns or blisters which may indicate physical abuse. Untreated bed sores, the need for medical or dental care, dirty clothing, poor hygiene and grooming and unusual weight loss are possible signs of self-neglect or neglect by a caregiver.

Emotional abuse or neglect may cause a person to withdraw from normal activities, be less alert or behave unusually. Exploitation may be signified by sudden changes in a person's finances and accounts, altered wills and trusts, unusual bank withdrawals or loss of property, according to the National Center on Elder Abuse.

A person may be abusive if they seem to control an elder's actions, isolate the elder from family and friends and be emotionally or financially dependent on the elder. Abusers also may appear indifferent to the elder, seeming apathetic or hostile, call the elder names or threaten the elder's pet.

Although it's been difficult to pinpoint how many older adults are abused, research suggests only one in 14 elder abuse incidents in the home are reported to authorities.

Preventing Abuse

Competent older adults can take a number of steps to prevent themselves from being mistreated. These include staying busy and engaged in life, cultivating a strong network of family and friends and taking care of themselves to stay as independent as possible.

Older adults also should refuse to allow anyone to add their name to the person's bank account without their consent and should never make financial decisions under pressure or sign over money or property to anyone without getting legal advice, according to recommendations from the National Center on Elder Abuse.

Elder abuse within the home can be averted by proactive family choices, such as seeking counseling or help change long-time patterns of behavior, conflict or addictions or deal with current stresses, recommends the American Psychological Association.

Concerned citizens can prevent or end abuse by reaching out to vulnerable neighbors, friends or family members, especially those isolated because of physical, cultural or geographical circumstances. They also may volunteer with community programs that provide older adults companionship and help in their homes...

Source: Tamera Manzanares, *Pilot & Today* (Steamboat Springs, CO, June 1 2009), http://www.steamboatpilot.com/news/2009/jun/01/aging_well_awareness_key_stopping_elder_abuse/.

A number of studies have been completed in an attempt to estimate the incidence of **courtship violence** and gender differences in abuse. In a study of college students, at least one-third of those who dated had experienced physical aggression at some point in their dating history.[54] As expected, the incidence of courtship violence "known of" by students greatly exceeded what had been directly experienced. Also,

---

[54]Gordon E. Barnes, Leonard Greenwood, and Reena Sommer, "Courtship Violence in a Canadian Sample of Male College Students," *Family Relations* 40 (January 1991), 37–44; and James M. Makepeace, "Gender Differences in Courtship Victimization," *Family Relations* 35 (July 1986), 383–388.

as expected, extreme forms of violence, such as assault with an object or weapon, were less common than milder forms, such as pushing and slapping. Nearly two-fifths of the students knew of instances of threats, pushing, or slapping.

Consistent with studies of college students, a national representative sample of never-married persons between the ages of 18 and 30 found that women were at least as likely, if not more likely, to be physically aggressive than men.[55] This finding led the authors to note that, when developing a theory of dating aggression, the mechanisms that bring about both male and female aggression must be considered. Thus, patriarchy may help explain dating aggression among men, but it does not explain why women are aggressive. The same source noted that people who are young, from the lower class, and who drink before a conflict are more prone to physical aggression. Thus, once again, it seems that verbal aggression may be the seed of physical aggression and that both verbal and physical aggressive behavior are reciprocated in kind.

Simons and others found a significant link between experiences in the family of origin and dating violence.[56] Frequent exposure to corporal punishment increased the risk of dating violence but did not predict it. Rather, low support and involvement by parents was associated with adolescent delinquency and drug use, which in turn, predicted involvement in dating violence.

Date Rape and Sexual Coercion

Forced sexual contact constitutes a particular kind of violence among intimates. Estimates of unwanted sexual assaults against female students, committed by acquaintances as well as by strangers, have been in the range of 20 to 25 percent. A study at the University of New Hampshire revealed that 39 percent of the women had experienced some forced contact, 20 percent had experienced forced attempted intercourse, and 10 percent had experienced forced completed intercourse (rape).[57]

A study of males at a small liberal arts college revealed that 34 percent of the respondents admitted to some proclivity to rape and/or forced sex.[58] Similarly, a study of Canadian male students showed that those who were sexually aggressive also tended to be physically aggressive, traditional in sex role beliefs, accepting of interpersonal violence, and members of fraternities.[59] Fraternity members are

---

[55]Jan E. Stets and Debra A. Henderson, "Contextual Factors Surrounding Conflict Resolution while Dating: Results from a National Study," *Family Relations* 40 (January 1991): 29–36; and Jan E. Stets, "Interactive Processes in Dating Aggression: A National Study," *Journal of Marriage and the Family* 54 (February 1992), 165–177.

[56]Ronald L. Simons, Kuei-Hsiu Lin, and Leslie C. Gordon, "Socialization in the Family of Origin and Male Dating Violence: A Prospective Study," *Journal of Marriage and the Family* 60 (May 1998), 467–478; and Vangie A. Foshee, Karl E. Bauman, and G. Fletcher Linder, "Family Violence and the Perpetration of Adolescent Dating Violence: Examining Social Learning and Social Control Processes," *Journal of Marriage and the Family* 61 (May 1999), 331–342.

[57]Sally K. Ward, Kathy Chapman, Ellen Cohn, Susan White, and Kirk Williams, "Acquaintance Rape and the College Social Scene," *Family Relations* 40 (January 1991), 65–71.

[58]Julie A. Osland, Marguerite Fitch, and Edmond E. Willis, "Likelihood to Rape in College Males," *Sex Roles* 35 (1996), 171–183.

[59]Leandra Lackie and Anton F. de Man, "Correlates of Sexual Aggression among Male University Students," *Sex Roles* 37 (1997), 451–457.

more likely to be reinforced by their friends for engaging in sexual coercion and aggression.

The occurrence of violence during childhood or adolescence, whether exhibited toward parents or during courtship, seems to be a foundation for marital and parental violence. Unfortunately, the experience of violence between spouses and between parents and children is seldom the perpetrator's first experience.

Treating and Preventing Family Violence

Application of the ABCX model to violence in families and among intimate partners suggests the various types of violence that take place may or may not represent crisis events. As previously stated, a crisis event depends on (B) the resources available to members and (C) the meanings or definitions attached to the acts.

It has been clearly shown in previous discussions that many acts between siblings, parents and children, and partners are perceived as expected and normal behaviors. Even a Gallup poll in 1994 indicated that almost one person in four (23 percent) said he or she could imagine approval of a wife slapping her husband.[60] People were more cautious about the opposite situation, however, as only 10 percent said they would ever approve of a husband slapping a wife.

The response of the abused persons—to endure, to fight back, or to escape—will depend on the meanings and perceptions of the event as well as the resources available to those abused: strength, peer support, friends and kin, money or services, police and crisis intervention centers, and, particularly, self-esteem.

When Gelles and Straus asked women who had experienced violence how they reacted to the most recent incidence, more than half said they cried. Other responses, in order of frequency, were to run to another room, hit back, run out of the house, and call a friend or relative; the response in last place was to call the police.[61]

Gelles and Straus suggested that an important and beneficial way of helping battered women would be to empower them to negotiate with their husbands to end the violence. A particularly important intervention service (resource) would be education in mediation or conflict-resolution techniques. Other important resources for battered women include sources of help, such as police, social workers, shelters, medical services, and so forth.

Gelles and Straus argued that prevention policies and programs must be directed at the two factors that make it possible for people to abuse and maltreat those whom they love.[62] First, eliminate cultural norms and values that accept violence as a means of resolving conflict and problems in families. Second, develop programs and policies that support families and reduce internal and external stresses and inequalities. How can these goals be accomplished?

The first goal—to eliminate cultural norms and values that support violence—necessitates establishing a moral code that loved ones are not to be

---

[60]David W. Moore, "Approval of Husband Slapping Wife Continues to Decline," *The Gallup Poll Monthly* 341 (February 1994), 2.

[61]Gelles and Straus, *Intimate Violence*, Figure 10, p. 258.

[62]Ibid., 194.

hit. This means banning spanking and corporal punishment. Sweden and all other Scandinavian countries, for example, have taken the lead in this regard by banning capital punishment, outlawing corporal punishment of children in schools, and passing legislation prohibiting spanking. Firearm ownership is also rigorously controlled. Violent programming on Swedish television is severely restricted.

In contrast, most people in the United States are less sensitive to the controversies and more accepting of capital punishment; corporal punishment; spanking; minimal control over sale and registration of firearms; and violence on TV, in movies, in sports, and in children's games. A review of 217 studies dating back to 1957 revealed a positive and significant correlation between television violence and aggressive behavior.[63] This held true regardless of age, suggesting that the influence of violent television portrayals is not confined to young children or adolescents. Violence, in general, including family, marital, parental, and sibling violence, will remain prevalent as long as the society in which it occurs glorifies killing, shooting, beating, hitting, and abusing.

The second goal of developing programs and policies that support families is closely related to the first goal of changing norms and values. Policies and programs have been enacted in many states to address child abuse, spouse abuse, and marital rape. Additional efforts to eliminate poverty and unemployment; to provide adequate medical and hospital care to all families; to support effective planned parenthood; to reduce sexual, class, and racial inequality, both in the home and community; and to promote kin and community linkages and support networks would likely result in lowering levels of family violence.

---

[63]Haejung Paik and George Comstock, "The Effects of Television Violence on Antisocial Behavior: A Meta-Analysis," *Communication Research* 21 (August 1994), 516–546.

Summary

1. The central issues of this chapter—stress and violence—are not unique to any given point of the family life course or any particular family structure. A stressor, or crisis-provoking, event includes any situation that threatens the status quo and well-being of the system or its members. These events may come from sources both within and outside the family. Certain events may solidify the unit, while others may be very disruptive.

2. The ABCX model refers to some event (A) interacting with the family's crisis-meeting resources (B) and the definition or meaning given to the event (C), resulting in the level or degree of crisis (X). When and if B and C are adequate, the levels of stress and crisis will be minimal. If they are inadequate, the levels of stress and crisis will be high.

3. A common stressor event in many marriages and intimate relationships is that of abuse and violence. Various myths about violence tend to attribute it to deviants within the society rather than to acknowledge it as an outgrowth of and component of a given society.

4. Considerable research attention has been focused on the abuse of children. Traditional modes of discipline grant legitimacy to spanking and other forms of physical punishment of children. Since most of such punishment occurs behind closed doors, most abuse never comes to the attention of the public.

5. Violence is sometimes directed by children, particularly adolescents, toward parents. Research has shown that parental assault is extensive, occurring among both males and females and directed at both mothers and fathers.

6. Wife and female partner abuse may involve common couple violence or patriarchal terrorism. Like child abuse, abuse toward women is not always viewed as inappropriate, particularly in contexts of male authority and dominance. As with child abuse, abuse of female intimates may have decreased in recent years, despite a public perception that both types of abuse are on the rise. Many female partners do not or cannot leave their violent male partners due to economic dependency and lack of alternatives and sometimes due to positive perceptions of other aspects of the relationship.

7. Rape, or forced coitus without consent, is another form of violence against wives and women. Many states have changed their laws concerning rape, but the issue remains a point of controversy when occurring between spouses or intimate partners.

8. Husband and male partner abuse is granted far less attention than the abuse of children and wives; however, physical violence seems to be one aspect of intimate relationships that approaches equality between spouses.

9. Sibling abuse is the most frequent and accepted form of violence within families, often centering around sibling rivalry and jealousy. Supposedly, one sibling resents something the other has, or tensions center around differences over the availability of limited resources.

10. Abuse of people who are elderly frequently involves aging parents, particularly mothers. The mistreatment of elders ranges from positive or active neglect to verbal and physical abuse.

11. Other forms of violence among intimates include adolescents and young adults in the dating/courtship process. Such violence may take the form of threats or physical injury or may frequently involve sexual aggression, coercion, or date rape.

This chapter focused on marital and family stress and violence. Chapter 14 turns to terminations of marriages, particularly through divorce, and the subsequent pattern of remarriage.

Key Terms and Topics

Stressor events p. 493

ABCX model p. 493

Variations of the ABCX model p. 495

Violence in families and among intimates p. 497

Myths of family violence p. 499

Causes of family violence p. 500

Child abuse and violence p. 502

Corporal punishment p. 502

Cultural spillover theory p. 502

Child sexual abuse p. 504

Parent abuse and violence p. 505

Wife and female partner abuse and violence p. 506

Common couple violence p. 506

Patriarchal terrorism p. 506

Rape among intimates p. 508

Rape p. 508

Husband and male partner abuse and violence p. 509

Mutual abuse and violence in couples p. 510

Sibling abuse and violence p. 511

Elder abuse and violence p. 512

Violence among other intimates p. 512

Courtship violence p. 512

Date rape and sexual coercion p. 514

Treating and preventing family violence p. 515

Discussion Questions

1. List five stressor events for families. How could families prepare for events such as these? How is it possible that certain events strengthen families whereas others tear them apart?

2. What factors enhance crisis proneness and crisis preparedness? Using the ABCX formula given in the chapter, show how *resources* and *meanings* lead to family adequacy or inadequacy in facing potential crisis situations.

3. Select any personal or family problem. How could or does the availability of resources affect one's ability to address the problem? What types of resources are significant to families or individuals? How does one's definition of the problem affect the level of stress experienced?

4. Examine the seven myths of family violence. How many seem to be partially true? With which ones do you agree or disagree? Why?

5. What family and social circumstances put children at greater risk for abuse, physical and sexual? What are the long-term effects of abused individuals?

6. Consider the position that marital and intimate relationships (including abuse and rape) are private and personal matters. If so, should the community or state get involved in what lovers, couples, and families do to each other? Why or why not?

7. Why don't many abused wives or female partners leave abusive situations? What factors make a difference in women's decision making?

8. Is it necessary to be concerned about, or do research on, violence toward husbands or between siblings? Can't husbands take care of themselves? Aren't fights among children natural? Explain.

9. Think of personal childhood experiences of violence. What experiences do you recall? With whom? For what reasons?

10. Discuss various forms of abuse within families toward elderly parents. What types of action or programs might lessen the severity of or even resolve the problem?

11. Are you aware of abuse or violence in dating and nonmarital interactions? What forms does it take? Is sexual aggression or coercion actually violence? Why or why not?

12. What is the relationship of factors such as alcoholism, drug addiction, unemployment, and lack of money to violence and abuse? How might a pregnancy, birthday, or holiday affect the likelihood of violence?

Further Readings

Abraham, Margaret. *Speaking the Unspeakable: Marital Violence Among South Asian Immigrants in the United States*. New Brunswick, NJ: Rutgers University Press, 2000.

> A look at violence among immigrants to the United States from countries such as India, Pakistan, Bangladesh, Sri Lanka, and Nepal.

Boss, Pauline. *Family Stress Management: A Contextual Approach*. Thousand Oaks, CA: Sage Publications, Inc. 2nd ed., 2002.

> An emphasis on understanding and managing stress in terms of perceptions and meanings with a larger social context.

Cossins, Anne. *Masculinities, Sexualities, and Child Sexual Abuse*. The Hague, Netherlands: Kluwer Law International, 2000.

> An examination of explanations of child sexual abuse with a focus on sociological theories of masculinities and sexualities and a test of the power/powerless theory.

Flowers, R. Barri. *Domestic Crimes, Family Violence and Child Abuse: A Study of Contemporary American Society*. Jefferson, NC: McFarland, 2000.

> An overview of the types of intrafamilial and intimate violence that fall under the broad umbrella of domestic violence.

Goodman, Lisa A. and Deborah Epstein, *Listening to Battered Women: A Survivor-Centered Approach to Advocacy, Mental Health, and Justice*. Washington, DC: American Psychological Association, 2008.

> An examination of responses to domestic violence by community advocacy groups, mental health professionals and the justice system using a feminist model.

Haley, Shawn D., and Braun-Haley, Ellie. *War on the Homefront: An Examination of Wife Abuse*. New York: Berghahn Books, 2000.

> A study of the impact of abuse, breaking away from it, preventive measures, and a look at the future.

Hammer, Rhonda. *Antifeminism and Family Terrorism: A Critical Feminist Perspective*. Lanham, MD: Rowman and Littlefield, 2001.

> A focus on a feminist activism that links colonization, global capitalism and poverty, and the prevalence of family violence.

Hines, Denise and Malley-Morrison, Kathleen. *Family Violence in the United States: Defining, Understanding, and Combating Abuse*. Thousand Oaks, CA: Sage Publications, 2005.

> An overview of theory and research in the area of family violence across a wide span of relationships, from husband–wife violence to child abuse, to intimate partner violence and elder abuse.

Johnson, Michael P. *A Typology of Domestic Violence: Intimate Terrorism, Violent Resistance, and Situational Couple Violence*. Boston: Northeastern University Press, 2008.

> An extensive elaboration of his typology of domestic violence and the theoretical implications of viewing domestic violence as not a unitary phenomenon but as a broad category capturing several distinct relationship conditions.

Loseke, Donileen R., Gelles, Richard, and Cavanaugh, Mary M. *Current Controversies on Family Violence*, 2nd Edition. Thousand Oaks, CA: Sage Publications, 2005.

A collection of chapters written by family scholars, practitioners, and policy makers discussing major controversies around family violence issues.

Malley-Morrison, Kathleen and Hines, Denise. *Family Violence in a Cultural Perspective: Defining, Understanding, and Combating Abuse.* Thousand Oaks, CA: Sage Publications, 2005.

A look at family violence across four major ethnic categories in the United States.

Straus, Murray A., Richard J. Gelles, and Suzanne K. Steinmetz. *Behind Closed Doors: Violence in the American Family*, 2nd Edition. New York: Doubleday/Anchor Books, 2006.

An updated revision of one of the most important books on domestic violence published in the past three decades.

14

Divorce and Remarriage

Divorce Following a Lengthy Marriage

Nancy was married nearly twenty years. She had two daughters, ages 18 and 9. She was a wife, mother, and homemaker to a husband who had a successful business. What went wrong? Here is a brief overview of the situation as told by Nancy.

"I was 26 when I got married, and my husband was six years older. I had dated him for several years. I had doubts about marrying him but was tired of dating, tired of being single, thought he would change after we got married, and did think I loved him. I remember sitting down with my dad and making out a list of pros and cons about marrying. My dad always was a good listener and still is one of my best friends. My parents had provided a good example of how marriage could be, so I decided to marry him.

"Since he was divorced previously, I couldn't get married in the church, as we were both Catholic. A relative who was a priest performed a civil ceremony in a hospital chapel. I took my vows seriously and accepted the fact that he had two girls from his first marriage. They lived with their mother and never spent much time with us. Since their grandmother lived in our town, when they would come to visit they would spend most of the time with her. My husband supported them financially but was emotionally distant from them.

"Within months after our marriage, I recognized problems. My husband had been single for seven years between marriages and he continued as a 'married single.' He would go golfing with the boys, spend a lot of time at the bar, and would come home very late. Over the years, I became more and more unhappy but yet felt I had everything. He was nice to me, we were financially stable, and I had a daughter that I loved dearly. But he was emotionally distant. We only talked about surface stuff and were never able to talk about our problems. We never took vacations because he was always too busy with the business. I was looking for more from my marriage, particularly an emotional connection.

"My husband never helped out at home, but that wasn't a big issue. I was a traditional homemaker and didn't go to work until my daughter entered school. Even then, I worked only part time as a substitute teacher at the school my daughter attended. Nine years after our first daughter was born, we had another daughter. But my husband and I were seldom affectionate with one another and the marriage continued to deteriorate.

"I considered leaving him for years but that was too big a step for me. We had two daughters and I had become very close to his family and even his two daughters from his first marriage. In fact, I'd likely be married to him today if he hadn't developed a relationship with another woman. I found a receipt for flowers and confronted him about it. I later discovered he had been seeing her for two years. He seemed pleased that he had kept it very secret from almost everyone and only a few of his friends knew.

"To me, that was the final straw. So two years ago I left him, and last year we got a divorce. Financially I'm O.K. but I'm still trying to understand and come to grips with it. My 18-year-old daughter is in school and lives with her dad but my 9-year-old daughter is with me. Her dad sees her when it is convenient but is emotionally distant from her too.

"As it now stands, I will probably stay single the rest of my life. I don't deliberately avoid men but all of my close friends are women. I know so many unhappy married people and I don't think I can ever be as happy in a marriage as I can be without it."

Questions to Consider

Given the fact that Nancy was Catholic, took vows "until death do we part," and felt she had everything—including two lovely daughters and financial stability, was she wrong in getting a divorce? Why or why not?

Early in her marriage, Nancy knew there were serious problems. Why did she, and why do many couples, remain married for many years before getting a divorce? Why do some couples never take that step?

*A*ll societies provide one or more ways for husbands, wives, or both to deal with unsatisfactory marital relationships. Highly patriarchal, male-dominant societies are likely to permit men to have mistresses or concubines while they are married. In many societies, including the United States, marriage may be regarded as a civil contract, in which the state specifies how old people have to be to get married, how many spouses they may have, and the conditions under which marriages can be dissolved.

In some countries, often in conformity with the Canon Law of the Roman Catholic Church, marriage was, until recently, indissolvable except by death. This was true in countries such as Argentina, Brazil, Chile, and Colombia in Latin America; the Philippines in Southeast Asia; and Italy, Ireland, and Spain in Western Europe. In some countries, such as the United States, France, Switzerland, Russia, Poland, and the Scandinavian countries, a divorce is granted if one or both parties have been guilty of a grave violation of marital obligations or if it is shown that the marriage has completely broken down. Finally, the official laws of Islam and of Judaism grant free power of the husband to terminate his marriage by repudiating his wife. In reality, this occurs infrequently, and movements exist to provide power to wives to bring about dissolution of their marriages as well.

In the United States, divorce is the best-known and most common means of ending an unsatisfactory marital relationship; thus, most attention in this chapter will be devoted to divorce. Desertions, legal separations, informally agreed upon separations, and annulments are other means that people use to get out of a marriage, at least temporarily, if not permanently.

Desertion and Marital Separation

Desertion is the willful abandonment, without legal justification, of one's spouse, children, or both. Little is known about desertion, and few studies have considered this issue. It is a legal ground for divorce by the nondeserting spouse in about twenty-eight states after, typically, a one-year absence (the range is from six months in West Virginia to seven years in Vermont).

Traditionally, it has been assumed that desertion applied only to men. Today, there are reports on "runaway wives," as well. Unlike men, who may want out of a marriage, women who desert are more likely to seek escape from child rearing and home responsibilities that have become unbearable. For both sexes, it appears that desertion is a response to one issue or many that seem unsolvable: children, marital conflicts, alcoholism, infidelity, inability to support a family, and the like.

Unlike divorce, desertion is not institutionalized. No registration takes place with the courts or any other official body, and the deserting and nondeserting spouses cannot remarry. Exactly what constitutes desertion and what roles are appropriate in legal, economic, and social situations are not very clear. For example, how many days' absence constitutes desertion? When a spouse leaves and returns on multiple occasions, do marital and parental role patterns resemble those of the one- or two-parent family? Is one spouse legally responsible for the expenses and activities of the other? Because of the lack of institutionalized norms and the ambiguity of events surrounding desertion, it is believed that desertion has far more negative effects than divorce.

What about **marital separation**? A widely held assumption is that marital separation is a stepping-stone to divorce, sometimes soon followed by another marriage. While divorce follows separation for many couples, others use separation as a time to work out a reconciliation, ending marital difficulties. Still other couples remain married but live in long-term, unresolved separations.

The U.S. Census distinguishes between people who are *married, spouse present, married, spouse absent*, and those who are *separated*. The category for **separated** includes people with legal separations, those living apart with intentions of obtaining a divorce, and other persons permanently or temporarily separated because of marital discord. The category for **married, spouse-absent** includes people married but living apart due to employment or serving away from home in the armed forces or residing apart for any reason except separation, as just described. According to *The 2009 Statistical Abstract of the United States*, in 2007, 1.8 percent of men and 1.3 percent of women 18 years of age or older were classified as married, spouse absent. Rates were highest for those between 30 and 40 and for those 75 and above (most likely due to health). Separated status was reported for another 1.8 percent of men and 2.6 percent of women, with the highest rates occurring for those between the ages of 35 and 45.[1]

In cases of **legal separation,** the husband and wife are legally authorized to live apart, and formal agreements specify visiting patterns, support, and so forth. These separations are sometimes referred to as *limited divorce, partial dissolution*, or *divorce from bed and board.*

The majority of separations are not legalized. An **informal separation** often is an arrangement between husband and wife whereby one or both decide to live separately. Unlike cases of desertion, each knows the whereabouts of the other, and unlike cases of divorce, the couple is legally married and cannot remarry. These couples seem to be overrepresented among low-income families; thus, informal separation has been referred to as the "poor man's divorce."

One of the few studies of marital separations was done in the metropolitan Cleveland area with a random sample of over 1,100 residents.[2] It was found that one in six couples was likely to separate for at least forty-eight hours at some point in their relationship because of arguments or disagreements. Some separations were a step on the way to permanent separation or divorce. Other separations were used as a conflict-resolution technique or a dramatic gesture to force some action on the part of the spouse. Those most likely to separate were blacks, women, and those with low incomes and minor children. For most people, separations were associated with a high sense of emotional distress.

What about separations, temporary or permanent, for reasons other than marital discord? One source concluded that marital noncohabitation does not make the heart grow fonder.[3] Couples living in separate households—most often because of military service or incarceration (confined in prison)—were nearly twice as likely to divorce within three years compared to persons cohabiting with their spouses.

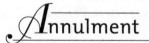

Annulment

The word *annul*, legally defined, means to reduce to nothing, to obliterate, to make void and of no effect, to abolish, to do away with, to eradicate. When a marriage has been annulled, a court, acting under the law of the state, has found

---

[1]U.S. Census Bureau, *The 2009 Statistical Abstract*, "Table 56—Marital Status Of The Population by Sex and Age: 2007," http://www.2010census.biz/compendia/statab/cats/population/marital_status_and_living_arrangements.html.

[2]Gay C. Kitson, "Marital Discord and Marital Separation: A County Survey," *Journal of Marriage and the Family* 47 (August 1985), 693–700. Note also Stephen B. Kincaid and Robert A. Caldwell, "Marital Separation: Causes, Coping, and Consequences," *Journal of Divorce and Remarriage* 22 (1995), 109–128.

[3]Ronald R. Rindfuss and Elizabeth Hervey Stephen, "Marital Noncohabitation: Separation Does Not Make the Heart Grow Fonder," *Journal of Marriage and the Family* 52 (February 1990), 259–270.

that causes existed *prior* to the marriage that render the marriage contract void. The court concludes that the marriage, when performed, was in fact no marriage at all. By annulling the marriage, the court, in effect, says that it never existed.

Generally, the distinction between divorce and annulment lies in the time in which certain actions occurred. Divorce generally involves an action that occurred *after* the date of marriage—irreconcilable differences, incompatibility, cruelty, adultery, desertion, nonsupport, alcoholism, and the like. Annulment generally involves an action that occurred *before* the date of marriage—being underage, already being married, insanity, incurable impotence, an incestuous relationship, and the like.

Divorce around the World

In the Western world, divorce traditionally has been viewed as an unfortunate event for the persons involved and as a clear index of failure of the family system. But over the past few decades, in the United States and other Western countries, attitudes toward separation and divorce have changed. An examination of divorce laws in the United States, England and Wales, France, and Sweden revealed that divorce has become increasingly easy to obtain, spousal support has become less common, efforts have been made to increase child-support awards and improve payment compliance, and shared parental decision-making authority has become increasingly encouraged.[4]

Divorce is not unique to Western countries, however, but it is a factor in nearly all the world's nations and has traditionally been common in most tribal societies. In addition, in the past, a few nations have had higher divorce rates than currently in the United States, such as Japan in the period 1887–1919, Algeria in 1887–1940, and Egypt in 1935–1945.

At present, the United States has one of the highest divorce rates in the world, but not the highest. Divorce rates are particularly high for Russia and the countries of the former Soviet Union. Based on the latest figures (2005–2006) available from Eurostat, the Organisation for Economic Cooperation and Development (OECD), and the United Nations,[5] the U.S. rate of divorce per 1,000 persons in the population was about 3.7 compared to 4.5 in Russia, 3.8 in Ukraine, 3.5 in Moldova, 3.3 in Belarus, 3.4 in Lithuania, 3.2 in Latvia, and 3.1 in the Czech Republic. Cuba also has a high divorce rate (3.8). Divorce rates range between 2.0 and 2.5 throughout most of Northern, Central and Western Europe, Oceania, Canada, the United Kingdom, and Japan and Korea. Rates are less than 2.0 throughout most of Southern Europe (Spain, Italy, Greece, and Slovenia) and other major Catholic countries such as Poland, Ireland and Mexico (at 0.7, the lowest rate of divorce among the 36 OECD countries reporting rates). Divorce rates also are extremely low throughout the Middle East.

---

[4]Mark A. Fine and David R. Fine, "An Examination and Evaluation of Recent Changes in Divorce Laws in Five Western Countries: The Critical Role of Values," *Journal of Marriage and the Family* 56 (May 1994), 249–263.

[5]United Nations Statistics Division, Marriage and Divorce, "Table 25. Divorces and crude divorce rates by urban/rural residence: 2002–2006," http://unstats.un.org/unsd/demographic/products/dyb/dyb2006/Table25.pdf; and OECD Family Database "Chart SF8.5: The increase in crude divorce rates in all OECD countries from 1970 to 2006/2007," http://www.oecd.org/dataoecd/4/19/40321815.pdf.

CROSS-CULTURAL *Perspectives*

Divorce in China

Divorce cases in China are typically of two types: those where both husband and wife desire divorce and those where only one partner desires it. Procedures for divorce in the first category, referred to as *divorce by agreement*, are simple and without cost to the applicants. The couple simply goes to the local marriage registration office and completes an application. If no coercion is involved and the couple is able to reach agreement on custody of the children and the division of family property, a divorce certificate is issued. When only one partner wants a divorce, he or she will go to the marriage registration office and apply. Application is followed by mediation, attempting reconciliation. If that fails, the case goes to the People's Court, which decides for or against the divorce and, if there are children, who gets custody.

Have the marriage laws and changes in family size and gender roles led to an upsurge in divorce? In percentage terms, yes, but the numbers involved appear to be very small. For example, an increase from 341,000 divorces in 1980 to 800,000 in 1990 is an increase of 135 percent. But in China, a country of 1.2 billion people, this is equal to 0.8 cases per 1,000 population. Viewed from a global perspective, this rate is very low, particularly when compared with rates of most countries in the industrialized West. Without a doubt, today most marriages in China are stable, most individuals expect to stay married for life, and both the local kinship structure and government policy favor such stability.

Source: Sheryl WuDunn, "Divorce Rate Soars as Chinese Decide Love Is Part of Marriage," *The New York Times*, April 17, 1991, p. B1.

In terms of rate of change, most OECD countries have seen increases in their divorce rates since 1970, with the United States and Mexico changing the least and traditionally Catholic countries such as Portugal, France, Spain, Italy, and Ireland experiencing the largest increases (both in absolute and relative terms).

How are variations in the rate or frequency of divorce explained? Obviously, religion and restrictions placed on divorce in highly religious societies explains large differences between countries. Other factors are also predictive, however. One study sampled sixty-six countries to investigate societal-level correlates of divorce.[6] Four variables were shown to bear a significant relationship to the likelihood of divorce. Associated with lower divorce rates were (1) a high sex ratio, indicating a relative undersupply of women, and (2) a late average age at marriage for women. Significantly but nonlinearly related to divorce were (3) level of socioeconomic development and (4) female labor force participation rate. Both of these variables exhibited U-shaped associations with divorce. This suggests that socioeconomic development and increased female labor force participation in the early stages of industrialization tend to reduce the rate of divorce, but at later stages of industrialization and modernization, they tend to increase the incidence of divorce.

Many societies in the Western world, including the United States, rate high in socioeconomic development and female labor force participation. Thus, with an erosion of traditional patriarchal patterns and a heavy emphasis on the individual and small nuclear family in contrast to an emphasis on extended kin, one could expect high rates of divorce. The following sections will examine how divorce rates are determined and will explore trends in the United States.

---

[6]Katherine Trent and Scott J. South, "Structural Determinants of the Divorce Rate: A Cross-societal Analysis," *Journal of Marriage and the Family* 51 (May 1989), 391–404.

CROSS-CULTURAL *Perspective*

Divorce in Sweden

In Sweden, given the incidence of nonmarital cohabitation, the divorce rate is not a very adequate indicator of marital dissolution. A better measure is one that shows the breakup rate of couples who are either married or living in a consensual union.

As one might suspect, if it is difficult to know how many consensual unions form, it is even more difficult to know how many break up. What does seem clear is that, in Sweden and around the world, nonmarital cohabitation does not have the stability of marital cohabitation. Thus, to add a nonmarital cohabitation dissolution rate

to the divorce rate in Sweden (about one-half that of the United States) may give Sweden the highest breakup rate in the industrialized world.

Data by Andersson show that the risk of divorce is lower for women with one child than for childless women and again substantially lower for women with two children than one child. As in the United States, having a young child reduces the divorce risk, suggesting that small children "protect" families against divorce, at least for a time.

See: Gunnar Andersson, "The Impact of Children on Divorce Risks of Swedish Women," *European Journal of Population* 13 (1997), 109–145.

ivorce in the United States

Divorce Rates

Divorce rates are likely to be calculated in one of three ways:

1. *Crude Divorce Rate:* The number of divorces that take place per 1,000 persons in the total population
2. *Refined Divorce Rate:* The number of divorces per 1,000 married females or males
3. The ratio of divorces granted in a given year to the number of marriages contracted in that same year

Note the differences in rate, depending on which figure is used. For instance, the *crude divorce rate* in the United States in 2007 was 3.6.[7] This means that for every 1,000 persons in the population (men, women, children, adults, married, single), 7.2 persons became divorced, or 3.6 *marriages* ended in divorce (or annulment). Or said another way, in a city of 100,000, a divorce rate of 3.6 means that 360 divorces would have been granted in 2007. Because the American system is monogamous (two persons per divorce), 720 individuals in this city would have experienced divorce that year. Note how this divorce rate can be influenced by factors such as the age distribution or the proportion of the married to the single population. In a country or city with a large family size, a low life expectancy, a late age at marriage, a sizable proportion of the population being children or single teenagers, or a disproportionate number of the population unmarried, a sizable percentage of those married could get divorced, yet the country or city would have a seemingly low divorce rate.

Although a better estimate of the chances of a married person experiencing divorce in a given year, the *refined divorce rate* typically is not calculated in official government reports. Using vital statistics data from *The 2009 Statistical Abstract,*

---

[7]U.S. Census Bureau, *The 2009 Statistical Abstract*, "Table 56—Marital Status of the Population by Sex and Age: 2007," http://www.2010census.biz/compendia/statab/cats/population/marital_status_and_living_arrangements.html.

however, it is possible to make such a calculation (at least for those 18 years old and older).[8] In the United States in 2007, the number of divorces per 1,000 married women 18 and older was approximately 16.7 and for men it was 16.8. Unlike the first rate described, single persons and children are excluded from this calculation. Since it is based on only one partner in the marriage, it also does not have to be adjusted any further. The refined divorce rate is a direct expression of the likelihood that a woman (or man) will be susceptible to divorce in the year calculated. This figure could be used to compare divorce rates cross-culturally without being influenced by the number, age, or marital status of the total population.

The ratio of *divorces granted in a given year to the number of marriages in that year* was about .49 in 2007. This is a rate commonly used to make arguments concerning the "breakdown in the U.S. family." Nearly one out of two marriages ends in divorce—or does it?

Although it may be accurate to speak of twice as many divorces as marriages occurring in a given year, using this method of calculation does not support the conclusion that one-half of all marriages will end in divorce. The inaccuracy is due to at least three reasons:

1. The marriages that occurred that year are not the ones that ended in divorce; those marriages began perhaps one, eight, or thirty years ago. There is no relevant link between the number of marriages begun and ended in 2007.

2. Approximately 45 percent of all marriages are remarriages for one or both spouses, which is not taken into account. Persons who divorce and remarry in the same year contribute to both the number of marriages and the number of divorces, producing a ratio of 1 to 1—as many divorces as marriages. To redivorce in the same year would produce the impossible result of having more divorces than marriages.

3. It is also possible to calculate a number of marriages that is smaller than the number of divorces. Note an example using census figures.

Perhaps a question of greater interest than a divorce rate in any given year is "Of all marriages, how many will eventually end in divorce?" A study by the National Center for Health Statistics based on 1995 data from the National Survey of Family Growth (NSFG) used life table methods to calculate the likelihood of divorce based on the divorce behaviors of previous cohorts of married individuals.[9] This analysis yielded figures close to the ratio of divorces to marriages in a given year. That is, about one-half of all marriages begun today or over the past decade will end in divorce. Specifically, after five years, 20 percent of all first marriages had disrupted due to separation or divorce. By ten years, 33 percent had disrupted; and, by twenty years, 50 percent had disrupted.

The problem with this method of estimation, however, is that divorce rates do not remain fixed over time and in recent decades have been declining. Thus, marriages that began twenty years in the past (relative to the study year of 1995) were exposed to the extremely high divorce rates of the mid- to late 1970s. As a result,

---

[8]Calculated based on data on divorce rates, population, and marital status of population in 2007 from the U.S. Census Bureau, *The 2009 Statistical Abstract*, "Table 123—Marriages and Divorces—Number and Rate by State," http://www.2010census.biz/compendia/statab/cats /births_deaths_marriages_divorces.html; and "Table 7—Resident Population by Age and Sex," and "Table 56—Marital Status of the Population by Sex and Age: 2007," http://www.2010census. biz/compendia/statab/cats/population/marital_status_and_living_arrangements.html.

[9]National Center for Health Statistics, *First Marriage Dissolution, Divorce, and Remarriage: United States* (Hyattsville, MD: Department of Health and Human Services, May 31, 2001), Tables 3 and 4, no. 323, pp. 5 and 6.

Divorced from Reality

news item

The great myth about divorce is that marital breakup is an increasing threat to American families, with each generation finding their marriages less stable than those of their parents.

Last week's release of new divorce statistics led to a smorgasbord of reporting feeding the myth. This newspaper warned readers, "Don't stock up on silver anniversary cards" because "women and men who married in the late 1970s had a less than even chance of still being married 25 years later." And apparently things are getting worse, as "the latest numbers suggest an uptick in the divorce rate among people married in the most recent 20 years covered in the report, 1975–1994." Other major newspapers ran similar articles.

The story of ever-increasing divorce is a powerful narrative. It is also wrong. In fact, the divorce rate has been falling continuously over the past quarter-century, and is now at its lowest level since 1970. While marriage rates are also declining, those marriages that do occur are increasingly more stable. For instance, marriages that began in the 1990s were more likely to celebrate a 10th anniversary than those that started in the 1980s, which, in turn, were also more likely to last than marriages that began back in the 1970s.

Why were so many analysts led astray by the recent data? Understanding this puzzle requires digging deeper into some rather complex statistics.

The Census Bureau reported that slightly more than half of all marriages occurring between 1975 and 1979 had not made it to their 25th anniversary. This breakup rate is not only alarmingly high, but also represents a rise of about 8 percent when compared with those marriages occurring in the preceding five-year period. But here's the rub: The census data come from a survey conducted in mid-2004, and at that time, it had not yet been 25 years since the wedding day of around 1 in 10 of those whose marriages they surveyed. And if your wedding was in late 1979, it was simply impossible to have celebrated a 25th anniversary when asked about your marriage in mid-2004. If the census survey had been conducted six months later, it would have found that a majority of those married in the second half of 1979 were happily moving into their 26th year of marriage. Once these marriages are added to the mix, it turns out that a majority of couples who tied the knot from 1975 to 1979—about 53 percent—reached their silver anniversary.

The narrative of rising divorce is also completely at odds with counts of divorce certificates, which show the divorce rate as having peaked at 22.8 divorces per 1,000 married couples in 1979 and to have fallen by 2005 to 16.7.

Why has the great divorce myth persisted so powerfully? Reporting on our families is a lot like reporting on the economy: statistical tales of woe provide the foundation for reform proposals. The only difference is that conservatives use these data to make the case for greater government intervention in the marriage market, while liberals use them to promote deregulation of marriage. But a useful family policy should instead be based on facts. The facts are that divorce is down, and today's marriages are more stable than they have been in decades. Perhaps it is worth stocking up on silver anniversary cards after all.

Source: Betsey Stevenson and Justin Wolfers, *The New York Times,* September 29, 2007. http://www.nytimes.com/2007/09/29/opinion/29wolfers.html?_r=1

much fewer of them survived than would likely be the case for more recent marriage cohorts. Therefore it would be misleading to say that marriages begun today have a 50 percent likelihood of ending in divorce sometime in the next 20 years. In reality, the risk of divorce for today's newlyweds is likely to be quite a bit less.

Perhaps more important is what the results of this study say about the likelihood of divorce for certain subgroups. If the wife was a teenager at first marriage, the marriage was more likely to dissolve than if the wife was at least 20 years of age. After ten years, 48 percent of the women who married under age 18 were disrupted, a figure that rose to 67 percent after twenty years. Comparable figures for the 18- to 19-year-olds were 40 percent after ten years and 56 percent after twenty years. By race/ethnicity, the disruption rate after ten years was 32 percent for white, 34 percent for Hispanic, 47 percent for black, and 20 percent for Asian.

Regardless of the manner of calculation, statistics on divorce are not perfect. Even data reported by the National Office of Vital Statistics are based on estimates obtained from states participating in the divorce-registration area (DRA). Thus, actual data from all fifty states are not available. Although the accuracy of divorce rates and statistics is improving, divorce data are not perfect. The best available information is presented with the recognition that the figures are based on estimates from selected available data.

Trends in Divorce

As shown in Table 14.1, the number of divorces and annulments granted in the United States increased during every five-year interval between 1960 and 1990, both in terms of absolute numbers (from 393,000 to 182,000) and in terms of crude and refined rates (from 2.2 to 4.7 and from 9.2 to 20.9, respectively). Since 1990, however, the number of divorces have been declining almost as dramatically (from 1,182,000 to 1,086,000) as has the crude and refined rates of divorce (from 4.4 to 3.6 and from 20.9 to 16.7, respectively). The 1981 figure of 1,213,000 divorces—involving more than 2.42 million divorced persons—was the highest national total ever observed for the United States. During the 1970s and until 1981, the number of divorces increased more rapidly than the total population and the married population of the United States.

When looked at over a longer term, divorce rates show a sensitivity to long-term changes in the socioeconomic system and shorter term changes and events such as economic depressions, wars, women's labor force participate, on and changes in divorce laws. As can be seen in Figure 14.1, the divorce rate has shown a long term trend of increasing over the 20th century. This trend is likely due to rapid industrialization and

Table 14.1

Number of Divorces and Divorce Rates: United States, 1960–2007

| YEAR | NUMBER OF DIVORCES | DIVORCE RATE PER 1,000 | |
		TOTAL POPULATION	MARRIED WOMEN
2007	1,085,000 (est.)	3.6	16.7 (est.)
2000	1,125,000 (est.)	4.1	(N.A.)
1995	1,169,000	4.4	19.8
1990	1,182,000	4.7	20.9
1985	1,190,000	5.0	21.7
1980	1,189,000	5.2	22.6
1975	1,036,000	4.8	20.3
1970	708,000	3.5	14.9
1965	479,000	2.5	10.7
1960	393,000	2.2	9.2

Source: National Center for Health Statistics, *Monthly Vital Statistics Reports*, vol. 49, no. 6 "Births, Marriages, Divorces, and Deaths: Provisional Data for January–December 2000" (Hyattsville, MD: Public Health Service, August 22, 2000); *Statistical Abstract of the United States: 2001*, 121st ed. (Washington, DC: Government Printing Office, 2001), no. 117, p. 87; and U.S. Census Bureau, *The 2009 Statistical Abstract*, "Table 123—Marriages and Divorces—Number and Rate by State," http://www.2010census.biz/compendia/statab/cats/births_deaths_marriages_divorces.html.

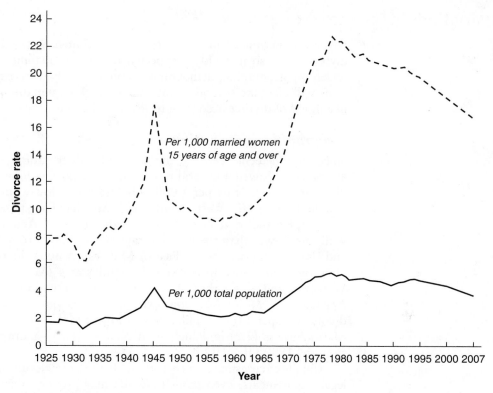

Figure 14.1

Divorce Rates: 1925–2007

Source: U.S. Census Bureau. *The 2009 Statistical Abstract.* "Table 123—Marriages and Divorces—Number and Date by State." http://www.2010Census.biz/compendia/statab/cuts/births_deaths_marriages_divorces.html.

urbanization and changes in cultural values that have broken down community solidarity, increased levels of stressors that marriages are exposed to, and shifted the focus of marriage from an instrumental institution to one that has to serve individual emotional and psychological needs for development and fulfillment.

Within the context of this longer term trend, shorter spells of divorce have occurred as a result of economic depressions (see the changes between 1925–1935) as individuals lack the financial security and means for divorce. Rates recover after these periods, however. Rates of divorce also rise steeply after major wars and then plummet during the period following the rise (see changes around the start and end of WWII—between 1940 and 1950). Following a hiatus in divorce from 1950 through 1960, rates again began to rise sharply, especially in the late 1960s through the 1970s. Much of this increase might be attributed to the greater independence, power and autonomy of women whose participation in the labor force was also increasing sharply during this time, giving them resources to find alternatives to poor marriages as well as to the liberalization of divorce laws (specifically, the institution of no-fault divorce) that began in New York state in 1970 and spread throughout the country in the following decade. Similar to the effect of opening the flood gates of a dam, this liberalization of laws suddenly made it possible for many women in poor and abusive marriages to get a divorce. Interestingly, once this period of increase in women's participation in labor and increased liberalization of laws concluded, divorce rates subsided and have even decreased.

Variations in Divorce

Divorce is permitted in every state in the United States. Each state has its own divorce code, so it could be expected that the probability of divorce would vary widely by geographic, demographic, and social characteristics. The following sections will examine several variations and seek explanations for a higher or lower likelihood of divorce according to selected characteristics.

Geographic Distribution

Since the nineteenth century, the geographic distribution of divorce in the United States has followed a general trend, increasing as one moves from east to west. In 2007, the divorce rate per 1,000 population was lowest in the East and Midwest and highest in the West, South, and Appalachian states (e.g., Virginia, West Virginia, Kentucky, Tennessee, and North Carolina). Among the twenty-one states with rates lower than the national rate of 3.6, only three—South Carolina, Texas, and Utah—were outside the East or Midwest. Among the twenty-eight states with rates over 3.6, only three New England states (Maine, New Hampshire, and Vermont) and one other state (Delaware) were outside the West, South, or Appalachia.[10] Major variations exist among individual states as well. In 2007, the divorce rate per 1,000 population was lowest in the District of Columbia (1.6) and Massachusetts (2.2) and highest in Nevada (6.5)—a dramatic decline, however, from the 1990 rate of 11.4.

Unique circumstances such as those that exist in Nevada are greatly influenced by legal requirements. Even though Nevada may produce a small fraction of the total divorces granted nationally (about 1.7 percent), the divorce rate per 1,000 population within that state can be affected significantly by a relatively small number of couples who come there from other states to get divorced. Except for Nevada and a few other states, it is unlikely that migratory divorce has a major effect on divorce rates.

How can these geographical variations be explained? Different factors likely operate in different areas, but in general, the probability of divorce is believed to be lower in culturally homogeneous rather than heterogeneous communities and in communities with primary, face-to-face interactions in contrast to communities with anonymous relationships, segmentalized relationships, or both. In traditional Durkheimian social structural terms, this pattern can be explained by a social integration hypothesis of fewer divorces in areas of high consensus on rules of behavior (norms) and effective social controls to ensure conformity. Communities or areas (regions, states) that are highly integrated socially would tend to exert stronger social pressures against nontraditional behaviors (which divorce generally is perceived to be) and exert both formal and informal pressures for conformity to community norms.

The levels of social integration and pressure toward conformity are likely influenced by residential mobility as well. High levels of residential movement are related to both higher levels of divorce and lower levels of social integration. What about neighborhood stress and divorce? Scott South focuses on the role that neighborhood socioeconomic disadvantage plays on the likelihood of divorce and separation.[11] He suggests that distressed neighborhoods, rather than disrupting existing marriages

---

[10]U.S. Census Bureau, *The 2009 Statistical Abstract*, "Table 123—Marriages and Divorces—Number and Rate by State," http://www.2010census.biz/compendia/statab/cats/births_deaths_marriages_divorces.html.

[11]Scott J. South, "The Geographic Context of Divorce: Do Neighborhoods Matter?" *Journal of Marriage and Family* 63 (August 2001), 755–766.

among couples with children, increase the prevalence of single-parent families by increasing rates of out-of-wedlock childbearing. That is, no support was found for a causal relationship between neighborhood socioeconomic disadvantage and the risk of marital dissolution, but neighborhoods do have an effect on the development of single-parent families and nonmarital fertility.

Ages of Husbands and Wives

Divorce is very common among young couples. Census data reveal that for women, divorce rates are at their peak for teenagers ages 15 to 19 and decline with increasing age. For men, divorce rates are highest in the 20 to 24 age category and then decline with increasing age (see Figure 14.2). Overall, women who marry as teenagers are two to four times as likely to divorce as those who marry later, and men who marry below age 25 are twice as likely to divorce as those who marry later.

Explanations for these high rates may include emotional immaturity, inability to assume marital responsibilities, greater incidences of early marriage in lower socioeconomic statuses (where divorce is more likely), more premarital pregnancies (also related to higher incidences of divorce), and similar factors. An increase in the age at marriage appears to be a significant factor in the decline in divorce rates over the past two decades in the United States and elsewhere. A study in Indonesia revealed that trends such as delayed marriage and educational expansion accounted

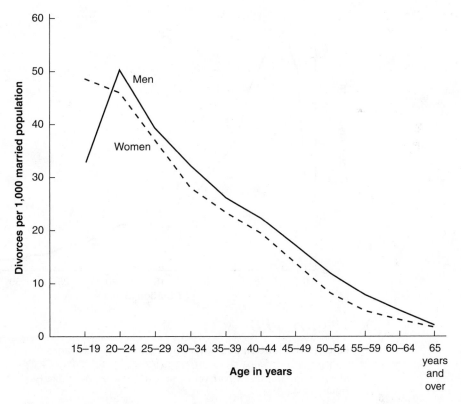

Figure 14.2

Age-Specific Divorce Rates for Men and Women

Source: National Center for Health Statistics, "Advance Report of Final Divorce Statistics, 1989 and 1990" *Monthly Vital Statistics Reports*, vol. 43, no. 9 (Hyattsville, MD: Public Health Service. 22 March 1995), Figure 3, p. 3.

for about one-third of the decline in marital dissolution.[12] A macro-level analysis suggests that one way to reduce divorce rates is to marry at a later age.

Duration of Marriage

The largest number of divorce decrees are granted one to four years after marriage, and that number declines relatively consistently with increased duration (see Figure 14.3). The second, third, and fourth years of marriage appear to be the modal (most common) years for divorce. Few divorces (about 3 percent) occur within the first year of marriage, due partly to requirements by many states that couples be separated for at least one year before obtaining a divorce. One-third of divorcing couples (31.7 percent) had been married one to four years, and about one-fourth (28.3 percent) had been married five to nine years. The remaining one-third of divorcing couples had been married ten years or more, including 6.2 percent who had been married twenty-five years or more.[13]

Divorce occurs regardless of age or length of marriage; no evidence shows an increase in mid-life divorce over earlier ages or of shorter durations. It is not, however, a rare phenomenon. Of those divorces that do occur in midlife, women's growing economic independence was found to be the principal factor in separation and

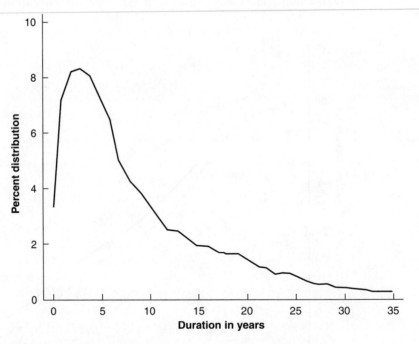

Figure 14.3

Percent Distribution of Divorces by Duration of Marriages

Source: National Center for Health Statistics, "Advance Report of Final Divorce Statistics, 1989 and 1990" *Monthly Vital Statistics Report*, vol. 43, no. 9 (Hyattsville, MD: Public Health Service, 22 March 1995), Figure 3, p. 4.

---

[12]Tim B. Heaton, Mark Cammack, and Larry Young, "Why Is the Divorce Rate Declining in Indonesia," *Journal of Marriage and Family* 63 (May 2001), 480–490.

[13]National Center for Health Statistics, *Monthly Vital Statistics Report*, vol. 43, no. 9, March 22, 1995, Table 11, p. 20.

divorce over the life course.[14] On the other hand, a college education was found to reduce the risk of divorce both in the second decade of marriage and later. This may be due to factors such as having married later or having married husbands with more education and higher earnings, or to marital investment effects: having too much to lose from divorce, employment status, home ownership, and the like.

As of a decade ago, the average interval between the first marriage and divorce was about eleven years. For those who remarried and got another divorce, the median interval between the second marriage and divorce was 7.3 years. For the third marriage or more, the median interval was about five years. It would appear that the average length of each succeeding marriage that ends in divorce is shorter than the previous one. Most likely, the first divorce experience is the most difficult one. Having been through a divorce, accepting divorced status, and later remarrying may tend to make divorce a more acceptable solution to an unsuccessful second, third, or fourth marital relationship.

The duration of remarriages is influenced by many factors not at issue in first marriages: ex-spouses, ex-in-laws, stepchildren, and so on. For example, national data suggest that bringing stepchildren into a second marriage appears to weaken the marital unit; child bearing prior to remarriage increases the risk of marital dissolution; and having a child in the second marriage reduces the probability of dissolution.[15] In addition, perhaps, remarriages are composed disproportionately of people who have problems that make having stable marriages difficult: alcoholism, abusiveness, or instability. Whatever the reason, the timespan of remarriages that end in divorce is shorter than in first marriages.

Many marriages that never end in divorce are seriously disrupted in all but the legal sense. This observation leads to a point made at various times throughout this book: length of marriage is not necessarily an index of marital success or adjustment, and divorce is not necessarily a good index of marital breakdown. Divorce may simply indicate a couple's willingness to provide a legal ending to their marital relationship.

Race, Religion, and Socioeconomic Status

The success levels of interracial and interfaith marriages were discussed in Chapter 6. The discussion turns now to how rates differ by race, religion, and socioeconomic level in nonmixed (endogamous) marriages. Is the probability of divorce different for blacks and whites, Protestants and Catholics, and people of lower and higher socioeconomic levels?

The likelihood of divorce by race usually differs within a state as well as within the same racial group among different states. As discussed earlier in the chapter, the probability of first marriage disruption after ten or twenty years was highest for blacks, followed by Hispanics, then non-Hispanic whites, and lowest for Asians. These racial differences may be partly explained by urban residence, mobility patterns, social-class differences, and differing accessibility to various types of social and economic resources. Generally, the greater the accessibility to such resources, the lower the incidence of divorce.

What about religion? Do divorce rates differ by major religious affiliation? Data from seven U.S. national surveys by Norval Glenn and Michael Supancic showed that marital dissolution is moderately higher for Protestants, considered as

---

[14]Bridget Heidemann, Olga Suhomlinova, and Angela O'Rand, "Economic Independence, Economic Status, and Empty Nest in Midlife Marital Disruption," *Journal of Marriage and the Family* 60 (February 1998), 219–231. Note also Zheng Wu and Margaret J. Penning, "Marital Instability after Midlife," *Journal of Family Issues* 18 (September 1997), 459–478.

[15]Howard Weinberg, "Childbearing and Dissolution of the Second Marriage," *Journal of Marriage and the Family* 54 (November 1992), 879–887.

a whole, than for Catholics, and lower for Jews than for Catholics.[16] The highest divorce rates are among persons with no religious affiliation. This finding is consistent with the data on frequency of attendance at religious services; religiosity is an important deterrent to divorce and separation.

Contrary to what one might expect, the Glenn and Supancic study, as well as others, showed that Protestant fundamentalists—the most conservative Protestant denominations (for example, Nazarene, Pentecostal, Baptist)—have relatively high dissolution rates, in spite of their strong disapproval of divorce. Factors associated with conversion to these fundamentalist denominations were found to be important in producing the high dissolution rates.[17] Conversion may signify the cultural conflict that results from the radical transition from one context to another. It may also indicate a lack of normative integration in the antiseparation/divorce doctrine, on the one hand, while urging acceptance and tolerance of the converted "sinner" on the other. The higher divorce/separation rate may also reflect the lower than average socioeconomic status of persons in these denominations; the strong demands these groups make on the time, energy, and money of their adherents (which may negatively affect marriages); the inflexibility or rigidity of their theological position; or even the focus and emphasis on the next life rather than the current one.

What about socioeconomic level? The divorce rate has increased at all socioeconomic levels, yet the proportion of persons ever divorced remains highest among relatively disadvantaged groups. When education, occupation, or income is used as an index of socioeconomic level, the divorce rate goes up as the socioeconomic level goes down.

One exception to this relationship exists among professional women who have five or more years of college education. Generally, compared to women of similar age groups, professional women were more likely never to have married, were more likely to divorce if they had married, and were less likely to remarry if they divorced. This may be due to their lessened dependence on men, to the viable alternatives they have to marriage, and to the strain resulting from their efforts to balance both work and family roles.

It appears that economic independence on the part of wives does have a positive effect on the risk of divorce. In a panel study of income dynamics of more than 3,500 married couples, Scott South revealed that the impact of wives' employment on marital dissolution has become increasingly positive over time.[18] Moreover, as marriages age, the effect of wives' employment on divorce becomes even stronger. He suggests three societal changes that might account for the increasingly destabilizing impact of wives' employment on marriage: (1) the development of institutional supports for unmarried mothers, (2) a reduced tendency for working wives to adopt traditional gender roles, and (3) the growing exposure of working women to spousal alternatives. (This alternative factor was discussed in Chapter 9 and is considered again later in this chapter.)

Regardless of these exceptions, there generally remains greater marital instability and higher divorce rates at lower socioeconomic levels. This may stem from a number of factors, including the frustrations that come from having difficulty meeting

---

[16]Norval D. Glenn and Michael Supancic, "The Social and Demographic Correlates of Divorce and Separation in the United States: An Update and Reconsideration," *Journal of Marriage and the Family* 46 (August 1984), 563–575.

[17]S. Kenneth Chi and Sharon K. Houseknecht, "Protestant Fundamentalism and Marital Success: A Comparative Approach," *Sociology and Social Research* 69 (April 1985), 351–375.

[18]Scott J. South, "Time-Dependent Effects of Wives' Employment on Marital Dissolution," *American Sociological Review* 66 (April 2001), 226–245.

TRANSNATIONAL FAMILIES

Divorce Experience in Hong Kong

Hong Kong is a transnational context for its millions of inhabitants and their families. Existing at the nexus of traditional Chinese culture, contemporary globalization, the entry of Mainland China into the world capitalist system, and the influence of British colonialism, families in Hong Kong face conflicting expectations and develop complex systems of adaptation that can complicate the divorce process. In a study of thirty-five women who were participants in empowerment workshops for divorced or divorcing women, Winnie Kung, Suet-Lin Hung, and Cecilia Chan explored the pressures that these women faced as a result of the context within which they lived.

The cultural context of Hong Kong is a mixture of traditional Confucian beliefs about the central role of family life in society (and the generational and gender hierarchies implied), romantic ideals, and marriages based on love, companionship and equality that were introduced over the past century as a result of British colonization. This mixture has led to increased ambiguity about marriage and divorce norms. In addition, the socioeconomic context complicates marriage and divorce as proximity to Mainland China, combined with the expansion of Chinese manufacturing in large suburbs, has resulted in many resident men from Hong Kong working and living during the week apart from their spouses.

The extreme economic differences between these men and Mainland Chinese women, the tradition in Mainland China of condoning men's extra-marital relationships, and the removal of community constraints has led to increased opportunities for extramarital affairs. In addition, for low-income single men in Hong Kong, the extreme economic differences between Hong Kong and Mainland China and the relative proximity of the Mainland contribute to the formation of transnational marriages that involve high levels of inequality, high levels of economic and immigration stress, and isolation of the wife once she immigrates to Hong Kong. As a result of these and other forces, the divorce rate in Hong Kong has increased dramatically in recent decades from .76 in 1984 to 2.0 in 2005.

With the rise in divorce has come a more visible struggle between traditional Chinese culture and the modern culture. Four intersection points cause difficulties for women who are divorcing their husbands. The first is the wife's own extended family that still expresses concern over how her divorce will affect her and the extended family financially and how it could lead to social stigma. As a result, they often exert pressures on her to reconcile and tolerate her husband's infidelities, blame her for being too emotional and intolerant, and even intervene by apologizing to her husband's family for her intolerance. Second, the husband's extended family often colludes with the husband in trying to hide his infidelities and this can create additional strains in what is typically an already strained in-law relationship. Third, the informal social system still assigns blame and shame unequally to the wife in a divorce. Although these women agreed that people in Hong Kong are more accepting of divorce, this acceptance did not pertain to their own personal spheres of interaction. Finally, the formal system of institutions is still in a state of conflict about divorce. Legal procedures in divorce and applications for social welfare are lengthy and complicated and lawyers and social workers in the system still maintain old prejudices and patriarchal/paternalistic approaches.

Winnie W. Kung, Suet-Lin Hung, and Cecilia L. W. Chan, "How the Socio-Cultural Context Shapes Women's Divorce Experience in Hong Kong," *Journal of Comparative Family Studies*, 35 (2004), 33–50.

---

expenses, the upper strata being more tied to long-term investment expenditures, and the more tightly knit kin and family networks among higher strata couples that make divorce more difficult.

The alert reader may note what appears to be a contradiction in the data. For example, it was shown in Figure 14.1 and mentioned in the text that divorce rates tend to decrease during times of economic depression and rise during times of prosperity. And it was just mentioned that the incidence of divorce increases as the socioeconomic level goes down. How is it possible that divorce rates decrease during depression, when times are hard, and also increase among the lower strata, where times are also hard?

Several factors are involved. During economic depression, divorce rates drop at all class levels. During the Great Depression of the 1930s, the lower classes still had the highest divorce rate. Many of the marriages that survived the 1930s ended in divorce in the 1940s. Also, general lifestyle, sense of loyalty, linkages with kin, occupational and income security, and group support all affect rates of divorce. These factors were different in the 1930s for Depression families than they are now for lower-class families. Once again, the powerful influence of the social network is evident in something perceived as individualistic and personal as divorce.

Other social factors beyond geographic, demographic, and socioeconomic variations may contribute to the likelihood of divorce. For example, a *family change hypothesis* suggests that multiple parental structural transitions make things worse for children and increase the likelihood that offspring will divorce later in life.[19] Couples who have parents, siblings, or friends who have divorced are themselves more likely to divorce. Adult children of divorced parents are more likely to have been exposed to poor models of dyadic behavior and may not have learned the skills and attitudes that facilitate successful functioning within marriage. Having divorced peers may release inhibitions and reduce pressure to remain in an unhappy marriage, or it may actually encourage individuals to seek out more attractive partners.

Are there factors that enable us to predict the likelihood of divorce? One longitudinal study found that marital problems at one point in time such as jealousy, drinking, spending money, moodiness, not communicating, and anger increased the odds of divorce ten and twelve years later. Extramarital sex was a particularly powerful predictor of divorce.[20]

Another study showed that wives' traditional attitudes are associated with lower odds and husbands' traditional attitudes with higher odds of marital dissolution.[21] The same source indicated that physical violence is a prime hardship that influences divorce and that nonviolent relationships are associated with lower odds of marital dissolution. Obviously, the list of factors associated with the likelihood of divorce is not complete. Let us examine still other factors by turning our attention to some of the grounds on which divorce occurs: legally and socially.

Legal and Social Grounds for Divorce

As previously discussed, the legal grounds for divorce vary somewhat for each state.[22] Apart from "no-fault" divorce, the most widely accepted legal grounds for divorce are breakdown of marriage, incompatibility, cruelty, and desertion. In all states, adultery is either grounds for divorce or evidence of incompatibility, irreconcilable differences, or breakdown of the marriage. Other legal grounds in at least ten states include nonsupport, alcoholism or drug addiction, felony conviction or imprisonment, impotence,

---

[19]Nicholas H. Wolfinger, "Beyond the Intergenerational Transmission of Divorce," *Journal of Family Issues* 21 (November 2000), 1061–1086; and Du Feng, Roseann Giarrusso, Vern Bengtson, and Nancy Frye, "Intergenerational Transmission of Marital Quality and Marital Instability," *Journal of Marriage and the Family* 61 (May 1999), 451–463.

[20]Paul R. Amato, "Explaining the Intergeneratinal Transmission of Divorce," *Journal of Marriage and the Family* 58 (August 1996), 628–640; and Paul R. Amato and Stacy J. Rogers, "A Longitudinal Study of Marital Problems and Subsequent Divorce," *Journal of Marriage and the Family* 59 (August 1997), 612–624.

[21]Laura Sanchez and Constance T. Gager, "Hard Living, Perceived Entitlement to a Great Marriage, and Marital Dissolution," *Journal of Marriage and the Family* 62 (August 2000), 708–722.

[22]See *The World Almanac and Book of Facts: 2001* (Mahwah, NJ: World Almanac Books, 2001), 746.

insanity, mental or physical cruelty, nonsupport, abandonment (desertion), fraud, force or duress, and bigamy. California, Colorado, and Oregon have procedures whereby a couple can obtain a divorce without an attorney and without appearing in court, provided certain requirements are met (such as being married less than two years and having no children, no real estate, and few debts).

The adversary divorce system in the United States, in which one party must be innocent and the other guilty, has been replaced in all fifty states with **no-fault divorce.** Traditional fault grounds were abolished in favor of dissolution of marriage based on **irreconcilable differences**—defined as any grounds determined by the court to be substantial reasons for not continuing the marriage.

Under no-fault divorce law, consent of both spouses is not required. The law is gender neutral in that both spouses are responsible for alimony and child support and both spouses are eligible for child custody. Financial awards such as child support and property distribution are not linked to "fault" but rather to the spouses' current financial needs and resources. The basic goals of no-fault divorce were intended (1) to make divorce less restrictive by reducing the legal and economic obstacles to divorce, and (2) to improve the social-psychological and communication climate of divorce by abolishing the concept of fault. Some states have even replaced the term *divorce* with *dissolution of marriage.*

What have been the consequences of no-fault divorce laws? Have fewer restrictions resulted in increased divorce rates? Do mothers and women fare better under the no-fault system? The answer to the first question appears to be yes and to the second no. An analysis of pre-no-fault and post-no-fault divorce rates of all fifty states revealed that all but six states had an increase in the rate of divorce following the enactment of the law.[23] Nevada, for example, had a large *decrease* that may be attributed to the fact that divorce in Nevada was no longer any less restrictive or more accessible than in other states. This reduced the need for couples to travel to Nevada for a quick and expedient divorce. Glenn, however, cautions us against reaching such strong and untentative conclusions about cause and effect, suggesting that adoption of no-fault divorce *in itself* had very little direct effect on divorce rates.[24]

In response to the second question, studies of property settlements have suggested consistently that divorcing mothers are faring more poorly under the no-fault system than they did under the former adversary system. The no-fault system reduced the bargaining power of spouses who did not want to divorce, which led to substantial declines in the financial settlements received by women.

Divorce proceedings under the no-fault system are relatively routine. Where cases are contested, they can become drawn-out affairs, resulting in much bitterness and expense. Attempts to decrease such conflict have led to **divorce mediation.** Mediation is a conflict resolution process in which the divorcing couple meets with a neutral third-party intervener (mediator) who helps them negotiate an agreement about property distribution, support, and child custody. The emphasis is on direct communication, openness, attention to emotional issues and the underlying causes of the disputes, and avoidance of blame. Proponents of mediation stress that it relieves court dockets clogged with matrimonial actions, reduces the alienation that couples experience in court, inspires durable consensual agreements, helps couples resume workable relationships to jointly rear their children, and translates into savings in

---

[23]Paul A. Nakonezny, Robert D. Shull, and Joseph Lee Rodgers, "The Effect of No-Fault Divorce Law on the Divorce Rate across the 50 States and Its Relation to Income, Education, and Religiosity," *Journal of Marriage and the Family* 57 (May 1995), 477–488.

[24]Norval D. Glenn, "A Reconsideration of the Effect of No-Fault Divorce on Divorce Rates," *Journal of Marriage and the Family* 59 (November 1997), 1023–1030.

time and money. The mediation process works on building and strengthening relationships, whereas the adversary process tends to weaken and destroy them.

Most divorce settlements are the result of a negotiation process in which parents make decisions concerning child support, custody, visitation, and marital property without bringing any contested issue into court for adjudication (judicial settlement). The modal or standard divorce package is one in which the mother has custody of the children and is awarded child support, and the father pays child support and has visitation rights.[25]

Generally, the reasons marriages dissolve and force these settlement and custody issues can be explained as "push" factors that drive persons apart, such as adultery, abusiveness, drunkenness, or interpersonal conflict. However, a more open systems perspective on marital dissolution looks as well at "pull" factors: conditions in the environment that pull persons away from their current spouses or partners. These factors, as described in Chapter 9, can be referred to as **marital alternatives**. Consciously or not, people compare their current relationships with alternative ones. If internal attractions and forces that keep a couple together become weaker than those from a viable alternative, the consequence is likely to be breakup.

Support for this idea comes from various sources. South and others, for example, found the risk of dissolution is highest where either partner encounters alternatives to the existing relationship.[26] They note that a sizable percentage of recently divorced persons had been romantically involved with someone other than a spouse prior to the divorce. This suggests that many married persons continue to be open to the possibility of an intimate (extramarital) relationship. Thus, a married woman who works in an occupation or environment having relatively many men and few women is more likely to find an attractive alternative to her current husband or partner. In other words, spouses' structural opportunities to form alternative opposite sex relationships are an important factor in explaining why some couples divorce. Esterberg and others found that the increase in women's options outside of marriage such as returning to school and consequent increased self-esteem are more important than attitudinal factors in hastening the transition to divorce.[27]

This approach is highly similar to that adopted by exchange theorists; the decision to divorce clearly contains important reward/cost considerations. The rewards (attractions) may include love, goods, services, security, joint possessions, children, sexual enjoyment, and so forth, and the costs (barriers) may include feelings of obligation or inadequacy, fears of family/friend reactions, religious prohibitions, financial costs, and the like. The probability for divorce increases as alternatives are perceived that provide greater rewards or lower costs than exist in marriage.

Impact of Children on Parental Divorce

Are children a deterrent to divorce? The answer appears to be both yes and no. Data have shown that firstborn and other children increase the stability of marriage

---

[25]Jay D. Teachman and Karen Polonko, "Negotiating Divorce Outcomes: Can We Identify Patterns in Divorce Settlements?" *Journal of Marriage and the Family* 52 (February 1990), 129–139.

[26]Scott J. South and Kim M. Lloyd, "Spousal Alternatives and Marital Dissolution," *American Sociological Review* 60 (February 1995), 21–35; and Scott J. South, Katherine Trent, and Yang Shen, "Changing Partners: Toward a Macrostructural-Opportunity Theory of Marital Dissolution," *Journal of Marriage and Family* 63 (August 2001), 743–754.

[27]Kristin G. Esterberg, Phyllis Moen, and Donna Dempster-McClain, "Transition to Divorce: A Life Course Approach to Women's Marital Duration and Dissolution," *The Sociological Quarterly* 35 (1994), 289–307.

Divorce is a common experience throughout the world. Although proceedings under a no-fault system are quite routine in the United States, contested cases may become lengthy legal battles involving competing attorneys and a judge who decides what the financial and child custody arrangements will be.

through their preschool years.[28] At least in the short run, young preschool children tend to keep couples together who would otherwise divorce. (Consider the braking hypothesis from Chapter 10.) However, older children and children born before marriage significantly increase chances of marital disruption. It is possible that the inhibiting effect of children on keeping couples together fades and that, as children get older, the strains of parenthood augment the strains of marriage, leading to increased risks of disruption.

Data from more than 11,000 divorcing families in northern California clearly support the relationship between the duration of marriage and the presence of children.[29] Explanations for children delaying (not preventing) divorce included the following: children make divorce more costly than continuation of the marriage; there is a cost of having the wife confined to the home and less free to take employment; older children are more articulate about their feelings; people who have children may be more secure in the marriage than their childless counterparts; couples may feel a stigma toward parents who divorce; and there may be anticipated complications attending divorce action (child custody, coparenting, single-parent problems). Note that all the couples in this study got divorced; thus, it provided no support for the myth that children prevent divorce. The study did support the notion of a longer duration of marriage before divorce when children were present.

---

[28]Linda J. Waite and Lee A. Lillard, "Children and Marital Disruption," *American Journal of Sociology* 96 (January 1991), 930–953.

[29]Robert M. Rankin and Jerry S. Maneker, "The Duration of Marriage in a Divorcing Population: The Impact of Children," *Journal of Marriage and the Family* 47 (February 1985), 43–52.

Consequences of Divorce for Adults

Consequences of divorce are evident at both the individual and interpersonal (micro) levels as well as at the organizational and societal (macro) levels.[30] Most research has focused on the micro levels. But one macrolevel finding from several countries— including the United States, Finland, Norway, and Canada—supported the proposition of a direct relationship between divorce and suicide.[31] Divorced people are more likely to commit suicide than married people. This proposition is consistent with the work on suicide originally published in 1897 by Emile Durkheim, who theorized that societies with low degrees of social integration typically share high rates of suicide.

A seventeen-year longitudinal study examined factors that predicted adjustment to divorce and marital disruption.[32] Adjustment was positively associated with income, dating someone steadily, cohabitation or remarriage, and being the partner who initiated the divorce. Clearly, leaving is preferable to being left. And younger individuals showed evidence of better adjustment than older individuals.

The economic consequences of divorce differ dramatically by gender. In short, the economic situation improves for men and declines for women. California data in the 1970s showed a radical change in the standard of living just one year after a legal divorce. Men experienced a 42 percent improvement in their postdivorce standard of living, while women experienced a 73 percent loss.[33] A reanalysis of these data produced estimates of a 27 percent (not 73 percent) decline in women's and a 10 percent (not 42 percent) increase in men's standard of living after divorce.[34]

Not all divorced men gain in economic status. One study suggested that with more households relying on dual incomes, a primary source of economic decline for men after union dissolution was an inability to compensate for the loss of their partner's income.[35]

Regardless of the magnitude of the male–female differences, the gender gap is real and seems to have changed very little over the past two decades. Apparently, this is not merely a phenomenon in the United States but holds true in other countries as well. In Germany, women experienced an even bigger drop in economic status following divorce than their U.S. female counterparts. German men fared about as well as their U.S. male counterparts.[36] In both countries, men were more likely than women to work and to earn more in the labor market both before and after a divorce. In both countries, mothers were more likely than fathers to care for children after a divorce. These and other factors pose a greater economic hardship for divorced women than for divorced men.

---

[30]Paul R. Amato, "The Consequences of Divorce for Adults and Children," *Journal of Marriage and the Family* 62 (November 2000), 1269–1287; and Frank F. Furstenberg Jr., "Divorce and the American Family," *Annual Review of Sociology* 16 (1990), 379–403.

[31]Steve Stack, "The Effect of Divorce on Suicide in Finland: A Time Series Analysis," *Journal of Marriage and the Family* 54 (August 1992), 636–642; Steven Stack, "The Impact of Divorce on Suicide in Norway, 1951–1980," *Journal of Marriage and the Family* 51 (February 1989), 229–238; and Frank Trovato, "The Relationship between Marital Dissolution and Suicide: The Canadian Case," *Journal of Marriage and the Family* 48 (May 1986), 341–348.

[32]Hongyu Wang and Paul R. Amato, "Predictors of Divorce Adjustment: Stressors, Resources, and Definitions," *Journal of Marriage and the Family* 62 (August 2000), 655–668.

[33]Lenore J. Weitzman, "The Economics of Divorce: Social and Economic Consequences of Property, Alimony, and Child Support Awards," *UCLA Law Review* 28 (August 1981), 1251.

[34]Richard R. Peterson, "A Re-Evaluation of the Economic Consequence of Divorce," *American Sociological Review* 61 (June 1996), 528–536.

[35]Patricia A. McManus and Thomas A. DiPrete, "Losers and Winners: The Financial Consequences of Separation and Divorce for Men," *American Sociological Review* 66 (April 2001), 246–268.

[36]Richard V. Burkhauser, Greg J. Duncan, Richard Hauser, and Roland Berntsen, "Wife or Frau, Women Do Worse: A Comparison of Men and Women in the United States and Germany After Marital Dissolution," *Demography* 28 (August 1991), 353–360.

National longitudinal surveys showed that 40 percent of widows and over 25 percent of divorced women fall into poverty for at least some time during the first five years after being single.[37] It is little wonder that more divorced women report that they are in constant financial crisis, are perpetually worried about not being able to pay their bills, have more stress, and feel less satisfied with their lives than any other group in the United States. In contrast, most men who divorce or separate are immediately better off. They retain most of their labor incomes, typically do not pay large amounts of alimony and child support to their ex-wives, and no longer have to provide for their former families. Although writers frequently refer to *his* and *her* marriages, those differences appear minor when comparing *his* and *her* divorces.

There appear to be several routes to economic recovery for women and mothers following divorce: (1) increasing their own earnings by entering the paid labor force or increasing their work hours, (2) obtaining or increasing child support from the father, and (3) remarriage or cohabitation: marrying or living with a person who can provide additional economic resources. Evidence supports the latter as the most promising route to economic recovery. Findings show that in absolute terms, remarriage is economically more advantageous than cohabitation, but both are equivalent in their ability to restore family income to prior levels.[38] Over the long term however, cohabitation, when it doesn't lead to marriage, is a poor mechanism for maintaining a child's economic well-being.

Consequences for Children of Divorced Parents

An estimated 1 million children are the victims of divorce each year. Therefore, a question of great concern is, What are the consequences of divorce for children? Should couples, although unhappily married, stay together for the sake of the children?

Laypeople assume that the psychological, economic, and social effects of divorce on children are predominantly negative, and these negative assumptions influence how people think about particular children. Research found that this negative prototype of children of divorce leads people to recall unfavorable information and to fail to recall favorable information about such children.[39] This may lead to a self-fulfilling prophecy when teachers, counselors, social workers, and parents expect children from divorced families to have more than their share of problems and treat them in ways that exacerbate or even generate these very problems.

Few people would argue that children are better off in happy, stable families than in divorced or unhappy, unstable families. As previously indicated, evidence has shown that divorce diminishes the economic and social resources available to children, which has negative consequences for educational attainment, marital timing, marital probability, and divorce probability.[40]

---

[37]Leslie A. Morgan, "Economic Well-Being Following Marital Termination," *Journal of Family Issues* 10 (March 1989), 86–101.

[38]Donna Ruane Morrison and Amy Ritualo, "Routes to Children's Economic Recovery after Divorce: Are Cohabitation and Remarriage Equivalent," *American Sociological Review* 65 (August 2000), 560–580.

[39]Paul R. Amato, "The 'Child of Divorce' as a Person Prototype: Bias in the Recall of Information about Children in Divorced Families," *Journal of Marriage and the Family* 53 (February 1991), 59–69.

[40]Gary D. Sandefur, Sara McLanahan, and Roger A. Wojtkiewicz, "The Effects of Parental Marital Status during Adolescence on High School Graduation," *Social Forces* 71 (September 1992), 103–121; and Norval D. Glenn and Kathryn B. Kramer, "The Marriages and Divorces of the Children of Divorce," *Journal of Marriage and the Family* 49 (November 1987), 811–825.

Divorce during a child's adolescence may be particularly disturbing. When children of divorce ages 7 to 11 were contrasted with adolescents ages 11 to 16, the results suggested more deleterious effects on the older children.[41] In addition, when compared to married partners, adolescent children of divorced parents are less likely to graduate from high school, tend to marry at an earlier age, have a lower probability of ever marrying, and have a higher probability of getting divorced. Other evidence has shown that adolescents from divorced homes are more prone to commit delinquent acts, experience problems in peer relations, and are highly associated with family-related offenses, such as running away and truancy.[42] These findings confirm the popular notion that divorce is bad for children, and particularly so for adolescent children.

The negative consequences of divorce appear to extend well beyond adolescence. One clearly defined consequence of divorce is its influence on the adult well-being of children involved. Data from more than thirty-seven studies revealed that having one's parents divorce (or permanently separate) has broad negative consequences for an individual's quality of life in adulthood.[43] Adult characteristics affected by parental divorce included psychological well-being (depression, low life satisfaction), family well-being (lower marital quality and stability, more frequent divorce, poorer relationships with parents), socioeconomic well-being (low educational attainment, income, and occupational prestige), and physical health. These highly negative findings are somewhat tempered when community samples rather than clinical samples are used, when more recent studies rather than earlier studies are used, and when statistical controls (such as parental education and occupational status) are used rather than simple zero-order differences.

Are the findings just presented the result of a divorce or separation as the central event in shaping the lives of children? Furstenberg and others note that to focus on the impact of divorce itself makes it easy to overlook the circumstances leading up to the separation.[44] These circumstances and processes that often end in divorce may be harmful to children whether the parents stay together or separate. Even before the disruption, both male and female adolescents from families that subsequently dissolved exhibited more academic, psychological, and behavioral problems than peers whose parents remained married. High levels of marital conflict, poor parenting practices, or persistent economic stress may compromise children's economic, social, and psychological well-being in later life regardless of a divorce or separation.

---

[41]P. Lindsay Chase-Lansdale, Andrew J. Cherlin, and Kathleen E. Kierman, "The Long-Term Effects of Parental Divorce on the Mental Health of Young Adults: A Developmental Perspective," *Child Development* 66 (1995), 1614–1634.

[42]L. Edward Wells and Joseph H. Ranken, "Families and Delinquency: A Meta-Analysis of the Impact of Broken Homes," *Social Problems* 38 (February 1991), 71–93; and David H. Demo and Alan C. Acock, "The Impact of Divorce on Children," *Journal of Marriage and the Family* 50 (August 1988), 619–648.

[43]Paul R. Amato and Bruce Keith, "Parental Divorce and Adult Well-Being: A Meta-analysis," *Journal of Marriage and the Family* 53 (February 1991), 43–58. See also Andrew J. Cherlin, P. Lindsay Chase-Lansdale, and Christine McRae, *American Sociological Review* 63 (April 1998), 239–249; and Paul R. Amato and Juliana M. Sobolewski, "The Effects of Divorce and Marital Discord on Adult Children's Psychological Well-Being," *American Sociological Review* 66 (December 2001), 900–921.

[44]Frank F. Furstenberg Jr. and Julien O. Teitler, "Reconsidering the Effects of Marital Disruption: What Happens to Children of Divorce in Early Adulthood," *Journal of Family Issues* 15 (June 1994), 173–190; and Yongmin Sun "Family Environment and Adolescents' Well-Being before and after Parents' Disruption: A Longitudinal Analysis," *Journal of Marriage and Family* 63 (August 2001), 697–713.

Jekielek makes similar arguments.[45] Using national data, she finds that both parental marital conflict and marital disruption increase the later anxiety/withdrawal of children ages 6 to 14. But she finds as well that children remaining in high-conflict environments exhibit lower levels of well-being than children who experienced high levels of parental conflict but whose parents divorced or separated. Given this, it may make little sense to argue that, for the sake of the children, partners in unhappy marriages should stay together. Unhappy families have choices, neither of which is ideal or highly favorable for children. Both the intact home with persistent conflict and the divorced home are likely to cause varying degrees of stress, pain, and difficulty, but divorce may be the better choice.

Some support for the idea that divorce may be the better choice, particularly in high-conflict marriages, comes from two separate national longitudinal studies of parents and their adult children.[46] The dissolution of high-conflict marriages appeared to have beneficial effects on their offspring's lives. These children were better off in the long run, if their parents divorced than if they remained married. The one study that compared low- and high-conflict marriages indicated that dissolution of low-conflict marriages had negative effects on offspring's lives. Why did low-conflict couples get divorced in the first place? These couples were less integrated into the community, had fewer impediments to and more favorable attitudes toward divorce, and were more predisposed to engage in risky behavior. Children from these divorced parents experienced inordinate adversity, both psychologically and socially.

Child Custody

If children are minors, **child custody** and economic support become issues of major concern. As of the early 2005, 13.5 million women and men were custodial parents of children under 21 years of age with the other parent living elsewhere.[47] A majority of these parents (11.4 million, or 84.4 percent), were women. Mothers living with children from an absent father had a poverty rate of 27.8 percent, approximately two-and-one-half times the poverty rate of their male counterparts (11.1 percent) and more than four times the rate for all married-couple families with children (8 percent).

Joint custody generally is defined as an arrangement in which the child spends at least 30 percent of the time with each of two parents. It appears to be on the increase, but about only one in five decisions are of this type. This arrangement generally is perceived the most ideal from the perspective of parent–child relationships. A review of the literature seems to suggest that parents and children in joint custody arrangements are more likely than those in sole custody arrangements to express high levels of satisfaction with their situation.[48] These findings are particularly clear with fathers, but evidence shows that mothers benefit from joint custody as well.

---

[45]Susan M. Jekielek, "Parental Conflict, Marital Disruption and Children's Emotional Well-Being," *Social Forces* 76 (March 1998), 905–935.

[46]Alan Booth and Paul R. Amato, "Parental Predivorce Relations and Offspring Postdivorce Well-Being," *Journal of Marriage and Family* 63 (February 2001), 197–212; and Donna Ruane Morrison and Mary Jo Coiro, "Parental Conflict and Marital Disruption: Do Children Benefit When High-Conflict Marriages Are Dissolved," *Journal of Marriage and the Family* 61 (August 1999), 626–637.

[47]U.S. Census Bureau, *The 2009 Statistical Abstract*, "Table 549—Child Support—Award and Recipiency Status of Custodial Parent: 2005," http://www.2010census.biz/compendia/statab/cats/social_insurance_human_services/child_support_head_start_child_care.html.

[48]James A. Twaite, Daniel Silitsky, and Anya K. Luchow, *Children of Divorce: Adjustment, Parental Conflict, Custody, Remarriage, and Recommendations for Clinicians* (Northvale, NJ: Jason Aronson Inc., 1998), 49–51.

In spite of having higher incomes than women and evidence that men can "mother," only about 14 percent of men are awarded custody of their children. Here, at a rally supporting divorced husbands' custody rights, a man makes his views known outside a courthouse.

Part of the satisfaction appears to be related to *respite care*, those periods of time separate from the children when the parents can catch up on their obligations and engage in activities they enjoy.

Although contradictory evidence exists, it appears that in general, children from joint-custody families may have fewer emotional and behavioral problems than children from sole-custody families. Joint-custody arrangements tend to be agreed on by parents who can establish a reasonable working relationship with respect to coparenting activities. The absence of parental conflict may be a critical factor in determining the adjustment of the child. In addition, children may be better able to accept the reality of the divorce and be less preoccupied with the dream that parents will get together again.

Research exists that shows joint-custody fathers to be more in compliance with financial child support obligations, to be more involved in making parental decisions, to share responsibilities, and to make contact and participate in activities with their children than noncustodial fathers.[49]

Custodial Fathers and Mothers

Custodial fathers represent about one case in five. An analysis of custodial fathers indicated that single fathers are more likely to be black, younger than thirty, and less educated than custodial fathers, who are more likely to be white, older, and more highly educated.[50] Custodial fathers had much higher incomes than single fathers or custodial mothers (but less than married fathers). Consistent with their higher incomes, only about 20 percent of custodial fathers received assistance from at least one welfare program. About 30 percent of these fathers obtained a child support award through the courts. Compare these figures with those of mother-only families, 45 percent of whom received welfare assistance and 80 percent of whom received child support awards. Even among the fathers who got a child support award, about half of the noncustodial mothers paid nothing.

Custodial mothers represent about 81 percent of reported cases. As was shown in Chapter 4, in a female-headed and single-parent household, the likelihood of being at poverty level is very great. The figures of nearly 40 percent of Hispanic and African American single parents below the poverty level included the never-married, widowed, married-but-absent husband, as well as the divorced. But even among the divorced, more than one-third of single-parent women are below the poverty level.

[49]Judith A. Seltzer, "Relationships between Fathers and Children Who Live Apart: The Father's Role after Separation," *Journal of Marriage and the Family* 53 (February 1991), 79–101; and William N. Bender, "Joint Custody: The Option of Choice," *Journal of Divorce and Remarriage* 21 (1994), 115–131.

[50]Daniel R. Meyer and Steven Garasky, "Custodial Fathers: Myths, Realities, and Child Support Policy," *Journal of Marriage and the Family* 55 (February 1993), 73–89.

One primary reason for this poverty status following divorce is the father's noncompliance with child support awards. The severity of this problem has been well documented by U.S. Census and other reports, which have shown that in 2005 less than one-half (47.3 percent) of all children for whom child support has been decreed actually receive the full amount.[51] Another one-third (30.3 percent) of the children receive less than the specified amount, and just over one-fifth (22.5 percent) receive no support at all. Given the public attention given to the problem of "deadbeat dads" one would expect the number of full payers to be much higher, but in fact, it is lower than it was in 1990 when it was about 51.1 percent.

Reasons for nonsupport or insufficient support extend well beyond court enforcement and even ability to pay. Interpersonal reasons are likely issues, such as the level of attachment between former spouses, the quality of their relationship, and the frequency of visits by noncustodial parents to their children. It has been clearly documented that divorced noncustodial fathers have little contact with their children. Fathers are particularly unlikely to provide assistance that requires direct participation, such as helping their children with homework or attending school events.[52]

Split Custody

What about split custody of children? **Split custody** involves the separation of siblings so that each parent has at least one child. Arguments against such an arrangement include depriving children of important sibling support and caregiving, promoting unhealthy parent–child alliances, further disrupting already disrupted families, and even that parents adopt such an arrangement to avoid paying child support or to punish the other parent.

A study from Australia based on questionnaires and interviews with approximately 50 split custody arrangements provided a general picture of such cases.[53] Compared to sole custody families, split custody children had more siblings, were older, and the oldest children were more likely to be male and living with their father. The research results raised doubts about the predicted dire consequences of the children in that there was no significant weakening of sibling bonds, children were not alienated from noncustodial parents, and most children enjoyed regular access to both sets of parents and separated siblings for some years after separation. Also, rather than parents choosing this to avoid **child support** or to punish the other parent, children's wishes contributed to the adoption of this arrangement in most cases.

Homosexual Parents

What about granting custody and visitation rights to homosexual parents? Courts claim to determine custody and visitation on the basis of the "best interests of the child," and most rulings assume that a child's best interest is not with a homosexual parent. The available quantitative literature was reviewed to compare the impact of heterosexual and homosexual parents on children. The conclusion was that no difference existed on any measures between the heterosexual and homosexual parents

---

[51]U.S. Census Bureau, *The 2009 Statistical Abstract*, "Table 549—Child Support—Award and Recipiency Status of Custodial Parent: 2005," http://www.2010census.biz/compendia/statab/cats/social_insurance_human_services/child_support_head_start_child_care.html.

[52]Jay D. Teachman, "Contributions to Children by Divorced Fathers," *Social Problems* 38 (August 1991), 358–371.

[53]Bruce Hawthorne, "Split Custody as a Viable Post-Divorce Option," *Journal of Divorce and Remarriage* 33 (Numbers 3/4, 2000), 1–19.

Family Diversity

Gay Marriage Also Means Gay Divorce

In her essay, "Gay Divorce: Thoughts on the Legal Regulation of Marriage," Claudia Card reflects on the potential positive and negative consequences of advocating for what she terms the "legal regulation of marriage for same-sex partners" (25). At the core of her reflections are the entanglements that legal marriage creates that make it difficult to leave unhappy, exploitive or abusive relationships.

On the side of advocating for legalizing same-sex marriage, she notes how benefits and rights are tied to marriage in American society and that continued denial of marriage to same-sex couples means continued denial of those benefits and rights and the continued delegation of same-sex persons as second class citizens. On the side of *not* advocating for legalizing same-sex marriage, she cites the constraining nature of marriage and the potential consequences of divorce. Even though "no-fault" divorce is an option throughout the United States, she notes that if one's partner does not want a divorce it still remains difficult to end one's marriage and escape abusive situations. As a result, she cautions that those who romanticize about the possibilities of same-sex marriage should also

"[c]ontemplate the prospect having to sue for divorce because your spouse does not agree to it...[and] the likely legal battles over property, custody, and visitation rights that often underlie a spouse's unwillingness to agree" (28). She goes on to state: "Marriage and divorce can be such nightmares that I have difficulty wrapping my mind around the evident fact that so many same-sex couples in the United States have demonstrated their desire to marry by participating in public ceremonies" (28).

After weighing the pros and cons of advocating for same-sex marriage, Card concludes that it would be better to put same-sex marriage advocacy on the "back burner" and fight for policies such as universal health care and social security benefit eligibility detached from marital status. In other words, she advocates for disentangling marriage from the delivery of health care and other rights and benefits. Once this occurs, then state intervention in relationships is no longer required and deregulation can begin. Such deregulation, she argues, would benefit both same-sex and heterosexual relationships by freeing them from the "trap" that marriage creates for those who are exploited and abused within it.

Source: Claudia Card, "Gay Divorce: Thoughts on the Legal Regulation of Marriage," *Hypatia*, 22 (Winter 2007), 24–38.

---

on parenting styles and practices, the emotional adjustment and well-being of the child, or the sexual orientation of the child or children.[54] In other words, the findings failed to support any justification for the continuation of a bias against homosexual parents by any court.

Child Support and Remarriage as Economic Factors

Two key determinants of economic well-being for divorced custodial mothers are child support and **remarriage.** It has already been noted how few mothers get regular or full child support. Research found that about 50 percent of all nonblack, ever-divorced mothers eligible for child support remarried within the first five to six years after divorce. Mothers who received child support and mothers who received above-average amounts of child support were less likely to have remarried within five or more years after divorce. Receiving child support may be a negative factor in the remarriage of divorced mothers.[55]

---

[54]Mike Allen and Nancy Burrell, "Comparing the Impact of Homosexual and Heterosexual Parents on Children: Meta-Analysis of Existing Research," *Journal of Homosexuality* 32 (1996), 19–35.

[55]Karen Fox Folk, John W. Graham, and Andrea H. Beller, "Child Support and Remarriage," *Journal of Family Issues* 13 (June 1992), 142–157.

Remarriages and Stepfamilies

The United States is recognized as a monogamous society. Yet it is likely that a greater number—as well as a larger proportion—of people in the United States have multiple spouses than in many countries recognized as polygamous. This "distinction" is especially true for U.S. women, because elsewhere polyandry occurs rarely. (The marriage of one man to several women is common in a number of cultures; however, the marriage of one woman to several men is infrequent.) In the United States, more than anywhere else in the world, women are likely to experience multiple husbands—albeit only one at a time.

Couples who remarry are likely to do so for reasons of love, to be monogamous, and to expect the marriage to last until death—just as they did the first time. Yet remarried couples face life experiences and engage in lifestyles that, in many ways, differentiate them from couples in first marriages. People who remarry are older, on average, than those who marry for the first time; are presumably more mature; and are more likely to have children.

People Who Remarry

The United States has the highest remarriage rate in the world: over 45 percent of marriages are remarriages for one or both partners.[56] An estimated two-thirds of all divorced persons in the United States remarry, but the rate of remarriage has declined over the past two decades. A decline has occurred in Canada and Western Europe, as well. One explanation for this decline is the rising rate of nonmarital cohabitation after divorce.[57] And although women are less likely than men to remarry, they are just as prone to cohabit as men. As one might expect, younger people remarry and cohabit more quickly than older people.

Obviously, since widowhood increases with age, the median age of widows who do remarry is more than twenty years greater than the remarriage age of those divorced. Interestingly, the mean age at remarriage after widowhood for women was ten years less than the mean age at widowhood. This paradox suggests that, even though the probability of remarriage following widowhood is small for females, the youngest widows are most likely to remarry. Remarriage among older widows is compounded by the declining supply of potential husbands due to higher male mortality rates.

It is assumed that, in all countries in which remarriage occurs at all, the likelihood of remarriage varies, depending on social and demographic characteristics. In the United States, Canada, and most Western countries, the likelihood of remarriage may be categorized:

By gender—Remarriage is more likely for males than females.

By race and ethnicity—Remarriage is both more likely and more timely for white than for black women; however, both are more likely to remarry than women of Hispanic origin.

By age—Remarriage is more likely for those who married at a relatively young age and who are under age 30 at the time of divorce.

---

[56]For a good overview of this topic of remarriage, see Marilyn Coleman, Lawrence H. Ganong, and Mark Fine, "Re-investigating Remarriage: Another Decade of Progress," *Journal of Marriage and the Family* 62 (November 2000), 1288–1307.

[57]Zheng Wu and T. R. Balakrishnan, "Cohabitation after Marital Disruption in Canada," *Journal of Marriage and the Family* 56 (August 1994), 723–734.

By children—Remarriage is more likely for those who have no children or who have only a small number of children in their first marriage.

By education—Remarriage is more likely for those who have less than a college education.

By employment—Remarriage is more likely if the woman is not in the labor force.

By income—Remarriage is more likely for men with higher incomes and for women with lower incomes.

In analyzing remarriage according to the financial condition of women, Anne-Marie Ambert suggested that financially secure women display behavior considered dysfunctional on the "remarriage market."[58] Although these women have more opportunities to meet men, have more dates, and have more steady relationships, they are also more likely to break up relationships that do not suit them, less likely to tolerate abusive male behavior toward them, and less likely to flatter a man's ego. In brief, consistent with an exchange-theory model, high-status women have less to gain from remarriage than low-status women.

Similar patterns of remarriage were found in Japan but with some interesting differences. As in the United States, Japanese men were more likely than women to remarry (although in far greater proportions), and the supply of available husbands decreased with age (a declining sex ratio). But inconsistent with women in the United States, the percentage of Japanese women who said they "do not want to remarry" was high, even among young women, and it increased with age. A result is that Japanese women actually are much less likely to remarry than their American peers.[59] This was explained by suggesting that, in a society where there is little divorce and where marriage is treated more as a practical relationship than as a romantic one, divorced women are more likely to be completely unenamored with both their partners and the institution of marriage itself. When asked why they have not remarried, Japanese widows and divorcees both frequently responded, "I'm fed up with it."

Marriage among the Remarried

Remarriage offers many benefits to those who experienced the ending of a previous marriage. It offers those involved "another chance." Remarriage is likely to involve older persons, which implies greater maturity, improved finances, and prior experiences from which to benefit. Yet, the probability of a disruption in a second marriage is higher than in a first marriage. As was stated earlier, 33 percent of first marriages had disrupted after ten years. For second marriages, the proportion disrupted after ten years was 39 percent (48 percent for blacks).[60] Also stated earlier was that the length of the typical remarriage that ends in divorce is less than that of the average first marriage. Why? Is there a difference in marital satisfaction for those in first marriages compared with those in remarriages? The answer from a review of sixteen studies that addressed this question was yes.

---

[58]Anne-Marie Ambert, "Separated Women and Remarriage Behavior: A Comparison of Financially Secure Women and Financially Insecure Women," *Journal of Divorce* 6 (Spring 1983), 43–54.

[59]Laurel L. Cornell, "Gender Differences in Remarriage after Divorce in Japan and the United States," *Journal of Marriage and the Family* 51 (May 1989), 457–463.

[60]National Center for Health Statistics, *First Marriage Dissolution, Divorce, and Remarriage: United States* (Hyattsville, MD: Department of Health and Human Services, May 31, 2001), Table 10, number 323, p. 12.

Alan Booth and John Edwards addressed the issue of why remarriages are more unstable.[61] From a national sample of married persons, they found that those in remarriages were more likely to be poorly integrated with parents and in-laws, more willing to leave the marriage, more likely to be poor marriage material, have lower socioeconomic status, and more likely to be in age-heterogamous marriages.

Remarriages alone show tremendous variations, as well. Considerable research over the past decade has noted the special problems of remarriage when adolescent children from prior marriages are present. These children appear to have a destabilizing effect on the husband–wife relationship. Remarried couples with adolescent stepchildren experience higher rates of divorce than other remarriages. These stepfamilies also move teenagers out of the home faster than first-married families.[62] Adolescents living in stepfamilies also report difficulties. Divided loyalty and discipline are particularly stressful problems for these youth. The nature and problems of remarried couples with stepchildren will be considered more closely in the following section.

Remarried Couples with Stepchildren: Reconstituted Families

Most children who experience their parents' divorce also experience their custodial parent's remarriage and thus, the creation of a stepfamily. Traditionally, remarriages and stepfamilies were formed primarily when a spouse died; today, their formation results primarily from divorce. Terms including *remarried*, *reconstituted*, *binuclear*, *blended*, and *stepparent families* have been used to describe what constitutes significant nontraditional marital and family arrangements that present unique circumstances and relationships. A stepfamily may include a stepfather plus a mother and her children; a stepmother plus a father and his children; or a mother and father joining two sets of children.

Stepfamilies differ structurally from first families in a number of ways. First, one biological parent does not presently live in the household. Second, the parent–child relationship predates the new marriage. And, third, even though a legal relationship binds the remarriage, none binds the stepchildren and stepparents.

These structural elements of stepfamilies have altered parenting practices in major ways. One national sample of children between the ages of 7 and 11 found that, in a majority of families, marital disruption effectively destroyed the relation-

The majority of people who divorce or end an intimate relationship eventually enter another marriage or exclusive relationship. Those people who have children create stepfamilies, in which multiple sets of parents interact with and assume responsibility for multiple sets of children. The step- or binuclear family may include the children of one or both partners.

[61]Alan Booth and John N. Edwards, "Starting Over: Why Remarriages Are More Unstable," *Journal of Family Issues* 13 (June 1992), 179–194.

[62]Lynn K. White and Alan Booth, "The Quality and Stability of Remarriages: The Role of Stepchildren," *American Sociological Review* 50 (October 1985), 689–698.

news item

Blended Families Can Overcome Daunting Odds

As soon as 5-year-old Nate sees the two girls hop from their father's car, he starts squealing. He dashes through the empty house as Shayla, 12, tears off after him, tackling him with hugs of affection. While they play, Simone, 17, examines the room that will soon be hers.

The girls' father, Tom Staley, and Nate's mother, Jakey Hoffman, have been working on the Rochester Hills home since purchasing it earlier this month. The couple plan to marry in August, officially joining the ranks of more than 12.2 million blended American families...

For every 100 marriages, 46 involve a remarriage for one or both partners...Of the remarriages, 24 are a remarriage for both people. About 65% of remarriages involve children under 19...

More than 60% of remarried or recoupled families break up when children are involved, according to the Stepfamily Foundation, a research and support network based at Westbrook University in New York City. "Yes, these families have lots of challenges," says Stephanie Coontz, a spokeswoman for the Council on Contemporary Families, "but they can be healthy to the extent that they're seen as an extension of the family instead of a break from one family to another."

However, sometimes unrealistic expectations of blissful Brady Bunch bonding get in the way of reality.

"One of the biggest things that hurt us in the beginning was our kids weren't getting along," says Amy Retsel, 37, who married Jamie Retsel, 39, two years ago...

Typical children's squabbles about little things like who gets to sit where in the family van and where to go on family outings became major battles with cries of unfairness coming from children on both sides. "We learned to say, 'This is where we're going and next time maybe it'll be your turn,'" Amy Retsel says.

"You had seven different personalities put into one household. There's just no way for it to be peace and quiet and delightful all the time," she says. "I think if anything in the long run, they'll all be better because it's teaching them to be open-minded, flexible and tolerant."...

Jakey Hoffman and Tom Staley are optimistic about their future as a blended family...

"I was glad when I found out they were getting married," Simone says. "I really liked her right away."

Shayla agrees.

"Nate, he's like a real little brother. We're just like brothers and sisters. We've gotten along ever since we've gotten to know them."

Tom Staley grew up in a blended family and says he has learned lessons that will help his new family.

"You have to earn respect. You don't just walk in and take it," says Staley, who was raised by his biological mother and stepfather...

"I am so blessed because we all get along with each other and with each other's ex-spouses," says Hoffman..."If our kids didn't like one or the other person, we wouldn't have planned to marry."

The girls' mother, Valeriece Staley, says she's glad her daughters will have another person in their lives who cares about them.

"I think Jakey's great," she says. "For me to be threatened or intimidated would be silly. It's not like people have a limited amount of love to give. Bringing someone else into their lives who loves them can only be a good thing."

Source: Cassandra Spratling, "Blended families can overcome daunting odds," *Detroit Free Press*, May 31, 2009, http://m.freep.com/BETTER/news.jsp?key=469324&rc=fe&p=1.

ship between the children and the biological parent living outside the home.[63] Nearly half of all children had not seen their nonresident fathers in the past year. Contrary to the picture painted by the media, children of divorce rarely have two homes, and only a minority ever sleep over at their fathers' houses. It was suggested that perhaps a majority have never set foot in the houses of their nonresident fathers.

---

[63]Frank F. Furstenberg Jr. and Christine Winquist Nord, "Parenting Apart: Patterns of Childrearing After Marital Disruption," *Journal of Marriage and the Family* 47 (November 1985), 893–904.

The claim has been made that fathers "swap" families when they form new ones—that is, they shift allegiances from nonresident children to new residential children. Manning and Smock say that fathers do swap families but only when the trade-off is between new biological children living inside fathers' households and existing biological children living outside fathers' households.[64] Fathers do not appear to actually swap children, because on average, many continue to financially support nonresident children. But biological parenthood, when combined with coresidence, appears to take precedence over nonresident parenthood.

A puzzling finding in the literature on disrupted families is the absence of a remarriage benefit for children in stepfamily households. Although the remarriage of parents increases a family's economic security and brings an additional parental figure into the household, children in stepfamilies exhibit about the same number of adjustment problems as children in single-parent families and more problems than children in original, two-parent families. Even outside the United States, a large sample of nearly 14,000 adolescents in the Netherlands showed that those from one-parent and stepparent families reported lower self-esteem, more symptoms of anxiety and loneliness, and even more suicidal thoughts and attempts.[65]

It appears that parents who cohabit before marriage have less negative parent–child relationships after marriage.[66] Cohabitation may provide a more gentle transition to remarriage, gradually incorporating the future stepfather into family routines. It was also found that the earlier the courtship for remarriage was introduced after divorce, the less the disruption of family and individual functioning. It seems that, with a more rapid transition to a new marriage, there is less time for children to adjust to living in a custodial mother household. In any case, these findings have called into question the idea that considerable time between divorce and remarriage is desirable or beneficial for the adjustment of children.

Many structural variations of remarriage have the potential to create **boundary ambiguity**: the uncertainty of family members as to who is part of the family and performs, or is responsible for, certain roles and responsibilities within the family system. This uncertainty of boundaries is likely to increase both family stress and the risk of behavior problems in children.[67] This is true not only in cases with alcoholic parents or missing husbands but also in cases where it is not clear who *really* is a member of the family and what roles or tasks should be performed (such as between a stepmother and her nonresidential children or grandparents with the children of their stepson).

Ambiguity and difficulty with children may be heightened when children visit rather than live with a stepparent. The stepparenting experience, particularly for

[64]Wendy D. Manning and Pamela J. Smock, "Swapping Families: Serial Parenting and Economic Support for Children," *Journal of Marriage and the Family* 62 (February 2000), 111–122. Note also Lynn White and Joan G. Gilbreth, "When Children Have Two Fathers: Effects of Relationships with Stepfathers and Noncustodial Fathers on Adolescent Outcomes," *Journal of Marriage and Family* 63 (February 2001), 155–167.

[65]Nadia Garnefski and Rene' F. W. Diekstra, "Adolescents from One Parent, Stepparent, and Intact Families; Emotional Problems and Suicide Attempts," *Journal of Adolescence* 20 (1997), 201–208.

[66]Marilyn J. Montgomery, Edward R. Anderson, E. Mavis Hetherington, and W. Glenn Clingempeel, "Patterns of Courtship for Remarriage: Implications for Child Adjustment and Parent–Child Relationships," *Journal of Marriage and the Family* 54 (August 1992), 686–698.

[67]B. Kay Pasley and Marilyn Ihinger-Tallman, "Boundary Ambiguity in Remarriage: Does Ambiguity Differentiate Degree of Marital Adjustment and Integration," *Family Relations* 38 (January 1989), 46–52.

stepmothers, is likely to be more positive with live-in stepchildren. Most research has suggested that the role of stepmother is more difficult than that of stepfather, in large part because most stepmothers do not have live-in stepchildren. In contrast, most stepfathers do. When stepchildren visit, it is usually the stepmother and not the children's father who has to do the extra housecleaning, shopping for food, and cooking. Women often perceive this work as a burden because they receive little emotional benefit from the visits. Similarly, stepsiblings' relations were found to be more positive when the children lived together rather than just visited.

Stepmothers often are viewed with trepidation in remarried families with children. Most of us have experienced the "Cinderella" story of the evil, uncaring stepmother or read fairy tales about witches and stepmothers. Yet, why are stepmothers expected to immediately assimilate into a family and instantly love the children as if they were their own? Statements about the "evil stepmother" and "instant love" represent myths (falsehoods) that show no signs of losing strength and that negatively affect the experiences of stepmothers.[68] Empirical evidence does support some of the cultural stereotypes. Stepmothers are less satisfied with their relationships with stepchildren and display more negative behaviors toward them than stepfathers. A point of particular difficulty for stepmothers often centers around accepting the attachment between the stepchild and the stepchild's biological mother. Becoming "another" mother (stepmother) often is difficult.

What happens to parent–child relationships when stepfamilies include children from both parents (**complex stepfamilies** rather than from just one parent (**simple stepfamilies**)? A study of Australian couples revealed that the complex stepfamily had lower agreement scores on areas dealing with financial management, communication, personality scores, adjustments, and parenting.[69] In general, persons in complex stepfamilies experienced greater dissatisfaction and stress than did those in simple stepfamilies. Perhaps complex stepfamilies are well named in that they must deal with more complexities in discipline and external relationships than simple stepfamilies.

The unique structural elements of stepfamilies clearly raise a variety of questions not likely relevant to the traditional nuclear unit: how does the ex-spouse affect the children's relationship with the new spouse? Which parent gets the child for birthdays, holidays, and special events? Do parents compete in giving the children expensive gifts? Do gifts come equally from parents and stepparents? Is discipline likely to be equal and consistent coming from a mother and stepfather or a father and stepmother? Are incestuous and other types of sexual abuse issues of concern, particularly between stepfathers and stepdaughters? Are children the messengers or communication links between the mother and father, who may or may not be on cordial terms? Are children living in homes with stepparents at risk for increased emotional and behavioral problems? What socialization difficulties occur in the process of stepparenting?

These and other questions will likely be the subject of future research, given the predominance of stepfamilies in U.S. society today.

---

[68]Marianne Dainton, "The Myths and Misconceptions of the Stepmother Identity," *Family Relations* 42 (January 1993), 93–98.

[69]Noel C. Schultz, Cynthia L. Schultz, and David H. Olson, "Couple Strengths and Stressors in Complex and Simple Stepfamilies in Australia," *Journal of Marriage and the Family* 53 (August 1991), 555–564.

Summary

1. In the United States, divorce is the best-known and most common means of ending an unsatisfactory marital relationship. Desertion, marital separation, and annulment are other means of escaping a marriage, even if only temporarily.

2. When viewed crossculturally, lower divorce rates are associated with a high sex ratio and a late average age at marriage. A curvilinear relationship exists between the level of socioeconomic development and the rate of participation of females in the paid labor force.

3. The rate of divorce may be calculated in a number of ways such as (a) divorces per 1,000 persons in the total population, (b) divorces per 1,000 women ages 15 and over, or (c) the ratio of divorces to the number of marriages in a given year.

4. Within the United States, divorce varies according to a wide range of geographic, demographic, and social characteristics. Divorce rates are higher for young couples than for those who marry when in their late twenties and older. By race, divorce rates are higher for blacks than for whites; by religion, divorce rates are higher for Protestants than for Jews and Catholics; and by socioeconomic level, divorce rates tend to go up as educational level, income, and occupational position go down. One exception to this relationship exists among educated, professional women.

5. The legal grounds for divorce vary somewhat for each state; the most widely accepted grounds are marital incompatibility and evidence of irreconcilable differences. In the past few decades, "no-fault" divorce has been adopted in most states to resolve many of the difficulties traditionally associated with proving "fault." Studies have suggested, however, that economically, women fare more poorly under no-fault than under the former adversary system.

6. Social grounds for divorce often differ considerably from legal grounds. Divorce mediation, as a conflict-resolution process, has grown rapidly as a means of diminishing the bitterness and divisiveness that usually accompany divorce. Reasons for staying in or ending a marriage constitute attractions (rewards) and barriers (costs). The decision whether to divorce is made in light of available alternatives.

7. The consequences of divorce for adults are evident at both macro and micro levels, as reflected by factors such as higher rates of suicide and depression. The economic consequences differ dramatically for males and females; men usually do much better and women much worse following divorce.

8. Children are a primary concern in considering divorce. Research does not support the idea that unhappy or unsuccessful marriages should remain intact for the sake of the children; however, research does acknowledge that children of divorced parents go through periods of stress and major readjustment. Mothers tend to get custody of children; the underpayment or nonpayment of child support by fathers creates hardships for many women and children.

9. Most persons who end one marriage eventually enter another. The remarriage rate climbs with the divorce rate. Remarriage is, in general, more likely for men than for women, for divorcees than for widows, for younger persons than for older persons, for whites than blacks or those of Hispanic origin, for the childless than those with children, for those with less education and lower incomes than those with higher levels, and for women not in the paid labor force.

10. Remarriages appear more unstable than first marriages. Compared to first-married people, remarried people have poorer integration with parents and in-laws, are more willing to leave the marriage, and report more difficult events.

11. The complexities of remarriage are compounded by the presence of children. Stepfamilies are structurally different from traditional nuclear families. Elements such as one biological parent not living in the home, the child predating the new marriage, and the lack of legal, binding relationships between stepchildren and stepparents alter parenting in dramatic ways.

This chapter focused on divorce and remarriage and addressed issues relevant to the contemporary U.S. family. As such, these issues are also relevant to society. To offer programs and establish policies that support marriages and families is, at least in terms of rhetoric, the goal of government and community units. The final chapter will consider this issue of the family and social policy.

Key Terms and Topics

Desertion p. 523

Marital separation p. 523

Separated p. 523

Married, spouse absent p. 524

Legal separation p. 524

Informal separation p. 524

Discussion Questions

1. What are some of the reasons for desertion, separation, and annulment versus divorce? How does each situation affect husbands, wives, and children?

2. Compare the divorce rates of different countries. Why are some much higher than others? What social factors might cause the likelihood of divorce to increase or decrease?

3. How are divorce rates determined? In this chapter, three different divorce rates were calculated for the same year. What does each mean? What factors influence each rate even when the number of divorces remains constant?

4. Divorce rates were found to differ by duration of marriage and by race, religion, socioeconomic status, and the like. What differences have been supported, and how can these variations be explained?

5. Research has shown that conservative and fundamentalist Protestant religious groups that oppose divorce tend to have high divorce rates. Why?

6. Visit a local court that handles divorce cases. Arrange to meet with a judge to discuss the legal process, the legal grounds for divorce compared to the nonlegal reasons for divorce, and his or her views on divorce mediators, joint custody, grandparents' rights, and other legal issues. What legal changes does the judge view as necessary? Why?

7. Discuss the implications and consequences of "no-fault" divorce. What are its pros and cons? What effect is it likely to have on divorce rates, long-term trends, and the like?

8. What do you believe are the primary reasons that marriages end? Could any of these factors be discovered and perhaps influenced prior to marriage? If so, how? Why do many unsatisfactory marriages not end?

9. Examine some of the consequences of divorce for adults. Why are the consequences so different for males and females?

10. What are the consequences of divorce for children? What are the consequences for children who live in unbroken but unhappy homes?

11. How do remarriages differ from first marriages? Address duration of marriage, likelihood of divorce, roles and boundaries, and common problems.

12. How do stepchildren affect a marriage? Discuss some of the advantages and problems that characterize reconstituted families or stepfamilies.

Further Readings

Arendell, Terry. *Fathers & Divorce*. Thousand Oaks, CA: Sage Publications, 1995.

Based on interviews with seventy-five divorced fathers, the author examines the masculine discourse of divorce, relationships with former wives, and parenting behaviors.

Booth, Alan, and Dunn, Judy. *Stepfamilies: Who Benefits? Who Does Not?* Hillsdale, NJ: Lawrence Erlbaum Associates, 1994.

Seventeen chapters cover marriages that create stepfamilies, test how they function as child-rearing organizations and as sources of support, and detail needed research and policy agendas.

Ganong, Lawrence, and Coleman, Marilyn. *Changing Families, Changing Responsibilities: Family Obligations Following Divorce and Remarriage*. Mahwah, NJ: Lawrence Erlbaum Associates, 1999.

A book that addresses intergenerational family obligations following divorce and remarriage.

Hetherington, E. Mavis, and Kelly, John. *For Better or for Worse: Divorce Reconsidered*. New York: W. W. Norton, 2002.

Following more than 2,500 children over several decades, the author challenges the writings about the total negative effects of divorce.

Lawson, Erma Jean, and Thompson, Aaron. *Black Men and Divorce*. Thousand Oaks, CA: Sage Publications, 1999.

An exploration of black men's experience with divorce including divorce-related stressors, postmarital relationships, strategies for coping, and fatherhood.

Pryor, Jan, and Rodgers, Bryan, eds. *Children in Changing Families: Life after Parental Separation*. Malden, MA: Blackwell Publishers, 2001.

A documentation of demographic changes in select countries and a summary of known outcomes for children affected by parental separation and stepfamily formation.

Smart, Carol, Neale, Bren, and Wade, Amanda. *The Changing Experience of Childhood: Families and Divorce*. Malden, MA: Blackwell Publishers, 2001.

An exploration of children's own accounts of family life after divorce and as participating agents in decision making about their own lives.

Thompson, Ross A. and Amato, Paul R., eds. *The Postdivorce Family: Children: Parenting, and Society*. Thousand Oaks, CA: Sage Publications, Inc., 1999.

A look at parents' responsibilities after divorce including custody issues, child support orders, and nonresidential parenting.

Wallerstein, Judith, Lewis, Julia, and Blakeslee, Sandra. *The Unexpected Legacy of Divorce*. New York: Hyperion, 2000.

A longitudinal study of the effects of divorce on ninety-three children covering a span of more than twenty-five years.

chapter 15

Family Social Policy

Family Policy and Programs in Action

John and Chris are married and have two teenage children. John has a Ph.D. in social work from Virginia Commonwealth University, and Chris has a master's degree in social work from the same institution. John is the director of the social work program at a state university in North Carolina and Chris is a school social worker in a rural county in the western part of the state. In addition to administrative and grant-writing responsibilities, John teaches courses in social policy with a major concentration in social welfare. Chris, on the other hand, is on the front line of social work practice: providing assistance to children and families, working with community service agencies, and providing training to teachers and parents.

A major concern of John's centers around children. Even though the United States has the highest rate of child poverty among westernized and industrialized countries, there is no coherent policy directed at families and especially toward children. He wonders how long a civilized country can go without investing in its children without suffering serious consequences. Social Security and Medicare exist for seniors but few precise and well-established programs or policies provide housing, medical care, nutrition, or minimum standards of living for children. He would like to see an allowance without a means test for all children under age 5 with a reduction in benefits as children get older: a proposal actually advocated by George McGovern when he was running for president of the United States.

John adds that, at present, each person earning less than a specific amount gets an earned income tax credit. But tax credits are not equitable. If you pay no taxes, you get no credit. And a high percentage of the eligible poor don't receive the credit because they don't know about it or are not aware of other existing programs.

Another one of his concerns centers around the replacement of AFDC (Aid to Families with Dependent Children) with TANF (Temporary Assistance for Needy Families). TANF is a means-tested, income-based program that did away with the entitlement to public assistance and added time limits to receiving benefits. Welfare rolls have dropped, but what are the consequences for children? And with additional resources going to fight terrorism, provide public security, build a "Star Wars" program, and provide other military support, even less attention will be directed toward children who get no assistance at present or will not when their time limit expires.

As a school social worker, Chris deals directly with children and families on a daily basis. Children with behavioral problems, mental health needs, attention deficit disorders, inadequate supervision, neglect or abuse at home, special financial needs, and the like are some of her child concerns.

One of her primary duties is finding out the children's needs and accessing the resources to meet them. Many of the parents of these children are the working poor. They frequently hold two or three jobs, often do seasonal work, and usually receive no benefits. If these families don't have insurance or Medicaid, they can't afford to get medical services. Chris is heavily involved in raising money, much of which goes directly to these families to pay fuel bills, prescriptions, food, transportation costs, and so forth. Churches and private donors are sources she calls upon frequently to provide the needed funds.

Chris spends additional time contacting and working with community agencies and in preventive activities. These include talking to classes about drug prevention, alerting teachers to a child's special needs, informing them about existing programs and policies, and working with and educating parents.

Questions to Consider

John wonders how long a civilized country can go without investing in its children without suffering serious consequences. In what ways might countries invest in children? What kind of consequences might result without these investments?

Many families experience problems with abuse, alcohol and drugs, unplanned young pregnancies, unemployment, poverty, and the like. What kind of programs might be effective in assisting them? Are these public or private matters? Who should pay for them?

*M*ost persons, married and single, recognize that intimate relationships and families are significant and important in their own lives and the lives of others. In fact, one could argue the value-laden position that, across cultures and throughout history, no single institution has had greater influence than the family has in shaping the lives of persons, in affecting interpersonal relationships, and even in determining national stature.

Why then doesn't the United States have an explicit national policy (or policies) for families? Among all the agencies overseeing education, health, commerce, labor, energy, transportation, defense, agriculture, and the like, no U.S. agency is devoted specifically to the family. Recent administrations, while proclaiming the importance of the family and even campaigning on the issue of family values, vetoed family-leave bills, cut funding for family-planning programs, and punished persons or groups who didn't conform to a particular marital and family lifestyle. Former President Clinton made efforts to establish governmental policies that would support a range of individual and family needs and interests: minimum wage increases, gay rights, pro-choice, parental leave, health care, and child protection. An increase in the minimum wage, a selective parental leave bill, and other legislation affecting families were passed, but many other efforts were defeated in congress. At the beginning of this century, the Bush administration focused efforts on fighting terrorism and tax cuts but expressed little or no interest in issues such as those just mentioned or in spending for social programs other than education.

Even the current Obama administration has failed to put forward a comprehensive policy aimed specifically at strengthening and enhancing the quality of family life, although many initiatives have been put forward to strengthen and extend existing programs and policies that support families such as: the expansion of the earned income tax credit aimed at working parents and fathers who pay child support, the expansion of the Family and Medical Leave Act to cover more circumstances facing families and more workers, the expansion of the Child and Dependent Care Tax Credit, greater enforcement of the Equal Employment Opportunity Commission guidelines against caregiver discrimination, and the expansion of the Nurse-Family Partnership program to all low-income, first-time mothers. In addition, new initiatives are expected to strengthen responsible fatherhood, support domestic violence prevention programs, require paid sick leave benefits and encourage similar policies in the states, and make the government a model for a flexible workplace.[1] Whether or not political and economic conditions will allow these initiatives to come to fruition is debatable. There is considerable rhetoric espousing the importance of strengthening families, but there is less agreement in the population about what that means and entails. As a result, family policy in the United States is likely to remain more of a patchwork than a comprehensive set of initiatives.

Meaning and Use of Family Policy

Many illustrations of family policy—from a one-child policy in China to policies establishing a legal age for marriage or grounds for divorce—have been presented throughout the text. But what is meant by **family policy?**

In this chapter, *family policy* will be used very broadly to include a set of goals or objectives for families that governmental bodies and social organizations try to achieve through structured programs or activities. Note that the policy is not the program. Policies are objectives and goals that are more or less deliberate, intended, and desirable. Programs are the practical applications used to achieve or fulfill the goals. As a result, it is possible, and often likely, that policies exist without any specific program to carry them out. Similarly, many programs continue year after year

---

[1]Jeremy Adam Smith, "President Obama's Family Policy Agenda," *Daddy Dialectic: A Blog for Twenty-First-Century Parents.* http://daddy-dialectic.blogspot.com/2009/03/presidents-obamas-family-policy-agenda.html.

without any coherent or specifically designed policy. Like a governmental bureaucracy that has outlived its purpose but is ongoing, so, too, do many programs continue that fail to fulfill any specific policy goals or that have outlived their original intent or purpose.

Shirley Zimmerman noted that family policy constitutes a collection of separate but interrelated policy choices that aim to address problems that families are perceived as experiencing in society.[2] These problems are likely to include many of the topics covered in this text: adoption, child care, abortion, unwed parenthood, intimate violence, family breakup, AIDS, poverty, welfare, minority families, home/work demands, later-life families, and the like.

Zimmerman's goal of family policy is to maximize the well-being of families.[3] She defines family well-being as a value that includes the state of being healthy, happy, and free from want as well as achieving satisfaction with marriage, work, leisure, housing, and so forth. The goal of her family policy is to assist families in attaining these values.

Family policy goals may be explicit or implicit. The goals or objectives of **explicit family policy** are directed specifically at families with the intent to achieve precise family outcomes or objectives. These goals are "stated explicitly" such as the federal legislation that requires insurance companies to provide forty-eight hours instead of twenty-four hours of hospital coverage to new mothers and their babies. The goals of **implicit family policy** are often left unstated. The policies may not even be addressed to families but may have significant consequences for them.

An example of implicit family policy would be legislation that requires teenagers to attend school until a certain age. Families are affected, but the specific objective is left implicit or unstated. This type of policy can be defined so broadly that it incorporates everything that touches the lives of family members and is subsumed under policy headings such as health, taxation, employment, the environment, or education. Most family policies are more implicit than explicit, but both have consequences for families—some intended (*manifest*) and others unintended (*latent*).

The approach in this book is to deal with family policy in general terms, particularly in defining both *family* and *policy*. *Families* will refer to both traditional and legal forms as well as to intimately bonded relationships that may neither be legally recognized or conform to traditional norms. *Policies* will refer to any laws, goals, or objectives and their accompanying programs or activities to carry them out that affect families and influence the activities of family members.

Research on Family Policy

Within the social sciences, an issue frequently contested is the extent to which social research can or should be "value free." This issue becomes particularly acute when dealing with family policy research. One side of the issue argues for value neutrality, objectivity, and basic research apart from any policy objective. The opposite side of the issue argues that value-free research is impossible, even if desired, and that trained social researchers need to apply their expertise to constructive ends.

One solution to this debate is to acknowledge both positions by "wearing two hats": one of researcher and one of citizen/advocate. The researcher provides empirical

---

[2]Shirley L. Zimmerman, *Understanding Family Policy: Theories and Applications* (Thousand Oaks, CA: Sage Publications, 1995), 3.
[3]Ibid., 8.

evidence of what exists, and the citizen/advocate works for goals he or she deems important. The *researcher* attempts to maintain objectivity throughout the research endeavor and ideally is open to all sides of an issue. This includes a willingness to accept findings that may contradict one's personal positions. In **family policy advocacy,** the *advocate/citizen* endorses and actively works for a course of action that improves family life. The advocate takes one side of an issue, usually consistent with his or her own value system, with the intent of influencing an action or decision viewed as beneficial to families and their members.

In the 1990s, the lines between the researcher and the advocate/citizen had become extremely blurred. The Family Research Council, a title that sounds quite "scientific" and "objective" in its approach, is comprised of persons who advocate a traditional and very conservative stance on family issues. In a similar vein, sociologist scholars such as David Popenoe and Norval Glenn have expressed dismay over out-of-wedlock childbearing, single parenthood, and divorce and have joined a "Council on Families" to express their concerns.

As mentioned in Chapter 1, Popenoe wrote of marriage as an institution in decay. He and other members of the Family Research Council wrote a book about the decline in families. In 1997, Norval Glenn conducted a review of twenty very diverse textbooks on marriage and the family.[4] Although Glenn's methodology and value stance can be criticized concerning the manner in which his research was

Family policy and formal legislation take place at local, state, and national levels. The United States has no national family policy per se; traditionally, the federal government has allocated funds to state governments, which set specific policies and provide services for families, often through local agencies.

---

[4]Norval D. Glenn, "A Critique of Twenty Family and Marriage and Family Textbooks," *Family Relations* 46 (July 1997), 197–208.

conducted, a more serious matter is what an organization called "The Institute of American Values" did with his research. This group disseminated widely a highly selective, highly distorted view of Glenn's research article on textbooks in a booklet titled *Closed Hearts, Closed Minds: The Textbook Story of Marriage.* Specific sentences from a few of the textbooks that did not support the perspective or values of the "Institute" were selected for dissemination. Little attention was devoted to, or examples given of, the vast amount of material in these textbooks that supported or confirmed the value stance of the Institute. The point here is the blurring of lines between objective research and political advocacy.

Research with a policy focus can take a number of directions: (1) to establish family policy, (2) to evaluate existing family policy, and (3) to analyze the impact of family policy. Karen Bogenschneider[5] includes these three research positions (described in the sections that follow) as models of professional roles for building family policy. In addition, she views family policy advocacy as an appropriate professional role when considered within the context of a new role of family policy, alternatives education.

Unlike the advocate's approach, the alternatives educator does not lobby for a particular policy but rather clarifies the potential consequences of various policy alternatives. This position is based on the premise that when individuals have sufficient knowledge, they can make judgments for themselves better than others can make judgments for them. This knowledge of the consequences of policy alternatives is based on an objective integration and dissemination of research findings.[6] Following are three selected directions that research with a policy focus can take.

Research to Establish Family Policy

There are various ways to establish family policy. Steven Wisensale noted that four "think tanks," in particular, are actively involved in both family research and advocacy: The Brookings Institution, The American Enterprise Institute, The Urban Institute, and The Heritage Foundation.[7] Members of these institutes and foundations publish books, special reports, and position papers; testify before congressional committees; and hold seminars and conferences to disseminate their information. Some, such as The Heritage Foundation, spend less than half of their total expense budget on research, defining their primary role as providing conservative policymakers with arguments to bolster their views. Others, such as The Urban Institute, have guidelines that direct them to sharpen thinking about society's problems, improve government decisions, and increase citizens' awareness about important public issues.

Much of the research done in think tanks is focused on the first purpose mentioned, that is, research to establish family policy. Typically, research to establish policy starts with a general hypothesis that some kind of social action may be desirable. Such research does not necessarily assume that a problem exists, does not evaluate an existing policy or program, and does not assess the

---

[5]Karen Bogenschneider, "Roles for Professionals in Building Family Policy," *Family Relations* 44 (January 1995), 5–12.

[6]Note, for example, Karen Bogenschneider, Jonathan R. Olson, Kirsten D. Linney, and Jessica Mills, "Connecting Research and Policymaking: Implications of Theory and Practice from the Family Impact Seminars," *Family Relations* 49 (July 2000), 327–339.

[7]Steven K. Wisensale, "The Family in the Think Tank," *Family Relations* 40 (April 1991), 199–207.

consequences of a policy or program. Rather, given some nontraditional family patterns (cohabitation, dual-career marriages, female-headed households, reconstituted families, never-married parents, and so forth), research for family policy examines a certain structural arrangement and seeks to discover the outcome of that way of life for the individuals involved as well as for society as a whole. The research may find that all is well and nothing needs to be done, or it may recommend that laws need to be changed, programs developed, or action taken to fulfill specific needs.

Research to Evaluate Existing Family Policy

A second type of policy research is done to evaluate existing family policy. Family-policy evaluation research is conducted at a programmatic level to determine the degree to which social programs have achieved or are achieving the stated goals of a public policy or resultant program.

The need for family-policy evaluation research is evident with an issue such as parental leave. Connecticut passed a law (effective July 1, 1988) that provides up to twenty-four weeks of unpaid parental/family leave within any two-year period, with a guaranteed return to the same or comparable job. Thus, after a few years, it was possible to check Connecticut businesses to see if any of the arguments stated against family leave had empirical support. A task force surveyed a randomly drawn sample of 2,000 firms with ten or more employees. The survey revealed that less than 15 percent of Connecticut firms provided job-guaranteed parental leave. Where leave did exist, excessive leave-taking was not a problem, and most firms exhibited the resourcefulness and flexibility to deal with leaves without incurring substantial direct costs.[8]

Research on the Impact of Family Policy

A third type of policy research is family-impact analysis. Here, the attempt is to assess the intended and unintended consequences, to families, of public policy and social programs. For example, what is the impact of mortgage interest deductions on those who cannot afford to purchase homes? What are the effects of a program such as Head Start on mothers as well as children? What are the employment and income consequences of a policy that prohibits a woman from terminating a pregnancy?

Unlike evaluation research, which is focused on whether the goals or objectives are being met, family-impact analysis looks at how families are affected beyond the explicit intentions or goals of the policy or program. As a result, evaluation research may show that intended goals are being met, but impact analysis may show the goals are counterproductive, producing unintended but negative consequences for families.

For example, in Chapter 14, it was mentioned that two key determinants of economic well-being for divorced mothers are remarriage and child support. Evaluation research of child support showed that those mothers who get support are better off economically than those who do not. This is an obvious result. But

---

[8]Elizabeth Trzcinski and Matia Finn-Stevenson, "A Response to Arguments against Mandated Parental Leave: Findings from the Connecticut Survey of Parental Leave Policies," *Journal of Marriage and the Family* 53 (May 1991), 445–460.

CROSS-CULTURAL *Perspectives*

Parental Leave Policy in Sweden

In 1974, Sweden became the first country to institute parental leave for both mothers and fathers. The parental leave program is highly flexible in how and when it is taken, and who takes it. As of 1995, the parents of a newborn child are entitled to ten months' leave at 80 percent income compensation, one non-transferable month for each parent compensated at 90 percent, and three additional months at a flat rate. Benefits can be used full time or part time (25, 50, or 75 percent of full time) and saved and used any time before the child is 8 years old. Use of benefits on a part-time basis can be combined with part-time work or with unpaid leave. Multiple births give a right to six months extra benefits for each additional child. A return to the original job is guaranteed.

Even maternal care practices have changed to encourage participation of fathers in prenatal care, parental education, and delivery. In employment, fathers get two weeks off with pay at the time of childbirth, sixty days off per year with pay (shared with mothers) to care for sick children, two days off to visit day-care centers and schools (again, with pay), and the right to reduce the workday to six hours for child-care purposes. Benefits are paid out directly from social insurance offices rather than from employers. Mainly employers, through payroll taxes on all employees, however, pay for the leave program.

By providing support for families, Sweden has made it more possible for men to remain with their biological children, either in a union or not, while maintaining their traditional roles as providers. In the United States, the private costs of families have escalated to such an extent that men have been turning away from family relationships involving children.

Sources: M. Sundstrom, "Determinants of the Use of Parental Leave Benefits by Women in Sweden in the 1980s," *Scandinavian Journal of Social Welfare* 5 (1996), 76–82; Linda Haas, "Family Policy in Sweden," *Journal of Family and Economic Issues* 17 (Spring 1996), 47–92; and Eva M. Bernhardt and Frances K. Goldscheider, "Men, Resources, and Family Living: The Determinants of Union and Parental Status in the United States and Sweden," *Journal of Marriage and Family* 63 (August 2001), 793–803.

what other consequences (impact analysis) does child support have? For one, child support was shown to negatively affect the remarriage of divorced mothers, the other key determinant of economic well-being.[9]

Overview of Research

Effective family policy is highly dependent on all three types of research: research to determine what type of policy is needed, research to evaluate an existing program or policy, and research to assess the impact or consequences of a program or policy beyond its specific intent. The formulation and enforcement of policies affecting families will be addressed in the next section, where some key issues are presented.

*I*ssues Surrounding Family Policy

Policy matters usually are characterized by a divergence of ideas, conflicts over positions, and opposing recommendations. When policy is made, it seldom satisfies all interest groups or gets the endorsement of all social and political organizations. At

[9]Karen Fox Folk, John W. Graham, and Andrea H. Beller, "Child Support and Remarriage," *Journal of Family Issues* 13 (June 1992), 142–157.

times, policy differences relate to different basic philosophies of life, perceptions of the role of government, and images of what the family is or should be.

In the following sections, several of these differences will be examined. Although each is presented in dichotomous terms, remember that both views exist simultaneously. Rarely can an issue be resolved into an "either/or" position.

Goals and Objectives of Family Policy

The first issue addresses questions of goals and objectives of family policy: namely, the type of family or families desired. Should policy be directed toward the traditional family or toward a diversity of lifestyles, relationships, and families? Also, should policy be directed at preventing the family from change and at maintaining the status quo, or at supporting change, flexibility, and creativity? This issue is at the heart of Scanzoni's differentiation of "conventionals" from "progressives."[10]

Conventionals are those who believe the normal family is conjugal. A male, as husband and father, is head of the household and the sole economic provider. A female, as wife and mother, is a helpmate to her husband and a homemaker responsible for household duties, domestic care, and the socialization of the children. Children are helpless and dependent.

Conventionals, represented by political and religious conservatives, want to save this traditional image of what families should be. They view family change as a breakdown of morality and disintegration of the family. Conventionals have demonstrated substantial political power in crippling sex-education programs, halting the Equal Rights Amendment, and electing persons who oppose abortion. They were instrumental in enacting legislation such as the Family Protection Act, which requires that parents be notified when an unmarried minor receives contraceptive devices or abortion services from a federally supported organization. They have restricted the federal government from "interfering" with state statutes pertaining to child abuse and have changed the definition of "abuse" to *exclude* corporal punishment (so spanking is OK). Conventionals led a national fight against the legalization of same-sex marriages and, in fact, were successful in enacting the Defense of Marriage Act (DOMA) in 1996 that defines marriage as "a legal union between one man and one woman as husband and wife" and grants states the authority to ignore same-sex marriages that may have been performed legally elsewhere.[11] Conventionals have opposed legal services for groups such as homosexuals or the poor and also opposed educational materials that do not espouse traditional and conservative values. The function of policy, from the perspective of conventionals, is to maintain the status quo or return to some idealized image of what the family once was and should be.

Progressives are those who believe a normal family can take many forms. The view is not of *the* family but of a *variety* of families and close relationships. A progressive model is a pluralistic one that allows many options. At the core of this model is the notion that involved adults should strive to become equal partners and to achieve equity among family members. Scanzoni stated that, given their pluralistic view of society, progressives accept the notion that alternative views of

---

[10]John Scanzoni, *Shaping Tomorrow's Family: Theory and Policy for the 21st Century* (Beverly Hills, CA: Sage Publications, 1983); and John Scanzoni, "Reconsidering Family Policy: Status Quo or Force for Change?" *Journal of Family Issues* 3 (September 1982), 277–300.

[11]A discussion of the Defense of Marriage Act can be seen in Julie K. Kohler and Shirley L. Zimmerman, "Policy Issues and Families over the Life Course," in Sharon J. Price, Patrick C. McHenry, and Megan J. Murphy, *Families across Time: A Life Course Perspective* (Los Angeles: Roxbury Publishing Co., 2000), 231–233.

family should be allowed to compete in the marketplace, allowing nonaligned persons to gravitate toward those patterns suiting them best. Conservatives cannot accept this notion.[12]

Theoretically, Scanzoni linked the functionalist approach with conventionals. The emphasis is on structure and stability. Thus, couples who stay together are successful and represent stability, and those who divorce are failures and represent breakdown. Out-of-wedlock births and female-headed households represent disorganization. In contrast, progressives are linked more closely with the conflict approach, where the emphasis is on process and change. A wide variety of goals are legitimate and result from complex negotiations between interest groups, each with preferred patterns and relationships. From this view, any number of nontraditional patterns are acceptable: childless marriages; egalitarian relationships; divorce; marriage in middle or old age; diverse family forms among people who are minorities or poor; cohabitation without marriage; homosexual relationships; access to abortion; women, wives, and mothers in the employed labor force; and males as housekeepers and child rearers.

Scanzoni noted that, in spite of the unified and influential efforts of conventionals, the major weakness of their model is that it is out of step with the times. Their theory does not conform to reality—what is actually happening. Society is not static, families are not uniform, and goals are not unanimous.

Levels of Policy Control

A second issue for family policy concerns the level—federal, state, or local—at which family policy should be formulated and enforced. Under the Reagan and both Bush administrations as well as the Republican-controlled Congress of the Clinton administration, this issue was central to funding activities. Traditionally, the federal government position has been that states, upon receiving grants from the federal government, should determine how and for what purposes the money should be spent.

As indicated earlier, the United States has no federal family policy. Looking back, between 1990 and 1993, the federal government passed a child care and development block grant to help states improve child care, a child support recovery act that made it a federal crime to willfully fail to pay child support awarded in another state, a family and medical leave act that provided twelve weeks of unpaid leave for a serious illness or to care for an ailing family member, a family preservation and support act that provided almost $1 billion for community-based family services, an international parental kidnapping act that established international parental abduction as a felony, and a national child protection act that encouraged states' criminal background checks on child care providers.

Between 1994 and 1998, the federal government passed (1) an educate America act that promoted parental involvement in their children's schooling, (2) a full faith and credit of child support orders act that required states to enforce child support orders established in other states, (3) a violence against women act that increased funding for battered women and established a national domestic violence hotline, (4) a debt collection and improvement act that authorized interception of federal payment to parents owing child support, (5) a defense of marriage act (DOMA, mentioned previously) that defined marriage as a union between one man and one woman, (6) a personal responsibility and work opportunity reconciliation act that eliminated public assistance as an entitlement if certain eligibility criteria were not met, (7) a telecommunications reform law requiring new television sets to include a

---

[12]Scanzoni, *Shaping Tomorrow's Family*, 153.

CROSS-CULTURAL *Perspectives*

Child Care Policy in Ireland

With the tremendous growth that has occurred in the Irish economy in recent decades (a period known as the "Celtic Tiger"), an increase in work opportunities for women has been inevitable. According to Jo Murphy-Lawless, married women's labor force participation in Ireland rose from 14 percent in 1971 to 45 percent in 1997. There has also been a significant increase in women's educational attainment. What has this meant for families and child care arrangements in this traditionally Catholic country with a strong ethos that children should be cared for by their mothers?

Although there have been some pilot schemes to help employed women with children find the child care they need, the country still operates on a "maximum private responsibility" model leaving women to rely on informal child care arrangements such as family members and child-minders (a growing informal economy of usually foreign workers). Most citizens in Ireland believe that quality and affordable child care is needed, but it has yet to materialize. This condition has been challenged by women's political groups such as the National Women's Council and their political action led to the creation of a governmental "Expert Working Group." Unfortunately, when this group proposed a series of steps to reduce the child care burden on working mothers in 1999, only a single recommendation was enacted—a capital tax allowance to businesses who invested in workplace child care facilities. This failure to relieve the pressures on modern families through more comprehensive policy changes and initiatives was attributed to the pressure of "back benchers" in parliament who relied upon the rhetoric of preserving traditional Irish values by preserving the traditional Irish family model.

Source: Jo Murphy-Lawless, "Changing Women's Lives: Child Care Policy in Ireland," *Feminist Economics*, 6 (2000), 89–94.

V-chip to screen out programs that parents may deem inappropriate for their minors, (8) an adoption and safe family act that promoted adoption, (9) a balanced budget act that provided a $500 child tax credit, and (10) a deadbeat parents act that made it a felony for anyone to cross a state line to evade child support.[13]

In spite of all these federal acts and laws, family matters such as marriage, divorce, distribution of property, and child welfare have traditionally been the responsibility of state governments. Discussions in previous chapters noted that the legal control of marriage and divorce in the United States currently resides with the states rather than the federal government. Even though no state permits polygamy per se, states differ considerably as to grounds for divorce and the ease of remarriage. Even though all states have a welfare reform program, states set different standards as to the conditions of eligibility and the amounts of payment. Similarly, even though no state permits the marriage of preteenage children, states vary as to the age at which youth may legally marry.

Involvement at the federal level becomes evident when one notes how certain restrictions set at the state level—such as the prohibition of miscegenation (marriage between members of different races), abortion, and the distribution of contraceptives—were ruled unconstitutional by the Supreme Court. So even though marriage laws are formulated and enforced by the states, federal courts have, at times, declared various practices to be unconstitutional.

---

[13]For a more thorough review of these acts and their provisions, see Karen Bogenschneider, "Has Family Policy Come of Age? A Decade Review of the State of U.S. Family Policy in the 1990s," *Journal of Marriage and the Family* 62 (November 2000), Table 1, p. 1143.

This issue, like all others, is not an "either/or" question. There are both advantages and disadvantages to the establishment of family policies at either a national or a state level. Some advantages of family policies at the federal level include:

- Making the family and family-related issues visible nationally
- Giving family issues a national priority
- Setting uniform standards for a nation
- Providing large-scale funding of programs and research

In contrast to the distinct advantages of family policy at the federal level, inherent problems also exist. One problem is having national-level policies that impact negatively on select groups of the population. For example, one writer assessed the impact of the "supply-side economics" of the Reagan administration on family-support services, food-related programs, employment, education, and housing.[14] The policies of the Reagan administration were shown to have affected people who are poor (many of whom are African American) more negatively than people who are in a better economic position.

A second problem with setting policies at the national level centers around adapting policies to local issues and to the special needs of specific racial, ethnic, regional, and cultural groups and families.

Public versus Private Positions

A third issue for family policy revolves around the extent to which intimate relationships and families are *public* or *private*. Many times, the family is seen, even revered, as a private institution, separate from and closed to public scrutiny. A contrasting position demands that the family be open to public view and subject to public scrutiny.

The *privacy position* argues that certain behaviors are legitimately off-limits to others. The family or an intimate relationship, in this perspective, is a matter of personal concern; a haven for privacy; a place of unconditional affection and love; a network for sharing fears, anxieties, and joys; a place to grieve over a loss; and a source of protection and security free from "Big Brother" and public dominance. Cannot husbands and wives or cohabiting couples decide for themselves when, where, and how they desire to show affection; the manner in which they control the number of children they want; how they discipline, educate, clothe, and feed these children; and how they resolve intrafamily conflict?

The *public position* argues that the state and community have the right (and even the obligation) to establish boundaries on what happens in private. If children are hungry, wives are raped, or families are homeless, should not state or public agencies intervene? If so, when and to what extent? What about issues such as minimum income, day care, discipline and corporal punishment, abortion, alcohol and drug dependency, health care, and housing?

Fox states that the social functions of public scrutiny include (1) an instructive function that has the capacity to teach what is and is not acceptable behavior; (2) a regulatory function that serves as a means of social control, often by means of embarrassment or shame; and (3) a restorative function that may lead to an outpouring of compassion and concern.[15] As was clearly evidenced following the terrorist

---

[14]Maurice A. St. Pierre, "Reaganomics and Its Implications for African-American Family Life," *Journal of Black Studies* 21 (March 1991), 325–340.

[15]Greer Litton Fox, "Families in the Media: Reflections on the Public Scrutiny of Private Behavior," *Journal of Marriage and the Family* 61 (November 1999), 821–830.

bombing of the World Trade Center and the Pentagon in September 2001, people do respond to the tragedies of others. But for them to do so, these personal and family losses and hurts need to be made public.

Interestingly, some people who advocate the privacy position on certain issues, such as child care and a minimum family income, often advocate a public position, or governmental intervention, in other areas, such as sex-role behavior or prohibiting abortion. For example, right-wing religious and political groups have led organized efforts in the past two decades *against* passage of the Equal Rights Amendment but *for* the passage of antiabortion and antigay laws.

Preventive or Ameliorative Policy

Assuming that certain policies are necessary, a fourth issue for family policy is whether policies should be directed toward (1) *all* families and intimate relationships in an attempt to prevent abuse, divorce, or any family-type problem, or (2) only families and relationships that already have problems.

A preventive policy for *all* families or intimate relationships focuses on issues that affect everyone: employment, health, minimum wages, housing, gender and racial/ethnic equality, tax equity, and the like. This type of policy perspective includes two-parent as well as middle- and upper-class families. They too have children, face conflicts in the home and workplace, and experience divorce and stepfamilies.

The ameliorative, or *need*, position focuses on select groups or behaviors that are defined as problems: unwed parenthood, abortion, child and spouse abuse, single parenthood, divorce, homelessness, and the like.

Perhaps a medical analogy is relevant. Traditionally, medical care in the United States was directed toward people who were sick. Physicians were seen only when colds, diseases, or broken bones created the need for medical care. An emerging view is directed at prevention, at a holistic orientation to care, and toward maintaining a high level of health for everyone.

The ameliorative, problem, or need position includes an added dimension of *deserving* or *undeserving*. Poor children and elderly persons who are ill have special needs. But in addition, they *deserve* help. Why? Because their condition or circumstances exist through no fault of their own. Thus, child support and Medicare are considered "legitimate" programs because a need exists for them and the recipients deserve help. Likewise, Social Security is a worthwhile income-support program, without stigma, because the benefits were earned; working people paid into the program and deserve the payback. That many people have other income and do not really need Social Security, or that most people get back what they paid in the first eight or ten years, becomes irrelevant, according to this view. Certainly, Social Security is not labeled or stigmatized as welfare because people deserve and are entitled to it. In contrast, welfare and AFDC or TANF carry negative connotations. Why? Although people receiving this aid may need the support, they are considered "undeserving." They "should" be able to work, be thrifty, be independent, and support themselves, and they should not have had those children out of wedlock in the first place. What's more, they never paid into any plan that would make them worthy recipients.

It is interesting to note that labeling specific types of relationships or structures as *problematic*, *pathological*, or *ill* may, in itself, affect the types of policies directed toward them. Consider single parenthood as an example. If this form of structure— one parent with children—is viewed as pathological, then policy will likely focus on preventing the formation of single-parent family structures and providing services

news item

Welfare Reform in a Recession

WASHINGTON—At a time when unemployment has risen sharply and many American families need help, experts and legislatures say the country's welfare system needs an overhaul to target the current problems. "In the 2001 recession, the number of families receiving assistance also remained flat, but the current recession has involved a much more rapid increase in unemployment," said Mark Greenberg, director at the Georgetown University Center on Poverty, Inequality and Public Policy. "Overall, the story has been the program has been very unresponsive at a time when unemployment has gone up and more families need help."

Temporary Assistance for Needy Families (TANF), the nation's direct cash assistance program for families that mostly serves single mothers, was created in 1996 as part of a federal effort to revamp the welfare system.

Two fundamental components of the program are time limits and work requirements, which operates by giving block grants to states to organize their own programs. The strict requirements imposed on states by the federal program is a key problem.

A Need for Reform?

According to the Center of Budget and Policy Priorities, in 2005, an average of 2.1 million families per month received TANF cash assistance, serving 40 percent of eligible families. If these programs served 80 percent, the number of families receiving assistance would be 4.2 million. TANF caseloads have declined markedly since then, dropping in some states, flattening in others and slowly rising in others.

Greenberg said the share of eligible families getting help in the mid-90s was about 85 percent and that now it's down to 40 percent. The share of poor children receiving assistance had been 60 percent and today it has dropped below 25 percent.

The stimulus package passed by Congress made an additional $5 billion available for states if states increase their spending on basic assistance, subsidized employment or short-term help for families. The states would be required to put up 20 percent of the cost, but even that may be hard for a number of states with so many states struggling with budget problems.

Ron Haskins of the Brookings Institution...said as the rolls plummeted in the 90s and people became employed, states were left with extra funds. States diverted the welfare money to other programs, such as child care and child protection.

"Once you allocate the money to various organizations, it's hard to get it back because then you can't leave them in a lurch," he said. "That was an unanticipated consequence of the welfare reform bill...

Structural Issues

Part of the problem is the structure of TANF itself. It is difficult for an eligible family to receive help because many states have complex eligibility rules that make it hard to get through the initial application process. States also have extensive requirements imposed on families already receiving assistance, making it difficult to continue to receive assistance even though a family may still be in need.

The program may also discourage states from helping more people because of the additional penalties the state might incur. The easiest way for states to meet federal requirements can be by cutting the caseload.

Expert say the programs need to give states more flexibility and get rid of prescriptive rules that make it difficult for states to provide access to extended education and individualized services.

States also need to focus more on strategies that will provide people with stable sustainable employment and that will make a dent in poverty and child poverty, according to Greenberg.

Source: Inyoung Hwang, "Welfare Reform in a Recession," *Medill Reports*, June 04, 2009. Story URL: http://news.medill.northwestern.edu/washington/news.aspx?id=133473 Story Retrieval Date: 6/5/2009 2:26:27 AM CST.

designed to facilitate reconstitution of these "less than complete" families. On the other hand, if single-parent families are simply considered one of many accepted family lifestyles, the policy will likely focus on what is necessary for all families: minimum incomes, adequate housing, inexpensive child care, employment opportunities, support services, and the like.

Who holds responsibility for the homeless? What kinds of social policies or programs, if any, are directed to these persons or families? Does government have any obligation to provide assistance, is this the responsibility of private agencies and individual citizens, or are they to blame for their own plight?

Biological or Relationship Policy

A fifth issue for family policy is whether policy should focus on *biological* (birth ties) or *social* relationships and intimate attachments. The biological focus emphasizes the birth parent as the one most suited to raise a child. It emphasizes a heterosexual marriage in which couples can conceive and give birth. The relationship focus emphasizes the "best interest of the child." It emphasizes a marriage or relationship that might involve a male and a female or it might involve persons of the same sex.

Today, most legal policies focus on the biological. This biological slant reflects widespread assumptions about ties based on birth and genes that make family bonds "natural." Who is not familiar with the saying that "blood is thicker than water," implying that family birth bonds are stronger than bonds based on social relationships? What is less widely recognized or assumed is the extent to which family and kinship are themselves social constructs. The definitions of family and kin are culturally determined.

In the United States, a biological focus is evident in child custody decisions. Children are most frequently placed with the mother, followed in frequency by placement with the father, and at times another relative by birth or marriage. Unless a birth parent is found to be unfit or to have abandoned the child, this parent will predominate over others. This biological focus is also highly evident in the emphasis on heterosexual marriage and parenting.

Skolnick, in describing this biological bias most explicitly, notes that in recent years the traditional biological concept of family in American culture and law has been joined by what she calls "a new biologism." This includes a growing sense that:

the true essence of a person is rooted in the primordial differences of gender, race, ethnicity, genes. It's true that the recent advances in genetic research have made biological information about one's family background an important part of a person's medical history. But the new biologism is a much broader cultural phenomenon that encompasses identity politics and the emphasis on ethnic roots, the search movement among adoptees, and the antiadoption movement which has emerged in recent years.[16]

In contrast, policies based on *relationships* place the focus on attachments and interpersonal connections rather than biological ones. In cases of child custody and adoption, the focus is on the best interest of the child. Skolnick speaks of "psychological parenthood," meaning that the "parent" is the adult who best fills the child's needs for adult nurturance, through day-to-day interaction, companionship, interplay, and mutuality.[17] This role often is filled by a biological parent—but not always so. Thus, in a case like the widely publicized Baby Jessica case, custody of the child would go not to the biological birth parent(s) but to the parents who had raised her since birth. (The 1993 Baby Jessica case involved a Michigan Supreme Court ruling that returned an adopted child to her birth mother. The birth mother and the man she first named as the father had signed adoption papers. Later, the mother changed her mind, claiming that the man she was soon to marry was the biological father. The court awarded custody of Jessica to the birth mother, who took a screaming toddler from the arms of the mother who had adopted and raised her since shortly after birth.)

Micro- versus Macro-Level Policy

A sixth issue for family policy is whether policy should operate at primarily the micro-level or macro-level. **Micro-level policy** focuses on persons and patterns of personal interactions that characterize everyday life. **Macro-level policy** focuses on the social patterns and forms of social organization that shape an entire society, which are beyond the control of any individual yet play a powerful role in affecting families and influencing personal lives.

At the *micro level*, the individual or set of individuals in interaction is the unit of analysis and focus of attention. To deal with a marital problem, counsel the husband or wife. To deal with unwed mothers, delinquent youth, abused children, or people who are elderly, ill, or mentally retarded, provide housing (or institutionalization), personal counseling, and individual attention. This micro-level position is well understood and highly emphasized in terms of social policy and specific courses of action. The unwed mother or the person who is sick or mentally retarded is the one with the problem and in need of treatment or attention.

In contrast, at the *macro level*, the organization, system, or society is the unit of analysis and focus of attention. At this level, individuals or relationships are affected by how society is structured and by the nature of social systems within that society. Policies related to areas such as taxation, military service, health care, employment, housing, education, and leisure all affect persons and

---

[16]Arlene Skolnick, "Solomon's Children: The New Biologism, Psychological Parenthood, Attachment Theory, and the Best Interests Standard," in *All Our Families: New Policies for a New Century*, eds. Mary Ann Mason, Arlene Skolnick, and Stephen D. Sugarman (New York: Oxford University Press, 1998).

[17]Ibid., 244.

TRANSNATIONAL FAMILIES

International Adoption

Increased globalization since World War II has not only characterized the economy and marital relationship markets but also has extended to the adoption market. This is particularly true for the United States, where, according to Madeline Engel, Norma Phillips, and Frances Dellacava, citizens have adopted more children from outside the country than have the citizens of any other country (in fact more than all other countries combined). This high international adoption rate was initially fueled by feelings of obligation and concern following World War II, the Korean War, and the Vietnam War, but then later reinforced through the media, Internet, and an increase in the perceived risks and choices associated with adoptions within the United States. Between 1990 and 2005, the number of international adoptions in the United States increased three-fold, from 7,093 to 22,728. The vast majority of international adoptions today come from China, Russia, and Guatemala.

How do other countries and the international community view these adoptions and what policies have they put in place to regulate and/or control them? There are a number of factors that influence countries policies. One factor is the perception that international adoption is just one more practice of "imperialism, arrogance, and exploitation" (263). A second is the sense of national shame that can come about when a country has extremely high rates of adopting out its children internationally. This was the case recently in South Korea, which has been a major source of adopted children in the United States since just after the Korean War. A third factor is the perception that a country is "marketing" its children and orphans, as occurred with respect to Romania in the early 1990s. This perception led to the institution of policies in Romania requiring long residencies for adopting parents. Fourth, concerns about the illegal trafficking of children have led both adopting countries and international bodies to implement tighter controls over international adoptions. Finally, strong cultural beliefs and concerns about cultural integrity and identity often lead countries to restrict international adoptions even when disasters occur that swell the number of orphans (as occurred in the 2004 tsunami in Indonesia and the 2005 earthquake in Pakistan).

Source: Madeline Engel, Norma K. Phillips, and Frances A. Dellacava, "International Adoption: A Sociological Account of the U. S. Experience," *International Journal of Sociology and Social Policy*, 27 (2007), 257–270.

families, but the focus of such policies is not on a given person or family with a specific problem.

For instance, if poverty status is characterized by lower levels of commitment to marriage and if high rates of marital dissolution are related to the frequency of unwed parenthood, to child abuse, and to low levels of mental and marital health, then it seems imperative that social policy be directed not merely at counseling the mother or the abused wife or child but at the conditions maintaining poverty. If welfare policies force men to live separately from their spouses and children, or if federal tax laws or Social Security requirements impose penalties on marriage, then these policies—operating at a macro level—need to be reexamined. If sexual or racial inequality in society prevents wives from establishing credit or owning property and prevents African American families from living in certain neighborhoods or attending certain schools, then these practices and conditions need to be addressed at a level beyond any given individual or family.

The differential distribution and unequal sharing of the costs of unemployment across families highlights the plight of African American families, single parents, and parents of young children as well as how unemployment and its financial repercussions are shaped by broad social, economic, and political forces operating at the macro-level. Even with a healthy economy with "full employment," some portion of the labor force remains jobless.

Keep in mind that employment—or lack of it—affects men, women, and families. Policies that include conditions such as flexible work patterning, daycare, nondiscriminatory hiring, and decent wages help families—including two-earner households and single parents—make ends meet; however, the policies are developed and implemented slowly.

Scanzoni presented the argument that macro-level, family-related objectives have rarely addressed fundamental issues, since it is impossible to define a family in concrete terms while not excluding many of the nontraditional forms, as described throughout this text.[18] Likewise, he suggested that micro-level responses have been inadequate because a gap often exists between the demands of contemporary society and the capabilities of conventional families and individuals to grapple with those demands. Thus, he argued for policy at a **meso level,** an alternative between the macro and micro levels.

The meso level involves *mediating structures,* that is, groups and organizations that extend beyond the person or family but don't encompass an entire state or nation. These include community groups and agencies; churches and temples; local chapters of national organizations such as the National Organization for Women (NOW), the American Civil Liberties Union (ACLU), Planned Parenthood, and Family Service Associations; veterans associations; unions and political action groups; and so forth. These groups could mediate, train, and support the diverse range of family structures and concerns found in the pluralistic U.S. society.

Future of the Family System

The underlying issue in this chapter on issues relating to family policy is that of the future of the family system. Will it survive? What types of intimate relationships, families, and societies will exist in the next ten, fifty, or one hundred years? How can people prepare for them? What types of training do people need to provide for their children and grandchildren (assuming they will be "their" children)? What types of structures will exist in the family realm? What functions will be expected of this institution? Will families be necessary? Will marriages exist? Will women have equal status with men? Will marriage and children be allowed only for heterosexual partners?

In reviewing the current status and future prospects of families in the United States, Mark Fine summarizes a number of strengths and weaknesses.[19] Strengths of families include their durability, their diversity, and their resilience. Families remain the basic institution in which individuals aggregate socially, and family life remains as important to individuals as it ever was. Diverse family forms have achieved a greater level of acceptance with a recognition that they do not necessarily impact negatively on the members' well-being. In spite of problems, most families are resilient and tend to function relatively well. *Weaknesses* of families include their lessening potency as socializing agents, the decreasing level of role clarity, the intensive value placed on individualism, the declining status of some aspects of children's well-being, and a lack of involvement by some fathers in several areas of family life.

---

[18]Scanzoni, *Shaping Tomorrow's Family*, 97–118 and 225–227. Note also Frances G. Pestello and Patricia Voydanoff, "In Search of Mesostructure in the Family: An Interactionist Approach to Division of Labor," *Symbolic Interaction* 14 (1991), 105–128.

[19]Mark A. Fine, "Families in the United States: Their Current Status and Future Prospects," *Family Relations* 41 (October 1992), 430–435.

Family Diversity

Family Diversity: A Challenge to Public Policy

After a review of some of the major changes in American families over the past century, Andrew Cherlin argues that policymakers need to reevaluate the American tradition of basing aid to individuals and children on conditions of marital status and family structure. He argues that changes such as increased age at marriage, lower marriage rates, high single parenting rates, high divorce and remarriage rates, and short and multiple cohabitations have systematic roots in the changing socioeconomic system and are unlikely to be affected by policies that simply try to promote marriage and leave family and child welfare contingent on marital status. As a result, many children today and in the future will be left behind and not have their basic needs attended to because they live in situations outside the normative two-married-parent model.

Unfortunately, American sentiments strongly favor a traditional, two-married-parent family model, making any attempt to unlink benefits and welfare from this status—and instead link benefits to parents regardless of partnership status—doomed to failure. Any such attempts are likely to be seen as undermining the traditional and distinctive American family by "rewarding" people for living in alternative arrangements and divesting marriage of its "incentives." As he concludes: "The dilemma for policymakers is how to make the trade-off between marriage-based and marriage-neutral programs. A careful balance of both is needed to provide adequate support to American children" (50).

Source: Andrew J. Cherlin, "American Marriage in the Early Twenty-First Century," *The Future of Children*, 15 (Autumn 2005), 33–55.

But what about the future of the family system? Can it be predicted? The following observations are made in predicting its future:

1. Changes that take place (and will take place) in society at large or among people in intimate relationships are not necessarily pleasing or regrettable, good or bad, or constructive or destructive. Changes are likely to be welcomed or rejected depending largely on one's own frame of reference, the groups with which one identifies, and the value orientations to which one adheres. For example, rising divorce rates may be viewed either as a problem or as a solution to other problems. Homosexuality may be viewed as an illness or as a right to love whomever one chooses. War may be viewed as vital to national defense or as an immoral destruction of life and property. This is not meant to imply that changes are never disruptive to the social order; rather, that social matters must be seen in the context in which they occur.

2. Although many people see the family as the core of society and as the most basic of all institutions, it must be clear that (as has been stated time and again) the family cannot be understood as an isolated phenomenon. The family must be viewed in relation to economic, educational, religious, and political institutions. In addition, factors such as population density, mobility patterns, and stratification divisions must be taken into account. It is not by chance that agricultural societies tend to emphasize extended families, parental involvement in partner selection, and often plural marriage. Neither is it by chance that the United States places an emphasis on romantic love, separate households, and monogamous marriages. The central point is that, if accurate predictions are to be made, it is essential to understand what is likely going to take place in other social systems.

3. The family is not a uniform entity. Change will occur, almost without question. But to speak of the changing family as if it were a uniform entity or as if only one particular form or structure is appropriate is both misleading and unrelated to the real world. From the very beginning of U.S. society, the cultural base of the population was diverse and varied. Then, as today, one could expect to find variations in intimate relationships and family patterns when considering such factors as rural/urban residence, region of the country, religious affiliation, racial and ethnic identity, social-class background, and age. One could also expect to find variations in the number of spouses, number of children, and size of the kinship network. Finally, there will be variations in employment patterns of both men and women, in the household tasks they perform, and in how they rear and discipline their children. One must recognize the tremendous differences that exist in family structures and interpersonal relationships. At the same time, it must be realized that, within this diversity, strands of unity belie heterogeneous origins.

Having provided these qualifications, permit the authors to state unequivocally, that, as long as society exists, some form of family system will exist. We agree with DaVanzo and others[20] that, over the next few decades, certain demographic trends will continue, such as:

> Women, including those who are mothers of young children, will likely continue to work outside their homes. Policies that would increase the compatibility of working and caring for children, or reduce the costs of child care, are likely to lead to even higher rates of labor force participation by mothers of young children.

> Economic opportunities for women will reduce the incentive to marry and have children, or will at least delay marriage and child bearing, and may keep divorce rates fairly high. It is unlikely that we will see important reversals in the trend toward cohabitation.

> There will be continued shifts in the proportions of children and older people in the population, with fewer of the former and more of the latter.

The passing of the traditional family has caused a great deal of trauma and left a good number of loose ends. But the rebuilt family will include many variations of primary, intimate, close relationships that will fulfill family-type functions. Most Americans will continue to find marriage and family interactions basic sources of emotional and psychic stability. Families will continue to be the primary sources of socialization, security, affection, and meaning. Families are likely to remain the largest collective social service agency in the nation and world—responsible for the care of children and people who are sick, disabled, and elderly, and responsible for the economic welfare of their members. The nature of partners who comprise a relationship or marriage may change, the expectations of men and women may change, sexual codes and practices may change, and general family lifestyles may be vastly different.

But change by itself does not necessarily bring decay, immorality, and general deterioration of families. Rather, destruction of society and the family is more likely to result because of an inability to change.

---

[20]Julie DaVanzo, M. Omar Rahman, and Kul T. Wadhwa, "Current Items: American Families: Policy Issues," *Population Index* 59 (Winter 1993), 547–566.

Summary

1. All areas of marriage and family life are affected by certain economic, political, and social policies. It seems safe to assume that, while most social policies have an effect on families, few were developed or formulated with marriages and families in mind.

2. As used in this chapter, *family policy* refers to objectives concerning family well-being that are met through specific courses of action. The intent of social policy is to guide, influence, or determine the structure, functions, behavior, ideas, and values of its members.

3. Three types of family policy research were discussed in this chapter. Research to establish family policy examines some particular family structure or lifestyle to determine if certain policies or programs are necessary and to make recommendations as to what they should be. Family-policy evaluation research attempts to determine the degree to which social programs achieve their stated goals. Family-policy impact analysis assesses the intended and unintended consequences of public policy and social programs.

4. Policy matters usually are characterized by a divergence of ideas, conflicts over positions, and opposing recommendations. At a general level of analysis, six of these issues or differences were examined in this chapter:

a. *Goals and objectives*—the extent to which policies are aimed at maintaining the status quo or serve as forces for change. *Conventionals* seek the status quo, as idealized in the traditional conjugal family, whereas progressives seek change and multiple family forms more consistent with a pluralistic society.

b. *Levels of control*—the extent to which policies should be established, enforced, and paid for at the federal, state, or local level.

c. *Public versus private positions*—the extent to which families and intimate relationships are public or private institutions, meaning the extent to which there should be a separation of family and governmental or legal intervention.

d. *Preventive or ameliorative policy*—the extent to which policies should be directed toward all close relationships and aimed at prevention, or only toward traditionally defined families with problems.

e. *Biological or relationship policy*—the extent to which policies should be based on biological and birth ties or based on social relationships and intimate attachments.

f. *Micro versus macro level*—the extent to which policies should operate at primarily the micro level or macro level, that is, focusing on small-group and interpersonal relationships, or focusing on social patterns or forms of social organization that shape entire societies.

5. What is the future of the family? Social policies will, without doubt, affect the future patterns of intimate and family relationships. The family is changing and will continue to change. In sum:

a. These changes are not good or bad, per se.

b. The future of the family cannot be understood separate from other institutions and systems.

c. The family of the future will not be a uniform entity.

d. Any type of social projection must be made cautiously.

6. Given these qualifications, the author predicts unequivocally that, as long as a society exists, some form of family system will survive. It will include many differing structural arrangements, perform a variety of functions, and fulfill a range of personal and social needs.

Key Terms and Topics

Family policy p. 561
Explicit family policy p. 562
Implicit family policy p. 562
Research on family policy p. 562
Family policy advocacy p. 563
Research to establish family policy p. 564

Research to evaluate existing family policy p. 565
Research on the impact of family policy p. 565
Issues surrounding family policy p. 566
Goals and objectives of family policy p. 567
Conventionals p. 567
Progressives p. 567

Discussion Questions

1. Differentiate among *policy*, *social policy*, and *family policy*. Can social policy exist independently of and have no impact on families? Why or why not?

2. Can or should family policy research be value-free? Can or should policy *research* be separated from policy *advocacy*? How can family policy researchers integrate knowledge of *what is* with concern over *what should be*?

3. Describe the different goals of (a) research to establish family policy, (b) research to evaluate family policy, and (c) family-policy impact analysis.

4. What arguments can be made for establishing policy to maintain the status quo as opposed to policy that permits or forces change and diversity? Is it possible to talk about the family in the Western world? Why or why not?

5. Contrast the stances taken by conventionals and progressives. How do these stances translate into policy directives on issues such as teenage sexual behavior and contraceptive usage, sex education, abortion, day-care facilities, cohabitation, divorce, remarriage, the employment of mothers of young children, and so forth? (Select three issues.)

6. What arguments can be made for establishing family policy at a federal as opposed to a state or local level? What arguments can be made against this idea? Is a national U.S. family policy possible or realistic? Why or why not?

7. Most family policy initiatives are carried out with programs and activities instituted at the local level. Should federal or state tax money be used to provide school vouchers for parochial schools, for

"faith-based" social programs, or to assist religious organizations in their efforts to improve the well-being of families and children?

8. What arguments can be made for and against the separation of family and state? In which areas does the government clearly have no right to get involved? In which areas is government involvement mandatory?

9. What arguments can be made for directing policy toward *prevention*, in all intimate relationships? Toward only helping families with problems? What are some effects of labeling certain structural arrangements "problems"?

10. Discuss the issue of biological or birth ties versus ties based on social relationships. For example, should abusive parents or parents who gave up their child for adoption but later change their minds have legal and social rights to their birth children over loving nonbirth parents or the parents who adopted?

11. Is effective family change more likely to occur within society by directing programs and policies at individuals and interpersonal relationships (at a micro level) or at social patterns and organizations (at a macro level)? Explain.

12. What predictions can be made about families and intimate relationships in the twenty-first century? Describe their probable structures and functions, the impact made on them by new technologies, changing parent–child relationships, the division of marital roles and tasks, the status of women, and sexual norms. Are any areas likely to remain static, stable, and relatively unchanged? Why or why not?

Further Readings

Bogenschneider, Karen. "Has Family Policy Come of Age? A Decade Review of the State of U.S. Family Policy in the 1990s," *Journal of Marriage and the Family* 62 (November 2000), 1136–1159.

Bogenschneider, Karen. *Taking Family Policy Seriously.* Mahwah, NJ: Lawrence Erlbaum Associates, 2002.

A perspective on what family policy is, why it is needed, and whether policymaking would be more effective if approached from a family rather than an individual perspective.

Kamerman, Sheila B., and Kahn, Alfred J., eds. *Family Change and Family Policies in Great Britain, Canada,*

New Zealand, and the United States. New York: Oxford University Press, 1997.

A focus on the historical roots of family policy in areas such as employment, health care, and social services in the four countries mentioned.

Mason, Mary Ann, Skolnick, Arlene, and Sugarman, Stephen. *All Our Families: New Policies for a New Century.* New York: Oxford University Press, 1998.

An interdisciplinary exploration of selected topics including teen pregnancy, divorce, child abuse, step-families, and others, with a focus on policy reform.

Mercier, Joyce M., Garasky, Steven B., and Shelley, Mack C., eds. *Redefining Family Policy: Implications for the 21st Century.* Ames: Iowa State University Press, 2000.

An examination of a range of family policy issues including welfare reform, child and health care, housing, and others.

Parcel, Toby L., and Cornfield, Daniel L., eds. *Work and Family: Research Informing Policy.* Thousand Oaks, CA: Sage Publications, Inc., 2000.

A look at the juggling act of work and family, with a focus on how policies might alleviate pressures that parents express in managing both.

Wisensale, Steven K. *Family Leave Policy: The Political Economy of Work and Family in America.* Armonk, NY: M.E. Sharpe, Inc. 2001.

This volume addresses the changing American family and its connectedness to labor and employment concerns.

Zimmerman, Shirley L. *Family Policy: Constructed Solutions to Family Problems.* Thousand Oaks, CA: Sage Publications, Inc., 2001.

A comprehensive look at policy frameworks and the implications of policy decisions for family well-being.

Glossary

ABCX model   A model of family crisis in which A (an event or situation) interacts with B and C (the resources available and the definition or meaning of the event) to produce X (the level or degree of crisis).

Acculturation   A process whereby an ethnic group adopts or adapts to the cultural belief system of the dominant group.

Achieved status   One's position in a group or society and the rights and responsibilities associated with it, based on individual accomplishments.

Affluent polygyny   A type of polygyny widely practiced among middle- and upper-class males in Arab countries and containing many elements of control and exploitation of women.

Agape   A type of love based on the spiritual/cognitive/relationship dimension of rationality, intellectualism, and selfless duty to others.

Age-specific fertility rate   The fertility rate for all women in the population of a given age.

Anal stage   Developmental stage in Freud's construct in which sensations relating to excretion interest the child.

Analytical definition   A definition that highlights the key elements of group structure and relationships that make life in families different from life in other types of groups.

Androgynous or confluent love   Love relationships based on equality between the partners.

Androgyny   The condition of no sex-role differentiation; androgynous individuals are those who are capable of expressing both or either masculine or feminine behavior.

Annulment   The process of ending a marriage because of conditions that existed prior to it, in effect making the marriage nonexistent.

Arranged marriage   The pattern in which marital partners are selected by persons other than the couple themselves (parents, matchmakers, etc.).

Ascribed status   One's position in a group or society and the rights and responsibilities associated with it, based on family connections and determined at birth.

Asian American   The diverse collection of Americans with ethnic ties to Asia, such as the Chinese, Japanese, Filipinos, Asian Indians, Koreans, and others.

Assimilation   A process whereby an ethnic group is integrated into the system of social relationships of the dominant group.

Assortive marrying   The idea that people marry those like themselves more often than could be due to chance.

Assumption   The central core of a theory that states the fundamental truths about the world from which all other aspects of the theory derive their meaning.

Attachment style   A pattern of interaction with others reflecting a desire for closeness and a comfort with proximity.

Authoritative parenting style   A style of parenting that involves high levels of expectations and demand, but also involves high levels of support and responsiveness.

Authoritarian style   A style of parenting that involves high levels of expectation and demand, but low levels of supportiveness and responsiveness.

Authority   Legitimate power.

Autonomous marriage   A system of marriage in which partners select each other rather than have partners selected for them.

Avunculocal residence   A system of residence where a man goes to live with his mother's eldest brother when he attains adulthood, where he continues to live with his new wife after marriage. Their male child then goes to live with his wife's brother when he attains adulthood. The man's sister lives with her husband after marriage, but her children return to her brother's home when they reach maturity. Thus, the female line is preserved, but in the context of male dominance.

Baby boom   The dramatic rise in the number of births following World War II until about 1960.

Baby boomlet/baby boom echo   An increase in the number of live births in a given year brought about because of an increase in the number of women in the population of child-bearing age (a result of a baby boom one generation earlier).

Barriers to dissolution   Conditions that create high structural commitment in a relationship by lowering alternatives or increasing the costs of leaving.

Bidden wedding   A type of wedding in which the expenses are paid for by the guests, who are recruited from surrounding areas by young men called bidders.

Bigamy   The marriage of one person to two persons of the opposite sex; similar to polygamy but restricted to two spouses.

Bilateral   Describes a family system that traces descent and inheritance through both the male and the female lines.

Bilocal   Describes a family system in which a newly married couple lives near the parents of either spouse.

Birth order   Sibling position based on order of birth.

Birthrate   The number of births per one thousand population in a given year.

Bisexual   The lack of sexual preference; that is, sexual involvement with both sexes.

Blue-collar   An occupational classification made up of individuals classified in the U.S. Census as employed in precision production, craft, and repair; machine operating, assembling, and inspecting; transportation and material moving; and handling, equipment cleaning, helping, and laboring.

Boundary ambiguity   The uncertainty of family members as to who is part of the family and performs, or is responsible for, certain roles and responsibilities within the family system; a common issue in stepfamilies.

Bourgeoisie   The class, or social group, of people who control the means of production and use capital, natural resources, and labor to generate profit.

Braceros   Individuals living in Mexico brought into the United States specifically as guest workers to provide cheap labor for agricultural industries.

Braking hypothesis   The notion that spouses may delay getting divorced or approach the decision to divorce more cautiously when they have children.

Bride's price   The goods, services, or money a family receives in exchange for giving their daughter in marriage.

Capital   The accumulated goods or resources that can be used to satisfy human needs, respond to stressor events or crises, and acquire additional resources in the future. It can be economic, human, social, or cultural in form.

Capitalism   A primarily industrial system in which ownership of the means of production is concentrated in the hands of those who can most successfully produce profit and in which the production of profit is the primary motivation for economic activity.

Causal ordering   The specification of which variable is the cause and which is the effect when examining the relationship between two variables.

Causal validity   The trust one has that an observed relationship between two variables occurs because one is causal to the other (i.e., one exerts a force on the other that brings about a certain systematic and predictable change).

Chicano   A Mexican American.

Child custody   The legal arrangement (usually following divorce) providing parental responsibility for the care of a child. Under sole custody, one parent has this responsibility; under joint custody, both parents share this responsibility; and under split custody, each parent assumes responsibility for certain children.

Childless marriage   A marriage in which the couple has no children, either voluntarily or involuntarily.

Choice theory   A focus on decision making and how individuals choose what to do.

Classical conditioning   A response is linked to a known stimulus, as with Pavlov's famous dog experiment. Contrast with *operant conditioning*.

Collectivism/communalism   Refers to the belief that each member of the society has an obligation to the whole of society and places the common good over their own individual needs.

Commitment   A motivation or desire to maintain a belief, behavior, or relationship.

Common couple violence   Conflict between couples with occasional violent outbursts by either partner.

Compadre, comadre, compadrazgo   In the Mexican tradition, coparents or godparents.

Companionate love   A type of love based on secure and trusting attachments.

Comparison level   The standard that individuals develop for what constitutes the maximum profit they can expect in any given situation or relationship.

Comparison level for alternatives   The maximum expected profit to be gained from participating in an alternative behavior or relationship.

Complementary needs theory   A theory of mate selection based on the idea that people marry those providing maximum need gratification; needs tend to be complementary rather than similar.

Conceptual framework   A cluster of interrelated concepts used to describe and classify phenomena.

Conjugal family   A nuclear family that always includes a husband and wife (the conjugal unit) and may or may not include children (see nuclear family).

Consanguine families   Extended families based on blood relationships—namely, descent from the same ancestors.

Conservative welfare regime   A welfare system that focuses attention on the family as a provider of support, but attempt to equalize support across families through income redistributive tax policies and supplements for needed supports such as child care.

Control variables   Variables whose values are statistically held constant (nonchanging) when looking for causal relationships between other variables.

Conventional   Denoting groups and persons who want to maintain the status quo and adhere to a traditional image of what the family should be.

Corporal punishment   The use of physical force to correct or control a person's behavior.

Correlational techniques   Statistical analysis techniques based on the idea that if two variables are related (either causally or noncausally), when comparing the scores for both variables across a set of units, change in the score on one variable will be systematically related to change in the score on the other one.

Courtship violence   Physical aggression expressed during the dating stage that suggests the likelihood of future marital violence on the part of the aggressive partner.

Cross-sectional designs   A type of research design in which units are studied at only one point in time.

Crude divorce rate   The number of divorces that take place per 1,000 population.

Crude marriage rate   The number of marriages per 1,000 population.

Cult of domesticity   A cultural norm in which women are seen as the protectors of morality, both in terms of their husbands and their children, and in which women are expected to care for the home and those in it.

Culture of poverty   A system of values and beliefs that arises in high poverty areas characterized by a lack of faith that hard work will improve one's chances in life and that it is good to be self-sufficient.

Cultural capital   The cultural experiences (e.g., travel to foreign countries, visits to museums, attendance at concerts, etc.), language usage and linguistic styles, knowledge of topics deemed important by powerful groups in society, and lifestyle preferences that are symbols of social exclusiveness and status.

Cultural resource theory   Conjugal power can be explained only if one considers the cultural context as well as the relative resources of the partners.

Cultural scenario   An instructional guide for how to behave in particular roles that exists at the level of collective life and that forms a basis for the creation of roles at the interpersonal level.

Cultural spillover theory Violence in one sphere of life tends to engender violence in other spheres.

Deduction A logical process involving the derivation of particular and concrete predictions from general and abstract principles or theories of realty.

Democratic welfare regimes A welfare system that provides benefits based on citizenship alone. Be it income security, health care, child care, elder care, or any other type of support, all members of society are eligible for the same level of benefit regardless of their ability to pay for it.

Descriptive family A description of family life extracted from an analysis of individual families interacting and adapting in their natural environments. This is the family we live with in our day-to-day lives.

Desertion Willful abandonment, without legal justification, of a spouse or children.

Developmental frame of reference A theoretical perspective on the family that emphasizes the process by which earlier family life events influence later family interactions.

Developmental task A set of prerogatives for social action within families, brought about by changing conditions of life resulting from changes in family structure, changes in normative prescriptions, and/or individual developmental changes experienced by family members.

Discrimination The systematic exclusion of one or more groups of individuals from participation and full rights and benefits of society based on their physical and social characteristics.

Disorganized attachment style An interaction style reflecting neither a desire for closeness nor a distress by distance. These individuals experience a high level of approach-avoidance anxiety in close relationships

Distributive justice theory A theory that predicts individuals' perceptions of fairness in their relationship based on the actual level of equality in outcomes, the inward versus outward comparison of outcomes, and the justifications that can be made for unequal outcomes.

Division of labor The way in which a group divides up, or specializes the completion of, essential survival and maintenance tasks.

Divorce mediation Conflict resolution mechanism in which a divorcing couple meets with a third party who helps negotiate the terms of the split.

Double standard The use of one set of norms and values for females and a different set for males.

Dowry The sum of money, property, and possessions brought to marriage by a female.

Ecological validity The extent to which the conditions under which research results were obtained can be generalized within the natural setting of human behavior.

Economic capital The economic resources one has accumulated such as savings accounts, houses, credit lines, stocks and bonds, and other forms of wealth.

Economic determinism A belief that the fundamental logic of the economic system of a society sets in motion social processes that determine all other aspects of social systems, from political to religious to familial to cultural.

Empty-nest syndrome A postparental stage of family life in which children leave the "nest" and the family household contracts in size to the couple or individual member.

Endogamy A marriage pattern in which persons marry others within their own social groups.

Emotional work Activities or behaviors engaged in by actors to manage their own emotions and/or those of their partner in a way that facilitates the relationship.

Equilibrium assumption An assumption that social structures (i.e., the system of positions, role relationships, power hierarchies, etc.) will always try to maintain themselves and will resist change.

Eros A type of love based on the physical/emotional dimension of relationships and tied to sexuality.

Ethnic group A group distinguished by their national origin or distinctive cultural patterns, such as religion, language, or region of the country.

European marriage pattern   A pattern of low marriage rates and high age at marriage first seen in the middle ages and in the northern sections of Western Europe.

Euthanasia   Deliberate ending of a loved one's life to spare him or her the suffering that accompanies an incurable disease.

Exogamy   A marriage pattern in which individuals marry outside their own group.

Expected intermarriage rate   The percentage of people who would have selected a mate outside their own group if they had chosen their marriage partners randomly; the rate is based on the frequency distribution of the particular groups in the population.

Experience effect   Refers to the idea that a particular status (e.g., cohabitation) implies that one has experienced something that has altered one's self, the nature of one's interactions with another, or one's life circumstances and environment in a way that creates a difference in outcomes when compared to others with alternative statuses.

Experiment   A research design in which units of study (individuals) are brought into a standardized and highly controlled setting where they are usually randomly assigned to two or more groups (a process called randomization). One group (the experimental or treatment group) receives a treatment or stimulus designed to bring about some predicted outcome. The other group (the control group) does not receive the stimulus (or receives some other stimulus not expected to bring about the same outcome).

Explanatory research   Research designed to test, in an unbiased manner, the validity of hypotheses logically deduced from abstract theories.

Exploratory research   Research designed to discover new knowledge and construct new theories by not making a priori assumptions and by utilizing a process of logical induction.

Expressive roles   Social roles that require emotional involvement and expressiveness, such as caring for children, preparing meals to sustain health, and generally meeting the emotional needs of family members.

Expressive self   A self-concept based on one's individuality, emotional and psychological need fulfillment, and maintenance of a system of informal intimate relationships.

Extended family   A family in which two or more generations of the same kin group live together; extension beyond the nuclear family.

Extramarital sex   Sexual intercourse between a man and a woman, at least one of whom is married to someone else.

Familism   Philosophy under which the needs or interests of the family take precedence over those of the individual.

Family   A kinship/structural group of persons related by blood, marriage, or adoption; usually related to the marital unit and including the rights and duties of parenthood.

Family binary   A belief system that involves a contrast between "real" families defined by the presence of a father and a mother and "pseudo" families defined by undesirable conditions such as single parenting and cohabitation.

Family lifecycle   The social sequence of events (such as marriage, children, "empty nest," retirement, and death) that are repeated by successive generations of families.

Family of orientation   The nuclear family into which one was born and reared; consists of self, siblings, and parents.

Family policy   A definite course or method of action with the intent of influencing or determining present and future forms of family organization, behaviors, and decisions; may be implemented and enforced at local, state, and national levels. Explicit family policies are intended to achieve specific outcomes. The goals of implicit family policy are often left unstated.

Family policy advocacy   Endorsing and actively working for a course of action that improves family life.

Family of procreation   The nuclear family formed by marriage; consists of self, spouse, and children.

Family system   A configuration of interdependent parts (social positions) with characteristic organizations and patterns of interdependence.

Family systems frame of reference   A theoretical perspective that views families as living systems that respond to environmental pressures but are affected by the perceptions and motivations of individual family members. Each family system must adapt to its environmental conditions in order to survive, but must also change its structure and modify its processes of adaptation to account for the needs and desires of its members.

Family-work spillover   A condition where the stresses and conditions of family life alter the performance of work roles.

Feedback   The process by which families monitor their outputs relative to goals and then incorporate those outputs as inputs and react to them by making system adjustments, either in terms of members' behaviors, structured processes, or the goals themselves.

Feminism   A theoretical paradigm based on the principle that women's lived experiences and perceptions should be given greater significance in understanding social life.

Feminization of poverty   A societal-level process over time in which the poor are increasingly made up of women and children.

Fertility rate   The number of births in a given year relative to the number of women in the population between the ages of 15 and 44.

Feudalism   A primarily agricultural system in which ownership was concentrated in the hands of a few elite groups and commoners worked the land to support the elites and provide for their own subsistence.

Fictive kinship   Exchange patterns resembling those of kin in which nonrelated friends offer services, support, and goods.

Functional equivalence   The idea that there are many ways a society might choose to fulfill any particular functional need.

Gay   A term generally used to refer to men with a same-sex orientation.

Gender   The umbrella term that refers to the totality of being male or female, which may or may not correspond precisely with one's sex.

Gesellschaft societies   Urban societies characterized by high levels of social differentiation and individualism.

Gemainschaft societies   Rural societies where relationships are primary and communal in nature.

Gender binary   A belief that men and women are naturally different from each other; this difference defines not only the nature and purpose of sexuality but also sustains other inequalities that exist based on gender.

Gender identity   The way one defines or perceives oneself in terms of his or her sex, male or female; sexual identity.

Gender role   The expected behaviors appropriate to one's gender that are assigned by a given culture.

Generalized other   According to Mead, in child development, a milestone at which the child can recognize the expected behaviors of other people and respond accordingly.

General marriage rate   A rate based on the number of persons in the population who are eligible to get married in a given year that corrects for the fact that two people are involved in every marriage.

Genital phase   Development period in Freud's construct when adult responsibilities and family formation occur.

Grand narrative   A story about some aspect of social life expressed broadly in a culture through various avenues of cultural expression. The grand narrative is a social construction and can only be detected through an analysis of various vehicles of cultural expression (e.g., art, music, novels, advertising, television, etc.).

Group marriage   The marriage of two or more women to two or more men at the same time.

Hegemony   The dominance of one cultural group's value system over other cultural groups' value systems.

Heterogamy   A pattern of partner selection in which the partners have different social characteristics.

Heteronormativity   A social process whereby the rules or scripts for acceptable social behavior are constructed by labeling unacceptable sexual behaviors and attaching negative images and sanctions to those labels.

Heterosexual   Having a sexual preference for members of the opposite sex.

Hispanic American   An American of any race who has a Spanish or Latin American origin or background.

Homogamy   A marriage pattern in which people marry others with similar social characteristics.

Homosexual   Having a sexual preference for members of the same sex.

Hospice   A therapeutic environment for the terminally ill where pain and grief management are stressed.

Household   The group of persons who occupy a housing unit.

Human capital   The skills and abilities one has accumulated such as abilities to read, write, and perform quantitative operations. It also includes general and specialized knowledge one has accumulated that can be used to facilitate social outcomes (e.g., more effective parenting, greater communication and conflict management, etc.) as well as economic ones (e.g., performance in specialized occupational careers).

Human poverty index for developing countries   A measure of poverty based on three factors: the probability of a birth not surviving to age 40, the adult literacy rate, and a combined measure comprised of access to improved water sources and the proportion of children underweight for their age.

Human poverty index for developed countries   A measure of poverty based on four factors: the probability of a birth surviving to the age of 60, the adult functional literacy rate, the proportion of the population with disposable household incomes in the lowest 25 percent for the country as a whole, and the rate of long-term unemployment lasting 12 months or more.

Human sexuality   According to Ira Reiss, erotic and genital responses produced by the cultural scripts of a society.

Hypergamy   A marriage pattern in which the female marries upward into a higher social stratum (male marries downward).

Hypogamy   A marriage pattern in which the female marries downward into a lower social stratum (male marries upward).

Hypothesis   A statement of a relationship between variables that can be put to an empirical test.

Ideal-type constructs   Hypothetical models of opposite extremes that provide contrasting (polar) qualities with which to characterize any social phenomenon.

Identity   A set of roles and role expectations associated with one's position in a relationship or social structure. For the symbolic interactionist, there is not one identity but as many identities as there are systems of relationships.

Identity hierarchy   An organization of identities in the self-concept in which the expectations associated with different identities are given different priorities.

Ideology   A value system linked to a position in the power structure of society.

Incest   Socially forbidden sexual relationships or marriage with certain close relatives.

Incidence   The extent to which members of a population have experienced some status or event in their lifetime.

Incomplete institution   A set of practices and relationships increasingly accepted and engaged in by the population but lack clear role expectations to govern the behaviors of their participants.

Indian reservations   Native American areas established by treaty, statute, or court order and recognized as territories in which the tribes have jurisdiction.

Induction   A logical process involving the derivation of general and abstract knowledge from particular and concrete observations.

Indifferent/uninvolved parenting style   A type of parenting characterized by low levels of expectations and demand and low levels of supportiveness and responsiveness.

Inferential statistics   A branch of statistics involving the estimation of how well a sample represents the larger population from which it was drawn.

Influence   The ability to model the thinking and behavior of persons who hold authority.

Insecure-avoidant attachment style   An attachment style where the individual has a strong desire for closeness but is uncomfortable with any distance for fear of losing the attachment figure.

Insecure-resistant attachment style   An attachment style reflecting discomfort with proximity and a strong desire for distance.

Institution   A specific area of human social life that has become broadly organized into discernible patterns and supported by agreed upon expectations or standards for goals and behavior.

Institutional definition   A definition of a social group based on how members of a particular society define the group's structure, function, and nature of relationships. It is a socially constructed definition.

Institutionalize   A process through which behaviors become patterned and predictable.

Instrumental roles   Social roles that require nonemotional, rational behavior such as working outside the home, managing money, and fixing machinery.

Instrumental self   A self-concept based on what one has done or one's status in the community and broader society.

Intermarriage   A marriage between persons of different groups; exogamy.

Intermarriage rate   The percentage of marriages that are mixed relative to all marriages involving individuals in a specific category. It is a rate per couple.

Intermarriage rate for individuals   The percentage of individuals in a specific category who enter into mixed marriages.

Internal social control   Social control brought about by learning rules and principles for behavior and maintained by internal psychological processes rather than outside pressures or threats of punishment.

Interpersonal script   The behaviors and reactions to others developed through interactions in a relationship over time and shaped by the context of cultural scenarios.

Intervention polygyny   A type of polygyny where women choose to enter into polygynous marriages or to accept polygynous marriages because doing so resolves marital problems stemming primarily from the failure to produce male children.

Intrapsychic scripting   An internal dialogue, a world of fantasy, in which interpersonal scripts and cultural scenarios are played out in the mind.

Irreconcilable differences   Any grounds a court determines as substantial reasons for dissolving a marriage.

Joint custody   The legal arrangement (usually following divorce) in which both parents share the responsibility for the care of a child or children.

Joint family   One type of extended family in which brothers share property but do not always live in a single household.

Kinkeeper   Usually a female who works at keeping the family members in touch with one another.

Kinship systems   Patterns of rights, obligations, and constraints that govern the relationships between individuals in societies based on ties of blood, marriage, or adoption.

Latency phase   Developmental stage in Freud's construct in which a child's earlier erotic impulses are repressed.

Latent function   The hidden aspects of what a system does, or the unintended consequences of a given form of social structure on the functioning of the larger system.

Legal separation   The state in which legally married couples maintain separate residences but have established legal responsibilities of support, rights of visitation, and so on.

Lesbian   A female sexually oriented toward other females.

Levirate   The marriage of a widow to the brother of her deceased husband.

Liberal welfare regime   A welfare system that places responsibility for social support on a free market system. In liberal regimes, taxation and state-provided support are low.

Individuals are expected to contract for support and insurance against problems through private sources. Only those in extreme need can receive assistance from the state.

Life expectancy   The average number of years a person in a given population cohort can expect to live.

Lifespan   The maximum length of life possible in a given society.

Longitudinal design   A type of research design in which the same units are studied at multiple points in time.

Macho or Machismo   As used popularly in the United States, macho means very masculine; as used in traditional Spanish or in Latin America, machismo is an ideal of manliness, characterized by strength, daring, virility, and authoritarianism.

Macro-level policy   A policy that focuses on large-scale units, such as social categories, systems, and forms of social organization that affect families (taxation, medical care, employment, housing, education, laws, and so forth).

Macro theories   Theories most widely applicable to problems of family change and stability across societal contexts that see individual behavior in families as determined by the structures within which those individuals are embedded.

Manifest function   The expressed and self-evident aspects of what a system does or the intended consequences of a given form of social structure on the functioning of the larger system.

Marianism   A cultural belief in Hispanic culture that mothers are sacred and should be respected.

Marital alternatives   People's perceptions of how much better or worse their life would be without their current spouse and how easily that spouse could be replaced with one of comparable or better quality.

Marital happiness or satisfaction   The degree to which an individual evaluates his or her relationship as equal to, or greater than, expectations.

Marital quality or adjustment   The extent to which the interactions between partners in a relationship meet some standard of quality or contain generally positive elements.

Marital separation   The state in which individuals are legally married but do not share a common household or residence.

Marital stability   The likelihood of a marriage to end in separation or divorce.

Marital success   The extent to which a couple is able to achieve one or more goals (permanence, companionship, fulfilling expectations of the community, etc.).

Marriage protection hypothesis   Partners intimately bonded may be buffered against physical and emotional pathology.

Marriage squeeze   The effects of an imbalance between the number of males and females in the prime marriage ages due to rising or falling birthrates and the median age difference at marriage.

Mating gradient   The tendency for women to seek men of similar or higher status and men to seek women of similar or lower status; the result is that high-status women and low-status men are less likely to date and marry.

Matricentric   A family system where the wife/mother is at the center of social interactions, although she may or may not have power to make important decisions for the family.

Matrilineal   Describes a family system that traces descent and inheritance through the mother's line.

Matrilocal   Describes a family system in which a newly married couple is expected to live with the wife's family.

Measurement reliability   The extent to which measurement results obtained from one observer or at one point in time can be replicated by a second observer or second observation at a later point in time (assuming no change has occurred between measurement time points).

Measurement validity   The extent to which a measure correctly assesses what it was intended to measure.

Mechanical solidarity   A form of social solidarity found in preindustrial societies and based on the commonality of life experiences and values.

Mesalliance   Marriage with a person of a lower social position.

Meso-level policy   A policy that focuses on groups and organizations as mediating structures between the large-scale macro units and the small-scale micro units.

Micro-level policy   A policy that focuses on small-scale units, such as individuals and small-group interaction.

Micro theories   Theories that factor in individual motivations and see marital and family phenomena as the direct outcome of individuals negotiating with one another to realize desired goals.

Minority group   Any group subordinate to another group.

Miscegenation   Marriage and interbreeding between members of different races, as in the United States between blacks and whites.

Modernity   A historical period in which social relationships and cultural expressions are governed by the principle of rationality rather than traditional or emotional action.

Modified-nuclear and modified-extended families   Nuclear families that retain considerable autonomy yet maintain a coalition with other nuclear families with whom they exchange goods and services.

Monogamy   A marriage pattern in which one male is married to one female at a time.

Moral commitment   A desire to stay in a relationship, not because it is rewarding or because one cannot leave, but because it is the right thing to do.

Morphogenesis   Ongoing change and adjustment in a social system resulting from continuous feedback processes.

Moynihan report   A report written for the U.S. Congress in the 1960s by sociologist Daniel Patrick Moynihan that explored the historical origins of African American family life and concluded that African American families were dysfunctional and in crisis due to the emergence of a matricentric household.

Multi-level theories   Theories that attempt to incorporate both macro-level and micro-level processes.

Native American   The native or indigenous people to North America, sometimes referred to as American Indians.

Negative feedback   A "deviation-attenuating loop" in which system deviance is corrected and behaviors are brought into conformity with preexisting rules and procedures.

Negative relationship   A relationship between two variables where change on one variable in one direction occurs systematically across units with change on another variable in the opposite direction.

Neolocal   Describes a family system in which a newly married couple is expected to establish a new place of residence, separate from their parents.

No-fault divorce   The legal dissolution of marriage based on irreconcilable differences in which neither party is at fault.

Nonmarital cohabitation   An arrangement in which an unmarried male and female share a common dwelling.

Norm of reciprocity   An expectation in all societies that when one receives rewards from another, one is obligated to return them in future exchanges in equal or greater value.

Normative/collective efficacy   The degree to which neighborhoods are characterized by conditions of social organization versus disorganization (e.g., levels of unemployment, poverty, crime, and geographical mobility among neighborhood residents, crime rates and levels of victimization, presence of deviant subcultures in the community, etc.).

Nuclear family   Any two or more persons of the same or adjoining generation, related by blood, marriage, or adoption, and sharing a common residence.

Oedipus complex   The unconscious desire of the male to marry his mother.

Operant conditioning   Skinner's term for instrumental conditioning: a response is not related to any known stimuli. Contrast with *classical conditioning*.

Operational definitions   Definitions of concepts expressed in terms of procedures for their measurement.

Operationalization   The process of translating abstract meanings of concepts into procedures for measurement.

Oral stage   Development period in the first year of life in which gratification is centered on sensations in the mouth.

Orderly replacement   The notion that successive generations are duplicates of or similar to preceding generations.

Organicism   A philosophical position that the whole is more than the sum of its parts and, like the body, the parts serve the whole.

Organic solidarity   A type of social solidarity found primarily in industrial societies in which individuals have become so differentiated in their role responsibilities that the only basis for cooperation is a sense of their interdependence.

Pacific Islanders   Categories of people residing on islands in the Pacific such as Hawaii, Samoa, Guam, or Fiji.

Parental investment theory   A theory that argues that it is in males' interest to maximize their sexual behavior with the "fittest" of the females of the species. The more children produced with females possessing traits signifying health and the predisposition to nurture children, the greater their chances of having more of their offspring survive into adulthood and be successful reproducers themselves. Females of the species, however, will be more interested in limiting their fertility so as to invest more of their psychological, emotional, and physical resources in nurturing each child and assuring their survival.

Parenting styles   A typology of four general types of parenting—authoritative, authoritarian, and permissive/indulgent, and indifferent/uninvolved—based on the degree to which parents expect or demand behavioral standards from their children and the degree to which parents are supportive and responsive to their children's needs.

Passionate love   A type of love characterized by high levels of emotional intensity.

Patriarchy   A system of beliefs and practices that establishes male members of a society as having more authority and decision-making power than females.

Patriarchal terrorism   Systematic use of violence by a man to "control" a wife, involving physical and/or psychological force.

Patrilineal   Describes a family system that traces descent and inheritance through the father's line.

Patrilocal   Describes a family system in which a newly married couple is expected to live with the husband's family.

Permissive/indulgent parenting style   A style of parenting characterized by low levels of expectations and demand and high levels of supportiveness and responsiveness.

Personal commitment   A desire to stay in a relationship because it is highly rewarding.

Personality   Within symbolic interaction theory, refers to an individual's self-concepts, self-perceptions, self-worth, and self-esteem, together with a predisposition to behave consistently.

Phallic stage   Developmental period in Freud's construct in which a child becomes preoccupied with the genitals.

Pluralism   Many and varied forms of family and marital organization.

Polyandry   The marriage of one woman to more than one man at the same time.

Polygamy   The marriage of one man or one woman to more than one wife or more than one husband at the same time.

Polygyny   The marriage of one man to more than one woman at the same time.

Positive feedback   A process in which deviances from established rules and procedures are monitored by the system and reacted to with changes to the system to accommodate the deviance rather than depress it.

Positive relationship   A relationship between two variables in which change on one variable in one direction occurs systematically across units with change on another variable in the same direction.

Positivism   A philosophical position that all phenomena, including social phenomena, have certain regularities and uniformities that operate independently of the researcher or observer and that these patterns can be discovered and knowledge-tested through objective observation.

Post-modernism   A variety of perspectives across disciplines that generally involve a rejection of rationality and science as the foundation for knowledge. Post-modernists see scientific knowledge (and theories) as simply "grand narratives" that have been socially constructed to give meaning to a diversity of individual human experiences.

Postparental period   The stage of the family lifecycle in which children typically leave home and are legally and socially recognized as adults; the conjugal family returns to a two-person, married-couple household and the single parent to a one-person household.

Poverty guidelines   Simplified versions of poverty thresholds used for program administration purposes.

Poverty threshold   A level of income used to classify individuals and families as living in poverty and based on three times the USDA's Economy Food Plan cost. It is based solely on money income and does not reflect noncash assistance or government benefits.

Power   The ability to control or influence the behavior of others, even without their consent.

Prejudice   A negative perception of and bias toward a group of individuals based on their physical or social characteristics.

Prescriptive family   A description of family life extracted from an analysis of cultural narratives that represents the normative expectations of a cultural group and may or may not accurately represent the actual organization of families among all members of the group. The family that we live by.

Premarital sexual intercourse   Coitus involving at least one partner who is single and has not been previously married. It does not imply that the relationship is intended to lead to marriage.

Prevalence   The number of people in the population currently experiencing a certain status or event.

Primary group   A small group of people who interact in personal, direct, and intimate ways.

Principle of least interest   The notion that the partner with the least interest in a relationship is in a position to exploit the other.

Private sphere   The world of interactional processes occurring within the context of the home.

Progressive   Denoting groups and persons who view families as pluralistic and accept change and nontraditional lifestyles as legitimate.

Proletariat   The class, or social group, of people who labor and serve as the instrument of production for the *bourgeoisie*.

Pronatalism   A belief that having children (and many children) is highly desirable.

Proposition   A statement of the relationship between two or more concepts.

Public assistance   Popularly used to refer to welfare and other government support for the poor such as food stamps, Medicaid, and public housing. Often overlooked are benefits that the middle and upper class receive, such as lower tax rates for capital gains than for income, and interest deductions for home mortgages.

Public sphere   The world of transactional processes occurring between the home and other institutions.

Qualitative   Describes a process in which the researcher doesn't know ahead of time which factors will be important to observe and cannot, therefore, use any specific measures to quantify (put into numbers) those factors. Descriptions are given in the observer's words and are shaped by his or her perceptions.

Quantitative   Describes a process in which the researcher already knows what he or she wants or needs to observe. As a result, specific measures can be used or developed for use in doing these observations in an unbiased way. Phenomena are described in the form of numbers on a scale.

Racial group   An aggregation of individuals in a society who share a common genetic heredity based on skin color.

Randomization   A process of assigning research subjects to groups in an experiment using random or probability processes (e.g., flipping a coin, throwing a die, drawing straws, picking a card). Randomization occurs after subjects have been selected from a larger population and improves the causal validity of results. Compare to *random sample*.

Random sample   A subset of a larger population chosen for study by using random or probability processes (e.g., flipping a coin, throwing a die, drawing straws, picking a card, etc.). Random sampling occurs before subjects are asked questions on a questionnaire or are assigned to groups in an experiment. Random sampling increases sample generalizability and sample representativeness. Compare to *randomization*.

Rational mode of action   Social action based on logical means–ends relationships.

Reconstituted family   A family, including a man and a woman, at least one of whom has been previously married, and the children from one or both prior marriages; a stepfamily.

Reference group   A group with which persons psychologically identify and to whom people refer when making evaluations of themselves and their behavior.

Refined divorce rate   The number of divorces per 1,000 married females or males.

Reflexivity   A process of self-examination in which one's own actions are observed and reacted to internally and provide the foundation for future actions.

Religious authority homogamy   A shared belief between marital partners in the authority of religion in shaping behavior and one's life course.

Remarriage   Marriage by anyone who has previously been married.

Replacement threshold   The total fertility rate required to "replace" the population through natural reproductive means (i.e., without in-migration).

Residential segregation   A condition where minority group members live together in communities separate from those of the dominant group as a result of discriminatory housing and lending practices and the movement of dominant groups out of those communities.

Resource   Any commodity, material or symbolic, that can be transmitted through interpersonal behavior and gives one person the capacity to reward another.

Resource dilution hypothesis   Fewer family resources are available to individual children in large families, adversely affecting educational performance and achievement levels.

Resource theory   (Actually, a proposition rather than theory.) An explanation of power based on resources: The more a partner controls resources of value in the conjugal relationship, the greater that partner's relative power. See also *cultural resource theory*.

Role   The social expectations or behaviors that accompany a particular status.

Role conflict   A condition where the expectations for behavior in one role interfere with one's ability to fulfill the expectations and demands of another role.

Role theory   Propositions about expectations associated with statuses that explain consensus, conflict, strain, ambiguity and so forth, personally and interpersonally.

Romantic love   A cultural construction of a type of relationship involving intense emotions capable of transforming life circumstances, exclusivity, possessiveness, and an obsessive state of cognition.

Sample generalizability   The extent to which a scientific sample was selected in a way that allows the researcher to say the results found for the sample would have a high likelihood of being found if he or she studied the whole population.

Sample representativeness   The extent to which a scientific sample has included a true cross-section of the larger population from which it was drawn.

Sampling   A scientific process through which units of observation (things, people, relationships, groups, or whole societies) are selected from a larger population of similar units.

Sandwich generation   Middle-aged people with dependent children and aging parents to care for.

Scientific approach   An approach to the discovery and verification of knowledge about the real world. It involves the discovery of new knowledge through open-ended observation and the ongoing testing of existing knowledge through a priori prediction and unbiased observation to determine the validity of the prediction.

Scripting theory   An attempt to explain what we perceive to be sexual, and how we construct our ideas, thoughts, and fantasies.

Secondary group   A group whose members interact in an impersonal manner, have few emotional ties, and come together for a specific, practical purpose.

Secure attachment style   An attachment style where individuals feel comfortable with both proximity and some distance, although too much distance (outside the range of eye contact and rapid access to parent) causes distress.

Selection effects   Noncausal relationships brought about by systematic self-selection of individuals into a sample.

Self-concept   A definition of who one is that individuals carry with them and continuously re-create through interactions with others. It includes information about how they expect themselves to act and how others expect them to act in various situations.

Self-selection bias   A bias introduced into studies when individuals are allowed to volunteer for a study or when they fall into a single category of the independent variable because they share some characteristic or trait that could cause them to differ systematically on the outcome variable and thereby be a source of spuriousness.

Sequential or serial monogamy   Marriage to a succession of partners but only one at a time.

Seven generations   A term used in Native American culture to refer to how decisions an individual makes in his/her life will affect the tribe over the following seven generations. As such, it conveys strong cultural values of collectivism/communalism and generational piety.

Sex   The biological condition of being male or female.

Sex control   The ability to control the sex of an unborn offspring.

Sex education   Formal instruction on topics relating to sexuality, in classes, seminars, workshops, and clinics. Note that informal sex education also occurs, through the growing child's exposure to sexual issues through the family, the media, and peers.

Sex ratio   The number of males per one hundred females in a population.

Sex roles   Learned and expected patterns of behavior associated with being biologically of one sex or the other.

Sexualization   Sexual socialization; the process by which individuals acquire their sexual self-concepts, values, attitudes, and behaviors.

Sexual orientation   An aspect of one's identity reflecting the gender of others toward whom one is emotionally and sexually attracted.

Sexual permissiveness   An increased willingness to engage in and a more lenient expression of sexual behavior. Generally accompanies an increase in the level of commitment to a relationship.

Sexual script   The learned designation of the who, what, when, where, and why of one's sexuality.

Sexuality binary   Contrasts "natural" sex with "unnatural" sex and attempts to constrain sexual behavior to heterosexual intercourse. This belief that heterosexual intercourse is natural while other sex acts are not often is sustained by references of biological and physiological differences between men and women.

Shared religious practices   Joint attendance at religious rituals and services by marital partners.

Sibling   One's brother or sister.

Significance   The extent to which the observations of a sample can be generalized to the larger population from which it was drawn. It is expressed in terms of the probability of making a false generalization based on sample results (low probabilities indicate a high level of significance).

Significant other   A person with whom one psychologically identifies and whose opinions are important.

Social capital   The network of social relationships (e.g., kinship networks, friendship networks, community networks, political networks, etc.) that one has developed and that can be used to help monitor external environment, find assistance in times of need, and create opportunities for enhancing or expanding goals and outcomes.

Social class   One's position within a system of social stratification based on achievement (such as in capitalism), in which that position has implications for rights, responsibilities, and access to resources. In a purely Marxist sense, there are two social classes—the *proletariat* (workers) and the *bourgeoisie* (owners).

Social conflict frame of reference   A perspective of society that views conflict as natural, permanent, and inevitable and as a significant source of social change.

Social constructions   Classifications of reality that are agreed upon by members of a social group.

Social differentiation   The extent to which individuals in society have separate and distinct roles. This distinctiveness comes about when societies specialize, or divide up, the tasks necessary for survival.

Social exchange frame of reference   A perspective that seeks to explain personal and social behaviors based on reciprocity of rewards and costs.

Socialization   The process of learning the rules of and expectations for behavior for a given society.

Social generontology   The study of older persons and the aging process.

Social network theory   A focus on the sexual dyad embedded in a larger network of social relationships.

Social norm   A rule that tells members of a society how to behave in a particular situation.

Social script   A set of culturally defined procedural norms and expectations that guide the behaviors of actors in some activity.

Social self   The organization of internalized roles developed in interaction with others.

Social solidarity   The extent to which individuals participate in a social system and are motivated to fulfill their role responsibilities.

Social status   A socially defined position occupied by a person; may be ascribed (age, race, sex) or achieved (husband, father, teacher).

Social stratification   The ranking of people into positions of equality and inequality; the arrangement of social classes.

Social theories of sexual behavior   A focus on socialization and social control factors involved in human sexual behavior.

Socioeconomic status   A classification of one's position in a modern system of inequality based on levels of education, occupational prestige, and income.

Sociology   The study of human society and social behavior.

Sororate   The marriage of a widower to the sister of his deceased wife.

Split custody   The legal arrangement (usually following divorce) in which the siblings are separated and each parent has the responsibility for at least one child.

Spurious relationship   A noncausal association or systematic covariation between two variables.

Stem family   An extended-family type consisting of two families in adjacent generations joined by economic and blood ties.

Stepfamily   A family including a man and a woman, at least one of whom has been previously married, and often including children from that previous marriage. Simple stepfamilies include children from just one remarried parent; complex stepfamilies include children from both remarried parents.

Stepmother   Woman married to a man with children from a previous marriage.

Stereotype   A widely held belief about the character and behavior of all members of a group that seldom corresponds to the facts.

Strength of relationship   The degree to which two variables covary systematically across a set of cases.

Stressor events   Crisis-provoking events and situations for which families have little or no preparation.

Structural commitment   A condition leading to a desire to stay in a relationship because one has few alternative sources of rewards and/or the costs of leaving the relationship are very high.

Structural-functional frame of reference   A perspective that emphasizes the units of organization plus the consequences of that particular structural arrangement.

Structured conflict   The existence of differences in interests and values among members of a group regardless of whether they are recognized or expressed openly.

Subfamily   A family unit (married couple or parent with child) living in a household headed by someone else (parent, relative, nonrelative).

Surveys   A research methodology in which the researcher selects an entire population or a subset of the population to study and then has them answer a predetermined set of questions either by selecting answers on a questionnaire (on paper or on the internet) or by verbally responding to an interviewer on the telephone or face-to-face.

Symbolic interaction frame of reference   A perspective that stresses interaction among people as well as the social processes that occur within individuals made possible by language and internalized meanings.

Total fertility rate   An estimate of how many births each woman of child-bearing age in the population in a given year would experience in her lifetime if her childbearing followed the same age pattern present in the population in that year.

Traditional mode of action   Social action based on previously established standards rather than emotional impulse or rational calculation.

Tribal-designated statistical areas   Statistical areas on which census data are tabulated based on concentrations of Native Americans regardless of the type of land they are living on.

Trust lands   Native American lands associated with a particular tribe but located outside reservation boundaries and are held in trust by the federal government.

Typology   A type of concept that combines several traits to convey a more complex aspect of reality.

Uncertainty reduction theory   All people seek to reduce uncertainty in their lives. For parents, depending on the culture, this may involve having more children to provide financial and other support as the parents age.

Underclass   The group of families within the U.S. population characterized by persistent poverty and a variety of associated problems such as welfare dependency, joblessness, substance addiction, and crime.

Unilineal   Describes a family system that traces descent and inheritance through either the male line or the female line.

Universal permanent availability   The notion that any individual is a potential mate, available for marriage with any other individual at any time.

Value theory   A theory of mate selection: interpersonal attraction when the people share (or perceive themselves as sharing) similar value orientations.

Variable   A concept that represents degree or value; a characteristic such as age, class, or income that can vary from one person or context to another.

Wedding tour   A wedding custom of the past practiced by the elite that involved a trip after the wedding to visit foreign locations and extended kin.

Welfare regime   A system for classifying countries based on how they distribute resources for the needy.

White-collar   An occupational position where jobs usually are salaried positions requiring higher levels of educational training. They typically are professional or managerial positions in business, education, or government.

Widowhood   The state of having lost one's spouse through death.

Work-family spillover   A condition where the stresses and conditions of work alter the performance of family roles.

Name Index

Subject Index

Photo Credits

Page 2: © Trudi Unger 6: © Jim West/Photolibrary 22: © Erich Schlegel/Dallas Morning News/Corbis 31: Photo courtesy of Richard A. Bulcroft 42; © Hulton Archive /Getty Images 47: Photo courtesy of Richard A. Bulcroft 75: © Michael Newman / PhotoEdit, Inc. 87: © I Love Images/Photolibrary 94: © David Young-Wolff / PhotoEdit 138: © AP/Wide World Photos 144: © Joseph A Rosen/Photolibrary 153: © Alan Carey/The Image Works 155: © Dean Abramson/Stock Boston 167: © Lionel Delvingne/Stock Boston 188: © BananaStock/PictureQuest 201: © Bettmann/CORBIS 206: © Gary Buss/Getty Images 207: © Bill Bachman/PhotoEdit 208: © Aldo Murillo/iStockphoto.com 217: © Bob Daemmrich/PhotoEdit 219: © Simon Marcus/Flirt Collection/Photolibrary 224: © Will Hart / PhotoEdit 234: © Alan Abraham/Corbis 243: © Danny Lehman/Corbis 262: © Michael J. Doolittle/The Image Works 264: © Laureen Middley/Iconica/Getty 272: © Tim Wimborne/ Reuters /Landov 285: © Marc Asnin/Corbis SABA 292: © Albert Callju/SuperStock 301: © Image Source/Getty 310: © Dougal Waters/Digital Vision/Getty 320: © Ariel Skelley/Corbis 327: © Mike Goldwater/Alamy 338: © Zena Holloway/Getty Images 343: Photo courtesy of James D. van Hoevenberg. Used with permission. 345: © Larry Williams/Larry Williams and Associates/Corbis 360: Photo courtesy of J. Ross Eshleman 374: © Radius Images/Alamy 382: © Buccina Studios/Photodisc/ Getty 399: © Medicimage Ltd./Photolibrary 401: © Jonathan Nourok/PhotoEdit 411: © Rob Lewine 415: © Owen Franken/Stock Boston 420: Photo courtesy of J. Ross Eshleman 434: © Rachel Epstein/The Image Works 437: Photo courtesy of J. Ross Eshleman 450 (girl): © Myrleen Ferguson Cate/ PhotoEdit 450 (boy): © iStockPhoto.com/Nataliia Sdobnikova 453: © Christina Kennedy/PhotoEdit 458: © Yuri Arcurs/ Shutterstock.com 468: Photo courtesy of J. Ross Eshleman 474: © Dennis MacDonald/PhotoEdit, Inc. 482: © Jonathan Blair/ Corbis 490: © EJWhite/Shutterstock.com 504: © BananaStock/ SuperStock 507: © Yellow Dog Productions/Stone/Getty 512: © iStockphoto.com/Eduardo Jose Bernardino 520: © RubberBall/ SuperStock 541: © John Neubauer/PhotoEdit 546: © Eryrie/ Alamy 551: © Donn Thompson/DK Stock/Getty 558: ©Alex Wong/Getty 563: © Stock Connection Distribution/Alamy 573: © Photodisc/SuperStock